ICSE Exams 2026

AF814172

All in One

BIOLOGY

Class 9

ICSE Exams 2026

All in One®

BIOLOGY

Class 9

Authors

Dr. Anamika Tripathi

Sanubia

arihant

SUCCESS AND NOTHING LESS

arihant
SUCCESS AND NOTHING LESS

ARIHANT PRAKASHAN
(School Division Series)

卐 ADMINISTRATIVE & PRODUCTION OFFICES

Regd. Office

'Ramchhaya' 4577/15, Agarwal Road, Darya Ganj, New Delhi -110002
Tele: 011- 47630600, 43518550; Fax: 011- 23280316

卐 *Head Office*

Kalindi, TP Nagar, Meerut (UP) - 250002, Tel: 0121-7156203, 7156204

卐 SALES & SUPPORT OFFICES

Agra, Ahmedabad, Bengaluru, Bareilly, Chennai, Delhi, Guwahati, Hyderabad, Jaipur, Jhansi, Kolkata, Lucknow, Nagpur & Pune.

PO No : TXT-XX-XXXXXXX-X-XX

Published By Arihant Publications (India) Ltd.

For further information about the books published by Arihant, log on to www.arihantbooks.com or e-mail at info@arihantbooks.com

Follow us on

卐 PRICE ₹295.00

PRODUCTION TEAM

Publishing Managers	Cover Designer	Inner Designer
Mahendra Singh Rawat & Keshav Mohan	Salman Shaikh	Ankit Tyagi
Project Head	**Page Layouting**	**Proof Reader**
Yojna Sharma	Amit Bansal, Vikas Kumar	Apoorvi

Index *cum* Study Planner

One Book- Endless Features
to Help you Succeed

Chapter Inside

At the start of each chapter, all the Chapter topics have been listed, so that students may know what they are going to study.

CHAPTER
01

Cell : The Unit of Life

Chapter Inside

• Discovery of Cell • Structural Organisation of a Cell
• Cell Organelles • Plant Cell and Animal Cell

Plant Tissues

There are different types of plant tissues which perform different functions like photosynthesis, transport of food, absorption of water from soil, etc. On the basis of the dividing capacity, plant tissues can be classified into two fundamental types as follows

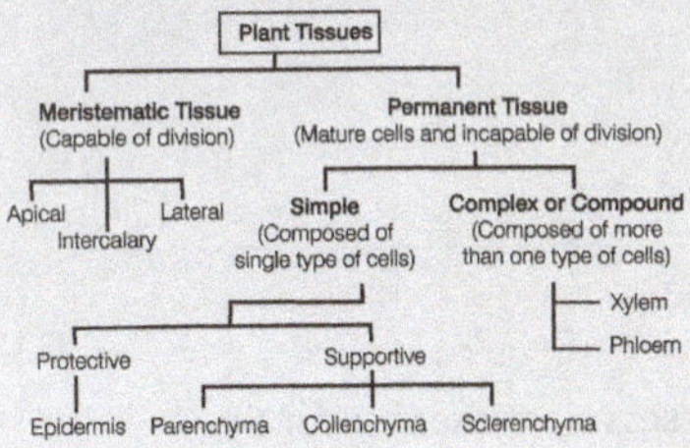

Check Your Learning

A set of 3-5 Questions given in between the text, helps students to remain connected with the text while studying. They can instantly assess themselves for their understanding.

Simplified Theory

It contains the necessary study material well supported by Definitions, Facts, Figures, Flowcharts, etc.

Eukaryotic Cells

These cells possesses membrane bound nucleus and other cell organelles, which are well-defined and well-developed. A variety of locomotory structure and cytoskeleton are also present in them, e.g. plant cell and animal cell (discussed later in this chapter).

Check Your LEARNING...

1 Who first discovered the living cells?
2 Who postulated that all cells arise from pre-existing cells?
3 What is the average size of ***Mycoplasma***?
4 Name any two unicellular organisms.
5 Give any two examples of cells with no definite shape.
6 Expand the term BGA and PPLO.

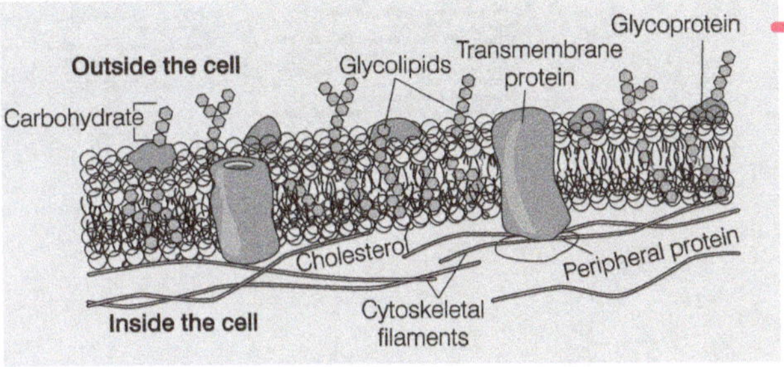

Illustrative Figures

To make the concepts completely visible, illustrative diagrams have been given at various place.

One Book- Endless Features
to Help you Succeed

QUICK Revision

At the end of each chapter, QUICK Revision is given. It contains crux of the chapter in pointer form.

QUiCK Revision

- **Cell** It is the basic structural and functional unit of life.
- **Cell theory** This was formulated by Schleiden and Schwann and includes following three statements, i.e.
  - (i) All organisms are composed of one or more cell and cell products.
  - (ii) Cells are the structural and functional unit of living organisms.
  - (iii) Cells arise from pre-existing cells (*omnis-cellula-e-cellula*) as given by **Virchow**.
- **Prokaryotic cells** These cells have incipient nucleus that is devoid of membrane. They do not have membrane bound cell organelles.
- **Eukaryotic cells** These cells consist of outer cell wall (only in plants and fungi), plasma membrane, cytoplasm, membrane bound nucleus and within cytoplasm cell organelles are suspended.

Chapter Practice

Section-I

1 Mark Questions

1. Name the following.
   (i) The scientist who discovered nucleus.
   (ii) A cell with primitive nucleus.
   (iii) The non-living structure present only in plant cell.
   (iv) The area of cellular activities in plant and animal cells.
   (v) The cells of human body that do not contain nucleus at maturity.
   (vi) The part of cell which is concerned with liberation of energy.
   (vii) The type of plastid involved in photosynthesis.
   (viii) The organelle that contains its own genetic material.
   (ix) Organelle responsible for making cell wall in plant cell.
   (x) Organelle rich in hydrolytic enzymes.
   (xi) The organelle of cell responsible for the synthesis of protein.
   (xii) Membrane that covers the vacuole.
   (xiii) An organelle present in the animal cell, but not in plant cell.

Ans. (i) Robert Brown
(ii) Prokaryotic cell
(iii) Cell wall
(iv) Cytoplasm
(v) Red blood corpuscles
(vi) Mitochondria
(vii) Chloroplast
(viii) Chloroplast and mitochondria

Ans. (i) Robert Hooke discovered the cell.
(ii) The three components of a cell include cell membrane, nucleus and cytoplasm.
(iii) Nucleolus is known as the factory of ribosomes.
(iv) The functional segments of DNA are called genes.
(v) Chloroplasts are the green-coloured plastids found in plants.

3. Give biological reasons for the following.
   (i) The shape of the cell usually affects its functions.
   (ii) Plasma membrane is called selectively permeable membrane.
   (iii) Mitochondria are known as powerhouse of the cell.
   (iv) Plastids are able to make their own protein.
   (v) Lysosomes are known as suicidal bags.

Ans. (i) The shape of a cell plays an important role in the functions performed by it. For example, white blood cells do not have any fixed shape. Thus, they can easily squeeze out from thick blood vessels by changing the shape and come to the body fluid to kill the invading pathogen. Similarly, RBCs have concave shape and lacks cell organelles, so that they can carry maximum oxygen.
(ii) Plasma membrane selectively allows the entry and exit of some materials in and out of the cell. Therefore, it is called selectively permeable membrane.
(iii) Mitochondria are known as powerhouse of the cell because these are associated with cellular respiration and energy generation of the cell.
(iv) Plastids like chloroplast have their own DNA and ribosomes. Therefore, they are able to make their own proteins.

Chapter Assessment

It is the Assessment exercise for the complete chapter. With this exercise, students can assess their understanding of the chapter and can prepare for it accordingly.

Chapter Practice

The Exercise contains questions in that format in which these are asked in the examinations. Questions have been categorised as 1 mark questions, 2 marks questions, 3 marks questions and structured based questions. All the questions given here are fully solved.

Chapter Assessment

Section-I

1 Mark Questions

1. Name the following.
   (i) Process used by lysosomes to digest stored food contents during starvation.
   (ii) Largest cytoplasmic organelle in a plant cell.
   (iii) Scientist who coined the term protoplasm.
2. Correct and rewrite the following statements by changing the underlined word.
   (i) Plastids are also called the suicidal bags of the cell.
   (ii) 78 chromosomes are found in cray fish.
   (iii) The single-celled organisms are called multicellular organisms.
3. Give biological reasons for the following.
   (i) Organ and organelles are two different structures in organism.
   (ii) Plant cell possesses large-sized vacuoles.

6. (i) Fill in the blanks with suitable words.
   (a) Cell wall is made up of .... in plant cells.
   (b) .... are largely involved in the synthesis of fats.
   (c) Vacuole contains ....
   (d) The semi-permeable membrane which surrounds vacuole is called ....
   (e) The fluid part between plasma membrane and nucleus is ....
   (ii) Fill in the blanks (*A-E*) with appropriate words in the following table.

Structures	Whether found in animal or plant cell or both	Functions
A	B	Photosynthesis
C	Animal cell	Spindle formation during cell division
Cell wall	D	E

One Book- Endless Features

to Help you Succeed

Olympiad Section

It includes some special questions based on the pattern of Olympiad and other competitions to give the students a taste of the questions asked in competitions. These are not meant for school examinations.

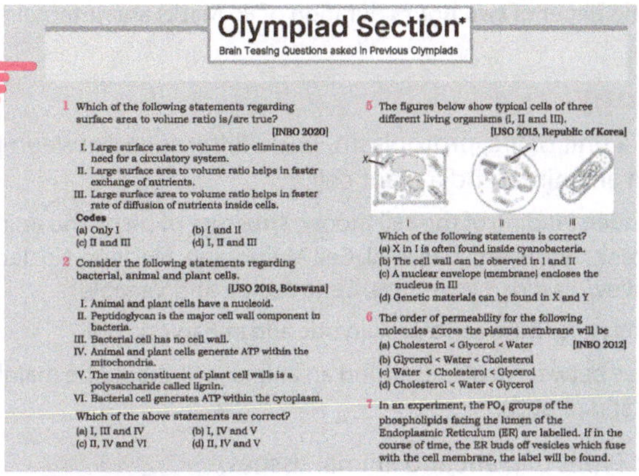

Olympiad Section*

Brain Teasing Questions asked in Previous Olympiads

1 Which of the following statements regarding surface area to volume ratio is/are true? [INBO 2020]

I. Large surface area to volume ratio eliminates the need for a circulatory system.
II. Large surface area to volume ratio helps in faster exchange of nutrients.
III. Large surface area to volume ratio helps in faster rate of diffusion of nutrients inside cells.

Codes
(a) Only I (b) I and II
(c) II and III (d) I, II and III

2 Consider the following statements regarding bacterial, animal and plant cells. [IJSO 2018, Botswana]

I. Animal and plant cells have a nucleoid.
II. Peptidoglycan is the major cell wall component in bacteria.
III. Bacterial cell has no cell wall.
IV. Animal and plant cells generate ATP within the mitochondria.
V. The main constituent of plant cell walls is a polysaccharide called lignin.
VI. Bacterial cell generates ATP within the cytoplasm.

Which of the above statements are correct?
(a) I, III and IV (b) I, IV and V
(c) II, IV and VI (d) II, IV and V

5 The figures below show typical cells of three different living organisms (I, II and III). [IJSO 2015, Republic of Korea]

X Y
I II III

Which of the following statements is correct?
(a) X in I is often found inside cyanobacteria.
(b) The cell wall can be observed in I and II
(c) A nuclear envelope (membrane) encloses the nucleus in III
(d) Genetic materials can be found in X and Y

6 The order of permeability for the following molecules across the plasma membrane will be [INBO 2012]
(a) Cholesterol < Glycerol < Water
(b) Glycerol < Water < Cholesterol
(c) Water < Cholesterol < Glycerol
(d) Cholesterol < Water < Glycerol

7 In an experiment, the PO_4 groups of the phospholipids facing the lumen of the Endoplasmic Reticulum (ER) are labelled. If in the course of time, the ER buds off vesicles which fuse with the cell membrane, the label will be found.

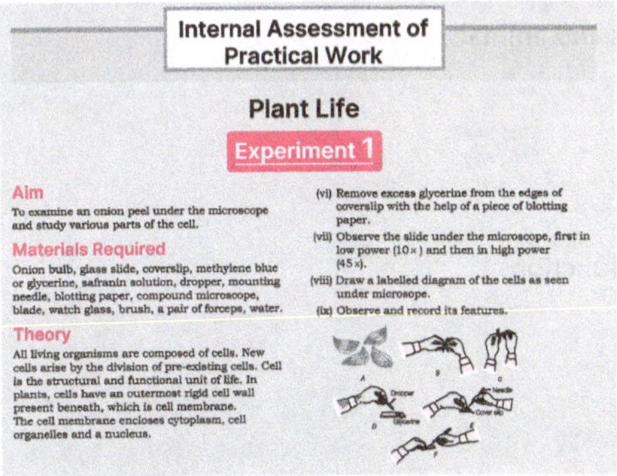

Internal Assessment of Practical Work

Plant Life

Experiment 1

Aim
To examine an onion peel under the microscope and study various parts of the cell.

Materials Required
Onion bulb, glass slide, coverslip, methylene blue or glycerine, safranin solution, dropper, mounting needle, blotting paper, compound microscope, blade, watch glass, brush, a pair of forceps, water.

Theory
All living organisms are composed of cells. New cells arise by the division of pre-existing cells. Cell is the structural and functional unit of life. In plants, cells have an outermost rigid cell wall present beneath, which is cell membrane. The cell membrane encloses cytoplasm, cell organelles and a nucleus.

(vi) Remove excess glycerine from the edges of coverslip with the help of a piece of blotting paper.
(vii) Observe the slide under the microscope, first in low power (10×) and then in high power (45×).
(viii) Draw a labelled diagram of the cells as seen under microsope.
(ix) Observe and record its features.

A B C D E F
Dropper Glycerine Needle Cover slip

Sample Question Papers

To make students practice of examination in real sense, there are 3 Sample Question Papers at the end. All these Sample Questions Papers are exactly prepared on the latest syllabus & pattern of examination.

Internal Assessment of Practical Work

To make this book complete in all aspects, experiments based on latest syllabus have been given.

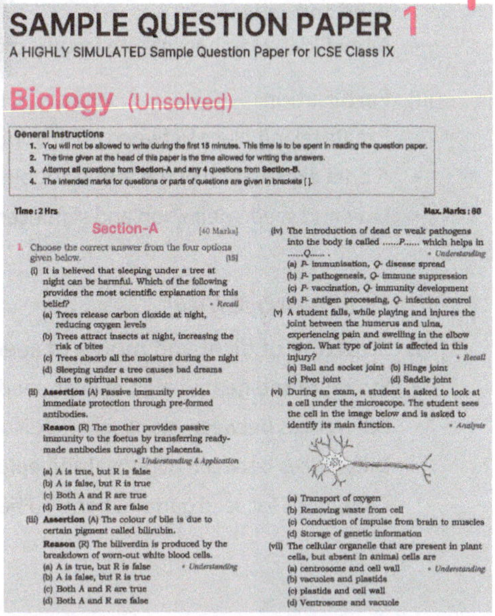

SAMPLE QUESTION PAPER 1

A HIGHLY SIMULATED Sample Question Paper for ICSE Class IX

Biology (Unsolved)

General Instructions
1. You will not be allowed to write during the first 15 minutes. This time is to be spent in reading the question paper.
2. The time given at the head of this paper is the time allowed for writing the answers.
3. Attempt all questions from **Section-A** and any 4 questions from **Section-B**.
4. The intended marks for questions or parts of questions are given in brackets [ ].

Time : 2 Hrs **Max. Marks : 80**

Section-A [40 Marks]

1. Choose the correct answer from the four options given below. [15]

(i) It is believed that sleeping under a tree at night can be harmful. Which of the following provides the most scientific explanation for this belief? • *Recall*
(a) Trees release carbon dioxide at night, reducing oxygen levels
(b) Trees attract insects at night, increasing the risk of bites
(c) Trees absorb all the moisture during the night
(d) Sleeping under a tree causes bad dreams due to spiritual reasons

(ii) **Assertion** (A) Passive immunity provides immediate protection through pre-formed antibodies.
Reason (R) The mother provides passive immunity to the foetus by transferring ready-made antibodies through the placenta. • *Understanding & Application*
(a) A is true, but R is false
(b) A is false, but R is true
(c) Both A and R are true
(d) Both A and R are false

(iii) **Assertion** (A) The colour of bile is due to certain pigment called bilirubin.
Reason (R) The biliverdin is produced by the breakdown of worn-out white blood cells. • *Understanding*
(a) A is true, but R is false
(b) A is false, but R is true
(c) Both A and R are true
(d) Both A and R are false

(iv) The introduction of dead or weak pathogens into the body is called ......*P*...... which helps in ......*Q*...... . • *Understanding*
(a) *P*- immunisation, *Q*- disease spread
(b) *P*- pathogenesis, *Q*- immune suppression
(c) *P*- vaccination, *Q*- immunity development
(d) *P*- antigen processing, *Q*- infection control

(v) A student falls, while playing and injures the joint between the humerus and ulna, experiencing pain and swelling in the elbow region. What type of joint is affected in this injury? • *Recall*
(a) Ball and socket joint (b) Hinge joint
(c) Pivot joint (d) Saddle joint

(vi) During an exam, a student is asked to look at a cell under the microscope. The student sees the cell in the image below and is asked to identify its main function. • *Analysis*

(a) Transport of oxygen
(b) Removing waste from cell
(c) Conduction of impulse from brain to muscles
(d) Storage of genetic information

(vii) The cellular organelle that are present in plant cells, but absent in animal cells are • *Understanding*
(a) centrosome and cell wall
(b) vacuoles and plastids
(c) plastids and cell wall
(d) Ventrosome and vacuole

Latest Course Structure

There will be one paper of **two hours** duration of 80 Marks and Internal Assessment of Practical Work carrying 20 Marks.

Basic Biology

(i) The cell, a unit of life, protoplasm, basic difference between prokaryotic and eukaryotic cell; differences between an animal and a plant cell.

- A basic understanding of the cell theory, structure of plant and animal cell with functions of various cell organelles. (Protoplasm, Cytoplasm, Cell Wall, Cell Membrane, Nucleus, Nucleolus, Mitochondria, Endoplasmic Reticulum, Ribosome, Golgi bodies, Plastids, Lysosomes, Centrosome and Vacuole).
- Major differences between a prokaryotic and eukaryotic cell.
- Differences between a plant cell and an animal cell should be mainly discussed with respect to cell wall, centrosome, vacuoles and plastids.

(ii) Tissues : Types of plant and animal tissues.

- A brief understanding of their location, basic structure and functions with examples.
- A brief understanding of their role in different physiological processes in plants and animals.

Flowering Plants

(i) Flower : Structure of a bisexual flower, functions of various parts.

- A brief introduction to complete and incomplete flowers.
- Essential and non-essential whorls of a bisexual flower; their various parts and functions.
- Inflorescence and placentation (meaning only)
  (Charts or actual specimens may be used to help enhance clarity of concepts.)

(ii) Pollination : Self and cross-pollination.

- Explanation, advantages and disadvantages of self and cross-pollination.
- Agents of pollination and the characteristic features of flowers pollinated by various agents such as insects, wind and water.
- A brief idea as to how nature favours cross-pollination.

(iii) Fertilisation

- Events taking place between pollination and fertilisation leading to the formation of zygote in the embryo sac.
- A brief explanation of the terms double fertilization and triple fusion.
- Fruit and seed - definition and significance.

Plant Physiology

(i) Structure of dicot and monocot seeds, Germination of seeds, types and conditions for seed germination.

- Structure and germination of Bean seed and Maize grain.
- Differences between monocot and dicot seeds.
- Differences between hypogeal and epigeal germination.
- Conditions for seed germination - To be explained and supported by experiments.

(ii) Respiration in plants : Outline of the process, gaseous exchange.

- A brief outline of the process mentioning the terms Glycolysis, Krebs' cycle and their significance.
- A reference to be made to aerobic and anaerobic respiration with chemical equations in each case.
- Experiments on gaseous exchange and on heat production.

Diversity in Living Organisms

(i) A brief outline of the five kingdom classification.

- Main characteristics of each kingdom with suitable examples:
  - Monera, Protista, Fungi.
  - Plantae - Thallophyta, Bryophyta, Pteridophyta and Spermatophyta.
  - Animalia - non-chordates from Porifera to Echinodermata and Chordates - all five Classes.

(ii) Economic importance of Bacteria.

(a) Useful role of bacteria:

- Medicine: antibiotics, serums and vaccines.
- Agriculture: nitrogen cycle (role of nitrogen fixing, nitrifying and denitrifying bacteria)
- Industry -curing of tea, tanning of leather.

(b) Harmful role of bacteria - spoilage of food, diseases in plants and animals, bio-weapons.

(iii) Economic importance of Fungi.

A brief idea of the useful role of Fungi in breweries, bakeries, cheese processing and mushroom cultivation (Processes of manufacture are not required).

Human Anatomy and Physiology

(i) Nutrition

(a) Classes of food; balanced diet. Malnutrition and deficiency diseases.

- *Functions of carbohydrates, fats, proteins, mineral salts (calcium, iodine, iron and sodium), vitamins and water in proper functioning of the body.*
- *Sources of vitamins, their functions and deficiency diseases.*
- *Meaning and importance of a 'Balanced Diet'.*
- *Role of cellulose in our diet.*
- *Causes, symptoms and prevention of Kwashiorkor and Marasmus.*

(b) The structure of a tooth, different types of teeth.

- *Structure of a tooth to be discussed with the help of a diagram.*
- *Functions of different types of teeth.*
- *Dental formula of an adult.*

(c) Digestive System: Organs, digestive glands and their functions (including enzymes and their functions in digestion, absorption and assimilation of digested food).

- *Organs and glands of the digestive system and their functions with reference to digestion, absorption and assimilation.*
- *Brief idea of peristalsis.*

(ii) Skeleton - Movement and Locomotion

- Functions of human skeleton.
- Axial and Appendicular Skeleton.
- Types of joints with reference to their location:
  - *immovable joints*
  - *slightly movable joints*
  - *freely movable (hinge joint, ball and socket joint, gliding joint, pivot joint).*

(iii) Structure and functions of skin.

- *Various parts of the skin and their functions.*
- *Special derivatives of the skin with reference to sweat glands, sebaceous glands, hair, nails and mammary glands.*
- *Heat regulation - vasodilation and vasoconstriction.*

(iv) Respiratory System: Organs; mechanism of breathing; tissue respiration, heat production.

- *Structures of the respiratory system.*
- *Differences between anaerobic respiration in plants and in man.*
- *Role of diaphragm and intercostal muscles in breathing to provide a clear idea of the breathing process.*
- *Brief idea of gaseous transport and tissue respiration.*
- *Brief understanding of respiratory volumes.*
- *Effect of altitude on breathing; asphyxiation and hypoxia.*

Health and Hygiene

(i) A brief introduction to maintaining good health.

General idea of personal hygiene, public hygiene and sanitation.

(ii) A brief introduction to communicable, non – communicable, endemic, epidemic, pandemic and sporadic diseases; modes of transmission.

- *Meaning of each of the above with examples.*
- *Modes of transmission: air borne, water borne; vectors (housefly, mosquito, cockroach).*

(iii) Bacterial, Viral, Protozoan, Helminthic diseases:

- *Bacterial: Cholera, typhoid, tuberculosis.*
- *Viral: AIDS, Chicken pox, Hepatitis.*
- *Protozoan: Malaria, Amoebic dysentery, Sleeping sickness.*
- *Helminthic: Ascariasis, Taeniasis, Filiariasis.*

(symptoms and measures to control the above diseases.)
(Scientific names of causative agents not required).

(iv) Aids to Health: Active and passive immunity.

- *Meaning of Active and passive immunity.*
- *An understanding of the use and action of the following – vaccination, immunization, antitoxin, serum, antiseptics, disinfectants, antibiotics.*
- *An idea of the local defense system and its merits, difference between antiseptics and disinfectants.*

(v) Health Organisations: Red Cross, WHO.
Major activities of the Red Cross and WHO.

Waste Generation and Management

(i) Sources of waste - domestic, industrial, agricultural, commercial and other establishments.

- *Domestic waste: paper, glass, plastic, rags, kitchen waste, etc.*
- *Industrial: mining operations, cement factories, oil refineries, construction units.*
- *Agricultural: plant remains, animal waste, processing waste.*
- *Municipal sewage: Sewage, degradable and non-degradable waste from offices, etc.*
- *e-waste: brief idea about e-waste.*

(ii) Methods of safe disposal of waste.

- *Segregation, dumping, composting, drainage, treatment of effluents before discharge, incineration, use of scrubbers and electrostatic precipitators.*
- *Segregation of domestic waste into biodegradable and non-biodegradable by households: garden waste to be converted to compost; sewage treatment plants.*

Internal Assessment of Practical Work

The practical work is designed to test the ability of the candidates to make accurate observations from specimens of plants and animals.

Plant Life

(i) The examination of an onion peel under the microscope to study various parts of the cell.

(ii) A cross-pollinated flower to be examined and identified and the parts to be studied and labelled e.g. Hibiscus.

(iii) Specimens of germinating seeds with plumule and radicle (the bean seed and maize grain) for examination, identification, drawing and labelling the parts.

Animal Life

(i) The examination of a human cheek cell under the microscope to study various parts of the cell.

(ii) Identification of sugar, starch, protein and fat. through conduct of relevant tests.

(iii) Examination and identification of specimens belonging to the following groups of animals:

Non Chordata - Porifera, Coelenterata, Platyhelminthes, Nemathelminthes, Annelida, Arthropoda, Mollusca and Echinodermata.

Chordata- Pisces, Amphibia, Reptilia, Aves, Mammalia.

Identification of the structure of the following organs through specimens/models and charts: Lung and skin.

(iv) Experiments to show the mechanism of breathing.

Bell jar experiment should be discussed. Comparison should be made with the human lungs and respiratory tract to show the mechanism of breathing.

(v) Visit a few establishments in the locality such as motor repair workshops, kilns, pottery making units, fish and vegetable markets, restaurants, dyeing units. Find out the types of wastes and methods prevalent for their disposal. On the basis of the information collected prepare a report, suggest measures to improve the environmental conditions.

(vi) Visit a water treatment plant, sewage treatment plant or garbage dumping or vermi composting sites in the locality and study their working.

CHAPTER 01

Cell : The Unit of Life

Chapter Inside

- Discovery of Cell • Structural Organisation of a Cell
- Cell Organelles • Plant Cell and Animal Cell

Cell is the fundamental, structural and functional unit of living organisms. All organisms including plants and animals are composed of cells. Each and every cell arises from its pre-existing cell and becomes specialised for performing different functions after division.

All organisms including humans are produced from a single cell. In this chapter, we will study about the complex structure of a cell, its various organelles and their functioning inside the cell.

Discovery of Cell

Robert Hooke (1665) was the first scientist who discovered cell. He examined the slice of cork under the self-designed microscope having two lenses.

He observed that cork consists of small box-like structures, resembling honeycomb and he called them cells. The cork cells which Hooke saw were actually dead cells.

Major Landmarks Related to Cell Discovery

Scientists	Years	Works
Robert Hooke	1665	Discovered cells for first time in cork slice with the help of a primitive microscope.
Antonie van Leeuwenhoek	1674	Discovered free-living cells in pond water by his improved microscope.
Robert Brown	1831	Discovered nucleus in cell.
Schleiden and Schwann	1838-1839	Presented cell theory, which states that all plants and animals are composed of cells and the cell is the basic unit of life.
Purkinje	1839	Coined the term 'protoplasm' for the jelly-like semifluid substance of cell.
Rudolf Virchow	1855	Expanded the cell theory by suggesting that all cells arise from pre-existing cells.
Knoll and Ruska	1932	Built an electron microscope that made understanding of the complex structure of cell and its organelles possible.

Cell Theory

MJ Schleiden (1838), a German botanist and **Theodor Schwann** (1839), a German zoologist after studying plant cells and animal cells independently said that all plants and animals are made up of cells. In 1855, **Rudolf Virchow**, a German pathologist further expanded it by saying that cell arises from pre-existing cells (*Omnis-cellula-e-cellula*).

Observations made by these scientists gave rise to the concept of cell theory which can be concluded as follows

(i) All living organisms are made up of cells.
(ii) Cell is the smallest structural and functional unit of life.
(iii) All cells arise from pre-existing cells.

During chemical observations and after studying functions of different parts, it was concluded that all cells are similar in chemical constituents and metabolic activities.

Note
- The first simple microscope was constructed by Antonie van Leeuwenhoek.
- The invention of electron microscope helped to view cells more precisely.

Size of the Cells

The size of the cells varies significantly from the smallest cell of *Mycoplasma* (0.01-0.5 μm) to very large egg cells of the ostrich (15 cm in diameter).

The longest cell of human body are the nerve cells which may reach up to the length of 90 cm. Cells are usually small in size because large surface area relative to volume ensures greater diffusion of substances as well as aids in better cell-to-cell communication.

Shape of the Cells

The shape of the cells is also variable and depends upon the functions as well as internal and external pressures of the cell. It can be elliptical (e.g. fat cell), spherical (e.g. ovum), spindle-shaped (e.g. smooth muscle cell), knobbed thread (e.g. sperm), discoidal or oval (e.g. RBC), elongated (e.g. nerve cells), bean-shaped (stomata), star-shaped (bone cells), etc.

The shape of cells of *Amoeba* and white blood cells keeps on changing and hence, they do not have definite shapes.

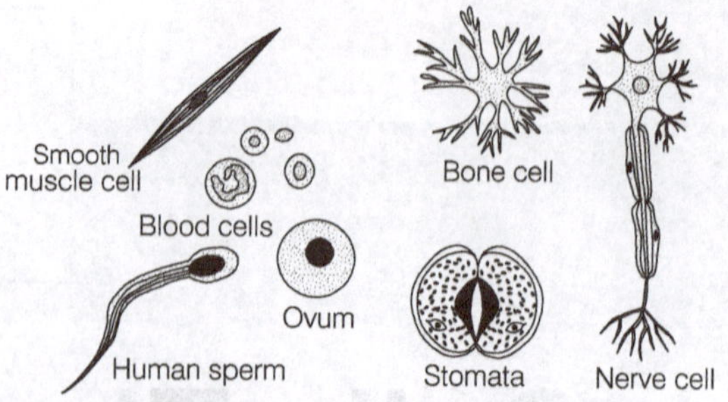

Different shapes of cells from human body

Significance of Cell Shape

When maturity is attained, cells acquire specific shape and structure according to their functions. This can be understood by the following examples

(i) The human red blood corpuscles have concave surface on two sides to increase surface area for gaseous exchange (CO_2 and O_2). They also lack nucleus.
(ii) The nerve cell possesses an elongated and extended shape. It transmits the nerve impulse to distant parts of body from brain and *vice-versa*.
(iii) The White Blood Cells (WBCs) do not have any specific shape. These are *Amoeba*-like structures. These cells squeeze out from blood vessels (one cell thick) by changing their shape and come to the body fluid (**diapedesis**) at the site of infection to kill the invading pathogen.
(iv) In plants, guard cells take specific bean-shape for performing the function of opening and closing of stomata. Similarly, elongated xylem and phloem cells help in the conduction of water and nutrients in plants.

Cellular Composition of Different Organisms

The discovery of microscopes has established the fact that organisms are both single-celled and many-celled. The single-celled organisms are called **unicellular organisms**, e.g. *Amoeba, Paramecium, Euglena, Chlamydomonas*, bacteria, *Mycoplasma*, unicellular fungi like yeast, etc.

On the other hand in many organisms, cells work together to form tissues which ultimately form organs. When many organs work together, they form the body. Such organisms are **multicellular organisms**, e.g. flowering plants, *Hydra*, worm, monkey, humans, etc.

Types of Cells

The cells can be of following two types depending on their structural organisation, *viz*

(i) Prokaryotic cells

(ii) Eukaryotic cells

Prokaryotic Cells

These cells have primitive undefined nucleus called **nucleoid** (*Pro*–primitive, *karyon*–nucleus), i.e. these cells do not have a well-developed nucleus and cell organelles. All bacterial cells are prokaryotic cells. Other examples include Blue-Green Algae (BGA) and Pleuro Pneumonia-Like Organism (PPLO).

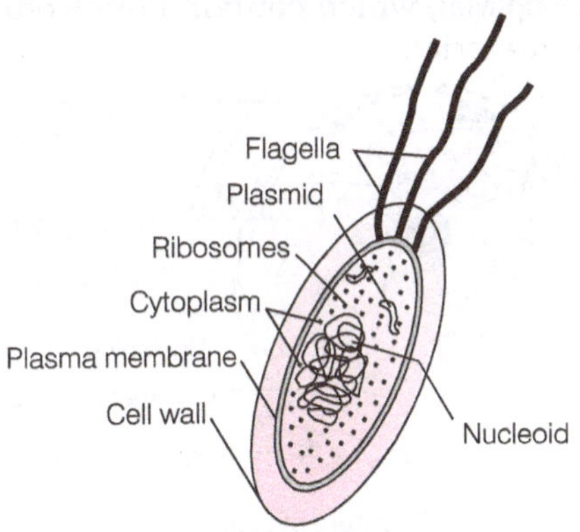

Prokaryotic cell

Eukaryotic Cells

These cells possesses membrane bound nucleus and other cell organelles, which are well-defined and well-developed. A variety of locomotory structure and cytoskeleton are also present in them, e.g. plant cell and animal cell (discussed later in this chapter).

Check Your LEARNING...

1 Who first discovered the living cells?
2 Who postulated that all cells arise from pre-existing cells?
3 What is the average size of ***Mycoplasma***?
4 Name any two unicellular organisms.
5 Give any two examples of cells with no definite shape.
6 Expand the term BGA and PPLO.

Structural Organisation of a Cell

All the components of a cell are immersed in a self perpetuating jelly like liquid called **protoplasm**. It was called physical basis of life by Huxley.

Protoplasm

Protoplasm is jelly-like viscous and colourless. It is the living part of a cell, i.e. it can perform all the vital activities. Protoplasm can be differentiated into two regions, namely **nucleoplasm**, i.e. protoplasm in the nucleus and **cytoplasm**, i.e. extranuclear protoplasm.

These components can be broadly categorised into following three categories

(i) **Outer covering**, i.e. **cell wall** (non-living) and **cell membrane** (living).

(ii) **Cytoplasm** that contain many specialised cell organelles.

(iii) **Nucleus** is a double-membraned organelle that contains the genetic material.

The detailed study of cell components is discussed below

Plasma Membrane or Cell Membrane

This is the outermost covering of cell that separates the contents of the cell from its external environment. Plasma membrane is made up of lipids and proteins.

Structurally the lipids are present as continuous bilayer in which proteins and other chemicals are placed randomly.

The presence of lipids (as phospholipids) and proteins provides flexibility to plasma membrane and enables the cell to engulf food and other materials from external environment.

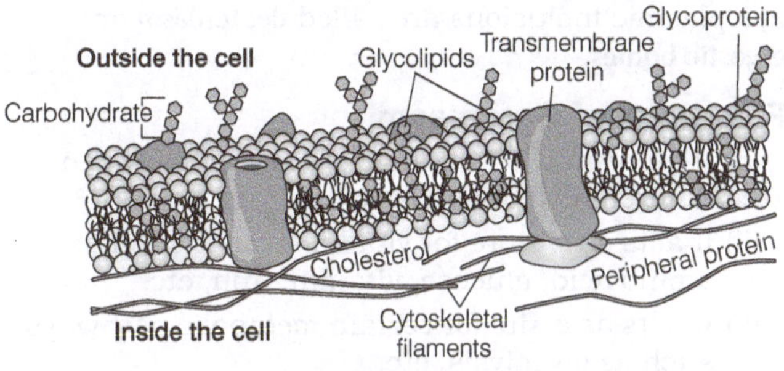

Plasma membrane

Functions of Plasma Membrane

(i) It permits the entry and exit of some selective materials in and out of the cell. The cell membrane therefore, acts as semipermeable or selectively permeable or partially permeable or differentially permeable membrane.

(ii) It helps to maintain the shape of the cell.

(iii) It acts as a mechanical barrier and protects the internal contents of the cell from leaking out.

(iv) It provides protection against microbes and foreign substances.

(v) It gets modified to perform different functions, e.g. microvilli in intestine of human beings for absorption.

Cell Wall

It is a tough, non-living covering present outside the plasma membrane. It is found only in plant cells and is freely permeable. It is mainly made up of cellulose, a complex non-living substance that provides structural strength to plants.

Functions of Cell Wall

(i) It is freely permeable, i.e. it allows the movement of molecules into and out of the cell without hinderance.

(ii) It provides rigidity to the plant cell and maintains the shape of cells.

Note Fibres of cotton, jute and coconut which are of great economic value are the cell walls of dead cells.

Cytoplasm

The large region of each cell enclosed by cell membrane is filled with cytoplasm. It is dense, viscous and colloidal solution of organic compounds like minerals, carbohydrates, proteins, lipids and vitamins. All metabolic biological reactions take place in the cytoplasm.

Cytoplasm of all living organisms possesses various living and non-living structures which are referred to as **cytoplasmic inclusions.** The living cytoplasmic inclusions are called **cell organelles** and non-living cytoplasmic inclusions are called **deutoplasm** or **ergastic bodies.**

Functions of Cytoplasm

(i) It helps in the exchange of material between different cell organelles.

(ii) It acts as a store for vital molecules such as amino acid, glucose, vitamin, iron, etc.

(iii) It acts as a site for certain metabolic pathways such as glycolysis, etc.

Check Your LEARNING...

1 Name the components of plasma membrane.
2 Which structural component provides flexibility to plasma membrane?
3 Name the carbohydrate that forms the cell wall.
4 What are cytoplasmic inclusions? Give example.
5 Name any two vital molecules found in cytoplasm.

Cell Organelles

Large and complex cells, including cells of multicellular organisms need a lot of chemical activities to support their complicated structure and function. To keep these activities separated from each other, these cells use small membrane bound structures within themselves called cell organelles or cell inclusions. They carry out many crucial functions of the cell. Detailed account of these organelles is as follows

Nucleus

It is the largest cell organelle in animal cell and popularly called as the **brain of cell.** It is composed of a double-layered covering called **nuclear membrane.** It has numerous pores called **nuclear pores** for the transfer of materials from inside the nucleus to cytoplasm. It encloses a liquid ground substance called **nucleoplasm,** which contains nucleolus and chromatin material.

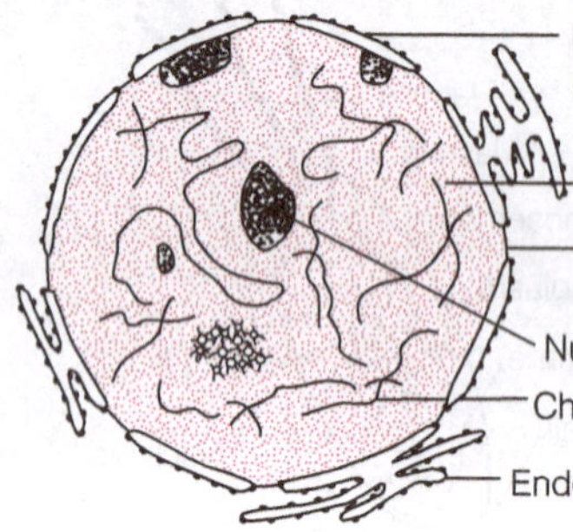

Structure of a nucleus

Nucleolus is a more or less rounded structure found inside the nucleus and does not have covering membranes. It is known as **factory of ribosomes.** As ribosomes are ribonucleoprotein (RNA + protein) particles, hence it has the ability to synthesise both, i.e. RNA and proteins.

Nucleus also contain **chromatin** which is long, thread-like structure. It condenses to form chromosomes during cell division.

Chromosomes are rod-shaped structure that contain information for the inheritance of features from parents to next generation.

They are composed of two components, i.e. DNA and protein. The DNA molecules contain information necessary for constructing and organising cells. The functional segments of DNA are called **genes.**

Number of chromosomes in some plants and animals are given in the table below.

Chromosome Numbers in Some Plants

Garden pea	14
Onion	16
Maize	20
Wheat	42
Potato	48

Chromosome Numbers in Some Animals

Human	46
Gorilla	48
Mouse	40
Honeybee	32
Lion	38
Tiger	38
Cat (domestic)	38
Chicken	78
Dog	78
Ascaris (worm)	4
Cray fish	176

Functions of Nucleus

(i) Nucleus plays an important role in cellular reproduction, in which a cell divides to form two new cells.

(ii) It also determines the cell development and maturity by directing the chemical activities of the cell.

(iii) It helps in the transmission of hereditary traits from parents to offspring.

(iv) It controls all metabolic activities of cell and if it is removed, the cell dies.

Mitochondria

These were first observed by **Kölliker** in 1857. It is a **double membrane** bound cell organelle. The outer membrane is very porous and freely permeable while the inner membrane is selectively permeable and deeply folded into finger-like projections called **cristae**. The latter create large surface area for ATP generating chemical reactions and contains respiratory enzymes.

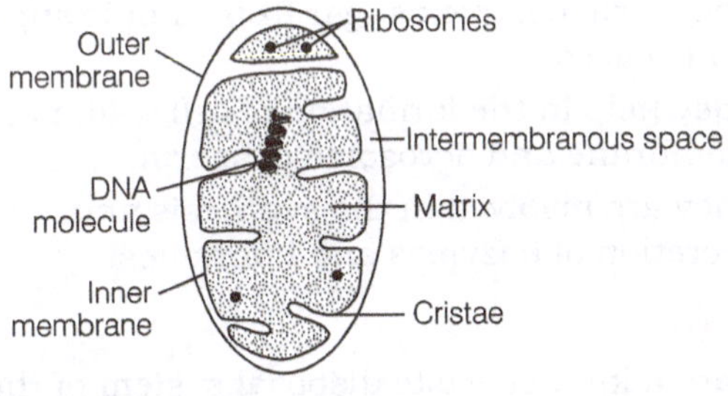

Internal structure of mitochondria

Space between outer and inner membrane is called **intermembranous space.**

Functions of Mitochondria

(i) They generate energy for various activities of cell and are known as the **powerhouse of the cell.** Mitochondria are sites of cellular respiration and release the energy required by the cell in the form of ATP (Adenosine Triphosphate) molecules.

(ii) Whenever the cell requires energy, ATP molecules are broken down and generate energy which is used for metabolic activities within body. Thus, ATP is known as **energy currency of the cell.**

(iii) Mitochondria are strange cell organelles in the sense that they have their own DNA and ribosomes hence, they are able to make some of their own proteins. Thus, these are known as **self-replicating** or **semi-autonomous organelle.**

Plastids

These are large cytoplasmic organelles. They are found in the cells of plants and algae only. Plastids often contain various coloured pigments. On the basis of colour, i.e. type of pigments found in them, plastids are of following types

(i) **Chloroplasts** These are the green plastids that function as the site of photosynthesis, i.e. help in the synthesis of organic food. These are capable of trapping solar energy for photosynthesis with the help of green pigment called **chlorophyll** in them.

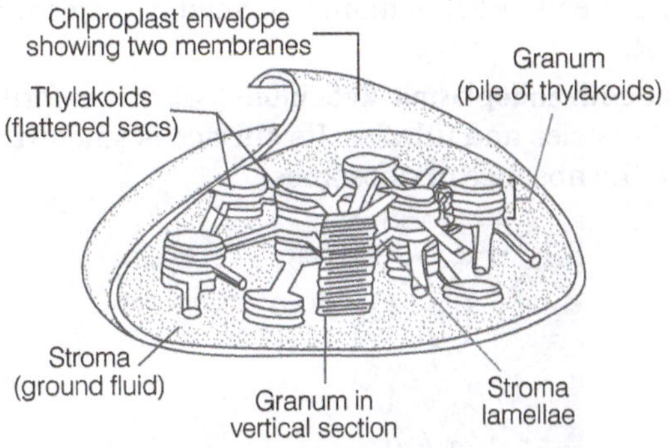

A diagram showing internal structure of chloroplast as revealed by electron microscope

Chloroplast is a double membranous structure and contains its own DNA. It contains a proteinaceous matrix of fluid called **stroma** and the membrane system called **lamellae** or **thylakoids.** At some places, the thylakoids get aggregated to form stacks of discs, called **grana** or granum.

(ii) **Chromoplasts** These are coloured plastids. They contain coloured pigments such as xanthophyll (yellow), carotene (red-orange), etc.
They provide colour to the plant parts (flowers and fruits) thereby, helping them in pollination and dispersal of fruits and seeds.

Note The colouring pigments like blue, violet and purple are not associated with plastids. These colours are attributed by anthocyanin pigments which remain dissolved in cell sap.

(iii) **Leucoplasts** They are colourless plastids. Their main function is to store food materials. They are not involved in the synthetic activities. The leucoplasts are further of three types as follows
   (a) **Amyloplast** It stores starch and thus, found in tubers, cotyledons and endosperm.
   (b) **Elaioplast** It stores oil (lipids) and found in the epidermal cells of oilseeds, anther, etc.
   (c) **Proteinoplast** It stores protein and found in seeds and nuts.

Endoplasmic Reticulum

It is a large network of single membrane-bound tubes and sheets extending from outer nuclear membrane to cell membrane. The ER membrane is similar in structure to the plasma membrane. It occurs in three forms, i.e. **cisternae, vesicles** and **tubules.** ER appears in varying forms in different cells, but it always forms a network system of vesicles and tubules. Depending upon the nature of its membrane, ER is of two types

(i) **Rough Endoplasmic Reticulum** (RER) It contains ribosomal particles, due to which its surface is rough. The ribosomes are the site of protein synthesis. RER is mainly formed of cisternae of ER.

(ii) **Smooth Endoplasmic Reticulum** (SER) It is formed of vesicles and tubules. Its surface is smooth due to the absence of ribosomes.

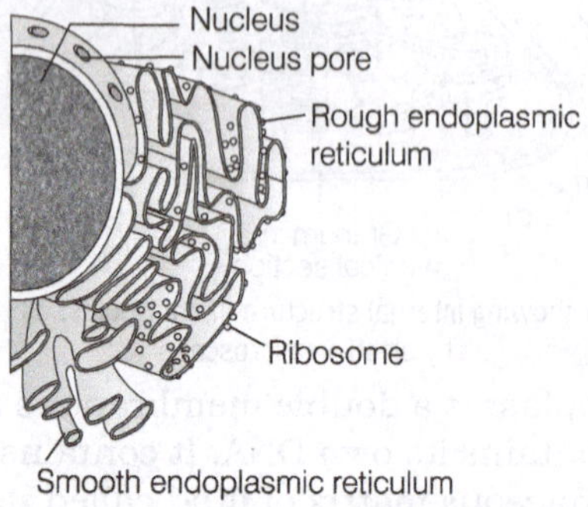

Structure of endoplasmic reticulum

Functions of Endoplasmic Reticulum

(i) It forms a network system and provides a channel for the transport of materials between various regions of cytoplasm or between cytoplasm and nucleus.

(ii) Smooth endoplasmic reticulum helps in the manufacture of fat molecules or lipids. Some of these lipids and proteins help in building cell membrane. This process is called **membrane biogenesis.**

(iii) SER plays crucial role in detoxification of poisons and drugs.

(iv) The ER gives mechanical support to the cytoplasm by providing a kind of cytoskeleton to maintain the shape of cell.

Golgi Bodies

They consist of a system of single membrane bound vesicles arranged parallel to each other in stacks called **cisternae**. These membranes often have connection with the membranes of endoplasmic reticulum and form another portion of a complex cellular membrane system.

The material that is synthesised near Endoplasmic Reticulum (ER) is packaged and dispatched to various parts, i.e. inside and outside the cell through Golgi complex. Golgi complex occurs in all cells except prokaryotes such as PPLO, bacteria and cyanobacteria and some eukaryotes such as human RBCs, sieve tubes of plants, etc. In plants, these are known as **dictyosomes.**

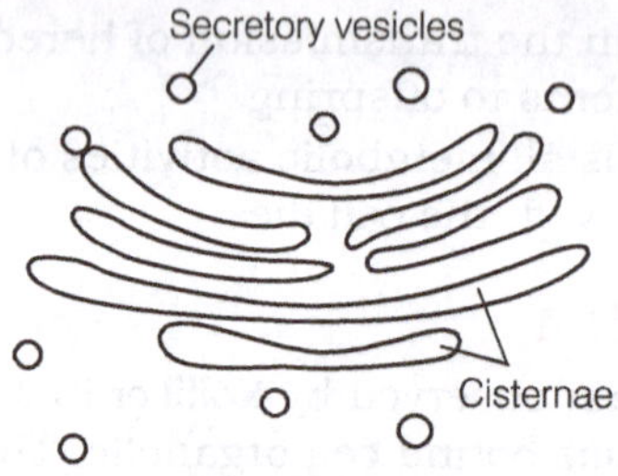

Golgi apparatus

Functions of Golgi Bodies

(i) They are involved in the formation of lysosomes.
(ii) They help in the packaging of materials, storage and modification in vesicles.
(iii) They form complex sugar from simple sugar in some cases.
(iv) They help in the formation of cell wall, plasma membrane and acrosome of sperm.
(v) They are involved in the synthesis and secretion of enzymes and hormones.

Lysosomes

These are a kind of waste disposal system of the cell. Lysosomes are single membrane-bound sacs that are filled with digestive enzymes. These enzymes are made by rough endoplasmic reticulum. Lysosomes are also called the **suicidal bags** of a cell because during the disturbance in cellular metabolism or when the cell gets damaged, lysosomes may burst and the enzymes can digest their own cell. This proces is called **autolysis.**

Functions of Lysosomes

(i) They help to keep the cell clean by digesting any foreign material that enters the cell as well as worn out cellular organelles. Hence, lysosomes are called **scavengers** and **cellular housekeepers**.

(ii) They remove bacteria or any foreign material entering the cell by breaking it into small pieces through its powerful digestive enzymes, which can breakdown all organic materials.

(iii) During starvation, the lysosomes digest stored food contents by **autophagy** and supply energy to the cell.

Ribosomes

These are small sub-spherical granular organelles, that are not bounded by any membrane. They are usually scattered freely in the cytoplasm or attached to the membrane of endoplasmic reticulum. They contain RNA and proteins.

Functions of Ribosomes

They are primarily involved in the synthesis of proteins. Thus, these are called **protein factories**.

Vacuoles

They are the fluid-filled organelles bounded by a membrane called **tonoplast**. In animal cells, these are small and numerous in number. In plant cells, these are large-sized and fewer (usually one) in number.

Functions of Vacuole

(i) Vacuoles are full of cell sap and provide turgidity and rigidity to cells in plants.

(ii) In plants, they store mineral, salts, sugars, water, etc.

(iii) In animals (specially unicellular like protozoan), they perform the function of osmoregulation.

Centrosome

This cell organelle is present only in animal cell and not in plant cell. It is present near the nucleus of the animal cell. It contains two microbodies called **centriole** in its centre.

Both the centrioles in a centrosome lie perpendicular to each other in which each has an organisation like the cartwheel and together they are called **diplosome**.

Functions of Centrosome

(i) It initiates and regulates cell division in animal cells.

(ii) It forms cilia and flagella in ciliated and flagellated cells of organisms.

Plant Cell and Animal Cell

The basic structure in all plant and animal cells is same. However, there exist some important differences between the two. These differences are summarised in the table below.

Differences between Plant and Animal Cells

Cell organelles	Plant cells	Animal cells
Cell wall	It is present on the outer side of plasma membrane.	It is absent.
Centrosomes	They are absent.	They are present near nucleus.
Plastids	These are present which include leucoplast, chromoplast and chloroplast.	These are absent.
Vacuole	One big vacuole is present, covering maximum area of cell.	Many small vacuoles are present.

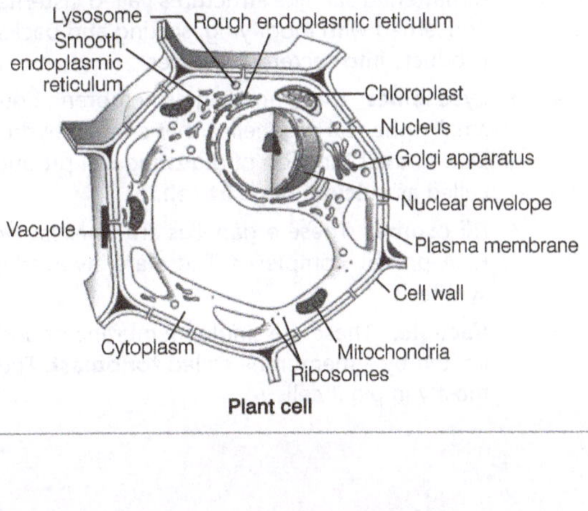

Plant cell

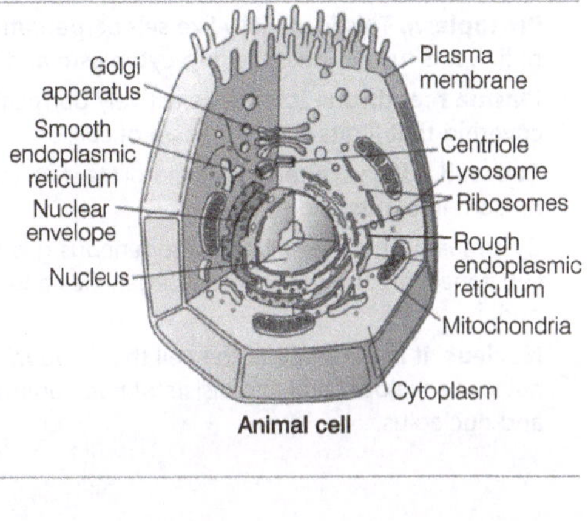

Animal cell

Differences between Prokaryotic and Eukaryotic Cells

Features	Prokaryotic cells	Eukaryotic cells
Size	Generally small (1-10 μm)	Generally large (5-100 μm)
Nuclear region	Poorly developed, no nuclear membrane hence called nucleoid.	Well-defined, surrounded by nuclear membrane.
Chromosome	Single	Multiple
Nucleolus	Absent	Present
Cell organelles	Membrane bound cell organelles are absent.	Cell organelles are present, e.g. mitochondria, plastids, endoplasmic reticulum, etc.
Centriole	Absent	Present in animal cells.
Organisms	Found in bacteria, blue-green algae, etc.	Found in fungi and plant cell.
Cell division	Takes place by fission or budding.	Takes place by mitotic or meiotic cell division.

Check Your LEARNING...

1. Give/state the function of nuclear pores.
2. What is the energy currency of cell?
3. What is the function of cristae in mitochondria?
4. What does the colourless plastids called?
5. Name the particles found on the surface of RER.
6. Name a eukaryotic cell that lacks Golgi complex.
7. How does our body get energy even if we are starving from quite a while?

QUiCK Revision

- **Cell** It is the basic structural and functional unit of life.
- **Cell theory** This was formulated by Schleiden and Schwann and includes following three statements, i.e.
  - (i) All organisms are composed of one or more cell and cell products.
  - (ii) Cells are the structural and functional unit of living organisms.
  - (iii) Cells arise from pre-existing cells (*omnis-cellula-e-cellula*) as given by **Virchow**.
- **Prokaryotic cells** These cells have incipient nucleus that is devoid of membrane. They do not have membrane bound cell organelles.
- **Eukaryotic cells** These cells consist of outer cell wall (only in plants and fungi), plasma membrane, cytoplasm, membrane bound nucleus and within cytoplasm cell organelles are suspended.
- **Protoplasm** This is the jelly like self perpetuating substance of life. It is further divisible into cytoplasm and nucleoplasm.
- **Plasma membrane** It is the selectively permeable outer covering that limits the cytoplasm of cell.
- **Cell wall** It is the outermost, rigid protective covering present in plants and fungi.
- **Cytoplasm** It is a jelly-like homogeneous ground substance. It contains both cell organelles and deutoplasmic bodies.
- **Nucleus** It is the brain of the cell that is bounded by a nuclear envelope. It also consists of nucleoplasm, chromatin and nucleolus.
- **Mitochondria** These are organelles involved in ATP generation in cell. They contain double membranes, i.e. an outer and inner membrane. They contain their own DNA.
- **Plastids** These are double membrane-bound organelles used for trapping solar radiations and storage of food.
- **Chloroplast** It is a chlorophyll containing plastid. It contains an outer and inner membrane. The matrix inside the membrane is stroma in which membranous sacs, i.e. thylakoids are present. In these thylakoids, chlorophyll is found. Chloroplast also contains their own DNA. It is involved in photosynthesis.
- **Endoplasmic reticulum** It consists of interconnected membranes in the form of cisternae, vesicles and tubules. It is of two types, **rough endoplasmic reticulum** and **smooth endoplasmic reticulum.**
- **Golgi apparatus** It is also membranous organelle consisting of flattened sac-like structures called cisternae. These are concerned with modifying, sorting and packaging of cell products into secretory vesicles.
- **Lysosomes** These are single-membrane bound small-spherical organelles that contain hydrolytic enzymes. Due to their function of digesting cell products, these are also called as **suicidal bags of cell.**
- **Ribosomes** These organelles are smallest, non-membranous, RNA-protein complexes. These are involved in protein synthesis.
- **Vacuoles** These are single membrane bound organelles limited by a membrane called **tonoplast**. They are found mostly in plant cells.

Chapter Practice

Section-I

1 Mark Questions

1. Name the following.
   (i) The scientist who discovered nucleus.
   (ii) A cell with primitive nucleus.
   (iii) The non-living structure present only in plant cell.
   (iv) The area of cellular activities in plant and animal cells.
   (v) The cells of human body that do not contain nucleus at maturity.
   (vi) The part of cell which is concerned with liberation of energy.
   (vii) The type of plastid involved in photosynthesis.
   (viii) The organelle that contains its own genetic material.
   (ix) Organelle responsible for making cell wall in plant cell.
   (x) Organelle rich in hydrolytic enzymes.
   (xi) The organelle of cell responsible for the synthesis of protein.
   (xii) Membrane that covers the vacuole.
   (xiii) An organelle present in the animal cell, but not in plant cell.

Ans. (i) Robert Brown
(ii) Prokaryotic cell
(iii) Cell wall
(iv) Cytoplasm
(v) Red blood corpuscles
(vi) Mitochondria
(vii) Chloroplast
(viii) Chloroplast and mitochondria
(ix) Golgi bodies
(x) Lysosomes
(xi) Ribosomes
(xii) Tonoplast
(xiii) Centrosome

2. Correct and rewrite the following statements by changing the underlined words.
   (i) <u>Purkinje</u> discovered the cell.
   (ii) The three components of a cell include cell membrane, nucleus and <u>Golgi bodies</u>.
   (iii) <u>Centrosome</u> is known as the factory of ribosomes.
   (iv) The functional segments of DNA are called <u>chromatin</u>.
   (v) <u>Leucoplasts</u> are the green-coloured plastids found in plants.

Ans. (i) Robert Hooke discovered the cell.
(ii) The three components of a cell include cell membrane, nucleus and cytoplasm.
(iii) Nucleolus is known as the factory of ribosomes.
(iv) The functional segments of DNA are called genes.
(v) Chloroplasts are the green-coloured plastids found in plants.

3. Give biological reasons for the following.
   (i) The shape of the cell usually affects its functions.
   (ii) Plasma membrane is called selectively permeable membrane.
   (iii) Mitochondria are known as powerhouse of the cell.
   (iv) Plastids are able to make their own protein.
   (v) Lysosomes are known as suicidal bags.

Ans. (i) The shape of a cell plays an important role in the functions performed by it. For example, white blood cells do not have any fixed shape. Thus, they can easily squeeze out from thick blood vessels by changing the shape and come to the body fluid to kill the invading pathogen. Similarly, RBCs have concave shape and lacks cell organelles, so that they can carry maximum oxygen.
(ii) Plasma membrane selectively allows the entry and exit of some materials in and out of the cell. Therefore, it is called selectively permeable membrane.
(iii) Mitochondria are known as powerhouse of the cell because these are associated with cellular respiration and energy generation of the cell.
(iv) Plastids like chloroplast have their own DNA and ribosomes. Therefore, they are able to make their own proteins.
(v) Lysosomes are called suicidal bags because they contain digestive enzyme, which help in digesting the dead cell organelles and foreign particles.

4. (i) Match the following columns.

Column I		Column II	
A.	Rudolf Virchow	1.	Built an electron microscope
B.	Leewenhoek	2.	Cell theory
C.	Knoll and Ruska	3.	Cell theory expansion
D.	Schleiden and Schwann	4.	Coined the term protoplasm
E.	Purkinje	5.	Discovered free-living cell

Ans. A–3, B–5, C–1, D–2, E–4

(ii) Match the following columns.

	Column I		Column II
A.	Smooth endoplasmic reticulum	1.	*Amoeba*
B.	Lysosome	2.	Nucleus
C.	Nucleoid	3.	Bacteria
D.	Food vacuoles	4.	Detoxification
E.	Chromatin material	5.	Suicidal bags

Ans. A-4, B-5, C-3, D-1, E-2

(iii) Match the following columns.

	Column I		Column II
A.	Vacuoles	1.	Intracellular digestion
B.	Nucleolus	2.	Respiratory enzymes
C.	Lysosomes	3.	Covered by tonoplast
D.	Plastids	4.	Chloroplast
E.	Cristae	5.	Forms Ribosomes

Ans. A-3, B-5, C-1, D-4, E-2

5. Choose the correct answer from the four options given below.

(i) Which part of a plant cell is dead?
(a) Plasma membrane (b) Plastids
(c) Cell wall (d) All of these

Ans. (c)

(ii) Largest cell organelle present in animal cell is
(a) nucleus
(b) chloroplast
(c) endoplasmic reticulum
(d) mitochondria

Ans. (a)

(iii) Well-defined nucleus is absent in
(a) plant cell (b) animal cell
(c) eukaryotic cell (d) prokaryotic cell

Ans. (d)

(iv) An undefined nuclear region in prokaryotic cell is known as
(a) nucleus (b) nucleolus
(c) nucleic acid (d) nucleoid

Ans. (d)

(v) Mitochondrial infoldings are known as
(a) cristae (b) matrix
(c) grana (d) cisternae

Ans. (a)

(vi) Coloured plastids are known as
(a) leucoplast (b) chromoplast
(c) stroma (d) None of these

Ans. (b)

(vii) Secretory organelles of the cell are
(a) dictyosome (b) lysosome
(c) peroxisome (d) ribosome

Ans. (a)

(viii) Which cell organelle helps in protein synthesis?
(a) Nucleus
(b) Golgi apparatus
(c) Ribosomes
(d) Plastids

Ans. (c)

(ix) Plant cell lacks
(a) centrosome (b) mitochondria
(c) plastids (d) nucleus

Ans. (a)

(x) The plant and animal cells differ from each other in
(a) nutrition (b) growth
(c) movement (d) respiration

Ans. (a)

6. (i) Fill the paragraph with the help of words given in box.

Plastid, chlorophyll, animal cell, cell wall, vacuoles, plasma membrane, mitochondria, DNA, storage, chloroplast

An 1. .... is a type of eukaryotic cell. It is distinct from other eukaryotes, most notably plant cell as they lack 2. .... and 3. .... They also have smaller 4. .... Due to the presence of a 5. ...., these cells permit the movement of substances selectively. 6. .... are organelles found in nearly all eukaryotes. They are surrounded by two membranes. Mitochondria contain their own 7. .... Plants have 8. .... Again, these have their own DNA content and 9. .... which produce organic compounds through photosynthesis. Other plastids in plants are involved in 10. .... of materials.

Ans. 1. animal cell
2. cell wall
3. plastid
4. vacuoles
5. plasma membrane
6. Mitochondria
7. DNA
8. chloroplast
9. chlorophyll
10. storage

(ii) The nucleus present in prokaryotic cells is primitive and is called 1. .... This is not well-developed unlike 2. .... cells which possess a well-defined nucleus. 3. .... is a well-known example of prokaryotic cells. Apart from the nuclear region, the number of chromosome in 4. .... is only one.

Ans. 1. nucleoid
2. eukaryotic
3. Blue-green algae
4. prokaryotic cells

7. Choose the odd one out from the following terms given below and name the category to which other three belong.
(i) *Amoeba, Paramecium, Euglena, Hydra*
(ii) Yeast, *Mycoplasma*, Bacteria, Mushroom
(iii) Chloroplast, Chromoplast, Leucoplast and Protoplasm
(iv) Nucleus, Mitochondria, Chloroplast, Golgi apparatus
(v) Nuclear membrane, Nucleolus, DNA and Cytoplasm

Ans. (i) **Odd term** *Hydra* (a multicellular organism)
Other three are unicellular organisms.
(ii) **Odd term** Mushroom (multicellular)
Other three are unicellular organisms.
(iii) **Odd term** Protoplasm
Other three are type of plastids in plant cell.
(iv) **Odd term** Golgi apparatus
Other three are double membrane bound organelles.
(v) **Odd term** Cytoplasm
Other terms are related with structure of nucleus.

8. Given below are sets of five terms each. Rewrite the terms in correct order of logical sequence.
(i) Cell membrane, Cytoplasm, Cell wall, Nuclear membrane, Nucleolus
(ii) Genes, Nuclear membrane, Nucleolus, Chromosome, Nucleoplasm

Ans. (i) Cell wall, Cell membrane, Cytoplasm, Nuclear membrane, Nucleolus
(ii) Nuclear membrane, Nucleoplasm, Nucleolus, Chromosomes, Genes

9. Expand the following biological abbreviations.
(i) DNA (ii) RNA
(iii) ATP (iv) RER
(v) SER

Ans. (i) Deoxyribonucleic Acid
(ii) Ribonucleic Acid
(iii) Adenosine Triphosphate
(iv) Rough Endoplasmic Reticulum
(v) Smooth Endoplasmic Reticulum

10. State whether the following statements are true or false. Correct and rewrite the false statement.
(i) All living organisms originate from a single cell.
(ii) All cells have cell wall.
(iii) Cell membrane is living.
(iv) Golgi bodies are the storehouse of energy.
(v) Chromoplast contains chlorophyll.
(vi) Vacuole contains cell sap.
(vii) Chromosomes are present in the cytoplasm.

Ans. (i) True
(ii) False, only plant cells have cell wall.
(iii) True
(iv) False, mitochondria are the storehouse of energy.
(v) False, chloroplast contains chlorophyll.
(vi) True
(vii) False, chromosomes are present in the nucleus.

11. Mention the exact location of the following.
(i) Cell organelles (ii) Nucleolus
(iii) Genes (iv) Stroma
(v) Centrosome

Ans. (i) Cell organelles are present in the cytoplasm.
(ii) Nucleolus is found inside the nucleus.
(iii) Genes are present on the chromosome.
(iv) Stroma is the proteinaceous matrix of fluid present in chloroplast.
(v) Centrosomes are present near the nucleus of the animal cell.

12. Give one example of each.
(i) Smallest cell
(ii) Largest cell
(iii) Longest cell
(iv) A cell that show diapedesis
(v) Unicellular fungi
(vi) Eukaryotic one-celled organism
(vii) Coloured plastids

Ans. (i) *Mycoplasma*
(ii) Ostrich's egg
(iii) Nerve cell
(iv) White Blood Corpuscles (WBCs)
(v) Yeast
(vi) *Paramecium*
(vii) Chromoplast/Chloroplast

13. State the main function of the following.
(i) Plasma membrane
(ii) Nucleus
(iii) Nucleolus
(iv) Centrioles
(v) Mitochondria
(vi) Chloroplasts
(vii) Rough endoplasmic reticulum
(viii) Smooth endoplasmic reticulum
(ix) Golgi body
(x) Lysosomes

Ans. (i) **Plasma membrane** It acts as a semipermeable membrane and allows only selective substances to pass through it.
(ii) **Nucleus** It is the controlling centre of a cell. It contains the DNA (genetic information) in the form of genes.
(iii) **Nucleolus** It helps in ribosome synthesis.
(iv) **Centrioles** They initiate cell division in animal cells.
(v) **Mitochondria** The main function of mitochondria in aerobic cells is the production of energy by the synthesis of ATP.
(vi) **Chloroplasts** These are the sites of photosynthesis within plant cells.

(vii) **Rough ER** It acts as the site of protein synthesis.

(viii) **Smooth ER** It acts as the site of lipid synthesis.

(ix) **Golgi body** It is involved in the formation of lysosomes and helps in storage, modification and packaging of materials in vesicles.

(x) **Lysosomes** They help to keep the cell clean by digesting dead cells and foreign particles.

14. Differentiate between the following pairs on the basis of what is given in bracket.

(i) Unicellular and Multicellular organisms (structure)

(ii) Prokaryotic and Eukaryotic cells (presence and absence of nucleus)

(iii) Cell wall and Cell membrane (location)

(iv) Cytoplasm and Protoplasm (structure)

(v) Organ and Organelle (function)

(vi) Chloroplast and Chromoplast (colour and function)

Ans. (i) Difference between unicellular organisms and multicellular organisms is as follows

Unicellular organisms	Multicellular organisms
These organisms consist of only one cell, e.g. *Amoeba*, bacteria.	These organisms consist of more than one cell, e.g. plants, human beings.

(ii) Difference between prokaryotic and eukaryotic cells is as follows

Prokaryotic cell	Eukaryotic cell
Nuclear region is poorly defined due to the absence of nuclear envelope and is called nucleoid.	Nuclear region is well-defined and nucleus is surrounded by a nuclear membrane.

(iii) Difference between cell wall and cell membrane is as follows

Cell wall	Cell membrane
It is the outer covering of plant cell.	It is the outer covering of animal cell.

(iv) Differences between cytoplasm and protoplasm are as follows

Cytoplasm	Protoplasm
A viscous semi-transparent jelly-like substance present in the cell.	It is a translucent living substance of a cell.
It excludes nucleus.	It includes nucleus.

(v) Difference between organ and organelle is as follows

Organ	Organelle
It is a multicellular structure that performs specific functions in the body.	It is a part of a cell that performs specific functions within the cell.

(vi) Differences between chloroplast and chromoplast are as follows

Chloroplast	Chromoplast
It is the green-coloured plastid.	It is yellow or orange coloured (other than green) plastid.
It helps in photosynthesis.	It gives colour to fruits and flowers and helps in pollination.

15. Give appropriate biological/technical terms for the following.

(i) The controlling centre of a cell.

(ii) 'Powerhouse' of a cell.

(iii) Colourless plastids

(iv) Suicidal bags of a cell.

(v) Protein factories of the cell.

Ans. (i) Nucleus (ii) Mitochondria

(iii) Leucoplasts (iv) Lysosomes

(v) Ribosome

16. Briefly explain the following terms.

(i) Protoplasm (ii) Nucleoplasm

(iii) Chromatin (iv) Chromoplast

(v) Tonoplast

Ans. (i) Protoplasm is an aggregate of various organic and inorganic substances in the form of granular fluid where all the biological reactions take place.

(ii) Nucleoplasm is a liquid ground substance in the nucleus which contains nucleolus and chromatin material.

(iii) Chromatin is thin thread-like structures made up of DNA and protein. It condenses during cell division to form a thick rod-like structure called chromosomes.

(iv) The coloured plastids in plant cells are known as chromoplasts, which give colour to flowers and fruits.

(v) Tonoplast is a membrane surrounding a vacuole in plant cell.

17. Answer the following questions briefly.

(i) Who discoverd cell and how?

(ii) Who proposed cell theory?

(iii) What is membrane biogenesis?

(iv) Write the name of different plant parts in which chloroplast and leucoplast are present.

(v) Name some common features of both plant and animal cells.

Ans. (i) Robert Hooke discovered cell with the help of his self-designed microscope. He examined a thin slice of cork and saw that the cork resembled the structures of a honeycomb having many compartments.

(ii) Cell theory was proposed by Schwann and Schleiden in 1839. Rudolf Virchow in 1855 made an addition to the cell theory by saying that all cells arise from pre-existing cells.

(iii) Lipids and cholesterol formed by SER and some proteins synthesised by RER helps in building the cell membrane. This process is called membrane biogenesis.

(iv) Chloroplast is present in mesophyll cells of the leaves. These are the green plastids which act as the site for protein synthesis.
Leucoplasts are the colourless plastids and they play a major role in storage of materials. They are found in tubers, cotyledons and endosperm.

(v) Some common features of both plant and animal cells are as
 (a) Organelles like nucleus, mitochondria, endoplasmic reticulum, plasma membrane, cytoplasm, ribosomes and Golgi apparatus are found in both type of cells.
 (b) Both type of cell undergo cell division.
 (c) Cellular respiration occurs in both type of cells.

2 Marks Questions

18. Why are the cells called the structural and functional unit of life?

Ans. Living cells have certain specific components within it known as cell organelles. Each kind of cell organelle performs a specific function, such as making new materials in the cells, release of waste, transportation, etc. Thus, a cell can perform all its functions with the help of these organelles. That is why, the cells are called structural and functional unit of life.

19. Draw a diagram of prokaryotic cell and label cell wall, ribosomes, nucleoid and plasma membrane.

Ans.

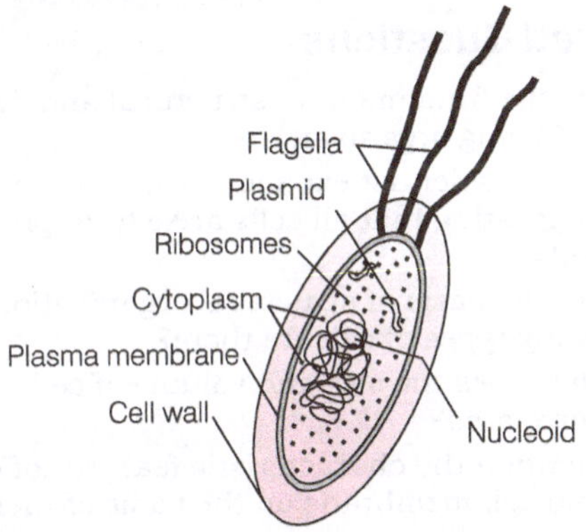

20. What are the different types of endoplasmic reticulum? Write the functions of each.

Ans. There are two types of Endoplasmic Reticulum (ER)
Rough ER (RER) Ribosomes present on its surface are the site of protein synthesis.
Smooth ER (SER) Ribosomes are absent on their surface. These act as a site of lipid synthesis.

21. How is endoplasmic reticulum important for membrane biosynthesis?

Ans. Importance of ER in membrane biosynthesis are
 (i) RER synthesises proteins, which are passed to Golgi apparatus.
 (ii) The SER helps in the manufacture of fat and lipids, which along with protein helps in building of cell membrane.
 (iii) Endoplasmic reticulum helps in transporting proteins to various places.

22. What is the significance of vacuole in a plant cell?

Ans. The vacuole is membrane bound space found in the cytoplasm. It contains water, sap, excretory product and other materials that are not useful for the cell. In plant cells, vacuoles occupy 90% of the volume of the cell. They help in maintaining cell fluid balance and shape of the cell by maintaining turgor pressure against the cell wall.

23. If the organisation of a cell is destroyed due to some physical or chemical influence, what will happen?

Ans. Living cells are capable of performing certain basic functions due to the presence of cell organelles present in it. If this organisation of cell is destroyed, then cell will not be able to perform its basic functions and it will die after some time.

3 Marks Questions

24. Briefly give the contributions of the following scientists in formulating the cell theory
 (i) Rudolf Virchow
 (ii) Schleiden and Schwann

Ans. (i) Rudolf Virchow (1855) He was the first to explain that the cells divide and new cells are formed from the pre-existing cells (*omnis cellula-e-cellula*). He demonstrated that the cell theory applies to diseased tissue as well as to healthy tissue. He also engaged his research in the fields of Archaeology and Anthropology.
 (ii) Schleiden and Schwann (1839) They observed animal and plant cells and then proposed cell theory. This theory explains that all animals and plants are composed of cells, which serve as the structural and functional unit.

25. What are the disadvantages of multicellularity?

Ans. The disadvantages of multicellularity are
 (i) Specialised cells often lose power of division, so that injury is not repaired, e.g. nerve cells.
 (ii) Regeneration ability of multicellular organisms decreases with specialisation.
 (iii) Specialised cells may lose vital functions in order to carryout specific activity, e.g. RBCs and sieve tube cells.

26. Multicellular organisms show division of labour. Explain.

Ans. The body of a multicellular organisms contains cell as a basic structural unit. The cells are organised to form tissues such as blood, bone, etc. The tissues are organised to form organs such as heart, kidney, etc. The organs are further organised to form organ systems such as digestive system, reproductive system, respiratory system, etc. Hence, various organ systems of organism get arranged to form a complete individual which shows division of labour.

27. Mention the differences between prokaryotic and eukaryotic cells.

Ans. Refer to table on page no. 8.

28. Write a short note on plasma membrane.

Ans. Cell membrane is the outer boundary of a cell. It is a thin, elastic and living membrane. It has fine pores through which materials enter or exit the cells. It allows certain materials to pass through it, hence called as semipermeable membrane. It is composed of a lipids bilayer and proteins.

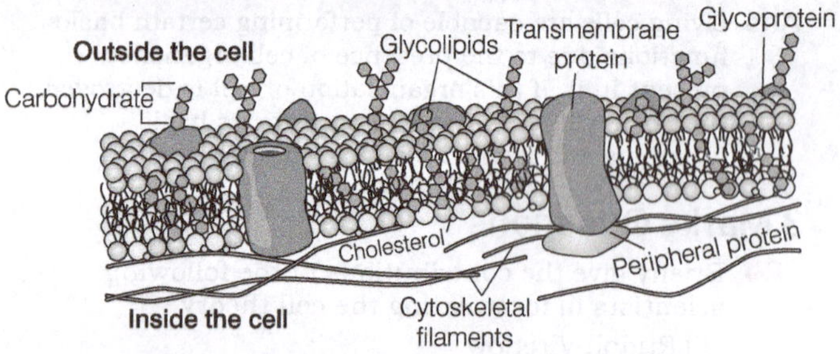

29. What would happen if the plasma membrane ruptures or breaks down?

Ans. In case plasma membrane ruptures or breaks down

(i) All the useful substances will move out of the cell because plasma membrane is selectively permeable.

(ii) There will be no difference between cell content and its external environment.

(iii) The cell will lose its normal shape.

30. Explain the structure of nucleus.

Ans. Robert Brown discovered nucleus in the cell in 1831. The nucleus is the control centre of a cell.

Structure of Nucleus

(i) **Nuclear membrane** The nuclear membrane encloses nucleus in the eukaryotes. The nuclear membrane is penetrated by large nuclear pore complexes, which selectively transport molecules into or out of the nucleus.

(ii) **Nucleoplasm** It is the protoplasm in the nucleus that contains genetic material (DNA), chromosomes and nucleolus.

(iii) **Chromatin** The chromatin material inside the nucleus is an organisation of DNA and protein. As a cell prepares to divide, the chromatin condenses and becomes thick enough to form specialised structures called chromosomes.

(iv) **Nucleolus** It is the most important site of ribosome synthesis. The nucleolus was first recognised by Fontana in 1874.

31. State the chief functions of mitochondria.

Ans. Mitochondria perform the following major functions

(i) Mitochondria are the main site of aerobic respiration, where respiratory substrates are completely oxidised into carbon dioxide and water.
The energy liberated in this process is utilised in synthesising energy rich molecules called ATP.

(ii) They have a group of enzymes that carryout elongation of fatty acids by adding acetyl Co-A and subsequently reducing the keto-acids.

(iii) The matrix of mitochondria contains enzymes for the synthesis of fatty acids.

32. What would happen to the life of a cell, if there were no Golgi apparatus ?

Ans. If Golgi body is absent in a cell, then following activities will not take place.

(i) Storage, modification and packaging of different materials.

(ii) Synthesis and secretion of enzymes, hormones, etc.

(iii) Formation of cell plate during cell division.

(iv) Formation of lysosomes, acrosome and peroxisomes.

Section-II [5 Marks]

Structured Questions

1. Cell is the fundamental, structural and functional unit of living organisms.

(i) Which scientist expanded the cell theory by suggesting that all cells arise from pre-existing cells?

(ii) On the basis of structural organisation, how many types of cell are there?

(iii) How does the size and volume of cell correlated?

(iv) Mention the characteristic features of cell wall and cell membrane on the basis of their permeability.

(v) Define the term protoplasm.

Ans. (i) Rudolf Virchow expanded the cell theory by suggesting that all cells arise from pre-existing cells.

(ii) Two types, i.e. prokaryotic and eukaryotic cells.

(iii) The small-sized cells possess large surface area to volume ratio. This relationship is *vice-versa* for large cells.

(iv) Cell wall is freely permeable and plasma membrane is selectively permeable membrane.

(v) Protoplasm is the total living substance of a cell, i.e. the cytoplasm and the nucleus.

2. The cell consists of three essential parts, i.e. cell membrane, nucleus and cytoplasm.

(i) Give the composition of plasma membrane.

(ii) Which structure in nucleus is known as 'factory of ribosomes'?

(iii) Which component of nucleus contain hereditary material?

(iv) Is plasma membrane living or non-living?

(v) State one function of plasma membrane.

Ans. (i) Plasma membrane consists of lipids and proteins.

(ii) Nucleolus

(iii) The chromatin in nucleus contains DNA which transmits characters from parents to offspring and thus, acts as hereditary material.

(iv) Plasma membrane is living membrane.

(v) Plasma membrane provides and maintains shape of a cell and regulates transportation of material in and out of the cell.

3. Observe the figure shown below and answer the questions that follows.

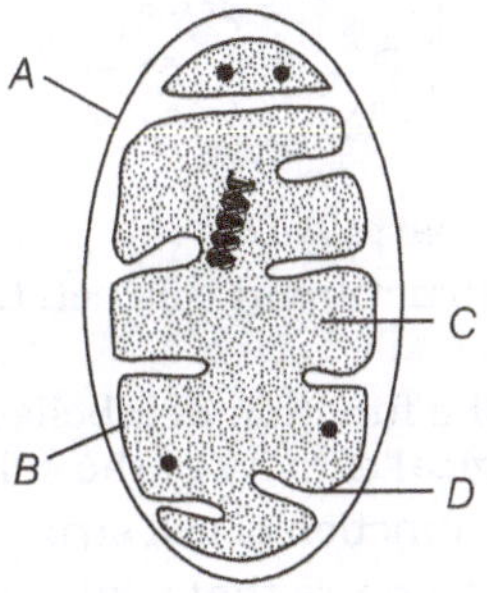

(i) Label the parts marked *A-D*.

(ii) What does this figure represent?

(iii) Mention the role performed by this structure in the cell.

(iv) The inner membrane of this structure is deeply folded. What are the advantage of these folds?

(v) Why these are known as semi-autonomous organelles?

Ans.(i) The parts marked *A–D* are labelled as

A– Outer membrane

B– Inner membrane

C– Matrix

D– Cristae

(ii) This figure represents the structure of mitochondrion.

(iii) This structure participates in cellular respiration and produces energy.

(iv) These folds create the large surface area for ATP generating chemical reactions.

(v) These are regarded as semi-autonomous organelles due to the presence of their own DNA that can replicate independently and synthesise their own proteins.

4. The figure given below shows an organelle.

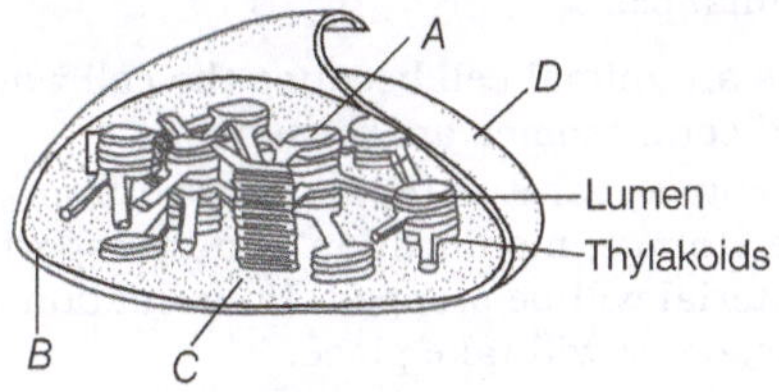

(i) Name the organelle.

(ii) In which cell, this structure is present?

(iii) What is the function of this structure?

(iv) Label the parts *A-D*.

(v) Name two other types of plastids.

Ans. (i) The given organelle is chloroplast.

(ii) In eukaryotic plant cell, this structure is present.

(iii) Chloroplast helps to carryout photosynthesis in plant cells.

(iv) The parts *A–D* are labelled as

A– Grana or granum

B– Inner membrane

C– Stroma

D– Outer membrane

(v) Chromoplasts and leucoplasts are the other types of plastids.

5. Given below is the diagram of a cell. Study the same and answer the questions that follows.

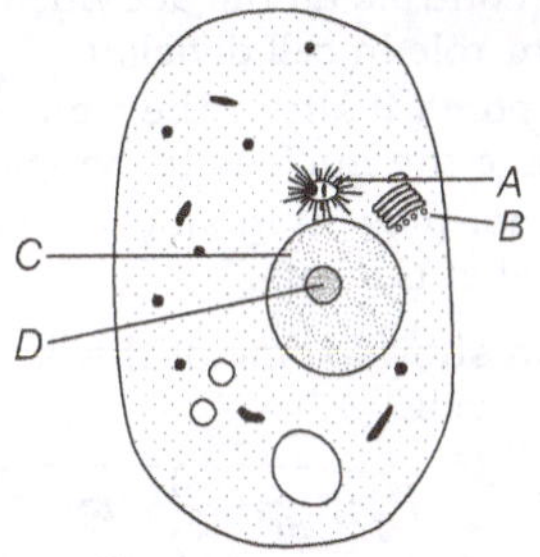

(i) Name the parts *A, B, C* and *D* indicated in the diagram.

(ii) State the functions of parts *B* and *C*.

(iii) State the function of *A*.

(iv) Is it an animal cell or plant cell? Give a logic reason to support your answer.

(v) What would happen if part labelled as *B* will be removed from this cell?

Ans. The parts *A, B, C* and *D* indicated by the guidelines are as

(i) *A*– Centrosome *B*– Golgi body
C– Nucleus *D*– Nucleolus

(ii) *B* – Golgi body helps in storage, modification and packaging of material in vesicles.
C– It is nucleus which controls cell activities and contains hereditary material.

(iii) *A*– It is centrosome which helps in divison of animal cell.

(iv) It is an animal cell because the cell wall is absent and centrosomes are present.

(v) If Golgi apparatus (*B*) is removed from the cell, the storage, modification and transport of the material will be stopped. No formation of lysosomes will take place.

6. The figure shows a certain structure of a cell.

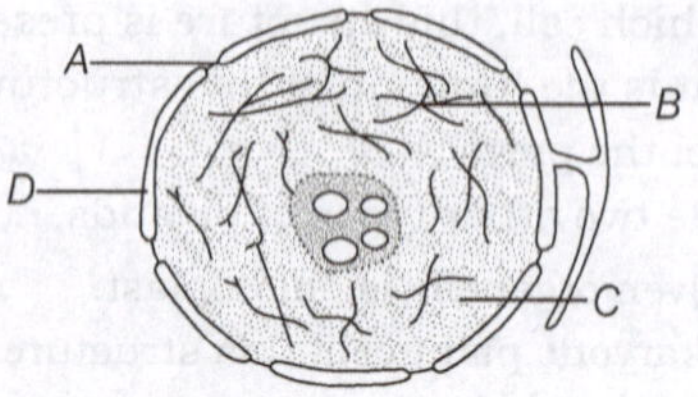

(i) Label the parts *A* to *D*.
(ii) Name the structure.
(iii) Why is it important to the cell?
(iv) Give the function of part labelled as *A*.
(v) Is this structure present in all the cells? Justify your answer.

Ans. (i) The labelled parts as *A*–*D* are
A–Nuclear pore, *B*–Chromatin,
C–Nucleoplasm, *D*–Nuclear envelope
(ii) The given structure is of nucleus.
(iii) Nucleus controls all the activities of cell and plays important role in cell division.
(iv) Nuclear pore (*A*) allows the transfer of material from inside the nucleus to cytoplasm.
(v) No, it is not present in all cells. Prokaryotic cells are devoid of nucleus.

7. The diagram shows some of the structures present in an animal cell.

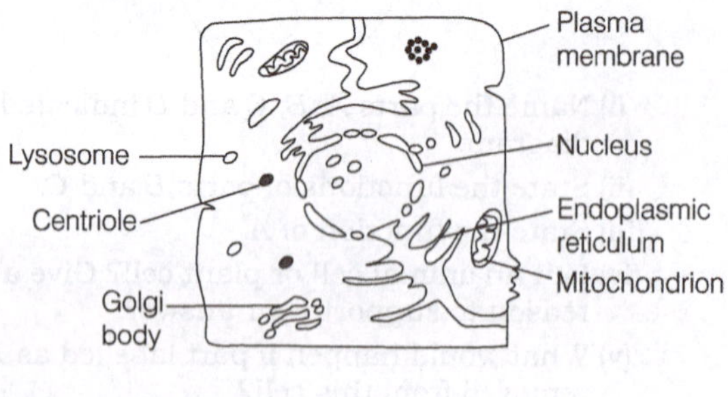

Which of these structures is responsible for
(i) Manufacture of lipids and steroids
(ii) Release of energy
(iii) Manufacture of hormones and digestive enzymes
(iv) Production of spindle fibres in cell division
(v) Endo and exocytosis

Ans. (i) **Golgi body** It is responsible for the manufacture of lipids and steroids.
(ii) **Mitochondrion** It generates energy for various activities of cell.
(iii) **Lysosomes** They are responsible for the production of hormones and digestive enzymes.
(iv) **Centrioles** They are responsible for the production of spindle fibres.
(v) **Plasma membrane** It is responsible for endo and exocytosis.

8. Study the given figure of an animal cell and answer the following questions.

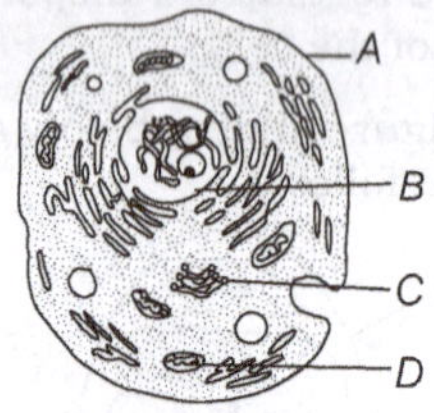

(i) Label the parts *A*-*D*.
(ii) Name a structure in this cell that is absent in plant cell.
(iii) What is the function of labelled part *B* in the physiological activity of the cell?
(iv) Write one function of cell structure labelled *D*.
(v) Name a structure that is absent in this cell but present in plant cell.

Ans. (i) The labelled parts *A*–*D* are as
A– Cell membrane *B*– Nucleus
C– Golgi body *D*– Mitochondrion
(ii) Centriole is absent in plant cell but present in animal cell shown in diagram.
(iii) *B*-Nucleus regulates and controls the various cellular activities.
(iv) *D*-Mitochondrion is the powerhouse of a cell and produces energy by respiration.
(v) Plastids and cell wall are absent in animal cell, but present in plant cell.

Chapter Assessment

Section-I

1 Mark Questions

1. Name the following.
   (i) Process used by lysosomes to digest stored food contents during starvation.
   (ii) Largest cytoplasmic organelle in a plant cell.
   (iii) Scientist who coined the term protoplasm.

2. Correct and rewrite the following statements by changing the underlined word.
   (i) Plastids are also called the suicidal bags of the cell.
   (ii) 78 chromosomes are found in cray fish.
   (iii) The single-celled organisms are called multicellular organisms.

3. Give biological reasons for the following.
   (i) Organ and organelles are two different structures in organism.
   (ii) Plant cell possesses large-sized vacuoles.

4. Match the following columns.

Column I	Column II
A. Mitochondria	1. Protein synthesis
B. Ribosomes	2. Photosynthesis
C. Centrosome	3. Powerhouse of the cell
D. Chloroplast	4. Cell division

5. Choose the correct answer from each of the four options given below.

(i) Which of the following is found in both, *Chlamydomonas* and *Amoeba*?
   (a) Chloroplasts (b) Centrioles
   (c) Cell membrane (d) All of these

(ii) Organelle without a cell membrane is
   (a) ribosome (b) Golgi apparatus
   (c) chloroplast (d) nucleus

(iii) The cell organelle which is not found in plant is
   (a) lysosome (b) ribosome
   (c) centriole (d) mitochondria

(iv) Which of the following is not a function of vacuole?
   (a) Storage
   (b) Providing turgidity and rigidity to the cell
   (c) Waste excretion
   (d) Locomotion

6. (i) Fill in the blanks with suitable words.
   (a) Cell wall is made up of .... in plant cells.
   (b) .... are largely involved in the synthesis of fats.
   (c) Vacuole contains ....
   (d) The semi-permeable membrane which surrounds vacuole is called ....
   (e) The fluid part between plasma membrane and nucleus is ....

   (ii) Fill in the blanks (*A–E*) with appropriate words in the following table.

Structures	Whether found in animal or plant cell or both	Functions
A	B	Photosynthesis
C	Animal cell	Spindle formation during cell division
Cell wall	D	E

7. Chosse the odd one out from the following terms and name the category to which other belong.
   (i) Nucleus, Nuclear membrane, Nucleoid, Nucleolus
   (ii) Grana, Thylakoid, Stroma, Vacuoles
   (iii) Cisternae, Vesicles, Tubules, Ribosomes
   (iv) *Chlamydomonas, chloroplast, Euglena, Amoeba*

8. Expand PPLO.

9. State whether the following statements are true or false. Correct and rewrite the false statements.
   (i) Schleiden and Schwann gave the cell theory, which was further expanded by Rudolf Virchow.
   (ii) Leeuwenhoek discovered the free-living cells in pond water for the first time.
   (iii) Most mature plant cells have a large central vacuole that stores important substances including wastes.
   (iv) The root word 'karyon' in the terms 'prokaryotic' and 'eukaryotic' refers to the presence of a cell wall.
   (v) Endoplasmic reticulum functions as cytoplasmic framework by providing a surface for some of the biochemical activities of the cell.

10. Give the exact location of the following.
   (i) Cytoplasm
   (ii) Chromosomes

11. Give one example of each.
    (i) Amoeboid shape cells in human body.
    (ii) Cell organelle found only in animal cell.
    (iii) Scavengers and cellular housekeeper of cell.
12. State the main function of the following.
    (i) Vacuoles (ii) Cell wall
    (iii) Chromosomes
13. Differentiate between the following pairs on the basis of what is given in bracket.
    (i) Mitochondria and Lysosomes (function)
    (ii) Chromoplast and Leucoplast (colour of plastids)
    (iii) Chromosome and Centrosome (location)

2 Marks Questions

14. How are chromatin, chromatid and chromosome related to each other?
15. What are lysosomes and centrosome? Write their functions.

3 Marks Questions

16. Why do plant cells possess large-sized vacuoles?
17. What are the facts which prove that all cells are autonomous?

Section-II [5 Marks]

Structured Questions

18. Study the figure given below and answer the questions that follows.

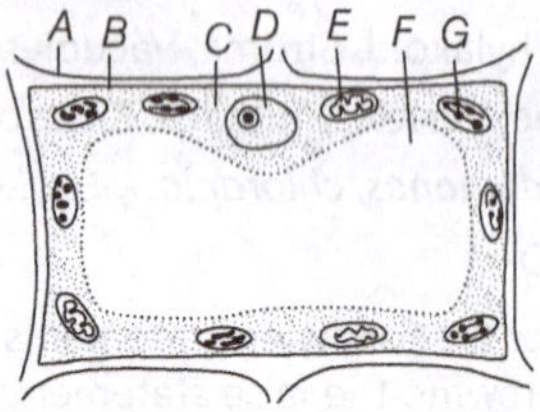

    (i) Identify the figure.
    (ii) Label the parts A-G.
    (iii) Is it a plant cell or an animal cell? Give reason in support of your answer.
    (iv) State the functions of the parts A, D and G.
    (v) Name the cell organelle concerned with the following functions.
    (a) Production of energy
    (b) Protein synthesis
19. The diagram given below is a mitochondria. Study the diagram and then answer the questions that follows.

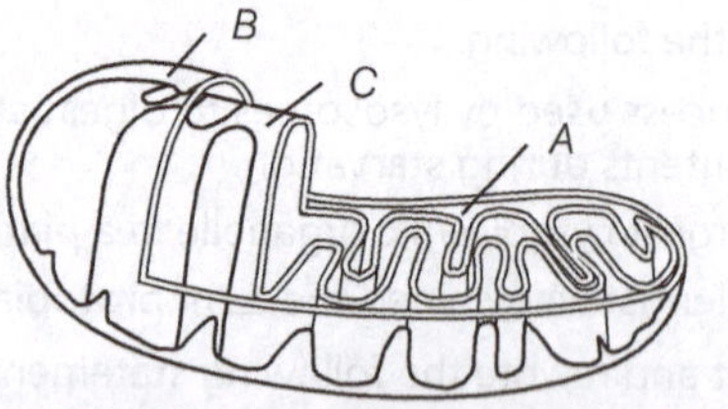

    (i) Label the parts A, B and C.
    (ii) In what form, mitochondria release energy?
    (iii) Give the structural difference between B and C.
    (iv) Why mitochondria are able to make its own protein?
    (v) Is this structure present in both plant and animal cell? Give reason for your answer.
20. The cellular components are called cell organelles. They are present in eukaryotic cells.
    (i) Which organelle is the storage sac of solid and liquid materials?
    (ii) Which organelles other than nucleus contain DNA?
    (iii) Name the nucleic acid which contain genes.
    (iv) Name one organelle present in plant that can make some of its protein.
    (v) Name the plastids which stores starch, oils and protein granule.

For explanations scan the given QR Code

Olympiad Section*

Brain Teasing Questions asked in Previous Olympiads

1 Which of the following statements regarding surface area to volume ratio is/are true? **[INBO 2020]**

I. Large surface area to volume ratio eliminates the need for a circulatory system.
II. Large surface area to volume ratio helps in faster exchange of nutrients.
III. Large surface area to volume ratio helps in faster rate of diffusion of nutrients inside cells.

Codes

(a) Only I
(b) I and II
(c) II and III
(d) I, II and III

2 Consider the following statements regarding bacterial, animal and plant cells. **[IJSO 2018, Botswana]**

I. Animal and plant cells have a nucleoid.
II. Peptidoglycan is the major cell wall component in bacteria.
III. Bacterial cell has no cell wall.
IV. Animal and plant cells generate ATP within the mitochondria.
V. The main constituent of plant cell walls is a polysaccharide called lignin.
VI. Bacterial cell generates ATP within the cytoplasm.

Which of the above statements are correct?

(a) I, III and IV
(b) I, IV and V
(c) II, IV and VI
(d) II, IV and V

3 Which of the following statements is incorrect about a prokaryote? It has .... **[IJSO 2016, Indonesia]**

(a) nucleoid, a region where the cell's DNA is located (not enclosed by a membrane)
(b) fimbriae-attachment structures on the surface of some prokaryotes
(c) plasma membrane enclosing the cytoplasm
(d) centrosome, a region where the cell' microtubules are initiated, contains a part of centrioles

4 The nuclear membrane disappears during cell division. After completion of cell division, it reappears during the interphase. Which of the following contributes towards formation of the nuclear membrane? **[INBO 2016]**

(a) Spindle fibre proteins
(b) Cytoskeletal elements
(c) Endoplasmic reticulum
(d) Golgi bodies

5 The figures below show typical cells of three different living organisms (I, II and III). **[IJSO 2015, Republic of Korea]**

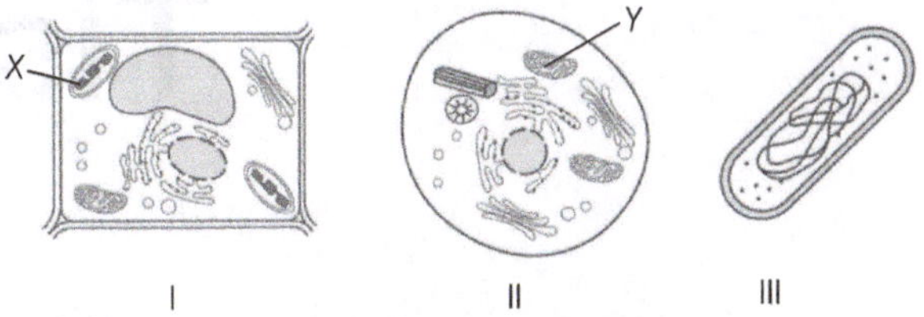

Which of the following statements is correct?

(a) X in I is often found inside cyanobacteria.
(b) The cell wall can be observed in I and II
(c) A nuclear envelope (membrane) encloses the nucleus in III
(d) Genetic materials can be found in X and Y

6 The order of permeability for the following molecules across the plasma membrane will be **[INBO 2012]**

(a) Cholesterol < Glycerol < Water
(b) Glycerol < Water < Cholesterol
(c) Water < Cholesterol < Glycerol
(d) Cholesterol < Water < Glycerol

7 In an experiment, the PO_4 groups of the phospholipids facing the lumen of the Endoplasmic Reticulum (ER) are labelled. If in the course of time, the ER buds off vesicles which fuse with the cell membrane, the label will be found. **[INBO 2011]**

(a) on the PO_4 groups of cell membrane facing extracellular fluid
(b) on the PO_4 groups of cell membrane facing cytosol
(c) only on inner lumen of ER
(d) on both inner and outer laminae of ER

8 Which of the following, primarily contribute to the 'cytomembrane system' of a cell? **[INBO 2011]**

I. Endoplasmic reticulum
II. Vesicles
III. Microtubules
IV. Mitochondria
V. Golgi apparatus

Codes

(a) I and V
(b) I, II, III and V
(c) I, II and V
(d)I, II, III, IV and V

Answers

1. (b) **2.** (c) **3.** (d) **4.** (c) **5.** (d) **6.** (b) **7.** (a) **8.** (c)

**These questions may or may not be asked in the examination, have been given just for additional practice required for olympiads, scholarship exams etc. For detailed explanations refer Page No. 230.*

CHAPTER

02

Tissues

Chapter Inside

• Tissues • Plant Tissues • Animal Tissues

All living organisms are made up of **cells**. Unicellular organisms perform all the functions, such as digestion, respiration, excretion, reproduction etc., by a single cell, e.g. *Amoeba*.

However, multicellular organisms have several cells, which are grouped together to form **tissues**. These tissues further gets specialised to carryout different functions. In this chapter we will study about different tissues found in plants and animals.

Tissues

A group of similar cells, performing the same function and having a common origin are called tissues. The term tissue was given by **Bichat**. The microscopic study of tissues and their functions is known as **histology** (term was given by **Meyer**).

The structural and functional organisations are different in plants and animals both, i.e. plants remain stationary while animals move as per their needs. Thus, each of them possesses different feeding methods and are differently adapted. Based on these habits, the tissues in plants and animals are strikingly different.

So, it tissues are further classified as **plant tissue** and **animal tissue**.

Plant Tissues

There are different types of plant tissues which perform different functions like photosynthesis, transport of food, absorption of water from soil, etc.

On the basis of the dividing capacity, plant tissues can be classified into two fundamental types as follows.

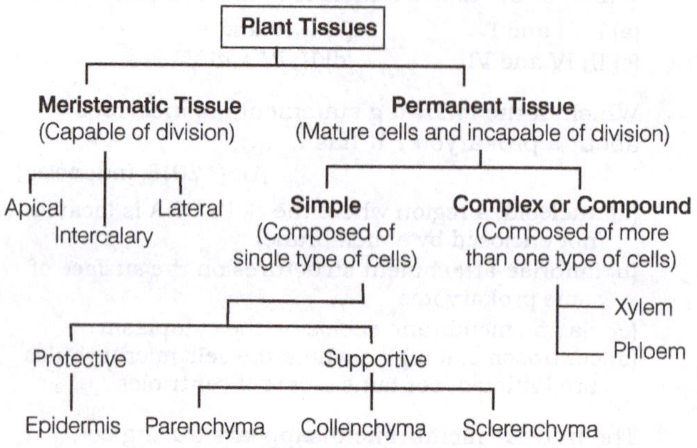

1. Meristematic Tissue or Meristem

The tissues in which cells always keep on dividing and give rise to new cells are called meristematic tissues. Plants grow only in those regions where meristematic tissues are present and active, e.g. root and shoot tips. Thus, meristematic tissue are also called **growth tissue**.

Characteristics of meristematic tissue are as follows

(i) The shape of cells is spherical, polygonal or rectangular.

(ii) Cells forming this tissue are very active, have dense cytoplasm, thin cellulose walls and prominent nuclei.

(iii) Meristematic tissues lack vacuoles.

(iv) Cells are tightly packed with no intercellular spaces.

(v) These tissues divide to form new cells, which differentiate to give rise to pemanent tissues.

Types of Meristematic Tissue

On the basis of the region where they are present in the plant, meristematic tissues are of following types

(i) **Apical** (terminal) **meristems** These are present at the growing tips of stems, roots and on the tips of axillary buds. Thus, these are helpful in increasing the length of stems and roots.

(ii) **Intercalary meristems** These are present at the base of the leaves or internodes (on either sides of the node) of stem. It helps in longitudinal growth of plants by adding primary tissues.

(iii) **Lateral meristems** (cambium) These are present below the bark and on the lateral sides of roots and stems.
They help in increasing the girth of root and stem.

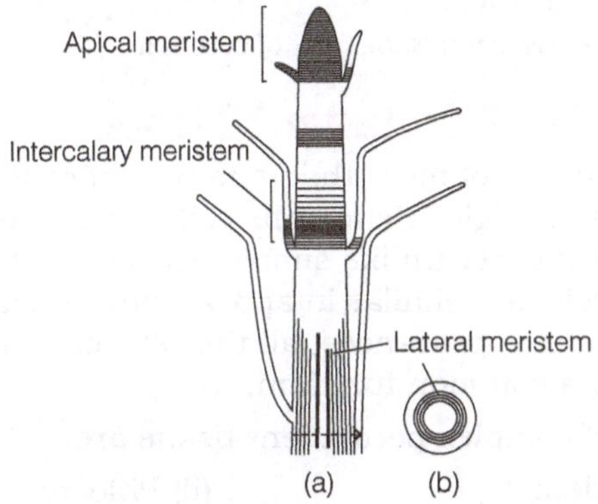

Meristematic tissue in plant body : (a) Location, (b) Transverse section of lateral meristem

2. Permanent Tissue

These tissues are formed from the meristematic tissue when they loose the ability to divide. A permanent tissue is a group of cells in which growth is stopped, either completely or for the time being.

Characteristics of permanent tissue are as follows

(i) These tissues may be dead or living.

(ii) They have a definite shape, size, thickness and function.

On the basis of structure, permanent tissues are of two types, i.e. simple and complex permanent tissues.

Simple Permanent Tissues

They are made up of only one type of cells, i.e. the cells forming these tissues are similar in structure and function. Simple permanent tissues are further classified as follows

(i) Protective Tissue

These tissues cover the surface of roots, stems and leaves. The upper and lower epidermis of leaves, stems, cork cells in bark, etc., are examples of protective tissues. Their cells possess thick cell walls. This tissue is further categorised to

(a) **Epidermis** This is the outermost layer of cell in plants and it is usually made up of a single layer of cells. It is meant to provide protection to all the parts of the plant. During secondary growth, epiderm gets replaced by periderm.

(b) **Cork or Phellem** In older roots and stems, tissues at the periphery become cork cells or phellem cells. These cells are dead and compactly arranged, i.e. have no intercellular spaces. They form the bark of trees.

(ii) Supporting Tissue

These tissues provide support to the plants and perform other functions also.

These are of following three types

(a) **Parenchyma** These are simple living cells with little specialisation, thin cell wall and single large vacuole. Cells of these tissues are usually loosely pa/cked with large spaces between them (intercellular spaces).

They are present in the cortex and pith of stems, roots and in the mesophyll of leaves. Parenchyma is the most abundant tissue in plants.

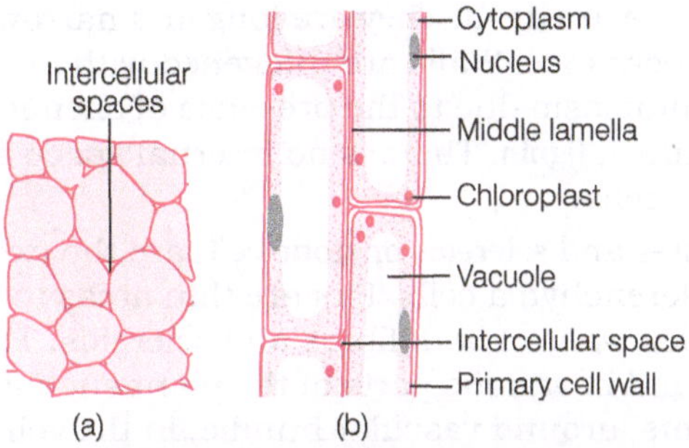

Parenchyma tissue : (a) Transverse section (b) Longitudinal section

Functions of Parenchyma Tissue

- This tissue provides temporary support to plants and also stores food, e.g. starch in potato.
- In some situation, the parenchyma cell contains chlorophyll and performs photosynthesis. Such type of tissue is called **chlorenchyma.**
- In aquatic plants, large cavities are present in parenchyma cells in order to give buoyancy to plants, which help them to float. Such type of tissue is called **aerenchyma**, e.g. water hyacinth.
- Parenchyma in roots and stems store nutrients and water.

(b) **Collenchyma** These cells are living, elongated and irregularly thickened at the corners. They have very little intercellular spaces. These tissues are generally found in leaf stalks and below the epidermis of stems. These are absent in roots, stems and leaves of monocot plants.

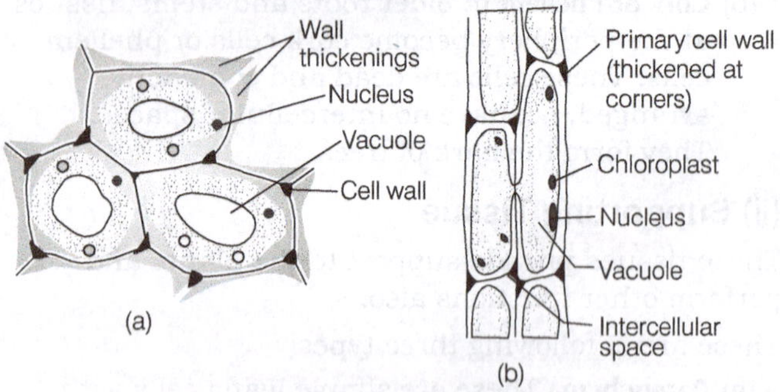

Collenchyma tissue: (a) Transverse section, (b) Longitudinal section

Functions of Collenchyma Tissue

- It provides mechanical support and elasticity (flexibility) to plants.
- It allows easy bending in various parts of plant (leaf and stem) without breakage.

(c) **Sclerenchyma** The cells of sclerenchymatous tissue are dead. They are long and narrow in appearance. Walls are thickened with no protoplasm due to the presence of chemical named, **lignin**. There is no internal space between the cells.

Fibres and **sclereids** or **stone cells** are the two sclerenchyma cells. Pits are thin areas in the thick walls of both fibres and sclereids. They are found in various parts of the plant such as stem, roots, around vascular bundle, in the veins of leaves, hard covering of seeds and nuts, etc.

The grit in the pulp and skin of some fruits develop due to the presence of sclereids in it.

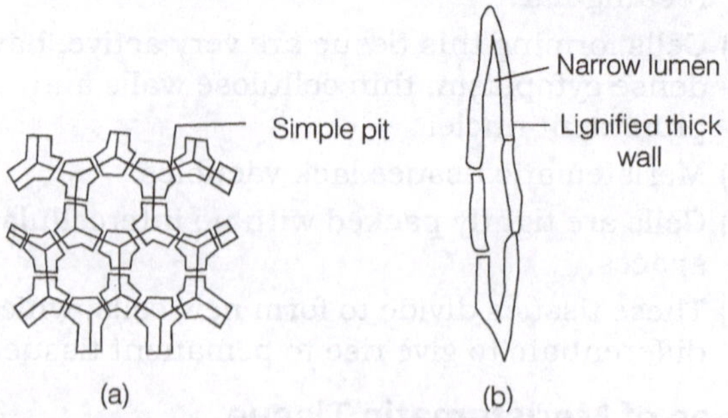

Sclerenchyma tissue : (a) Transverse section, (b) Longitudinal section

Functions of Sclerenchyma Tissue

- It is known to be the chief mechanical tissue which makes plant hard and stiff, e.g. husk of coconut.
- It is used for the manufacturing of certain mats, ropes and textile fibres.

Check Your LEARNING...

1 Which two simple tissues provide mechanical support to the plants?
2 Which tissue provides flexibility to the plants?
3 State the location of collenchyma in plants.
4 Which chemical is present in thickened corners of sclerenchyma? .
5 Which tissue forms the husk of coconut?

Complex Permanent Tissue

It is made up of more than one type of cells having a common origin. Hence, the cells look different from each other unlike simple permanent tissue in which cells are similar in appearance. Regardless of different appearances, all the cells coordinate to perform a common function.

Types of complex permanent tissue are

(i) Xylem (ii) Phloem

Both of them are **conducting tissues** and constitute the **vascular bundle**. This is a distinctive feature of the complex plants, which provide them the possibility of surviving in the terrestrial environment.

(i) Xylem

It is a vascular and mechanical tissue. The cells of xylem have thick walls and many of the them are dead. These cells are found in the form of tubular passages in the centre of vascular bundles. Xylem consists of various elements, these include

(a) **Tracheids** are long tubular dead cells with large cavities, lignified walls and tapering ends.They allow transportation of water and minerals from roots to leaves. They also provide mechanical support.

(b) **Vessels** are long tube-like structures, formed by a row of cells placed end to end. Their walls are hard, thick and lignified. They also help in transportation of water and dissolved minerals.

(c) **Xylem parenchyma** These are the only living cells with thin cell wall. They store food (sugar and starch) and helps in the sideways conduction of water.

(d) **Xylem fibres** They have elongated dead cells with tapering ends and thick cell walls. They have narrow cavities.
They help in transportation of water and provide mechanical support.

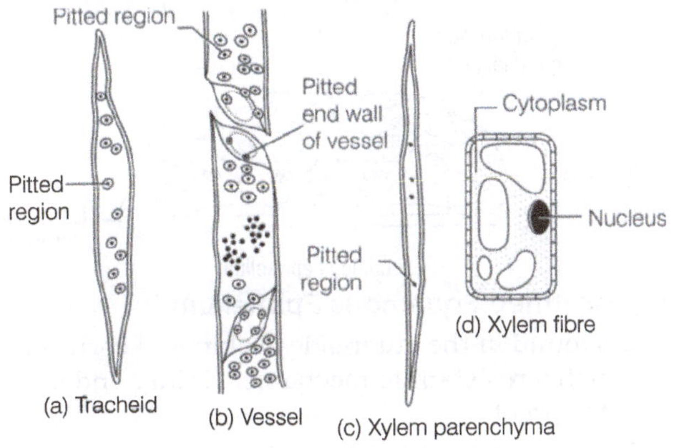

Components of xylem

Functions of Xylem

- Xylem transports water, mineral and salts upward from the roots to different parts of the plant. Older xylem tissue forms the wood which does not help in transport.
- It provides mechanical strength to the plant body.

(ii) Phloem

It is a living vascular conducting tissue. It is also known as **bast**. It is located on the outer side of vascular bundle.

Phloem is made up of following four types of elements

(a) **Sieve tubes** These are tubular cells with end walls perforated by numerous pores called **sieve plates.** Nucleus is absent and they have thin layer of cytoplasm.
They help in the transport of food from leaves to storage organs and other parts of the plants.

(b) **Companion cells** These are thin and small elongated cells. They have dense cytoplasm and prominent nucleus. They control the activities of sieve tubes.

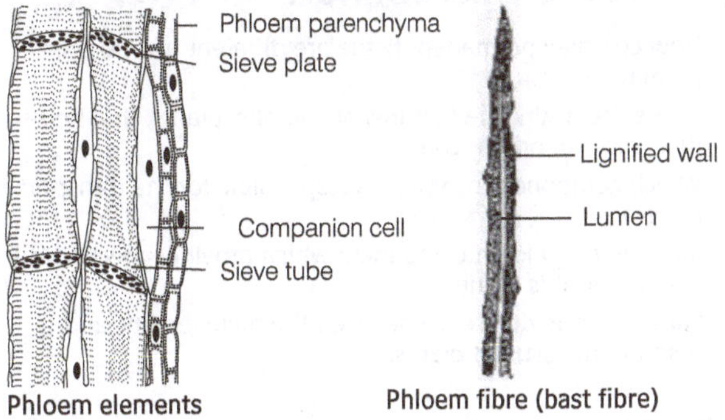

(c) **Phloem parenchyma** These are thin-walled, living parenchymatous cells. They help in the storage of fat, starch, etc., and transportation of food.

(d) **Phloem fibres** These are thick-walled, dead, sclerenchymatous cells. They provide mechanical strength to the plant.

Functions of Phloem

- It helps in translocation of food materials from leaves to other parts of the plant.
- It helps in the storage of food.

Differences between Xylem and Phloem Tissues

Xylem	Phloem
It conducts water or sap.	It conducts organic food.
All the conducting cells are non-living, except xylem parenchyma.	All the conducting cells are living, except phloem fibres.
It contains three types of dead cells , i.e. vessels, tracheids and xylem fibres.	It contains three types of living cells, i.e. phloem parenchyma, companion cell and sieve cell.
Xylem constitutes bulk of the plant body.	Phloem always forms a small part of the plant body.

Differences between Meristematic and Permanent Tissues

Meristematic tissue	Permanent tissue
Cells divide repeatedly.	Cells are differentiated from the meristematic tissue and normally do not divide.
Cells are undifferentiated and intercellular spaces are absent.	Cells are fully differentiated and intercellular spaces are present.
Vacuoles are absent.	Vacuoles are present.

Meristematic tissue	Permanent tissue
Cells have dense cytoplasm.	Cells have thin-layered cytoplasm around the vacuoles.
Cells are always living.	Cells may be living or dead.

Check Your LEARNING...

1 How complex permanent tissue are different from simple permanent tissue?
2 Name the distinctive features of complex plants, that helped in their survival on the Earth.
3 Which component of xylem is responsible for the transport of minerals?
4 Identify the phloem component which provides mechanical strength to this tissue.
5 State any one difference between the meristematic and permanent tissue of plants.

Animal Tissues

On the basis of their structure and functions, animal tissues are classified into four basic types, *viz.* epithelial, connective, muscular and nervous tissue.

These tissues are further categorised as given below

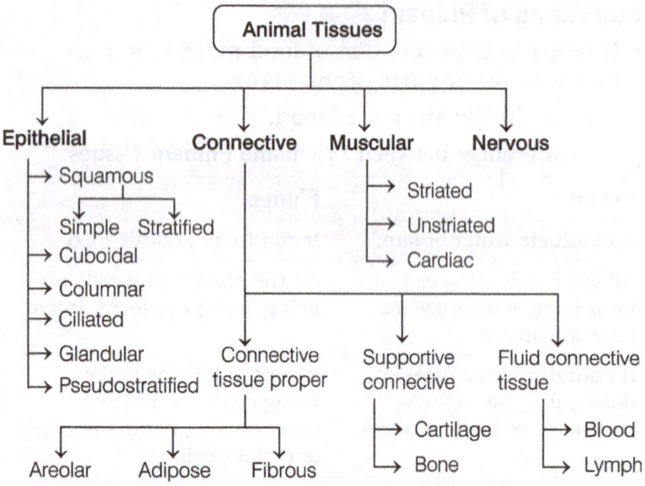

1. Epithelial Tissue

It is the protective tissue of animal body, which covers the most organs of the body. It also forms a barrier to keep different body systems separated from each other.

Characteristics of epithelial tissue are given below

(i) Cells of epithelial tissues are tightly packed and form a continuous sheath, i.e. there is no intercellular space between them.

(ii) Epithelial tissues may be flat, cuboidal or columnar.

(iii) Skin, lining of mouth, lining of blood vessels, alveoli and kidney tubules, are all made up of epithelial tissue.

On the basis of shape of the cells and their arrangement, epithelial tissues are further classified as follows

i. Squamous Epithelium

Squamous epithelial tissue constitutes the skin which protects the body. It is further categorised as

(a) Simple Squamous Epithelium

- It is single-layered and closely fitted. The cells are very thin or flat and appear as tiles over a floor.
- It forms a delicate lining of blood vessels and lung alveoli, where transport of various substances occurs through a selectively permeable membrane.
- It also covers oesophagus and lining of mouth.

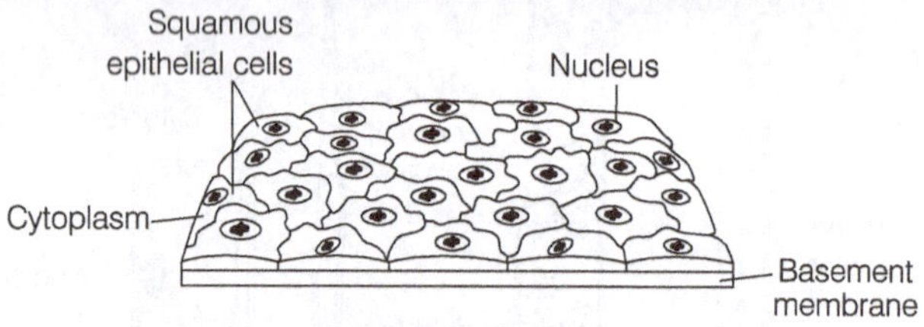

Squamous epithelium

(b) Stratified Squamous Epithelium

- It is found in the outer side of skin and cornea as it is highly resistant to mechanical injury and is water-proof.
- Cells are arranged in many layers to prevent their wear and tear.

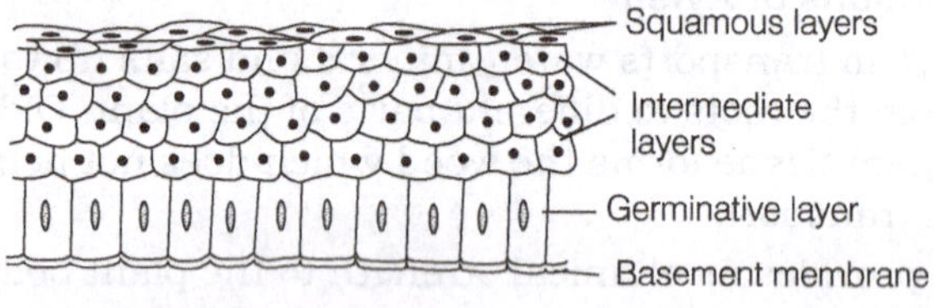

Stratified epithelium

ii. Cuboidal Epithelium

- It is made up of cube-shaped cells which have rounded nuclei.
- It forms lining of kidney tubules and ducts of salivary glands, where it provides protection and mechanical support. It also forms germinal epithelium of gonads.

- It helps in absorption, excretion and secretion.

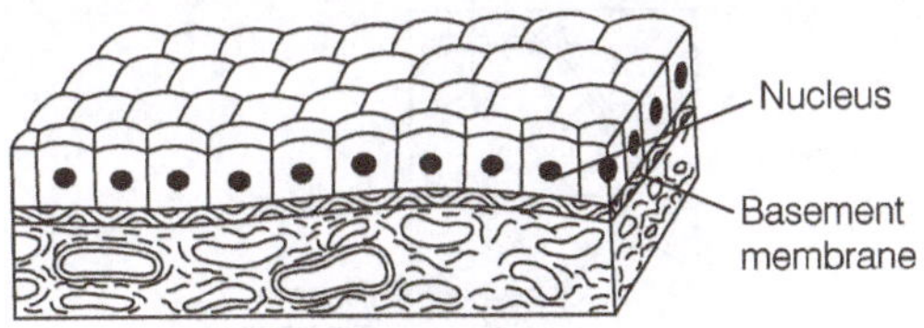

Cuboidal epithelium

iii. Columnar Epithelium

- It is made up of tall, cylindrical or pillar-like cells with elongated nuclei.
- It is usually found in the inner lining of stomach and intestine.
- Its main function is absorption and secretion.

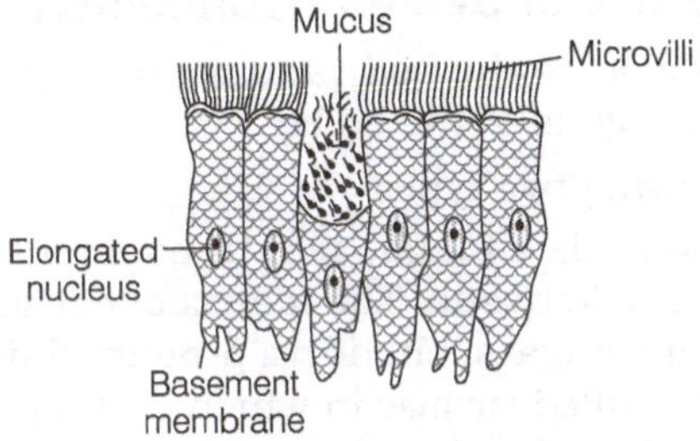

Columnar epithelium

iv. Ciliated Columnar Epithelium

- When columnar epithelial cells possess cilia (hair-like projections), they are called **ciliated epithelium**.
- The cilia have the ability to move. Their movement pushes substances like mucus, forward to clear the passage.
- It is found in the respiratory tract and also lines oviducts, sperm ducts, kidney tubules, etc.

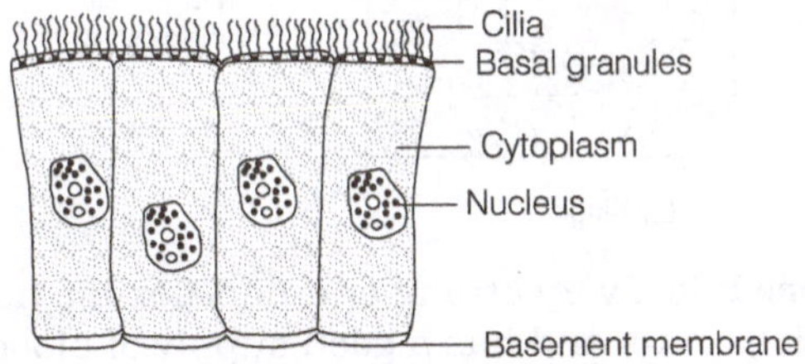

Ciliated columnar epithelium

v. Glandular Epithelium

- It is a kind of epithelium whose cells gets modified to secrete certain chemical sustances.
- Such cells are found in the lining of the stomach and intestine.
- Sometimes, portions of epithelial tissue fold inward and results in the formation of a multicellular gland, e.g. sweat gland.

vi. Pseudostratified Epithelium

- It is a type of epithelium which comprises only a single layer of columnar cells, but it appears two-layered because some cells are shorter than the others.
- It covers the inner lining of trachea and bronchi. It is protective in nature.

Functions of Epithelial Tissue

(i) These tissues protect the underlying cells from drying, injury, bacterial or viral infection and from harmful effects of chemicals. Inside the body, they form lining of organs and protect them.

(ii) Permeability of epithelium cells plays a vital role in regulating the exchange of materials between the body and external environment.

(iii) Epithelial tissues help in absorption of water and nutrients. They also help in the diffusion of gases (epithelium of alveoli).

(iv) Epithelial tissues help in the elimination of waste products from body.

(v) Some epithelial tissues secrete variety of substances like sweat, saliva, enzymes, etc.

2. Connective Tissue

This tissue is specialised to connect various body organs with each other, e.g. it connects two or more bones to each other, muscles to bones, binds different tissues together and also gives support to various parts of the body.

Characteristics of connective tissue are given below

(i) The cells of connective tissues are loosely packed.

(ii) The cells are living and are embedded in an intercellular matrix that may be either jelly-like fluid, dense or rigid in nature.

Connective tissues are further classified as follows

i. Fluid or Vascular Tissue

It is the fluid tissue that keeps on moving in the body. It helps in the transport of various materials such as nutritive elements, gases, excretory products, hormones, etc. It is of two types, i.e. blood and lymph.

(a) **Blood** It is an alkaline fluid tissue containing matrix called plasma and blood corpuscles. Different cells like **RBCs** (Red Blood Corpuscles), **WBCs** (White Blood Corpuscles) and **platelets** are found suspended in the plasma of the blood.

Plasma is straw coloured fluid which contains 90% of water along with proteins, salts and hormones.

Different blood corpuscles function differently in the body. These are as follows

- **RBCs** are biconcave, enucleate and disc-like in humans. They help in the transport of respiratory gases, i.e. oxygen and carbon dioxide with the help of haemoglobin.
- **WBCs** fight with disease causing pathogens by producing antibodies.
- **Blood platelets** are spindle-shaped and help in the clotting of blood.

Note The colour of blood is red due to the presence of haemoglobin in RBCs. Iron or haem (Fe) is an integral part of this pigment. Oxygen tends to bind with this pigment and is then transported to various parts of the body.

(b) **Lymph** It is pale yellow in colour and its composition is similar to plasma but without plasma proteins. It contains only WBCs. It plays an important role in the defence of the body especially against invading organisms.

ii. Connective Tissue Proper

It is a supporting and packaging tissue found between the organs lying in body cavity. It is the most abundant type of connective tissue. It serves for packing and binding the organs.

It is further divided as follows.

(a) **Areolar tissue** It is located between skin and muscles, around blood vessels and nerves in the bone marrow. It is a loose and cellular tissue. It consists of two kinds of fibres, e.g. **white collagen fibre and yellow elastic fibre**. It helps in the repair of damaged tissues.

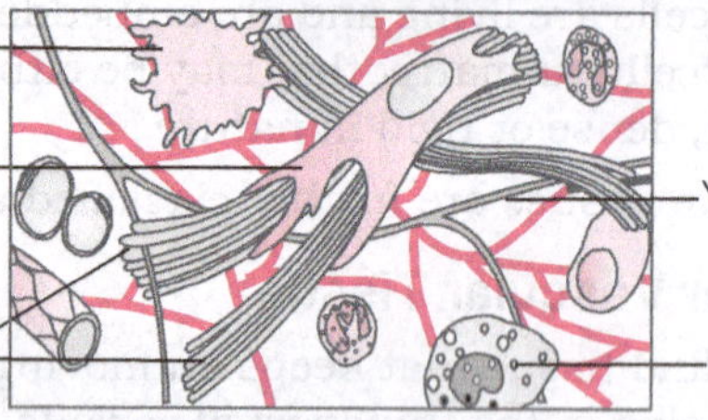

Areolar tissue

(b) **Adipose tissue** It is located below the skin and in between internal organs around kidney and eyeball. It serves as a fat reservoir and keeps visceral organs in position. It also acts as an insulator due to storage of fats and prevent the loss of heat from body.

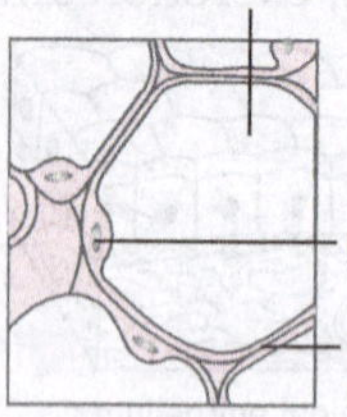

Adipose tissue

(c) **Fibrous or Dense connective tissue** It consists of a densely packed fibres bounded together by areolar tissues. They form the **tendons** which connect muscles to bones and **ligaments** which connect one bone to another bone.

iii. Supportive or Skeletal Connective Tissue

It gives support to the body and provides protection to the vital organs of the body.

It is of following two types

(a) **Cartilage** It is a tough, semitransparent elastic and flexible tissue. The matrix of cartilage contains sugars, chondrin protein, fluid-filled spaces called **lacunae** in which cartilage forming cells called **chondrocytes** are present.

Cartilages are found in the tip of nose, external ears, trachea and bronchial tubes, between vertebrae and at the end of long bones.

They provide smoothness to the bone surfaces at the joints.

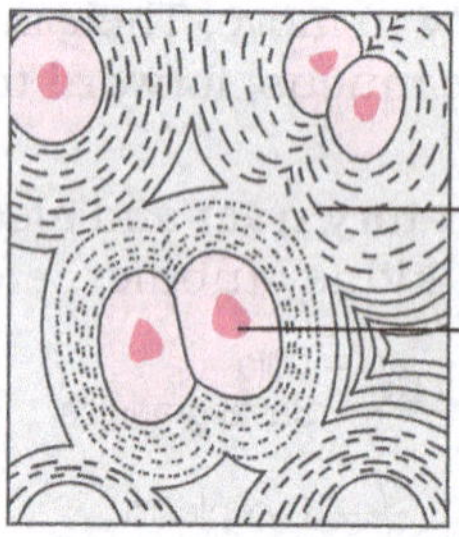

Cartilage

(b) **Bone** It is a very strong and non-flexible tissue. It is porous and has a good supply of blood vessels and nerves. Its matrix is made up of **ossein proteins** and rich in inorganic salts of calcium and phosphorus.

The matrix of bone contains fluid-filled spaces called **lacunae** in which bone forming cells called **osteocytes** are present. It forms the framework that supports the body. It also anchors the muscles and supports the main organs.

Functions of Connective Tissue

(i) Connective tissue binds different structures with one another, e.g. muscles with skin, muscles with bones etc.
(ii) It forms a supporting framework of cartilage and bones in the body.
(iii) It forms shock proof cushions around kidneys, ovaries and eyeballs.
(iv) It forms protective sheaths around delicate organs such as spleen, kidneys, testes, etc.
(v) White blood corpuscles of blood and lymph act as phagocytes and provide protection against infections.
(vi) Collagen fibres of connective tissue help in the repair of injured tissues.

Check Your LEARNING...

1 How epithelial tissue is further classified on the basis of cell shape and arrangement?
2 The sites where cuboidal epithelium is present, would be specialised in which type of functions?
3 In which type of epithelium, cilia are present? What is their role in this epithelium?
4 Why are connective tissue named so?
5 Why is blood called as a connective tissue?
6 Through which tissue two bones are attached to each other?

3. Muscular Tissue

Muscular tissues are soft tissue that makeup the different types of muscles in the body.

Characteristics of muscular tissue are as follows

(i) It contains long, fibre-like cells called **muscle fibres**.
(ii) The muscle fibres are held together by the connective tissue to form muscles.
(iii) It contains special type of proteins called **contractile proteins** which cause movement of muscles by contraction and relaxation.

Different types of muscular tissue are given below

i. Striated Muscle or Skeletal Muscle

It is also called as **voluntary muscles** as we can move them by conscious will. The cells of these muscles are long, cylindrical, unbranched and multinucleate.
Under microscope, these muscles show alternate light and dark bands or striations. Hence, they are also called **striated muscles**.

It is mostly attached to bones and helps in body movement, e.g. muscles of limbs.

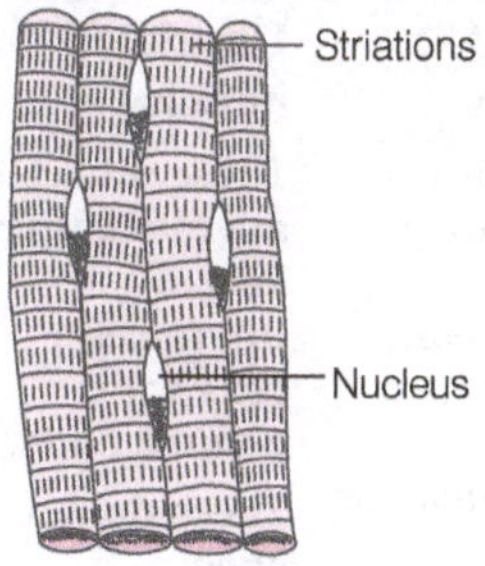

Striated muscle or Skeletal muscle

ii. Unstriated Muscle or Smooth Muscle

It is an involuntary muscle, as we cannot move them according to our will. They are found in alimentary canal, lining of blood vessels, iris of eye, ureters and bronchi of lungs.

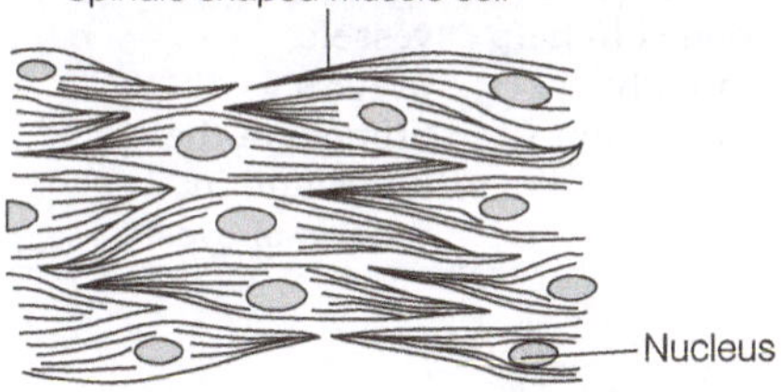

Unstriated muscle or Smooth muscle

The cells of smooth muscles are long with pointed end (spindle-shaped) and are uninucleated. These muscles do not show any dark or light bands. Hence, they are called as **unstriated muscles**.

iii. Cardiac Muscle

It is involuntary muscles present only in our heart. The cells of cardiac muscles are cylindrical, striated, uninucleated and branched. It performs rhythmic contraction and relaxation throughout the life and never get tired.

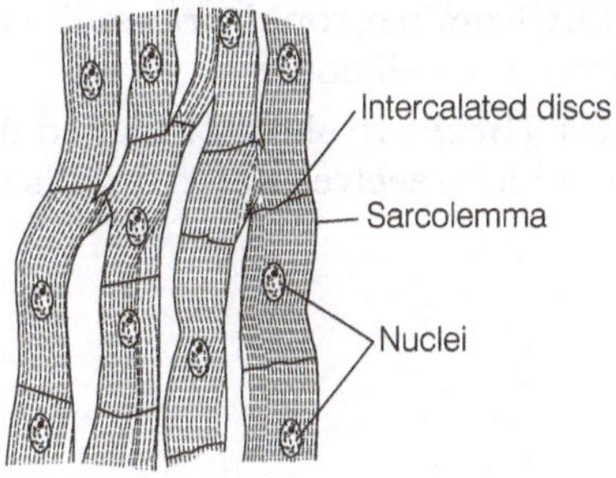

Cardiac muscle

Differences between the Structure of Different types of Muscular Tissues

Types	Striated muscles	Unstriated muscles	Cardiac muscles
Structure	These are made up of long, cylindrical, unbranched and multinucleate cells. These show alternate light and dark striations.	These muscles are made up of long uninucleate cells with pointed ends. These do not show striations.	These are made up of cells, which are cylindrical, branched and uninucleate. These muscles show striations and intercalated discs.
Site/ Location	These are located in limbs and are mostly attached to bones to help in body movement.	These are mostly present in walls of alimentary canal, blood vessels, ureters, bronchi of the lungs and in the iris of eyes.	These are present only in the walls of heart.

4. Nervous Tissue

It is highly specialised tissue and due to this the animals are able to perceive and respond to the stimuli. It contains specialised elongated cells called **nerve cells or neurons.**

Neurons have the ability to respond according to the stimuli received. Brain, spinal cord and nerves are composed of nervous tissues. An individual nerve cell may be up to several metre long.

It is composed of three major parts.

(i) **Cell body or Cyton** It consists of cytoplasm, nucleus and cell membrane.

(ii) **Axon** It is a single long conducting fibre extending from neuron. It transmits impulse away from the cell body.

(iii) **Dendrites** These are short branched fibres of neuron which receives nerve impulses.

Many nerve fibres bound together by connective tissue and forms a nerve. Combination of nerve and muscle tissue in animals causes rapid movement in response to stimuli.

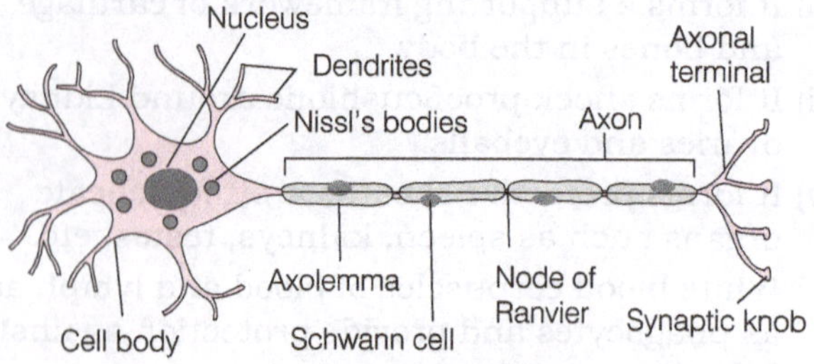

Structure of a neuron

Functions of Nervous Tissue

(i) This tissue is specialised to receive and transmit nerve impulses in the body.

(ii) Dendrites receive impulse and axon transmits the impulse away from the cell body.

Differences between Animal and Plant Tissues

Animal tissue	Plant tissue
Tissue organisation is based on active locomotion.	Tissue organisation is based on stationary or fixed habit in plants.
Organisation is more complex.	Organisation is comparatively simple.
Growth is not limited to a region.	Growth is limited to certain region.
Most of the tissues are living.	Most of the tissues are dead.

Check Your LEARNING...

1 Why striated muscles are also called skeletal muscles?

2 Name the type of muscles present in

(i) Iris of eye

(ii) alimentary canal

(iii) bronchi of lungs

3 Smooth muscles are also called unstriated muscles. Why?

4 Where are cardiac muscles present?

5 Name the type of cells, which form nervous tissue.

6 What are the three main parts of neuron?

QUiCK Revision

- **Tissues** Group of cells that are similar in structure and work together to achieve a particular function forms a tissue.
- **Plant tissues** These are based on their dividing capacity and mainly provide support to the plants.
- **Meristematic tissue** These tissues have actively dividing cells. They are found in the growing regions of plant. These include
  - **Apical meristem** Present at growing tips of stems and roots.
  - **Intercalary meristem** Present at the base of leaves or internodes on twigs.
  - **Lateral meristem** Present on the lateral sides of stems and roots.
- **Permanent tissue** These tissues do not divide. They take up permanent shape, size and function. These are formed from meristematic tissue when they lose the ability to divide.
- **Simple permanent tissue** It is made up of only one type of cell. These are
  - **Parenchyma** Simplest form of tissue with little specialisation. These provide support to plants and also store food.
  - **Collenchyma** Cells are living, elongated and irregularly thickened at the corners, generally found in leaf stalks below the epidermis. These provide mechanical support and elasticity to plant tissues.
  - **Sclerenchyma** Present in stems around vascular bundles in the veins of leaves and in the hard covering of seeds and nuts. These provide strength and enable the plant to bear various stresses.
- **Complex permanent tissue** It is made up of more than one type of cell. It is further of two types
  - **Xylem** A vascular and mechanical conducting tissue, also known as wood. Responsible for transport of water and minerals from roots to other parts.
  - **Phloem** A vascular tissue also known as bast, responsible for transport of food from leaves to other parts of the plant.
- **Animal tissues** Their organisation is based on their structure and function.
- **Epithelial tissue** It is covering and protective tissue, which is tightly packed. It is present in skin and lining of mouth. It is of following types
  - **Squamous epithelium** Simple flat cells as in trachea or may be several layers thick (stratified) as in skin.
  - **Cuboidal epithelium** Cube-shaped cells, have rounded nuclei, provide mechanical support.
  - **Columnar epithelium** Tall, pillar-like cells, have elongated nuclei.
  - **Ciliated columnar epithelium** Cells have hair-like projections cilia.
  - **Glandular epithelium** Certain epithelial cells acquire additional specialisation known as **gland cells** that can secrete substances at the epithelial surface.
- **Connective tissue** It connects various body organs. It is of following types
  - **Fluid or Vascular tissue** Links different parts of the body and maintains the continuity of body, e.g. blood and lymph.
  - **Connective tissue proper** This tissue serves for packing and binds the organs; further divided into areolar (packing) tissue, adipose (fat) tissue and fibrous connective tissue (tendon and ligament).
  - **Supportive or Skeletal connective tissue** Forms endoskeleton of vertebrate body and provides protection to the vital organs of the body, e.g. bone and cartilage.
- **Muscular tissue** It consists of elongated cells and is responsible for movement. It is of following types
  - **Striated muscles** Mostly attached to bones and help in body movement, exhibit voluntary movements.
  - **Unstriated muscles** They cannot be moved according to will (involuntary).
  - **Cardiac muscles** Present in heart, show rhythmic contraction and relaxation throughout the life involuntarily.
- **Nervous tissue** It enables body to respond to stimulus. They transmit stimuli from one place to another within body through neurons.

Chapter Practice

Section-I

1 Mark Questions

1. Name the following.
   (i) Tissue capable of cell division.
   (ii) The tissue present at the apex of roots.
   (iii) The type of plant tissue which is fully differentiated.
   (iv) A supporting tissue which consists of isodiametric living cells.
   (v) Parenchyma cells that contain chloroplast.
   (vi) The plant tissue that is mainly mechanical and protective in function.
   (vii) Collective name of xylem and phloem.
   (viii) Tissue which forms wood in plants.
   (ix) Tissue concerned with the conduction of food materials.
   (x) Tissue that forms the inner lining of the mouth.
   (xi) Tissue present in the inner lining of intestine .
   (xii) Tissue that transports CO_2 and O_2 in animals.
   (xiii) Connective tissue with a fluid matrix.
   (xiv) The pigment which imparts red colour to the red blood cells.
   (xv) Tissue that stores fat in our body.
   (xvi) Tissue that joins bone to bone.
   (xvii) Tissue that joins muscles to bone.
   (xviii) The flexible supporting tissue in animals.

Ans. (i) Meristematic tissue (ii) Apical meristem
(iii) Permanent tissue (iv) Parenchyma
(v) Chlorenchyma (vi) Sclerenchyma
(vii) Vascular bundle (viii) Xylem
(ix) Phloem
(x) Simple squamous epithelium
(xi) Columnar epithelium
(xii) Blood (xiii) Blood
(xiv) Haemoglobin (xv) Adipose tissue
(xvi) Ligament (xvii) Tendon
(xviii) Cartilage

2. Correct and rewrite the following statements by changing the underlined words.
   (i) <u>Cambium</u> meristem is present on the either side of the nodes of stem.
   (ii) Xylem consists of tracheids, <u>sieve tubes</u>, xylem parenchyma and xylem fibres.
   (iii) <u>WBCs</u> helps in transport of respiratory gases.
   (iv) The matrix of bone is made up of <u>fat</u>.
   (v) Cardiac muscles are cylindrical, uninucleated and <u>unbranched</u>.

Ans. (i) Intercalary meristem is present on the either side of the nodes of stem.
(ii) Xylem consists of tracheids, vessels , xylem parenchyma and xylem fibres.
(iii) RBCs helps in transport of respiratory gases.
(iv) The matrix of bone is made up of ossein protein.
(v) Cardiac muscles are cylindrical, uninucleated and branched.

3. Give biological reasons for the following.
   (i) Water hyacinth floats on water sufrace.
   (ii) Branches of tree move and bend freely in high wind velocity.
   (iii) Intercellular spaces are absent in sclerenchyma tissue.
   (iv) It is difficult to pull out the husk of coconut.
   (v) The cells of stratified squamous epithelium are arranged in many layers.

Ans. (i) Aerenchyma is present in swollen petiole of water hyacinth, which encloses a lot of air and makes the plant lighter than water. Hence, it is able to float on the surface of water.
(ii) Branches of tree move and bend freely in high wind velocity because of the presence of collenchyma tissue which provides flexibility to the branches of tree.
(iii) Intercellular spaces are absent in sclerenchyma tissue because their walls are lignified and form bundles of mechanical functions.
(iv) Husk of coconut is made up of sclerenchymatous fibres, which are closely packed. So, it is difficult to pull out the husk of coconut.
(v) The cells of stratified squamous epithelium are arranged in many layers to prevent their wear and tear.

4. (i) Match the following columns.

Column I	Column II
A. Collenchyma	1. Heart
B. Sclerenchyma	2. Perceive and respond to stimuli
C. Cardiac muscles	3. Dead cells with thick deposit of lignin
D. Phloem	4. Transportation of food
E. Nervous tissue	5. Living cells, usually elongated with thick corner

(ii) Match the following columns.

	Column I		Column II
A.	Striated muscle	1.	Fibrous
B.	Tendon	2.	Stomach
C.	Smooth muscle	3.	Trachea
D.	Ciliated epithelium	4.	Axon
E.	Neuron	5.	Skeletal

(iii) Match the following columns.

	Column I		Column II
A.	Thin-walled cells	1.	Phloem
B.	Present in the leaf stalk	2.	Xylem
C.	Lignin deposition on cell walls	3.	Parenchyma
D.	Tracheids	4.	Collenchyma
E.	Sieve tube present	5.	Sclerenchyma

(iv) Match the following columns.

	Column I		Column II
A.	Fluid connective tissue	1.	Smooth muscles
B.	Striated muscle	2.	Cartilage
C.	Surface of joints	3.	Adipose tissue
D.	Storage of fat	4.	Blood
E.	Unstriated muscles	5.	Skeletal muscle

Ans. (i) A–5, B–3, C–1, D–4, E–2
(ii) A–5, B–1, C–2, D–3, E–4
(iii) A–3, B–4, C–5, D–2, E–1
(iv) A–4, B–5, C–2, D–3, E–1

5. Choose the correct answer from the four options given below.

(i) Girth of stem increases due to
(a) apical meristem (b) lateral meristem
(c) intercalary meristem (d) vertical meristem

Ans. (b)

(ii) Which is not a function of epidermis?
(a) Protection from adverse condition
(b) Gaseous exchange
(c) Conduction of water
(d) Transpiration

Ans. (c)

(iii) Parenchyma cells are
(a) relatively unspecified and thin-walled
(b) thick-walled and specialised
(c) lignified
(d) None of the above

Ans. (a)

(iv) The tissue which contain photosynthetic pigment is
(a) chlorenchyma (b) aerenchyma
(c) sieve tubes (d) sieve elements

Ans. (a)

(v) The only living component of xylem is
(a) tracheids (b) vessels
(c) xylem parenchyma (d) xylem sclerenchyma

Ans. (c)

(vi) Hair-like projections present in the respiratory tract are
(a) cilia (b) squamous epithelium
(c) mucus (d) neuron

Ans. (a)

(vii) Which of the following helps in the repair of tissue and fills up the space inside the organ?
(a) Tendon (b) Adipose tissue
(c) Areolar tissue (d) Cartilage

Ans. (c)

(viii) Apart from storing fat globules, adipose tissue also acts as
(a) muscle (b) cartilage
(c) covering tissue (d) insulator

Ans. (d)

(ix) Tendon and ligaments are examples of
(a) fibrous connective tissue
(b) cartilage
(c) muscular tissue
(d) adipose tissue

Ans. (a)

(x) Cartilage is not found in
(a) nose (b) ear
(c) kidney (d) larynx

Ans. (c)

(xi) 'Cardiac' is a term related to the
(a) intestine (b) heart
(c) nose (d) brain

Ans. (b)

(xii) Intercalated discs are found in
(a) striped muscle cells (b) cardiac muscle fibres
(c) nerve cells (d) ligaments

Ans.(b)

(xiii) The cytoplasmic projections arising from the cyton is
(a) pseudopodia (b) dendrons
(c) cilia (d) flagella

Ans. (b)

6. Fill in the blanks by using suitable words.

(i) The plant tissue containing a single type of cell is called ....
(ii) The plant tissue which is found in growth region is called ....
(iii) The girth in the skin of some fruits develop due to the presence of ....
(iv) .... tissue is composed of different types of cells.
(v) .... conducts water and minerals in plants.
(vi) .... conducts food materials in plants.

(vii) The lining of stomach and intestine are composed of .... epithelium.
(viii) .... has no blood vessels or nerves.
(ix) Blood is an example of .... tissue.
(x) Axons of .... cell are very long.

Ans. (i) simple tissue (ii) meristem
(iii) Sclereids (iv) Complex
(v) Xylem (vi) Phloem
(vii) columnar (viii) Cartilage
(ix) connective (x) nerve

7. Choose the odd one out from the following terms given below and name the category to which other three belong.
(i) Parenchyma, Cartilage, Collenchyma, Sclerenchyma
(ii) Xylem fibres, Tracheids, Vessels, Companion cells
(iii) Squamous epithelium, Adipose tissue, Columnar epithelium, Cuboidal epithelium
(iv) Bone, Blood, Areolar tissue, Columnar epithelium.
(v) Skeletal muscles, Cardiac muscles, Smooth muscles, Neuron

Ans. (i) **Odd term** Cartilage
Rest three are examples of plant tissue.
(ii) **Odd term** Companion cell
Rest three are parts of xylem.
(iii) **Odd term** Adipose tissue
Rest three are type of epithelial tissues.
(iv) **Odd term** Columnar epithelium
Rest three are examples of connective tissue.
(v) **Odd term** Neuron
Rest three are the type of muscle tissue.

8. State whether the following statements are true or false. Correct and rewrite the false statements.
(i) A group of similar cells forms an organ.
(ii) Vacuoles are absent in meristematic tissue.
(iii) Lateral meristems are responsible for the increase in the diameter of a plant.
(iv) Parenchyma cells are thin-walled.
(v) Aerenchyma encloses large air spaces in aquatic plants for exchange of gases.
(vi) Xylem fibres are living.
(vii) Glandular epithelium is present in the lining of trachea.
(viii) Stratified epithelium is found in cornea and skin.
(ix) The cells of the adipose tissues are filled with lymph.
(x) Adipose tissue is a type of connective tissue meant for storage of fats.
(xi) Cardiac muscle is branched.

Ans. (i) False. A group of similar cells forms a tissue.
(ii) True
(iii) True
(iv) True
(v) True
(vi) False. Xylem fibres are dead cells.
(vii) False. Glandular epithelium is present in the lining of stomach and intestine.
(viii) True
(ix) False. The cells of adipose tissue are filled with fats.
(x) True
(xi) True

9. State the exact location of the following.
(i) Apical meristem
(ii) Lateral meristem
(iii) Parenchyma tissue
(iv) Squamous epithelial cells
(v) Cuboidal epithelium
(vi) Ciliated epithelium
(vii) Unstriated muscle
(viii) Axons

Ans. (i) Apical meristem is present at the tip of stems and roots.
(ii) Lateral meristems is present below the back and on the lateral sides of roots and stems.
(iii) Parenchyma tissue is present in the cortex, pith and roots.
(iv) Squamous epithelial cells are present in oesophagus and lining of mouth.
(v) Cuboidal epithelia are found in the lining of kidney tubules and ducts of salivary gland.
(vi) Ciliated epithelia are found in the respiratory tract.
(vii) Unstriated muscles are found in iris of eye.
(viii) Axons are the parts of neurons in brain and spinal cord.

10. Give one example of the following.
(i) Supporting tissue
(ii) Connective tissue propor
(iii) Fluid tissue
(iv) Unstriated muscles
(v) Cells that can contract and relax
(vi) Cells that can conduct impulses

Ans. (i) Parenchyma
(ii) Areolar tissue
(iii) Blood
(iv) Uterus
(v) Muscle cells
(vi) Neurons

11. State the main function of the following.
(i) Epithelial tissue (ii) Parenchyma
(iii) Sclerenchyma (iv) Areolar tissues
(v) Blood (vi) Bone
(vii) Cardiac muscle (viii) Neurons

Ans. (i) Epithelial tissue is the protective covering of most of the organs. It protects the underlying cells from drying, injury, infection and chemical effects.
(ii) Parenchyma provides support to plants and also stores food.
(iii) Sclerenchyma provides mechanical support to plant. It provides strength and rigidity to the plant body.
(iv) Areolar tissue holds various tissues together. It helps in the repair of damaged tissues.
(v) Blood transports oxygen and nutrients to the lungs and tissue. It carries cells that fight infection.
(vi) Bone forms supporting framework of body and anchors the muscles and support the main organs.
(vii) Cardiac muscle helps in the rhythmic contraction and relaxation of heart.
(viii) Neurons receive and transmit signals to different parts of the body.

12. Mention one difference between each of the following pairs on the basis of what is given in the bracket.
(i) Simple tissue and Complex tissue (structure)
(ii) Parenchyma and Sclerenchyma (cell wall)
(iii) Meristematic tissue and Permanent tissue (dividing capacity)
(iv) Blood and Lymph (composition)
(v) Tendon and Ligament (location)

Ans. (i) Difference between simple tissue and complex tissue is as follows

Simple tissue	Complex tissue
It is made up of only one type of cells which resemble each other, e.g. parenchyma.	It is made up of more than one type of cells which look different from each other, e.g. xylem.

(ii) Difference between parenchyma and sclerenchyma is as follows

Parenchyma	Sclerenchyma
Cell wall is very thin and made up of cellulose.	Cell wall is uniformaly thick due to the deposition of lignin.

(iii) Difference between meristematic and permanent tissue is as follows

Meristematic tissue	Permanent tissue
Cells divide repeatedly to form new cells.	Cells normally do not divide and attain specialised functions.

(iv) Difference between blood and lymph is as follows

Blood	Lymph
It consists of plasma, RBCs, WBCs and platelets.	It consists of blood plasma and white blood cells.

(v) Difference between tendon and ligament is as follows

Tendon	Ligament
It attaches muscles to bone.	It attaches bone to bone.

13. Give the biological/technical terms for the following.
(i) Dividing cells at the tip of roots and stems.
(ii) The category of plant tissues that have lost their ability to multiply.
(iii) The kind of plant cells with thin walls and a single large vacuole.
(iv) Elongated cells which are thickened at corners.
(v) Tissues which provide the upward movement of water and dissolved materials from the roots to other parts of the plant.
(vi) The type of tissue that lines the respiratory tract.

Ans. (i) Apical meristem (ii) Permanent tissue
(iii) Parenchyma cells (iv) Collenchyma
(v) Tracheids and vessels (vi) Epithelial tissue

14. Briefly explain the following terms.
(i) Tissue (ii) Tracheids
(iii) Ligaments (iv) Bone
(v) Dendrites

Ans. (i) Group of similar cells, having same origin and perfom a specific function is known as tissue.
(ii) Tracheids are long, tubular dead cells with lignified walls and tapering ends.
(iii) Ligaments are dense connective tissue that connects one bone to another bone.
(iv) Bone is strong and non-flexible tissue. It is made up of protein and is rich in salts of calcium and phosphorus.
(v) Dendrites are short branched fibres of neuron which recieves nerve impulses.

15. Answer the following questions briefly.
(i) How does the cork act as a protective tissue?
(ii) Why are xylem and phloem called complex tissue?
(iii) Give three features of cardiac muscles.
(iv) Name two types of process present in neuron.

Ans. (i) Cork is several layers thick and known as the bark of tree. The cells of cork are dead and compactly arranged without intercellular spaces. They have a chemical substance called suberin in their walls. The suberin makes cork cell impervious to gases and water. Thus, it protects the underlying tissue from desiccation.

(ii) Xylem and phloem are made up of more than one type of cell, which coordinate to perform a common function. So, they are called complex tissue.

(iii) Features of cardiac muscles are
- (a) Cardiac muscles are involuntary.
- (b) They show rhythmic contraction and relaxation.
- (c) Their cells are cylindrical, branched and uninucleate.

(iv) Two types of process present in neuron are
- (a) **Axon** It carries impulses away from the cell body.
- (b) **Dendrite** It carries impulses towards the cell body.

2 Marks Questions

16. 'The tissue system in multicellular organisms promotes division of labour'. Justify the statement.

Ans. There is a division of labour in multicellular organisms. Different functions like digestion, respiration, excretion, etc., are taken up by different group of cells or tissues. In multicellular organisms each tissue or organ carryout one particular function and carry the specialised ability to perform the same hence, they do it more efficiently, e.g. xylem is specialised to conduct water and minerals. Similarly, for food translocation phloem is responsible.

17. What is epithelial tissue? State the type of epithelial tissue present in the lining of blood vessel.

Ans. The outermost covering or protective tissue in animal body is called epithelial tissue. Simple squamous epithelium tissue forms the lining of blood vessels.

18. What type of tissue blood is? Give the name of its various components.

Ans. Blood is a type of fluid connective tissue.

Various components of blood include
- (i) RBCs
- (ii) WBCs
- (iii) Platelets

19. Explain the structure of striped muscle.

Ans. The striped muscles are long, unbranched and multinucleate fibres. These fibres are surrounded by a membrane called sarcolemma. These muscle fibres contain alternate dark and light bands due to which these appear striated.

20. What is the specific function of the cardiac muscles?

Ans. Cardiac muscles are involuntary muscles present in heart. They help in the rhythmic contraction and relaxation of heart. This means that the pumping of blood through heart results from the continuous relaxation and contraction of cardiac muscles.

3 Marks Questions

21. What happens when,
- (i) formation of cork in older stem does not occur.
- (ii) apical meristem is damaged in plants.
- (iii) ligament gets overstretched.

Ans. (i) If the formation of cork does not occur in older stem then the outer tissue will rupture due to increase in girth and plant will get infected by an invasion of parasites.

(ii) If apical meristem gets damaged in plants, then growth of plant will not occur.

(iii) Overstretching of ligament causes sprain.

22. List three characteristics of parenchyma.

Ans. Major characteristics shown by parenchyma are as follows
- (i) The cells of parenchyma are living and possess the power of division.
- (ii) The cells are loosely packed with large intercellular spaces in between them.
- (iii) Parenchyma are found in soft parts of plant such as cortex of roots, ground tissue in stem and in the mesophyll cells of leaves.
- (iv) They serve as a packing tissue to fill the space in between other tissue and maintain the shape of plants.
- (v) They store waste products of plant such as tannin, gum, crystals, etc. [Any three]

23. Explain the structure of parenchyma and collenchyma with the help of diagrams.

Ans. Parenchyma cells are homogeneous with thin cell walls made up of cellulose. Their cells have intercellular spaces and a large vacuole is also present.

Collenchyma cells are bounded by thick walls, i.e. thickened at the corners by the deposition of pectin.

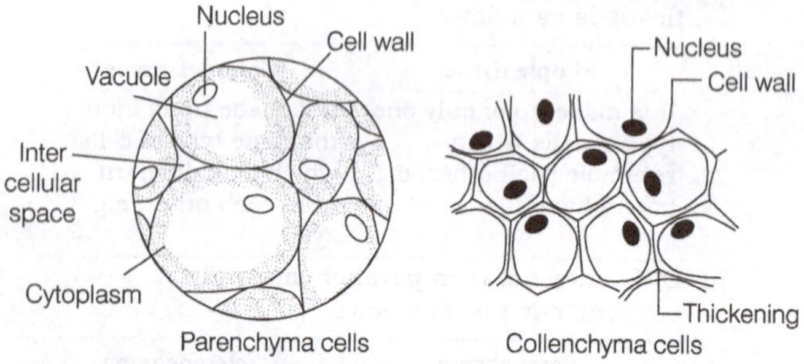

24. List the constituents of phloem. What will happen if the phloem at the base of a branch is removed?

Ans. Major constituents of phloem include sieve tubes, companion cells, phloem fibres and phloem parenchyma.

If the phloem at the base of branch is removed, then lower area of the branch will not receive food from the leaves. But the plant will not die, because it will continue to receive food from other branches as food can move in both the directions in phloem.

25. What are neurons? Where are they found in the body? What function do they perform in the body of an organism?

Ans. Neurons are structural and functional unit of nervous system. These are found in brain and spinal cord.

Functions

(i) This tissue is specialised to receive and transmit nerve impulses in the body.

(ii) Dendrites receive impulse and axon transmits the impulse away from the cell body.

Section-II [5 Marks]

Structured Questions

1. Study the diagram given below and answer the questions that follows.

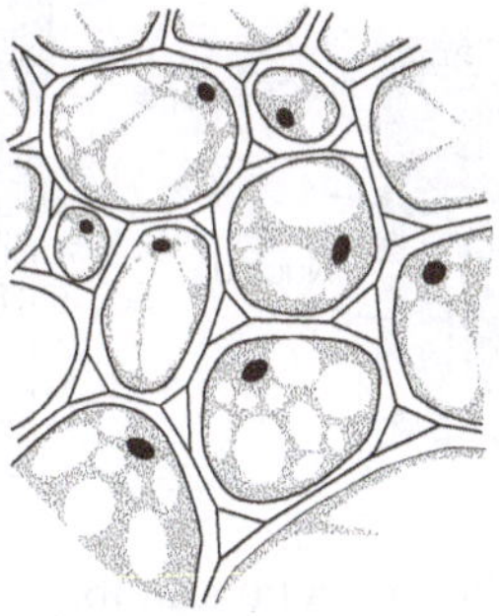

(i) Identify the given tissue.

(ii) Infer the characteristic features of these cells.

(iii) Suggest any two parts of the plant where such cells are present.

(iv) Give one function of given tissue.

(v) Give the name of different modification of the given tissue.

Ans. (i) The given tissue is parenchyma.

(ii) The characteristic features of parenchymatous cells are: They consists of thin-walled unspecialised cells which are loosely packed, e.g. having simple intercellular spaces. Each cell has a prominent nucleus.

(iii) Parenchymatous cells are found in

(a) Root

(b) Stem

(iv) This tissue provides support to plants and also stores food.

(v) Aerenchyma and chlorenchyma are the different modification of the given tissue.

2. Study the diagram given below and anwer the questions that follows.

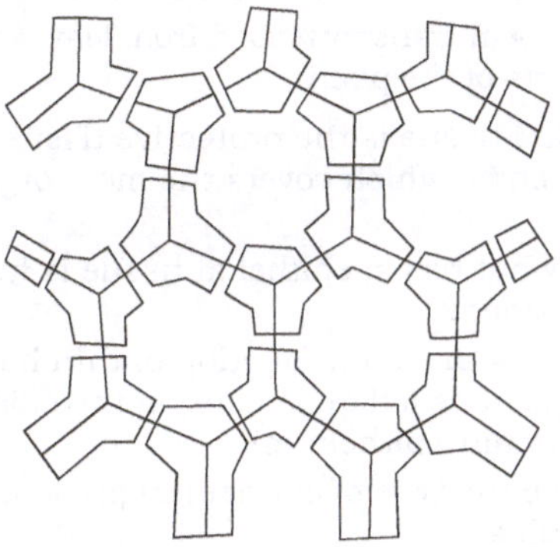

(i) Identify the tissue shown in the figure.

(ii) Specify any parts of the plant where such cells are present.

(iii) Give any two characteristic features of these cells.

(iv) Give one use of this tissue.

(v) Which tissue forms the husk of coconut?

Ans. (i) Sclerenchyma tissue is shown in the figure.

(ii) Sclerenchymatous cells are found in

(a) vascular bundles (b) veins

(iii) Two characteristic features of these cells are as

- The cells of sclerenchymatous tissue are dead.
- They are long and narrow in appearance.

(iv) This tissue is used in the manufacturing of certain mats, ropes and textile fibres.

(v) Sclerenchymatous tissue forms the husk of coconut.

3. Complex permanent tissue is made up of more than one type of cells having a common origin.

(i) What are the different types of complex tissue?

(ii) Give the role of xylem parenchyma.

(iii) Which element of phloem is made up of dead cells?

(iv) Give the name of living component of xylem.

(v) Highlight the function of xylem and phloem.

Ans. (i) Xylem and phloem are the different types of complex tissue.

(ii) Xylem parenchyma stores food and helps in the sideways conduction of water.

(iii) Phloem fibres are made up of dead cells.

(iv) Xylem parenchyma is the living component of xylem.

(v) The functions of xylem and phloem are as
- Xylem transports water and minerals from roots to leaves of the plant.
- Phloem transports food from leaves to other parts of the plant.

4. Epithelial tissue is the protective tissue of the animal body, which covers the most organ of the body.
(i) On what basis, epithelial tissue is further classified?
(ii) What is the main function of thin hair-like projections (cilia) persent on the ciliated columnar epithelium?
(iii) Name the type of epithelium present in kidney tubules.
(iv) Which type of epithelium secretes certain chemical substances?
(v) Give role of squamous epithelium.

Ans. (i) On the basis of shape of the cells and their arrangement.
(ii) The cilia have the ability to move. Their movement pushes the mucus forward to clear the passage.
(iii) Ciliated columnar epithelium is present in kidney tubules.
(iv) Glandular epithelium secretes certain chemical substances.
(v) Squamous epithelium protects the underlying parts from injury, entry of germs, harmful chemicals and drying up.

5. Observe the following figure and answer the following questions.

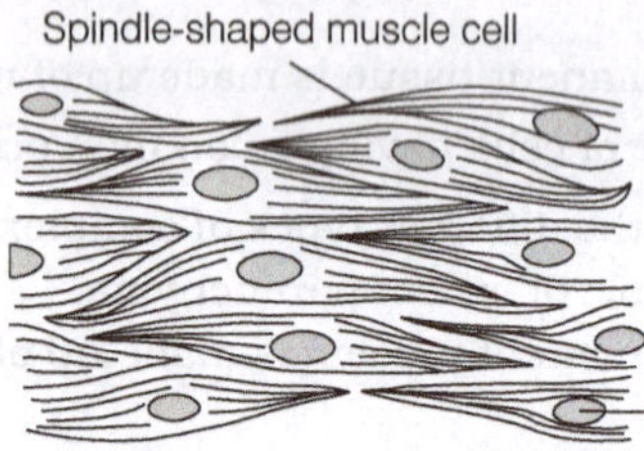

(i) What is shown in figure?
(ii) What is the function of this tissue?
(iii) Name some organs where this tissue is located.
(iv) Give the characteristic features of given tissue.
(v) What type of muscle , smooth or striated is found in the iris of eye?

Ans. (i) The figure shows smooth muscle cells.
(ii) Smooth muscle tissue facilitates the movements in involuntary organs.
(iii) Smooth muscles are found in alimentary canal, lining of blood vessel, bronchi of lungs, etc.
(iv) The characteristic features of given tissue (smooth muscle cells) are as follows
- The cells of smooth muscles are long with pointed ends and are uninucleated.
- They do not show any striations.

(v) Smooth muscles are found in the iris of eye.

6. Study the diagram given below and answer the questions that follows

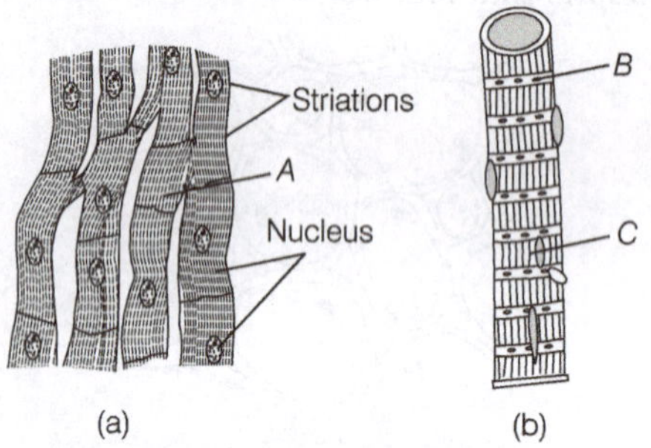

(i) Identify diagrams (a) and (b).
(ii) Label the parts *A*, *B* and *C*.
(iii) Which one of them acts as impulse booster?
(iv) Which one of them is under control of our will?
(v) Give the location of the (a) and (b).

Ans. (i) Figure (a) is cardiac muscle fibres.
Figure (b) is skeletal or striated muscle fibres.
(ii) The parts *A*, *B* and *C* are labelled as
A-Intercalated disc; *B*-Light band; *C*-Dark band
(iii) Intercalated disc acts as an impulse booster.
(iv) Skeletal or striated muscle i.e. (b) is under the control of our will. Therefore, these muscles are called voluntary muscles.
(v) Cardiac muscle (a) are found in heart and skeletal muscles (b) are found in limbs.

Chapter Assessment

Section-I

1 Mark Questions

1. Name the following.
   (i) The tissue responsible for growth in plant.
   (ii) One-celled thick outermost layer of leaves.
   (iii) The protective tissue in plants with lignin deposition.
   (iv) The tissue of plant in which companion cells and sieve tubes are located.
   (v) The tissue attached to the limbs.
   (vi) The long and unbranched extension of neurons.

2. Correct and rewrite the following statements by changing the underlined words.
   (i) Sclerenchyma cells are loosely packed with large intercellular spaces in them.
   (ii) The conducting cells of xylem are non-living except xylem fibres.
   (iii) Cartilage is a porous and a non-flexible tissue.

3. Give biological reasons for the following.
   (i) Growth of plants occurs only in certain specific region.
   (ii) Adipose tissue acts as insulator in the body.

4. (i) Match the following columns.

	Column I		Column II
A.	Blood and lymph	1.	Transport tissue
B.	Bone and cartilage	2.	Epithelial tissue
C.	Tendon and ligament	3.	Dense connective tissue
D.	Ciliated and cuboidal	4.	Skeletal connective tissue
E.	Xylem and phloem	5.	Fluid connective tissue

(ii) Match the following columns.

	Column I		Column II
A.	Axons and dendrites	1.	Xylem
B.	RBCs and WBCs	2.	Phloem
C.	Vessels and tracheids	3.	Neurons
D.	Sieve tubes and companion cells	4.	Muscular tissue
E.	Contractile protein	5.	Blood

5. Choose the correct answer from each of the four options given below.
   (i) All phloem components are living except
   (a) companion cells (b) phloem fibres
   (c) sieve tubes (d) phloem parenchyma
   (ii) Which of these is not an example of connective tissue?
   (a) Blood (b) Bone
   (c) Epithelium (d) Ligament
   (iii) Fats are stored in
   (a) areolar tissue (b) adipose tissue
   (c) nervous tissue (d) cartilage
   (iv) Tendons and ligaments are examples of
   (a) fibrous connective tissue (b) cartilage
   (c) muscular tissue (d) adipose tissue
   (v) The muscular tissue which functions throughout the life continuously without fatigue is
   (a) skeletal muscle (b) cardiac muscle
   (c) smooth muscle (d) voluntary muscle

6. Fill in the blanks by using suitable words.
   (i) The example of protective tissue in plant is ....
   (ii) There are .... kinds of supportive tissue in plants.
   (iii) The term tissue was given by ....
   (iv) .... is the structural element of xylem.
   (v) .... is the most widely spread, occurs beneath the epidermis of the skin.
   (vi) Areolar tissue consist of two types of fibres, i.e. .... and ....

7. Choose the odd one out of the following terms given below and name the category to which other three belong.
   (i) Tracheids, Sieve tube, Companion cells, Phloem parenchyma
   (ii) Areolar tissue, Cartilage, Adipose tissue, Fibrous connective tissue

8. State whether the following statements are true or false. Correct and rewrite the false statements.
   (i) Blood platelets help in clotting of blood.
   (ii) Haemoglobin is present in RBCs.
   (iii) Cartilage is porous in nature.
   (iv) Smooth muscles show dark and light bands under microscope.
   (v) Axons are small-sized and always branched.

9. State the exact location of the following.
   (i) Collenchyma
   (ii) Areolar tissue
   (iii) Neuron
   (iv) Striated muscles
   (v) Unstriated muscles
10. Give one example of the following.
    (i) Epithelial tissue in animal body.
    (ii) Components of blood
    (iii) Multicellular gland
11. State the main function of the following.
    (i) Collenchyma
    (ii) Cilia
    (iii) Cartilage
12. Mention one difference between each of the following pairs on the basis of what is given in the bracket.
    (i) Xylem and Phloem (function)
    (ii) Voluntary and Involuntary muscles (structure)
13. Give the biological/technical terms for the following.
    (i) Dividing cells at the base of the leaves.
    (ii) The tissue which conducts water in a plant.
    (iii) The types of tissue that line the stomach and intestine.
14. Briefly explain the following terms.
    (i) Histology (ii) Lateral meristem
15. Answer the following questions briefly.
    (i) Mention any one characteristic feature imparted by collenchyma tissue to the plants.
    (ii) What is the feature of muscular tissues?
    (iii) How many parts are found in neurons?

2 Marks Questions

16. The functional combination of nerve and muscle tissue is fundamental to most animal, comment.
17. How connective tissue is different from other tissues?

3 Marks Questions

18. Discuss the different types of plant meristem?
19. What is the role of epidermis in plants?

Section-II [5 Marks]

Structured Questions

20. Given diagram shows the longitudinal section of phloem elements.

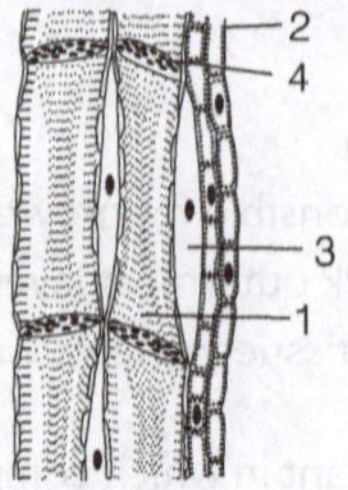

    (i) Label the parts numbered 1 to 4.
    (ii) What is the function of part labelled 2?
    (iii) Which are living cells in the given figure?
    (iv) Why is phloem kept under complex permanent tissue?
    (v) Why are complex permanent tissue also called as conducting tissues?
21. Study the given figure below and answer the questions that follows.

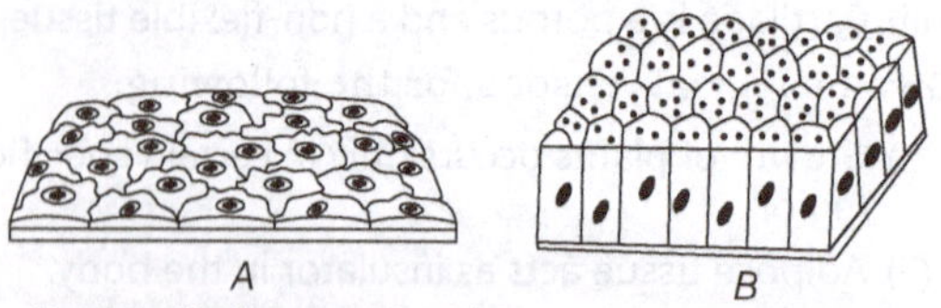

    (i) Identify figures *A* and *B*.
    (ii) Which epithelium forms the outer layer of the skin and lines of cavities or ducts?
    (iii) Give one characteristic function of tissue '*B*'.
    (iv) Where is *B* found in our body?
    (v) What is the role of *A* ?

For explanations scan the given QR Code

Olympiad Section*

Brain Teasing Questions asked in Previous Olympiads

1 Toluidine is a metachromatic stain that can impart different colours to different plant tissues. The primary cell walls turn pink while secondary cell walls turn blue. Which of the following is likely to result? [INBO 2020]

(a) Collenchyma cell walls will turn pink
(b) Xylem vessels will turn pink
(c) Phloem walls will turn blue
(d) Chlorenchyma wall will turn blue

2 Plant tissues where carbon fixation occurs are known as 'source'. The product(s) formed is/are then transported to different parts of the plant body for its further utilisation or storage, which is known as 'sink'. Which of the following can be categorised as 'source (P)'and 'sink (Q)'? [INJSO 2018]

(a) (P) endodermis of root; (Q) phloem cells of root
(b) (P) epidermal region of assimilatory root; (Q) meristematic region of assimilatory root
(c) (P) parenchyma of beet tuber; (Q) phloem cells of root
(d) (P) xylem tissue of a green leaf; (Q) phloem tissue of the adjacent green leaf

3 In a hypothetical experiment, the outer tissue of the woody part of the stem of a dicotyledonous plant is removed in the form of a ring, leaving only the xylem and pith intact. Which one of the statements is most likely to be correct? [INJSO 2017]

(a) Water transport from the root to leaves will be obstructed but food transport from leaves to stem will be unhindered
(b) Water transport from root to leaves will not be obstructed but food transport from stem to leaves will be hindered
(c) Water transport from root to leaves will not be obstructed but food transport down the leaves stops at the ring
(d) Water transport from leaves to root is obstructed but food transport down from the leaves stops at the ring

4 Cartilage is a connective tissue that smoothens bone surfaces at the joints. It is also present in nose, ear, trachea and larynx. Matrix of hyaline cartilage is predominantly composed of [INJSO 2013]

(a) proteins and sugars
(b) calcium and phosphorous
(c) calcium and fibres
(d) sugars and calcium

5 The transitional epithelium lines inner surface of urinary bladder and ureter. This epithelial layer is thinner and more stretchable as compared to the stratified epithelium. The best possible explanation for such a structural feature of transitional epithelium is that it [INJSO 2013]

(a) prevents infection to the organs
(b) accommodates fluctuation of volume of the liquid in an organ
(c) enables reabsorption of salts from urine
(d) helps in micturition (process of urination)

6 Read the following description of a plant cell type. 'These are elongated tapering cells with cross walls, secondary thickenings with pits and are dead at maturity'. [INBO 2012]
Which of the following is the correct statement about the function of cells described?

(a) They are the main food conducting cells of flowering plants
(b) They are the main water conducting cells of flowering plants
(c) They serve to protect the plants and retard water loss
(d) They conduct water in all vascular plants

7 Mark the odd pair out. [INBO 2010]

(a) Totipotency: Parenchyma
(b) Secondary growth: Cambium
(c) Dermal cells: Trichomes
(d) Periderm: Collenchyma

Answers

1. (a) **2.** (b) **3.** (c) **4.** (a) **5.** (b) **6.** (d) **7.** (d)

**These questions may or may not be asked in the examination, have been given just for additional practice required for olympiads, scholarship exams etc.* *For detailed explanations refer Page No. 230.*

CHAPTER 03

The Flower

Chapter Inside

• Structure of Bisexual Flower • Parts of a Flower • Types of Flowers • Placentation • Inflorescence

The flower is an attractive, brightly coloured reproductive part of the flowering plants. It is a modified shoot in which internodes are highly condensed and leaves are modified into floral parts. By undergoing sexual reproduction, it helps in the formation of fruit and seeds. In this chapter, we will study about the different parts of flowers, their inflorescence, types and placentation.

Structure of Bisexual Flower

A flower arises at the axil of a leaf-like structure called **bract**. It may be either green or differently coloured (e.g. *Bougainvillea*, lily, etc). Flowers with bracts are called **bracteate** and those without bracts are called **ebracteate**, (e.g. China rose, sunflower, etc) The stalk of the flower is also called **pedicel**. It provides support to the flower. A flower that lacks a stalk is known as **sessile**.

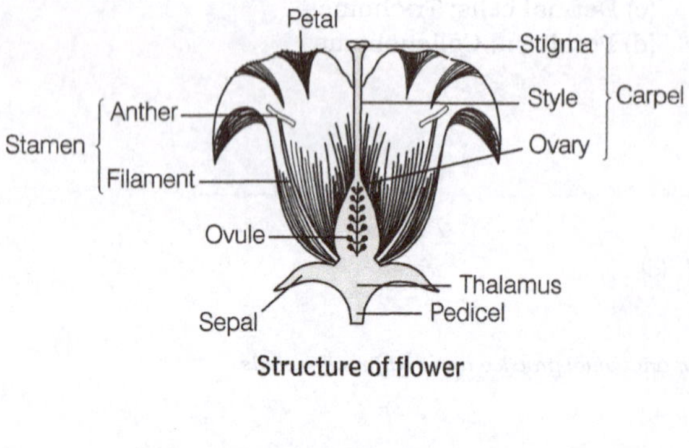

Structure of flower

The terminal and swollen part of the axis of the flower is the **receptacle** or **thalamus** or **torus**. The flower contains four different types of whorls, *viz.* **sepals, petals, stamen** and **pistil**. These are discussed in detail further in this chapter.

Parts of a Flower

A typical flower consists of four distinct parts (whorls), i.e. the **calyx**, the **corolla**, the **androecium** and the **gynoecium**. Out of these, the calyx and corolla are considered as **non-essential parts** whereas the androecium and gynoecium are considered as **essential parts** because they take part in the process of reproduction.

1. Calyx

It is the outermost whorl of a flower. It is made up of units called **sepals** (usually 5 in number). The sepals are generally green, leaf-like structure which protect the flower in the budding stage.

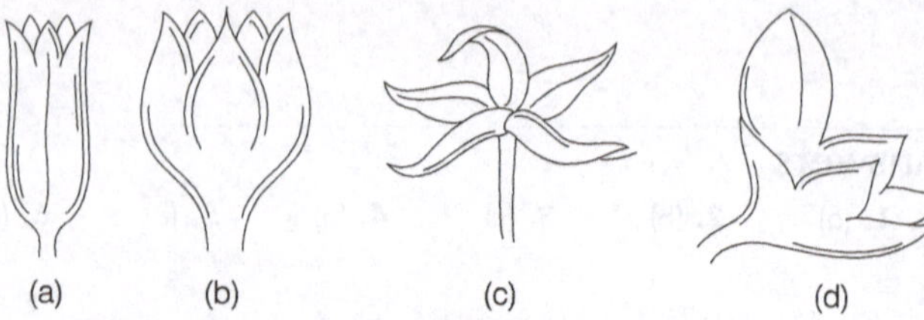

(a) (b) (c) (d)

Gamosepalous Polysepalous Epicalyx

These sepals can be fused with each other thus, called **gamosepalous** (e.g. marigold, China rose, sunflower and *Petunia*) or may be free from each other and are called **polysepalous** (e.g. *Brassica*). Additional floral whorl outside the calyx is called **epicalyx** (e.g. *Hibiscus* or shoe flower).

Functions

(i) They protect inner whorls of the flower in bud stage.

(ii) In gulmohar, these are coloured (red) thus, called **petaloid sepals** which attract pollinators like birds, insects, etc.

(iii) The green sepals carryout photosynthesis, as they contain chlorophyll.

2. Corolla

Corolla is regarded as second whorl of the flower. It is composed of **petals** which are coloured and leaf-like structures. Petals arise inner to and above the sepals on thalamus. They are generally arranged in a single whorl, but there may be double whorl (poppy) or a spiral whorl (water lily). Just like calyx, corolla may also be **gamopetalous** (petals united, e.g. *Petunia*) or **polypetalous** (petals free, e.g. *Hibiscus*).

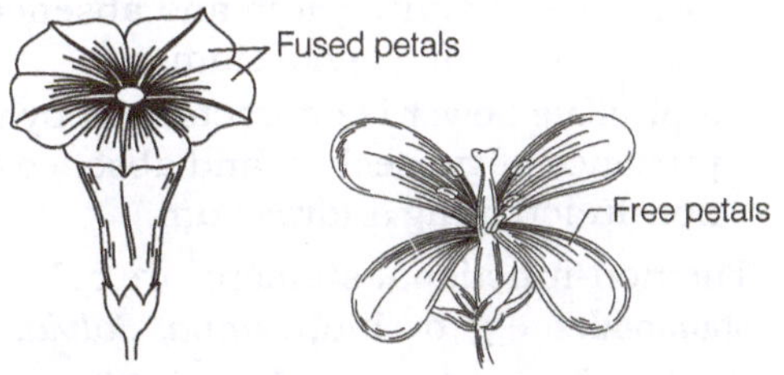

(a) **Gamopetalous** (b) **Polypetalous**

Sometimes corolla bears outgrowth such as, **spur** (beak-like, tube-shaped structure, e.g. larkspur), **nectary** (special nectar glands developed at base of flower, e.g. nasturtium) and **corona** (an additional whorl having lobes, scales or hairs which add beauty to flower, e.g. *Narcissus*).

Functions

(i) These constitute the specialised part of the flowers to attract pollinators.

(ii) These are brightly coloured and sometimes strongly scented with nectary base which produces nectar.

(iii) The corolla encloses and protects stamens and pistils.

Note In some flowers like *Asparagus*, there are no clear cut differentiated sepals and petals. Instead, these are greenish or whitish leaf structures. These are called **perianth** and individual perianth are called **tepals**, which can be greenish (sepaloid) or beautifully coloured (petaloid), e.g. spider lily.

3. Androecium

This third whorl of flower is composed of **stamens**. Each stamen, which represents the male reproductive organ consists of a **stalk** or a **filament** and an **anther**. Each anther is usually bilobed (*bi*-two, *lobes*-chamber). Its both the lobes are attached at the back by a sterile band called **connective.** Each lobe of anther has two chambers, called as pollen sacs. The pollen grains are produced in pollen sacs.

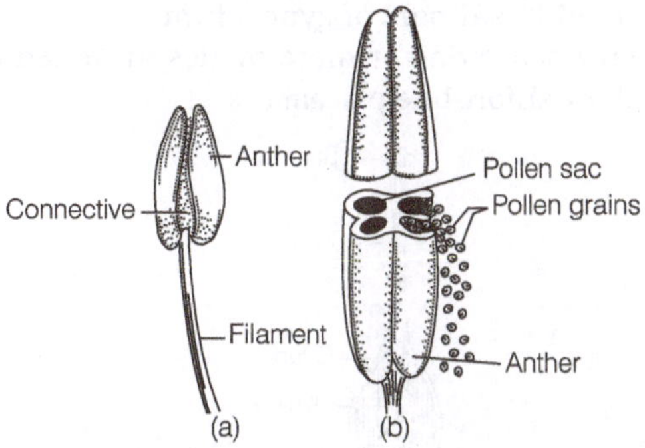

(a) A typical stamen, (b) Anther showing pollen grains

Stamens get organised inside androecium in the following ways.

(i) **Polyandrous** All the stamens are free from each other. Their filaments may be of same or different sizes, e.g. *Brassica*.

(ii) **Monadelphous** Only anthers are free but their filaments are united to form one group, e.g. China rose (shoe flower), cotton.

(iii) **Diadelphous** The filaments of stamens are united in two bundles but their anthers are free, e.g. pea, *Sesbania*, etc. In this, one of the several filaments is free and others are fused. However, the anthers remain free.

(iv) **Polyadelphous** The filaments of the androecium unite to form several groups, e.g. *Bombax*, *Citrus*, etc.

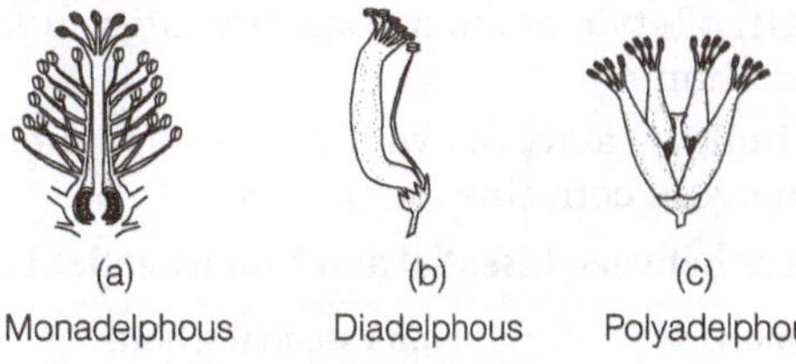

Forms of stamens

Note Sometimes filaments are free but anthers are united together, such condition is called **syngenesious**, e.g. sunflower.

Functions

(i) The anthers produce pollen grains containing male gametes.

(ii) The filaments attached to anthers help in making it more accessible for pollination.

4. Gynoecium

Pistil or gynoecium is the fourth whorl which constitutes female reproductive part of the flower. It is made up of one or more **carpels** (single female unit). A carpel consists of three parts, i.e. stigma, style and ovary.

The **stigma** is usually present at the tip of style and is the receptive surface for pollen grains. **Style** is a slender stalk that bridges ovary to stigma. **Ovary** is the enlarged basal part of gynoecium.

Each ovary bears one or more ovules attached to a flattened, cushion-like **placenta**.

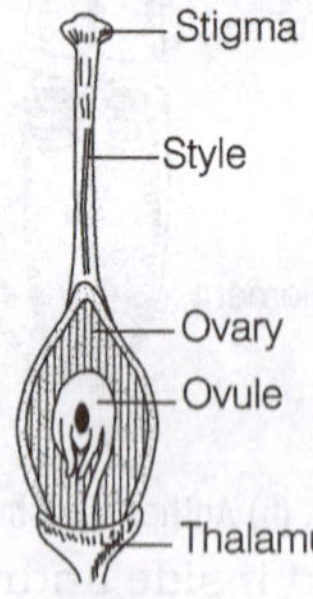

Gynoecium (Single carpel)

When gynoecium contains one carpel, it is **monocarpellary**, if it contains two carpels, then it is **bicarpellary** and if more than two carpels, then it is **polycarpellary**. If the carpels are free, the gynoecium is called **apocarpous** and if the carpels are united, it is called **syncarpous**.

Ovary having single chamber is called **unilocular** and that having many chambers is called **multilocular**. Each ovule have large sac-like structure known as **embryo sac**.

Functions

(i) Stigma helps in receiving pollens and in their germination.

(ii) Length of style helps in exposing stigma for pollination.

(iii) The hollow cavity of ovary contains ovules. Each ovule contains an egg cell.

Differences between Essential and Non-essential Whorls

Essential whorls	Non-essential whorls
Whorls that are directly involved in reproduction are called essential whorls.	Whorls which are not directly involved in reproduction but are helping parts, which either protect the flower or make it more attractive for pollination.
Androecium (stamens) and gynoecium (pistils) are the essential whorls of a flower.	Calyx (sepals) and corolla (petals) are the non-essential whorls of a flower.

Check Your LEARNING...

1 Name the condition in which the petals are free.
2 Give two contrasting traits between calyx and corolla.
3 What term is given to stamens united in one group?
4 When the stamens are united in two bundles, but anthers remain free, what does the flower called?
5 Name the type of gynoecium in which carpels are free.

Types of Flowers

1. On the basis of the presence or absence of whorls, flowers are of following two types

   (i) **Complete flower** The flower which has all four whorls is called complete flower, e.g. rose, *Petunia, Hibiscus,* etc.

   (ii) **Incomplete flower** Flower in which any of the four whorls is missing is referred to as incomplete flower, e.g. *Begonia,* orchid, etc.

2. On the basis of type of reproductive part present, flower is of following types

   (i) **Unisexual flowers** (imperfect flower) These flowers have either androecium or gynoecium in them, e.g. *Cucurbita.*

   - A **staminate** flower is characterised by the presence of androecium and absence or non-functioning gynoecium.
   - A **pistillate** flower is characterised by the presence of gynoecium and absence or non-functioning androecium.

   The non-functional stamens are called **staminodes**, e.g. orchid, *Canna, Salvia,* etc.

   (ii) **Bisexual flowers** (perfect flower), These flowers having both male and female reproductive parts (androecium and gynoecium). These are also called **intersexual** or **hermaphrodite**, e.g. mustard, *Petunia, Hibiscus,* etc.

   (iii) **Neuter flowers** A flower is said to be neuter if both the androecium and gynoecium are absent, e.g. ray florets of sunflower.

   (iv) **Monoecious flowers** If both male and female flowers are present on same plant, they are called monoecious plants, e.g. maize, gourd, cucumber, etc.

   (v) **Dioecious flowers** If male and female unisexual flowers are borne on different plants, then they are called dioecious plants, e.g. papaya, palm mulberry, etc.

Note
- A flower is called **naked**, if both sepals and petals are lacking, e.g. betel. They are also called **achlamydeous**.
- The smallest flower is *Wolffia arrhiza*, whereas the largest flower is *Rafflesia* which is pollinated by elephants.

Placentation

Each chamber of the ovary of a flower contains cushion-like structure called **placenta**. The arrangement of ovules within the ovary is known as **placentation**. The placenta is a tissue, which develops along the inner wall of the ovary. The ovules remain attached to the placenta.

Inflorescence

The arrangement and distribution of flowers over a plant is called inflorescence. The plant axis bearing flowers is called **peduncle** or **rachis**. The flowers are borne either single or in bunch. If the flowers are borne singly are called **solitary flowers**. The grouping of flowers makes them more attractive for pollination by insects or animals. The longest inflorescence is found in *Agave*.

The inflorescence can be of following types

(i) **Racemose inflorescence** Here, the main axis never ends and continues to grow. Here, the flowers are borne laterally.

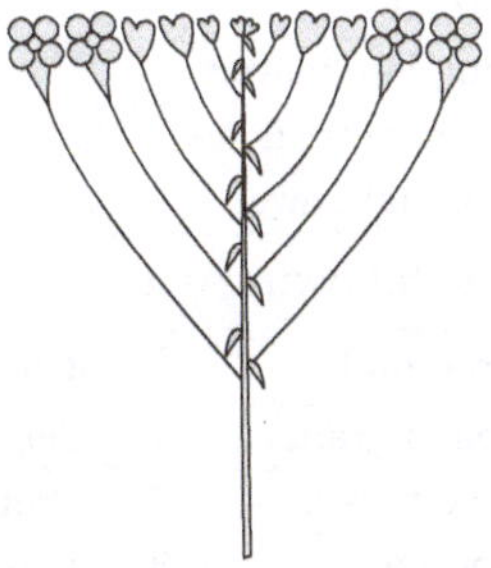

Racemose inflorescence

The older flowers are found at the base whereas the and younger ones are present at the apex. Thus, flowers are borne in acropetal succcession, e.g. mustard, radish, *Sesbania*, *Trifolium*, etc.

(ii) **Cymose inflorescence** In this, the tip of the main axis gets terminated into a flower. Further growth continues by one or more lateral branches, which also behaves like the main axis.
In this type, younger flowers occupy basal position while older flowers are found towards the apex. Flowers are arranged in basipetal order. e.g. *Solanum*, *Begonia*, teak, etc.

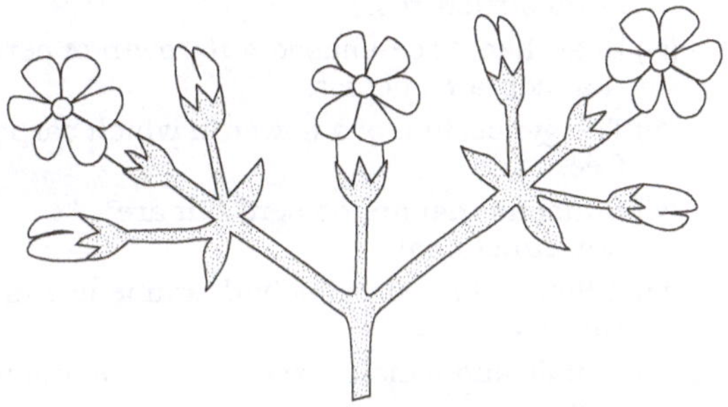

Cymose inflorescence

Check Your LEARNING...

1. Name a pistillate flower.
2. Why is papaya called dioecious?
3. Give one example each of a monoecious and dioecious flower.
4. Name the cushion-like structure in the ovary.
5. What is rachis?

QUiCK Revision

- Flower is a compressed shoot in which the leaves are modified into floral parts. It is comprised of four whorls.
- **Calyx** or **Sepals** are the outermost and lowermost whorl of flower. They are usually green but in some cases, they are brightly coloured.
- **Corolla** or **Petals** are coloured, leafy structure that attract insects for pollination.
- **Androecium** or **Stamen** represents the male reproductive structure of flower. Each stamen consists of a long filament and an anther.
- **Gynoecium** or **Carpel** is the female reproductive structure. It possesses a stigma, style and ovary.
- **Essential parts** of a flower include the stamens and the carpels.
- **Non-essential parts** include the non-reproductive structures like petals and sepals.
- On the basis of whorls, flowers are referred to as **complete flower** containing all the four floral structures and **incomplete flower**, where one or more floral structures are missing.
- On the basis of reproductive structures, flowers can be
  - **Unisexual** Flowers in which either the androecium or gynoecium is present.
  - **Bisexual** Flowers in which both the androecium and gynoecium are present.
  - **Neuter** Flowers in which both androecium and gynoecium are absent.
  - **Monoecious** are plants which bear both the staminate and pistillate flowers.
  - **Dioecious** plants have either staminate or pistillate flowers.
- **Placentation** is the arrangement of ovules within the ovary.
- **Inflorescence** is the arrangement of flowers on the plant. It can be of racemose or cymose type.

Chapter Practice

Section-I

1 Mark Questions

1. Name the following.
   (i) A specialised shoot having leaves modified into floral structures.
   (ii) The two parts of a flower which play a key role in reproduction.
   (iii) Special glands developed on or at the base of floral structures.
   (iv) Beak-like, tube-shaped outgrowth of perianth that contains nectar.
   (v) The gynoecium of a flower in which carpels are free.
   (vi) Stamens that are present but are non-functional.
   (vii) A flower that contains both stamens and carpels.
   (viii) If male and female flowers borne on different plants.
   (ix) The arrangement of ovules within the ovary.
   (x) The common axis of the plant that bears flowers.

Ans. (i) Flower (ii) Androecium and gynoecium
(iii) Nectary (iv) Spur
(v) Apocarpous (vi) Staminode
(vii) Bisexual/Hermaphrodite
(viii) Dioecious plant (ix) Placentation
(x) Peduncle

2. Correct and rewrite the following statements by changing the underlined words.
   (i) The essential whorls of a flower play a vital role in <u>transportation</u>.
   (ii) *Hibiscus* shows <u>diadelphous</u> condition.
   (iii) The pistil is made up of units called <u>rachis</u>.
   (iv) A flower lacking one or more sets of floral whorls is a <u>complete</u> flower.
   (v) Ray florets of sunflower is an example of <u>staminate</u> flower.

Ans. (i) The essential whorls of a flower, i.e. androecium and gynoecium play a vital role in reproduction.
(ii) *Hibiscus* or China rose represents monadelphous condition with free anthers and fused filaments.
(iii) The pistil is made up of units called carpels.
(iv) A flower lacking one or more sets of floral whorls is an incomplete flower.
(v) Ray florets of sunflower is an example of a neuter flower.

3. Give biological reasons for the following.
   (i) Sepals are able to photosynthesise.
   (ii) Petals are brightly coloured.
   (iii) Some plants have nectaries.
   (iv) Stigma covers the top of style.

Ans. (i) Sepals, in a way similar to leaves, contain chlorophyll, thus they can perform photosynthesis.
(ii) Petals are brightly coloured to attract pollinators such as animals, birds and insect to carryout pollination.
(iii) Plants have nectaries for providing nectar to insect pollinators.
(iv) Stigma acts as a landing platform for pollens, thus acquires the topmost position.

4. (i) Match the following columns.

Column I	Column II
A. Corona	1. *Narcissus*
B. Complete flower	2. Rose
C. Incomplete flower	3. Mustard
D. Bisexual flower	4. Orchid

(ii) Match the following columns.

Column I	Column II
A. Pollen grains	1. *Bombax*
B. Free petals	2. Protect stamens
C. Corolla	3. Polypetalous
D. Polyadelphous	4. Pollen sac

(iii) Match the following columns.

Column I	Column II
A. Epicalyx	1. pollens
B. Fused sepals	2. Present inside ovary
C. Ovules	3. Marigold
D. Stamen	4. Shoe flower

Ans. (i) A–1, B–2, C–4, D–3
(ii) A–4, B–3, C–2, D–1
(iii) A–4, B–3, C–2, D–1

5. Choose the correct answer from the four options given below.
   (i) The reproductive unit of angiosperms is
   (a) inflorescence (b) floral buds
   (c) flower (d) flower meristem

Ans. (c)

(ii) The presence or absence of bract in a flower is respectively indicated of
(a) bracteolate, ebracteolate
(b) bracteate, ebracteate
(c) ebracteate, bracteate
(d) ebracteolate, bracteolate

Ans. (b)

(iii) The bracts are large and colourful in
(a) *Bougainvillea* (b) shoe flower
(c) lily (d) mustard

Ans. (a)

(iv) The expanded tip of pedicel from where floral parts arise is called
(a) thalamus (b) receptacle
(c) Both (a) and (b) (d) None of these

Ans. (c)

(v) Which of these is essential part of the flower?
(a) Anther (b) Calyx
(c) Petal (d) Sepal

Ans. (a)

(vi) In a flower, the parts that produce male and female gametes are
(a) stamen and anther (b) filament and stigma
(c) anther and ovary (d) stamen and style

Ans. (c)

(vii) Monadelphous stamens mean the filament of stamens are arranged in ...... bundle(s).
(a) one (b) three (c) four (d) two

Ans. (a)

(viii) Gynoecium is the
(a) female reproductive part of flower made up of one carpel
(b) female reproductive part of flower made up of many carpels
(c) female reproductive part of flower made up of two carpels
(d) Any of the above

Ans. (d)

(ix) A plant having both the female and male parts on the same flower is
(a) *Cucurbita* (b) maize
(c) mustard (d) papaya

Ans. (c)

(x) Which of the following statements is false for flowers?
(a) Flowers are always bisexual
(b) They are the sexual reproductive organ
(c) They are produced in angiospermic plants
(d) Flowers also have non-essential whorls

Ans. (a)

6. Fill in the blanks by using suitable words.
(i) Thalamus is the extended part of the ....
(ii) Calyx and corolla form .... whorls of the flower.
(iii) The term ...... is used for fused sepal and petal.
(iv) In .... condition, filaments of stamens are united in a bundle of two.
(v) A carpel consists of ......, ... and ....
(vi) A .... pistil has multiple carpels.
(vii) .... is an example of a complete flower .
(viii) A flower which contains only male parts is called ....
(ix) Arrangement of flower on plant axis is called ....
(x) Flowers borne singly are called ....

Ans. (i) flower axis
(ii) non-essential
(iii) perianth
(iv) diadelphous
(v) stigma, style, ovary
(vi) polycarpellary
(vii) *Hibiscus*
(viii) staminate
(ix) inflorescence
(x) solitary flowers

7. Choose the odd one out from the following terms given below and name the category to which other three belong.
(i) Petals, Calyx, Corolla, Androecium
(ii) Style, Stigma, Stamen, Ovary
(iii) Marigold, Sunflower, *Petunia, Brassica*
(iv) Calyx, Androecium, Gynoecium, Thalamus
(v) Coconut, Papaya, Gulmohar, Maize

Ans. (i) **Odd term:** Androecium
Rest three are not essential whorls of the flower.
(ii) **Odd term:** Stamen
Rest three are the parts of carpel.
(iii) **Odd term:** *Brassica* (polysepalous)
Rest three exhibit gamosepalous condition where sepals are fused with each other.
(iv) **Odd term:** Thalamus
Rest three are distinct whorls of a flower.
(v) **Odd term:** Gulmohar
Rest three are examples of unisexual flower.

8. State whether following statements are true or false. Correct and rewrite the false statements.
(i) Flowers are always produced in a bunch.
(ii) Corolla is an essential whorl of a flower.
(iii) Flower with colourful and undifferentiated perianth is called sepaloid.
(iv) Androecium does not play any role in reproduction.
(v) Flowers can be complete or incomplete.
(vi) *Salvia* is a staminate flower.
(vii) Papaya is monoecious plant.

Ans. (i) False, flowers are either borne singly or in bunch.
(ii) False, both corolla and calyx are non-essential whorls of a flower.

(iii) False, flower with colourful and undifferentiated perianth is called petaloid.
(iv) False, androecium is an essential whorl that is important for reproduction as it contains pollens.
(v) True
(vi) False, in *Salvia*, the stamens are non-functional, thus it is called staminode.
(vii) False, papaya is dioecious plant.

9. State the exact location of the following.
(i) Thalamus (ii) Anther
(iii) Style (iv) Ovule
(v) Placenta

Ans. (i) **Thalamus** Tip of the flower stalk.
(ii) **Anther** Located at the tip of filament. They collectively form stamen.
(iii) **Style** Tube-like structure between stigma and ovary.
(iv) **Ovule** Inside the ovary.
(v) **Placenta** Cushion-like region within ovary.

10. Give one example of the following
(i) Gamosepalous condition
(ii) Monadelphous stamen
(iii) Polyadelphous
(iv) Complete flower
(v) Imperfect flower

Ans. (i) Marigold/China rose (ii) Cotton
(iii) Citrus (iv) *Petunia*
(v) *Cucurbita*

11. State the main function of the following.
(i) Sepal
(ii) Corolla
(iii) Androecium
(iv) Anther
(v) Style

Ans. (i) Sepal protects the flower in bud stage.
(ii) Corolla attract insects pollinators.
(iii) Androecium helps in the production of pollen grains. .
(iv) Anther produce and protect pollen.
(v) Style helps to convey pollens from stigma to ovary.

12. Differentiate between the following pairs on the basis of what is mentioned in brackets.
(i) Calyx and Corolla (function)
(ii) Gamopetalous and Polypetalous (condition of petals)
(iii) Style and Filament (function)
(iv) Apocarpous and Syncarpous (condition of carpel)

Ans. (i) Difference between calyx and corolla is as follows

Calyx	Corolla
It protects the inner parts of a flower.	It attracts insects for pollination.

(ii) Difference between gamopetalous and polypetalous is as follows

Gamopetalous	Polypetalous
Petals are fused fully or partially.	Petals are free from each other.

(iii) Difference between style and filament is as follows

Style	Filament
It is a part of carpel that holds stigma.	It is a part of androecium that holds anther.

(iv) Difference between apocarpous and syncarpous is as follows

Apocarpous	Syncarpous
More than one carpel, all of them are free from each other.	More than one carpel, all of them are fused with each other.

13. Give biological/technical terms for the following.
(i) Undifferentiated calyx and corolla.
(ii) When all the carpels are united.
(iii) A flower in which stamens are absent.
(iv) Non-functional stamens.
(v) When both sepals and petals are lacking in a flower.

Ans. (i) Perianth (ii) Syncarpous
(iii) Pistillate flower (iv) Staminodes
(v) Achlamydeous

14. Briefly explain the following terms.
(i) Bract
(ii) Corolla
(iii) Polyadelphous condition
(iv) Gynoecium
(v) Placenta

Ans. (i) The flower arises at the axil of a leaf-like structure called bract.
(ii) Corolla comprises of petals that are leaf-like structures.
(iii) Polyadelphous is a condition wherein filaments of stamens are united to form more than two bundles, e.g. *Bombax*.
(iv) Gynoecium is the female reproductive part of the flower which is made up of one or more carpels.
(v) Placenta is a cushion-like tissue that develops along the inner wall of ovary.

15. Answer the following questions briefly.
   (i) How are essential whorls more important than non-essential whorls?
   (ii) State the functions of androecium.
   (iii) Write a short note on gynoecium.
   (iv) How are the flowers classified on the basis of presence or absence of whorls?
   (v) Give any two characterstics of a complete flower.

Ans. (i) Essential or reproductive whorls of the flower help the flower to reproduce and thus, ensure maintenance of species number. Non-essential whorls, on the other hand have no role in reproduction.

(ii) Androecium represents the third whorl of the flower comprising of stamens. It performs two functions
- Anthers produce pollen grains that contain male gametes.
- Filaments are attached to anther and make it more accessible to pollination.

(iii) Gynoecium is the female reproductive part of the flower which is made up of one or more carpels. It is also known as pistil. It consists of three parts namely; stigma, style and ovary which perform specific functions.

(iv) On the basis of presence or absence of whorls, flowers are of the following types
- **Complete flower** Flowers having all the four whorls, i.e. calyx, corolla, androecium and gynoecium. e.g. *Hibiscus*.
- **Incomplete flower** Flowers lacking any of the four whorls, e.g. *Begonia*.

(v) Two characteristics of a complete flower are
- It contains four types of whorls namely; calyx, corolla, androecium and gynoecium.
- Corolla is usually brightly coloured and in some cases, strongly scented.

2 Marks Questions

16. For which basic feature, *Agave* and *Wolffia* are known different among flowers?

Ans. *Agave* and *Wolffia* are different among flowers because *Agave* possesses the longest inflorescence in flowers whereas *Wolffia* sp. is the smallest flower known till date.

17. Mention the type of sepals and petals found in *Petunia*.

Ans. In *Petunia*, the sepals are gamosepalous, i.e. they are fused together. The petals in *Petunia* are gamopetalous type, i.e. the petals are fully or partially fused with each other.

18. What is corona? What is its functions?

Ans. Sometimes, corolla gets split and an additional whorl consisting of lobes, scales or hair is formed. This additional whorl is called corona. It functions to add beauty to the flower.

19. Draw the diagram of a typical stamen.

Ans.

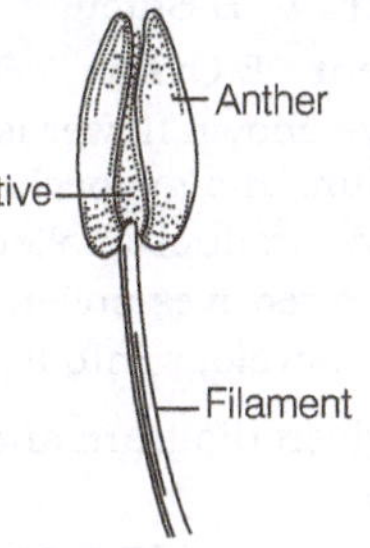

A typical stamen

20. Enlist the various features of cymose inflorescence.

Ans. The features of cymose inflorescence are as follows
   (a) Flowers are actually terminal.
   (b) Growing point or terminal bud always ends in flowers.
   (c) Younger flowers occupy the basal position while the older flowers are found towards the apex.

3 Marks Questions

21. Give a detailed account of gynoecium.

Ans. Refer to text on page no. 42.

22. How are flowers classified based on the carpels of ovary?

Ans. Refer to text on page no 42.

23. Write a short note on the types of flower on the basis of presence or absence of reproductive part.

Ans. Refer to the text on page no. 42.

Section-II [5 Marks]

Structured Questions

1. Study the given diagram and answer the questions that follows.

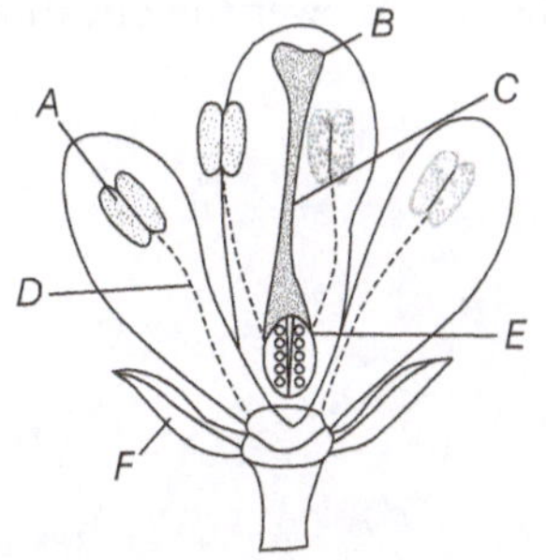

   (i) Name the parts marked as *A-F*.
   (ii) State giving reason whether the above shown flower is bisexual or unisexual.
   (iii) Which part produces pollen grains?
   (iv) Which part receives pollen grains?
   (v) Which part develops into fruit after fertilisation?

Ans. (i) The parts marked as *A–F* are
A-Anther *B*-Stigma *C*-Style
D-Filament *E*-Ovary *F*-Calyx
(ii) The above shown flower is bisexual since both androecium and gynoecium are present in it.
(iii) Anther (*A*) produces pollen grains.
(iv) Stigma (*B*) receives pollen grains.
(v) Ovary (*E*) develops into fruit after fertilisation.

2. Study the given diagram and answer the questions that follows.

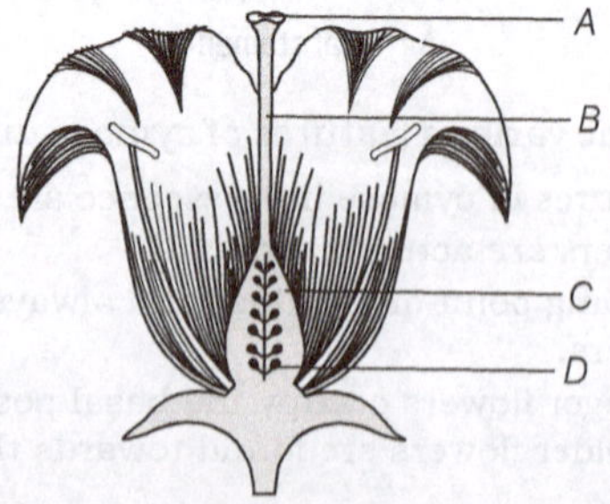

(i) What do parts labelled as *A*, *B* and *C* constitue?
(ii) Name the part labelled as *D*.
(iii) State any one characteristic feature of the flower shown above?
(iv) What role is played by *A* in pollination?
(v) Name the outermost whorl of the flower.

Ans. (i) The parts labelled as *A* (Stigma) and *B* (Style) and *C* (Ovary) constitute the carpel.
(ii) The part labelled as *D* is **Ovule.**
(iii) The flower given above is bisexual as it contains both stamens and carpels.
(iv) *A* (Stigma) acts as a landing platform for pollen grains.
(v) Calyx is the outermost whorl of the flower.

3. A typical flower consists of four distinct whorls, i.e. calyx, corolla, androecium and gynoecium. Such a flower with all the four whorls is known as complete flower. Answer the questions that follow.
(i) Which part of the flower is green, leaf-like but is present as an addition?
(ii) Which whorl constitute coloured leaf-like structures?
(iii) Name the structure that bears outgrowths like spur.
(iv) Which plant/flower shows filaments united in several groups?
(v) What does a gynoecium constitue?

Ans. (i) Epicalyx of the flower is green, leaf-like but is present as an addition.
(ii) Second whorl, i.e. corolla as petals constitute coloured leaf-like structures.
(iii) Corolla bears outgrowths like spur.
(iv) *Bombax* plant shows filaments united in several groups.
(v) A gynoecium consists of one or more carpels. A carpel consists of stigma, style and ovary.

4. An androecium represents the male reproductive part of the flower. It is a collection of stamens of variable sizes. Answer the questions that follow.
(i) What does androecium comprise of?
(ii) How many parts does androecium have?
(iii) Which type of androecium is found in case of pea?
(iv) Give the constituents of pollen grains.
(v) Arrange the four whorls of flower, beginning from the innermost whorl.

Ans. (i) Androecium comprises of male reproductive organs called stamens.
(ii) Androecium consists of multiple stamens, each having two parts, i.e. anther and filament.
(iii) Diadelphous condition is found in case of pea.
(iv) Pollen grains contain male gametes.
(v) The arrangement of the four whorls of flower, beginning from the innermost whorl is gynoecium, androecium, corolla and calyx.

Chapter Assessment

Section-I

1 Mark Questions

1. Name the following.
   (i) Attractive part of the flower.
   (ii) Condition in which the petals of a flower are united.
   (iii) An individual perianth that may or may not be coloured.
   (iv) An additional whorl with lobes, scales and hair.
   (v) Flower with an absent/non-functional gynoecium.

2. Correct and rewrite the following statements by changing the underlined words.
   (i) *Brassica* shows <u>gamosepalous</u> condition.
   (ii) Each anther representing male reproductive organ is <u>tetralobed</u>.
   (iii) <u>Ovary</u> is responsible for the germination of pollen grains.
   (iv) <u>Maize</u> is a dioecious flower/plant.

3. Give biological reasons for the following.
   (i) Calyx region of the flower is green in colour.
   (ii) Corolla is regarded as the second whorl of the flower.
   (iii) Betel is known as the naked flower.

4. (i) Match the following columns.

Column I		Column II
A. Carpels	1.	Non-essential whorl
B. Complete flower	2.	Date palm
C. Dioecious	3.	Ovary
D. Calyx	4.	Shoe flower
E. Sessile	5.	Flower with no stalk

   (ii) Match the following columns.

Column I		Column II
A. Monoecious	1.	Green
B. Peduncle	2.	Young flowers at the base
C. Calyx	3.	Plant axis bearing flowers
D. Racemose	4.	Gourd
E. Cymose	5.	Older flowers at the base

5. Choose the correct answer from each of the four options given below.
   (i) An incomplete flower is
   (a) rose (b) orchid
   (c) *Petunia* (d) *Hibiscus*
   (ii) A pistil with many carpels
   (a) monocarpellary (b) polycarpellary
   (c) bicarpellary (d) pentacarpellary

6. Fill in the blanks by using suitable words.
   (i) The four whorls of flower get attached and arranged on ....
   (ii) Androecium has two parts .... and .... which collectively form ....
   (iii) A pistil with five carpels is called ....
   (iv) A tissue that attaches ovules on the ovary wall is ... .

7. Choose the odd one out from the following terms given below and name the category to which other three belong.
   (i) Sepal, Petal, Perianth, Anther
   (ii) Pollen grain, Filament, Anther, Carpel

8. State whether the following statements are true or false. Correct and rewrite the false statements.
   (i) A typical flower has six floral whorls.
   (ii) Corolla is the outermost whorl of the flower.
   (iii) Flowers can be unisexual, bisexual or neuter.
   (iv) Bean is a monoecious plant.
   (v) Gynoecium is the only non-essential part of flower.

9. State the exact location of the following.
   (i) Petal
   (ii) Receptacle

10. Give one example of the following.
   (i) Colourful tepals
   (ii) Syngenesious condition
   (iii) Diadelphous condition

11. State the main function of the following.
   (i) Flower
   (ii) Pollen grains

12. Differentiate between the following pairs on the basis of what is mentioned in brackets.
    (i) Ovary and Anther (structure)
    (ii) Pistillate and Staminate flowers (presence or absence of pistil)
    (iii) Essential and Non-essential whorls (function)
13. Give biological/technical terms for the following.
    (i) Fused sepals
    (ii) More than one carpel free from each other.
    (iii) Male and female flowers on the same plant.
14. Briefly explain the following terms.
    (i) Syngenesious (ii) Diadelphous (iii) Syncarpous
15. Answer the following questions briefly.
    (i) What is a neutral or neuter flower? Give one example.
    (ii) Explain bract. Name a plant which has bract.
    (iii) What structure in the flower is called epicalyx?

2 Marks Questions

16. Explain different conditions of sepals found in various flowers with example.
17. How does a cucumber plant differ from the papaya plant in terms of sexuality?

3 Marks Questions

18. Give three functions of corolla.
19. Compare the conditions of stamens in China rose, pea and *Bombax*.

Section-II [5 Marks]

Structured Questions

20. The diagram shows position of floral whorls on the thalamus of a flower.

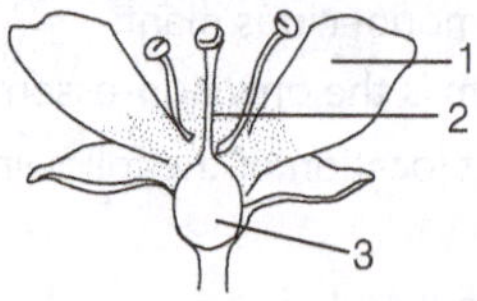

    (i) Label the parts numbered 1, 2 and 3.
    (ii) Give the function of part 3 labelled above.
    (iii) Give an example of the type of flower shown. What category does it belong to?
    (iv) Mention any two functions of the part labelled 2.
    (v) What do you call a flower with no stalk?
21. Sepals are collectively called the calyx. They are the outermost whorl of a flower. The development of sepals vary considerably among flowering plants. Answer the questions that follows.
    (i) Individual sepal constituting calyx, has a photosynthesis rate less than that in leaves. Give reason.
    (ii) What are polysepalous flower?
    (iii) Give one example of a flower having free sepals.
    (iv) *Hibiscus* is a gamosepalous or polysepalous. Justify your answer.
    (v) What does the coloured sepals called? Give example.
22. Study the figure and answer the quesitons that follows.

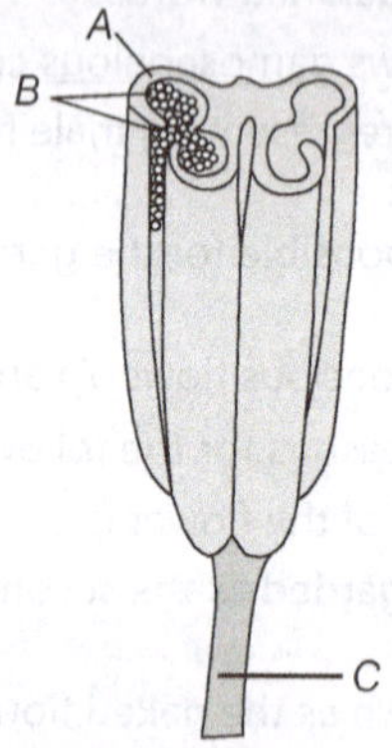

    (i) Identify the figure above.
    (ii) Name the parts labelled as *A*-*C*.
    (iii) State the function of the parts labelled above.
    (iv) How many chambers are there in an anther?
    (v) Give example of a condition wherein all stamens are free from each other .

For explanations scan the given QR Code

Olympiad Section*

Brain Teasing Questions asked in Previous Olympiads

1 The ABC model postulates that the organ identity in each whorl of a flower is determined by the combination of the following five genes, i.e. Apetala-1 (AP1) Apetala-2 (AP2) Apetala-3 (AP3) 6 Pistillata (PI) Agamous (AG).

The table indicates the normal expression pattern of these genes in the whorls of a wild flower. As shown in the table, the expression of AP1 or AP2 in a whorl leads to the suppression of AG in that same whorl and *vice-versa*. **[INBO 2015]**

AP3 or PI (B)			
AP1 or AP 2 (A)		AG (c)	
Sepals	Petals	Stamens	Carpels
1 Outermost whorl	2	3	4 Innermost whorl

Which of the following patterns will develop (from outermost whorl to the innermost whorl), if only the activity of genes AP3 and PI is lost?

(a) Sepals, Petals, Petals, Carpels
(b) Sepals, Stamens, Stamens, Carpels
(c) Sepals, Sepals, Carpels, Carpels
(d) Sepals, Sepals, Petals, Carpels

2 With reference to the table in the previous question (Question no. 2), which of the following patterns will develop (from outermost whorl to the innermost whorl) if only the activity of genes AP1 and AP2 is lost. **[INBO 2015]**

(a) Petals, Petals, Stamens, Carpels
(b) Carpels, Stamens, Stamens, Carpels
(c) Petals, Stamens, Stamens, Carpels
(d) Stamens, Stamens, Carpels, Carpels

3 In Mendoza flora, *Atriplex lampa* are an angiosperm with imperfect (unisexual) flowers.
These flowers are on separate plants, so in this case, we are referring to a plant type. **[IJSO, Argentina 2014]**

(a) Monoecious with flowers with stamens and carpels together
(b) Monoecious with staminate flowers and carpellate flowers
(c) Dioecious with staminate flowers and carpellate flowers
(d) Dioecious with flowers with stamens and carpels together

4 Identify the flower parts *A* to *E* in the given diagram.

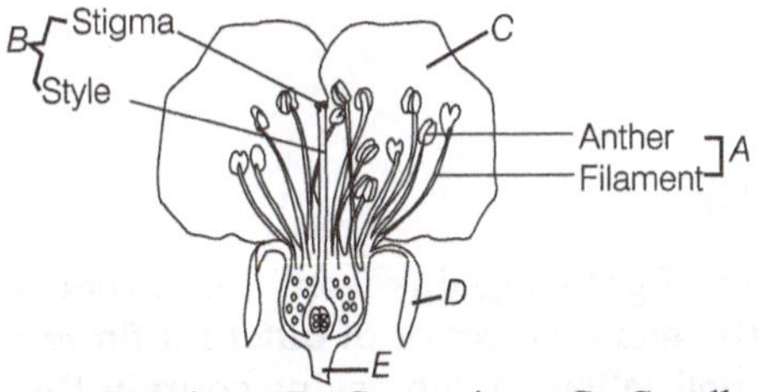

(a) *A* – Androecium, *B* – Gynoecium, *C* – Corolla, *D* – Calyx, *E* – Pedicel
(b) *A* – Gynoecium, *B* – Androecium, *C* – Corolla, *D* – Pedicel, *E* – Calyx
(c) *A* – Thalamus, *B* – Gynoecium, *C* – Pedicel, *D* – Corolla, *E* – Calyx
(d) *A* – Androecium, *B* – Gynoecium, *C* – Epicalyx, *D* – Calyx, *E* – Rachis

5 Which among the following statements are true for unisexual flowers?

I. They possess both stamen and pistil.
II. They possess either stamen or pistil.
III. They exhibit cross pollination.
IV. Unisexual flower possessing only stamens cannot produce fruits.

Codes

(a) I and IV
(b) II, III and IV
(c) III and IV
(d) I, II and IV

Answers

1. (c) **2.** (b) **3.** (c) **4.** (a) **5.** (b)

**These questions may or may not be asked in the examination, have been given just for additional practice required for olympiads, scholarship exams etc. For detailed explanations refer Page No. 230.*

CHAPTER 04

Pollination and Fertilisation

Chapter Inside

• Pollination • Agents of Cross-pollination • Fertilisation • Post-fertilisation Events

Pollination

The transfer of pollen grains from the anther to the stigma of the same flower or of different flowers is termed as **pollination.** Pollen grains contain the male gametes and ovary contains the female gamete. The fusion of these two gametes leads to **fertilisation** which result in the production of seeds and fruits.

Types of Pollination

There are two types of pollination, i.e. self-pollination and cross-pollination.

1. Self-pollination

When the pollen from the anther of a flower is transferred to the stigma of the same flower or to the stigma of another flower of the same plant, it is known as self-pollination. Generally, it is not dependent on any external agency for pollination.

Self-pollination can be of the following two types

(i) **Autogamy** It involves the transfer of pollen grains from anther to the stigma of same flower, e.g. wheat, rice, etc.

(ii) **Geitonogamy** It involves the transfer of pollen grains from the anther of a flower to the stigma of another flower of the same plant, e.g. *Cucurbita.*

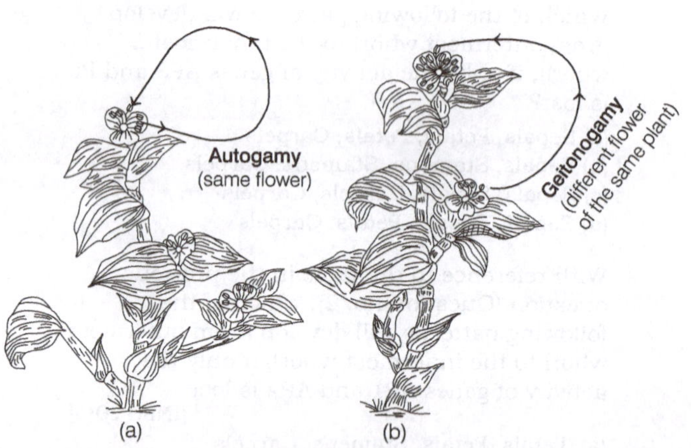

Self-pollination

Adaptations for Self-pollination

Plants require some adaptations to fulfil the needs for self-pollination.

These are as follows

(i) **Bisexuality** (Hermaphroditism) Self-pollination can take place only in bisexual flowers (those bearing both stamens and carpels). It is also seen in plants having both male and female flowers.

(ii) **Homogamy** In this condition, both the anther and the stigma of bisexual flowers should mature at the same time, to ensures self-pollination e.g. *Mirabilis*.

(iii) **Cleistogamy** In some plants, flowers never open up and the anthers dehisce inside the closed flowers to ensure self-pollination. Thus, there is no chance of cross-pollination in cleistogamous flowers, e.g. *Oxalis, Viola,* pea, etc.

Advantages of Self-pollination

These are as follows

(i) Purity of race is maintained as parental traits are preserved.

(ii) There are less chances of failure of pollination, if flowers show homogamy.

(iii) Production of nectar and scent by flowers is not required.

(iv) There is no wastage of pollen grains. Small number of pollens will ensure pollination.

Disadvantages of Self-pollination

These are as follows

(i) Repeated self-pollination decreases the vigour and vitality of future generations.

(ii) The weaker or defective characters are inherited and cannot be eliminated.

(iii) Production of new varieties and species of plants is not possible because the same genetic traits are passed on to the next or upcoming generation.

2. Cross-pollination or Allogamy

It involves the transfer of pollen grains from the anther of one plant to the stigma of another flower.

This is the only type of pollination which brings genetically different types of pollen grains to the stigma of same species, e.g. papaya, maize, etc. Cross-pollination or allogamy takes place in unisexual as well as in bisexual (monoecious) flowers.

Nature favours cross-pollination and the flowers in some way or other, are modified to prevent self-pollination.

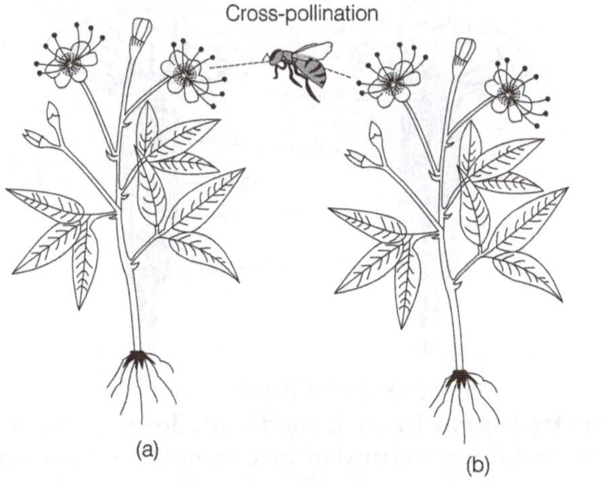

Cross-pollination

Adaptations for Cross-pollination

Some adaptations that favour cross-pollination are given below

(i) **Unisexuality** or **Dicliny** In this, separate male and female flowers are borne on different plants, e.g. papaya, palm.

(ii) **Self-sterility** or **Incompatibility** In this condition, the pollen grains of a flower fail to germinate on the stigma of the same flower. In such conditions, pollens from another plant of same species can complete the seed selfing process effectively, e.g. potato, tobacco, ray floret of sunflower, orchids, etc.

(iii) **Dichogamy** In some bisexual flowers, the anther and stigma do not mature at the same time. It is of two kinds

(a) **Protandrous** or **Protandry** The anthers mature earlier than the stigma, e.g. sunflower, sweet pea, *Salvia, Jasminum,* etc.

(b) **Protogynous** or **Protogyny** The stigma matures earlier than the anthers, e.g. *Magnolia,* custard apple, peepal, rose, etc.

(iv) **Heterostyly** Some flowers have style and anthers at different heights. Either the style is very long or anthers are at more height, so that self-pollination becomes impossible. This condition is known as heterostyly, e.g. *Oxalis*, *Primula*, *Linum*, etc.

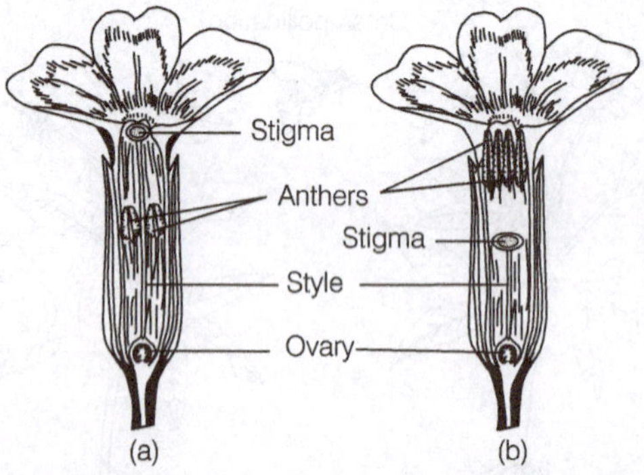

(a) Long-styled flower, (b) Short-styled flower

(v) **Herkogamy** In such condition, flower possesses certain structural or mechanical barriers which do not allow self-pollination. For example, in pansy and iris flower, a hood covering the stigma acts as a mechanical barrier.

Advantages of Cross-pollination

These are as follows

(i) Stronger and healthier offspring are produced.

(ii) Production of a large number of viable seeds.

(iii) New varieties with useful characters are produced.

(iv) Plants produced from cross-pollinated flowers are more resistant to diseases and other unfavourable conditions.

Disadvantages of Cross-pollination

These are as follows

(i) It does not ensure fertilisation as the landed pollen may not remain functional.

(ii) Cross-pollinating plants waste lots of their energy in the formation of
- large number of pollen grains.
- scent or odour.
- showy, bright-coloured petals.

(iii) It involves different external agencies, if somehow these agencies are absent then, there will be no pollination.

(iv) It may also lead to loss of vigour as some unwanted traits may also get inherited.

Check Your LEARNING...

1 What is being transferred during the process of pollination.

2 Name the two types of pollination.

3 Name the plant bearing both male and female parts on same flower.

4 Name a flower which shows cleistogamy.

5 What is protandrous condition?

6 Write one disadvantage of cross-pollination.

Agents of Cross-pollination

Pollen cannot be transferred from the anther to the stigma on its own. So, cross-pollination relies on other agents to transfer the pollen. The agents responsible for pollination in flowering plants have been grouped into two main categories as shown below

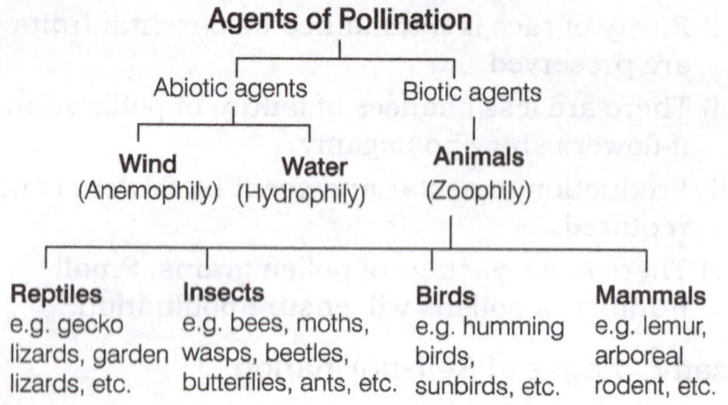

The adaptive features of flowering plants along with their agent of pollination are discussed below

1. Wind Pollination or Anemophily

It takes place through the wind. The flowers that are pollinated by wind show the following characteristics

- Flowers are small, colourless, inconspicuous, nectarless and are arranged as inflorescence, e.g. corncob.
- The anthers are well-exposed for the easy dispersal of pollen grains.
- Pollen grains are small, light, dry, dusty, non-sticky and sometimes even winged. They are produced in large numbers.
- The stigmas are large, hairy and feathery or branched to catch the air-borne pollen grains.

Common examples of wind pollinated flowers are grasses, sugarcane, bamboo, coconut, maize, pine etc.

Wind Pollination in Maize

In maize (a monoecious plant), the cluster of male flowers (tassel) are borne at the apex. The female flowers (cobs) are borne near the base in the axil of leaf on the plants. The male flowers produce large quantities of pollen grains. When mild wind shakes the plant, the male flower releases the pollens which fall down vertically.

Many of them land on the sticky and feathery stigma of neighbouring plant, hence bringing about cross-pollination.

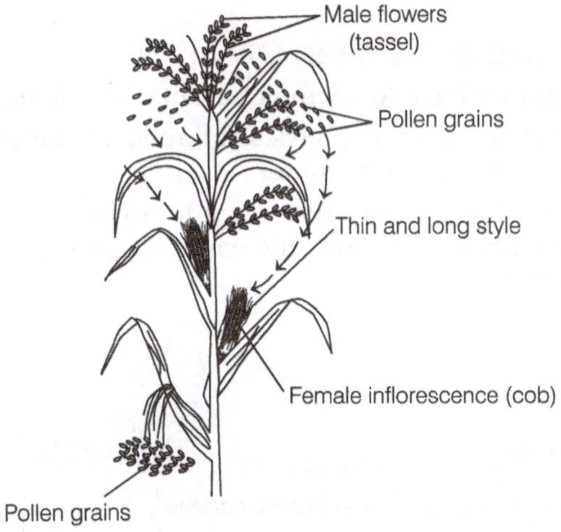

Anemophily in maize

2. Water Pollination or Hydrophily

It is seen in aquatic plants. The flowers that are pollinated by water show the following characteristics

- Flowers are small, colourless, inconspicuous, odourless and nectarless.
- The stigmas are long and sticky, e.g. *Vallisneria*, *Hydrilla* and *Zostera*.
- The pollen grains have the same specific gravity as that of water, so that they can float on water.
- Pollen grains are produced in large quantity and have mucilaginous covering.
- In some cases, the male flowers detach and float on water till they meet the female flowers, e.g. *Vallisneria*.

Water Pollination in *Vallisneria*

In *Vallisneria*, the female flowers reach the surface of water by the long stalk and male flowers or pollen grains are released on to the surface of water.

They are then carried passively by water currents.

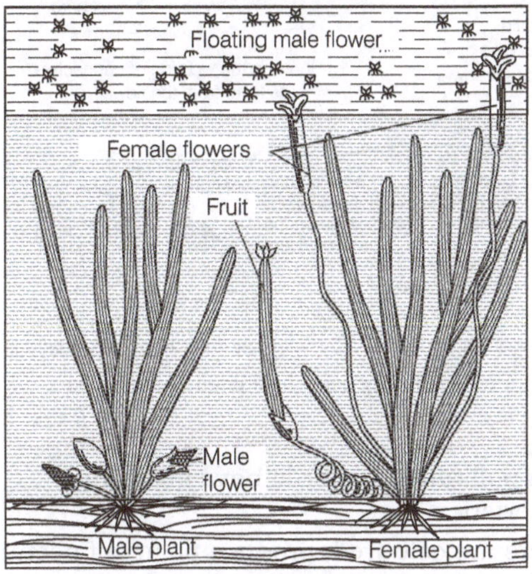

Hydrophily in *Vallisneria*

3. Insect Pollination or Entomophily

The flowers that are pollinated by insects show the following characteristics

- A number of flowers are clustered into an inflorescence to make them conspicuous, when the flowers are small, e.g. *Dahlia*.
- Flowers are large, colourful, fragrant and rich in nectar to attract insects, e.g. *Salvia*.
- The surface of both the pollen grains and the stigma is sticky, e.g. China rose, lotus, roses, etc.

Insect Pollination in *Salvia*

Each flower has two epipetalous stamens. These stamens have special modifications which help insects to pollinate flowers.

One of the anther lobes is sterile and the other is fertile. Both lobes are separated apart by a long connective tissue. The upper arm of connective tissue bears fertile anther and lower bears sterile anthers. When an insect lands on lower lip of flower to collect nectar, the sterile anther lobe is pushed down, which brings fertile lobe down in contact with the body of the insect thus, pollens get dusted on it.

In older flowers, the style brings the stigma in such a position that it brushes against the back of insect and collects pollen grains brought by the insect from a young flower.

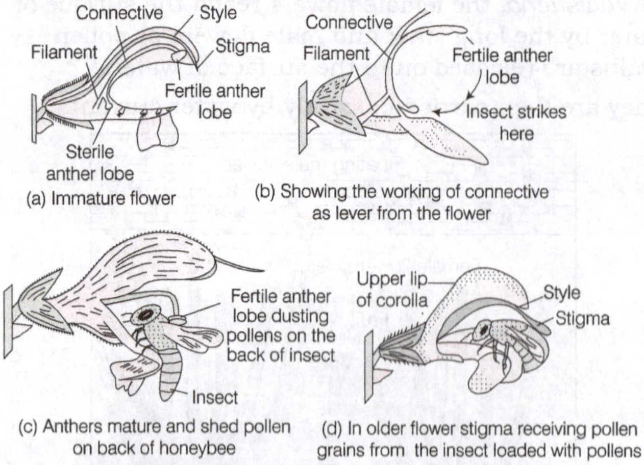

Salvia flower being pollinated by honeybee

4. Bird Pollination or Ornithophily

Flowers pollinated by birds have following characteristics

- Flowers are coloured, produce plenty of nectar with funnel-shaped corolla.
- Flowers are scentless as birds lack a good sense of smell, e.g. *Bignonia* flower is pollinated by humming bird.
- Pollen grains are produced in large quantity.

Note
- Pollination is also facilitated by elephants. This is called **Elephophily**. It is found in *Rafflesia*.
  Pollination by bats is called **chiropterophily** (e.g. *Bauhinia* and that by snails is **malacophily** (e.g. *Arisaema*)
- Man, practised **artificial pollination** wherein desired pollens were transferred in order to produce new varieties.

Differences between Self-pollination and Cross-pollination

Self-pollination	Cross-pollination
It is defined as the transfer of pollen grains from anther to the stigma of the same flower or to the stigma of another flower of same plant.	It is defined as the transfer of pollen grains from anther of one flower to stigma of another flower of another plant.
No external agent is required.	External agents like wind, water and insect are required.
Can occur in cleistogamous flowers (when flower is closed).	It occurs only in flowers which are open (chasmogamous).
Does not give rise to new varieties.	Give rise to new varieties.
Preservation of parental characters is possible.	Preservation of parental characters is not possible.
Involves maturation of male and female parts at the same time.	Involves maturation of male and female parts at different time intervals.

Check Your LEARNING...

1. What do you call the cluster of male flower in maize plant?
2. Which agency pollinate the flower of Vallisneria?
3. What are the scientific terms for pollination by wind and insects?
4. Write characteristics of flower of a water pollinated plant.
5. Name a plant pollinated by birds.

Fertilisation

It is the fusion of nuclei of male and female gametes. It results in the formation of a zygote or oospore. It occurs after successful pollination. In flowering plants, the pollen grain carries the male gamete while the female gamete is present in the ovule inside the ovary.

Structure of a Pollen Grain

Pollen grains have following characteristic features.

(i) Unicellular and spherical-shaped, about 25-50 micrometer in diameter.

(ii) Outer hard layer **exine** is made up of **sporopollenin** (no enzyme could degrade it, so far known).

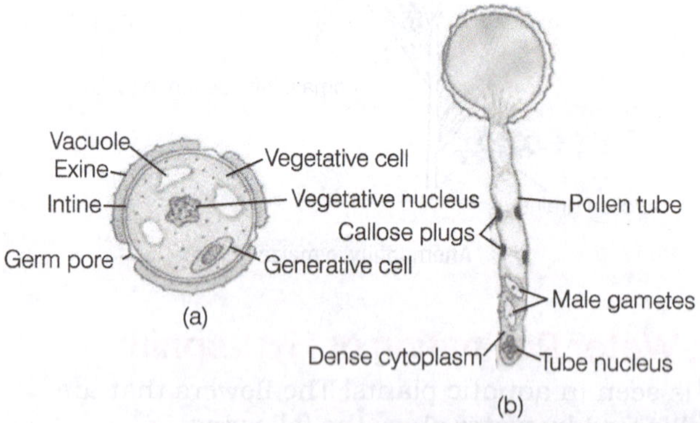

(a) Mature pollen grains, (b) Pollen germination

(iii) Germ pore is present on exine, where sporopollenin is absent. The pollen tube emerges out during germination through it.

(iv) The inner wall **intine** is made up of **cellulose** and **pectin**.

(v) Pollen grain has two nuclei called **tube nucleus** and **generative** (male) **nucleus**.

(vi) Once pollen grains deposit on stigma, they absorb sugar and water from the surface of stigma and swell up.

(vii) A mature pollen grain contains two cells, i.e. **vegetative cell** (bigger), which contains food reserves and **generative cell** (small), which floats on the cytoplasm of vegetative cell.

Structure of an Ovule

Ovule is a small structure present in the ovary. It has following characteristic features

(i) It is attached to the placenta by a stalk called **funicle.**

(ii) **Hilum** is a junction between ovule and funicle.

(iii) Each ovule has one or two protective envelopes called **integuments.**

(iv) **Micropyle** is an opening present at the tip, where integument is absent. Pollen tube enters through micropyle.

(v) The integuments enclose a mass of cells called the **nucellus**, which have food reserves.

(vi) **Embryo sac** or **female gametophyte** is located in the nucellus.

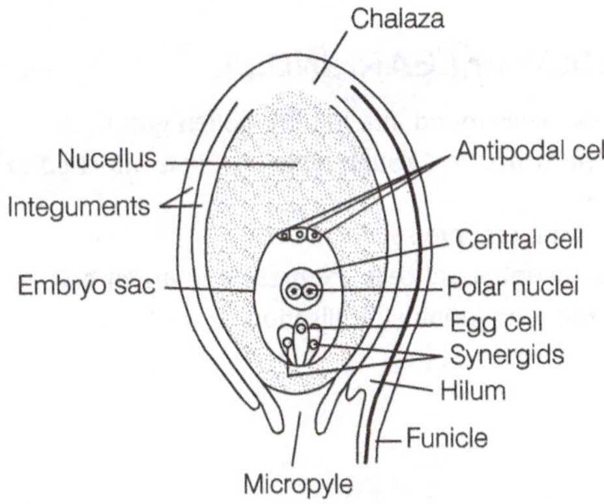

LS of ovule

The embryo sac contains the following structures

- A female gamete called **egg** cell.

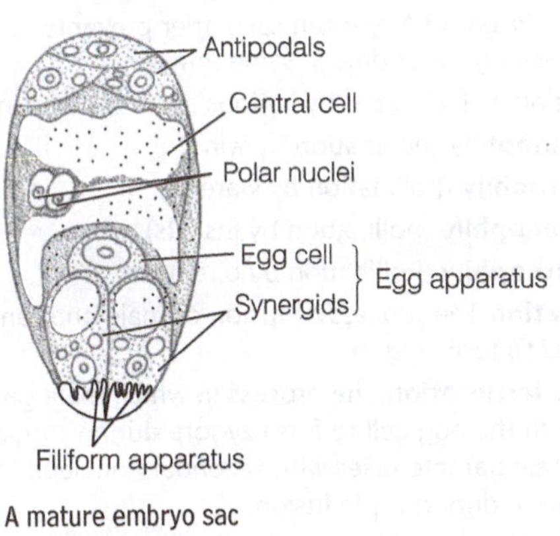

A mature embryo sac

- One large central cell that contains two **polar nuclei** which fuse to form the secondary nucleus in the centre.
- Two **synergids.**
- Three **antipodal cells.**

Events in Fertilisation

(i) After compatible pollination, the pollen grain germinates on the stigma by absorbing water and nutrients and produces a pollen tube through one of the germ pores.

(ii) The contents of the pollen grain containing a generative cell and a tube nucleus then move into this tube. The pollen tube grows through the tissues of stigma and style by secreting the enzymes that digest them.

(iii) The generative cell divides and forms two **male gametes** during the growth of pollen tube in the stigma.

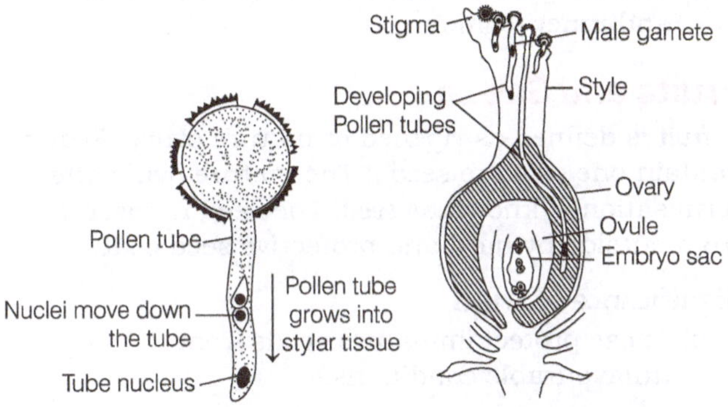

Germination of pollen grain on stigma

(iv) After reaching the ovary, the pollen tube enters the ovule *via* **micropylar end.**

(v) With the tip of the pollen tube getting dissolved, tube nucleus disintegrates and the two male gametes are released into the embryo sac.

(vi) One of the male gamete fuses with egg cell (syngamy) which results in the formation of zygote. Later on this, zygote develops into embryo and gives rise to a new plant.

(vii) Second male gamete fuses with two polar nuclei to form a triploid **Primary Endosperm Nucleus** (PEN). This is called **triple fusion.**

(viii) Since, two fusions, i.e. syngamy and triple fusion occur in an embryo sac, so this type of fertilisation is called **double fertilisation.**

The representation for double fertilisation is

- Egg cell (n) + Male gamete (n) = Zygote ($2n$) (syngamy).
- Secondary nucleus ($2n$) + Male gamete (n) = Endosperm ($3n$) (triple fusion).

(ix) After fusion, central cell and primary endosperm nucleus is called as **Primary Endosperm Cell** (PEC). It develops into the **endosperm** and zygote develops into an **embryo.**

Post-fertilisation Events

Post-fertilisation changes in floral parts are as follows

(i) Sepals fall down or persist in few.
(ii) Petals, stamen, stigma and style fall down.
(iii) Ovary changes into fruit, ovary wall forms pericarp.
(iv) Ovules become seeds.
(v) Synergids and antipodal cells degenerate.
(vi) Central cell becomes endosperm which may persist or get consumed.
(vii) The integument forms seed coat, i.e. outer testa and inner tegmen.

Fruits and Seeds

A **fruit** is defined as ripened or mature ovary. Fruits contain one or more seeds. The mature ovule after fertilisation is known as **seed**. The seed is covered from outside by hard and protective seed coat.

Significance of Fruits

(i) These protect immature seeds from unfavourable conditions.
(ii) These are colourful, attractive and tasty.
(iii) Many fruits are part of industries and are eaten as food.
(iv) These are rich source of vitamin, minerals and sugars, etc.
(v) Some fruits have medicinal properties such as watermelon helps in reducing blood pressure.

Significance of Seeds

(i) These help in the development of new flowering plants.
(ii) These can be stored as food source for long time.
(iii) These help in overcoming unfavourable conditions as they have adaptive strategies.
(iv) Seeds are the basis of agriculture.

Check Your LEARNING...

1 Name two cells found in a mature pollen grain.
2 Name the structure through which ovule is attached to the placenta.
3 Where is the embryo sac located?
4 How many antipodal cells are present in an embryo sac?
5 Define the term 'double fertilisation'.

QUiCK Revision

- **Pollination** is the transfer of pollen grains from the anthers of a flower to the stigma of the same flower or of another flower.
- **Self-pollination** (autogamy) is the transfer of pollen grains from the anthers to the stigma of either the same or genetically similar flower on same plant.
- Adaptations for self-pollination in plants include
  (i) **Cleistogamy** The flowers never open up and anthers dehisce inside these closed flowers.
  (ii) **Homogamy** Both the anthers and stigma in a bisexual flower mature at the same time.
- **Cross-pollination** is the transfer of pollen grains from the anther of flower of one plant to the stigma of the flower of another plant.
- Adaptations for cross-pollination in plants include
  (i) **Unisexuality** The stamens and carpels are present on different flowers.
  (ii) **Self-sterility or Incompatibility** The pollen grains cannot fertilise their own ovules.
  (iii) **Dichogamy** The male and female organs mature at different times. In **protandry**, anther matures earlier. In **protogyny**, stigma matures earlier.
  (iv) **Heterostyly** The difference in length of style and stigma prevents pollen from reaching the stigma in same flower.
  (v) **Herkogamy** A mechanical barrier prevents pollen from reaching the stigma in same flower.
- Pollination is facilitated by various agents, these include
  - **Anemophily** (pollination by wind)
  - **Hydrophily** (pollination by water).
  - **Entomophily** (pollination by insects)
  - **Ornithophily** (Pollination by birds), etc.
- **Fertilisation** The process of fusion of male and female gametes to form zygote.
- **Double fertilisation** The process in which male gamete fuses with the egg cell to form zygote during syngamy and other male gamete fuses with secondary nucleus ($2n$) to form endosperm during triple fusion.
- **Fruit** It is the ripened ovary after fertilisation.
- **Seed** It is mature ovule after fertilisation.

Chapter Practice

Section-I

1 Mark Questions

1. Name the following.
   (i) Transfer of pollen grains from anther to the stigma.
   (ii) The two processes required for sexual reproduction to take place.
   (iii) Condition in which anther and stigma attain maturity at the same time.
   (iv) The strategy evolved to prevent self-pollination in flowers.
   (v) Transfer of pollen grains from anther to stigma of another plant.
   (vi) Female flowers borne near the base in the leaf axil.
   (vii) The material that makes up the hard layer of pollen grain.
   (viii) A stalk that attaches the ovule to the placenta and provides nourishment to the ovule.
   (ix) Protective covering of ovule.
   (x) The part of pistil which develops into fruit.

Ans. (i) Pollination
(ii) Pollination and fertilisation
(iii) Homogamy
(iv) Self-incompatibility/Protogyny
(v) Cross-pollination or Allogamy
(vi) Cobs
(vii) Sporopollenin
(viii) Funicle or Funiculus
(ix) Integuments
(x) Ovary

2. Correct and rewrite the following statements by changing the underlined words.
   (i) Allogamy does not require any external agent.
   (ii) Showy and bright coloured petals do not play any role in cross-pollination.
   (iii) Pollen grains in ornithophilous flowers have a special mucilaginous covering.
   (iv) The secondary nucleus that participates in triple fusion is triploid in nature.
   (v) Antipodal cells along with central cell degenerate after fertilisation.

Ans. (i) Autogamy does not require any external agent.
(ii) Showy and bright coloured petals do not play any role in self-pollination.
(iii) Pollen grains in hydrophilous flowers have a special mucilaginous covering.
(iv) The secondary nucleus participates in triple fusion is diploid ($2n$) in nature.
(v) Antipodal cells along with synergids degenerate after fertilisation.

3. Give biological reasons for the following.
   (i) Repeated self-pollination is not preferred by the plant breeders.
   (ii) Some flowers are brightly coloured.
   (iii) Some pollen grains are rough, spiny and sticky.
   (iv) *Bignonia* flower does not have any fragrance.

Ans. (i) Plant breeders usually do not prefer repeated self-pollination as it leads to loss of vigour and vitality of the future generations.
(ii) Flowers like *Hibiscus* are brightly coloured to attract the insects for cross-pollination.
(iii) Some pollen grains are rough, spiny and sticky in nature so that they can easily stick to the body of the insect as well as to the stigma. This aids in the process of cross-pollination.
(iv) *Bignonia* and other flowers which get pollinated by birds do not have any fragrance since the birds lack a good sense of smell.

4. (i) Match the following columns.

Column I	Column II
A. Wind	1. Hydrophily
B. Water	2. Anemophily
C. Insects	3. Chiropterophily
D. Birds	4. Zoophily
E. Bats	5. Entomophily
F. Snails	6. Ornithophily
G. Larger animals including man	7. Malacophily

(ii) Match the following columns.

Column I	Column II
A. Self-pollination	1. *Magnolia*
B. Heterostyly	2. Entomophilous
C. Anemophily	3. *Hydrilla*
D. Protogyny	4. Preservation of parental traits
E. *Salvia*	5. Sunbirds
	6. Coconut
	7. *Oxalis*

(iii) Match the following columns.

	Column I		Column II
A.	*Jasminum*	1.	Strong and healthy offspring
B.	Rose	2.	Humming bird
C.	Dull coloured flowers	3.	Protandrous
D.	*Bignonia*	4.	Anemophilous
E.	Cross-pollination	5.	Protogynous

(iv) Match the following columns.

	Column I		Column II
A.	Generative nucleus	1.	Pollen tube
B.	Germ pore	2.	Endosperm nucleus
C.	Exine	3.	Testa
D.	Secondary nucleus	4.	Fertilisation
E.	Integument	5.	Male nuclei
F.	Egg nucleus	6.	Sporopollenin

(v) Match the following columns.

	Column I		Column II
A.	Outer integuments	1.	Fruit
B.	Inner integuments	2.	Perisperm
C.	Ovary	3.	Testa
D.	Ovules	4.	Seed
E.	Nucellus	5.	Tegmen
F.	Ovary wall	6.	Pericarp

Ans. (i) A–2, B–1, C–5, D–6, E–3, F–7, G–4
(ii) A–4, B–7, C–6, D–1, E–2
(iii) A–3, B–5, C–4, D–2, E–1
(iv) A–5, B–1, C–6, D–2, E–3, F–4
(v) A–3, B–5, C–1, D–4, E–2, F–6

5. Choose the correct answer from the four options given below.

(i) Transfer of pollen grains from anther to the stigma of another flower on the same plant is
(a) autogamy (b) cross-pollination
(c) geitonogamy (d) xenogamy

Ans. (c)

(ii) Stigmas are feathery and hang out of the flower to trap the pollen grains in
(a) Maize (b) *Hydrilla*
(c) *Bignonia* (d) China rose

Ans. (a)

(iii) Maize is pollinated by
(a) bird (b) wind (c) bees (d) water

Ans. (b)

(iv) Wind pollinated flowers often have
(a) single ovule in each ovary
(b) numerous flowers packed into inflorescence
(c) Both (a) and (b)
(d) None of the above

Ans. (c)

(v) Insect pollinated flowers are
(a) nectar producing (b) colourful
(c) fragrance producing (d) All of these

Ans. (d)

(vi) The number of antipodal cells in the embryo sac is
(a) 4 (b) 3 (c) 5 (d) 0

Ans. (b)

(vii) Double fertilisation is the fusion of
(a) egg cell and two male gametes
(b) one male gamete with egg and another with two polar nuclei
(c) Both (a) and (b)
(d) one polar nucleus with the other and with male gamete

Ans. (b)

(viii) After fertilisation in plant, the petals, stamens, style and stigma of flower
(a) change to fruit (b) change to seed
(c) fall off (d) remain intact

Ans. (c)

6. Fill in the blanks by using suitable words.

(i) ……. pollination is achieved within the same flower.
(ii) Cross-pollination takes place in all ……. plants.
(iii) Different timings for maturation of gynoecium and androecium is called …….. .
(iv) ……… is a water pollinated flower.
(v) The outer wall of pollen grain is called ……….., while the inner wall is ………. .
(vi) The pollen tube enters the ovule through the ….. .
(vii) The fusion product of male and female gametes is called ………… .
(viii) Double fertilisation is normally seen in ……… .
(ix) After fertilisation, the ovules change into ……. .
(x) The ovary changes into …….. after fertilisation and ovary wall forms ……… .

Ans. (i) Self (ii) monoecious
(iii) dichogamy (iv) *Vallisneria*
(v) exine, intine (vi) micropyle
(vii) oospore/zygote (viii) angiosperms
(ix) seeds (x) fruit, pericarp

7. Choose the odd one out from the following terms given below and name the category to which other three belong.

(i) Wheat, Rice, Papaya, Pea
(ii) Peepal, *Jasminum*, Rose, Custard apple
(iii) Grasses, Maize, Sugarcane, *Zostera*
(iv) Vegetative cell, Tube nucleus, Hilum, Pectin

Ans. (i) **Odd term** Papaya
Rest three show self-pollination.
(ii) **Odd term** *Jasminum*
Rest three are protogynous flowers.

(iii) **Odd term** *Zostera*
Rest three get pollinated by wind, i.e. anemophilous.

(iv) **Odd term** Hilum
Rest three are components of pollen grain.

8. Given below are sets of five terms each. Rewrite the terms in correct order of a logical sequence beginning with the term that is underlined.
(i) Flower, Seed, Bud, Pollination, Fruit
(ii) Pollen grain, Stigma, Ovary, Embryo sac, Style

Ans. (i) Bud, Flower, Pollination, Fruit, Seed
(ii) Pollen grain, Stigma, Style, Ovary , Embryo sac

9. Expand the following biological abbreviations.
(i) PEN (ii) PEC

Ans. (i) Primary Endosperm Nucleus
(ii) Primary Endosperm Cell

10. State whether the following statements are true or false. Correct and rewrite the false statements.
(i) Self-pollination occurs in unisexual flowers only.
(ii) Cleistogamy is found in self-pollinated flowers.
(iii) Heterostyly is found in self-pollinated flowers.
(iv) Anemophilous flowers are small and white.
(v) Entomophilous flowers are large and colourful.
(vi) Insects are the agents of pollination in *Salvia*.
(vii) PEN is formed by triple fusion.

Ans. (i) False, cross-pollination occurs in unisexual flowers only.
(ii) True
(iii) False, heterostyly is found in cross-pollinated flowers.
(iv) True
(v) True
(vi) True
(vii) True

11. State the exact location of the following.
(i) Intine (ii) Germ pore
(iii) Tube nucleus (iv) Micropyle
(v) Antipodal cells

Ans. (i) Inner wall of pollen grain.
(ii) Present on the exine of pollen grain where sporopollenin is absent.
(iii) Inside the pollen grain
(iv) Opening at the micropylar end of ovule
(v) Towards the chalazal end of ovule

12. Give one example for the following.
(i) Cleistogamous flower
(ii) Homogamous flower
(iii) Self-sterile plant
(iv) Protandrous flower
(v) Hydrophilous flower

Ans. (i) *Oxalis* (ii) *Mirabilis*
(iii) Potato (iv) Sweet pea
(v) *Hydrilla*

13. State the main function of the following.
(i) Pollen tube
(ii) Integuments
(iii) Polar nuclei

Ans. (i) Transfer of male gametes within the ovule.
(ii) Protection of ovule.
(iii) Fuse with one male gamete to form endosperm.

14. Mention one difference in each of the following pairs on the basis of what is given in the bracket.
(i) Autogamy and Geitonogamy (definition)
(ii) Protandry and Protogyny (maturation of anther and stigma)
(iii) Herkogamy and Heterostyly (presence or absence of barrier)
(iv) Anemophily and Hydrophily (type of stigma)
(v) Insect pollinated flowers and Wind pollinated flowers (essential whorls)

Ans. (i) Difference between autogamy and geitonogamy is as follows

Autogamy	Geitonogamy
It refers to the transfer of pollen grains from the anthers of a flower to the stigma of the same flower.	It refers to the transfer of pollen grains from the anther of a flower to the stigma of another flower of the same plant.

(ii) Difference between protandry and protogyny is as follows

Protandry	Protogyny
It is the maturing of anther earlier than stigma.	In this, the stigma matures earlier than anther.

(iii) Difference beteeen herkogamy and heterostyly is as follows

Herkogamy	Heterostyly
Mechanical barrier is present to prevent the pollen to reach the stigma of the same flower, e.g. pansy.	No mechanical barrier is present instead the stigma and anther are present at different heights, e.g. *Oxalis*.

(iv) Difference between anemophily and hydrophily is as follows

Anemophily	Hydrophily
Stigmas are large, hairy and feathery.	Stigmas are long and sticky.

(v) Difference between insect pollinated flowers and wind pollinated flowers is as follows

Insect pollinated flowers	Wind pollinated flowers
Essential whorls are not much exposed to air, e.g. *Salvia*.	Essential whorls are exposed to air, e.g. pea.

15. Give biological/technical terms for the following.
(i) Flowers that do not open
(ii) Flowers pollinated by elephant
(iii) Outer layer of pollen grain
(iv) Cell that forms the pollen tube
(v) Structure formed from a matured ovary

Ans. (i) Cleistogamous (ii) Elephophily
(iii) Exine (iv) Vegetative cell
(v) Fruit

16. Briefly explain the following terms.
(i) Pollination (ii) Hermaphroditism
(iii) Gamete (iv) Dichogamy
(v) Funicle

Ans. (i) **Pollination** It is the transfer of pollen grains from anther to the stigma of the same flower or of different flower.
(ii) **Hermaphroditism** Plants which bear both stamens and carpels, i.e. bear bisexual flowers show this condition.
(iii) **Gamete** It is a haploid cell that takes part in sexual reproduction.
(iv) **Dichogamy** It is the process in which the male and female organs of a bisexual flower mature at different times.
(v) **Funicle** A stalk that attaches the ovule to placenta and also provides nourishment to ovule.

17. Answer the following questions briefly.
(i) Mention two strategies involved to prevent self-pollination in flowers.
(ii) How do the pollen grains of *Vallisneria* protect themselves ?
(iii) What are the component cells of the egg apparatus in an embryo sac?
(iv) Write the fate of following parts after fertilisation.
(a) Synergids (b) Petals
(v) State the use of a seed.

Ans. (i) Flowers develop the following strategies to prevent self-pollination
(a) Protogyny or protandry (b) Self-incompatibility
(ii) Pollen grains of *Vallisneria* are protected from wetting by the mucilaginous covering.
(iii) The component cells of the 'egg apparatus' in an embryo sac include, two synergids, one egg cell and three antipodal cells.
(iv) (a) Synergids degenerate (b) Petals fall down
(v) Seeds contain embryo, which help to produce new plants.

2 Marks Questions

18. (i) Explain the two types of pollination.
(ii) Give two characteristic features of an ovule.

Ans. (i) Depending upon the source of pollen grains, pollination is of following types
(a) **Self-pollination** Pollens from the anther of a flower are transferred to stigma of same flower or of different flower on the same plant.
(b) **Cross-pollination** Pollens from the anther of one plant are transferred to the stigma of another plant of same species.
(ii) Ovule is a small structure present in the ovary. Its characteristic features are
(a) Each ovule has one or two protective envelopes called integuments.
(b) It is attached to the placenta by a stalk called **funicle**.

19. List two events which occur after penetration of pollen tube into the ovule.

Ans. After penetration, following events occur
(a) The tip of the pollen tube enlarges and ruptures.
(b) Its contents including two male gametes and vegetative nucleus are released.

20. List fate of different parts of ovary after fertilisation.

Ans. The fate of different parts of ovary after fertilisation are
(i) The ovary consists of ovules, which develop into seeds upon fertilisation.
(ii) The ovary itself enlarges to form fruit while the ovarian wall forms the fruits wall. The ovary wall can either be dry and hard or fleshy.

21. Mention any two economic importance of fruits.

Ans. Two economic importance of fruits are
(i) Fruits are good source of vitamins, minerals, organic acids and sugars.
(ii) Some fruits have medicinal properties such as watermelon helps in reducing blood pressure.

3 Marks Questions

22. (i) How is pollination brought about in *Salvia*? How does it take place?
(ii) Draw a neat diagram showing pollen germination and label any two parts.

Ans. (i) Pollination in *Salvia* is brought about by bees by a specialised floral mechanism.
While entering the corolla tube, the bee pushes the lower sterile anther lobe upwards. As a result of lever mechanism, the fertile lobe swings down and dusts the back of the bee with a cloud of pollens. When the bee visits another flowers, it transfers the pollens to a matured stigma, thus carrying out cross-pollination.
(ii) Pollen germination is represented by the following diagram

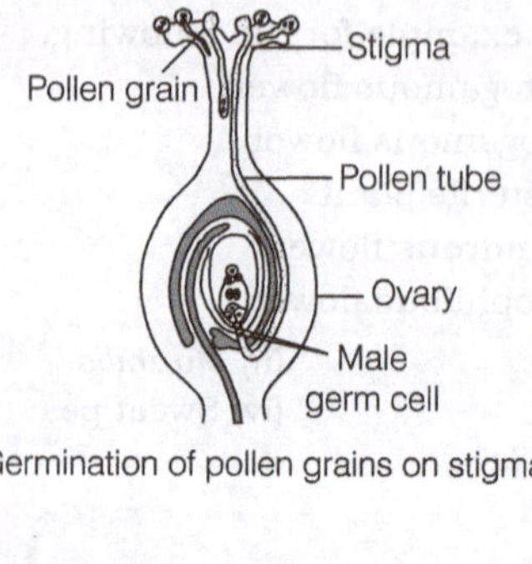

Germination of pollen grains on stigma

23. Explain the adaptations that a plant undergoes to fulfil its needs for self-pollination.

Ans. Adaptations that a plant undergoes to fulfil its needs for self-pollination are

(i) **Bisexuality** (Hermaphroditism) Self-pollination can take place only in bisexual flowers (those bearing both stamens and carpels). It is also seen in plants having both male and female flowers.

(ii) **Homogamy** In this condition, both the anther and the stigma of bisexual flowers should mature at the same time, e.g. *Mirabilis*. It ensures self-pollination.

(iii) **Cleistogamy** In some plants, flowers never open up and the anthers dehisce inside the closed flowers to ensure self-pollination. Thus, there is no chance of cross-pollination in cleistogamous flowers, e.g. *Oxalis, Viola*, pea, etc.

24. Distinguish between self-pollination and cross-pollination .

Ans. Refer to table on page no. 56.

Section-II [5 Marks]

Structured Questions

1. Study the figure given below and answer the questions that follows.

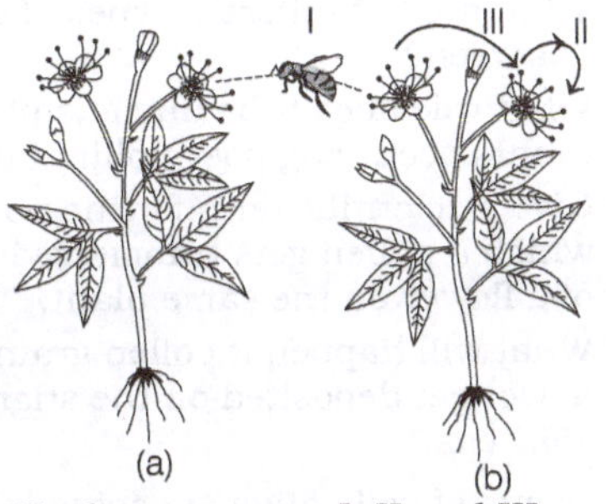

(i) Identify the processes I, II and III.

(ii) Which type of process occurs in a unisexual and cleistogamous flower, respectively?

(iii) State any two characteristic features of the type of flowers involved in process I.

(iv) By what other name is process I known?

(v) State any one disadvantage of the process labelled as II.

Ans. (i) The processes I, II and III are as I–Cross-pollination II–Self-pollination and III–Geitonogamy

(ii) In unisexual flower, process I (cross-pollination) occurs while in a cleistogamous flower, process II (self-pollination) occurs.

(iii) Two characteristic features of the type of flowers involved in process I are

- Well-exposed anthers
- Bright coloured flowers

(iv) Process I is also known as allogamy.

(v) One disadvantage of the process labelled as II is that the production of new varieties and plant species is not possible.

2. Study figure given below and answer the questions that follows.

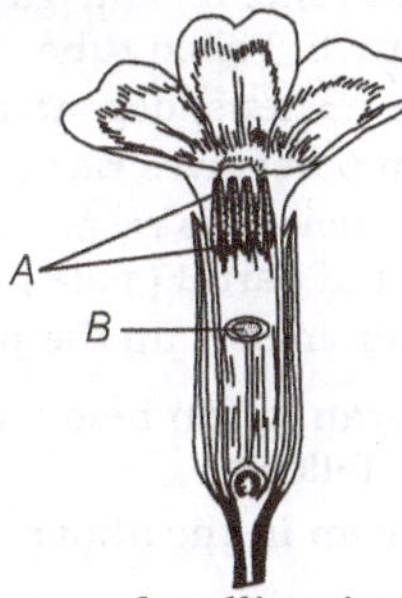

(i) Which type of pollination is most likely to occur?

(ii) Is there any one disadvantage of the process mentioned above?

(iii) What is the phenomenon shown in the figure above known as?

(iv) State any one point of difference between labels *A* and *B*.

(v) Give the consequences of the phenomenon shown above.

Ans. (i) In such flowers, cross-pollination is likely to occur.

(ii) Disadvantage of cross-pollination is that it involves different external agencies.

(iii) The phenomenon is known as heterostyly where the flowers may be of two or more types with regard to the length of the style and length of stamen.

(iv) Label *A* (anther) produces pollen grains whereas label *B* (stigma) is the receptive part or the landing part for those pollen grains.

(v) As a consequence of heterostyly (shown above), flowers are prevented from undergoing self-pollination, i.e. they cross pollinate.

3. The diagram shows a germinating pollen grain.

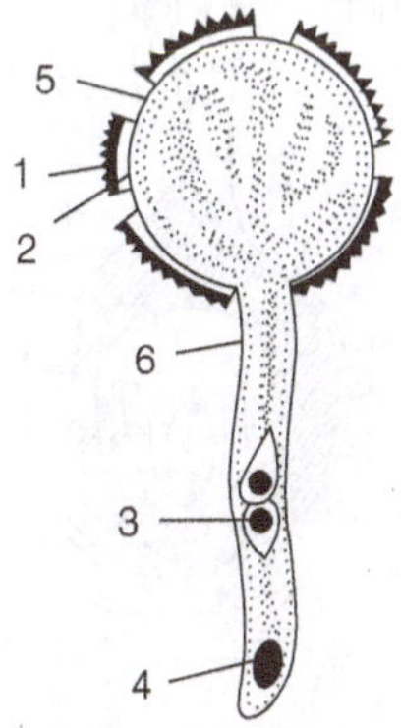

(i) Label the parts 1 to 6.

(ii) What happens to part 4 later in the stage?

(iii) What does part 5 give rise to?

(iv) Which structure is responsible for the development of part 3?

(v) Name the material that makes up part 1.

Ans. The parts 1 to 6 are labelled as

(i) 1. Exine, 2. Intine, 3. Male gamete, 4. Tube nucleus, 5. Germ pore, 6. Pollen tube

(ii) Part 4 (tube nucleus) degenerates later in this stage.

(iii) Part 5 (germ pore) gives rise to pollen tube.

(iv) Generative nucleus is responsible for the development of part 3 (male gamete).

(v) Sporopollenin makes up the part 1 (exine).

4. Study the diagram given below and answer the questions that follows.

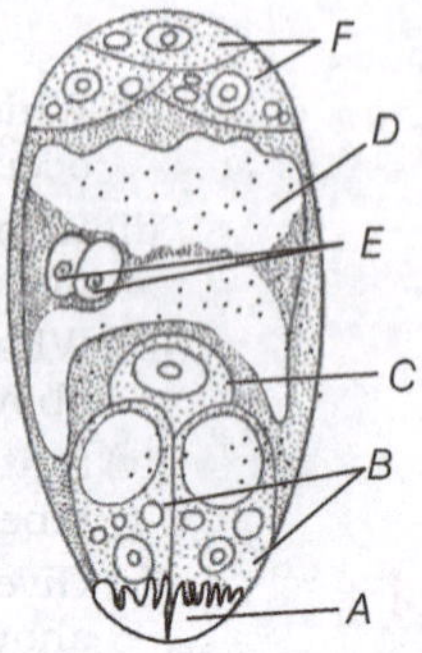

(i) What is shown in the above diagram?

(ii) Identify this labels *A*–*F* marked in the diagram.

(iii) Where is this structure located?

(iv) State the constituents of the structure shown along side.

(v) Give a collective term for labels *B* and *C*.

Ans. (i) The above diagram shows a mature embryo sac.

(ii) The marked parts *A*-*F* are labelled as *A*–Filiform apparatus, *B*–Synergids, *C*–Egg cells, *D*–Central cell, *E*–Polar nuclei, *F*–Antipodal cells

(iii) This structure (embryo sac) is located in the nucellus in female flower.

(iv) The embryo sac has an egg towards micropylar end, two polar nuclei, two synergids and three antipodal cells.

(v) Egg apparatus is a collective term for synergids (*B*) and egg cells (*C*).

5. Given below is a diagrammatic representation of the process of fertilisation. Study the same and then answer the questions that follows.

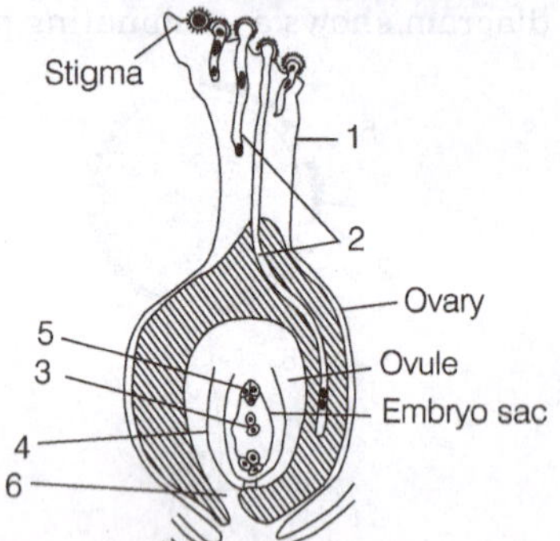

(i) Name the parts numbered 1, 2, 3, 4, 5 and 6.

(ii) What happens to (a) Ovary, (b) Ovule after fertilisation?

(iii) What is the function of the synergids?

(iv) What part does the stigma play in the process of fertilisation?

(v) What is egg apparatus?

Ans. (i) The parts numbered 1, 2, 3, 4, 5 and 6 are as 1–Style, 2–Pollen tubes, 3–Polar nuclei, 4–Embryo sac 5–Antipodal cells, 6–Micropyle

(ii) (a) Ovary changes to fruit after fertilisation.

(b) Ovule changes to seeds after fertilisation.

(iii) Function of synergids is to nourish the egg cell and guide the pollen tube towards egg.

(iv) During pollination, pollen grain is transferred to the stigma thus, stigma acts as the landing platform for pollens.

(v) Egg apparatus is a structure at the micropylar end which consists of one egg cell and two synergids.

6. Seeds are produced when pollen is transferred between flowers of the same species. Answer the questions that follows.

(i) What is meant by 'agents of pollination'?

(ii) What are the different types of pollination observed?

(iii) What role does tube nucleus play during events occurring post-pollination?

(iv) Give a scientific term for the pollination in which a pollen gets transferred to the stigma of a flower on the same plant.

(v) What will happen if pollen grains of rose flower get deposited on the stigma of *Hibiscus*?

Ans. (i) Agents of pollination are actually vectors which bring about pollination. Insects like wasps, bees, etc., wind and water are some agents of pollination.

(ii) The different types of pollination are insect pollination, wind pollination, water pollination, etc.

(iii) Tube nucleus directs the growth of pollen tube towards the micropylar end in order to proceed for fusion.

(iv) Geitonogamy

(v) In this case, germination of pollen will not take place because only the pollen of the flowers belonging to same species germinate to form pollen tube.

Chapter Assessment

Section-I

1 Mark Questions

1. Name the following.
   (i) A stalk that attaches the ovule to the placenta and provides nourishment to the ovule.
   (ii) The type of flower that favours cross-pollination.
   (iii) Type of pollination in flowers that are coloured with a funnel-shaped corolla.
   (iv) The part of flower that carries the female gamete.
2. Correct and rewrite the following statements by changing the underlined words.
   (i) The condition of homogamy can be observed in <u>peepal</u>.
   (ii) Herkogamy is usually seen in <u>*Oxalis*</u>.
   (iii) <u>Lotus</u> flower is pollinated by elephants.
3. Give scientific/biological reasons for the following.
   (i) Self-pollination does not result in introduction of new varieties.
   (ii) Cross-pollination does not occur in plants like *Oxalis*.
   (iii) Exine of the pollen is not a continuous layer.
   (iv) Process of fertilisation in angiosperms is called double fertilisation.
4. (i) Match the following columns.

Column I	Column II
A. Anemophily	1. *Vallisneria*
B. Hydrophily	2. *Salvia*
C. Entomophily	3. *Bignonia*
D. Ornithophily	4. Maize

(ii) Match the following columns.

Column I	Column II
A. Heterostyly	1. Cross-pollination
B. Cleistogamy	2. Chalazal end
C. External agency	3. Homogamy
D. Antipodal cells	4. *Viola*
	5. Micropylar end
	6. *Primula*

5. Choose the correct answer from the four options given below.
   (i) Which one of the following is one of the characteristics of self-pollinated flower?
   (a) Flowers are large and showy
   (b) Flowers produce nectar
   (c) Stigma and anthers mature at the same time
   (d) Pollen is produced in very large quantities
   (ii) Bisexual flowers may avoid self-pollination if
   (a) either anther or stigma is absent
   (b) anther and stigma do not produce enough eggs and pollens
   (c) anthers and stigma mature at different times
   (d) All of the above
   (iii) Exine and intine are the structural components of
   (a) embryo sac
   (b) pollen grain
   (c) stigma
   (d) seed
6. Fill in the blanks by using suitable words.
   (i) Pollination is the process of transfer of ....
   (ii) Self-pollination does not yield .... varieties.
   (iii) For cross-pollination, flowers should be .... and ....
   (iv) In .... pollination, there is wastage of ....
   (v) The .... provides nourishment to the growing embryo.
   (vi) .... comes out of pollen grain to transfer male gametes to the ovary.
   (vii) Embryo develops into .... in post-fertilisation event.
7. Choose the odd one out from the following terms given below and name the category to which other three belong.
   (i) China rose, Lotus, *Salvia*, *Zostera*
   (ii) Petals, Stigma, Ovary wall, Style
   (iii) Sunflower, Corn, Maize, Barley

8. State whether the following statements are true or false. Correct and rewrite the false statements.
   (i) Homogamy is an adaptation for self-pollination.
   (ii) Large number of pollens are produced for autogamy.
   (iii) Flowers are small and nectarless in wind pollination.
   (iv) Ornithophily is pollination by birds.
   (v) Endosperm is formed by zygote.
   (vi) Inner integument forms testa of seed.
9. State the exact location of the following.
   (i) Germ pore
   (ii) Female gamete
10. Give one example of the following.
   (i) A protandrous flower
   (ii) A flower showing herkogamy
11. State the main functions of the following.
   (i) Male gametes
   (ii) Nucellus
12. Mention one difference each of the following pairs on the basis of what is given in the bracket.
   (i) Ovule and Seed (function)
   (ii) Pollination and Fertilisation (immediate result)
13. Give scientific/biological terms for the following.
   (i) Condition which possess some structural barrier.
   (ii) Fusion of male gamete with two polar nuclei.
14. Explain the following terms briefly.
   (i) Elephophily
   (ii) Artificial pollination
   (iii) Allogamy
15. Answer the following questions briefly.
   (i) What is the disadvantage of continued self-pollination in plants?
   (ii) Name an insect pollinator.
   (iii) Write any two features of anemophilous flower.
   (iv) Write any two adaptations of insect pollinated flowers.

2 Marks Question

16. What is the need and significance of pollination in plants?

3 Marks Questions

17. What is anemophily? Write two features of anemophilous flowers.
18. Write any three adaptations in flowers of *Salvia* plant.

Section-II [5 Marks]

Structured Questions

19. Study the diagram given below that shows a flower pollinated by an insect and answer the questions that follows.

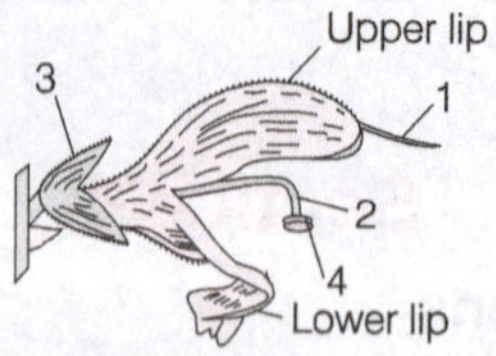

   (i) Label the parts 1 to 4.
   (ii) Name this flower.
   (iii) Name the insect that helps in pollinating this flower.
   (iv) What adaptation does the flower possess in order to carryout such type of pollination?
   (v) Does the above shown type of pollination possess any disadvantage? If yes, state any one.
20. Certain flowers have different timings for the maturation of anthers and stigma. Answer the questions that follows.
   (i) Give a scientific term for the above observation.
   (ii) Define protandry.
   (iii) Give two examples of flowers that show protogyny.
   (iv) Why do some flowers have style and anthers at different heights?
   (v) Name any two adaptations that prevent self-pollination and favour cross-pollination.
21. The figure shows the LS of ovary at the time of fertilisation. Study the figure and answer the questions that follows.

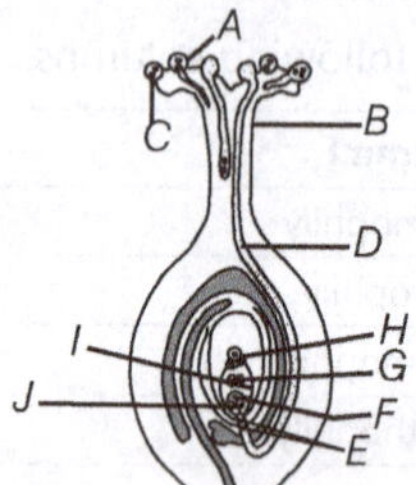

   (i) Label the parts *A*-*J*.
   (ii) Define triple fusion.
   (iii) What happens to the part *F* and *G* ?
   (iv) What is meant by syngamy?
   (v) What is the fate of structure labelled as *J*?

For explanations scan the given QR Code

Olympiad Section*

Brain Teasing Questions asked in Previous Olympiads

1 The following characters are found in many trees that grow in temperate forests. **[INBO 2018]**

(i) Pollens are shed at the beginning of growing season before the leaves develop.

(ii) Shedding of pollen in times to avoid high humidity and rain.

In such trees, the type of pollination is most likely to be

(a) Entomophilic (b) Anemophilic
(c) Ornithophilic (d) Chiropterophilic

2 Sexual reproduction in plants and animals involves the union of two gametes to form a single cell called zygote. Gametes include the egg and sperm cells. Zygote is formed after the sperm fertilises the egg, resulting in diploid chromosome. The zygote develops into ... . (Hint: The following figure indicates fertilised egg). **[INJSO 2016]**

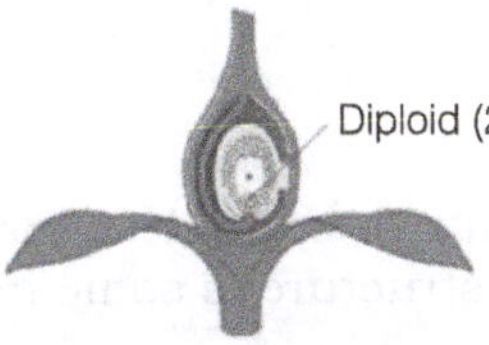

(a) Embryo (b) Endosperm (c) Carpel (d) Ovule

3 In angiosperms, double fertilisation provides the stimulus to the formation of seeds. Growth (measured as change in volume) of ovule, embryo and endosperm in *Pisum* is plotted in the graph. **[INBO 2016]**

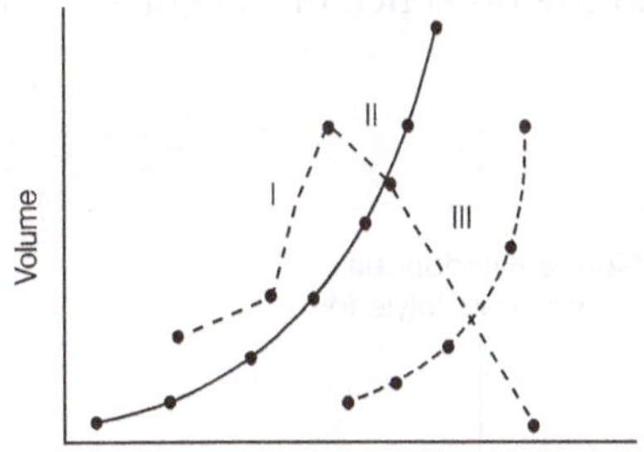

I, II and III respectively represent.

(a) Endosperm, Ovule and Embryo
(b) Ovule, Endosperm and Embryo
(c) Embryo, Ovule and Endosperm
(d) Endosperm, Embryo and Ovule

4 Which of the following statements regarding pollen grain is correct? **[INJSO 2014]**

(a) Tapetum nourishes the developing pollen
(b) Sporogenous tissue in the anther is haploid
(c) Endothesium produces the microspores
(d) Hard outer layer of pollen is intine.

5 A plant is fertilised by pollen grains from anther of another plant. Which of the following characteristics are expected to be found in its flowers?

I. Anthers and stigma mature at same time.
II. Male and female flowers are borne on two separate plants.
III. Flowers always remain closed.
IV. Styles are long while anthers are short.

Codes

(a) I and II (b) II and III
(c) III and IV (d) II and IV

6 Given below are few statements.

Read them carefully and classify them as characteristics of insect pollinated (I) and wind pollinated (II) flowers.

A. Produce scent and nectar.
B. Flowers are small and do not have showy petals.
C. Filaments are long to expose anthers in the air.
D. Stigmas are large and feathery.
E. Essential whorls are not much exposed.
F. Pollen grains are rough and sticky.

	I	II
(a)	B, C, F	A, D, E
(b)	B, D, E	A, C, F
(c)	A, E, F	B, C, D
(d)	A, C, D	B, E, F

Answers

1. (b) 2. (a) 3. (a) 4. (a) 5. (d) 6. (c)

These questions may or may not be asked in the examination, have been given just for additional practice required for olympiads, scholarship exams etc. For detailed explanations refer Page No. 230.

CHAPTER

05

Structure and Germination of Seed

Chapter Inside

• Seed • Seed germination

Seed

A seed is a mature ovule, which develops after fertilisation. It contains embryo which develops into a new plant. The seeds of different plants vary in size and shape but their basic structure is same in all plants. A mature seed mainly consists of three parts

(i) **Seed coat** Covering of the seed.

(ii) **Embryo** The miniature plant inside the seed.

(iii) **Cotyledons** These are the seed leaves which store food for the embryo.

Types of Seed

The seeds can be classified on the basis of number of cotyledons and the presence or absence of endosperm (nutritive tissue), as given below

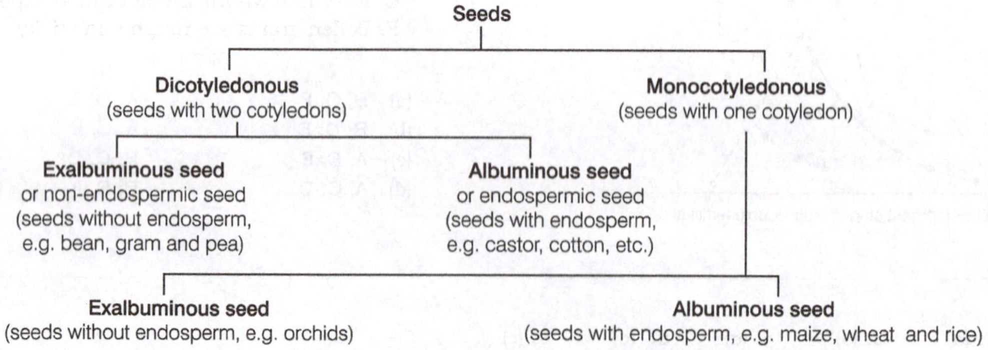

Structure of Dicotyledonous (Bean) Seed

Bean seeds are kidney-shaped which appear convex on one side and concave on the other. Bean seed contains two cotyledons so it is called **dicotyledonous.**

The detailed structure of a dicot seed (bean) is as follows

1. **Seed coat** Each seed is covered by a protective covering called seed coat. It develops from the integuments of ovule. The seed coat is differentiated as follows
   (i) **Testa** It is the outer, thick, protective layer. It protects the seed from pathogens like bacteria, fungi, insects, etc., and from injuries.
   (ii) **Tegmen** It is inner, thin membranous covering which protects the inner part of seed.
2. **Hilum** It shows the point of attachment of ovule to the ovary. It is just a mark (scar) on the concave side of the seed.
3. **Micropyle** It is a small pore near the hilum, through which oxygen, water, etc., enters into the seed. It also marks the opening *via* which pollen tube enters the ovule.
4. **Raphe** It is a ridge-like structure present around the median groove. It represents the portion of the stalk which remains fused with the testa.
5. **Embryo** It is defined as a young miniature plant along with cotyledons, enclosed within the seed coat.
   Thus, an embryo consists of two parts as described below
   (i) **Cotyledons** These are seed leaves. They are food laden, fleshy structures attached to the embryonal axis. They provide nourishment to the embryo in the early stages of development.
   (ii) **Embryonal axis** A young miniature plant is present between the two cotyledons. It is called the embryonal axis. It consists of the following parts
      (a) **Plumule** This is a leafy part of the embryo which give rise to shoot.
      (b) **Radicle** This is the lower end of the embryo which give rise to roots.
      (c) **Epicotyl** It is the part of the embryo over the plumule.
      (d) **Hypocotyl** It is the part of the embryo just above the radicle.

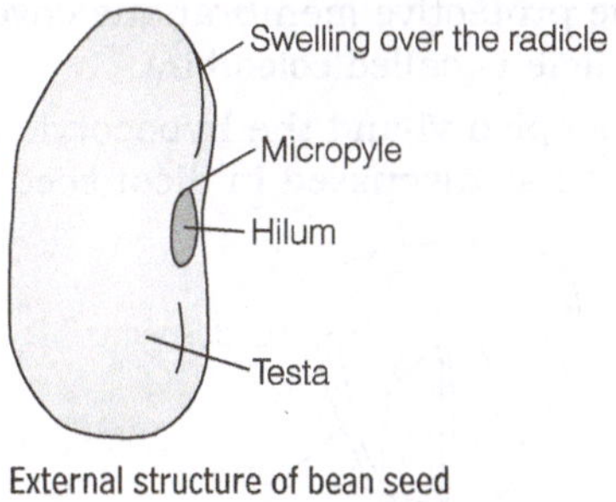

External structure of bean seed

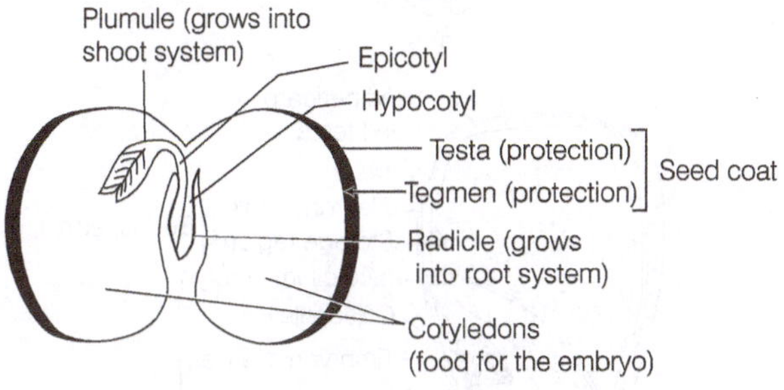

Internal structure of bean seed

Structure of Monocotyledonous Seed (Maize)

The maize seed contains only one cotyledon so it is called **monocotyledonous.** It is a single seeded fruit.

The maize grain is a flat, almost triangular structure. Externally it is differentiated into a large, upper area, which marks the position of endosperm and a small lower area that contains the embryo. These are separated by a prominent epithelial layer. In detail, its structural parts are as follows

1. **Seed coat** The seed coat in maize seed is not separable. It is fused with pericarp (fruit wall). Thus, it is called **grain.**
2. **Hilum and micropyle** These are not clearly visible in maize seed and are not distinguishable.
3. **Endosperm** It is the nutritive tissue of the seed. It contains starch as reserve food material which is surrounded by one cell thick **aleurone layer**. It is rich in protein and enzymes.
4. **Embryo** The embryo of maize seed consists of following parts
   (i) **Cotyledon** The maize grain contains a thin, papery, single cotyledon called **scutellum.** It does not contain food. It is present near the endosperm.
   (ii) **Plumule** It represents growing tip of the shoot along with embryonic leaves. It is covered with a sheath called **coleoptile.**

(iii) **Radicle** It is present at the lower base part of a seed and is covered by **root cap**. The protective membranous covering of radicle is called **coleorhiza**.

The epicotyl and the hypocotyl areas are same as discussed in dicot seeds.

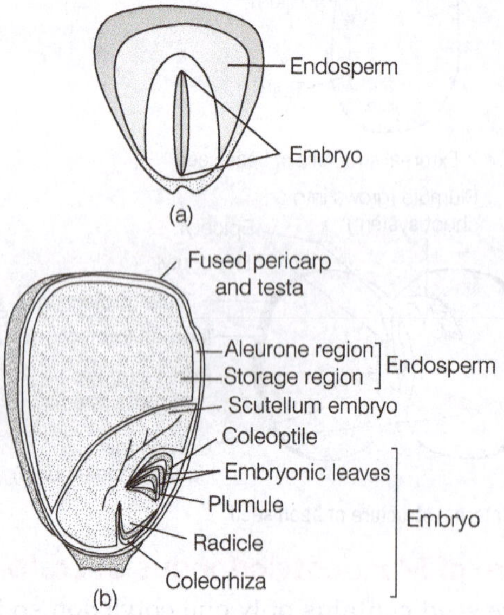

(a) External structure and (b) Internal structure of maize seed

Differences between Dicot Seed and Monocot Seed

Dicot seed (Bean)	**Monocot seed** (Maize)
Seed coat is thick and brown.	Seed coat is fused with pericarp.
Hilum and micropyle can be seen separately.	Hilum and micropyle cannot be differentiated.
Two cotyledons are present.	Only one cotyledon is present.
Endosperm is absent.	Endosperm is present and is well- developed.

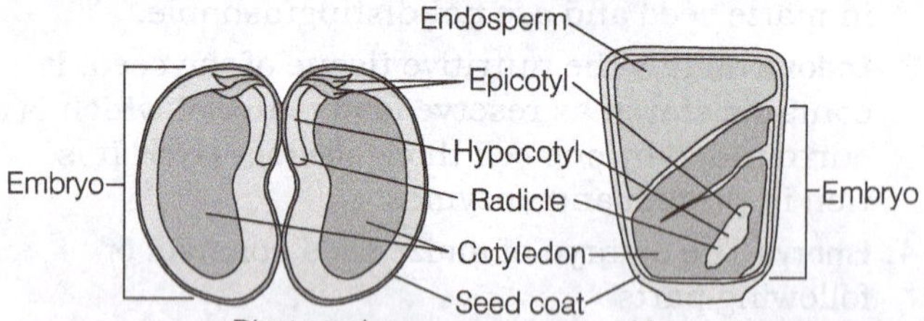

Check Your LEARNING...

1 Which part of flower forms seed?
2 Give two example of non-endospermic seeds.
3 State the function of testa.
4 What is hypocotyl?
5 Mention the name of covering which encloses plumule.
6 Name the protective covering of radicle in maize grain.

Seed Germination

Seed contains the embryo in a dormant state (resting phase) where all the chemical activities take place. A fresh seed has to pass through the period of dormancy to germinate.

Seed germination is a process in which seed embryo gets activated to grow into a seedling by using reserve food materials. This happens only when the seed gets suitable conditions needed for their germination. The process of germination is irreversible. Germination in any plant concludes with the formation of a seedling. It is a stage in the growth of a plant and persist till it become fully independent of the stored food.

Conditions Necessary for Seed Germination

The seeds germinate only when they get certain favourable conditions, which are as follows

1. **Water** Seed absorbs water through micropyle. Water accelerates the metabolic activities in the seed. The imbibition of water causes the seed to swell and helps in rupturing the seed coat. It also helps in the hydrolysis of stored food materials into soluble products and in translocation of soluble products to the embryo.
2. **Oxygen** All seeds respire during germination. More oxygen is necessary for respiration in the growing embryo due to rapid cell growth. Without oxygen, germination might fail.
3. **Temperature** Suitable temperature is must for the germination. Most of the seeds cannot germinate when the temperature is below 0°C or above 48°C. Optimum temperature range for seed germination is about 25-35°C.

Types of Seed Germination

The process of germination is categorised into two types depending upon the behaviour of cotyledons during germination, i.e. epigeal germination and hypogeal germination.

1. Epigeal Germination

Epigeal germination takes place above the ground and usually occurs in dicot seeds. The cotyledons are first pushed above the ground by the rapid elongation of hypocotyl. The length of epicotyl remains the same in epigeal germination.

Cotyledons soon turn green and start photosynthesising, e.g. *Phaseolus*, *Ricinus* (castor), *Dolichos* (bean), *Helianthus* (sunflower), *Brassica* (mustard), *Allium* (onion), etc.

Germination of Bean Seed

The various stages of epigeal germination of bean seed are as follows

- The seeds swell up after absorbing water.
- The radicle elongates, extends downward into the soil.
- Hypocotyl elongates, plumule reaches the surface of the soil.
- Cotyledons come out of the soil and thus seed germination takes place.

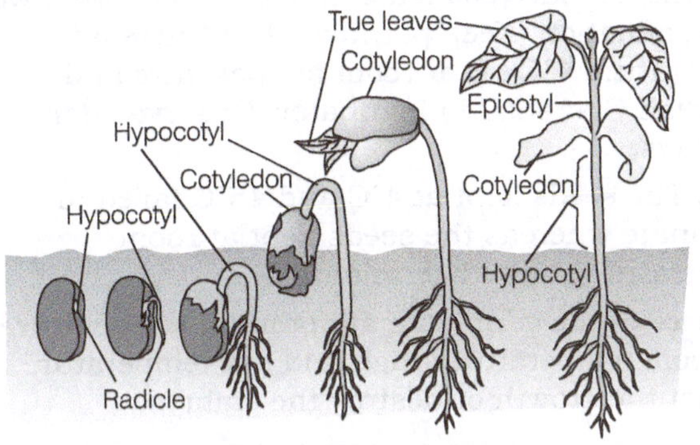

Germination in bean seed

2. Hypogeal Germination

In this type of germination, the epicotyl elongates faster than hypocotyl at the time of seed germination.

This keeps cotyledons inside the soil or may bring them just above the soil surface. However, they remain non-green, dry up gradually and fall off. Some dicot seeds like pea, mango, coconut and most of the monocot seeds like maize, rice show hypogeal germination.

Germination of Maize Grain

The various stages of hypogeal germination of maize grain are as follows

- The seed absorbs water and swells up. The epithelial layer of the scutellum secretes enzymes which convert starch in the endosperm into sugar and transfer it to the cotyledon.
- The radicle grows down and plumule grows up.

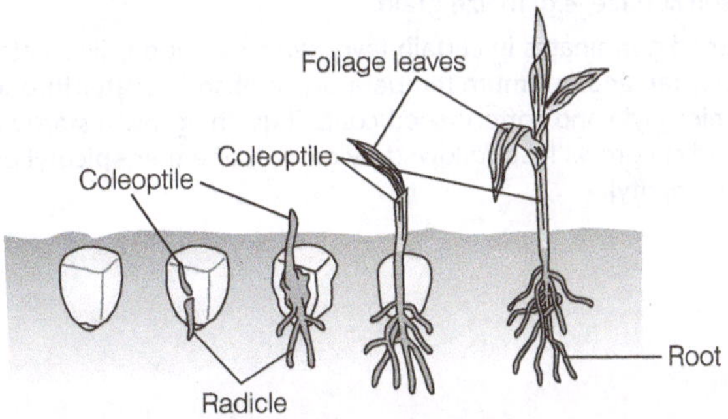

Germination in maize seed

- The epicotyl enlarges and cotyledons remain in the soil. So, the germination is hypogeal.

Note Vivipary involves a special mode of seed germination which takes place inside the fruit while it is still attached to the parent plant. It is observed in mangrove plants like *Rhizophora*.

Differences between Epigeal and Hypogeal Germination

Epigeal germination	Hypogeal germination
Hypocotyl elongates at a faster rate.	Epicotyl elongates at a faster rate.
Cotyledons are pushed above the ground.	Cotyledons remain under the ground.
Cotyledons play a role in photosynthesis.	Cotyledons have no role in photosynthesis.
Usually found in monocotyledonous seeds.	Usually found in dicotyledonous seeds.

Experiments Related to Seed Germination

There are few experiments by which we can understand the importance of factors which are necessary for seed germination.

Experiment 1

Aim To prove that water is necessary for seed germination.

Procedure Take four petridishes and mark them as A, B, C and D. Place cotton wool and seeds in each petridish as follows

Petridish A Keep seeds which have been soaked over night on wet cotton.

Petridish B Keep soaked seeds on dry cotton.

Petridish C Keep unsoaked seeds on dry cotton.

Petridish D Keep soaked seeds completely submerged in water.

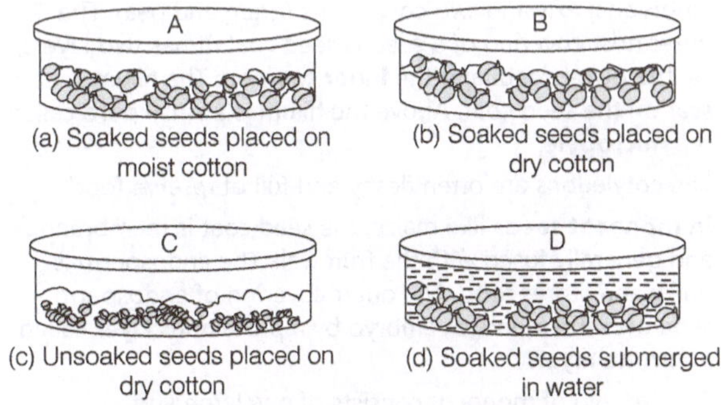

Experimental setup to show that water is necessary for seed germination

Result Seeds kept on petridish A germinate. In petridish B, seeds germinate but shrivel up and die. In petridish C, no change is seen in seeds. In petridish D, the seeds start germinating but eventually rot.

Inference Optimum water content needed for seeds to germinate was available only in petridish A.

Experiment 2

Aim To prove that oxygen is necessary for seed germination.

Procedure Take two conical flask and mark them as A and B. Spread moist cotton at the bottom of the flasks and place some soaked seeds on wet cotton. Hang a test tube containing **pyrogallic acid** dissolved in **sodium hydroxide** with the help of a thread in a flask marked as A and seal it with a cork. Seal the other flask marked as B, in the same way but with the test tube containing water. Place both the flasks at room temperature and observe them after 3-4 days.

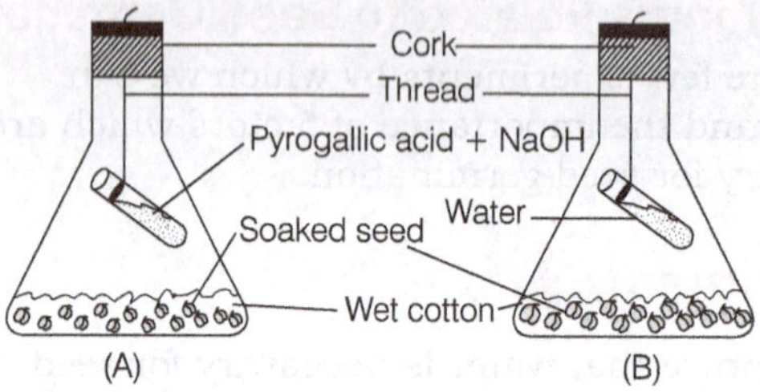

Experimental setup to show that oxygen is necessary for seed germination

Result The seeds in the flask A do not germinate, while the seeds in the flask B germinate.

Inference The seeds fail to germinate in flask A, because of the absence of O_2 (as Pyrogallic acid + NaOH absorbs O_2). The flask B has O_2 so seeds germinate in it.

Experiment 3

Aim To show that suitable temperature is necessary for the seed germination.

Procedure Take three petridishes and mark them as A, B and C. Place soaked seeds on a wet cotton wool for germination. Keep petridish A in fridge (at temperature 4°C), B at room temperature and petridish C at 45°C in incubator. Observe after 3-4 days.

Result The seeds kept at 4°C and 45°C failed to germinate whereas the seeds kept at room temperature showed germination.

Inference Seeds germinate at optimum temperature, i.e. room temperature. High and low temperature restrict the growth or destroy the embryo.

Check Your LEARNING...

1 Name a plant seed which show epigeal germination.
2 Name a plant seed which show hypogeal germination.
3 Name the conditions which affect seed germination.
4 What is the role of O_2 in a seed germination?
5 Name a chemical that can absorb oxygen.

QUiCK Revision

- Seed is ripened ovule which is developed after fertilisation.
- **In dicot seeds**, the embryo is made up of a radicle, an embryonal axis and two cotyledons (gram and pea). The outermost covering of a seed is seed coat. It has two layers, i.e. the **outer testa** and the **inner tegmen**. The hilum is a scar on the seed coat. Above the hilum is a small pore called the **micropyle**.
- The cotyledons are often fleshy and full of reserve food.
- **In monocot seeds** like maize, the seed coat is membranous and generally fused with the fruit wall. The endosperm is bulky and stores food. The outer covering of endosperm separates the monocot embryo by a proteinous layer called **aleurone layer.**
- The embryo of monocot consists of one large and shield-shaped cotyledon known as **scutellum** and a short axis with a plumule and a radicle. The plumule and radicle are enclosed in sheaths, which are called **coleoptile** and **coleorhiza**, respectively.
- **Epigeal germination** takes place above the ground. The cotyledons are first pushed above the ground by the rapid elongation of hypocotyl, e.g. *Ricinus* (castor).
- **Hypogeal germination** The epicotyl elongates faster than hypocotyl at the time of seed germination. This keeps cotyledons inside the soil or may bring them just above the soil surface, e.g. maize grain.
- Seed germinates in certain favourable conditions like water, oxygen and optimum temperature. It absorbs water through micropyle and softens seed coat. Thus, the growth starts. The radicle grows first, followed by growth of either epicotyl or hypocotyl.

Chapter Practice

Section-I

1 Mark Questions

1. Name the following
   (i) Structure that contains embryo and may or may not have a nutritive tissue.
   (ii) Protective covering that develops from integuments of ovule.
   (iii) Ridge-like structure present around the median groove.
   (iv) Young miniature plants having cotyledons and embryonal axis.
   (v) Part of embryo that gives rise to shoot.
   (vi) A protective sheath that covers plumule.
   (vii) Part of seed covered by root cap.
   (viii) Condition in which cotyledons remain under the soil or just on the ground during seed germination.

Ans. (i) Seed (ii) Seed coat
(iii) Raphe (iv) Embryo
(v) Plumule (vi) Coleoptile
(vii) Radicle (viii) Hypogeal germination

2. Correct and rewrite the following statements by changing the underlined words.
   (i) Seeds are formed after <u>pollination</u>.
   (ii) <u>Micropyle</u> is a scar present on the seed which denotes point of attachment of seed with its stalk.
   (iii) <u>Hilum</u> represents the part of stalk that remains fused with testa.
   (iv) <u>Plumule</u> is absent in dicot seeds.
   (v) Water <u>deaccelerates</u> the metabolic activities occurring inside the seed.

Ans. (i) Seeds are formed after fertilisation.
(ii) Hilum is a scar present on the seed which denotes point of attachment of seed with its stalk.
(iii) Raphe represents the part of stalk that remains fused with testa.
(iv) Endosperm is absent in dicot seeds.
(v) Water accelerates the metabolic activities occurring inside the seed.

3. Give biological reasons for the following.
   (i) Maize is called a grain and not a seed/fruit.
   (ii) Seeds have a hard protective covering around them.
   (iii) Seeds grown deep in soil fail to germinate.

Ans. (i) Maize is more precisely called a grain and not a seed/fruit because the fruit wall (pericarp) and seed coat are fused together to form a protective layer.
(ii) Seeds have a hard protective covering called seed coat around them because the seed coat helps to protect the embryo from any kind of injury and drying out and also from pathogens.
(iii) Seeds grown deep in the soil fail to germinate due to lack of oxygen for respiration.

4. (i) Match the following columns.

Column I	Column II
A. Radicle	1. Seed leaves
B. Plumule	2. Monocot abluminous seeds
C. Cereals	3. Future root
D. *Vallisneria*	4. Monocot exalbuminous seeds
	5. Future shoot

(ii) Match the following columns.

Column I	Column II
A. Bean seed	1. Dicot seed
B. Maize	2. Inner layer
C. Testa	3. Monocot seed
D. Tegmen	4. Outermost hard covering

(iii) Match the following columns.

Column I	Column II
A. Dormancy	1. 25 – 35° C
B. Optimum temperature	2. Occurs in monocots and dicots
C. Hypogeal germination	3. Period of rest
D. Epigeal germination.	4. Maize grain
	5. Bean seed

Ans. (i) A-3, B-5, C-2, D-4
(ii) A-1, B-3, C-4, D-2
(iii) A-3, B-1, C-4, D-5

5. Choose the correct answer from the four options given below.
   (i) An example of exalbuminous dicot seeds is
   (a) poppy (b) custard
   (c) apple (d) gram

Ans. (d)

(ii) In pea, castor and maize, the number of cotyledons are
(a) 2, 2 and 1, respectively
(b) 1, 2 and 2, respectively
(c) 2, 1 and 2, respectively
(d) 1 , 2 and 1, respectively

Ans. (a)

(iii) The part of a seed which grows and develops into root on germination is
(a) cotyledon (b) plumule
(c) follicle (d) radicle

Ans. (d)

(iv) In the monocotyledon seeds, the endosperm is separated from the embryo by a distinct layer known as
(a) testa (b) aleurone
(c) tegmen (d) epithelium

Ans. (b)

(v) Aleurone layer is rich in
(a) lipid (b) starch (c) protein (d) fatty acid

Ans. (c)

(vi) Endosperm is consumed by developing embryo in the seed of
(a) coconut (b) castor (c) pea (d) maize

Ans. (c)

(vii) The scutellum observed in a grain of wheat or maize is comparable to which part of the seed in other monocotyledons?
(a) Cotyledon (b) Endosperm
(c) Aleurone layer (d) Plumule

Ans. (a)

6. Fill in the blanks by using suitable words.
(i) Rice, wheat and maize are ...... seed.
(ii) Seed absorbs water through ....
(iii) Seed is a ...... ovule.
(iv) In albuminous seed, the food is stored in ....
(v) Fruit wall and seed coat are fused in ....
(vi) ...... is the protective layer of the radicle.
(vii) In hypogeal germination, ... elongates faster.
(viii) In ...... germination, the cotyledons are pushed above the soil.

Ans. (i) monocot (ii) micropyle
(iii) mature (iv) endosperm
(v) maize grain (vi) Coleorhiza
(vii) epicotyl (viii) epigeal

7. Read the following paragraphs and complete it by using proper words for *A*, *B* and *C*.

The maize seed consists of a single cotyledon called ...*A*..., a radicle and a plumule. Radicle is enclosed in ...*B*... and plumule is enclosed in ...*C*.... .

Ans. *A*-scutellum, *B*-coleorhiza, *C*-coleoptile

8. Choose the odd one out from the following terms given below and name the category to which other three belong.
(i) Mango, Maize, Bean, Groundnut
(ii) Seed coat, Hilum, Aleurone layer, Endosperm
(iii) Water, Oxygen, Sunlight, Temperature

Ans. (i) **Odd term** Bean
Rest three are show hypogeal germination.
(ii) **Odd term** Aleurone layer
Rest three are the parts of both monocot and dicot seeds.
(iii) **Odd term** Sunlight
Rest three are conditions necessary for seed germination.

9. Given below are sets of five terms. In each case, rewrite the terms in correct order in a logical sequence beginning with the term that is underlined.
(i) <u>Radicle</u>, Cotyledon, Plumule, Hypocotyl, Epicotyl
(ii) Embryo, First male gamete, Zygote, Egg cell, <u>Micropyle</u>

Ans. (i) Radicle, Plumule, Hypocotyl, Epicotyl, cotyledon.
(ii) Micropyle, First male gametes, Egg cell, Zygote, Embryo

10. State whether the following statements are true or false. Correct and rewrite the false statements.
(i) Wheat seed contains two cotyledons.
(ii) Micropyle is an opening in the seed.
(iii) Cotyledons are thin and fleshy in albuminous seeds.
(iv) Hilum provides the diffusion of respiratory gases for the embryo.
(v) In epigeal germination, epicotyl elongates at a faster rate.

Ans. (i) False. Wheat seed contains one cotyledon. Hence, it is monocotyledonous.
(ii) True
(iii) True
(iv) False. Micropyle provides the diffusion of respiratory gases for the embryo.
(v) False. Epicotyl elongates faster in hypogeal germination.

11. State the exact location of the following.
(i) Seed coat (ii) Raphe
(iii) Tegmen (iv) Aleurone layer

Ans. (i) **Seed coat** It is the protective covering around the seed.
(ii) **Raphe** Ridge-like structure around the median groove of seed.
(iii) **Tegmen** Inner thin membrane of seed next to testa.
(iv) **Aleurone layer** It surrounds the endosperm in a monocot seed.

12. Give one example of each of the following.
(i) Monocot albuminous seed
(ii) Seed with one cotyledon
(iii) Seed with fused seed coat and pericarp
(iv) Exalbuminous dicot seed
(v) Hypogeal germination

Ans. (i) Wheat (ii) Rice
(iii) Maize (iv) Bean
(v) Maize

13. State the main function of the following.
(i) Cotyledons
(ii) Testa
(iii) Micropyle

Ans. (i) **Cotyledons** These store food for the embryo within the seed.
(ii) **Testa** It protects the seed from various pathogens like bacteria, fungi, etc., and from injuries.
(iii) **Micropyle** It allows entry of oxygen, water, etc., into the seed so that it could respire and germinate efficiently.

14. Mention one difference in each of the following pairs on the basis of what is given in bracket.
(i) Hilum and Micropyle (location)
(ii) Testa and Tegmen (definition)
(iii) Epicotyl and Hypocotyl (location)

Ans. (i) Difference between hilum and micropyle is as follows

Hilum	Micropyle
It is a scar present on the concave side of the seed.	It is an opening present adjacent to hilum.

(ii) Difference between testa and tegmen is as follows

Testa	Tegmen
It is the outer, smooth thick and coloured protective layer of seed.	It is thin, white inner coat of seed.

(iii) Difference between epicotyl and hypocotyl is as follows

Epicotyl	Hypocotyl
Part of embryo over the plumule.	Part of embryo above the radicle.

15. Give suitable biological/technical terms for the following.
(i) Seeds without the endosperm.
(ii) Point of attachment of ovule to the funicle.
(iii) Thin, papery and single cotyledon present near endosperm in monocot seeds.
(iv) An irreversible process in which seed embryo gets activated to grow into a seedling with the help of reserve food.

Ans. (i) Exalbuminous seed
(ii) Hilum
(iii) Scutellum
(iv) Seed germination

16. Briefly explain the following terms.
(i) Seed (ii) Seed coat
(iii) Radicle (iv) Epicotyl
(v) Coleorhiza

Ans. (i) A seed is a mature ovule that develops after fertilisation.
(ii) Seed coat is a protective covering around seed which develop from integuments of the ovule.
(iii) Radicle is the lower end of the embryo that give rise to roots.
(iv) Epicotyl is the part of embryo over the plumule.
(v) Coleorhiza is the protective covering of the radicle.

17. Answer the following questions briefly.
(i) How are seeds broadly classified?
(ii) What do you call the seed having endosperm in them?
(iii) Why are orchid seeds called exalbuminous?
(iv) What is the shape of bean seeds?
(v) Which structure gives rise to seed coat?

Ans. (i) Seeds are broadly classified as monocots and dicots.
(ii) Endospermic or albuminous seeds.
(iii) Orchid seeds are termed as exalbuminous as they lack endosperm.
(iv) Bean seeds are kidney-shaped with one convex and one concave side.
(v) Integuments of ovule give rise to seed coat.

2 Marks Questions

18. (i) Maize grain is a one seeded fruit. Comment.
(ii) What does the seed constitute?

Ans. (i) Fruit is a ripened ovary wherein the ovarian wall develops to form fruit wall. Maize grains is referred to as one seeded fruit because it has only one cotyledon or seed leaf which store food for the embryo.
(ii) Seed consists of a tiny living plant called the embryo. It may also contain endosperm required for the nourishment of embryo during germination.

19. Give any two examples each of endospermic seed, and non-endospermic seeds in monocots and dicots both.

Ans. **Endospermic or Albuminous seeds**
(i) Monocots : Maize, wheat
(ii) Dicots : Castor, cotton

Non-endospermic or Exalbuminous seeds
(i) Monocots : Orchids, *Vallisneria*
(ii) Dicots : Bean, gram

20. (i) Write about any two structural components of a dicotyledonous seed.
(ii) What are the two types of seed germination?

Ans. (i) Two structural components of a dicot seeds are
- **Raphe** It is a ridge-like structure present around the median groove.
- **Seed coat** A protective covering that originates from the integuments of ovule. It is divided into testa and tegmen.

(ii) Two types of seed germination are
- Hypogeal seed germination
- Epigeal seed germination

3 Marks Questions

21. (i) Gram seed is used as dal as well as sprout due to its high nutritive value. Explain.
(ii) Give an account of seed germination.
(iii) What events occur during seed dormancy?

Ans. (i) Gram seed has good protein content in it. Germinated grams have active supply of nutrients to growing radicle and plumule. As a result, there is better availability of food which can be easily utilised by the body. Hence, there is strong belief that germinated gram seeds are of highly nutritive value.
(ii) Seed germination is defined as the fundamental process by which different plant species grow from a single seed into a plant. The complete process of seed germination is carried out in several steps. Certain external factors like oxygen, water and temperature affect the process of seed germination.
(iii) During seed dormancy, following events occur
- Seed coat that is resistant to water and gases, restricts water uptake and oxygen intake.
- Seeds with immature embryo do not develop.
- Some seeds may require more time for their germination.

22. With regard to germination in bean seed, answer the following questions.
(i) Name the seed part that grows into the seedling.
(ii) Name the seed part that provides nutrition for the growing seedling.
(iii) Draw a neat labelled diagram of a mature bean seed.

Ans. (i) The part of the seed that grows into the seedling is the embryo.
(ii) The part of the seed that provides nutrition to the growing seedling is called the cotyledon.
(iii) Refer to the diagram (internal structure of bean seed) from page no. 71.

Section-II [5 Marks]

Structured Questions

1. Observe the diagram given below and answer the following questions.

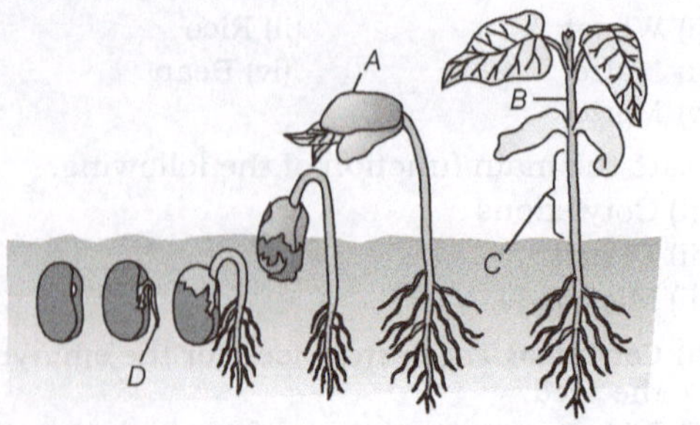

(i) Label the parts marked as *A-D*.
(ii) Which type of germination occurs in above diagram?
(iii) Name the seed shown in above diagram.
(iv) Name any two plants other than the one shown above that shows such type of germination.
(v) Define viviparity.

Ans. (i) The marked parts *A-D* are labelled as *A*–Cotyledon, *B*–Epicotyl, *C*–Hypocotyl, *D*–Radicle
(ii) Epigeal germination
(iii) Bean seed (Dicotyledon)
(iv) Castor and cotton
(v) Viviparity is the condition in which the seed germinates inside the fruit while being attached to the parent plant, e.g. *Rhizophora*.

2. Seeds are the product of ripened ovule after fertilisation by pollen.
Answer the questions that follows.
(i) What are the two basic parts of a seed?
(ii) In which seeds, does the embryo absorb the endosperm?
(iii) Where does the seed coat develop from?
(iv) Does micropyle helps in pollination? Comment.
(v) Why do large seeds have more energy reserves?

Ans. (i) Embryo and seed coat are the two basic parts of a seed.
(ii) Non-endospermic or exalbuminous seeds
(iii) Seed coat develops from the integuments of ovule.
(iv) Yes, micropyle helps in concluding the final steps of pollination by allowing entry of pollen tube.
(v) Large seeds have more energy reserves for the germination and growth of seedling.

Chapter Assessment

Section-I

1 Mark Questions

1. Name the following.
   (i) Seeds which do not germinate even when suitable conditions necessary for germination are available.
   (ii) A stage of plant growth from a seed before becoming fully independent of the food stored in it.
   (iii) Condition in which cotyledons remain under the ground (soil) or just on the ground during seed germination.

2. Correct and rewrite the following statements by changing the underlined words.
   (i) Tegmen protects the <u>outer</u> part of the seed.
   (ii) Epicotyl is the part of embryo <u>below</u> the plumule.

3. Give biological reason for the following.
   Cotyledons are referred to as seed leaves.

4. (i) Match the following columns.

	Column I		Column II
A.	Hypogeal	1.	Water absorption
B.	Epigeal	2.	Mango seed
C.	Micropyle	3.	Onion seed

   (ii) Match the following columns.

	Column I		Column II
A.	Aleurone layer	1.	Shoot giving part of seed
B.	Coleoptile	2.	Monocot seed
C.	Plumule	3.	Protein

5. Choose the correct answer from the four options given below.
   (i) Which of the following monocotyledonous seed is non-endospermic?
   (a) Maize (b) Wheat (c) Coconut (d) Orchid
   (ii) The plumule and radicle are enclosed in sheath which are called
   (a) aleurone layer, scutellum
   (b) aleurone layer, coleoptile
   (c) aleurone layer, coleorhiza
   (d) coleoptile, coleorhiza
   (iii) Scutellum represents
   (a) outermost layer of endosperm
   (b) a sheath that protects the radicle
   (c) the place where the seed gets attached to the raphe
   (d) a cotyledon
   (iv) In hypogeal seed germination, the structure that help to push the cotyledon inside the soil is
   (a) epicotyl
   (b) hypocotyl
   (c) plumule
   (d) radicle

6. Fill in the blanks by using suitable words.
   (i) Maize is an .... seed.
   (ii) ...... stores the food in seeds.
   (iii) An embryo has ...... and ....
   (iv) ...... is an example of non-endospermic seed.
   (v) The scar on the seed is called ....

7. Choose the odd one out from the following terms given below and name the category to which other three belong.
   Castor, Mango, Millets, Peanuts

8. Given below are sets of five terms each. Rewrite the terms in correct order in a logical sequence beginning with the term that is underlined.
   Tegmen, Cotyledon, <u>Testa</u>, Plumule, Radicle

9. State whether the following statements are true or false. Correct and rewrite the false statements.
   (i) In dry seeds, the embryo is not in active state.
   (ii) Rice seed is non-endospermic.
   (iii) Radicle is the future root of the plant.
   (iv) The bean seed has only one cotyledon.
   (v) Aleurone layer is present in pea seeds.

10. State the exact location of embryonal axis.

11. Give one example of the following
    (i) Viviparous germination
    (ii) Hypogeal germination
    (iii) Grain with single thick cotyledon

12. State the main function of the following.
Coleorhiza

13. Mention one difference in each of the following pairs on the basis of what is given in the bracket.
(i) Radicle and Plumule (future changes)
(ii) Cotyledon and Endosperm (definition)

14. Give biological/technical terms for the following.
Germination favouring a faster elongation of hypocotyl.

15. Briefly explain the following terms.
(i) Grain (ii) Viviparous germination

16. Answer the following questions briefly.
(i) How are seeds classified on the basis of presence or absence of endosperm?
(ii) The embryo growing inside the seed is able to 'respire'. Comment.
(iii) What happens when dry seed is kept under suitable conditions of water, light and temperature?
(iv) State the role of pyrogallic acid in germination experiments.

2 Marks Question

17. (i) What role does hypocotyl play in epigeal germination?
(ii) What do you observe when potatoes are kept in a basket for a long time during the rainy season? What is the cause behind this?

3 Marks Question

18. Certain seeds fail to germinate even after getting suitable conditions. What necessary conditions are being talked about?

Section-II [5 Marks]

Structured Questions

19. The diagram shows an experimental setup. Study the given setup carefully and answer the questions that follows.

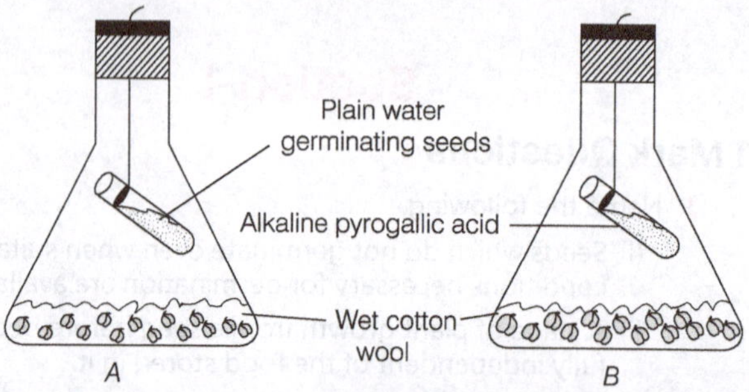

(i) What is the aim of the experiment?
(ii) Why are seeds not germinating in B?
(iii) How is pyrogallic acid made alkaline and why?
(iv) Why is wet cotton wool kept in flask A and B?
(v) What is germination?

20. Germination is a basic process in which seed undergoes certain physiological maturation. Answer the questions that follows.
(i) During the process of seed germination, rupturing of seed coat occurs. Why?
(ii) What is the proteinaceous part of monocotyledonous endosperm called?
(iii) What is meant by inactive seed?
(iv) Which gas is released by a dry seed?
(v) What does a seed contain?

For explanations scan the given QR Code

Olympiad Section*

Brain Teasing Questions asked in Previous Olympiads

1 If a plant is grown only in sand (S), only in clay (C) or only in humus (H), which of the following will be true? **[INBO 2010]**

I. Water availability to the roots will be more in C and H as compared to S.
II. Nutrient availability will be more in C and H as compared to S.
III. Oxygen availability will be low in C as compared to S and H.
IV. The ability of roots to penetrate S and H will be low as compared to C.

(a) Only I
(b) II and III
(c) I and IV
(d) I, II and III

2 A few normal seedlings of tomato were placed inside a dark room. After a few days, they were found to have turned white like albinos. Which of these can be used to describe them?

(a) Defoliated
(b) Etiolated
(c) Embolised
(d) Mutated

3 A process of breaking seed dormancy of some plants in which seeds are treated in moist medium at low temperature (5-10°C) for sufficient period of time is known as

(a) scarification
(b) stratification
(c) vernalisation
(d) None of these

4 Seed germination is the sprouting of a seed and growth of the embryo present inside the seed into a seedling or young plant capable of independent existence. Observe the given diagram showing seed germination and choose the incorrect option.

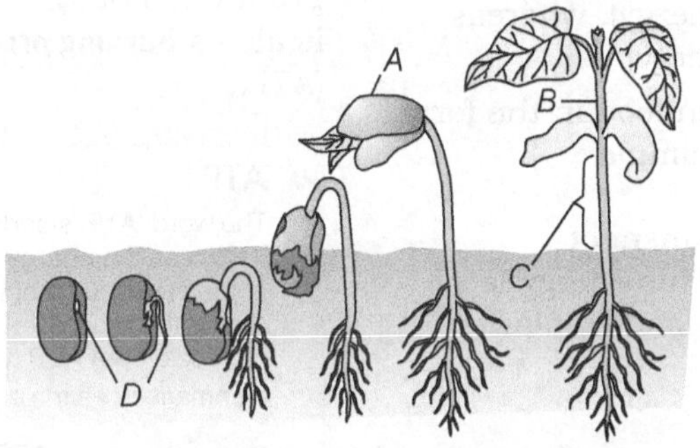

(a) Cotyledons are brought out of the soil by the greater growth of hypocotyl.
(b) This kind of germination is found in seeds of beans.
(c) Cotyledons become green and functional as first leaves of the seedling.
(d) The hypocotyl does not elongate much, instead the epicotyl grows and takes the plumule above the soil.

Answers

1. (d) **2.** (b) **3.** (a) **4.** (d)

**These questions may or may not be asked in the examination, have been given just for additional practice required for olympiads, scholarship exams etc. For detailed explanations refer Page No. 230.*

CHAPTER

06

Respiration in Plants

Chapter Inside

• Respiration • Experiments on Gaseous Exchange and Heat Production

All living cells perform various metabolic activities which require energy. Plants also require energy to carry out various **anabolic** (constructive biosynthesis) and **catabolic** (breaking up) activities. The former activities are **endergonic** (require energy), whereas the latter are **exergonic** (release energy).

This energy is made available when food in the form of glucose, is broken down into a simple carbohydrate.

This chapter deals with the mechanism of breakdown of food via **respiration.** This energy is further used in the preparation of food by plants.

Respiration

It is a catabolic process in which living cells oxidise organic substances like glucose, lipids, proteins, etc. either in **aerobic conditions** (requiring oxygen), producing CO_2, water and energy or in **anaerobic conditions** (not requiring oxygen), producing ethyl alcohol, CO_2 and energy.

$$\underset{\text{(Glucose)}}{C_6H_{12}O_6} + \underset{\text{(Oxygen)}}{6O_2} \longrightarrow \underset{\text{(Carbon dioxide)}}{6CO_2} + \underset{\text{(Water)}}{6H_2O} + \text{Energy}$$

(Aerobic condition)

$$\underset{\text{(Glucose)}}{C_6H_{12}O_6} \longrightarrow \underset{\text{(Ethyl alcohol)}}{2\,C_2H_5OH} + \underset{\text{(Carbon dioxide)}}{2\,CO_2} + \text{Energy}$$

(Anaerobic condition)

Combustion (Burning) vs Respiration

Combustion is the process of burning of substances like coal, wood, oil, etc. which result in the production of light and heat. Respiration in the cell is also a **burning process** which produces energy (ATP).

ATP

The word 'ATP' stands for Adenosine Triphosphate and is also known as the **energy currency of the cell** because it is an immediate source of energy in a living cell. The energy released during the process of respiration is used to buildup an ATP molecule from ADP and inorganic phosphate (Pi). This can be summarised as the equation given below

$$ADP + Pi \xrightarrow{\text{Energy}} ATP$$

Some major differences between combustion and respiration are tabulated below.

Combustion/Burning	Respiration
It is a fast oxidation of organic compounds.	It is a slow oxidation of organic compounds.
There is quick release of energy in the form of light and heat.	There is slow release of energy in the form of ATP.
It always occurs outside the cell.	It is a cellular process, occurs in the cell.
It is a physiochemical process.	It is a biochemical process.

Combustion/Burning	Respiration
It does not involve any enzyme.	It involves enzyme action.
It occurs at high temperature (at ignition point).	It occurs at body temperature.
No intermediate compounds are formed.	Many intermediate compounds are formed.

Types of Respiration

Respiration can be of the following two types

1. Aerobic Respiration

It is the process of complete oxidation of glucose in the presence of oxygen (air) forming CO_2 and water as byproducts. It is an exothermic process, i.e. huge amount of energy is released.

Aerobic (or oxybiotic) respiration can be summarised as the equation given below.

$$\underset{\text{(6 carbon molecule)}}{C_6H_{12}O_6 \text{ (Glucose)}} \xrightarrow{\text{In cytoplasm}} \underset{\text{(3 carbon molecule)}}{\text{Pyruvate}} + \text{Energy}$$

$$\xrightarrow[\text{In mitochondria}]{\text{Oxygen}} 6CO_2 + 6H_2O + 38 \text{ ATP}$$

This process starts in the **cytoplasm** and continues in the **mitochondria** of the cell. Each glucose molecule releases 38 ATP molecules.

Water and carbon dioxide are produced as the waste byproducts. The energy released during this process is used for all other life processes.

The release of energy in aerobic process is a lot greater than in the anaerobic process.

Mechanism of Aerobic Respiration

This involves the oxidation of food (glucose) in many steps. These steps are as follows.

(i) **Glycolysis** It occurs in the cytoplasm of the cell and does not require oxygen. During this, glucose is broken down into 2 molecules of pyruvic acid in a series of enzyme controlled biochemical reactions.

Glycolysis is also a part of anaerobic reaction in which pyruvic acid is produced in the cytoplasm.

$$\text{1 molecule of glucose} \xrightarrow[\text{Occurs in cytoplasm}]{\text{Various enzymes}} \text{2 molecules of pyruvic acid}$$

(ii) **Formation of acetyl Co-A** The pyruvic acid (3-carbon compound) formed earlier gets converted to acetyl Co-A (2-carbon compound) in the cytoplasm.

Then, it enters into the mitochondria for further oxidation. It is a connecting link between glycolysis and Krebs' cycle.

(iii) **Krebs' cycle** This pathway was discovered in 1937 by Sir **Hans Krebs** and he was awarded Nobel Prize for this in 1953. It is also known as **Tricarboxylic Acid Cycle** (TCA).

Krebs' cycle is a catabolic reaction that oxidises acetyl Co-A and organic acid into CO_2 and H_2O. It occurs in mitochondria.

Significance of glycolysis and Krebs' cycle are as follows

(a) Both of these are major pathways for the formation of ATP molecules.

(b) Citric acid cycle plays a role in both oxidation (catabolic) and synthetic (anabolic) processes.

2. Anaerobic Respiration

It is a process that involves breakdown of complex food substances into simpler ones in the absence of oxygen. This process results in the release of small amount of energy. Anaerobic (or anoxybiotic) respiration in any part of plant (fruit and seeds) cannot continue for more than a few days and the part ultimately dies.

Mechanism of Anaerobic Respiration

It takes place in yeast, bacteria and in human muscles.

The anaerobic respiration produces only two ATP molecules for each glucose molecule and carbon dioxide is released during this process.

It is termed as **fermentation** in microorganisms and it is of following types on the basis of the product formed.

(i) **Alcoholic fermentation** It is the incomplete breakdown of sugar into ethanol and carbon dioxide to release energy. This process occurs mainly in yeast, which is used to produce beer, wine, toddy, cheese, etc., by brewing. It can be summarised as

$$\underset{\text{(6 carbon molecule)}}{\text{Glucose}} \xrightarrow{\text{In cytoplasm}} \underset{\text{(3 carbon molecule)}}{\text{Pyruvate}}$$

$$+ \text{Energy} \xrightarrow[\text{In yeast}]{\text{Absenceof oxygen}} \underset{\text{(2 Ethanol)}}{C_2H_5OH} + 2CO_2 + 2 \text{ ATP}$$

(ii) **Lactic acid fermentation** It is the process of incomplete breakdown of sugar into lactic acid and energy in some bacteria, e.g. in yoghurt making, some bacteria cause milk to turn sour.

$$\underset{\text{(6 carbon molecule)}}{\text{Glucose}} \longrightarrow \underset{\text{(3 carbon molecule)}}{\text{Pyruvate}} + \text{Energy}$$

$$\xrightarrow[\text{In muscle cells}]{\text{Lack of oxygen}} \underset{\text{(3 carbon molecule)}}{\text{2 Lactic acid}} + 2\text{ ATP}$$

Note **Metabolism** It is the sum of all chemical reactions within the body. These reactions could be synthesising reactions (anabolic) or breaking down (catabolic) reactions, e.g. photosynthesis (anabolic) and respiration (catabolic).

Differences between photosynthesis and respiration are as follows

Photosynthesis	Respiration
It occurs only in green plants.	It occurs in all living cells.
It takes place in the presence of light only.	It is a continuous process independent of light.
Reactants are CO_2 and H_2O.	Reactants are glucose and oxygen.
O_2 is given out.	CO_2 is given out.
It is anabolic process.	It is catabolic process.
$6CO_2 + 12H_2O \xrightarrow[\text{Chlorophyll}]{\text{Light}} C_6H_{12}O_6 + 6H_2O + 6O_2$	$C_6H_{12}O_6 + 6O_2 \rightarrow 6CO_2 + 6H_2O + 38ATP$

Check Your LEARNING...

1. What is burning ?
2. Which compound is formed in first stage of aerobic respiration?
3. Which step of aerobic respiration is responsible for ATP formation?
4. Name the products formed by the breakdown of glucose anaerobically in yeast.
5. Define metabolism.

Experiments on Gaseous Exchange and Heat Production

Exchange of Gases in Plants

Plants do not have specialised organs for gaseous exchange like animals. Therefore, exchange of gases in them occurs differently through following parts

(i) **Roots** In plants, root hair helps in gaseous exchange. Also in mangrove plants, pores occur on roots, called **pneumatophores** (breathing pores). These roots are called **aerial roots**.

(ii) **Stem** Small pores called **lenticels** present on the stem also help in gaseous exchange.

(iii) **Leaves** Plant leaves are well-adapted for gaseous exchange. This occurs by a number of stomata present on their surface.

Note Roots of plants/trees are unable to respire in waterlogged conditions because of unavailability of O_2 in soil. This leads to death of roots and ultimately plants.

Experiment 1

Aim To demonstrate anaerobic respiration in germinating seeds.

Procedure Place few germinating gram seeds in a test tube. Pour mercury and fill it completely. Now place thumb on it and place it in a beaker filled with mercury in an inverted position. Make arrangements to keep the apparatus undisturbed for few days.

Observation After few days, the level of mercury falls in the test tube.

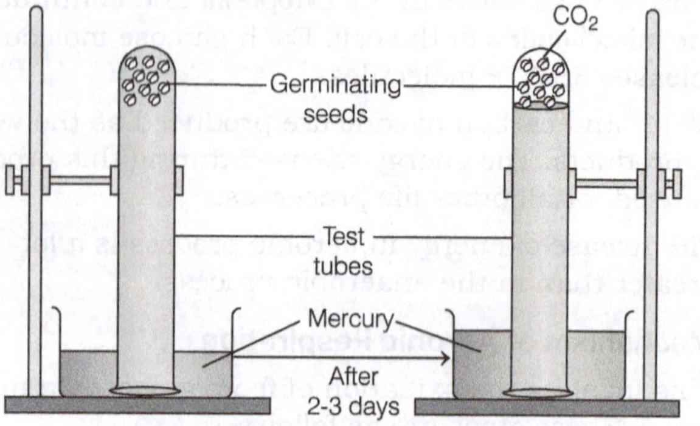

Demonstration of anaerobic respiration

Inference The level of mercury falls due to the presence of CO_2 gas released by germinating seeds. It exerts pressure on the mercury, thereby its level falls.

This can be proved by adding few KOH pellets in the tube, KOH will float up through mercury and on coming in contact with CO_2 it will absorb the gas and thus, the level of mercury will again rise.

Experiment 2

Aim To demonstrate that oxygen is used in respiration.

Procedure Take two test tubes A and B. Put some KOH solution in both. Now place germinating seeds in test tube A (supported by wire mesh) and heat-killed germinating seed in test tube B along with a disinfectant like formalin to avoid bacterial decay. Connect both test tubes A and B to a beaker containing coloured water.

The arrangement of experimental setup is done as shown in the figure.

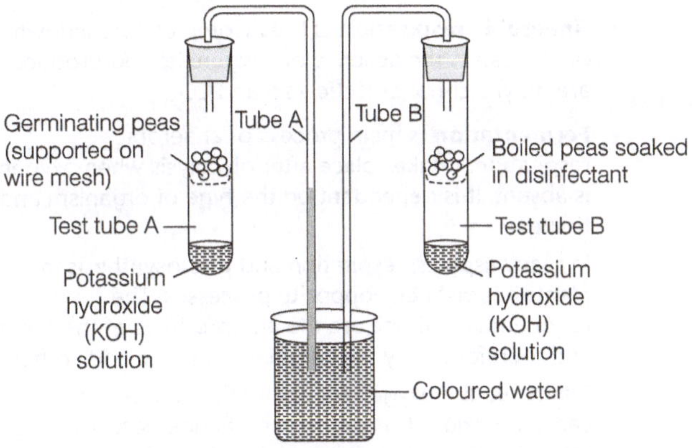

Experiment to demonstrate that oxygen is used up in respiration

Observation After few days, the coloured water rises up in tube A.

Inference The oxygen present in test tube A was used up by germinating seeds and CO_2 was produced. In turn, CO_2 produced by germinating seeds was absorbed by KOH, so vacuum was created in system A. This results in rise of water level in tube A. System B did not show this because seeds were boiled and killed.

Test tube B worked as a control as it did not show any rise in water level.

Experiment 3

Aim To prove that heat is produced during respiration.

Procedure Put germinating gram seeds in thermoflask A and germinated boiled seeds in thermoflask B. Place thermometer in both the flasks after plugging the mouth of both the flasks with cotton. Keep this setup undisturbed for few hours and record any change in temperature.

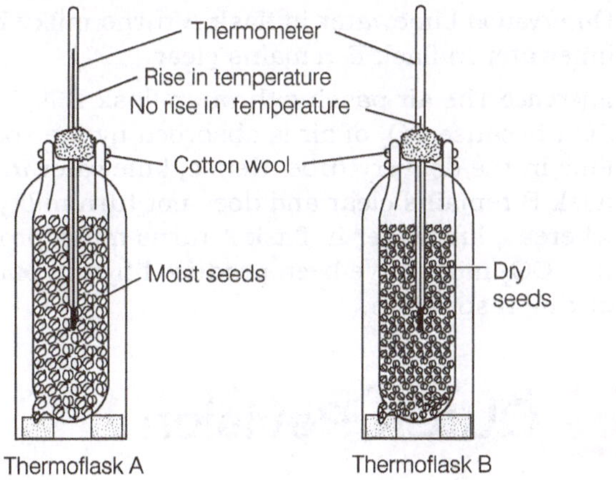

Experimental setup to demonstrate that heat is produced during respiration

Observation There is rise in temperature in flask A but not in flask B.

Inference The rise in temperature in thermoflask A occur because germinating live seeds respire and produce heat, whereas in flask B seeds are killed because of boiling. So, these are not respiring thus, no heat is produced.

Experiment 4

Aim To prove that carbon dioxide is produced by green plants during respiration.

Procedure Place a potted plant and cover it with the help of a bell jar. Apply vaseline on the rims of bell jar to make it airtight. Connect this bell jar with the two conical flasks A and B containing clear lime water with delivery tubes.

Insert one delivery tube in each flask with one side open towards outside. Add soda lime in the delivery tube of flask B.

Keep the setup in a dark room or cover the bell jar with a black cloth to prevent O_2 release.

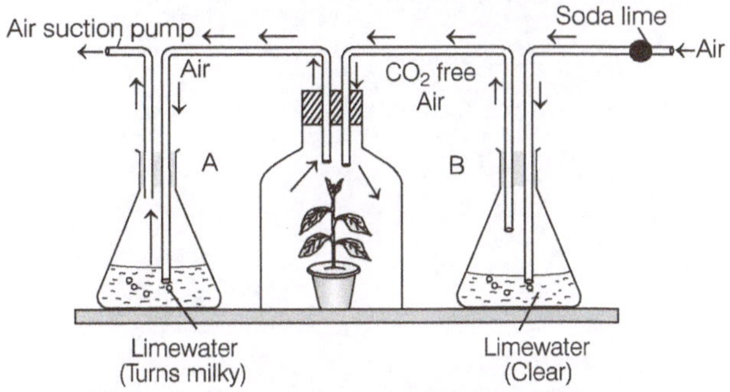

Experiment to show that carbon dioxide is produced by green plants during respiration

Observation Limewater in flask A turns milky but limewater in flask B remains clear.

Inference The air passing through flask B is free of CO_2, because CO_2 of air is absorbed by the soda lime in the delivery tube. Hence, limewater in flask B remains clear and does not turn milky, whereas, limewater in flask A turns milky proving that CO_2 must have been produced by the plant during respiration.

Check Your LEARNING...

1 Name the structure responsible for gaseous exchange in leaves of plants.
2 Which gas is produced during seed germination?
3 Does boiled peas also carryout respiration?
4 Is heat produced during respiration in plants?
5 What happens to limewater when it comes in contact with CO_2?

QUiCK Revision

- **Respiration** is defined as the process of stepwise oxidation of glucose in the living cells to release energy. It can be **aerobic** or **anaerobic**. Sometimes, respiration is compared with burning such as burning of coal. Both liberate energy and both give the end products CO_2 and water.
- **ATP** (Adenosine Triphosphate) is the chemical energy released during respiration.
- **Aerobic respiration** is the complete breakdown of glucose in the presence of oxygen. Its end products are CO_2, H_2O and energy.
- **Glycolysis** is an oxidative process in which glucose is converted into pyruvic acid and it is common in both aerobic and anaerobic respiration.
- **Krebs' cycle** occurs in mitochondria. It is a pathway in cellular respiration resulting in interconversion of molecules to release energy ATP.
- **Anaerobic respiration** is the incomplete breakdown of glucose in the absence of oxygen. Its end products are ethyl alcohol or lactic acid and CO_2.
- **Fermentation** is main process of anaerobic respiration. It takes place after glycolysis when oxygen is absent. It is dependent on the type of organism and tissue.
- In many aspects, respiration and photosynthesis in plants are distinctly opposite processes. The requirements of one are the end products of the other and therefore, they are complementary to each other.
- Plants require oxygen for respiration and release carbon dioxide. This gaseous exchange occurs through stomata, lenticels and general surface of root by diffusion.

Chapter Practice

Section-I

1 Mark Questions

1. Name the following.
   (i) A chain of chemical reactions that enable all living organisms to synthesise energy.
   (ii) A respiratory substrate other than glucose.
   (iii) Energy currency of the cell.
   (iv) Physiochemical process that does not require any enzyme.
   (v) Product obtained from the breakdown of glucose.
   (vi) Organisms in which alcoholic fermentation takes place.
   (vii) Organism that can live without oxygen.
   (viii) Partial oxidation of glucose in the absence of oxygen producing ethyl alcohol or lactic acid.
   (ix) A microorganism that produces lactic acid on fermentation.

Ans. (i) Respiration
(ii) Proteins
(iii) ATP (Adenosine Triphosphate)
(iv) Combustion
(v) Pyruvate
(vi) Yeast
(vii) Yeast
(viii) Fermentation
(ix) Bacteria

2. Correct and rewrite the following statements by changing the underlined words.
   (i) Energy obtained for life activities in an organism is obtained by <u>nutrition</u>.
   (ii) Respiratory gases undergo <u>osmosis</u> to move from one place to the other.
   (iii) Conversion of glucose to pyruvate occurs in the <u>nucleus</u> of a cell.
   (iv) Energy released in aerobic process is <u>equal</u> to that in anaerobic process.
   (v) Mangrove plants have pores occurring on their roots, called <u>lenticels</u>.

Ans. (i) Energy obtained for life activities in an organism is obtained by respiration.
(ii) Respiratory gases undergo diffusion to move from one place to the other.
(iii) Conversion of glucose to pyruvate occurs in the cytoplasm of a cell.
(iv) Energy released in aerobic process is much higher than that in anaerobic process.
(v) Mangrove plants have pores occurring on their roots, called pneumatophores.

3. Give biological reasons for the following.
   (i) Most of the organisms cannot survive without oxygen.
   (ii) Respiration is called energy releasing process.
   (iii) Glycolysis is considered as an important stage of respiration.

Ans. (i) Most of the organisms require oxygen for cellular respiration in order to produce energy and to carry out vital metabolic activities.
(ii) Respiration involves the breakdown of complex molecules (glucose) into simple ones (carbohydrates) with the release of a huge amount of energy. Thus, it is called an energy releasing process.
(iii) Glycolysis is considered as an important stage of respiration because it is a common process that occurs in both aerobic and anaerobic respiration.

4. (i) Match the following columns.

Column I	Column II
A. Lactic acid	1. Mitochondria
B. Ethyl alcohol	2. Yeast
C. Krebs' cycle	3. Energy currency
D. ATP	4. Muscle

(ii) Match the following columns.

Column I	Column II
A. Catabolism	1. Synthesis of molecules
B. Glucose	2. End product of glycolysis
C. Anabolism	3. Food substrate
D. Pyruvic acid	4. Breaking down reaction

(iii) Match the following columns.

Column I	Column II
A. Anaerobic respiration	1. Lime water
B. Lenticels	2. Fermentation
C. CO_2	3. Bark of old trees
D. Glycolysis	4. Cytoplasm

Ans. (i) A-4, B-2, C-1, D-3
(ii) A-4, B-3, C-1, D-2
(iii) A-2, B-3, C-1, D-4

5. Choose the correct answer from the four options given below.

(i) Respiration may be defined as
(a) exchange of oxygen in the tissue
(b) the oxidation of food substances to release energy
(c) the building up (synthesis) of complex substances
(d) getting rid of carbon dioxide that would accumulate in the tissue

Ans. (b)

(ii) Respiration is
(a) anabolic process
(b) catabolic process
(c) occurs when energy is required
(d) performed at intervals

Ans. (b)

(iii) The difference between respiration and combustion is related to the fact that respiration being
(a) multistep (b) enzyme controlled
(c) intracellular (d) All of these

Ans. (d)

(iv) The net gain of energy from 1 gram mole of glucose during aerobic respiration is
(a) 2 ATP (b) 4 ATP
(c) 38 ATP (d) 40 ATP

Ans. (c)

(v) The different steps of aerobic respiration are
(a) glycolysis and terminal oxidation
(b) glycolysis and Krebs' cycle
(c) glycolysis, Krebs' cycle and terminal oxidation
(d) Krebs' cycle and terminal oxidation

Ans. (c)

(vi) Which of the following is an end product of glycolysis?
(a) Pyruvic acid (b) $C_6H_{12}O_6$
(c) Oxygen (d) None of these

Ans. (a)

(vii) Respiration can occur in the absence of oxygen in
(a) potato (b) grass
(c) yeast (d) cockroach

Ans. (c)

(viii) Which of the following statements is correct?
(a) Pyruvate can be converted into ethanol and carbon dioxide by yeast
(b) Fermentation takes place in case of aerobic bacteria
(c) Fermentation takes place in mitochondria
(d) Fermentation is a form of anaerobic respiration

Ans. (d)

6. Fill in the blanks by using suitable words.
(i) Enzymes take part in ......, while no enzymes are involved in ....
(ii) During respiration, ... energy is used to produces ATP.
(iii) The byproducts of normal respiration are ...... and ....
(iv) The energy currency of a cell is ....
(v) The first phase of respiration is ....
(vi) The site of glycolysis is ....
(vii) Lack of oxygen in muscles often leads to cramps in the legs of sprinters. This is due to conversion of pyruvate to ....
(viii) The roots respire through ....
(ix) .... are the opening present on the stem (barks) of old trees that help in respiration.
(x) Germinating seeds need ...... for respiration.

Ans. (i) respiration, combustion
(ii) chemical (iii) CO_2, water
(iv) ATP (v) glycolysis
(vi) cytoplasm (vii) lactic acid
(viii) root hair (ix) Lenticels
(x) O_2

7. Choose the odd one out from the following terms given below and name the category to which other three belong.
(i) Fructose, Pure proteins, Glucose, Sucrose
(ii) Glucose, H_2O, CO_2, Energy
(iii) Oxygen, CO_2, Ethanol, Lactic acid

Ans. (i) **Odd term** Pure protein.
Rest three are carbohydrates preferred as primary respiratory substrates.
(ii) **Odd term** Glucose
Rest three are the products of aerobic respiration.
(iii) **Odd term** Oxygen.
Rest three are the products of anaerobic respiration.

8. Expand the following biological abbreviations.
(i) ATP (ii) Pi
(ii) TCA

Ans. (i) Adenosine Triphosphate
(ii) Inorganic Phosphate
(iii) Tricarboxylic Acid

9. State whether the following statements are true or false. Correct and rewrite the false statements.
(i) Respiration takes place in living cells.
(ii) Oxygen is released in respiration.
(iii) Site of respiration is ribosomes in plants.
(iv) Respiration is faster than combustion.
(v) Aerobic respiration can occur even in the absence of O_2.
(vi) A common phase of aerobic and anaerobic respiration is Krebs' cycle.

(vii) Anaerobic respiration occurs in the muscle cells of humans.
(viii) Fermentation occurs in muscles of animals.
(ix) In plants, gaseous exchange occurs through stomata.

Ans. (i) True
(ii) False, oxygen is not released during respiration.
(iii) False, site of respiration is stomata in case of plants.
(iv) False, respiration occurs at a slower rate than combustion.
(v) False, aerobic respiration takes place only in the presence of oxygen.
(vi) False, glycolysis is common to both aerobic and anaerobic respirations.
(vii) True
(viii) True
(ix) True

10. State the exact location of the following.
(i) Glycolysis (ii) Alcoholic fermentation
(iii) Pneumatophores (iv) Lenticles

Ans. (i) Glycolysis occurs in the cytoplasm of a cell.
(ii) Alcoholic fermentation in the yeast cell.
(iii) Pneumatophores are found in the roots of mangrove plants.
(iv) Lenticles are found on the stem of plants.

11. Give one example of the following.
(i) Organic substance which undergoes oxidative breakdown during respiration.
(ii) A substance that burns to produce high amount of heat and light.
(iii) 3-carbon molecule formed after breakdown of glucose.
(iv) Product obtained after sugar breaks down anaerobically.

Ans. (i) Glucose (ii) Coal
(iii) Pyruvate (iv) Ethanol

12. State the main function of the following.
(i) Yeast (ii) Stomata

Ans. (i) Yeast is used in the production of beer, toddy cheese, etc., as it undergoes alcoholic fermentation.
(ii) Stomata are tiny pores present on the leaf surface. They help in gaseous exchange during respiration.

13. Mention one difference in each of the following pairs on the basis of what is given in the bracket.
(i) Combustion and Respiration (enzyme involvement)
(ii) Respiration and Burning (intermediate products)
(iii) Anaerobic respiration and Fermentation (organisms involved)
(iv) Aerobic and Anaerobic respiration (end products)
(v) Photosynthesis and Respiration (occurrence)

Ans. (i) Difference between combustion and respiration is as follows

Combustion	Respiration
This process does not involve any enzyme.	This process involves enzyme action.

(ii) Difference between respiration and burning is as follows

Respiration	Burning
Several intermediate compounds are formed.	No intermediate compound is formed.

(iii) Difference between anaerobic respiration and fermentation is as follows

Anaerobic respiration	Fermentation
It occurs in the muscles of animals and bacteria.	It occurs in microorganisms like yeast.

(iv) Difference between aerobic respiration and anaerobic respiration is as follows

Aerobic respiration	Anaerobic respiration
End products are CO_2 and water.	End products are CO_2 and ethyl alcohol (plants) and CO_2 and lactic acid (animals).

(v) Difference between photosynthesis and respiration is as follows

Photosynthesis	Respiration
It occurs in green cells containing chlorophyll.	It occurs in all living cells.

14. Briefly explain the following terms.
(i) Combustion
(ii) Aerobic respiration
(iii) Lenticels

Ans. (i) Combustion is the process of burning of substances in the presence of O_2 resulting in the production of heat and light.
(ii) Aerobic respiration is an exothermic process of complete oxidation of glucose in the presence of oxygen (air) forming CO_2 and water as by products.
(iii) Lenticels are small pores which are present on the stem and aid in gaseous exchange.

15. Give biological/scientific terms for the following.
(i) Slow oxidation of organic compound.
(ii) Oxygen dependent, complete breakdown of respiratory substrates that yield a lot of energy.
(iii) Incomplete breakdown of sugar into ethanol and carbon dioxide.
(iv) An anabolic process that gives out oxygen.

Ans. (i) Respiration
(ii) Aerobic respiration
(iii) Alcoholic fermentation
(iv) Photosynthesis

16. Answer the following questions briefly.
(i) What happens to the energy released in respiration?
(ii) Write an equation of aerobic respiration in plants.
(iii) What are the different phases of aerobic respiration?
(iv) What is acetyl Co-A?
(v) How is tilling of soil useful for the crops?
(vi) Do all cells use oxygen to produce energy?

Ans. (i) Energy released in respiration is stored as ATP in mitochondria and later used for various metabolic activities in body.

(ii) $\underset{\text{(Glucose)}}{C_6H_{12}O_6} + \underset{\text{(Oxygen)}}{6\,O_2} \rightarrow \underset{\text{(Carbon dioxide)}}{6\,CO_2} + \underset{\text{(Water)}}{6\,H_2O} + \underset{\text{(Energy)}}{38\text{ ATP}}$

(iii) The different phases are glycolysis, Krebs' cycle and terminal oxidation.

(iv) Acetyl Co-A is a two carbon compound which acts a chemical intermediate between glycolysis and Krebs' cycle.

(v) Tilling of soil is useful for the crops as it helps in enhancing the porosity of the soil and makes it airy so that the underground parts of the plants gets sufficient oxygen.

(vi) No, cells do not always require oxygen to produce energy. For example, in muscle cells, energy is produced anaerobically is in the absence of oxygen.

2 Marks Questions

17. What are the two products obtained after anaerobic respiration?

Ans. The two products obtained after anaerobic respiration are ethyl alcohol and CO_2.

18. Anaerobic respiration is less efficient. Comment.

Ans. Anaerobic respiration involves the breakdown of glucose into simpler substances in conditions devoid of oxygen, i.e. it is an incomplete breakdown of glucose and thus it produces less energy. So, it is less efficient.

19. What is the similarity between aerobic and anaerobic respiration?

Ans. The two similarities between aerobic and anaerobic respiration are as
(a) Both use the same substrate, i.e. glucose for respiration.
(b) Both release energy.

3 Marks Questions

20. When a substrate is being metabolised, why does not all the energy that is produced get released in one step? It is released in multiple steps. What is the advantages of stepwise release?

Ans. The stepwise release of energy is advantageous to the cell because if all the energy from the glucose is released at once, most of it would be lost in the form of light and heat.

This energy is trapped in ATP which is utilised in various energy requiring processes of the organisms and for the synthesis of other biomolecules in the cell.

21. Write a short note on anaerobic respiration.

Ans. Anaerobic respiration is the incomplete breakdown of glucose into simpler substances in the absence of oxygen. This takes place in yeast, bacteria and human muscles.

It is termed as fermentation in microorganisms and is of two types

- **Alcoholic fermentation** In this, sugar breaks down into ethanol and CO_2 to release energy.
- **Lactic acid fermentation** It is the process of incomplete breakdown of sugar into lactic acid and energy.

Section-II [5 Marks]

Structured Questions

1. Energy required to perform various metabolic activities in the body comes from a vital process.
(i) Name the process responsible for providing energy as per above statement.
(ii) How is above process categorised?
(iii) How is energy liberated after the process?
(iv) How many molecules of ATP are released after oxidation of one molecule of glucose?
(v) Do enzymes play a role in the process?

Ans. (i) Respiration is the process responsible for providing energy.
(ii) The above process is categorised as aerobic and anaerobic.
(iii) Energy liberated after respiration can be in the form of heat and majority of it is also converted to chemical form, i.e. ATP.
(iv) 38 molecules of ATP are released after oxidation of one molecule of glucose.
(v) Yes, each breakdown step involves a particular enzyme.

2. The given figure represents an experimental setup.

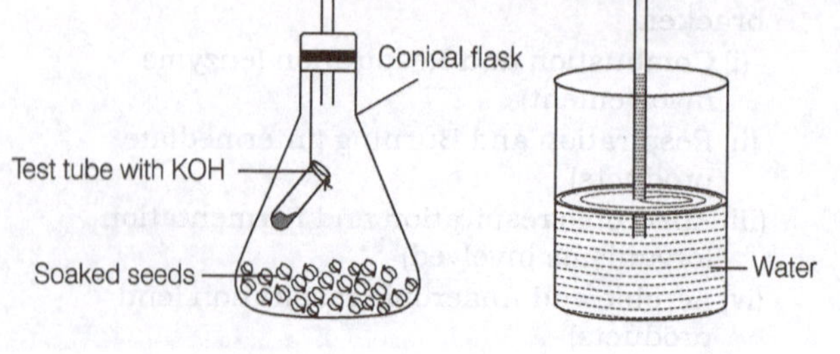

(i) What is the aim of the experiment?
(ii) Why has the water in the tube been risen?
(iii) What is the purpose of KOH?
(iv) Is there any control for this experiment? If so, mention it.
(v) What precaution should be taken for this experiment?

Ans. (i) The aim of the experiment is to show that respiration takes place in germinating seeds.
(ii) Seeds use oxygen for respiration which creates a vacuum in the tube and water level rises.
(iii) To absorb CO_2 released by the seeds.
(iv) Yes, take another conical flask with boiled seeds.
(v) The flask should be airtight.

3. To study and prove a particular physiological process in plants, the following experiment was setup.

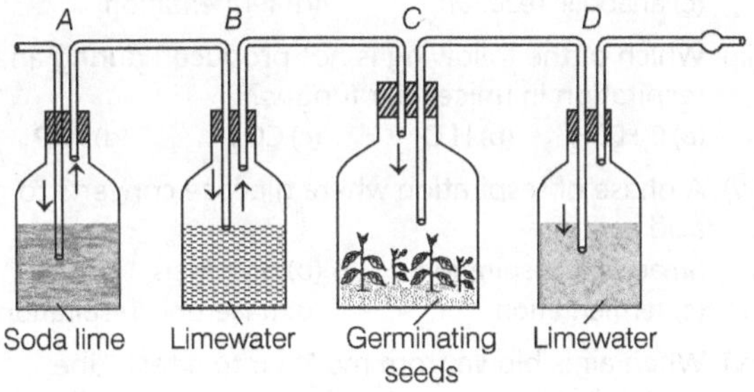

(i) Name the physiological process being studied.
(ii) What is the purpose of using soda lime in the bottle *A* and why is limewater placed in bottle *B*?
(iii) Would there be any change taking place in bottle *D*?
(iv) Represent the physiological process named in ques (i) above in the form of a chemical equation.
(v) If bottle *C* is fitted with a 3 holed rubber stopper and a thermometer was introduced in such a way that its bulb reaches close to the germinating seeds, what would you observe. Why?

Ans. (i) The physiological process being studied is aerobic respiration.
(ii) Soda lime in bottle *A* is used to remove the carbon dioxide from the incoming air. Limewater is placed in bottle *B* to ensure that all the CO_2 present in the air has been absorbed/air entering the bottle *C* is free from CO_2.
(iii) Limewater turns milky.
(iv) $C_6H_{12}O_6 + 6O_2 \rightarrow 6CO_2 + 6H_2O$ + Energy
(v) Temperature would rise proving that heat is produced during respiration.

Chapter Assessment

Section-I

1 Mark Questions

1. Name the following.
   (i) A catabolic process in which energy is released by breakdown of complex compounds during conversion into simpler ones.
   (ii) Waste products obtained as a result of aerobic respiration.
   (iii) Process of conversion of glucose to pyruvate.
   (iv) A process that occurs only in chlorophyllous cells resulting in formation of energy.
   (v) Chemical used to absorb CO_2 in respiratory experiment.
2. Correct and rewrite the following statements by changing the underlined words.
   (i) Digestion involves oxidation of nutrients to produce energy.
   (ii) Some organisms use oxygen to partially breakdown glucose into CO_2 and water.
   (iii) Respiration occurs in the cell to yield energy in the form of ADP .
   (iv) ATP stands for Adenosine Tetraphosphate.
   (v) Reactants for respiration are CO_2 and H_2O.
3. Give biological reasons for the following.
   (i) Pneumatophores are also called breathing pores.
   (ii) Roots of plants/trees fail to respire in water-logged conditions.
4. (i) Match the following columns.

	Column I		Column II
A.	Stomata	1.	Aerial roots
B.	Storehouse of energy	2.	Pyruvate
C.	Glycolysis	3.	Mitochondria
D.	Pneumatophores	4.	Leaves

   (ii) Match the following columns.

	Column I		Column II
A.	Burning	1.	Catabolic process
B.	Carbon dioxide	2.	Quick release of energy
C.	Respiration	3.	End product of respiration
D.	Photosynthesis	4.	Anabolic process

5. Choose the correct answer from the four options given below.
   (i) For the start of respiration, a living cell requires
   (a) glucose (b) glucose and oxygen
   (c) oxygen (d) glucose and ATP
   (ii) Anaerobic respiration is also called
   (a) complete oxidation (b) incomplete oxidation
   (c) anabolic reaction (d) fermentation
   (iii) Which of the following is not produced during anaerobic respiration in unicellular fungus?
   (a) C_2H_5OH (b) H_2O (c) CO_2 (d) ATP
   (iv) A phase of respiration where glucose converts to pyruvic acid is
   (a) aerobic respiration (b) glycolysis
   (c) fermentation (d) anaerobic respiration
   (v) When air is blown from mouth into a test tube containing limewater, the limewater turns milky due to the presence of
   (a) oxygen (b) carbon dioxide
   (c) nitrogen (d) water vapour
6. Fill in the blanks by using words.
   (i) During respiration, energy is released in the form of a chemical called ....
   (ii) Breathing roots are characteristics of plants growing in ...... areas.
   (iii) In young roots, the exchange of gases occurs between root hairs and ....
   (iv) During germination of seed, the gas produced is ....
   (v) In a young plant body, ... pores in epidermis helps in exchange of gases, whereas in a woody plant body, ... are the pores for exchange of gases.
7. State whether the statements are true or false. Correct and rewrite the false statements.
   (i) Anaerobic respiration produces large amount of energy.
   (ii) Aerobic respiration occurs in germinating seeds.
   (iii) Respiration is slower than combustion.
   (iv) Respiration can occur only in light.
   (v) There are certain bacteria which are completely anaerobic.
   (vi) Site of Krebs' cycle is mitochondria.

8. State the exact location of the following.
   (i) Tricarboxylic Acid Cycle
   (ii) Formation of Acetyl Co-A
   (iii) Lactic Acid Fermentation
9. Give one example of the following.
   A plant with pneumatophores.
10. State the main function of the following
   (i). Respiration (process)
   (ii) Bacteria (in lactic acid fermentation)
11. Mention one difference in each of the following pairs on the basis of what is given in the bracket.
   (i) Combustion and Respiration (release of energy)
   (ii) Burning and Respiration (temperature)
   (iii) Photosynthesis and Respiration (end product)
12. Give biological/technical terms for the following.
   (i) Organic substances which undergo oxidative breakdown during respiration.
   (ii) Connecting link between glycolysis and TCA.
13. Briefly explain the following terms.
   (i) Anaerobic respiration (ii) Fermentation
14. Answer the following questions briefly.
   (i) How does respiration differs from burning?
   (ii) Write an equation for aerobic respiration in plants.
   (iii) Write the chemical equation for anaerobic respiration.
   (iv) What common function is performed by stomata and lenticels?

2 Marks Questions

15. Respiration is a catabolic process. Comment.
16. Write a short note on ATP.

3 Marks Question

17. State the mechanism of aerobic respiration.

Section-II [5 Marks]

Structured Questions

18. Krebs' cycle is a catabolic reaction that occurs in mitochondria and carries out oxidation of acetyl Co-A and organic acid to CO_2 and H_2O.
   (i) State the other name for Krebs' cycle.
   (ii) What is the intermediate product formed prior to this process?
   (iii) Which form of energy conversion takes place in the cycle?
   (iv) How does it differ from glycolysis?
   (v) What is the significance of the process?
19. Given below is an experimental set up done by a candidate, to study the process of respiration in plants. The candidate failed to get the expected results, as two mistakes were made while setting up the experiment.

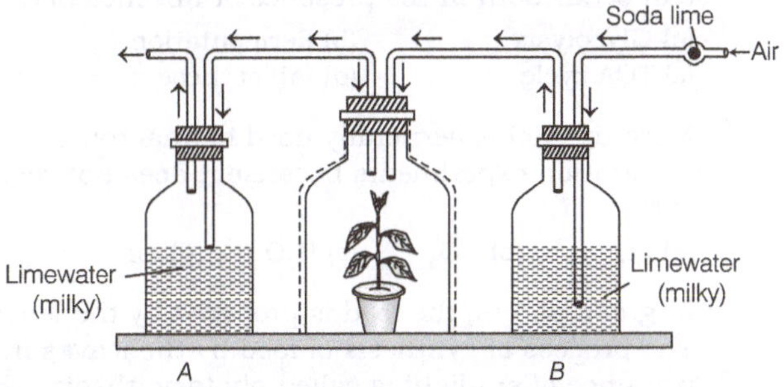

   (i) Identify and state one mistake made by the candidate.
   (ii) What is the role of soda lime in the experiment?
   (iii) What is the purpose of using limewater in flask A and B?
   (iv) Write the chemical equation to represent the process of respiration.
   (v) Why is vaseline applied on the rims of bell jar?

For explanations scan the given QR Code

Olympiad Section*

Brain Teasing Questions asked in Previous Olympiads

1 During aerobic respiration, energy is released in stepwise manner and ATP formation takes place with the help of this energy. What will happen if this energy is released at a single step instead of in parts? **[INJSO, 2010]**

(a) Incomplete oxidation of glucose takes place
(b) All the amount of energy can be utilised by the cell as more ATP molecules are produced
(c) maximum amount of this released energy is wasted in form of heat and cell may die
(d) Cell will follow anaerobic pathway of respiration

2 Which of the following cellular metabolic processes can occur both in the presence or absence of O_2?

(a) Glycolysis (b) Fermentation
(c) TCA cycle (d) All of these

3 Mercury (Hg) is gernerally used in anaerobic respiration experiments because it does not react with

(a) O_2 (b) CO_2 (c) H_2O (d) air

4 In green plants, the food is prepared by the leaves. The process of synthesis of food by the leaves in the presence of sunlight is called photosynthesis. The immediate product of photosynthesis is ....

(a) starch (b) protein
(c) glucose (d) Either (a) or (b)

5 Photosynthesis equation

Carbon dioxide + Water $\xrightarrow{\text{Sunlight}}$ Sugar + Oxygen

$6CO_2$	$6H_2O$	$C_6H_{12}O_6$	$6O_2$

Examine the illustration of the photosynthesis equation. How does the equation relate to both photosynthesis or cellular respiration and what is the connection between the two processes?

(a) Photosynthesis utilises energy to build carbohydrates, while cellular respiration metabolises carbohydrates
(b) Photosynthesis utilises energy to metabolise carbohydrates, while cellular respiration builds carbohydrates
(c) Photosynthesis and cellular respiration both utilise carbon dioxide and water to produce carbohydrates
(d) Photosynthesis and cellular respiration both metabolise carbohydrates to produce carbon dioxide and water

6 The given experimental setup demonstrates

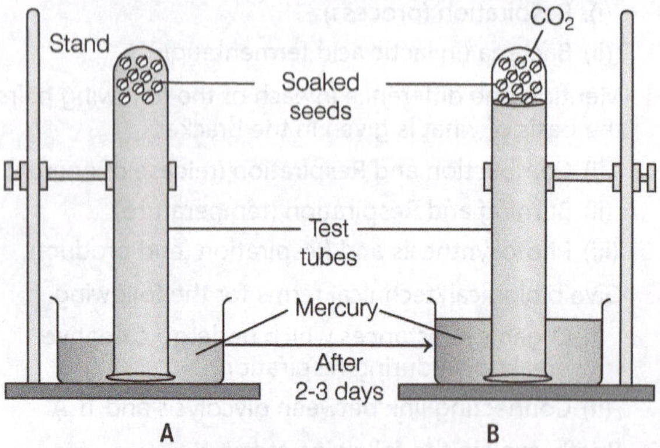

(a) photosynthesis
(b) aerobic respiration
(c) anaerobic respiration
(d) ascent of sap

7 What colour change is noticed when CO_2 is reacted with limewater?

(a) Limewater does not show any change in colour
(b) Limewater does not react with CO_2
(c) Limewater remains as such
(d) Limewater turns milky

8 In experiment on respiration, the seeds taken as control are boiled to avoid

(a) bacterial decay (b) release of O_2
(c) photosynthesis (d) reaction with KOH

9 Why there is slight increase in the level of water in the delivery tube of flask B in experiment to prove that oxygen is used up in respiration.

(a) O_2 was absorbed by KOH
(b) CO_2 was absorbed by KOH
(c) CO_2 was absorbed by boiled peas
(d) CO_2 was absorbed by germinating peas

10 Why germinating seeds are used in all the experiments of respiration instead of dry seeds?

(a) Germinating seeds are easy to handle
(b) Germinating seeds has faster rate of respiration than in dry seeds.
(c) Only germinating seeds can turn limewater milky
(d) Only germinating seeds respire aerobically

Answers

1. (c) **2.** (a) **3.** (b) **4.** (c) **5.** (a) **6.** (c) **7.** (d) **8.** (a) **9.** (b) **10.** (b)

*These questions may or may not be asked in the examination, have been given just for additional practice required for olympiads, scholarship exams etc. For detailed explanations refer Page No. 230.

CHAPTER 07

Diversity in Living Organisms

Chapter Inside

• Classification • Hierarchy of Classification • Types of Classification System • Kingdom-Plantae • Kingdom - Animalia

On Earth, there exists a large diversity of living organisms ranging from the massive blue whale of about 100 m to the microscopic bacteria, from transparent or colourless worms to the brightly coloured birds and flowers, from mosquitoes that live for few days to pine trees that survive for 100s of years. These variations amongst the living beings, which differentiate them from each other to a lesser or greater extent is known as **biological diversity** or **biodiversity**. The term biodiversity was coined by **Walter G Rosen** in 1986.

Classification

Greek scientist, **Aristotle** was earliest to attempt the scientific basis of classification. He used simple morphological characters to classify plants and animals. The method of arranging organisms into groups or sets on the basis of similarities and dissimilarities is called **classification**. It is based on characteristics, which occur in certain groups of organisms that makes them different from other groups.

Importance of classification is as follows

(i) It gives information regarding the existing diversity of plants and animals.

(ii) It makes the study of wide variety of organisms convenient.

(iii) It helps us to understand the pattern of evolution.

(iv) It forms the basis of the development of other biological sciences like ecology, biogeography, biochemistry and other disciplines of biology.

Note Binomial Nomenclature is a system of providing scientific names to organisms, each consisting of two words, first generic name (i.e. name of genus) and a second specific name (i.e. name of species).

Hierarchy of Classification

A system of arrangement for classification in which organisms are placed in order of logical sequence is called the **hierarchy**. A unit of classification of organisms which represents a definite category at any level of classification is called **taxon**, e.g. phylum.

Biologists, **Ernst Haeckel** (1894), **Robert Whittaker** (1969) and **Carl Woese** (1977) classified all organisms into broad categories called **kingdoms**.

Classification is done by naming the sub-groups at various levels as given in the scheme below

Kingdom
Phylum (for animals)/Division (for plants)
Class
Order
Family
Genus
Species

A brief idea of the taxonomic categories are given below

(i) **Species** Lowest taxonomic category capable of interbreeding to give birth to fertile offspring, e.g. *Domesticus* in *Felis domesticus* (house cat).

(ii) **Genus** It consists of closely related species and is ranked higher than species, e.g. dog and wolf are kept in the same genus–*Canis*.

(iii) **Family** Group of related genera having several common characters form a family, e.g. cat and lion belong to same family–Felidae.

(iv) **Order** Assemblage of a number of families having common characters make an order, e.g. tiger and wolf belong to the same order–Carnivora.

(v) **Class** Organisms of related order having similarity are placed together in a class, e.g. rats, camels and monkeys are all included in same class–Mammalia.

(vi) **Phylum** The different classes having some specific characters which are common in them are placed under the same phylum, e.g. phylum–Annelida.

(vii) **Kingdom** Highest category of taxonomic studies, consisting of set of distinguishing common characters. Under a kingdom, the organisms having same fundamental characteristics are grouped together, e.g. kingdom–Plantae and Animalia.

Note
- The science which deals with the identification, nomenclature and classification of organisms is called **taxonomy**.
- **Carolus Linnaeus** is known as the **Father of Taxonomy**.

Types of Classification System

Depending upon the types of system of classification, organisms are classified into various kingdoms.

Two Kingdom Classification

Linnaeus divided the living organisms into two kingdoms, i.e. Plantae (including all plants) and Animalia (including all animals). The two kingdom system of classification was accepted for a long time. However, some difficulties arose from this classification as several new living organisms had been discovered.

These are as follows

(i) Bacteria cannot be considered as a plant because they are prokaryotic organisms, some of them even possess flagella which help them to move.

(ii) Some single-celled organisms such as *Euglena* cannot be exclusively called plant or animal as they do not have chloroplasts (but have chlorophyll) like plants and a well defined mouth to feed like animals.

(iii) Fungi are also not plants as they neither have chlorophyll nor roots, stems or leaves.

So, the above three groups of organisms are now distinctly placed in the most accepted five kingdom system of classification.

Five Kingdom Classification

Whittaker classified organisms into five kingdoms on the basis of following three levels of organisation.

(i) Cell structure (prokaryotic or eukaryotic)

(ii) Modes and source of nutrition (autotrophic or heterotrophic)

(iii) Body organisation (unicellular or multicellular)

Five kingdom classification system of Whittaker is shown in flowchart below

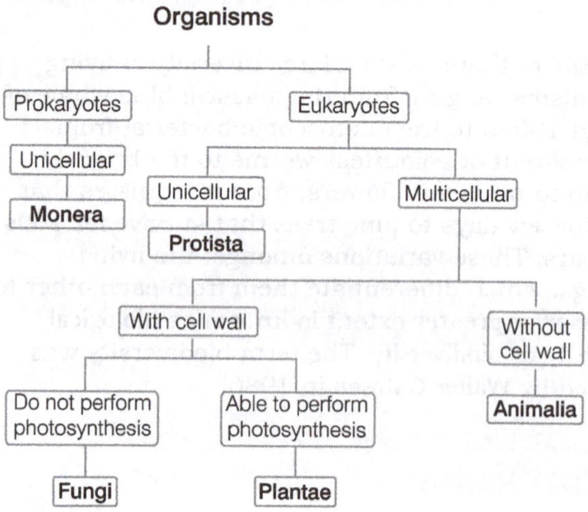

The important characteristics of these kingdoms are as follows

Kingdom–Monera

All unicellular and prokaryotic organisms are placed under kingdom–Monera.

Some common characteristics of kingdom–Monera are

(i) They are mostly single-celled.

(ii) Cell wall is normally present, which is made up of **murein or peptidoglycans** (other than cellulose) and motile flagellum is seen.

(iii) They have only one membrane called **plasma membrane** (cell membrane).

(iv) They do not have organised nucleus. It means the nuclear material (DNA) is distributed in the cell without being enclosed in a nuclear membrane. This condition of the cell is called **prokaryotic** (*pro*–primitive, *karyon*–nucleus).

(v) They lack all membrane bound cell organelles like mitochondria and chloroplast.

(vi) They may be either autotrophs (i.e. synthesise their own food) or heterotrophs (i.e. get their food from the environment).

(vii) They have three common shapes, i.e. rods, spirals and spheres. Also, they appear singly, in groups or in chains.
e.g. *Mycoplasma*, bacteria (*Escherichia coli*) and blue-green algae or cyanobacteria (*Anabaena* and *Nostoc*).

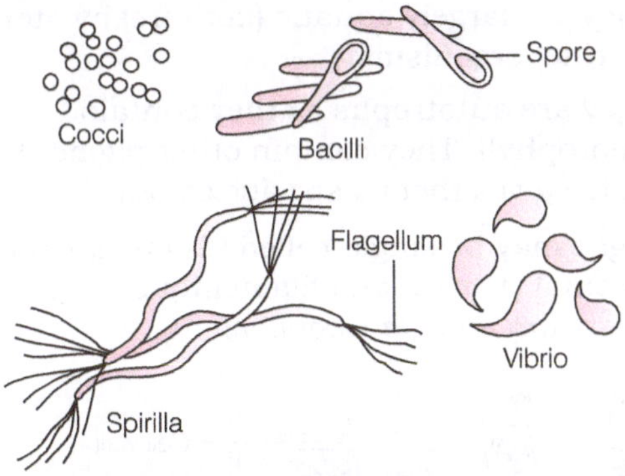

Bacteria of different shapes

Kingdom–Protista

All unicellular eukaryotes are placed under kingdom– Protista.

Some common characteristics of kingdom–Protista are

(i) They are unicellular (single-celled), as their body is not differentiated into cells.

(ii) Cell wall is generally absent, except in few of the members. The body is covered by cuticle or pellicle.

(iii) All membrane bound cell organelles are present.

(iv) They have a well-defined nucleus with a nuclear membrane. This condition of the cell is known as **Eukaryotic** (*Eu*–True, *karyon*–nucleus)

(v) Some of the members have pseudopodia, cilia or flagella as locomotory organelles.

(vi) They include both unicellular green autotrophic organisms (e.g. *Chlamydomonas*) as well as unicellular non-green heterotrophic organisms (e.g. *Euglena, Amoeba, Paramecium*).

Some multicellular photosynthetic plants like organisms such as *Pandorina* are also included in this kingdom.

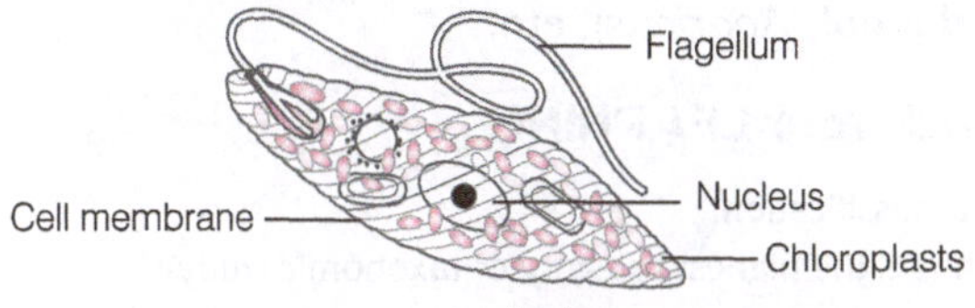

Euglena

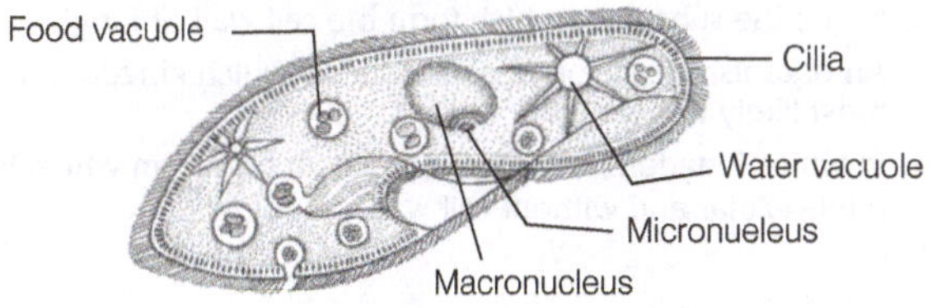

Paramecium

Kingdom–Fungi

It includes eukaryotic, multicellular, heterotrophic organisms. Some common characteristics of kingdom–Fungi are

(i) They are mostly filamentous (except yeasts, which are unicellular). Their bodies consist of long, slender, thread-like structures called **hyphae**. The network of hyphae is known as **mycelium**.

(ii) These hyphae are either multicellular or multinucleate (i.e. many nuclei distributed in the continuous cytoplasm).

(iii) The cell wall is made up of **chitin** and **polysaccharides**.

(iv) They are mostly heterotrophs and absorb soluble organic matter from dead substrates, hence also called **saprophytes**, e.g. *Mucor* and *Agaricus*.

(v) Some of these are parasites, e.g. *Puccinia, Albugo* and *Ustilago*.

(vi) They are achlorophyllous (i.e. lack chlorophyll in their cell).

(vii) They also live in symbiotic (mutually dependent) association with blue-green algae as **lichens** and with the roots of higher plants as **mycorrhiza**.

A mushroom

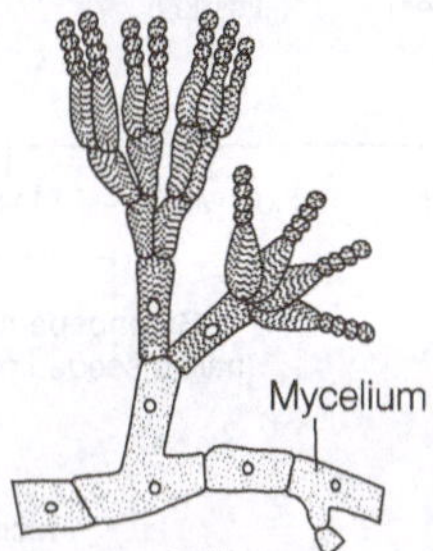

Penicillium

(viii) They appear like slow growing large coloured patches on the bark of trees, e.g. yeast, bread mould (*Rhizopus*), *Penicillium*, mushrooms (like toad stool, *Agaricus*), etc.

Check Your LEARNING...

1. Define classification.
2. Which is is the highest category of taxonomic study?
3. Name the kingdoms to which bacteria and Amoeba belongs.
4. Name the substance which form the cell wall of fungi.
5. An organism feeds on dead matter, to which kingdom it is most likely to belong.
6. In which kingdom, would you place an organism which is multicellular and without cell wall?

Kingdom–Plantae

It includes eukaryotic, multicellular and autotrophic (i.e. self-nourishing) organisms.

Some common characteristics of kingdom–Plantae are

(i) They have photosynthetic mode of nutrition (due to the presence of chlorophyll).

(ii) They grow indefinitely.

(iii) They show the presence of cellulosic cell wall.

(iv) Locomotion is absent except in some lower forms.

Depending on various characteristics, kingdom–Plantae is divided into Thallophyta, Bryophyta, Pteridophyta, Gymnosperms and Angiosperms, as shown in flowchart below

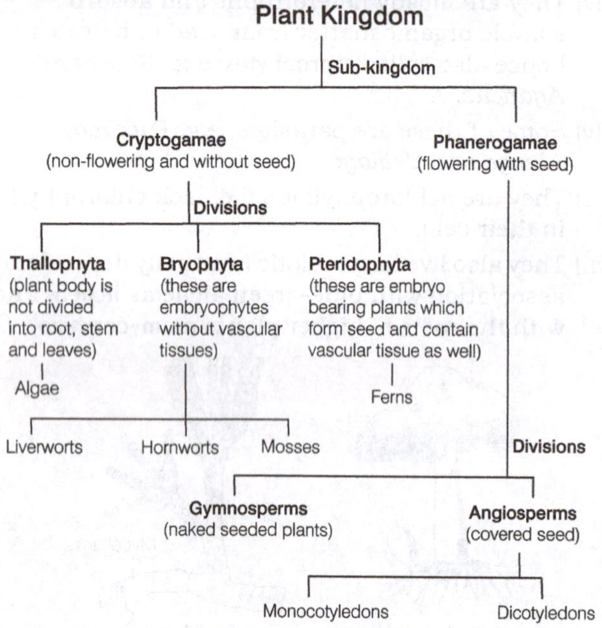

Cryptogamae

The thallophytes, bryophytes and pteridophytes do not have external flower or seeds and have naked embryo called **spores**.

These plants are called **cryptogams** because their reproductive organs are inconspicuous or hidden. It is further classified into following three divisions

Thallophyta

It includes algae as its representative organism.

Some common characteristics of thallophytes are

(i) They have **thallus-like** body, i.e. the plant body cannot be distinguished into roots, stems and leaves.

(ii) Their cell wall contains cellulose.

(iii) They are largely aquatic (both freshwater and marine) organisms.

(iv) They are autotrophs as they contain chlorophyll. They contain other pigments also which gives them a specific colour.

(v) Algae may be single-celled (*Chlamydomonas*), colonial (*Volvox*) and filamentous (*Ulothrix*, *Spirogyra* and *Oedogonium*).

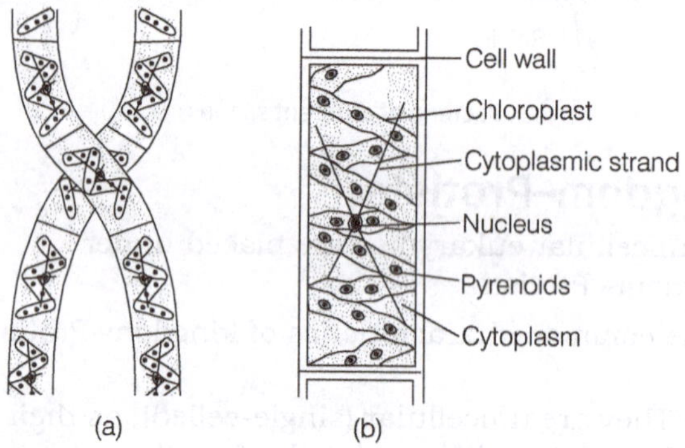

Spirogyra : (a) Two filaments, (b) Detailed structure of a cell

Bryophyta

The bryophytes include the various mosses and liverworts. Some common characteristics of bryophytes are

(i) The plant body is more differentiated than that of algae. They lack true roots, stems and leaves, but they may possess root-like, stem-like or leaf-like structures called **rhizoids**, **cauloid** and **phylloid**, respectively.

(ii) They usually occur in damp, humid and shaded localities. They are also called **'amphibians of plant kingdom'**.

(iii) However, there is no specialised tissue for the conduction of water and substance from one part of the plant body to another.

(iv) They reproduce usually by spore formation, e.g. *Riccia*, *Marchantia* (liverwort), *Funaria* (moss), *Sphagnum* (moss), etc.

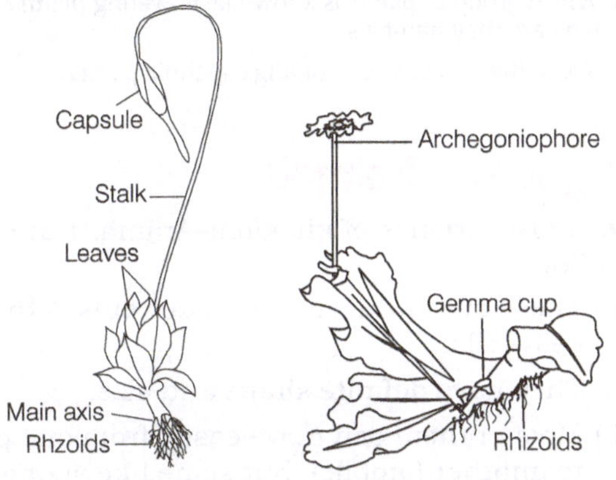

(a) *Funaria* (b) *Marchantia*

Pteridophyta

The pteridophytes include all the ferns.

Some common characteristics of pteridophytes are

(i) The plant body is differentiated into true root, stem and leaves and have specialised tissue for the conduction of water and other substances from one part of the plant body to another.

(ii) They usually occur in cool, damp, shady places, though some way flourish well in sandy soil condition.

(iii) The leaves are often made up of the leaflets bearing spores on the underside. Spores are the reproductive structures.

(iv) They are non-flowering plants, e.g. *Selaginella, Equisetum, Dryopteris,* ferns (*Marsilea*), *Adiantum*, etc.

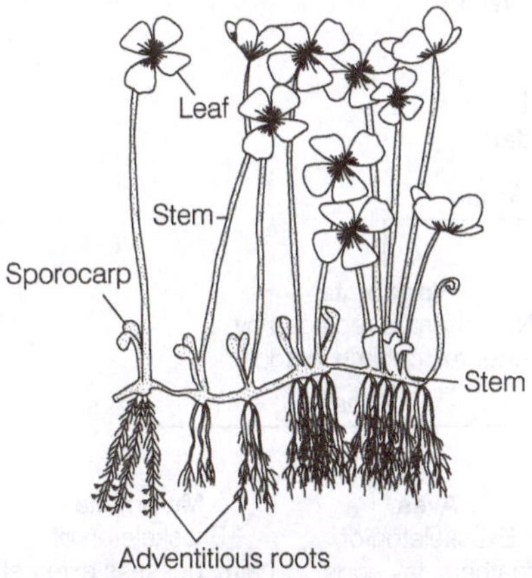

Marsilea

Phanerogamae

Some plants, which make seeds and have well-differentiated reproductive tissues are called **phanerogams**. These are also called as **spermatophytes**.

In these plants, seeds consist of embryo along with stored food. This stored food serves the purpose of initial growth of the embryo during germination.

On the basis of the presence or absence of naked seeds, these are divided into two groups.

- Gymnosperms
- Angiosperms

Gymnosperms

They include the woody plants with naked seeds. These plants are most primitive on Earth.

Some common characteristics of gymnosperms are

(i) The plant body is well-differentiated into root, stem and leaves.

(ii) They produce seeds but are not enclosed in fruits.

(iii) They bear seeds in structures called **cones**.

(iv) They bear both male and female cones containing pollen and ovules, respectively.

(v) They occur as woody trees, bushy shrubs or rarely as climbers.

(vi) They inhabit in the cold climates where snow, rather than rain, is the source of water, e.g. conifers (*Pinus*), etc. The only native gymnosperm which thrive in warmer areas are the cycads, e.g. *Cycas*.

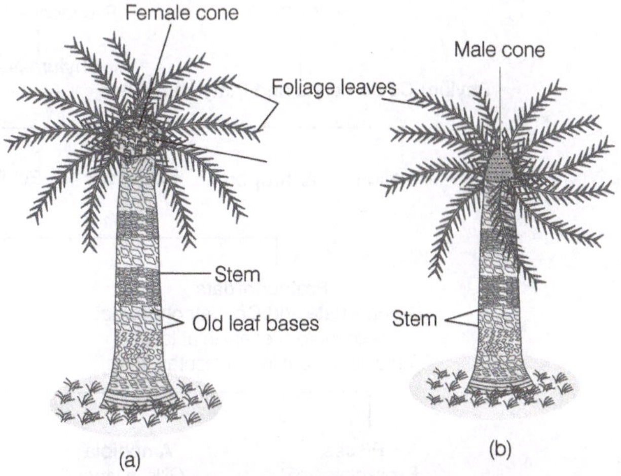

Cycas circinalis : (a) Female plant, (b) Male plant

Angiosperms

They include all the flowering plants.

The characteristics of angiosperms are as follows

(i) They produce seeds, flowers and fruits. Their seeds are enclosed inside the fruits.

(ii) They grow in almost every kind of habitat.

(iii) They reproduce sexually.

(iv) Plant embryo in seeds have structures called **cotyledons**. These cotyledons are called '**seed leaves**' because in many instances, they emerge and become green when the seed germinates. Thus, cotyledons represent a bit of pre-designed plant in the seed.

(v) They are mainly divided as **monocots** (with single cotyledon), e.g. cereals, maize, bamboo, sugarcane, etc., and **dicots** (with two cotyledons), e.g. hard wood trees, pulses, peas, spices, beverage crops, etc.

Differences between Monocot and Dicot

Monocot	Dicot
Have single cotyledon in seeds.	Have two cotyledons in seeds.
Leaves have parallel venation.	Leaves have reticulate venation.
Root system is fibrous.	Have tap root system.
Have weak stem.	Have strong stem.

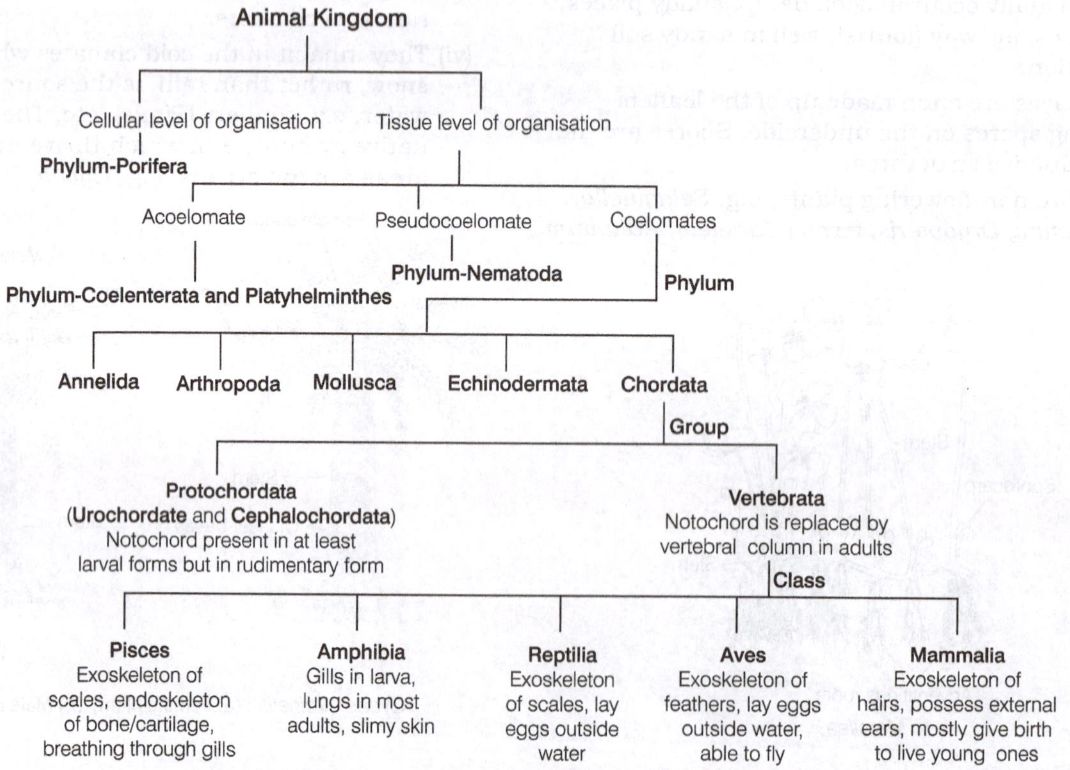

Check Your LEARNING...

1 Name the group of plant kingdom, whose body is differentiated into stem and leaf-like structure.

2 In which habitat, does pteridophytes occur?

3 Give an example of plant belonging to gymnosperms.

4 Which group of plants is known as flowering plants? Also, why are they named so?

5 Name the two divisions of angiospermic plants.

Kingdom – Animalia

The characteristics of kingdom–Animalia are as follows

(i) These are multicellular eukaryotes without cell walls.

(ii) They have definite shape and size.

(iii) Most of them can move easily from one place to another (mobile), but some like sponges and corals are non-mobile or sessile.

(iv) Their mode of nutrition is **heterotrophic** i.e. they depend on autotrophs or plants for their food.

Kingdom–Animalia is classified on the basis of the extent and type of body design as discussed below

All phyla are grouped under the category **invertebrates** (animals without backbone) except, the Vertebrata (animals with a back bone) of phylum–Chordata. In another explanation, we can also say that phylum from Porifera to Echinodermata are referred to as **non–chordates** and all five classes of vertebrates are referred to as **chordates**.

Phylum–Porifera

Some common characteristics of phylum–Porifera are

(i) These are primitive, multicellular, diploblastic and have cellular level of organisation.

(ii) Members of this phylum are commonly known as **sponges**. Their body consists of a hollow tube.

(iii) They are generally marine, except one or two freshwater sponges.

(iv) They contain pore or canals on the body surface through which water enters.

(v) The sponges usually have a skeleton of microscopic spicules or elastin spongin fibres.

(vi) The movement of water through these pores helps in food gathering, respiratory exchange and removal of waste.

(vii) They are sedentary (attached to solid support) and have a large body cavity called **spongocoel**.

(viii) They reproduce both sexually and asexually, e.g. *Euplectella, Sycon, Euspongia* (bath sponge), *Spongilla,* etc.

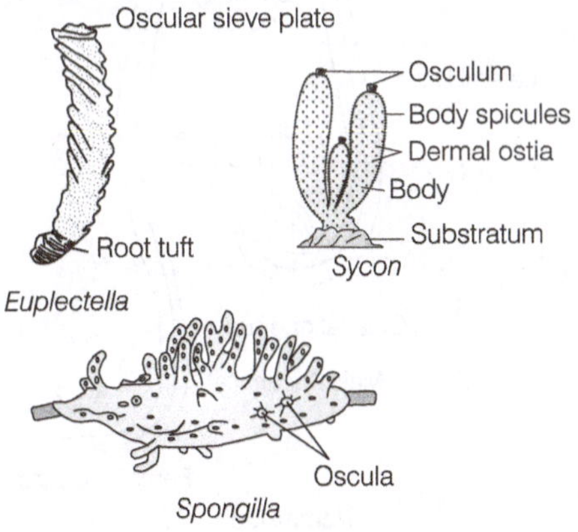

Poriferans

Phylum–Cnidaria (Coelenterata)

Some common characteristics of the phylum–Cnidaria are

(i) These are radially symmetrical, diploblastic animals and have tissue level of body organisation.

(ii) They possess **cnidoblasts** or **cnidocytes** (which contain the stinging capsules) on the tentacles and the body, that is why named as **Cnidaria**.

(iii) They are aquatic and mostly marine.

(iv) Some of them are corals which have skeleton composed of **calcium carbonate**.

(v) Their body cavity called **coelenteron**, have single opening, which is used for both ingesting food and removing waste.

(vi) Some of these species live in colonies (corals), while others have a solitary lifespan (*Hydra*), jellyfish (*Aurelia*) and sea anemone (*Adamsia*).

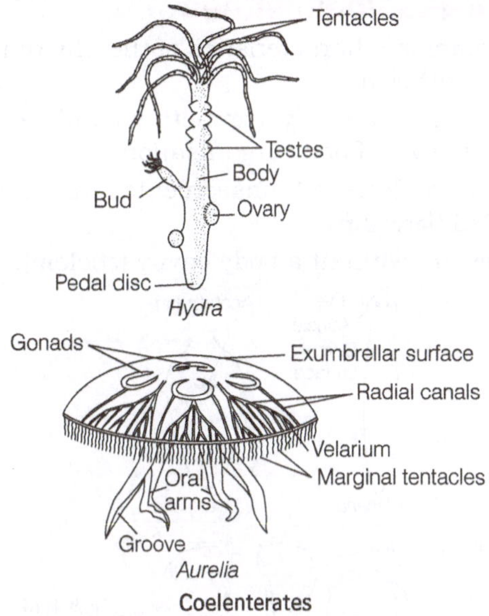

Coelenterates

Phylum–Ctenophora

Some common characteristics of the phylum–Ctenophora are

(i) These are radially symmetrical animals and have tissue level of organisation.

(ii) These animals are triploblastic with transparent body.

(iii) They have two tentacles and eight longitudinal rows of ciliary **comb-plates** for locomotion.

(iv) Adhesive cells called **colloblasts** are present in them, e.g. *Pleurobrachia* (comb jelly), *Cestum* (Venus girdle), *Ctenoplana, Beroe* (sea mitres), etc.

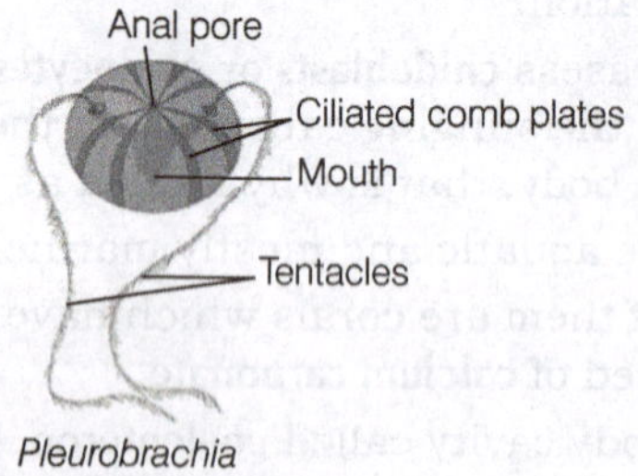

Ctenophores

Note The next three phyla–Platyhelminthes, Nematoda and Annelida include the animals collectively termed as 'worms'. This term is commonly used for creeping and crawling animals with relatively soft bodies.

Phylum–Platyhelminthes

Some common characteristics of the phylum–Platyhelminthes are

(i) They are bilaterally symmetrical and have organ level of body organisation.

(ii) They are flattened, unsegmented and therefore called **flatworms**.

(iii) They are without a body cavity (coelom).

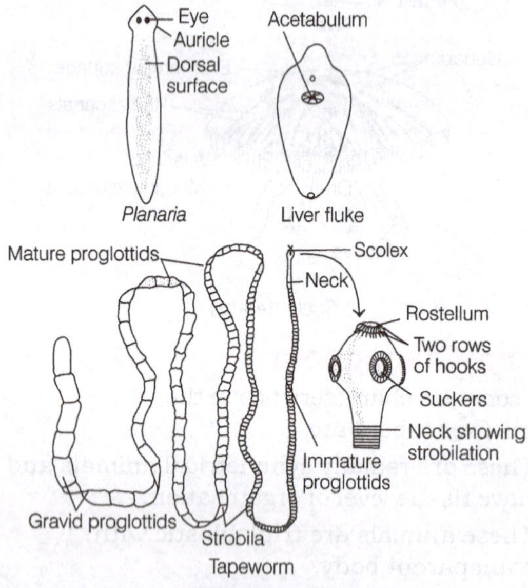

Platyhelminthes

(iv) Their free living forms are mostly marine, but few of them are freshwater species.

(v) They possess suckers and hooks for the attachment to the host.

(vi) Their body is triploblastic, i.e. body wall is made up of three layers of cells.

(vii) They have flame cells for excretion.

(viii) They can be free-living, e.g. *Planaria, Taenia solium* (tapeworm) or parasitic, e.g. *Fasciola* (liver fluke).

Phylum–Nematoda (Nemathelminthes or Aschelminthes)

Some common characteristics of the phylum–Nematoda are

(i) They are bilaterally symmetrical and have tissue level of body organisation.

(ii) They are long, cylindrical, triploblastic and unsegmented in shape.

(iii) They have a fluid-filled or false body cavity (without a true body cavity).

(iv) They are found in all types of habitat.

(v) Exchange of gases takes place through body surface.

(vi) Complete digestive system is present which opens at two ends i.e. mouth and anus.

(vii) Excretion occurs by one celled gland, called **renette cells** or by longitudinal excretory ducts.

(viii) They can be free-living or parasitic, e.g. *Ascaris* (roundworm), *Ancylostoma* (hookworm), *Wuchereria bancrofti* (filarial worm causes elephantiasis), *Enterobius* (pinworm of human), eelworm in potato plants, etc.

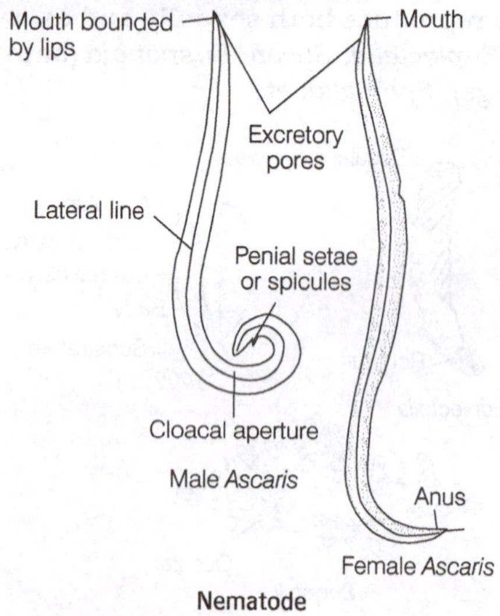

Nematode

Phylum–Annelida

Some common characteristics of phylum–Annelida are

(i) These are bilaterally symmetrical and have organ level of body organisation.

(ii) Body is divided into small segments, which are **metamerically segmented**.

(iii) They are free-living in soil or water and might be parasitic also. They are also found in fresh or marine water.

(iv) They are the first animals to develop true body cavity (coelom).

(v) Excretion occurs by paired segmental **nephridia**.

(vi) Respiration occurs through skin or gills.

(vii) They are **hermaphrodite** (i.e. male and female parts present in same organism) and reproduce sexually, e.g *Nereis* (sandworm), *Hirudinaria* (Indian cattle leech that sucks blood form its host), *Aphrodite* (sea mouse), *Pheretima posthuma* (earthworm), etc.

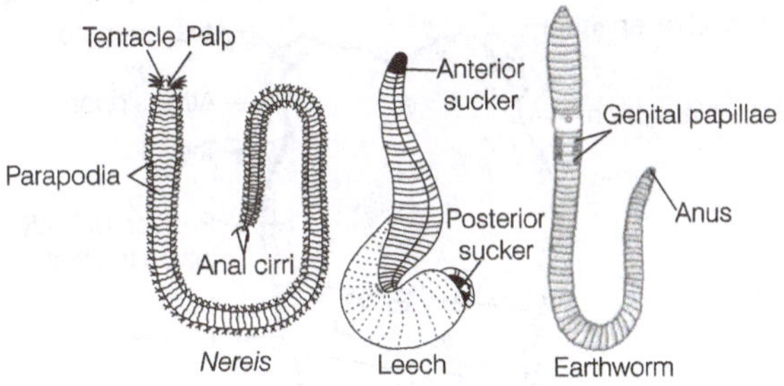

Annelids

Phylum–Arthropoda

Some common characteristics of phylum–Arthropoda are

(i) It is the largest animal phylum.

(ii) The animals are bilaterally symmetrical and have organ level of body organisation.

(iii) These are triploblastic and segmented animals.

(iv) Body is segmented and grouped into three regions, i.e. head, thorax and abdomen.

(v) Anterior part of the body forms a distinct head bearing sense organs and brain.

(vi) Body consists of exoskeleton, made up of **chitin**. They cast off their exoskeleton during growth in early life, which is regrown. This process is called **moulting**.

(vii) A body segment of these animals (somite) usually bears paired lateral and **jointed legs** or **appendages**.

(viii) Their body cavity is filled with blood (haemocoel).

(ix) In many arthropods, compound eyes are present with **mosaic vision** on the head, e.g. *Peripatus, Palaemon* (prawn), *Daphnia, Araneae* (spider), *Cyclops, Cancer* (true crab), *Scolopendra* (centipede), *Julius* (millipede), *Lepisma* (silverfish), butterflies, *Musca* (houseflies), etc.

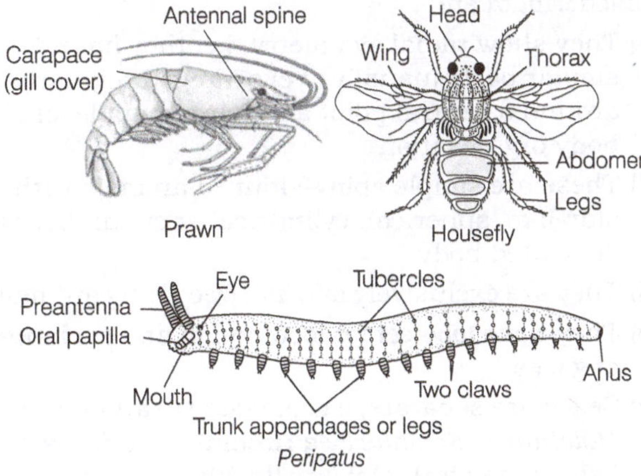

Arthropods

Phylum–Mollusca

Some common characteristics of phylum–Mollusca are

(i) They are bilaterally symmetrical and have organ level of body organisation and possess a soft body.

(ii) Their body is divided into head, visceral mass and foot.

(iii) They possess a body cavity (coelom).

(iv) Kidney-like structures or a pair of metanephridia are present for excretion.

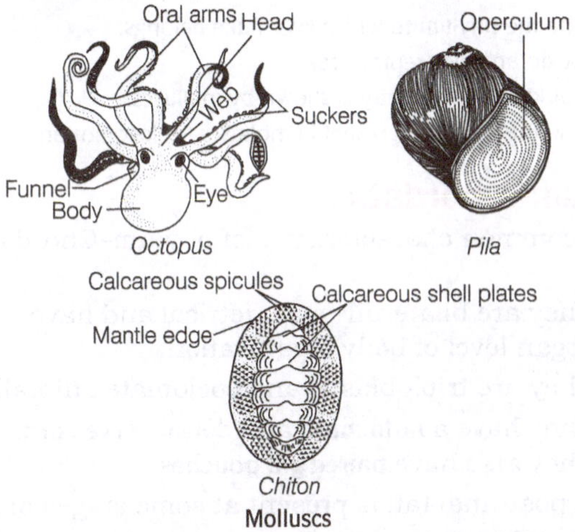

Molluscs

(v) They respire through gills (called **Ctenidia**) or mantle or a lung of mantle.

(vi) Sexes are usually separate.

(vii) Their body has a hard calcareous shell (made up of calcium carbonate).

(viii) A muscular foot is present for locomotion, e.g. *Dentalium* (tusk shell), *Pila* (apple snail), *Unio* (freshwater mussel), *Chiton, Octopus,* etc.

Phylum–Echinodermata

Some common characteristics of phylum–Echinodermata are

(i) They show radial symmetry, i.e. they have similar parts (usually five) arranged regularly around a central point and have organ level of body organisation.

(ii) These are simple spiny-skinned animals with star-like, spherical, cylindrical or cucumber or elongated body.

(iii) They are exclusively marine, free-living animals.

(iv) They have **tubefeet** for locomotion and exchange of gases.

(v) Sexes are separate, e.g. *Antedon* (feather star) *Holothuria, Echinus* (sea urchin), *Asterias* (star fish or sea star), *Ophiura* (brittle star), etc.

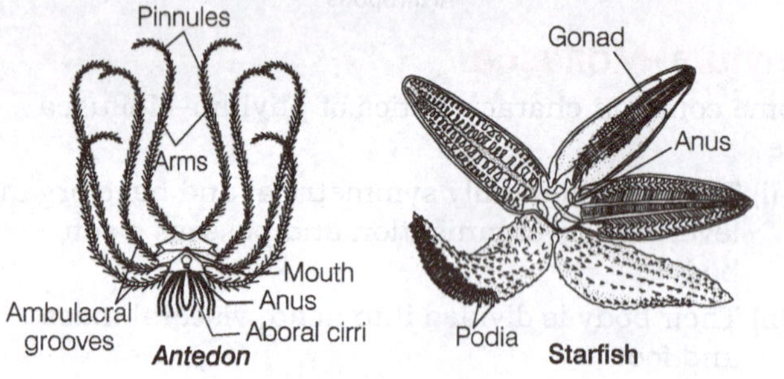

Echinodermata

Check Your LEARNING...

1 Name the phylum to which liver fluke belongs.
2 How do annelids reproduce?
3 What kind of symmetry is shown by molluscs?
4 Name the structure present in molluscs for locomotion.

Phylum–Chordata

Some common characteristics of phylum–Chordata are

(i) They are bilaterally symmetrical and have organ level of body organisation.

(ii) They are triploblastic and coelomate animals.

(iii) They have a **notochord** and **dorsal nerve cord**. They also have **paired gill pouches**.

(iv) A post-anal tail is present at some stages of life.

(v) They have segmented muscles in an unsegmented trunk (body).

(vi) Complete digestive system is present.

(vii) A cartilaginous or bony endoskeleton is present in majority of members.

Chordata is divided into two groups

- Protochordata (Acraniata)
- Vertebrata (Craniata)

Protochordata (Urochordata and cephalochordata)

The characteristics possessed by protochordates are as follows

(i) They are triploblastic, have bilaterally symmetrical body and a coelom.

(ii) They show notochord (a new feature of body design) at some stages of their lives.

Notochord is a long rod-like support structure that runs along the back of the animal separating the nervous tissue from the gut.

(iii) These are mostly marine animals, e.g. Herdmania, *Amphioxus* or *Branchiostoma* and *Doliolum*.

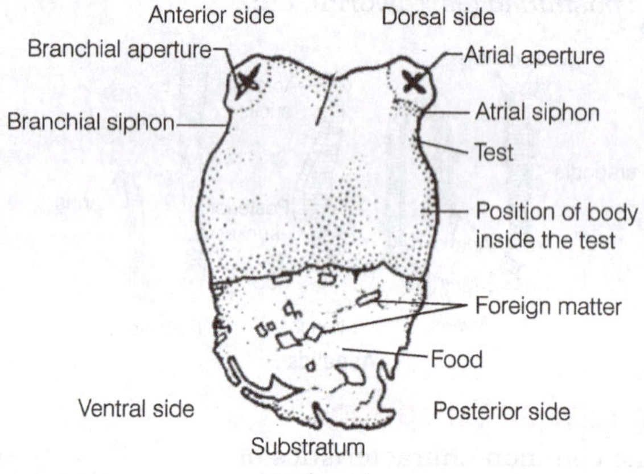

Herdmania

Vertebrata

The characteristics possessed by vertebrates are as follows

- They have a true vertebral column and internal skeleton which allows completely different distribution of muscle attachment points that help in movement.
- Their body is bilaterally symmetrical, triploblastic, coelomic and segmented.
- In these animals, complex differentiation of body tissues and organs is present.
- They have two pairs of limbs.
- Blood has haemoglobin and flows in closed blood vessels.

Vertebrata is further grouped into following five classes.

(i) Class–Pisces (Fishes)

The characteristics possessed by Pisces are as follows

- These are exclusively aquatic animals.
- They have stream-lined body covered with **scales** that ends in a muscular tail (which helps in movement).

- Fins are present, but limbs are absent.
- Respiration occurs by **gills** by taking oxygen dissolved from water.
- They are cold-blooded or poikilothermal (i.e. their body temperature fluctuates directly with the temperature of the environment) and have two-chambered heart.
- Most of them lay eggs.

Based on the nature of their skeleton, Pisces is divided into two classes as follows

(a) **Chondrichthyes** (cartilaginous fishes) Sharks, dogfish, skates.

(b) **Osteichthyes** (bony fishes) Carps (*Catla*), roaches, herrings, trouts, sea-horse, rohu, etc.

The gill slits in bony fishes are concealed under a gill cover (operculum), while those in cartilaginous fishes are exposed without a gill cover.

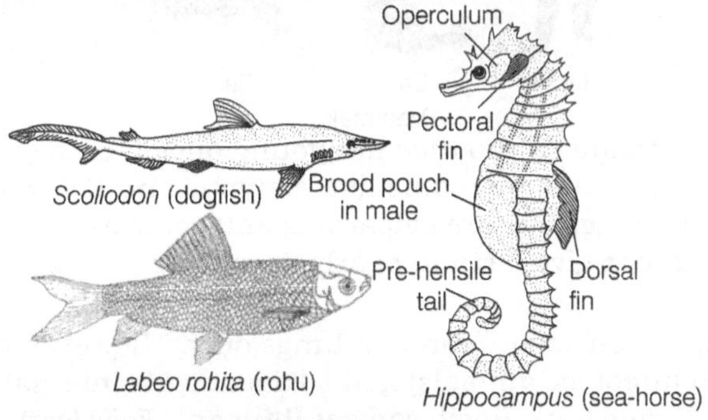

Some common fishes

(ii) Class–Amphibia

The characteristics possessed by amphibians are as follows

- They are amphibious in nature, *viz.* can live on land as well as in water. They were the first chordates to live on land.
- They lack scales and have mucous glands in their skin which secrete mucus that keeps the skin moist.
- The eardrum (tympanum) lies on the surface of the skin.
- Amphibians are cold-blooded and have three-chambered heart.
- They have distinct head and trunk. Neck and tail may or may not be present.
- Respiration occurs be either by skin, gills (in water) or by lungs (on land).
- Generally they require water for the completion of their life cycle as the eggs are laid in water and the larvae are aquatic.
- Limbs are tetrapods (four-limbed), pentadactyl type (five fingered). The digits do not possess claws.
- These have peculiar habit of **hibernation** (winter sleep) and **aestivation** (summer sleep) to overcome unfavourable conditions.
- Sexes are separate and fertilisation is external, e.g. *Rana* (frog), *Bufo* (toad), *Necturus* (mud puppy), *Salamandra* (salamander), *Hyla* (tree frog), etc.

Amphibian

(iii) Class–Reptilia

The characteristics possessed by reptiles are as follows

- These animals possess dry skin, with scales and mostly live in warmer regions. They are cold-blooded animals.
- They lay eggs with tough covering (leathery shell) on land.
- Lungs are the respiratory organs.
- Reptiles bear two pairs of pentadactyl (five digits) limbs (snakes and some lizards have no limbs).
- They have three-chambered heart (two auricles and one ventricle) except crocodile, with four-chambered heart.
- Sexes are separate. Fertilisation is internal, e.g. *Chelone* (turtle), *Chameleon, Naja* (cobra), *Hemidactylus* (house wall lizard), *Testudo* (tortoise), *Draco* (flying lizard), etc.

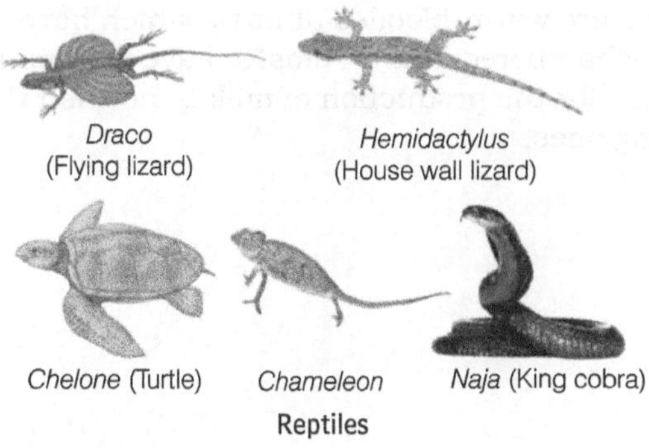

Reptiles

(iv) Class–Aves

The characteristics possessed by aves are as follows

- These are warm-blooded or homeothermal (i.e. they maintain an almost constant, relatively high body temperature irrespective of the temperature of the environment) animals.

- They have four-chambered heart.
- Their body is divisible into head, neck, trunk and tail.
- These are flying animals, having exoskeleton of feathers.
- Their forelimbs are modified into wings and jaws modified into horny toothless beak.
- Bones are light in weight because of air spaces (pneumatic bones) and body is streamlined to reduce air resistance during flight.
- Lungs with air sacs are present for double respiration.
- They have a sound producing organ called **syrinx**.
- Birds are egg laying with large amount of yolk and hard calcareous shell.
- Sexes are separate and fertilisation is internal, e.g. *Ciconia ciconia* (white stork), *Aythya fuligula* (male tufted duck), *Struthio camelus* (ostrich), pigeon, crow, sparrow, etc.

Aves

(v) Class–Mammalia

The characteristics possessed by mammals are as follows

- Body is divisible into head, neck, trunk and tail. Movable eyelids are present.
- These are warm-blooded animals which have four-chambered heart. Females have mammary glands for the production of milk to nourish the young ones.
- These are known to be the advanced group of animals with a very well-developed brain.
- Sweat glands and oil glands are present in their skin. Their skin is covered with hair.
- Mammalia is the first class to mark the presence of ear **pinna** (external fleshy ear). Middle ear is with three ossicles, i.e. malleus, incus and stapes.
- Different types of teeth are present in jaw socket.
- Each digit ends up with claws, hoofs or nails.
- Limbs are adapted for walking, running, swimming, burrowing and even flying (bats).

Mammals

- Most mammals produce live young ones (i.e. they are viviparous) but some like platypus and *Echidna* produce eggs (i.e. are oviparous) and some like kangaroos give birth to poorly developed young ones.
- Respiration occurs through lungs only. They excrete urea (ureotelic animals) and fertilisation is internal, e.g. *Rattus* (rat), *Homo sapiens* (human), *Felis* (cat), bat, *Canis* (dog), chimpanzee, *Macropus* (kangaroo), whale, dolphins, walrus (aquatic mammals).

Check Your LEARNING...

1. What is notochord?
2. Give one example of cartilaginous fish.
3. How many heart chambers are present in amphibians?
4. Name the sound producing organ in birds.
5. Give two visible features of mammals.

QUiCK Revision

- **Classification** is the arrangement of living organisms into groups created on the basis of similarities and dissimilarities among them.
- **Taxonomic hierarchy** is the sequence of taxonomic categories in an descending order of number of species as Kingdom → Phylum/Division → Class → Order → Family → Genus → Species
- **Kingdom** is the most prominent category of taxonomical hierarchy.
- **Linnaeus** (1758) proposed two kingdom classification on the basis of the presence or absence of cell wall.
- In 1969, **RH Whittaker** classified organisms into five kingdom classification. He classified them on the basis of complexity of cell structure or body structure, mode of nutrition, ecological lifestyle and phylogenetic relationships.
- **Kingdom–Monera** includes all prokaryotes, *viz*. mycoplasma, bacteria, cyanobacteria, etc.
- **Kingdom–Protista** includes all unicellular eukaryotic organisms like *Amoeba*, *Euglena*, *Paramecium*, etc.
- **Kingdom–Fungi** contains achlorophyllous, thalloid plants. They are usually saprophytic, parasitic or occasionally symbiotic,
  e.g. *Penicillium notatum*, *Aspergillus niger*, yeast, etc.
- **Kingdom–Plantae** includes all chlorophyllous organisms divided into algae (thallophytes), bryophytes, pteridophytes, gymnosperms and angiosperms.
- **Algae** include all chlorophyllous, photosynthetic, thalloid (no differentiation into roots, stems and leaves) plants. These are mostly aquatic plants.
- **Bryophytes** are the terrestrial plants, which require moisture or water for fertilisation. They lack true roots, stems and leaves. They are divided into liverworts and mosses.
- **Pteridophytes** are non-seeded plants having vascular tissue. These are dependent on water for fertilisation. Their body possess true root, stems and leaves, e.g. *Selaginella* and ferns.
- **Gymnosperms** are naked-seeded plants, e.g. *Cycas* and *Pinus*. These plants do not contain their sex organs in flowers.
- **Angiosperms** are the most advanced plants that dominate the entire land. These are found in almost all habitats. These bear flowers as their reproductive structures.
- **Kingdom–Animalia** is characterised by heterotrophic eukaryotic organisms that are multicellular and their cell lack cell wall. In animals, certain fundamental features are common to various individuals, which forms the basis of their classification.
- **Phylum–Porifera** Simplest multicellular organisms with pores, e.g. *Sycon*.
- **Phylum–Coelenterata** Two-layered body wall with central cavity, e.g. *Hydra*.
- **Phylum–Platyhelminthes** Flat, unsegmented worms without body cavity having parasitic nutrition, e.g. tapeworm.
- **Phylum–Nemathelminthes** Cylindrical, unsegmented worm without body cavity, e.g. *Ascaris*.
- **Phylum–Annelida** Segmented animals with true body cavity, e.g. earthworm.
- **Phylum–Arthropoda** Jointed limbs, exoskeleton made up of chitin. They include crabs, insects, spider, etc.
- **Phylum–Mollusca** Unsegmented body with hard shell, e.g. snail.
- **Phylum–Echinodermata** Unsegmented animals with spiny skin, e.g. starfish.
- **Phylum–Chordata** Animals having a notochord, a dorsal tubular nerve cord, paired pharyngeal gill slits. These are further divided into protochordates and vertebrates.
- **Vertebrates** are animals with vertebral columns. These are further divided into Pisces, Amphibia, Reptilia, Aves and Mammalia.
- **Pisces** Ectothermal, gills for breathing, two-chambered heart, e.g. cartilaginous fish, bony fish.
- **Amphibia** Ectothermal, live on land and water, three-chambered heart, gills, skin and lungs for breathing, e.g. frog.
- **Reptilia** Ectothermal, land animals, lungs for breathing, three-chambered heart, e.g. lizard.
- **Aves** Endothermal, lungs for breathing, four-chambered heart, e.g. crow.
- **Mammalia** Endothermal, lungs for breathing, give birth to young ones and females with mammary glands, e.g. man.

Chapter Practice

Section-I

1 Mark Questions

1. Name the following.
   (i) The method of arranging organisms into groups based on similarities and dissimilarities.
   (ii) Group of related genera which have certain common characters.
   (iii) Highest category of taxonomic studies.
   (iv) Kingdom of prokaryotes.
   (v) Reserve food material in fungi.
   (vi) Network of hyphae.
   (vii) Amphibians of the plant kingdom.
   (viii) The naked embryos present in Cryptogamae.
   (ix) Seed bearing structures in gymnosperms.
   (x) Name the division of plant to which monocots and dicots belong.
   (xi) Primitive, multicellular organisms having pores or canals on body surface.
   (xii) Organism having flame cells.
   (xiii) The phylum to which liver fluke and *Planaria* belong.
   (xiv) Advanced group of animals with a highly developed brain.

Ans. (i) Classification (ii) Family
(iii) Kingdom (iv) Monera
(v) Glycogen (vi) Mycelium
(vii) Bryophyta (viii) Spores
(ix) Cones (x) Angiospermae
(xi) Poriferans (xii) Flatworm
(xiii) Platyhelminthes (xiv) Mammals/Mammalia

2. Correct and rewrite the following statements by changing the underlined words.
   (i) <u>Binomial nomenclature</u> helps us to understand the pattern of evolution.
   (ii) A system of arrangement for classification in which organisms are placed in order of a logical sequence is called <u>nomenclature</u>.
   (iii) <u>Genus</u> is the lowest taxonomic category that can interbreed.
   (iv) <u>Carolus Linnaeus</u> classified organisms into five kingdoms based on certain characters.
   (v) Kingdom–Fungi includes eukaryotic, multicellular, <u>autotrophic</u> organisms.
   (vi) Mosses and liverworts are categorised under division–<u>Pteridophyta</u>.
   (vii) Monocots have <u>tap</u> root system.
   (viii) Alimentary canal is <u>absent</u> in nematodes.
   (ix) Fishes are cold-blooded with a <u>four-chambered</u> heart.
   (x) <u>Aves</u> is the first class to mark the presence of ear pinna.

Ans. (i) Classification helps us to understand the pattern of evolution.
(ii) A system of arrangement for classification in which organisms are placed in order of a logical sequence is called hierarchy.
(iii) Species is the lowest taxonomic category that can interbreed.
(iv) Whittaker classified organisms into five kingdoms based on certain characters.
(v) Kingdom–Fungi includes eukaryotic, multicellular, heterotrophic organisms.
(vi) Mosses and liverworts are categorised under division–Bryophyta.
(vii) Monocots have fibrous root system.
(viii) Alimentary canal is completely present in nematodes.
(ix) Fishes are cold-blooded with a two-chambered heart.
(x) Mammalia is the first class to mark the presence of ear pinna.

3. Give biological reasons for the following.
   (i) Organisms of kingdom–Monera are called prokaryotic.
   (ii) Fungi lack autotrophic mode of nutrition.
   (iii) Algae are a representative of Thallophyta.

Ans. (i) Kingdom–Monera consist of organisms that are single-celled and lack a well-defined nucleus. Thus, they are called prokaryotic.
(ii) Members of kingdom–Fungi lack chlorophyll and thus, fail to perform photosynthesis. Hence, they lack autotrophic mode of nutrition.
(iii) Algae have simple, undifferentiated body (thallus-like) with no differentiation of roots, stems or leaves. Thus, they are considered as a representative of Thallophyta.

4. (i) Match the following columns.

	Column I	Column II
A.	Gymnosperms	1. *Volvox*
B.	Pteridophyta	2. Mushroom
C.	Bryophyta	3. Moss
D.	Fungi	4. Fern
E.	Algae	5. *Cycas*

(ii) Match the following columns.

	Column I		Column II
A.	Starfish	1.	Arthropoda
B.	Housefly	2.	Mollusca
C.	Tortoise	3.	Echinodermata
D.	Snail	4.	Reptilian
E.	*Pheretima*	5.	Annelida

(iii) Match the following columns.

	Column I		Column II
A.	Kingdom–Monera	1.	Cell wall absent
B.	Kingdom–Fungi	2.	Cellulosic cell wall
C.	Kingdom–Plantae	3.	Peptidoglycan cell wall
D.	Kingdom–Protista	4.	Multicellular eukaryotes
E.	Kingdom–Animalia	5.	Chitinous cell wall

(iv) Match the following columns.

	Column I		Column II
A.	WG Rosen	1.	Phylum
B.	Linnaeus	2.	Kingdom
C.	Annelida	3.	Fungi
D.	Carnivora	4.	Coined the term biodiversity
E.	Protista	5.	Order
F.	*Ustilago*	6.	Father of Taxonomy

Ans. (i) A-5, B-4, C-3, D-2, E-1
(ii) A-3, B-1, C-4, D-2, E-5
(iii) A-3, B-5, C-2, D-1, E-4
(iv) A-4, B-6, C-1, D-5, E-2, F-3

5. Choose the correct answer from the four options given below.

(i) Which one of the following is the correct number of kingdoms proposed by Whittaker?
(a) 2 (b) 8 (c) 6 (d) 5

Ans. (d)

(ii) Bacteria belong to the kingdom
(a) Monera (b) Protista
(c) Fungi (d) Plantae

Ans. (a)

(iii) Identify the structure found in Protozoa for locomotion.
(a) Pseudopodia (b) Cilia
(c) Flagella (d) All of these

Ans. (d)

(iv) Which of the following division of plants show undifferentiated body?
(a) Thallophyta (b) Bryophyta
(c) Pteridophyta (d) Gymnosperms

Ans. (a)

(v) Which of these are known for producing seeds?
(a) Pteridophyta and gymnosperms
(b) Bryophyta and gymnosperms
(c) Gymnosperms and angiosperms
(d) Angiosperms and Pteridophyta

Ans. (c)

(vi) Under which of the following two categories animal kingdom (Kingdom–Animalia) is mainly grouped?
(a) Bilaterally symmetrical and radially symmetrical
(b) Coelomate and acoelomate
(c) Aquatic and terrestrial
(d) Vertebrates and invertebrates

Ans. (d)

(vii) Which of the following exhibits movement by crawling?
(a) Amphibians (b) Aves
(c) Mammals (d) Reptiles

Ans. (d)

(viii) Out of the following, which is an endothermal class of group–Vertebrata?
(a) Pisces (b) Amphibians
(c) Reptilia (d) Mammals

Ans. (d)

6. Fill in the blanks by using suitable words .

(i) A definite category at any level of classification is called ....
(ii) All .... lack nucleus.
(iii) The simplest group of Plantae is ....
(iv) Cone bearing plants are called ....
(v) The flowering plants belong to ....
(vi) The Platyhelminthes are also called ....
(vii) Excretory organ of earthworm is ....
(viii) In butterflies, circulatory system is of .... type.
(ix) Animals with backbone are called ... .
(x) Animals with hairy body are called .... .

Ans. (i) Taxon (ii) monerans
(iii) Thallophyta (iv) gymnosperms
(v) angiosperms (vi) flatworms
(vii) nephridia (viii) open
(ix) vertebrates (x) mammals

7. Choose the odd one out from the following terms given below and name the category to which other three belong.

(i) *Anabaena, Nostoc, Paramecium, Mycoplasma*
(ii) *Albugo, Puccinia, Mucor,* Mosses
(iii) *Ulothrix, Spirogyra, Volvox, Oedogonium*
(iv) *Marsilea, Funaria, Marchantia, Riccia*
(v) Housefly, Silverfish, Earthworm, Butterflies

Ans. (i) **Odd term** *Paramecium.*
Rest three belong to kingdom–Monera.
(ii) **Odd term** Mosses.
Rest three are categorised under kingdom–Fungi.
(iii) **Odd term** *Volvox.*
Rest three are filamentous forms of algae.
(iv) **Odd term** *Marsilea.*
Rest three are bryophytes.
(v) **Odd term** Earthworm.
Rest three are belong to phylum–Arthropoda.

8. Given below is a set of five terms each. Rewrite the terms in correct order of a logical sequence beginning with the term that is underlined.
(i) Kingdom, Class, Family, Order, <u>Species</u>
(ii) Cnidaria, Mollusca, Nematoda, <u>Porifera</u>, Annelida

Ans. (i) Species, Family, Order, Class, Kingdom.
(ii) Porifera, Cnidaria, Nematoda, Annelida, Mollusca

9. State whether the given statements are true or false. Correct and rewrite the false statements.
(i) Membrane bound cell organelles are absent in Protista.
(ii) Fungi show heterotrophic mode of nutrition.
(iii) All green plants are autotrophic.
(iv) Fungi is achlorophyllous.
(v) Algae have simple and undifferentiated body.
(vi) Gymnosperms can produce seeds.
(vii) Sponges have numerous pores in their body.
(viii) Most of the nematodes are parasites.
(ix) Reptiles are fully adapted to both terrestrial and aquatic life.
(x) Amphibians possess external ears.

Ans. (i) False, membrane bound cell organelles are present in Protista.
(ii) True (iii) True
(iv) True (v) True
(vi) True (vii) True
(viii) True
(ix) False, amphibians are fully adapted to both terrestrial and aquatic life.
(x) False, mammals possess external ears.

10. Give one example of the following.
(i) Organism having pseudopodia as locomotory organ.
(ii) A saprophytic fungi
(iii) A bryophyte
(iv) A ctenophore with colloblasts
(v) A marine protochordate

Ans. (i) *Amoeba* (ii) *Mucor*
(iii) *Riccia* (iv) Comb jelly
(v) *Balanoglossus*

11. State the main function of the following.
(i) Cilia
(ii) Spores
(iii) Pores (in poriferans)
(iv) Mucous glands (in amphibians)

Ans. (i) Cilia act as a locomotory organ in *Paramecium.*
(ii) Spores act as reproductive parts in bryophytes and pteridophytes.
(iii) Pores allow entry of water inside the body of poriferans.
(iv) Mucous glands (in amphibians) secrete mucus to keep skin moist.

12. Mention one difference in each of the following pairs based on what is given in the bracket.
(i) Bryophyta and Thallophyta (plant body)
(ii) Bryophyta and Pteridophyta (presence or absence of vascular tissues)
(iii) Gymnosperms and Angiosperms (seeds)
(iv) Nematoda and Arthropoda (body)
(v) Class–Pisces and Amphibia (respiratory organs)

Ans. (i) Difference between Bryophyta and Thallophyta is as follows

Bryophyta	Thallophyta
Plant body is differentiated into stems and root-like structures.	Plant body shows no differentiation and is simple.

(ii) Difference between Bryophyta and Pteridophyta is as follows

Bryophyta	Pteridophyta
They lack specialised vascular tissues.	They have vascular tissues that conduct water and minerals.

(iii) Difference between Gymnosperms and Angiosperms is as follows

Gymnosperms	Angiosperms
Plants of these group bear naked seeds.	Plants of these group bear seeds enclosed in a fruit.

(iv) Difference between Nematoda and Arthropoda is as follows

Nematoda	Arthropoda
They have long, cylindrical and unsegmented body.	They have segmented body made up of three layers of cells.

(v) Difference between Class–Pisces and Amphibia is as follows

Pisces	Amphibia
Respiratory organs are strictly gills.	Respiratory organs can be gills or lungs (as per present habitat).

13. Give biological/technical terms for the following.
    (i) Unicellular organisms whose body is not differentiated into cells.
    (ii) Mode of nutrition in which one organism depends on the other for food.
    (iii) A large body cavity that makes up a poriferan.
    (iv) Body wall made up of three germ layers.
    (v) Organisms which produce young ones.

Ans. (i) Acellular (ii) Heterotrophic
(iii) Spongocoel (iv) Triploblastic
(v) Viviparous

14. Briefly explain the following terms.
    (i) Binomial nomenclature
    (ii) Taxonomy
    (iii) Thallophytes
    (iv) Angiosperms
    (v) Class–Reptilia

Ans. (i) Binomial nomenclature is a system of providing scientific names to organisms each consisting of two words, first generic name (i.e. genus) and second specific name (i.e. species).
(ii) Science that deals with the identification, nomenclature and classification of organisms is called taxonomy.
(iii) Thallophytes are simple plants with no differentiation into stems, roots or leaves.
(iv) Angiosperms are a group of flowering plants that produce seeds, flower and fruits.
(v) Class–Reptilia is the first class of terrestrial animals having dry, scaly skin and which mostly live in warmer regions.

15. Answer the following questions briefly.
    (i) What is the need to classify animals?
    (ii) What are the units of classification?
    (iii) In which kingdom, will you place an organism that is unicellular, eukaryotic and photosynthetic?
    (iv) What are the major divisions of plant kingdom?
    (v) Which are the first land plants to have vascular tissues?
    (vi) State any one characteristic feature of members of class–Aves.

Ans. (i) Classifying animals or placing them into different categories based on similarities and dissimilarities, make their study systematic, easy and quick.
(ii) The units of classification are
Kingdom, Phylum/Division, Class, Order, Family, Genus, Species
(iii) Unicellular, eukaryotic and photosynthetic members are placed in kingdom–Protista.
(iv) Major divisions of plant kingdom include Thallophyta, Bryophyta, Pteridophyta, Gymnospermae and Angiospermae.
(v) Pteriodphytes are the first land plants to have vascular tissues.
(vi) Aves are warm-blooded animals with a four-chambered heart.

2 Marks Questions

16. Which scientist proposed the five kingdom classification for living organisms? Write the names of these five kingdoms in increasing order of complexity in their structure.

Ans. Robert Whittaker is 1969 proposed the five kingdom classification.
The five kingdoms are placed according to the increasing complexity in their structure as Monera, Protista, Fungi, Plantae and Animalia.

17. (i) What is symbiotic relationship?
    (ii) Name the symbiotic lifeform which grows on the bark of a tree as large coloured patches.

Ans. (i) Symbiotic relationship is a mutually dependent relationship between two living organisms in which both are benefitted.
(ii) Lichen is a symbiotic lifeform that grows on the bark of trees as coloured patches. It is an association between algae and fungi.

18. We start classification of plants on the basis of differentiation of plant body.
    (i) Which division lacks a well-differentiated body design?
    (ii) Where are such plants predominantly found?

Ans. (i) Thallophyta (algae) lack a well-differentiated body design.
(ii) These plants are predominantly found in both freshwater and marine habitats.

19. Write any two features of the group of plants referred to as amphibians of the plant kingdom.

Ans. Two characteristic features of the plant group referred to as amphibians of the plant kingdom are
- Plant body differentiated to form root, stem and leaf-like structures, they lack true roots, stems or leaves.
- They reproduce by spore formation.

20. (i) Which group of plants is known as 'flowering plants'?
    (ii) On the basis of seed, how is a maize plant different from a pea plant?

Ans. (i) Angiosperms are known as 'flowering plants'.
(ii) Maize plant has seed with one cotyledon, i.e. it is a monocot, whereas pea plant has seeds with two cotyledons, i.e. it is a dicot.

21. The cat, platypus and man are all mammals, yet one of the most unique feature of mammals when considered, helps to divide them into two groups. What is that feature? Mention one characteristic features which are common to all the three animals.

Ans. The features that divide mammals into two groups is whether they are egg laying, i.e. oviparous or give birth to young one, i.e. viviparous.

The four-chambered heart is the common feature.

3 Marks Questions

22. (i) Write any two major characteristics that are considered for classifying organisms into five major kingdoms. Name the five kingdoms.

(ii) Which kingdom do saprophytes belong to? What is the cell wall of fungi made up of ?

Ans. (i) Two major characteristics considered for classifying organisms are

(a) Cell structure (b) Mode of nutrition

The five kingdoms of classification are

- Monera
- Protista
- Fungi
- Plantae
- Animalia

(ii) Saprophytes belong to the kingdom–Fungi. Their cell wall is made up of tough, complex sugar, called chitin.

23. 'Lichens' show symbiotic lifeform between two organisms.

(i) Name the two organisms showing this relationship.

(ii) From which kingdoms do the above organisms belong?

(iii) Enlist the structural and nutritional features of the kingdoms involved in this association.

Ans. (i) Cyanobacteria (e.g. *Anabaena* and *Nostoc*) and Fungi are the organisms show symbiotic relationship.

(ii) Cyanobacteria belong to kingdom—Monera and fungus belong to kingdom—Fungi.

(iii) The organisms of kingdom—Monera are single celled possess a cell wall made up of peptidoglycans. They are either autotrophic or heterotrophic. In kingdom—Fungi, organisms are filamentous possess cell wall of chitin and are heterotrophic or saprotrophic.

24. Classify the following organisms based on the presence/absence of true coelom (acoelomate and coelomate).

Spongilla, sea anemone, *Planaria*, liver fluke, *Ascaris, Nereis*, earthworm, scorpion, birds, fishes and horses.

Ans. **Acoelomates** *Spongilla*, sea anemone, *Planaria*, liver fluke.

Coelomates *Ascaris, Nereis*, earthworm, scorpion, birds, fishes and horses.

25. State reasons why reptiles are successful on land.

Ans. Reptiles are successful on lands because

(i) They have dry and keratinised skin.

(ii) Their egg is surrounded by a shell.

(iii) Pulmonary respiration takes place.

(iv) Internal fertilisation takes place.

Section-II [5 Marks]

Structured Questions

1. Observe the diagram given below and answer the questions that follows.

(i) Identify the organism.

(ii) Name the group to which the above organism belongs.

(iii) State the mode of nutrition followed by the organism.

(iv) State one point that makes it different from kingdom–Plantae.

(v) What are hyphae?

Ans. (i) The given organism is *Agaricus*.

(ii) The given organism (*Agaricus*) belongs to the kingdom-Fungi.

(iii) The organism follows heterotrophic mode of nutrition.

(iv) The organism lacks chlorophyll. This makes it different from kingdom–Plantae.

(v) Hyphae are long, thread-like structures present on the body of a fungi.

2. Vertebrates show a variety in shape and size from small animal like frog to a big one like whale.

(i) By what other name is the group–Vertebrata called?

(ii) State one unique feature of vertebrates.

(iii) Name the class of Vertebrata that respire only by lungs.

(iv) Which vertebrates are called the 'first class of terrestrial animals'?

(v) Which vertebrate is warm-blooded and possesses an exoskeleton of feathers?

Ans. (i) Craniata is other name of the group–Vertebrata.

(ii) One unique feature of vertebrates is that they have a true vertebral column and an internal skeleton that helps in smooth muscle movement.

(iii) Class–Reptilia respire only by lungs.

(iv) Reptiles are called the 'first class of terrestrial animals'.

(v) Birds (Class-Aves) are warm-blooded and possess an exoskeleton of feathers.

Chapter Assessment

Section-I

1 Mark Quesitons

1. Name the following.
   (i) A group that includes unicellular eukaryotic organism.
   (ii) The substance that makes the cell wall of bacteria.
   (iii) A Phanerogamae plant.
   (iv) Division in which deodar and *Pinus* belong.
   (v) The animal class with forelimbs modified into wings.
2. Correct and rewrite the following statements by changing the underlined words.
   (i) Bacteria are <u>multicellular</u> organisms lacking all membrane bound organelles.
   (ii) Tiger and wolf belong to same order–<u>Felidae</u>.
   (iii) Coelenterates have skeleton composed of <u>calcium oxide</u>.
3. Give biological reasons for the following.
   (i) Fungi are not considered as plants.
   (ii) Thallophytes, bryophytes and pteridophytes are called cryptogams.
   (iii) Pteridophytes are also called vascular cryptogams.
4. (i) Match the following columns.

	Column I		Column II
A.	Species	1.	*sativum*
B.	Order	2.	Carnivora
C.	Family	3.	Plantae/Animalia
D.	Class	4.	Mammalia
E.	Kingdom	5.	Felidae

   (ii) Match the following columns.

	Column I		Column II
A.	Bread mould	1.	Parallel venation
B.	Bacteria	2.	Reticulate venation
C.	Monocots	3.	Devoid of mitochondria
D.	*Euglena*	4.	Kingdom-Fungi
		5.	Multicellular photosynthetic
		6.	Unicellular heterotrophic

5. Choose the correct answer from the four options given below.
   (i) Which one of the following represents the correct example of binomial scientific name?
   (a) Green algae (b) Rana tigrina
   (c) *Rana tigrina* (d) China rose
   (ii) Which of the following belongs to kingdom–Fungi?
   (a) *Amoeba* (b) Algae
   (c) Yeast (d) Mango
   (iii) Cauloid and phylloid are found in
   (a) *Marchantia* (b) *Cycas*
   (c) *Dryopteris* (d) All of these
   (iv) Hollow bones are present in
   (a) reptiles (b) aves
   (c) mammals (d) pisces
6. Fill in the blanks by using suitable words.
   (i) .... are a combination of algae and fungi.
   (ii) All plants are ....
   (iii) Bryophytes reproduce by ...... formation.
   (iv) ...... are fully adapted to both terrestrial and aquatic life.
   (v) Water canal system is well-developed in ....
   (vi) Sound producing organ in birds is ....
7. Choose the odd one out from the following terms given below and name the category to which other three belong.
   (i) Liverworts, *Cycas*, Mosses, *Equisetum*
   (ii) *Chlamydomonas*, *Selaginella*, *Equisetum*, *Marsilea*
8. Given below are sets of five terms each. Rewrite the terms in correct order in a logical sequence beginning with the term that is underlined.
   (i) Fungi, Animalia, Plantae, <u>Monera</u>, Protista
   (ii) Reptilia, Aves, <u>Pisces</u>, Mammalia, Amphibia
9. State whether the following statements are true or false. Correct and rewrite the false statements.
   (i) Bacteria belong to the kingdom-Monera.
   (ii) Cell wall is absent in fungi.
   (iii) Cilia is found in *Amoeba* for locomotion.
   (iv) All plants have roots, stems and leaves.
   (v) *Nereis* belongs to Phylum–Annelida.
   (vi) Aves have four-chambered heart.

10. Give one example of the following.

(i) A vascular cryptogam.

(ii) A woody plant with naked seeds.

(iii) A monocotyledonous plant.

(iv) A species belonging to Phylum–Mollusca.

(v) A species of the largest animal phylum.

(vi) A protochordate.

11. State the main function of the following.

(i) Suckers (in flatworm) (ii) Renette cells

(iii) Metanephridia

12. Mention one difference in each of the following pairs based on what is given in the bracket.

(i) Thallophyte and Pteridophyte (vascular tissue)

(ii) Annelids and Nematodes (body cavity)

(iii) Amphibia and Pisces (habitat)

13. Give biological/technical terms for the following.

(i) Symbiotic combination of root of higher plants and fungus.

(ii) Adhesive cells present in members of phylum-ctenophora.

(iii) Animals whose body is derived from two germ layers.

(iv) Hard parts present outside the body.

(v) Animals that lay eggs.

14. Briefly explain the following terms.

(i) Moulting

(ii) Cryptogams

(iii) Mammals

15. Answer the following questions briefly.

(i) Which kingdom include organisms lacking a well-defined nucleus and do not show multicellular body designs?

(ii) Which division among plants has the simplest body?

(iii) What do you call the animal group possessing backbone? Name any two classes under this group.

2 Marks Questions

16. List any two advantages of five kingdom classification over two kingdom classification.

17. Mention two advantages of seed producing plants over those which do not produce seeds.

18. List any two characteristic features based on which amphibians are said to be more advanced than Pisces.

19. Mammals are the most developed group of animals. Explain briefly.

3 Marks Questions

20. Mention any three features of chordates.

21. List three reasons why whales are not grouped under fishes?

Section-II [5 Marks]

Structured Questions

22. The evolution of plants has resulted in an increasing level of complexity.

(i) Which plant groups are called Cryptogamae?

(ii) Which plant group remains differentiated with rhizoids and phylloids?

(iii) Name the division to which *Dryopteris, Equisetum* belong.

(iv) What are phanerogams?

(v) What are seed leaves in angiosperms?

23. Observe the diagram given below and answer the questions that follows.

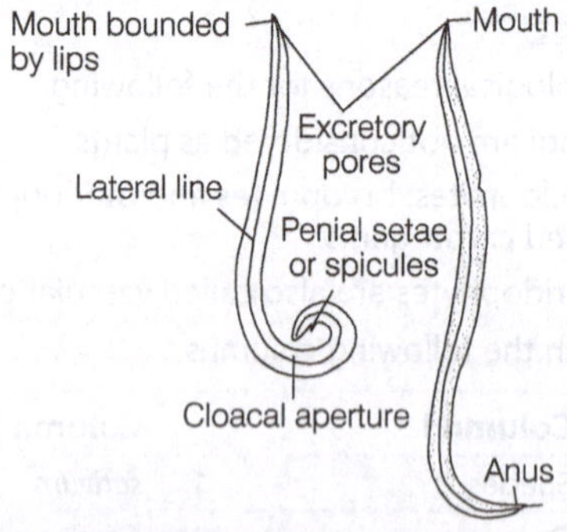

(i) Name the above shown organism.

(ii) Which phylum does the shown organism belong to?

(iii) What is the common name of the organism shown?

(iv) State any one characteristic feature of the organism shown.

(v) Name any two organisms belonging to same phylum.

For explanations scan the given QR Code

Olympiad Section*

Brain Teasing Questions asked in Previous Olympiads

1 The organism whose body develops from two germ layers are called diploblastic, whereas the organism developed from three germ layers are called triploblastic. In some triploblastic organism, the body cavity or coelom is formed from mesoderm and endoderm. Such an organism is called as ...(P)... and an example for it is ....(Q).... . Choose the correct option to fill in the blanks in the above statement. **[INJSO 2018]**

(a) P – coelomate; Q-*Hydra*
(b) P – coelomate; Q-*Planaria*
(c) P – pseudocoelomate; Q- *Pila*
(d) P – pseudocoelomate; Q- *Ascaris*

2 The chart represents the relationships between some plants. In the scheme, (P) to (S) represent characters which distinguish one example from the rest.

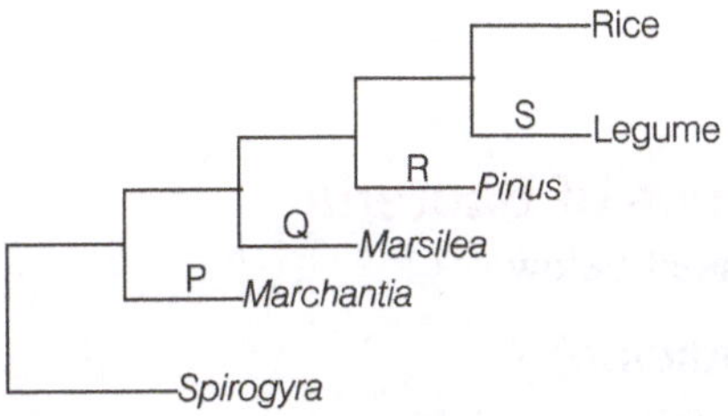

(I) to (V) below represent some characters related to (P)–(S), but not necessarily in that order. **[INJSO 2017]**

I. Without vascular tissue
II. Seeds have two cotyledons
III. Seeds have one cotyledons
IV. Do not produce seeds
V. Naked seeds

Which one of the following is a correct match between (P to S) with (I to V).

(a) P-I; Q-IV; R-V; S-II
(b) P-IV; Q-I; R-V; S-II
(c) P-I; Q-V; R-IV; S-III
(d) P-I; Q-IV; R-V; S-III

3 The given figures depict representative illustrations of three categories of animals with segmented bodies. **[INBO 2015]**

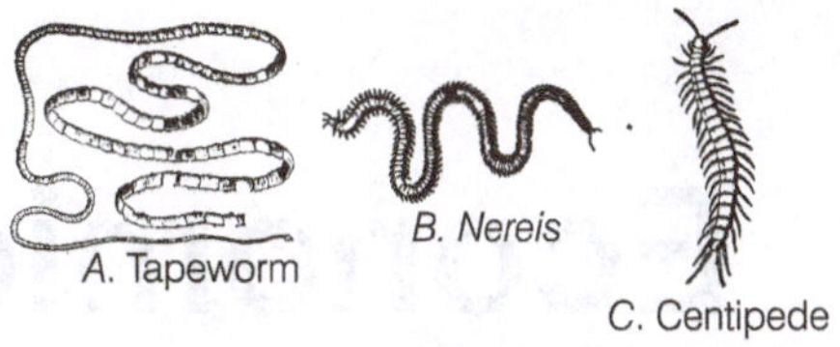

Which of these animal/s show metameric segmentation?

(a) Only *B*
(b) *A* and *B*
(c) *B* and *C*
(d) *A* and *C*

4 In the following table, Column I represents different taxa belonging to the Animal kingdom. Column II shows some excretory structures.

	Column I		Column II
A.	Mammalia (Vertebrata)	1.	No excretory organs
B.	Gastropoda (Mollusca)	2.	Kidneys
C.	Hexapoda (Arthropoda)	3.	Malpighian tubules
D.	Asteroidea (Echinodermata)	4.	Nephridia

[IJSO 2014, Argentina]

	A	B	C	D
(a)	1	2	3	4
(b)	2	4	3	1
(c)	2	1	4	3
(d)	3	2	4	1

5 Students of botany class expressed that their class is very boring. Next day, Smita madam brought a few botanical samples. She asked the class to group the plants according to some criteria. They classified the plants and tabulated their observations as in the table below. Looking at this information, she asked them to find out the correct set belonging to Pteridophyta and Algae, respectively. **[INJSO 2012]**

Criteria	I	II	III	IV	V
Seed production	Not seen	Not seen	Seen	Seen	Not seen
Vascular tissues	Absent	Present	Present	Present	Absent
Flowers	Absent	Absent	Absent	Present	Absent
Cones	Absent	Present	Present	Absent	Absent
Tissue differentiation	Absent	Present	Present	Present	Absent
Habit	Amphibious	Terrestria	Terrestria	Terrestria	Absent

(a) II and IV
(b) II and I
(c) III and V
(d) II and III

Answers

1. (d) **2.** (a) **3.** (c) **4.** (b) **5.** (b)

*These questions may or may not be asked in the examination, have been given just for additional practice required for olympiads, scholarship exams etc. For detailed explanations refer Page No. 230.

CHAPTER 08

Economic Importance of Bacteria and Fungi

Chapter Inside

- Bacteria • Useful Activities of Bacteria • Harmful Activities of Bacteria
- Fungi • Useful Activities of Fungi • Harmful Activities of Fungi

Bacteria

The term 'bacteria' was proposed by **Ehrenberg** in 1829. These are prokaryotic organisms without well-defined organelles like endoplasmic reticulum, mitochondria, etc.

These are the most primitive, simplest and smallest microorganisms with cell wall. Bacteria are cosmopolitan, i.e. found everywhere.

On the basis of shape, bacteria are divided into following types

(i) Coccus (spherical)
(ii) Bacilli (rod-shaped)
(iii) Spirilla (spiral-shaped with flagella)
(iv) Vibrio (comma-shaped)

Bacteria serve as both boon and bane to humankind. Therefore, their activities can be categorised into harmful as well as useful categories.

Useful Activities of Bacteria

These are discussed below

Bacteria in Medicine

They include the following fields

(i) **Antibiotics** These are the chemical substances produced by microbes that kill or retard the growth of other microbes. Several antibiotics prepared from bacteria are effective against other bacteria without causing any side effects.

Some of them are as follows

Antibiotics	Sources
Bacitracin	*Bacillus subtilis*
Terramycin	*Streptomyces rimosus*
Chloromycetin	*S. venezuelae*
Erythromycin	*S. erythreus*
Streptomycin	*S. griseus*
Neomycin	*S. fradiae*
Tetracycline	*S. aureofaciens*

(ii) **Serum** It is defined as blood plasma devoid of clotting factors (fibrinogen). It contains antitoxins for a particular pathogen.
Preparation of serum requires introduction of a small dose of bacterial toxin into a healthy animal, e.g. cow.
The body produces antitoxins to neutralise the effect of toxin. Blood of animal is taken after repeated introduction of the same toxin and after being chilled, it results in a clear straw coloured liquid (serum). Serum is used as a preventive measure against bacterial invasions.

(iii) **Vaccine** It is a biological preparation developed from weakened (attenuated) or killed forms of bacteria that provides active acquired immunity against a specific disease. Vaccines stimulate a persons body to produce antitoxins which provide immunity against future attacks from a specific pathogen. These are available for several diseases like cholera, typhoid, smallpox, etc.
e.g. **Living weakened bacteria** are used for the production of BCG vaccine for tuberculosis. Similarly, **killed bacteria** are used in preparation of TAB vaccine for typhoid.

(iv) **Steroids** These are the hormones usually obtained from the bodies of various animals. Steroids are used in the treatment of various diseases. These have been prepared by using bacteria (like *Corynebacterium* and *Streptomyces*) and various alkaloids (obtained from animals or plants).

Bacteria in Agriculture

Bacteria are used as biofertilisers to enrich the nutrient quality of the soil and play an important role in nitrogen cycle.

Nitrogen Cycle

The nitrogen cycle is the biogeochemical cycle by which free atmospheric nitrogen is converted into its various chemical forms.

The nitrogen cycle is mainly composed of four important processes, i.e. nitrogen-fixation, ammonification, nitrification and denitrification.

1. **Nitrogen-fixation** In this process, the atmospheric nitrogen is fixed which is used by the plants. In this step, the molecular nitrogen (N_2) is converted into inorganic nitrogenous compounds like nitrate, nitrite and ammonia. Nitrogen-fixation is of two types
   (i) **Physical nitrogen-fixation** The process of conversion of N_2 to inorganic nitrogenous compounds without the involvement of microorganisms.
   (ii) **Biological nitrogen-fixation** The process in which atmospheric nitrogen gets converted into inorganic nitrogenous compounds (nitrate, nitrite and ammonia) through microorganisms (bacteria, cyanobacteria, etc.) is called **biological nitrogen-fixation.**

   The organisms that fix nitrogen can be of two types
   (a) **Asymbiotic or Free-living bacteria** These are the bacteria which are not found in close relationship with another bacteria or organisms in order to convert atmospheric nitrogen into ammonia, e.g. number of cyanobacteria like *Anabaena* and *Nostoc.* The free-living bacteria can also be further divided as
   - **Free-living aerobic bacteria** These include microbes like *Azotobacter* and *Beijerinckia.*
   - **Free-living anaerobic bacteria** These include microbes like *Rhodospirillum* and *Clostridium.*

   (b) **Symbiotic bacteria** These are bacteria that can fix nitrogen by forming close associations with each other or with another organisms, e.g. relationship between *Rhizobium* bacteria with legumes.
2. **Ammonification** In next step, the organic matter (proteins and nucleic acids) of the dead remains is decomposed in order to produce ammonia (NH_3) by microorganisms (like *Clostridium*).
3. **Nitrification** It is the process in which ammonia produced by the degradation of manures is first oxidised to nitrite by the soil bacterium *Nitrosomonas* or *Nitrococcus.*
   This nitrite is then further oxidised to nitrate by another soil bacterium, i.e. *Nitrobacter.*
4. **Denitrification** It is the process in which the nitrate present in the soil is reduced back to free nitrogen (N_2). The process of denitrification is carried out by denitrifying bacteria (like

Thiobacillus denitrificans, Pseudomonas denitrificans, etc.).

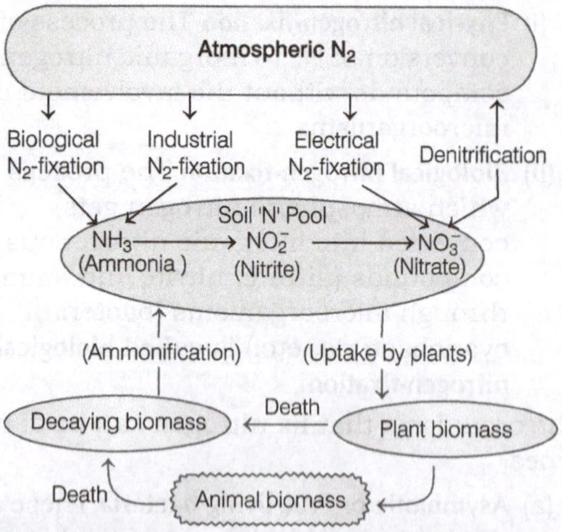

The nitrogen cycle showing relationship between the three main nitrogen polls, i.e. atmospheric, soil and biomass

Note
- **Decay** is the complete breakdown of organic matter by bacteria without giving out a foul smell.
- **Putrefaction** is the incomplete breakdown of organic matter by bacteria, emitting a foul smell.

Bacteria in Various Industries

The usefulness of bacteria for various industries include the following fields

(i) **Curing and ripening of tea and tobacco** Fermentation by bacteria is used for curing crude leaves of tea and tobacco. After harvesting, crude leaves are hung in shade and are permitted for the action of certain bacteria (*Bacillus megaterium*). This process helps in removal of bitterness, adds flavour and taste to tea and tobacco leaves increasing their market value.

(ii) **Tanning of hides and leather** Removal of fats, hair and other tissues from the hides of animals is also achieved through fermentation by bacteria. This process is called **tanning.**

(iii) **Manufacture of dairy products** Milk is inoculated by lactic acid bacterium (*Lactobacillus*) and is responsible for souring and coagulating it. Thus, it is used for making products such as cheese, curd, etc.

(iv) **Production of enzymes** Various enzymes are produced from bacteria that are used in food industry and in the manufacture of chemicals.

Enzymes	Sources
Amylase	*Bacillus* sp.
Proteases	*Bacillus subtilis*
Streptokinase	*Streptococcus pyogenes*

(v) **Production of vitamins** Several species of bacteria are used in the production of riboflavin (a kind of vitamin-B).
Clostridium butylicum, Propionibacterium shermanii and *Pseudomonas denitrificans* are used to produce cobalamin (vitamin- B_{12}).

(vi) **Manufacture of acetone and alcohol** Acetone, butyl alcohol and ethyl alcohol are some commercially obtained alcoholic products by distillation of molasses and fermentation by anaerobic bacteria.

Harmful Activities of Bacteria

These can be grouped under the following

(i) **Food spoilage** The bacteria like *Micrococcus, Salmonella, Staphylococcus, Clostridium,* etc., spoil the food stuffs. They can cause **botulism** (*Clostridium botulinum*) and **food poisoning** (*Clostridium perfringens, E. coli, Staphylococcus aureus*) by producing endotoxins and exotoxins. Marine foods such as sea weeds, oysters, crabs and fishes are destroyed by *Spirillum rectifiers.*
Therefore, preservation of food and making it free of disease causing germs is very necessary.
One such method is **pasteurisation.** It is a technique of partial sterilisation applied usually to milk.
Other methods include salting, refrigeration, adding preservatives, etc.

(ii) **Diseases** Bacteria cause various diseases of man, domesticated animals and of cultivated plants. These diseases are seen due to the poisonous products called **toxins** released by bacteria.

Some common diseases along with the causative bacteria are given in the table given below

Some Common Human Diseases Caused by Bacteria

Diseases in humans	Causative agents
Cholera	*Vibrio cholerae*
Diphtheria	*Corynebacterium diphtheriae*
Meningitis	*Streptococcus pneumoniae*
Tuberculosis	*Mycobacterium tuberculosis*
Pneumonia	*Diplococcus pneumoniae*
Typhoid	*Salmonella typhi*
Tetanus	*Clostridium tetani*
Plague	*Pasteurella pestis*

Some Common Plant Diseases Caused by Bacteria

Diseases in plants	Causative agents
Citrus canker	*Xanthomonas citri*
Angular leaf spot or black arm of cotton	*Xanthomonas malvacearum*
Leaf blight of rice	*Xanthomonas oryzae*
Red stripe of sugarcane	*Xanthomonas rubrilineans*
Wilt disease of potatoes	*Pseudomonas solanacearum*

Some Common Animal Diseases Caused by Bacteria

Diseases in animals	Causative agents
Anthrax of sheep and cattle	*Bacillus anthracis*
Vibriosis	*Vibrio tatus*
Fowl typhoid	*Salmonella gallinarum*
Black leg	*Clostridium chauvoei*
Brucellosis	*Brucella suis*
Dysentery	*Shigella dysenteriae*
Listeriosis	*Listeria monocytogenes*

(iii) **Bioweapons** Bioweapon or Biological weapon is a device that carries and delivers disease-causing biological agents (like bacteria, viruses, or genetically altered organisms) or a toxin derived from it to the target organism. Biological agents are used against humans, their crops and animals and this is termed as **biowar** or **biological warfare**. These agents are highly infectious which reproduce quickly and easily, and have high potency and low cost, e.g. *Bacillus anthracis* (anthrax), *Yersinia pestis* (plague), etc.

Check Your LEARNING...

1 Who gave the term bacteria?
2 Name the bacterial source of protease enzyme.
3 Which bacteria is involved in food spoilage?
4 Name the bacteria that cause wilt disease of potatoes.
5 Give two examples of biological agents.

Fungi

The term 'fungi' was coined by **Gaspard** and **Bauhin**. These are **eukaryotic** and **achlorophyllous** (i.e. without chlorophyll) organisms. They show heterotrophic mode of nutrition due to the absence of chlorophyll. Their plant body is thallus-like (thalloid) and non-vascular, i.e. without xylem and phloem. The study of fungi is known as **Mycology**.

The most common fungi are moulds that are seen growing on food, fruits and even tree bark.

Rhizopus is the common bread mould that grows on a variety of organic matter in warm and humid climate. *Rhizopus* can reproduce both sexually and asexually.

Similarly, yeasts are single-celled fungi found freely in the atmosphere. They are found readily growing in all kinds of sugary solutions, nectar of flowers, etc. They are of much importance to mankind.

Fungi are useful as well as harmful to humans in many ways as discussed below

Useful Activities of Fungi

These can be categorised as follows

As Food

Some fungi are edible and are used as delicious food. Mushrooms such as *Agaricus bisporus* (white button mushroom) and *A. campestris* are rich sources of vitamins (biotin, pantothenic acid and niacin) and minerals. Similarly, yeast is an important source of vitamin-B, E and proteins.

In Industries

Various industries, especially bakeries, breweries and cheese processing, depend upon fungi.

(i) **Breweries** Fungi especially yeasts (*Saccharomyces cerevisiae*) are utilised for the production of alcoholic beverages, such as beer, wine, whisky, rum and gin by the process of fermentation.

During fermentation (anaerobic respiration) of glucose in yeasts, ethyl alcohol (ethanol) and CO_2 are produced. Different raw materials are used for the production of alcoholic beverages, e.g. grape is used for the production of wine and barley maltose is used for the production of beer.

(ii) **Bakeries** Fluffiness in bread, cakes, etc., is due to the CO_2 released by yeast during the process of fermentation. It forms air spaces, giving it fluffy appearance.

(iii) **Cheese processing** Several species of *Penicillium* and *Aspergillus* impart different flavours to cheese, e.g. Roquefort cheese by *Penicillium roqueforti*.

(iv) **Chemicals** Many fungi are utilised for the commercial production of various chemicals.

Some Chemicals and their Related Products

Chemicals	Sources
Citric acid	*Aspergillus niger*
Fumaric acid	*Rhizopus stolonifer*
Orcein (stain)	*Rocella tinctoria* (lichen)
Perfumes	Lichens as *Evernia prunastri*

In Medicines

Fungi are used in various medicinal preparations such as

(i) **Antibiotics** These are substances of biological origin which, at low concentration, can inhibit the growth of bacteria and other microorganisms.

In 1919, **Sir Alexander Fleming**, for the first time, discovered the antibiotic named **penicillin** from the fungal colony of *Penicillium notatum.*

Some Antibiotics Derived from Fungi

Antibiotics	Sources
Penicillin	*Penicillium notatum* and *P. chrysogenum*
Clavicin	*Aspergillus clavatus*
Flavicin	*Aspergillus flavus* and *A. fumigatus*

(ii) **Vitamins** Many fungal metabolites are rich source of vitamins which are used as nutritional supplements and in medical therapy.

Vitamins	Sources
Vitamin-B	Yeasts such as *Saccharomyces cerevisiae*
Vitamin-A	*Rhodotorula gracilis*

(iii) **Enzymes** Different enzymes are synthesised on commerical scale by using different fungi.

Enzymes	Sources
Amylase, pectinase, protease	*Aspergillus oryzae*
Invertase	*Saccharomyces cerevisiae*

In Agriculture

Fungi increase the fertility of soil in different ways as follows

(i) Fungi can decompose organic compounds of dead plants, animals and excreta of animals and convert their essential elements into forms which can be used again as raw material by plants.

Some fungi, e.g. *Aspergillus* have soil binding properties due to the secretion of mucilaginous substances and polysaccharides. They absorb inorganic salts.

(ii) Fungi form symbiotic association with plants called **mycorrhiza**. The fungal symbiont absorbs phosphorus or other minerals and passes it into the plants.

Mushroom Cultivation

Mushrooms are multicellular, saprophytic fungi which grow on dead or decaying leaves, wood logs, etc. These are the important sources of proteins and vitamins. Mushrooms can be cultivated in little land areas throughout the year in hills and during winter in plains, in a temperature range of 16-18°C. Three kinds of mushrooms widely cultivated in India and abroad are

(i) White button mushroom (*Agaricus bisporus*)
(ii) Paddy straw mushroom (*Volvariella*)
(iii) Oyster mushroom (*Pleurotus*)

Major steps of mushroom cultivation are

(a) **Composting** It is made by mixing paddy or wheat straw, chicken manure and organic and inorganic fertilisers. The compost is filled in trays and kept at about 50°C for around one week.

(b) **Spawning** The seeds (mycelium) of mushroom are introduced into the compost.

(c) **Casing** A thin layer of soil is spread over the compost and temperature of 25°C is maintained for 3 days. Then, temperature is lowered to 16-18°C.

(d) **Cropping and harvesting** Growth occurs between 2-6 weeks. Full grown mushrooms are taken out.

(e) **Preservation** Vacuum cooling, storing at 15°C and freeze drying in a solution of brine are the important steps in preserving mushrooms to increase their shelf-life.

Harmful Activities of Fungi

These are as follows

(i) **Diseases** Fungi are responsible for a large number of diseases in plants, animals and human beings.

Some of them are given below

(a) **Animal diseases**

Athlete foot	*Trichophyton rubrum*
Penicillosis	*Penicillium* sp.

(b) **Human diseases**

Aspergillosis (lung disease)	*Aspergillus niger*
Ringworm	*Trichophyton, Microsporum*
Outomycosis (ear infection)	*Aspergillus flavus, A. nidulans*

(c) **Plant diseases**

Black wart disease of potato	*Synchytrium endobioticum*
White rust of crucifers	*Albugo candida* or *Cystopus candidus*
Late blight of potato	*Phytophthora infestans*

(ii) **Food spoilage** Food particles such as fruits, vegetables, meat, etc., are spoiled by fungi, which belong to moulds like *Rhizopus, Mucor, Penicillium* and *Aspergillus*.

(iii) **Decay and deteriorations** Saprophytic fungi grow on a number of articles of human use such as clothes, leather goods, optical instruments. The members of polyporales occur on living tree and cause wood rot, e.g. *Polyporus tomentosus*.

Check Your LEARNING...

1 Name the fungi used as a food.
2 What is the fungal source of citric acid?
3 Which mould was observed by Alexander Fleming and led to the discovery of antibiotics?
4 Give two examples of mushrooms that are widely cultivated in India.
5 Name the fungal species commonly associated with decay of wood.

QUiCK Revision

- Bacteria are primitive organisms consisting of single cell like structure and cell wall.
- Bacteria are the source of many antibiotics, serum, vaccines and steroids.
- **Antibiotics** are the chemicals produced by microorganisms, which inhibit or kill disease causing microbes.
- A **vaccine** is a preparation of dead or weakened pathogen, e.g. typhoid vaccine. When the vaccine is injected into the body of a person, it develops antitoxins and provides immunity.
- **Steroids** are the hormones obtained from the bodies of various animals which helps in the treatment of various diseases. These are also produced by uring bacteria and certain alkaloids.
- Bacteria also helps in **nitrogen-fixation**. Plants cannot absorb nitrogen from the atmosphere, but can absorb it from the soil in the form of nitrates. Bacteria convert nitrogen into nitrates.
- **Nitrification** is the process of conversion of ammonia into nitrites and then into nitrates by *Nitrosomonas*, while *Nitrobacter* bacteria convert nitrites into nitrates.
- **Denitrification** is the conversion of nitrates into free nitrogen. *Pseudomonas* bacteria helps in denitrification.
- Fermentation by bacteria is needed for curing of tea leaves which increase the flavour and taste of tea.
- Bacteria cause fermentation of cooked food, vegetable, fruits, etc. Some bacteria release toxic substances and cause food poisoning (botulism), e.g. *Clostridium botulinum*.
- Bacteria are a cause of many diseases in plants, animals and humans.
- **Bioweapons** are microorganisms (bacteria) which promote disease or death in people, animals and plants, e.g. anthrax and smallpox. These can be used against humans, plants and animals.
- **Fungi** are multicellular, undifferentiated organisms that do not contain chlorophyll.
- Fungi like yeast are used in breweries and bakeries.
- Fungi helps in the production of antibiotics. Penicillin was the first antibiotic obtained from *Penicillium notatum*.
- Mushroom cultivation involves composting, spawning, casing, cropping and harvesting or preservation.
- Fungi cause various diseases in animals (e.g. athlete foot), plants (e.g. late blight of potatoes) and humans (e.g. ringworm).
- Other harmful activities by fungi involves food spoilage, wood decay, etc.

Chapter Practice

Section-I

1 Mark Questions

1. Name the following.
   (i) The bacteria used for producing streptomycin and tetracycline.
   (ii) The bacterium responsible for botulism.
   (iii) Any one agent of biowar.
   (iv) The fungus is used for the commercial production of alcohol.
   (v) The fungus that yields pectinase.
   (vi) The fungi that forms symbiotic association with plants.
   (vii) One animal disease that is caused by fungal species.
   (viii) The fungi responsible for causing ringworm in human.
   (ix) The microbe that causes late blight of potato in plants.

Ans. (i) Streptomycin – *Streptomyces griseus.*
Tetracycline – *Streptomyces aureofaciens.*
(ii) *Clostridium botulinum*
(iii) *Bacillus anthracis*
(iv) *Saccharomyces cerevisiae*
(v) *Aspergillus oryzae*
(vi) Mycorrhiza
(vii) Athlete foot (*T. rubrum*)
(viii) *Trichophyton* and *Microsporum*
(ix) Fungus- *Phytophthora infestans*

2. Correct and rewrite the following statements by changing the underlined words.
   (i) Ehrenberg proposed the term <u>microorganism</u> in 1829.
   (ii) <u>Toxoids</u> are the hormones obtained from the bodies of various animals.
   (iii) *Bacillus subtilis* is the source of enzyme <u>invertase</u>.
   (iv) Yeasts, on undergoing anaerobic respiration, yield CO_2 and <u>methanol</u>.
   (v) Another name for vitamin-B_{12} is <u>riboflavin</u>.

Ans. (i) Ehrenberg proposed the term bacteria in 1829.
(ii) Steroids are the hormones obtained from the bodies of various animals.
(iii) *Bacillus subtilis* is the source of enzyme protease.
(iv) Yeasts, on undergoing anaerobic respiration, yield CO_2 and ethanol.
(v) Another name for vitamin-B_{12} is cobalamin.

3. Give biological reasons for the following.
   (i) Nitrogen cycle is an important part of many processes related to plants.
   (ii) Crude leaves of tobacco and tea are hung in shade and permitted for the action of certain bacteria post-harvesting.
   (iii) Bacteria are responsible for causing several diseases related to plants and animals.
   (iv) Fungi are eukaryotic organisms but show heterotrophic mode of nutrition.
   (v) Mushrooms are used as food.
   (vi) Tinned or canned food is safe to eat.

Ans. (i) Nitrogen is needed to make chlorophyll in plants. This chlorophyll is used in photosynthesis. Nitrogen cycle involves transformation of nitrogen from one of the chemical form to the other. Thus, it is an important part of many processes related to plants.
(ii) Crude leaves of tobacco and tea are hung in shade and permitted for the action of certain bacteria after harvesting for removing bitterness and adding flavour and taste to the leaves.
(iii) Bacteria are responsible for causing several diseases in plants and animals including humans. They are capable of doing so because they release toxins that are harmful for plants and/or animals.
(iv) Fungi are eukaryotic organisms but show heterotrophic mode of nutrition because they lack chlorophyll.
(v) Mushrooms are used as food because they are rich sources of vitamins (e.g. biotin, pantothenic acid and niacin) and minerals.
(vi) Tinned or canned food is generally safe to eat. However, there may be a possibility of few microbes surviving in it. Thus, people are generally advised to buy fresh food.

4. (i) Match the following columns.

	Column I		Column II
A.	Bacterial cell wall	1.	Streptomycin
B.	Alexander Fleming	2.	Bacteria occurring in pair
C.	Selman Waksman	3.	Spherical bacteria
D.	Diplococci	4.	Penicillin
		5.	Peptidoglycan

(ii) Match the following columns.

Column I	Column II
A. Diphtheria	1. *Salmonella typhi*
B. Typhoid	2. *Xanthomonas oryzae*
C. Vibriosis	3. *Vibrio tatus*
D. Leaf blight of rice	4. *Xanthomonas citri*
	5. *Corynebacterium diphtheriae*

(iii) Match the following columns.

Column I	Column II
A. Bread mould	1. *Mucor*
B. Roquefort cheese	2. *Penicillium*
C. Fumaric acid	3. *Aspergillus*
D. Amylase	4. *Rhizopus*
E. Vitamin-B	5. Yeast

(iv) Match the following columns.

Column I	Column II
A. Yeast	1. Weakened bacteria (living)
B. TAB vaccine	2. *E. coli*
C. Insulin	3. White button mushroom
D. *Agaricus bisporus*	4. *Saccharomyces cerevisiae*
E. Pasteurisation	5. Paddy straw mushroom
	6. Killed bacteria
	7. Milk

(v) Match the following columns.

Column I	Column II
A. *Saccharomyces cerevisiae*	1. Mycology
B. Study of fungi	2. Fungi
C. Thalloid body	3. Phycology
D. Vaccines	4. Biological preparations
	5. Vitamin-B

Ans. (i) A–5, B–4, C–1, D–2
(ii) A-5, B-1, C-3, D-2
(iii) A-1, B-2, C-4, D-3, E-5
(iv) A–4, B–6, C–2, D–3, E–7
(v) A–5, B–1, C–2, D–4

5. Choose the correct answer from the four options given below.

(i) Which of these is a free-living aerobic bacteria?
(a) *Clostridium* (b) *Nostoc*
(c) *Azotobacter* (d) *Rhizobium*

Ans. (c)

(ii) Alcohol is converted into vinegar by the action of microorganisms called
(a) viruses (b) yeast
(c) protozoan (d) bacteria

Ans. (d)

(iii) Which of these is treated by pasteurisation?
(a) Water (b) Oil
(c) Fruit juice (d) Milk

Ans. (d)

(iv) Which of the following disease is not caused by bacteria?
(a) Cholera (b) Typhoid
(c) Tuberculosis (d) Measles

Ans. (d)

(v) The process of conversion of sugar into alcohol is called
(a) nitrogen-fixation (b) moulding
(c) fermentation (d) infection

Ans. (c)

(vi) Production of ethanol (C_2H_5OH) occurs in one of the life processes of
(a) bread mould (b) yeast
(c) mushroom (d) *Penicillium*

Ans. (b)

(vii) The bread dough rises during baking because of
(a) increased heat (b) grinding of dough
(c) growth of yeast cells (d) kneading of dough

Ans. (c)

(viii) The first antibiotic called penicillin was extracted from
(a) a bacterium (b) a protozoan
(c) a fungus (d) an alga

Ans. (c)

(ix) Which of the following in an antibiotic?
(a) Sodium bicarbonate (b) Flavicin
(c) Alcohol (d) Yeast

Ans. (b)

(x) Source of the antibiotic clavicin is
(a) *Aspergillus flavus* (b) *Aspergillus fumigatus*
(c) *Aspergillus clavatus* (d) *Penicillium chrysogenum*

Ans. (c)

6. Fill in the blanks by using suitable words.

(i) .... is freely found in soil and is an anaerobe .
(ii) Streptokinase is an enzyme obtained from ....
(iii) The causative agent of bacterial meningitis is ....
(iv) Cholera is caused by ....
(v) Fumaric acid is obtained from fungus ....
(vi) The first antibiotic was obtained from the fungal colony of ....
(vii) White rust is a .... disease of plants.

Ans. (i) *Clostridium* (ii) *Streptococcus pyogenes*
(iii) *Streptococcus pneumoniae*
(iv) *Vibrio cholerae* (v) *Rhizopus stolonifer*
(vi) *Penicillium notatum* (vii) fungal

7. Choose the odd one out from the following terms given below and name the category to which the other three belong.
(i) Streptomycin, Neomycin, Flavicin, Erythromycin
(ii) *Nitrosomonas, Clostridium botulinum, Nostoc, Anabaena*
(iii) *Clostridium butylicum, Bacillus* sp., *Lactobacillus, Pseudomonas denitrificans, Clostridium botulinum*
(iv) Vibriosis, Dysentery, Athlete's foot, Black leg.

Ans. (i) **Odd term** Flavicin.
Rest three are antibiotics obtained from bacteria.
(ii) **Odd term** *Clostridium botulinum*
Rest three are bacteria which help in nitrogen cycle.
(iii) **Odd term** *Clostridium botulinum.*
Rest three are categorised under useful bacteria.
(iv) **Odd term** Athlete's foot.
Rest three are animal diseases caused by bacteria.

8. State whether the following statement are true or false. Correct and rewrite the false statements.
(i) Denitrifying bacteria convert ammonium components into nitrates.
(ii) *Lactobacillus* is a harmful bacterium.
(iii) Some bacteria are helpful in increasing soil fertility.
(iv) Decomposition of dead organisms increases soil fertility.
(v) *Bacillus anthracis* is used as a bioweapon.
(vi) All mushrooms are edible.
(vii) In bakeries, *Rhizopus* is used for baking of bread.
(viii) The first antibiotic penicillin was obtained from *Penicillium chrysogenum.*

Ans. (i) False, denitrifying bacteria convert nitrates into nitrogen.
(ii) False, *Lactobacillus* is useful bacterium that is used in dairy industry.
(iii) True
(iv) True
(v) True
(vi) False, some mushrooms are edible.
(vii) False, in bakeries, yeast is used for baking of bread.
(viii) False, first antibiotic was obtained from *Penicillium notatum.*

9. Give one example of the following.
(i) Antibiotic obtained from a bacteria.
(ii) Bacteria present in root nodules of legumes.
(iii) Nitrifying bacteria
(iv) An enzyme produced by a bacteria.
(v) Alcoholic products obtained from fermentation by anaerobic bacteria.
(vi) Any two antibiotics derived from a fungi.
(vii) An animal disease caused by a fungi.

Ans. (i) Neomycin (ii) *Rhizobium*
(iii) *Nitrobacter* (iv) Amylase
(v) Ethyl alcohol (vi) Flavicin, penicillin
(vii) Athlete's foot

10. State the main function of the following.
(i) Vaccines
(ii) Steroids
(iii) *Nostoc*
(iv) *Saccharomyces cerevisiae*

Ans. (i) Vaccines provide acquired immunity against a specific disease.
(ii) Steroids are used in the treatment of various diseases like arthritis.
(iii) *Nostoc* converts atmospheric nitrogen into ammonia.
(iv) *Saccharomyces cerevisiae* is used in the production of alcoholic beverages.

11. Mention one difference in each of the following pairs on the basis of what is given in the braket. .
(i) Erythromycin and Chloromycetin (source)
(ii) Terramycin and Bacitracin (source)
(iii) Nitrification and Ammonification (definition)
(iv) *Agaricus bisporus* and Fly agaric (nature)

Ans. (i) Difference between erythromycin and chloromycetin is as follows

Erythromycin	Chloromycetin
It is obtained from *Streptomyces erythreus.*	It is obtained from *Streptomyces venezuelae.*

(ii) Difference between terramycin and bacitracin is as follows

Terramycin	Bacitracin
It is obtained from *Streptomyces rimosus.*	It is obtained from *Bacillus subtilis.*

(iii) Difference between nitrification and ammonification is as follows

Nitrification	Ammonification
It is the conversion of ammonia and ammonium compounds into nitrates and nitrites.	It involves decomposition of organic matter to produce ammonia.

(iv) Difference between *Agaricus bisporus* and Fly agaric is as follows

Agaricus bisporus	Fly agaric
It is an edible mushroom.	It is poisonous in nature, and hence it is non-edible.

12. Give biological/technical terms for the following.
(i) Suspension of heat-killed pathogens which induce immunity.
(ii) Cyclic event in which atmospheric nitrogen changes from one form to another.
(iii) Incomplete breakdown of organic matter.
(iv) Device that carries and delivers a disease causing biological agent.
(v) Step in which seeds of mushroom are introduced into the compost.

Ans. (i) Vaccine (ii) Nitrogen cycle
(iii) Putrefaction (iv) Bioweapon
(v) Spawning

13. Briefly explain the following terms.
(i) Serum (ii) Nitrogen-fixation
(iii) Botulism (iv) Pasteurisation

Ans. (i) Serum is the plasma preparation with specific antibodies or antitoxins obtained from the blood of mammals and is devoid of clotting factors. .
(ii) Nitrogen-fixation is the process of converting free atmospheric nitrogen into soluble forms like nitrates.
(iii) Botulism is a rare condition of food poisoning caused by the bacterium *Clostridium botulinum.*
(iv) Pasteurisation is the heating of milk at a higher temperature of about 60°C for about 30 minutes followed by rapid and sudden cooling.

14. Answer the following questions briefly.
(i) Several antibiotics are sourced from bacteria. Justify giving example.
(ii) How does denitrification lead to reduction in soil fertility?
(iii) Which vitamins are produced using different bacterial species?
(iv) Can fungi be used as nutritional supplement? Explain.
(v) What is the black powder we see on stale bread?

Ans. (i) There are several antibiotics prepared from bacteria and are effective against other bacteria without causing any side effect.
e.g. Bacitracin obtained from *Bacillus subtilis.*
(ii) Denitrification is the process of transforming nitrates into nitrogen by bacteria. It leads to a decrease in the amount of nitrogen available for plants, thus causing reduced soil fertility.
(iii) Vitamin-B_{12} and riboflavin are produced using different bacterial species.
(iv) Yes, fungi species are utilised as food since, they are rich sources of vitamins and minerals. For example, *Agaricus bisporus* is an edible mushroom rich in vitamins and minerals.
(v) When a piece of bread is kept in a warm place, spores of moulds, like *Rhizopus* fall on it and germinate to form mycellium, which is seen as black powder on stale bread.

2 Marks Questions

15. State any two features of a good antibiotic.

Ans. A good antibiotic should have the following two features
(i) It should be able to kill several disease causing microorganisms.
(ii) It should not cause any side effect post usage.

16. Name the steps involved in the cycling of nitrogen in air.

Ans. The steps are
(i) Nitrogen-fixation
(ii) Ammonification
(iii) Nitrification
(iv) Denitrification

17. Describe the role of bacteria in the production of vitamins.

Ans. Several species of bacteria are used in the preparation of vitamins. *Clostridium butylicum*, is used in the production of riboflavin (a kind of vitamin-B). *Propionibacterium shermanii* and *Pseudomonas denitrificans* are used to produce cobalamin (vitamin-B_{12}).

18. State the importance of yeast in breweries and bakeries.

Ans. Yeast such as, *Saccharomyces cerevisiae* are used in brewing and baking industry. During anaerobic respiration of glucose in yeast, ethyl alcohol and CO_2 are produced.

3 Marks Questions

19. Write any three applications of bacteria in the field of medicine.

Ans. Three applications of bacteria in the field of medicine are
(i) **Antibiotics** These are chemical substances produced by some microbes that kill or retard the growth of other microbes. Several antibiotics prepared from bacteria are effective against other bacteria, e.g. bacitracin from *Bacillus subtilis* and streptomycin from *Streptomyces griseus.*
(ii) **Vaccine** It is a biological preparation that provides active acquired immunity to a particular disease. A number of vaccines have been developed from weakened or killed forms of the bacteria, e.g. living weakened bacteria-BCG vaccine for tuberculosis.
Killed bacteria -TAB vaccine for typhoid.
(iii) **Serum** It is the plasma preparation (having specific antibodies or antitoxins) from the blood of certain mammals, such as horse, monkey, etc. Serums are used as a preventive measure against bacterial invasion, e.g. blood clotting factor - VIII is used for the treatment of haemophilia-A and is produced by genetically modified bacteria.

20. Bacteria present in soil fix the nitrogen for plant use. What is this process known as? Write about these bacteria in brief.

Ans. The process is known as nitrogen-fixation. It is the process of converting free atmospheric nitrogen into suitable forms like nitrates which can be used by plants.

The nitrogen-fixing bacteria are of two types

(i) **Symbiotic nitrogen-fixation** The Gram-negative bacteria include symbiotic nitrogen-fixing bacteria like *Rhizobium. Rhizobium leguminosarum* are found in the root nodules of leguminous plants like pea, gram, etc. They are capable of fixing free nitrogen of atmosphere into amino acid. These bacterias are found in the root nodules. They show the phenomenon of symbiosis (reciprocal benefit).

(ii) **Free-living forms** like *Azotobacter* are found freely in soil as saprophyte. They also fix the atmospheric nitrogen into amino acids and proteins.

21. Define antibiotics. Who discovered the first antibiotic? Name atleast three more antibiotics derived from fungi, along with their source fungus.

Ans. Antibiotics are substances of biological origin which at low concentration, can inhibit the growth of bacteria and other microorganisms.

Sir Alexander Fleming discovered the antibiotic named penicillin from the fungal colony of *Penicillium notatum* for the first time.

Other antibiotics are

(i) Clavicin obtained from *Aspergillus clavatus*

(ii) Flavicin obtained from *Aspergillus flavus*

22. Apart from antibiotics, what other products useful for mankind are obtained from fungi? Explain.

Ans. Useful products obtained from fungi are

(i) **Vitamins** Many fungal metabolites are rich source of vitamins, which are used as nutritional supplement and in medical therapy, e.g. vitamin-B from yeasts such as *Saccharomyces cerevisiae* and vitamin-A from *Rhodotorula gracilis*.

(ii) **Enzymes** Different enzymes are synthesised on commercial scale by using different fungi, e.g. *Aspergillus oryzae* is used to produce amylase, pectinase, protease.

23. What are the major steps involved in mushroom cultivation?

Ans. Major steps of mushroom cultivation are

(i) **Composting** It is made by mixing paddy or wheat straw, chicken manure and organic and inorganic fertilisers. The compost is filled in trays.

(ii) **Spawning** The seeds (mycelium) of mushroom are introduced into the compost.

(iii) **Casing** A thin layer of soil is spread over the compost and temperature of 25°C is maintained for 3 days. Then, temperature is lowered to 16-18°C.

(iv) **Cropping and harvesting** Growth occurs between 2-6 weeks. Full grown mushrooms are taken out.

(v) **Preservation** Vacuum cooling, storing at 15°C and freeze drying in a solution of brine are the important steps in preserving mushrooms to increase their shelf-life.

Section-II [5 Marks]

Structured Questions

1. Soil bacterium plays an important role in the decomposition of organic matter.

(i) How are bacteria classified according to their shapes?

(ii) Why do bacteria find their use in agriculture?

(iii) What does organic matter comprise of?

(iv) Give another name of free-living bacteria.

(v) Name the bacterium that reduces nitrate of the soil back to free nitrogen.

Ans. (i) Bacteria vary in shape. They can be *Coccus* (spherical), *Bacillus* (rod-like), *Vibrio* (comma-shaped) and *Spirillum* (spiral-shaped).

(ii) Bacteria are used as biofertilisers to enrich the nutrient quality of soil. Thus, they are used in the field of agriculture.

(iii) Organic matter comprises of proteins and nucleic acids.

(iv) Asymbiotic bacteria is another name of free-living bacteria.

(v) *Pseudomonas denitrificans* reduces nitrate of the soil back to free nitrogen.

2. Observe the given figure carefully to answer the questions that follows.

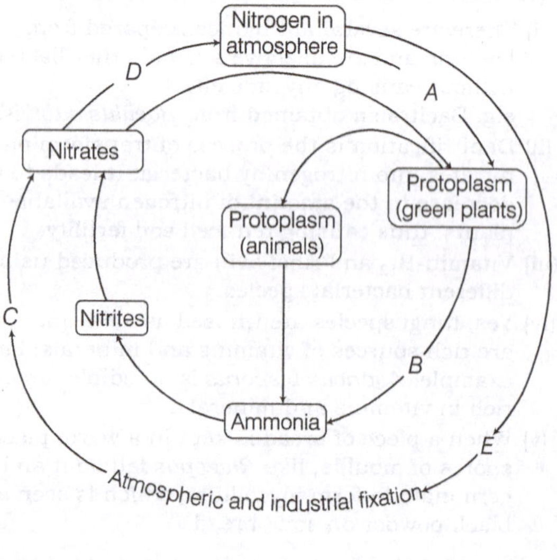

(i) Identify the process *A-E*.
(ii) Write the importance of this cycle.
(iii) What is meant by biological nitrogen-fixation?
(iv) Name the bacteria involved in the process *C*.
(v) What is the product obtained by the decomposition of organic matter of dead remains?

Ans. (i) The process *A–E* are as
A – Nitrogen-fixation
B – Ammonification
C – Nitrification
D – Denitrification
E – Nitrification

(ii) This process allows continuous flow of nitrogen in air, soil and water. It is important as nitrogen is an essential element for living organisms.
(iii) Biological nitrogen-fixation is a process in which atmospheric nitrogen is converted into inorganic nitrogenous compounds like nitrates, nitrites and ammonia with the help of microorganisms.
(iv) *Nitrosomonas* bacteria is involved in the process *C* (nitrification).
(v) Ammonia is obtained from the organic matter of the dead remains.

3. The diagram shows a fungus (mushroom).

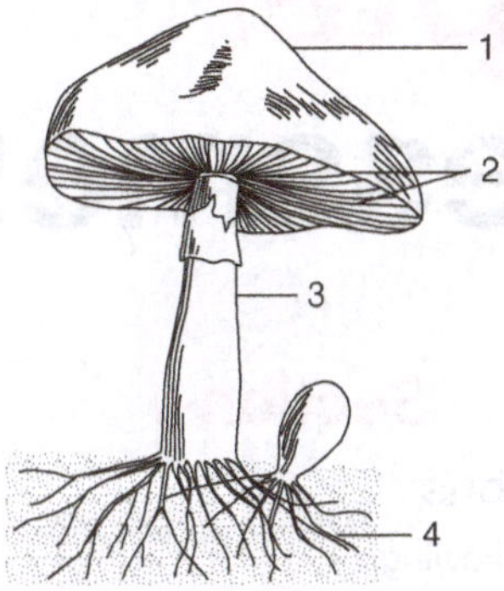

(i) Name the fungus.
(ii) Label the parts 1 and 2.
(iii) Why do they have high nutritive value?
(iv) What is its common name?
(v) Name any two vitamins that is generally present in mushrooms.

Ans. (i) The given fungus is *Agaricus bisporus*.
(ii) The parts 1 and 2 are labelled as
1. Cap, 2. Gills
(iii) They are rich in proteins and vitamins thus, possess high nutritive value.
(iv) White button mushroom is its common name.
(v) Niacin and biotin are generally found in mushrooms.

Chapter Assessment

Section-I

1 Mark Questions

1. Name the following.
   (i) Heat-killed diluted suspension of pathogenic bacteria of a specific disease.
   (ii) Bacteria used in curing and ripening of tea leaves.
   (iii) An association between two organisms mutually beneficial for each other.
2. Correct and rewrite the following statements by changing the underlined words.
   (i) An important antibiotic manufactured using bacteria is clavicin.
   (ii) Yeast is an important source of vitamin-C.
3. Give biological reasons for the following.
   (i) Bacteria are cosmopolitan in distribution.
   (ii) Salt acts as a preservative to pickles.
4. (i) Match the following columns.

Column I	Column II
A. Terramycin	1. *Bacillus subtilis*
B. Penicillin	2. *Aspergillus flavus*
C. Neomycin	3. *Streptomyces fradiae*
D. Flavicin	4. *Claviceps purpurea*
E. Bacitracin	5. *Streptomyces rimosus*
	6. *Penicillium notatum*

   (ii) Match the following columns.

Column I	Column II
A. *Clostridium butylicum*	1. Food poisoning
B. *Staphylococcus aureus*	2. Gaspard and Bauhin
C. Citrus canker	3. Vitamin-B_{12}
D. Fungi	4. Botulism
	5. *Xanthomonas citri*

5. Choose the correct answer from the four options given below.
   (i) Which of these microorganisms lives in the root nodules of leguminous plants?
   (a) *Clostridium* (b) *Rhizobium*
   (c) Yeast (d) *Aspergillus*
   (ii) Yeast is used in the production of
   (a) sugar (b) alcohol
   (c) hydrochloric acid (d) oxygen
   (iii) Which of these skin diseases is caused by fungus?
   (a) Prickly heat (b) Leukoderma
   (c) Ringworm (d) All of these
   (iv) Which one of the following characteristics is found in all fungi but not in all bacteria?
   (a) Aerobic respiration
   (b) Cell wall
   (c) Spore formation
   (d) A long circular DNA lying loose in cytoplasm
6. Fill in the blanks by using suitable words.
   (i) .... is a lactic acid bacterium.
   (ii) Tetracycline is an example of ....
   (iii) Pasteurisation is used for preserving......... .
   (iv) Concentrated solutions cause .... in cells of microorganisms.
7. Choose the odd one out from the following terms given below and name the category to which the other three belong.
   (i) *Salmonella typhi, Mycobacterium tuberculosis, Clostridium tetani, Xanthomonas rubrilineans.*
   (ii) *Micrococcus, Staphylococcus, Saccharomyces, Clostridium*
8. State whether the following statements are true or false. Choose and rewrite the false statements.
   (i) Milk is converted into lactic acid during the formation of curd.
   (ii) Vaccines have only killed forms of bacteria.
   (iii) Anaerobic decomposition is called putrefaction.

9. Give one example of the following.
   (i) Bacteria that produce bacitracin antibiotic.
   (ii) Fungi used as food.
   (iii) Fungi that can cause plant disease.
10. State the main function of the following.
   (i) *Streptomyces*
   (ii) *Thiobacillus denitrificans*
11. Mention one difference in each of the following pair on the basis of what is given in the bracket.
   Antibiotics and Serum (function)
12. Give biological/technical terms for the following.
   (i) Process of making food germ free by the addition of certain substances.
   (ii) Removal of fats, hair and other tissues from animal skin using bacteria.
13. Briefly explain the following terms.
   (i) Nitrification (ii) Bioweapons
14. Answer the following questions briefly.
   (i) State any two harmful activities of fungi.
   (ii) Mention any two characteristic features of pathogens used as bioweapons.
   (iii) Write any two uses of fungi.

2 Marks Questions

15. Making our food free from disease causing germs is essential. Explain. Mention any one technique of doing so.
16. Write a short note on symbiotic bacteria.

3 Marks Questions

17. The role of bacteria in industries is widespread. Justify.
18. How are different types of bacteria related to soil fertility?

Section-II [5 Marks]

Structured Questions

19. Study the diagram and answer the questions that follows.

   (i) Name the type of plant shown in the diagram.
   (ii) What are *X*?
   (iii) How is the structure mentioned above in question (ii), advantageous for the plant?
   (iv) What is nitrogen-fixation?
   (v) Name two bacteria which are found in the roots of these plants.
20. Fungi are highly evolved, multicellular organisms without chlorophyll.
   (i) Give two features of fungi.
   (ii) Name the fungi used for the production of wine.
   (iii) Which fungal species is used to impart different flavours to cheese?
   (iv) Give the common name of *Rhizopus*.
   (v) State the mode of reproduction found in *Rhizopus*.

For explanations scan the given QR Code

Olympiad Section*

Brain Teasing Questions asked in Previous Olympiads

1 Decompostion is an important process for nutrient recycling and ecosystem functionality. Nitrogen- fixing bacteria form an important part of the process. Choose the correct statement from the following. **[IJSO 2019 Doha, Qatar]**

(a) Decompose protein to ammonia
(b) Use atmospheric nitrogen to form nitric acid
(c) Use atmospheric ntirogen to form ammonium
(d) Change nitrates to N_2 that is then released into the atmosphere

2 If, in an experiment, all nitrogenase enzymes in a field are inactivated by irradiation, what will be the immediate vital effect of it? **[INBO 2014]**

(a) No fixation of nitrogen in leguminous plants of the field
(b) No fixation of atmospheric nitrogen at all
(c) No conversion of nitrate to nitrite in leguminous plants of the field
(d) No conversion of nitrates to ammonia in soil of the field

3 Plants having mutualistic relation with nitrogen-fixing bacteria would receive nitrogen in the form of .... from the bacteria. **[INBO 2014]**

(a) ammonium ions (b) amino acids (c) nitrates (d) nitrites

4 Observe the nitrogen cycle given below and answer the following questions. **[INJSO 2014]**

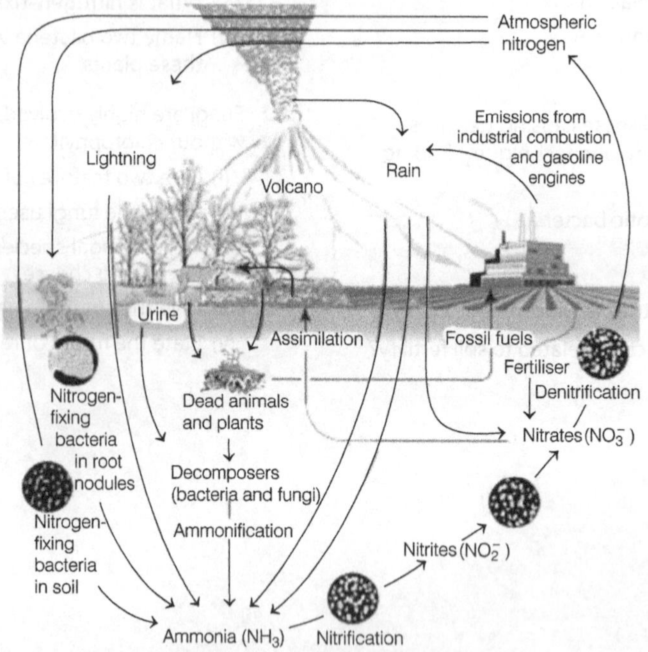

Beginning with free atmospheric nitrogen, which of the following marks the nitrogen cycle in proper order?

(a) Ammonification → Denitrification → Nitrogen-fixation → Nitrification
(b) Nitrogen-fixation → Ammonification → Nitrification → Denitrification
(c) Denitrification → Nitrification → Nitrogen-fixation → Ammonification
(d) Nitrification → Ammonification → Denitrification → Nitrogen-fixation

Answers

1. (c) **2.** (a) **3.** (a) **4.** (b)

**These questions may or may not be asked in the examination, have been given just for additional practice required for olympiads, scholarship exams etc. For detailed explanations refer Page No. 230.*

CHAPTER 09

Nutrition and Digestion in Humans

Chapter Inside

• Nutrients • Digestive System

The process by which an organism obtains its nutrients and utilises them to obtain energy and to build and repair the tissues is called **nutrition**.

Nutrients

The edible substances which we eat to obtain energy for growth, repair and maintenance of the body and to fight against occurrence of diseases, is called **food**. Each food item is usually made up of one or more ingredients, which we get from plants or animals. These ingredients contain **nutrients** which are needed by our body. **Nutrients** are the substances required for proper growth and maintenance of a living body. They can be classified as

- Carbohydrates
- Proteins
- Fats
- Vitamins
- Mineral salts
- Water

1. Carbohydrates

These are energy releasing compounds made up of oxygen, hydrogen and carbon with hydrogen and oxygen always in the ratio of 2:1. These are of three types depending upon their structure, that includes **monosaccharides, oligosaccharides and polysaccharides.** The main carbohydrates found in our food are in the form of starch and sugars. These provide energy to our body.

Some sources of carbohydrates are **wheat, rice, maize, pearl millet, potatoes, sugar, jaggery** (gud), **honey, fruits** (banana, mango and papaya), etc. Rice is a 'carbohydrate rich' source of food. The carbohydrates in our food are obtained mainly from plant sources.

Functions of Carbohydrates

The major functions of carbohydrates include

(i) The role of carbohydrates is to provide energy, as they are the main source of energy needed for physical and other activities.

(ii) They store energy in the form of starch in plants whereas in animals, these are stored as glycogen.

(iii) Cellulose is the structural form of carbohydrates in plants, which is a part of cell wall. In humans, roughage adds cellulose to diet.

Note Roughage is the part of food which does not have any nutritional value but helps in keeping faecal matter soft and prevents constipation.

2. Proteins

These constitute major part of our food. These are mainly used as the **building blocks** in our body. They contain carbon, hydrogen, oxygen and nitrogen.

Proteins are made up of amino acids. Proteins can be divided into two groups depending on their sources

(i) **Animal proteins** These are obtained from animal products like milk, cheese, egg, fish or meat.

(ii) **Vegetable proteins** These are obtained from plants like **gram, moong, tuar dal, beans, peas, soybeans,** etc.

Functions of Proteins

The major functions of proteins include

(i) They are essential for growth and repair of body.

(ii) They act as enzymes or chemical catalyst in metabolic reactions.

(iii) Antibodies are proteins which work for the defence system of the body.

3. Fats

These also provide energy to our body. Infact, fats provide twice as much energy as provided by the same amount of carbohydrates. Fats and oils are similar substances, the only difference being that fats are solid at room temperature, whereas oils are liquid at room temperature.

Fats can be obtained from plants as well as from animals. Some of the plant sources of fats are groundnut oil, mustard oil, coconut oil, sunflower oil, soybean oil, til oil and nut oil and some of the animal sources of fats are butter, ghee, milk, cream, cheese, eggs and meat.

Functions of Fats

The major functions of fats include

(i) They mainly act as reserve food and are the basic energy providers of our body.

(ii) They provide an insulating and protective covering. This covering is present over the entire surface of our body below the skin.

(iii) They provide insulation sheath for our nerves, **myelin sheath** is mainly made up of phospholipids.

4. Vitamins

These are a group of nutrients that our body requires in small quantities. These are essential for the proper functioning of the body but do not provide energy (protective food). If our diet is lacking in any vitamin, we suffer from certain diseases called **deficiency diseases.** Vitamins may be divided into two classes

(i) **Fat soluble vitamins** Vitamin-A, D, E and K.

(ii) **Water soluble vitamins** B-complex and vitamin-C.

An Overview of Various Vitamins

Name of vitamins	Sources	Functions	Deficiency diseases
Fat soluble vitamins			
Vitamin-A (Retinol)	Fish liver oil, egg yolk, milk, animal liver, yellow, red and green fruits. Vegetables like carrot, orange, etc.	Synthesis of retinal pigment, promotes normal vision, growth of bones and teeth, maintenance of epithelia.	**Xerophthalmia** (dryness of cornea and ulceration), **night blindness** (poor vision in dark)
Vitamin-D (Calciferol)	Fish liver oil, milk and its products, egg yolk, butter, UV rays of Sun.	It regulates metabolism of calcium and phosphorus for growth of bones and teeth.	**Rickets** in children, weak bones, bone deformities, **osteomalacia** in adults, dental caries, etc.
Vitamin-E (Tocopherol)	Vegetable oils, milk, green vegetables like lettuce, egg yolk, meat, cereals, nuts, etc.	Works as antioxidant, role in healing wound, etc.	Anaemia, sterility, muscular dystrophy.
Vitamin-K (Phylloquinone)	Green leafy vegetables, tomatoes, soybean, wheat, fish, liver, egg, etc.	Helps in the formation of prothrombin in liver for normal clotting of blood, also have role in formation of other blood clotting proteins.	**Haemorrhage** deficiency of prothrombin in blood (delaying in blood clotting).

Name of vitamins	Sources	Functions	Deficiency diseases
Water soluble vitamins			
Vitamin-B_1 (Thiamine)	Beans, peas, green vegetables, cereals, whole wheat, yeast, milk, egg yolk, rice, etc.	Helps in increasing appetite, promotes growth of the body.	**Beri-beri** (affects nervous system)
Vitamin-B_2 (Riboflavin)	Milk, liver, kidney, egg yolk, fish, yeast, germinating seeds, etc.	Required for cell growth and regulates oxidation of food.	**Cheliosis,** i.e cracking corners of mouth. **Dermatitis,** i.e. dryness of skin.
Vitamin-B_3 (Niacin)	Wheat bran, yeast, liver, vegetables, pulses, etc.	Promotes healthy skin and nervous system.	Pellagra, diarrhoea, indigestion, skin lesions, vomiting, dementia.
Vitamin-B_5 (Pantothenic acid)	Honey, egg yolk, tomatoes, sweet potato, yeast, etc.	Used in synthesis of fats, proteins coenzyme-A, helpful for healthy skin and hair.	Fatigue, insomnia, premature greying of hair, burning feet syndrome, retarded growth.
Vitamin-B_6 (Pyridoxine)	Meat, milk, egg yolk, fish, peas, whole grain, green leafy vegetables, liver, etc.	Involved in carbohydrate, lipid and proteins metabolism.	Anaemia, dermititis, paralysis, mental disorder.
Vitamin-B_9 (Folic acid)	Spinach leaves, wheat, peanuts, yeast, liver, kidney	Required in erythrocyte maturation, DNA and RNA synthesis	Inflammation of bowel, conditions involving ulceration of mouth, anaemia.
Vitamin-B_{12} (Cobalamin)	Liver and kidney are the richest sources. Other sources are egg, milk, fish, intestinal bacteria, etc.	Required for erythrocyte maturation, DNA synthesis, myelin formation.	Pernicious anaemia
Vitamin-C (Ascorbic acid)	Citrus fruits like lemon, grapes, cherry, tomato, green vegetables, etc.	Healing wounds and damaged bones, necessary for healthy teeth and gums.	Scurvy (Sailor's disease) delayed wound healing, loss of appetite.

5. Mineral Salts

These come next to vitamins under the category of protective foods. Minerals can be categorised into macroelements and microelements.

A brief introduction to these is given below

Macroelements

These are nutrients required in large quantities, e.g. Ca, Mg, Cl, etc. Two of these are given below.

(i) **Calcium** (Ca) is useful for bones and teeth formation. It is a major constituent for nerve functioning, muscle contraction, coagulation of blood, etc. It is found in dairy products, eggs, wheat, dark green vegetables and dates, etc. Its deficiency in blood causes **rickets, muscular spasm, haemorrhage** with more coagulation time, nervous disorders, **muscular cramps**, etc.

(ii) **Sodium** (Na) is most important for blood and nerve functioning. It is a principal cation of extracellular fluid (0-7%). In excitable tissues, it is responsible for the impulse transmission. It is found in table salt. Its deficiency causes **muscular cramps** along with neural disorders.

Microelements

These are nutrients required in smaller quantities and are given as

(i) **Iodine** (I) is a component of hormones of thyroid gland. It is present in salt (iodised salt), sea food, onions and drinking water. Its deficiency is associated with malfunctioning of thyroid gland. Its deficiency causes **goitre.**

(ii) **Iron** (Fe) is a component of respiratory pigments (like haemoglobin and myoglobin) and respiratory enzyme (like cytochromes). It is found in meat, dried nuts, cereals, beans, apple, banana, honey, dates, green leafy vegetables and pomegranate. Its deficiency causes **anaemia.**

Functions of Mineral Salts

The major functions of minerals include

(i) They are required for proper functioning, normal growth and good health.

(ii) They are needed to build bones and teeth, formation of blood, coagulation of blood and functioning of muscles, nerves, thyroid glands, etc.

(iii) They also control or affect the working of some glands like thyroid.

6. Water

It makes up almost 70% of our body weight and various life processes are impossible without it. We take in water not only directly by drinking, but also as part of the food we eat. Fresh fruits and vegetables, e.g. tomatoes, spinach, oranges, watermelons, etc. also provide a lot of water to our body.

Water helps our body to absorb nutrients from food. It also helps in throwing out some wastes from body as urine and sweat. The loss of lots of water from the body is called **dehydration**. It can happen due to diarrhoea, vomiting, burn or heat stroke. Acute dehydration can even cause death.

Balanced Diet

The total amount of food which a person eats during entire day is called their **diet. Balanced diet** is the diet that contains proper amounts of all the nutrients. It provides the body with all energy and fulfil various nutrient requirements needed for proper functioning. A balanced diet should include the foods that are

(i) **Energy rich** Fats and carbohydrates like butter, rice and chapaties.

(ii) **Tissue building** Proteins like pulses and peas.

(iii) **Protective** Vitamins, minerals like vegetables and fruits.

A balanced diet is not same for everyone. It depends on age, sex and type of work that one does. This can be explained by following examples

(i) In early childhood, the child grows rapidly. He or she needs more **proteins**.

(ii) Nursing mothers and pregnant women also need more protein to serve the needs of the growing baby.

(iii) A hard worker, labourer needs more energy which he can get by eating more **fats** and **carbohydrates**.

A Typical Balanced Diet

Carbohydrates	45–65%
Fats	20–35%
Proteins	10–35%

Trace amounts of other components like water, roughage, minerals and vitamins also constitute a balanced diet.

Cellulose also forms a major part of dietary fibre that is important for proper digestion. It cannot be broken down and it passes through our systems basically unchanged. It acts as bulk or roughage that helps in the movement of our intestines.

Lack or deficiency of any one or more essential elements of food in an individual diet leads to **malnutrition**.

Nutritional Disorders

Every organism requires adequate supply of nutrients in their diet for proper growth and development. Any change in this leads to either a nutritional imbalance or a digestive disorder. Some of the nutritional disorders are

(i) Kwashiorkor

It is a form of malnutrition caused by lack of protein in the diet. People who have kwashiorkor typically have an extremely emaciated (thin or weak) appearance in all body parts except their ankles, feet and belly, which swell with fluid.

Causes

Every cell in our body contains protein. We need protein in our diet for our body to repair cells and to make new cells. If the body lacks protein, growth and normal body functions will begin to shut down and kwashiorkor may develop.

Symptoms

The symptoms of kwashiorkor include

- Change in skin and hair colour (to a rust colour) and texture
- Fatigue
- Diarrhoea
- Loss of muscle mass
- Failure to grow or gain weight
- Oedema (swelling) of the ankles, feet and belly
- Damaged immune system, which can lead to more frequent and severe infections
- Irritability

Prevention

Kwashiorkor can be prevented by eating more protein and more calories overall, especially if treatment has started early. One may first be given more calories in the form of carbohydrates, sugars and fats. Once these calories provide energy, he will be given foods with proteins.

(ii) Marasmus

It can occurs in anyone who has severe malnutrition, but it usually occurs in children.

Causes

Nutrient deficiency is the main cause of marasmus. It occurs in children that do not ingest enough protein, calories, carbohydrates and other important nutrients. This is usually due to poverty and a scarcity of food.

Symptoms

The symptoms of marasmus include

- The main symptom of marasmus is being underweight. Children with this condition lose a lot of muscle mass and subcutaneous fat.
- Dry skin and brittle hair are also symptoms of marasmus.

In children with marasmus, the following can also occur

- Chronic diarrhoea
- Respiratory infections
- Intellectual disability
- Stunted growth
- Skin becomes loosely folded

Prevention

Initial treatment of marasmus often includes dried skim milk powder mixed with boiled water. Later, the mixture can also include a vegetable oil such as sesame, casein and sugar. **Casein** is a milk protein. The oil increases the energy content and density of the mixture.

Once a child starts to recover, they should take a more balanced diet that meets their nutritional needs.

Check Your LEARNING...

1. Name two sources of carbohydrates.
2. How are carbohydrates stored in plants?
3. Why proteins are called body building foods in human body?
4. Give one function of fats in human body.
5. Name the vitamin responsible for clotting of blood.
6. What is balanced diet?
7. How kwashiorkor can be prevented in young children?

Digestive System

Digestion is a **catabolic** process, in which complex and large components of food are broken down into their respective simpler and smaller forms with the help of various hydrolytic enzymes. These simpler forms are further taken up by different parts of body and are finally absorbed.

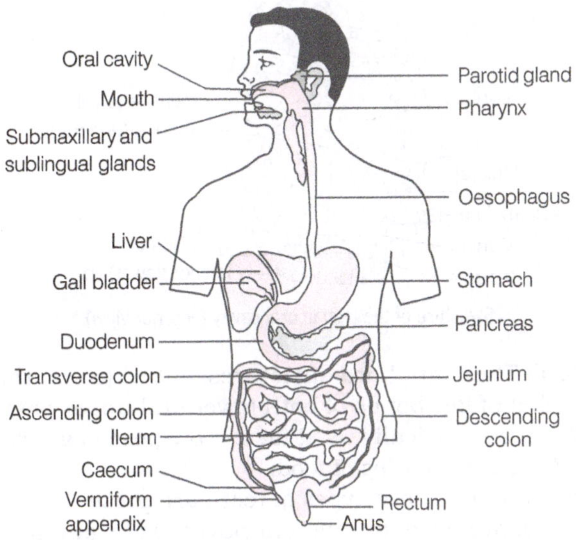

Human digestive system

The entire system, which performs this process of digestion is known as **digestive system**. In human beings, the digestive system constitutes a long tubular structure called **alimentary canal** (about 7-8 metres long) and **digestive glands** associated with it, which secrete various **digestive enzymes**.

Alimentary Canal

It is a long tube, where the entire process of digestion takes place. It is an internal coiled tube, which runs from anterior mouth to the posterior anus. The complete process of ingestion, digestion, absorption, assimilation and egestion of food material is done within the alimentary canal itself. The major portions of alimentary canal are discussed below

1. Mouth and Buccal Cavity

The first part of the digestive system from where the food enters into the alimentary canal. Mouth is a slit-like opening, bounded by two soft, movable **lips**. It opens into a small **vestibule** (space enclosed between lips and cheeks externally and gums and teeth internally), which in turn leads into the **buccal** or **oral cavity**.

Oral cavity further comprises of two main components

- **Tongue** It is a highly muscular, sensory organ present at the floor of buccal cavity. It bears several taste buds and helps in mixing food with saliva. Apart from this, it is also helpful in producing speech.

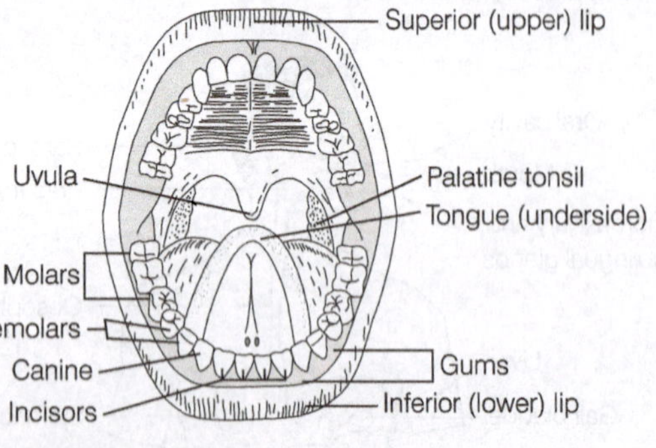

Structure of the human oral cavity (anterior view)

- **Teeth** These are hard structures embedded on the socket of jaw bones of both lower and upper jaws. Teeth are basically used for the purpose of **grinding, cutting** and **chewing** of food.
  In mammals, four types of teeth are present which are used for different purposes by animals, i.e.
  (i) **Incisors** present at the front of the mouth and are used for **cutting** or **clipping**.
  (ii) **Canines** are next to incisors and are used for puncturing or holding or **tearing** the food.
  (iii) **Premolars** and **molars** are the innermost and are used for crushing or grinding the food. The last molar of each side in each jaw is called **wisdom tooth**.

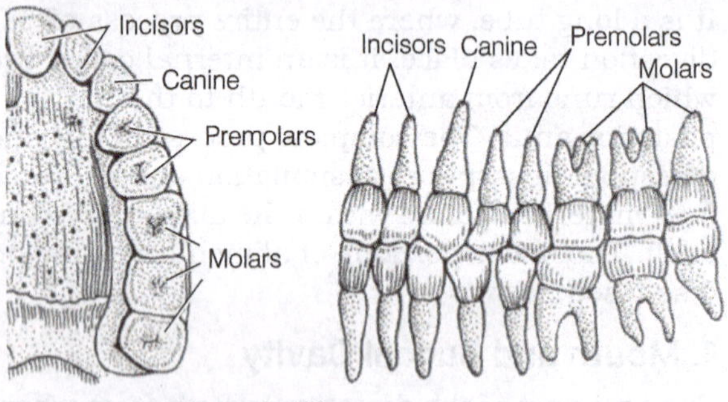

Human dentition

Thus, human teeth are different in shape and are called heterodont and other animals such as frogs and lizards have same kind of teeth and are called homodont.

However, the number of each type of teeth differs in different groups of animals.

Tooth Structure

The tooth have almost same structure in all the vertebrates. It is differentiated into three regions namely, **crown, neck** and **the root**. The part of tooth projecting above the gum line is called **crown.**

The **neck** is the part present inside the gums. The root is present inside the bony socket. The structure of tooth in its sectional view is given below

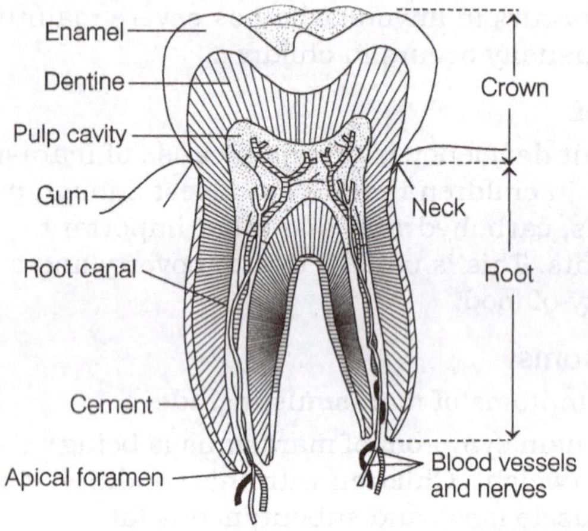

A section of a tooth

In the crown region, the outermost layer is called **enamel**. It is the hardest substance of human body. In the neck and root region, the outermost layer is called **cement layer**. In the centre of the tooth, a **pulp cavity** is present. It contains mass of cells, blood vessels, lymph vessels and nerves for nourishment of tooth.

The **pulp cavity** is surrounded by a layer of hard ivory-like substance called **dentine**. The fixation of tooth within the socket occurs with the help of thick bundles of collagen fibres covering the cementing layer.

Dental Formula

The number and the kinds of teeth in mammals are represented by an equation called dental formula. These are constant for every species.

Since, two halves of each jaw are identical, the teeth of only one side are recorded in this formula.

For vertebrates, this formula looks like $\frac{\text{I C Pm M}}{\text{I C Pm M}}$

Here, I = Incisors, C = Canines, Pm = Premolars, M = Molars.

The total number of teeth in jaw = number of teeth in dental formula × 2.

The dental formula in human

(i) Human (Adult) = $\frac{2123}{2123} \times 2 = 32$ (Permanent teeth)

(ii) Human (Child) = $\frac{2102}{2102} \times 2 = 20$ (Milk teeth)

Salivary Glands

These glands secrete saliva containing an enzyme called **salivary amylase** (ptyalin). It converts starch into sugar at an optimum pH of about 6.8. It is due to these salivary glands that our mouth waters when we eat or smell something we like. Three pairs of salivary glands that secrete saliva are **parotid** (present below the pinna, i.e. portion of outer ear), **submaxillary** (present on inner side of lower jaw) and **sublingual** (present below the tongue).

Saliva performs the following functions

1. Moisten and lubricates food which helps in swallowing.
2. Helps food particles to stick together to form bolus, so that they are easily swallowed.
3. Cleans the mouth and tends to destroy germs thus, preventing tooth decay.

Functions of Buccal Cavity

The buccal cavity shows two major functions

(i) **Mastication of food** It involves the movement of teeth, which helps in chewing food and the tongue, which helps the food to mix thoroughly with the saliva.

(ii) **Swallowing** (Deglutition) It is the process of passing bolus or mass of food in the oesophagus from the buccal cavity through pharynx.

Digestion in Buccal or Oral Cavity

Digestion starts in oral cavity by the chemical hydrolytic action of the carbohydrates splitting enzyme, salivary amylase (ptyalin). The saliva secreted inside oral cavity contains electrolytes and enzymes, i.e. salivary amylase and lysozyme. About 30% of the starch gets hydrolysed in the oral cavity by the action of salivary amylase (at optimum pH 6.8) into a disaccharide, i.e. maltose.

$$\text{Starch} \xrightarrow[\text{pH 6.8}]{\text{Salivary amylase}} \text{Maltose}$$

2. Pharynx

It is a small funnel-shaped chamber located behind the oral cavity. It serves as a common passage for both food and air, i.e. it communicates with both oesophagus (food pipe) and trachea (windpipe). The opening of trachea or windpipe is called **glottis**, which is guarded by a cartilaginous flap or lid called **epiglottis**. The glottis normally remains open, but during swallowing of food it gets covered by epiglottis to prevent the entry of food in trachea.

3. Oesophagus

It is a thin, long muscular tube that extends and leads into a J-shaped bag-like structure called **stomach**.

A muscular **gastro-oesophageal sphincter** regulates the opening of oesophagus into the stomach.

Peristaltic Movements

These are the necessary actions of the digestive process and are essential for moving food in a regulated manner along the digestive tube. The lining of the alimentary canal has muscles, which contract rhythmically in order to push the food forward. These movements are called peristaltic movements. They occur all along the gut, e.g. they occur in oesophagus when food is moved into stomach.

Check Your LEARNING...

1. Give one characteristic of incisors and premolars.
2. Name the material that covers the crown.
3. Give the dental formula of human child.
4. What is the role of buccal cavity in digestion of food?
5. What is peristaltic movement?

4. Stomach

It is the most dilated J-shaped part of the alimentary canal, which is situated between the oesophagus and the small intestine, below the diaphragm. It serves as a storehouse of food where partial digestion takes place through the secretions of gastric glands. The muscular walls of the stomach help in mixing the food properly.

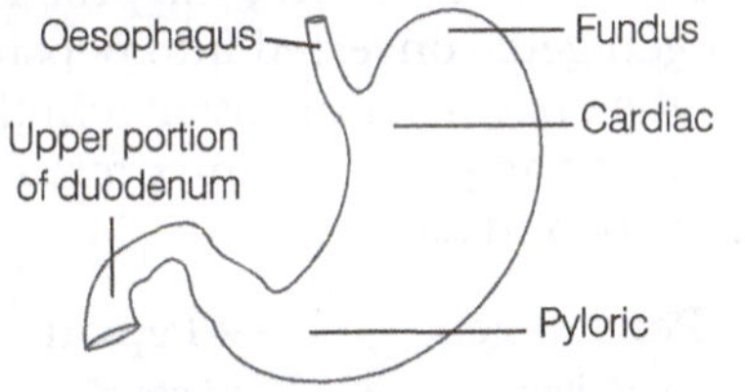

Anatomical regions of human stomach

Stomach has three major parts as given below

(i) **Cardiac stomach**, the upper portion into which the oesophagus opens.

(ii) **Fundic stomach**, the middle portion.

(iii) **Pyloric stomach**, the lower portion, which opens into the first part of small intestine, i.e. duodenum. It contains ring-like muscles called **sphincter** which regulates its opening.

Stomach serves the following functions

(i) It acts as a short term storage reservoir.

(ii) Substantial chemical and enzymatic digestion initiate in stomach (especially of proteins).

(iii) Gastric smooth muscles mix and grind the foodstuff by vigorous contractions with gastric secretions.

Gastric Glands

These are found in the wall of the stomach. The gastric glands release digestive juice containing HCl, pepsin, mucus, etc.

Hydrochloric acid (HCl) secreted by the oxyntic cells of stomach mucosa, kills the bacteria ingested with food. It creates an acidic medium of pH about 2, facilitating the action of **pepsin** enzyme, which acts on proteins present in food. Due to this highly acidic nature of HCl, the digestion of starch in stomach is prevented.

It also prepares the ingested food for further processing in the small intestine. The **mucus** protects the lining of the stomach from the action of the hydrochloric acid produced under normal conditions.

Digestion in Stomach

The stomach stores the food for around 4-5 hours. Internal mucosa of stomach contains gastric glands, which secrete gastric juices. The food mixes thoroughly with the acidic gastric juice secreted in the stomach by the **churning movements** of its muscles and becomes semi-digested, acidic, pulpy mass called **chyme**.

The enzymes of stomach and their actions are given below

(i) **Pepsin** On exposure to HCl, the proenzyme pepsinogen gets converted into pepsin (proteolytic enzyme of the stomach) that further converts proteins into proteases and peptones (peptides).

$$\underset{\text{(Inactive)}}{\text{Pepsinogen}} \xrightarrow{\text{HCl}} \underset{\text{(Active)}}{\text{Pepsin}}$$

$$\text{Proteins} \xrightarrow{\text{Pepsin (optimum pH 1-3)}} \text{Proteases + Peptones}$$

(ii) **Rennin** It is a proteolytic enzyme found in gastric juice of only infants, in its inactive form. Its secretion helps in the digestion of milk proteins.

$$\underset{\text{(Inactive)}}{\text{Prorennin}} \xrightarrow{\text{HCl}} \underset{\text{(Active)}}{\text{Rennin}}$$

$$\underset{\substack{\text{(Milk protein)}\\\text{(Soluble)}}}{\text{Casein}} \xrightarrow{\text{Rennin}} \underset{\substack{\text{(Peptide)}\\\text{(Insoluble)}}}{\text{Paracasein}}$$

(iii) **Gastric lipase** It acts on emulsified fats and also helps in digesting around 25% of milk fat (in infants). The amount of mucus and bicarbonates present in the gastric juice plays an important role in lubrication and protection of mucosal epithelium from excoriation by the highly acidic pH of stomach.

5. Small Intestine

The longest part of the alimentary canal, i.e. small intestine is fitted in a compact space as extensively coiled structure in our belly. The length of small intestine differs in all organisms depending upon their food habits, e.g. herbivores have long small intestine to facilitate cellulose digestion. Carnivores have shorter length of small intestine as meat is easily digestible.

It is divided into three parts

(i) Duodenum
(ii) Jejunum
(iii) Ileum

Small intestine is the site of complete digestion of food into different components. The inner lining of the small intestine has numerous finger-like projections called **villi**, which increase the surface area for absorption. Lacteals are lymphatic capillaries found in the villi of small intestine. They absorb and transport large molecules of fat and lipids.

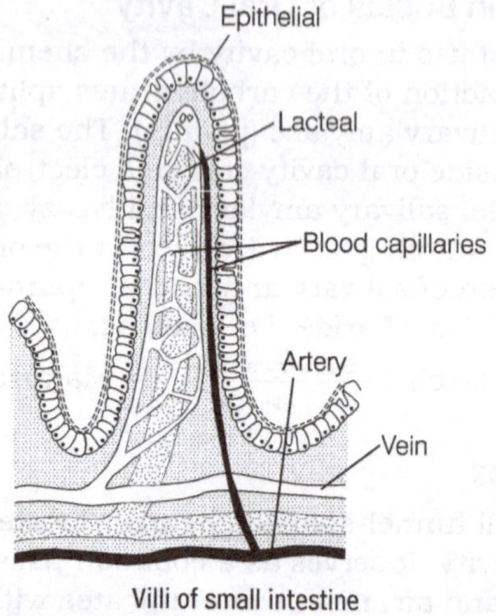

Villi of small intestine

Intestinal Glands

Walls of small intestine contain numerous glands that secrete intestinal juice containing **amylolytic** (digest carbohydrates), **proteolytic** (digest protein) and **lipolytic** (digest fats or lipids) enzymes.

Digestion in Small Intestine

To facilitate the digestion, muscularis layer of small intestine shows various movements which allow thorough mixing of food with various secretions from liver and pancreas in the intestine. The respective digestive juices from the pancreas (pancreatic juice), the liver (bile juice) and small intestine (intestinal juices) bring out the further chemical simplification of food.

Pancreas and their Enzymes

Pancreas secretes pancreatic juices into the small intestine through the duct called **pancreatic duct**. It joins the bile duct to form common **hepato-pancreactic duct** that opens into small intestine (duodenum).

The pancreatic juice secreted from the pancreas contains the various inactive enzymes.

These are given below

(i) Trypsinogen
(ii) Chymotrypsinogen
(iii) Procarboxypeptidases
(iv) Amylases
(v) Lipases
(vi) Nucleases

- **Trypsinogen** is activated by an enzyme **enterokinase** secreted by intestinal mucosa into active trypsin which in turn activates the other enzymes of pancreatic juice.

$$\underset{\text{(Inactive)}}{\text{Trypsinogen}} \xrightarrow[\text{pH (7 - 9)}]{\text{Enterokinase}} \underset{\text{(Active)}}{\text{Trypsin}}$$

- The proteins, proteases and peptones present in the chyme (reaching the intestine) are acted upon by the proteolytic enzymes of pancreatic juice. Further digestion proceeds as follows

$$\left.\begin{array}{r}\text{Proteins}\\ \text{Peptones}\\ \text{Proteases}\end{array}\right\} \xrightarrow[\text{Carboxypeptidase}]{\text{Trypsin / Chymotrypsin}} \text{Dipeptides}$$

- **Carbohydrates** in the chyme are hydrolysed by pancreatic **amylase** into disaccharides.

$$\text{Polysaccharides (starch)} \xrightarrow{\text{Amylase}} \text{Disaccharides}$$

- **Nucleases** in the pancreatic juice acts on nucleic acid to form nucleotides and nucleosides.

$$\text{Nucleic acids} \xrightarrow{\text{Nucleases}} \text{Nucleotides} \xrightarrow{\text{Nucleases}} \text{Nucleosides}$$

- **Steapsin** acts on emulsified fats to split them into fatty acids and glycerol.

$$\text{Emulsified fat} \xrightarrow{\text{Steapsin}} \text{Fatty acids + Glycerol}$$

Note Pancreas also secretes hormones, glucagon and insulin, which regulate glucose metabolism in body.

Liver and their Juices

Liver is the largest gland of the body, which secretes **bile juice** into the duodenum of small intestine.

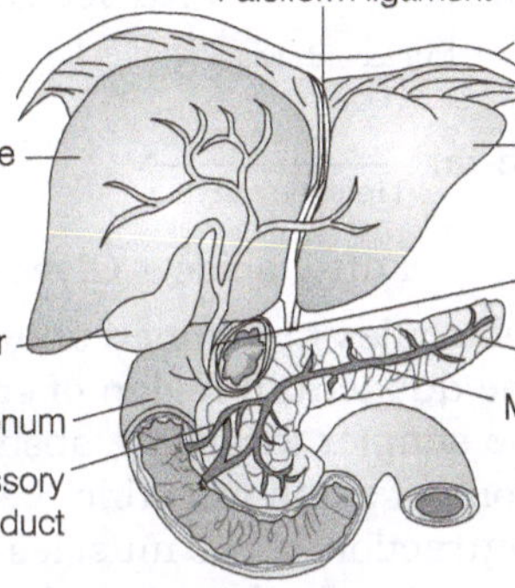

Liver and pancreas with associated structures

They act on large fat molecules to form smaller globules thus, increasing the efficiency of enzyme action. Gall bladder stores bile juices for the further use.

Bile contains the bile pigments, i.e. **bilirubin** and **biliverdin**, bile salts, cholesterol and phospholipids. Bile acts on food entering from stomach and makes it alkaline. This facilitates action of pancreatic secretions on food. Thus, fats are broken down into diglycerides and monoglycerides by the action of bile.

Note Bile does not contain any enzyme as gastric juice. It helps in emulsifying fats. The process of emulsification is basically carried out by the bile salts of bile.

Enzymes from Intestine

Intestinal mucosal epithelium has goblet cells (secrete mucus). The secretions of the brush border cells of mucosa together with the goblet cells secretions form the intestinal juice (also known as **succus entericus**). The succus entericus contains various enzymes

(i) Disaccharidases, e.g. maltase for digestion of maltose into glucose
(ii) Dipeptidases
(iii) Lipases
(iv) Nucleosidases

All enzymes act on the end products of below mentioned reactions in order to form their respective simpler forms.

$$\text{Dipeptides} \xrightarrow{\text{Dipeptidases}} \text{Amino acids}$$

$$\text{Maltose} \xrightarrow{\text{Maltase}} \text{Glucose + Glucose}$$

$$\text{Lactose} \xrightarrow{\text{Lactase}} \text{Glucose + Galactose}$$

$$\text{Sucrose} \xrightarrow{\text{Sucrase}} \text{Glucose + Fructose}$$

$$\text{Nucleotides} \xrightarrow{\text{Nucleotidases}} \text{Nucleosides}$$

$$\xrightarrow{\text{Nucleosidases}} \text{Sugars + Bases}$$

$$\text{Emulsified fat} \xrightarrow[\text{Lipolytic enzyme}]{\text{Lipases}}$$

$$\text{Fatty acids + Glycerol}$$

All the biomacromolecules mentioned above are broken down in the duodenum region of small intestine, while the simpler forms are absorbed in the other two regions of small intestine, i.e. jejunum and ileum. The contraction of the muscles in the small intestine allows the further churning and kneading of the chyme and finally pushing it into the large intestine.

6. Large Intestine

It is about 1.5 meter long. It is distinguishable into three main parts, i.e. **caecum, colon** and **rectum**.

(a) **Caecum** is present at terminal part of small intestine.

(b) **Colon** is the part of large intestine divided into ascending, transverse and descending colon.

(c) **Rectum** is the last part that stores the faecal matter temporarily.

Digestion in Large Intestine

The last stage of digestion of food occurs in large intestine. This is carried out by bacterial action. Glands of this region tend to secrete mucus, i.e. enzymes are not secreted into this part of the digestive system.

The undigested and the unabsorbed substances are finally passed on to the large intestine. Following functions are performed by the large intestine

(i) Absorption of water, minerals and certain drugs.

(ii) Secretion of mucus which helps in adhering the waste (undigested) particles together and lubricates it for an easy passage.

7. Anus

It is the end point of alimentary canal, which helps in the exit of waste materials. The exit of waste materials is regulated by anal sphincter.

Expulsion of undigested remains of food from the alimentary canal is called defaecation.

Absorption of Food

The food is absorbed in small intestine. Amino acids, simple sugars (like glucose, fructose), minerals, vitamins are absorbed through the villi, reach the blood capillaries and finally enter into the blood circulation and are distributed to the whole body.

Fatty acids and glycerol are absorbed into the lacteal or lymph vessel in order to enter the lymphatic system. Water is absorbed in large intestine.

Assimilation

It is the distribution of digested food products to various cells of the body. The villi in small intestine are richly supplied with blood vessels, which take the absorbed food to each and every cell of the body, where it is utilised for obtaining energy, building up new tissues and repairing the older ones.

Egestion

The elimination of undigested food formed in the colon of the large intestine through anus is called egestion. Peristalsis gradually pushes the undigested food from small intestine to large intestine. The remaining material after reabsorption of water and ions is stored in the rectum for some time and is ultimately removed from the body through anus.

Check Your LEARNING...

1. What purpose does the acidic nature of gastric juice serve?
2. Name two enzyme secreted by pancreas.
3. Which part of the stomach contains gastric glands?
4. Name any two enzymes found in succus entericus.
5. Maximum absorption of water takes place in which part of alimentary canal?

QUiCK Revision

- The basic requirement of all living beings is food. The major components of food are carbohydrates, fats, proteins, vitamins, minerals and water. **Minerals** are essential for growth and repair of tissues. All these are complex biomacromolecules and have to be broken down into simpler substances in digestive system by the process called **digestion**.
- **Teeth** in humans are thecodont, heterodont and diphyodont. They are differentiated into incisors, canines, premolars and molars. They are used in chewing and mastication of food.
- **Tongue** is a muscular movable organ present in buccal cavity. Small projections called **papillae** are present all over the surface of tongue for testing the tastes of food.
- **The buccal or oral cavity** is followed by the **pharynx**, which serves as a common passage of air and food.

Summary of Digestive System

Parts	Locations	Functions	Features
Mouth (Buccal cavity)	Lower half of the front of the skull.	To take in food. To breakdown food.	Contains teeth, tongue and lips. Salivary glands secrete into it.
Oesophagus	Stretches through the thoracic cavity from mouth.	Transports food from mouth to stomach.	Muscular tube which helps food to move onwards. Epiglottis prevents food entering into the trachea.
Liver	Found in the upper abdomen, under the diaphragm and mostly to the right-hand side.	Produces bile. Helps to detoxify the body, converts excess carbohydrates to fat. Stores vitamins and minerals. Makes cholesterol, which is needed to form hormones and makes plasma protein.	
Stomach	Under the diaphragm on the left-hand side of the abdominal cavity.	Digestion of food (proteins), converts pepsinogen into pepsin and helps to soften food for digestion.	The lining of the stomach (the mucosa) is heavily folded, forming millions of gastric glands.
Pancreas	Under the stomach on the left-hand side of the abdominal cavity.	Secretes digestive juices, neutralises chyme, secretes insulin and glucagon to help to regulate blood sugar levels.	A mixed gland's exocrine part has a duct to secrete enzymes. Endocrine part (ductless) is for insulin release.
		Small intestine	
Duodenum	In the abdominal cavity after the stomach.	Digestion of food, site of entry of products of pancreas and liver.	Contains many villi and microvilli
Jejunum and ileum	In the abdominal cavity after the duodenum.	Absorbs nutrients.	Contains many villi, walls only one cell thick. Rich blood supply. Villi contain lacteals for fat absorpton.
		Large intestine	
Caecum	Just below the junction of the small intestine and the large intestine.	Vestigial in humans. In herbivores, they contain bacteria that aid in the digestion of cellulose and synthesis of vitamin-B_{12}.	
Colon	In the abdominal cavity.	Reabsorbs water from undigested food.	
Rectum	Pelvic cavity connected to the colon.	Stores faeces.	
Anus	Pelvic cavity connected to rectum.	Site of egestion.	Controlled by the anal sphincter muscle.

- **Digestive glands** secrete digestive juices to convert the food into simpler substances. The major glands associated with digestion are salivary glands, liver and pancreas.
- **Salivary glands** are present in buccal cavity and secrete salivary juices. There are three pairs of salivary gland in man.
- **Gastric glands** are present in stomach. They contain secretory cells which help in digestion.
- **Liver** is the largest gland of body. It secretes bile which helps in breaking down of fats into small molecules.
- **Intestinal glands** are formed as a result of modification of epithelial cells present in intestine. These are located on villi.
- **Pancreas** is a mixed gland and secretes hormones-insulin and glucagon.
- **Absorption of food** takes place in small intestine while absorption of water takes place in large intestine.

Chapter Practice

Section-I

1 Mark Questions

1. Name the following.

(i) The undigestible, fibrous portion of food.
(ii) The fat soluble vitamin.
(iii) Deficiency of RBCs or haemoglobin in the blood.
(iv) A vitamin whose deficiency causes beri-beri.
(v) The disease caused by deficiency of iodine.
(vi) Mineral essential for haemoglobin formation.
(vii) One protein deficiency disease.
(viii) Phenomenon of wave-like contractions in the wall of alimentary canal.
(ix) The arrangement of teeth in the jaw.
(x) Chemical substance that changes pepsinogen into pepsin.
(xi) The enzyme involved in the breakdown of nucleotide into nucleoside.

Ans. (i) Roughage
(ii) Vitamin-A
(iii) Anaemia
(iv) Thiamine (vitamin-B_1)
(v) Goitre
(vi) Iron
(vii) Kwashiorkor
(viii) Peristalsis
(ix) Dentition
(x) HCl
(xi) Nucleotidase

2. Correct and rewrite the following statements by changing the underlined words.

(i) Saliva contains enzymes that digest <u>protein</u>.
(ii) Gastric glands of stomach mucosa have <u>chief cells</u> which secrete HCl.
(iii) Fats are broken down into di and monoglycerides with the help of <u>amylase</u>
(iv) Goblet cells are located in the intestinal mucosal epithelium and secrete <u>chymotrypsin</u>.

Ans. (i) Saliva contains enzymes that digest **starch**.
(ii) Gastric glands of stomach mucosa have **oxyntic cells** which secrete HCl.
(iii) Fats are broken down into di and monoglycerides with the help of **lipases**.
(iv) Goblet cells are located in the intestinal mucosal epithelium and secrete **mucus**.

3. Give biological reasons for the following.

(i) Fats are considered as the main energy producers. Why?
(ii) Vitamins are not digested by enzymes.
(iii) Humans cannot digest cellulose.
(iv) Some people complain about acidity.

Ans. (i) Oxygen is present in less amount in fats than in carbohydrates. So, the energy produced is more than carbohydrates. It produces approximately 9.4 kcal of energy.
(ii) Vitamins are directly absorbed in the body so these are not digested by enzymes.
(iii) Cellulose digesting enzyme (cellulase) is absent in humans. So, cellulose remains undigested in human alimentary canal.
(iv) In humans, HCl is secreted from the gastric glands. HCl is used for activating pepsinogen. Sometimes, its oversecretion causes acidity.

4. (i) Match the following columns.

Column I	Column II
A. Kwashiorkor	1. Formation of haemoglobin
B. Calcium	2. Deficiency of proteins
C. Iron	3. Synthesis of thyroxine
D. Iodine	4. Strong bones and teeth

(ii) Match the following columns.

Column I	Column II
A. Biomacromolecules of food	1. Alimentary canal and associated glands
B. Human digestive system	2. J-shaped bag-like structure
C. Stomach	3. Embedded in jaw bones
D. Thecodont	4. Converted into simple substances

Ans. (i) A–2, B–4, C–1, D–3
(ii) A–4, B–1, C–2, D–3

5. Choose the correct answer from the four options given below.

(i) Which of the following is a good source of carbohydrates?
(a) Meat (b) Almond
(c) Groundnut (d) Rice

Ans. (d)

(ii) Which of these is the best source of vitamin-A?
(a) Apple (b) Carrot
(c) Honey (d) Groundnut

Ans. (b)

(iii) Your grandmother always tells you to enjoy the sunshine; as it is good for our bones. Which vitamin changes to active form on exposure to sunshine?
(a) Vitamin-A (b) Vitamin-B
(c) Vitamin-C (d) Vitamin-D

Ans. (d)

(iv) Marasmus is caused due to deficiency of which of these?
(a) Vitamin-C
(b) Carbohydrates
(c) Minerals
(d) Iodine

Ans. (b)

(v) For a balanced meal, which of the following should be in the highest quantity in a thali?
(a) Rice (b) Dal
(c) Vegetable curry (d) Eggs

Ans. (a)

(vi) Hepato-pancreatic duct opens into the duodenum and carries
(a) bile (b) pancreatic juice
(c) Both (a) and (b) (d) saliva

Ans. (c)

(vii) Villi are located in
(a) large intestine (b) small intestine
(c) stomach (d) duodenum

Ans. (b)

(viii) Liver is the largest gland and is associated with various functions, choose one which is not correct ?
(a) Metabolism of carbohydrate
(b) Digestion of fat
(c) Formation of bile
(d) Secretion of hormone called gastrin

Ans. (a)

(ix) Mark the right statement among the following.
(a) Trypsinogen is an inactive enzyme
(b) Trypsinogen is secreted by intestinal mucosa
(c) Enterokinase is secreted by pancreas
(d) Bile contains trypsin

Ans. (a)

(x) The water from the digested food is mainly absorbed by which of these?
(a) Stomach (b) Duodenum
(c) Colon (d) Rectum

Ans. (c)

6. Fill in the blanks by using suitable words.
(i) Carbohydrates are stored in animals in the form of ....
(ii) Absence of roughage in diet leads to ....
(iii) .... are body building food.
(iv) .... is a protein deficiency disease.
(v) Vitamin .... deficiency causes pellagra.
(vi) In humans, the last three teeth are ....
(vii) .... covers the crown of the teeth.
(viii) Through mastication, the food is mixed with saliva and shaped into a soft, flexible mass called ....
(ix) .... is present in the stomach for protein digestion.
(x) Enzyme helps in .... of ingested food.
(xi) Pancreatic juice contains fat digesting enzyme called ....
(xii) End product of carbohydrate digestion is ....
(xiii) Removal of undigested food is called ....

Ans. (i) glycogen (ii) constipation
(iii) Proteins (iv) Kwashiorkor
(v) B_3 (vi) molars
(vii) Enamel (viii) bolus
(ix) HCl (x) digestion
(xi) lipase (xii) glucose
(xiii) egestion

7. Choose the odd one out from the following terms given below and name the category to which other three belong.
(i) Vitamin-A, Vitamin-C, Vitamin-D, Vitamin-E
(ii) Riboflavin, Thiamine, Folic acid, Iodine
(iii) Xerophthalmia, Marasmus, Pellagra, Scurvy
(iv) Amylase, Trypsin, HCl, Lipase

Ans. (i) **Odd term** Vitamin-C.
Rest three are belong to the category fat soluble vitamins.
(ii) **Odd term** Iodine.
Rest three are classified under vitamins.
(iii) **Odd term** Marasmus.
Rest three are belong to the diseases caused by vitamin deficiency.
(iv) **Odd term** HCl.
Rest three are the enzymes secreted by the pancreas.

8. Given below are sets of five terms each. Rewrite the terms in correct order in a logical sequence beginning with the term that is underlined.
(i) <u>Duodenum</u>, Colon, Caecum, Jejunum, Ileum
(ii) Rectum, <u>Pharynx</u>, Oesophagus, Duodenum, Stomach
(iii) <u>Mouth</u>, Stomach, Pharynx, Large intestine, Small intestine

Ans. (i) Duodenum, Jejunum, Ileum, Caecum, Colon
(ii) Pharynx, Oesophagus, Stomach, Duodenum, Rectum
(iii) Mouth, Pharynx, Stomach, Small intestine, Large, intestine

9. State whether the following statements are true or false. Correct and rewrite the false statements.
(i) Cellulose in our food passes out undigested from body.
(ii) Iron is required for the proper working of thyroid.
(iii) Mineral salts contribute in regulating body processes.
(iv) The major function of protein is to give energy.
(v) Saliva contains starch digesting enzyme.
(vi) Citrus fruits are the best sources of vitamin-C.
(vii) Absorption of water takes place in small intestine.
(viii) Pancreas secretes its juices in large intestine.
(ix) Bile is important for digestion of proteins.
(x) Maltose is digested by maltase.

Ans. (i) True
(ii) False, iodine is required for the proper working of thyroid.
(iii) True
(iv) False, proteins are building blocks in our body.
(v) True
(vi) True
(vii) False, absorption of water takes place in large intestine.
(viii) False, pancreas secretes its juices in small intestine.
(ix) False, bile is important for digestion of fats.
(x) True

10. State the exact loaction of the following .
(i) Liver (ii) Stomach
(iii) Jejunum (iv) Caecum
(v) Anus

Ans. (i) Liver is found in the upper abdomen, under the diaphragm and mostly to the right hand side.
(ii) Stomach is located under the diaphragm on the left hand side of the abdominal cavity.
(iii) Jejunum is located in the abdominal cavity after the duodenum.
(iv) Caecum is located at the junction of the small intestine and large intestine.
(v) Anus is located in pelvic cavity connected to rectum.

11. State one example of the following.
(i) Water soluble vitamin
(ii) Macroelements
(iii) The disease caused by the deficiency of tocopherol
(iv) Type of teeth
(v) One enzyme of stomach

Ans. (i) Vitamin-C (ii) Calcium
(iii) Deficiency disease (iv) Canines
(v) Pepsin

12. State the main function of the following.
(i) Carbohydrates
(ii) Riboflavin
(iii) Tongue
(iv) Cement in tooth
(v) Saliva
(vi) Small intestine
(vii) Liver

Ans. (i) Carbohydrates are good source of energy.
(ii) Riboflavin is essential for growth.
(iii) Tongue bears several taste buds and helps in mixing food with saliva.
(iv) Cement in tooth provides a protective layer around the pulp cavity.
(v) Saliva helps in lubricating the food for swallowing.
(vi) Small intestine completes digestion and absorption of digested food.
(vii) Liver secretes bile juice which acts on large molecules to form smaller globules.

13. Mention one difference in each of the following pairs on the basis of what is given in the bracket.
(i) Carbohydrates and Proteins (function)
(iii) Milk teeth and Permanent teeth (number)
(iv) Homodont and Heterodont (definition)
(v) Pepsin and Trypsin (mode of action)

Ans. (i) Difference between carbohydrates and proteins is as follows

Carbohydrates	Proteins
These provide energy.	These are required for growth and repair of the body tissues.

(ii) Difference between milk teeth and permanent teeth is as follows

Milk teeth	Permanent teeth
They are 20 in number.	They are 32 in number.

(iii) Difference between homodont and heterodont is as follows

Homodont	Heterodont
All the teeth are same, e.g. snake.	All the teeth vary in size, shape and function, e.g. man.

(iv) Difference between pepsin and trypsin is as follows

Pepsin	Trypsin
It acts in acidic medium.	It acts in alkaline medium.

14. Give the technical/biological terms for the following.
   (i) A protein found in milk that forms curd, it ends to be difficult for infants to digest.
   (ii) Enzyme that converts proteins into proteases and peptones.
   (iii) Fine microscopic, finger-like projections lining the small intestine that serve to increase the absorptive surface area.
   (iv) A lymphatic vessel in an intestinal villus, it aids in the absorption of fats.
   (v) Enzyme that hydrolyses proteins and peptones into polypeptides.
   (vi) Enzyme that hydrolyses lactose into glucose and galactose.

Ans. (i) Casein (ii) Pepsin
(iii) Villi (iv) Lacteal
(v) Trypsin (vi) Lactase

15. Briefly explain the following terms.
   (i) Food (ii) Balanced diet
   (iii) Dental formula (iv) Egestion

Ans. (i) A combination of organic and inorganic compounds that provides energy for metabolism and materials for repair or replacement of worn out tissues, growth, reproduction and regulation of metabolism is called food.
(ii) Balanced diet is the diet that contains proper amount of all the nutrients, i.e proteins carbohydrates, fats, vitamins, etc.
(iii) The number and kinds of teeth in mammals are represented by an equation called dental formula.
(vi) The elimination of undigested food formed in the colon of the large intestine through anus is called egestion.

16. Answer the following questions briefly.
   (i) Name the major nutrients present in the food.
   (ii) What happens if roughage is not included in the diet?
   (iii) What two roles are performed by buccal cavity?
   (iv) Name the indispensable protease of small intestine which does not directly take part in protein digestion.
   (v) Does gall bladder make bile?

Ans. (i) Major nutrients in food are carbohydrates, fats, proteins, vitamins and minerals.
(ii) If roughage is not included in diet, it may lead to constipation.
(iii) Two roles are performed by buccal cavity is mastication of food and mixing of food with saliva.
(iv) Enterokinase is the indispensable protease of small intestine, which does not directly take part in protein digestion.
(v) Gall bladder is not associated with the bile formation rather it is involved in the storage of bile. Bile is secreted from the hepatic cells of liver.

2 Marks Questions

17. State the importance of balanced diet in our daily intake of food.

Ans. A diet which has all nutritional components of food in an adequate amount is called balanced diet. We need carbohydrates in the highest amount followed by proteins and fats. Minerals and vitamins are required in minute amount. Intake of unbalanced diet for a long time leads to many nutritional disorders. Hence, balanced diet is important for us.

18. Cellulose is not digested in our body. Yet it is an important component of a balanced diet. Why?

Ans. Cellulose adds roughage in the food. Its sources are vegetables, wheat, fruits, etc. Roughage helps to move the food along the wall of the intestine and its absence leads to constipation. So, it must be included in the diet.

19. How are villi adapted for absorption?

Ans. Villi has the following features
(i) They have large surface area for absorption.
(ii) They have epithelial lining with a network of capillary and lacteals.

3 Marks Questions

20. Describe three main purposes of food requirement in our body.

Ans. The food is required by the body for the following purposes
(i) **Growth** Food provides raw materials for building up new protoplasm or cells for growth.
(ii) **Repair** Food provides raw materials for repair of worn out cells and for replacement of dead cells.
(iii) **Energy** Oxidation of food during respiration provides energy which is utilised by the body for various activities.

21. List the organs of human alimentary canal and name the major digestive glands with their location.

Ans. Human digestive system consists of two main parts, alimentary canal and digestive glands.

Alimentary canal comprises of following parts
(i) Mouth
(ii) Pharynx
(iii) Oesophagus
(iv) Stomach
(v) Small intestine
(vi) Large intestine
(vii) Rectum
(viii) Anus

Digestive glands include
(i) **Salivary glands** are situated just outside the buccal cavity and secrete salivary juice into it.
(ii) **Liver** is the largest gland in the body, situated in the abdominal cavity just below the diaphragm

and has two lobes. It secretes bile which helps in the digestion of fats.

(iii) **Pancreas** is the compound organ situated between the limbs of U-shaped duodenum acting as endocrine and exocrine organs. The exocrine portion secretes pancreatic juice whereas endocrine portion secretes hormones like insulin and glucagon.

22. Discuss the main steps in the digestion of proteins as the food passes through different parts of the alimentary canal.

Ans. Digestion of Protein in Stomach

The proenzyme pepsinogen on exposure to HCl, gets converted into active enzyme pepsin.

$$\text{Pepsinogen} \xrightarrow{\text{HCl}} \text{Pepsin}$$

$$\text{Protein} \xrightarrow{\text{Pepsin}} \text{Proteases + Peptones}$$

Pepsin always acts in acidic medium (pH 1.8). In infants, milk proteins are digested by rennin.

Digestion of Protein in Small Intestine

Pancreatic juice contains proenzyme, i.e. trypsinogen which gets activated by enterokinase, which is secreted by intestinal mucosa, into active trypsin. Trypsin acts in alkaline medium.

$$\text{Protein} \xrightarrow{\text{Trypsin/Chymotrypsin}} \text{Dipeptides}$$

The dipeptides get converted into amino acids by the enzyme succus entericus (intestinal juice).

$$\text{Dipeptides} \xrightarrow{\text{Dipeptidases}} \text{Amino acids}$$

Section-II [5 Marks]

Structured Questions

1. Nutrients are the substances required for proper growth and maintenance of a living body.
   (i) Which among all the nutrients required by an individual constitutes a major part of diet?
   (ii) State the role of fats in human.
   (iii) Deficiency of protein in diet of children causes serious disease. Name the disease.
   (iv) Give example of different minerals essential for our diet?
   (v) Name the vitamin responsible for scurvy.

Ans. (i) Proteins among all other nutrients consume a major part of diet (food).
(ii) Fats act as reserve food and are the basic energy providers of our body.
(iii) Kwashiorkor is caused due to protein deficiency in children.
(iv) Calcium, sodium, fluorine, iodine are the examples of different minerals essential for our diet.
(v) Vitamin-C is responsible for scurvy.

2. The figure shows alimentary canal of man.

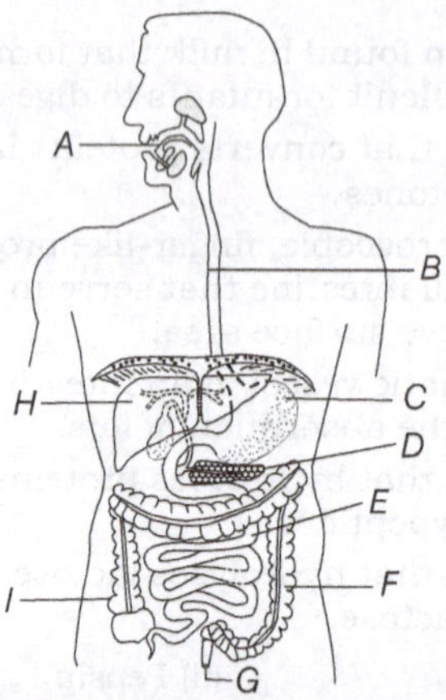

   (i) Label the parts *A* to *I*.
   (ii) What changes take place in part *E*?
   (iii) How does part *I* differ in man and rabbit?
   (iv) The food mixes thoroughly with the acidic gastric juice of the stomach by the churning movements of its muscular wall. What do we call the food at this stage?
   (v) Name the proenzymes found in pancreatic juice.

Ans. (i) The parts *A* to *I* are labelled as
A–Oral cavity *B*–Oesophagus, *C*–Stomach
D–Pancreas, *E*–Small intestine, *F*–Large intestine,
G–Anus, *H*–Liver, *I*–Caecum
(ii) ***E*-Small intestine** Complete digestion of food and absorption of digested food takes place here.
(iii) **Part-*I* is caecum.** In rabbit, it is longer as compared to that of human. In rabbit, the caecum contains some bacteria which produce some enzymes that digest cellulose. In human, cellulose is not digested due to the absence of enzyme cellulase.
(iv) The food at this stage is called chyme.
(v) Pancreatic juice contains proenzymes, trypsinogen, chymotrypsinogen and procarboxypeptidases.

3. Observe the given figure and answer the questions that follow.

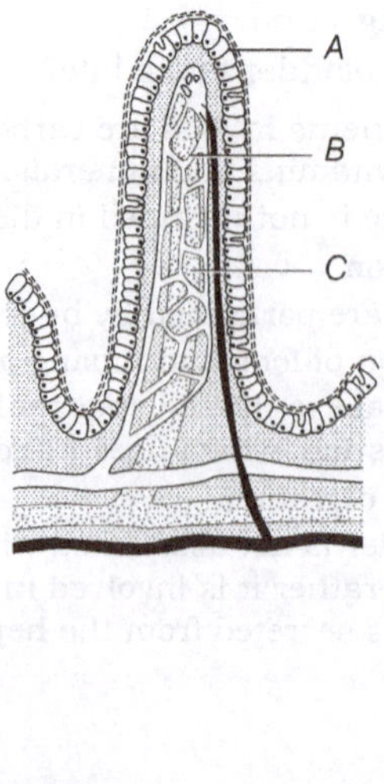

(i) What does the figure represent?
(ii) The above structure is present in which part of the digestive system?
(iii) Label the parts *A*-*C*.
(iv) Mention the role of part labelled as *C* in the figure.
(v) Name any two enzymes that are active in this portion.

Ans. (i) The figure represents villi.
(ii) Small intestine
(iii) The parts *A*–*C* are labelled as
A–Epithelium, *B*–Blood vessel, *C*–Lacteal
(iv) Lacteals are lymphatic capillaries found in the villi of small intestine. They absorb and transport large molecules of fats and lipids.
(v) Maltase and sucrase enzymes are active in this portion.

4. Study the figures given below and answer the questions that follows.
The figures show different kinds of teeth in man.

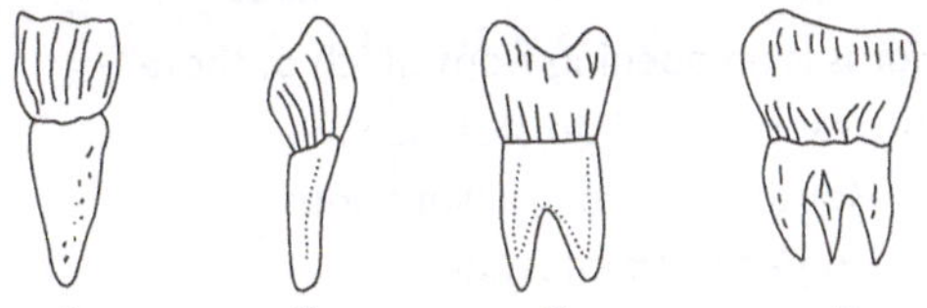

(i) Name the teeth labelled as *A* – *D*.
(ii) Write their functions.
(iii) Name two minerals present in teeth.
(iv) Give the dental formula of human adult.
(v) What is wisdom tooth ?

Ans. (i) The teeth *A*-*D* are labelled as
A-Incisor, *B*-Canine, *C*-Premolar and *D*-Molar
(ii) Their functions are
Incisor are used for biting, canines for tearing, premolars and molars for grinding purposes.
(iii) Two minerals present in teeth are calcium and phosphorus.
(iv) The dental formula of human adult is $\frac{2123}{2123} \times 2 = 32$.
(v) Wisdom tooth is the last molar of each side in each jaw attained on maturity.

5. The figure shows the section of a mammalian tooth.

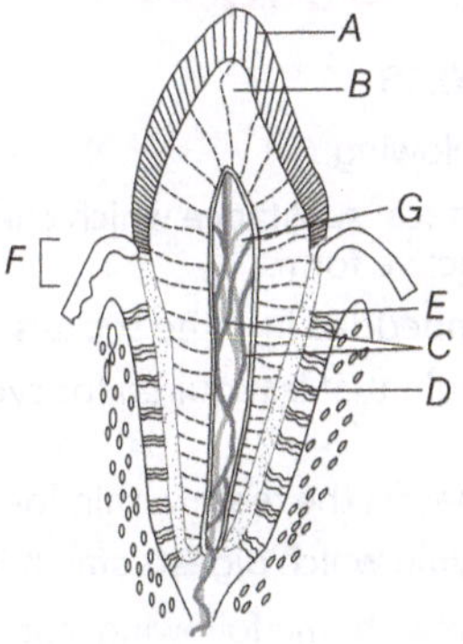

(i) Label the parts *A* to *H*.
(ii) What are the three main regions of tooth?
(iii) Which is the hardest part of it?
(iv) Which part of it is living?
(v) Which substance covers the pulp cavity?

Ans. (i) The parts *A* to *H* are labelled as
A–Enamel, *B*–Dentine, *C*–Blood capillaries, *D*–Gum, *E*–Cement, *F*–Neck, *G*–Pulp cavity.
(ii) The three regions of tooth are crown, neck and the root.
(iii) Enamel is the hardest part of tooth.
(iv) Pulp cavity is living which contain blood capillaries.
(v) Dentine covers the pulp cavity.

Chapter Assessment

Section-I

1 Mark Questions

1. Name the following.
   (i) The chemical substance which changes pepsinogen into its active form.
   (ii) Teeth embedded into the sockets of jaw bone.
   (iii) The vitamin that is required for synthesis of retinal pigment.
   (iv) Fibres that fix the teeth within the socket.
   (v) The enzyme which digests starch in the mouth.
2. Correct and rewrite the following statements by changing the underlined words.
   (i) Deficiency of vitamin-D causes <u>haemorrhage</u>.
   (ii) Dry skin is a symptom of <u>anaemia</u>.
   (iii) <u>Sodium</u> is the major constituent for nerve functioning.
3. Give biological reasons for the following.
   (i) Bone patients are advised to add more of milk and milk products in their everyday food.
   (ii) Mucus acts as a shield for stomach.
4. (i) Match the following columns.

Column I		Column II
A. Salad	1.	Protein
B. Butter	2.	Carbohydrates
C. Meat/Dal	3.	Fat
D. Chapati	4.	Vitamins and minerals

   (ii) Match the following columns.

Column I		Column II
A. Marasmus	1.	Protein
B. Vitamin-C	2.	Carbohydrate
C. Kwashiorkor	3.	Scurvy
D. Pernicious anaemia	4.	Vitamin-B_{12}

5. Choose the correct answer from four options given below.

(i) Which one of the following pairs of nutrients includes both the simple sugars (monosaccharides)?
(a) Sucrose and glucose (b) Glucose and maltose
(c) Fructose and glucose (d) Maltose and lactose

(ii) Which one of the following is the correct matching of a nutrient mineral element and its one rich source?
(a) Calcium–Potato
(b) Sodium–Citrus fruits
(c) Iodine–Dairy milk
(d) Potassium–Banana

(iii) What is the dental formula in human beings?
(a) $\frac{2033}{2033}$ (b) $\frac{2123}{2123}$
(c) $\frac{2122}{2122}$ (d) $\frac{2121}{2121}$

(iv) Pylorus is an opening from which of these?
(a) Oesophagus into stomach
(b) Mouth cavity into oesophagus
(c) Stomach into intestine
(d) Intestine into rectum

(v) Select what is not true for intestinal villi among the following.
(a) They possess microvilli
(b) They increase the surface area
(c) They are supplied with capillaries and the lacteal vessels
(d) They only participate in digestion of fats

6. Fill in the blanks by using suitable words.
   (i) Mammalian teeth are different in shape and are called ....
   (ii) .... mineral is important for the formation of haemoglobin.
   (iii) The exposed part of the tooth is called
   (iv) .... is the last part of the small intestine.
7. Choose the odd one out from the following terms given below and name the category to which other three belong.
   (i) Pepsin, HCl, Mucus, Amylases
   (ii) Iodine, Iron, Ascorbic acid, Sodium
8. Given below are sets of five terms each. Rewrite the term in correct order in a logical sequence beginning with the term that is underlined.
   (i) Assimilation, Egestion, <u>Ingestion</u>, Absorption, Digestion
   (ii) Oesophagus, <u>Mouth</u>, Stomach, Large intestine, Anus

9. State whether the following statements are true or false. Correct and rewrite the false statements.
   (i) Pulp cavity is surrounded by dentine.
   (ii) Intestinal villi have lymph vessels.
   (iii) Intestine is narrow for the fast movement of food.
   (iv) Pancreatic juice has enzymes to digest all the major components of food.
   (v) Liver stores glucose as starch.
10. State the exact location of the following.
   (i) Pancreas
   (ii) Duodenum
11. Give one example of the following.
   (i) Enzyme of pancreas
   (ii) Bile pigment
12. State the main function of the following.
   (i) Anal sphincter (ii) Pharynx
13. Mention one difference in each of the following pairs on the basis of what is given in the bracket.
   (i) Dentine and Enamel (definition)
   (ii) Sucrase and Maltase (function)
14. Give technical/biological terms for the following.
   (i) Space enclosed between lips and cheeks externally.
   (ii) Process of passing bolus from buccal cavity to oesophagus.
15. Briefly explain the following terms.
   (i) Digestion
   (ii) Churning movement
   (iii) Pulp cavity
16. Answer the following questions briefly.
   (i) What pH range is required for activity of trypsin?
   (ii) Name three salivary glands.
   (iii) What is the role of gastro-oesophageal sphincter?

2 Marks Questions

17. Why is small intestine considered the most important organ of the digestive system?
18. Write a short note on stomach.

3 Marks Questions

19. What are the end products of the digestion of starch, protein and fats, respectively?
20. How is chewing of food helpful in digestion? Also tell how is starch hydrolysed in buccal cavity (with reaction)?

Section-II [5 Marks]

Structured Questions

21. The figure represents a certain gland.
   (i) Name the gland.
   (ii) Label the parts *A*-*C*.
   (iii) State the role of the gland.
   (iv) What are the different enzymes present in the pancreatic juice?
   (v) State the role of amylopsin (pancreatic amylase)

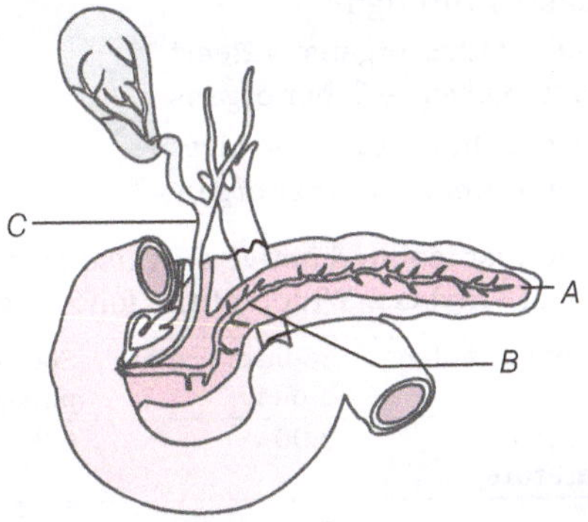

22. In human beings, the digestive system constitutes a long tubular structure called alimentary canal and digestive glands associated with it.
   (i) Which enzyme is present in saliva that breaks down starch?
   (ii) Where does digestion of fat take place in our body?
   (iii) Mention the site of complete digestion of carbohydrates and proteins in humans.
   (iv) Name two digestive glands associated with digestive system in humans.
   (v) Small intestine receives the secretion of which two organs.

For explanations scan the given QR Code

Olympiad Section*

Brain Teasing Questions asked in Previous Olympiads

1 The 'chief cells' of stomach secrete hydrochloric acid. Consider a hypothetical situation in which the 'chief cells' are destroyed resulting in complete inhibition of acid secretion in stomach. In comparison to a normal person, which one of the following is most likely to happen in the stomach during the above condition? [INJSO 2016]
(a) Digestion of proteins will increase
(b) Digestion of fats will start
(c) Digestion of carbohydrates will continue
(d) Digestion of fat will decrease

2 Ingestion, digestion, absorption, assimilation and egestion are the steps in food processing in our body. Majority of absorption takes place in small intestine (villi) which is transported to different organs through the circulatory system. Starting with villi, which of the following is the correct sequence of organs that the absorbed food passes through? [INJSO 2016]
(a) Liver → Other organs → Heart
(b) Heart → Liver → Other organs
(c) Heart → Other organs → Liver
(d) Liver → Heart → Other organs

3 A biochemist isolated active amylase enzyme from human saliva. She was interested in assaying the enzyme activity of amylase. Which of the following buffer will she be most likely choosing?

Name of the buffer	Sodium acetate buffer	Sodium phosphate buffer	Tris-HCl buffer	CAPS buffer
pH at room temperature	2.00	6.8	8.10	9.7

(a) Sodium acetate buffer
(b) Sodium phosphate buffer [INJSO 2015]
(c) Tris-HCl buffer
(d) CAPS buffer

4 Which of the following secretions of the alimentary canal in human do not contain any enzymes? [INJSO 2013]
(a) Salivary Juice
(b) Gastric juice
(c) Bile juice
(d) Pancreatic juice

5 A girl has undergone a surgery for removal of gall bladder. While being discharged from the hospital. Which of the following advise would you give her, being a doctor? She should .... [INJSO 2012]
(a) take food less in fats
(b) have a diet with less proteins
(c) take less sugary fruits
(d) take less quantity

Answers

1. (c) **2.** (d) **3.** (b) **4.** (c) **5.** (a)

These questions may or may not be asked in the examination, have been given just for additional practice required for olympiads, scholarship exams etc. For detailed explanations refer Page No. 230.

CHAPTER

10

Movement and Locomotion

Chapter Inside

• Skeleton • Human Skeleton • Joints

Movement is a change in posture or position of any body part of a living organism. It is an essential and significant feature of living organisms. When movement results in change of place or location by the organism, it is termed as **locomotion**. Animals show both movement and locomotion, while plants show movement only, locomotion is rare in them.

The movement and locomotion in human body is brought about by the following components

(i) Muscles (ii) Skeleton (iii) Joints

In this chapter, we will focus only on the skeleton and joints of human body.

Skeleton (Skeletal System)

The hard, supportive or protective elements of the animal body constitute the skeletal system or skeleton. It consists of a framework of bones and a few cartilages, both of them are specialised connective tissues.

Functions of Skeleton

These are as follows

(i) It gives **support** to softer body parts.

(ii) The bony framework is responsible for maintaining and providing **shape** to the body.

(iii) It **protects** the delicate internal organs like brain, heart, lungs, etc. For example, skull protects the brain, vertebral column protects the spinal cord, etc.

(iv) Skeleton provides surface for the **attachment of muscles.**

(v) The bones help in bringing about **movements** by forming levers with joints.

(vi) Tracheal rings, sternum and ribs are **helpful in breathing,** while ear bones (middle ear) **transmit sound vibrations.**

(vii) Bone maintains the calcium and phosphorus levels of blood.

(viii) Blood cells are formed in the bone marrow.

(ix) Bones, being hard are usually preserved as fossils. These fossils provide us a very authentic proof to trace the evolution of various animals.

Human Skeleton

Human body is made up of 300 bones at the time of birth. These get fused to form 206 bones in an adult. On the basis of the position of the skeletal structures in the body, the skeleton is divided into **axial** and **appendicular** skeleton.

Axial Skeleton

It comprises of 80 bones, which include skull, vertebral column, sternum and ribs, i.e. all the bones which are present along the median longitudinal axis of the body.

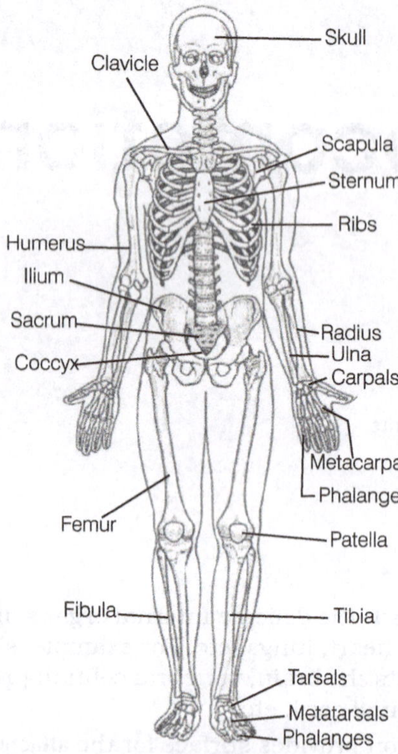

Human skeleton

Note
- According to size and shape, bones can be grouped in four categories, i.e. long, short, flat and irregular bones.
- Smallest bone is **stapes**.
- Longest and strongest bone is **femur**.
- Flat bones are **skull, sternum**, etc.
- Irregular bones are facial bones.

Skull

It is the bony framework of the head. It is composed of 29 bones.

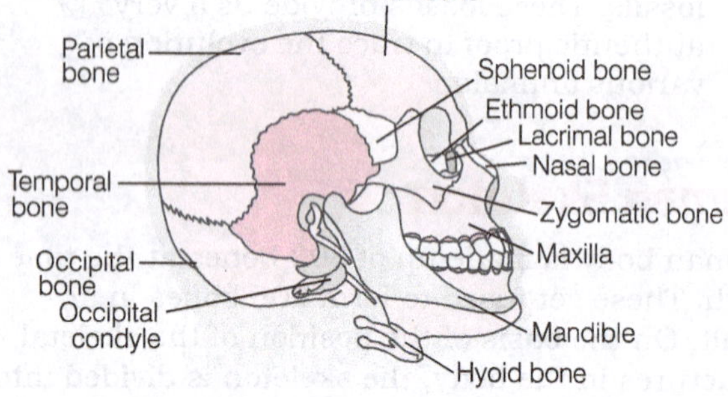

Diagrammatic view of human skull

Bones of skull are as follows

(i) **Cranium** (8) includes frontal (1), parietal (2), temporal (2), occipital (1), sphenoid (1) and ethmoid (1). They form the hard protective outer covering (cranium) for the brain, thus also called as **brain box**. These 8 flattened bones form immovable joints with separated margins called **sutures**.

(ii) **Facial bones** (14) include maxillae (2), palatine (2), mandible (1), vomer (1), nasal (2), zygomatic (2), lacrimal (2) and inferior turbinate (2). They form the front part of the skull.

(iii) **Ear ossicles** (6) include 2 malleus, 2 incus and 2 stapes. These three tiny bones belong to the middle ear.

(iv) **Hyoid** A U-shaped bone present at the base of buccal cavity. It is the only bone which is not in contact with any other bone. This is also called **tongue bone**.

Vertebral Column

It is also called **backbone** or **spine**. It is dorsally placed, curved, vertical rod extending from the base of the skull through a large hole, the **foramen magnum**. It is curved to maintain the balance of the body in an erect position.

It consists of ring-like bones called vertebrae. The vertebral column is composed of 33 vertebrae.

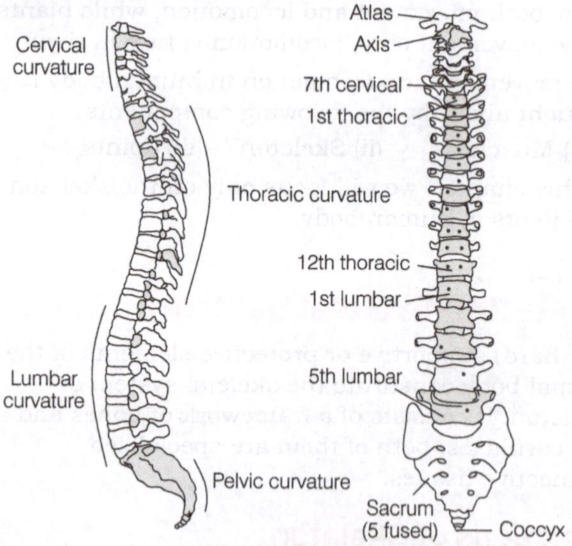

Vertebral column (human)

These are classified into following types

(i) **Cervical vertebrae** (7) They are found in the neck region and are 7 in number. The first cervical vertebra called the **atlas** and the second vertebra is the **axis**.

(ii) **Thoracic vertebrae** (12) They are found in the chest region. These 12 vertebrae form the dorsal side of ribcage to protect the heart and lungs.

(iii) **Lumbar vertebrae** (5) They are found in the waist region. These are the strongest vertebrae of human body.

(iv) **Sacral vertebrae** (5) They are fused together to form the sacrum in pelvis region. In humans, the female sacrum is wider than male sacrum.

(v) **Coccygeal vertebrae** (4) These are fused to form the coccyx in adults and found in the region of lower pelvis. In humans, it is considered as a vestigial tail.

Thus, vertebral formula for man is

$$C_{(7)}\ T_{(12)}\ L_{(5)}\ S_{(5)}\ C_{(4)} = 33$$

Structure of Typical Vertebra

The main body of the vertebra is called as **centrum**. Over the centrum is the **neural arch** that provides protection to the spinal cord which run beneath it. **Neural spine** is a flat longtitudinal ridge projecting upward from the meeting point of the two neural arches. The neural arch bears a median spinous process of the neural spine to which strong muscles are attached.

Two **transverse processes** project laterally from the base of the neural arch. It also bears **articular processes** (articular facets) which helps in articulation of one vertebra with another.

Each vertebra is separated from the adjacent vertebrae by **intervertebral discs** or gristle and are held together by ligaments that prevent it from dislocation.

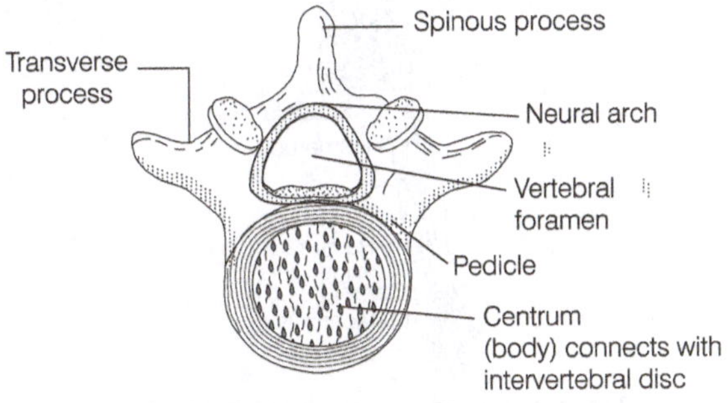

Structure of typical vertebra

Sternum (Breast Bone)

It is a flat dagger-shaped bone located on the ventral midline of thorax (i.e. in the middle of the front part of chest). It articulates with ribs and backbone.

Ribs

These are the thin, flat curved bones that form a protective cage around the organs of upper body. The ribs are composed of 24 bones arranged in 12 pairs.

These 12 pairs of ribs along with thoracic vertebrae and sternum constitute the bony cage or rib cage.

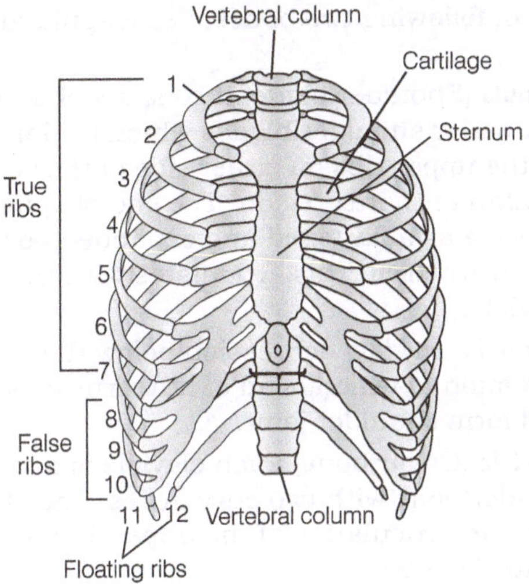

Sternum and ribs

Ribs are mainly categorised into following three types

(i) **True ribs** The first seven ribs are attached directly with the sternum with the help of hyaline cartilage and are called true ribs.

(ii) **False ribs** The 8th, 9th and 10th pair of ribs join the seventh rib with the help of hyaline cartilage. They do not articulate directly with sternum, hence are called false ribs.

(iii) **Floating ribs** The last two (11th and 12th) pair of ribs remain free anteriorly and are called floating ribs.

Note Some people have an additional 13th pair of ribs which is called as **gorilla ribs**.

Functions of Ribs

Ribs serve following functions

(i) They protect the heart, large blood vessels and lungs.

(ii) They bear respiratory muscles.

Check Your LEARNING...

1. Mention the total number of bones in axial skeleton.
2. How many bones comprise the backbone?
3. What is thoracic vertebrae?
4. Give the name of the flat dagger-shaped bone in humans.
5. How many pairs of false ribs are found in humans?

Appendicular Skeleton

It lies along the transverse (side) axis. It comprises of 126 bones, which include pectoral, pelvic girdles and limb bones, i.e. bones of arms and legs.

Pectoral (Shoulder) Girdle

It is present in the anterior part of the body. It consists of following two bones, i.e. scapula and clavicle.

(i) **Scapula** (Shoulder blade) It consists of a two flat triangular shoulder blades which lie dorsally on the upper ribs on either side of the vertebral column in thorax region. The end of spine projects as a flattened and expanded portion called **acromion**. This articulates with the clavicle.

Glenoid cavity is a depression below the acromion to which head of humerus articulates and form shoulder joint.

(ii) **Clavicle** (Collar bone) Each clavicle is a long slender bone with two curvatures. The clavicle helps in articulation of the upper limb with axial skeleton.

Therefore one end of clavicle articulates with scapula and other end articulates with the uppermost part of sternum.

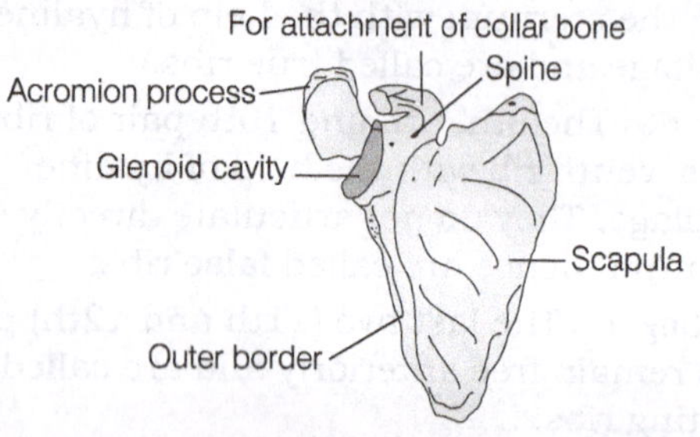

Pectoral (shoulder) girdle (left) as viewed from the back side

Functions of Pectoral Girdle

It provides an attachment point for numerous muscles that allow shoulder and elbow joints to move.

Pelvic (Hip) Girdle

It is located in the lower part of the trunk. It consists of two coxal (hip) bones. Each coxal is formed by the fusion of following three bones

(i) Upper ilium
(ii) Lower ischium
(iii) Inner pubis

The innominate at the middle of its lateral surface has a deep, cup-shaped **acetabulum**, where head of femur articulates. The two halves of the pelvic girdle meet ventrally to form pubic symphysis containing fibrous cartilage.

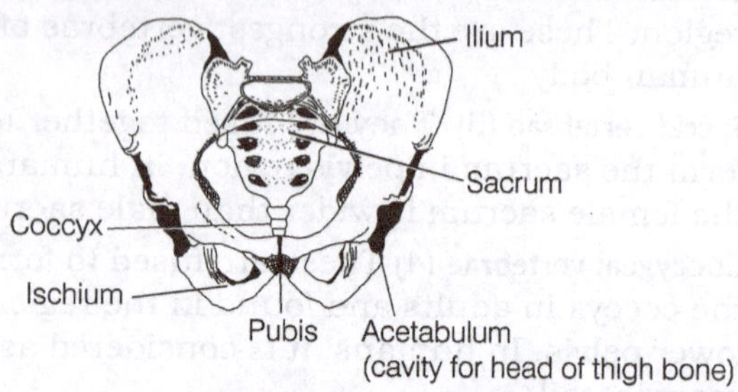

Pelvic (seen from the front)

Functions of Pelvic Girdle

It provides articulation to the bones of the leg, supports and protects abdominal viscera. It also provides
attachment to certain leg muscles. It is also responsible for protecting and supporting the abdominal organs.

Limbs

The bones of the limbs along with girdles constitute the appendicular skeleton. Each limb is made up of 30 bones.

Forelimb

The bones of the hand (forelimb) constitutes humerus (1), radius (1), ulna (1), carpals/wrist bones (8), metacarpal-palm bones (5) and phalanges/digits (14).

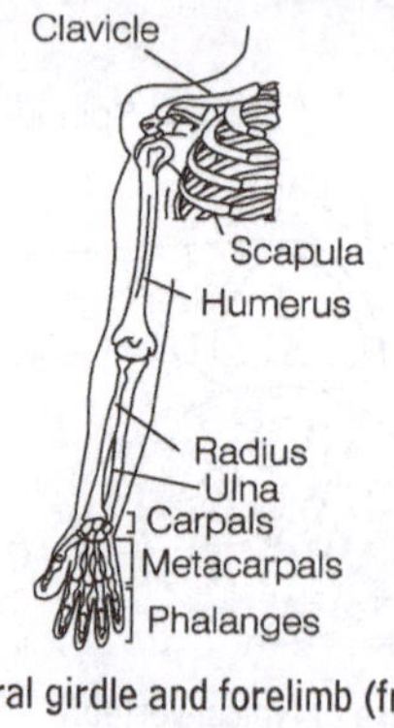

Right pectoral girdle and forelimb (frontal view)

The humerus and ulna together make up the elbow. The length of ulna is longer than the radius. The radius contributes to the movement of the wrist. The phalangeal formula for human hand is 2 (thumb), 3, 3, 3, 3.

Hindlimb

The bones of the leg (hindlimb) constitutes femur (1), tibia (1), fibula (1), patella (1), tarsals (7), metatarsals (5) and phalanges (14).

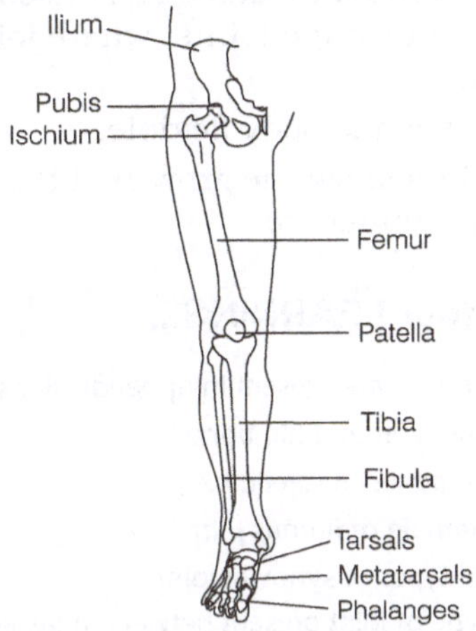

Right pelvic girdle and lower limb (frontal view)

A cup-shaped bone called **patella** cover knee ventrally. It is a sesamoid bone (bone embedded within a tendon). Femur, tibia and fibula bones together support the **shank** of leg. Tarsals form the ankle, metatarsals form the sole and phalanges form the digits of the foot. The phalangeal formula for human foot is 2 thumb, 3, 3, 3, 3.

Joints

The place of articulation between two or more bones or between a bone and a cartilage is called a joint. The study of joints is known as **Arthrology.**

Classification of Joints

There are three major structural types, i.e. fibrous, cartilaginous and synovial.

1. Fibrous (Immovable Joints)

They do not allow movement because the bones are held firmly by bundles of white fibrous tissue, made up of collagen. These joints are extremely strong, e.g. the **sutures** (joints between the bones of skull) and **syndesmosis** (joint between tibia and fibula).

2. Cartilaginous (Slightly Movable Joints)

They allow slight movement because of the elastic pads of fibrocartilage present between the ends of the bones,
e.g. the joint between sternum and ribs and the joints between the adjacent vertebrae in the vertebral column.

3. Synovial (Freely Movable Joints)

A considerable movement is allowed at all synovial joints. They are surrounded by tubular articular capsule.

The capsule consists of two layers, i.e. outer fibrous capsule and inner synovial membrane which secretes synovial fluid. The fluid lubricates and provides nourishment to articular cartilage.

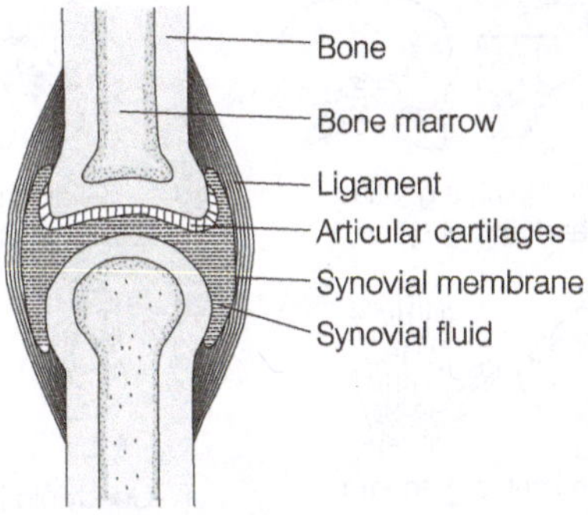

A typical synovial joint

In old age, stiffness of joints occurs due to decrease in synovial fluid that leads to **arthritis.**

Types of Synovial Joints

According to shape of bones and type of movement, the synovial joints are of following types

(i) **Ball and socket joint** In this type, a ball-like structure on one bone fits into a socket-like structure of another bone, e.g. shoulder joint (between pectoral girdle and head of humerus) and hip joint (between acetabulum and head of femur). It can move in all directions.

(ii) **Hinge** (knee) **joint** This joint allows the movement in one plane only. Spoon-like surface of one bone fits into the concave surface of another bone, e.g. elbow joint between humerus and ulna, interphalangeal joints and knee joint.

(iii) **Pivot joint** This joint is responsible for providing movement in one plane. Rounded or pointed bone fits into a shallow depression in another bone, e.g. joint between atlas and axis and radioulnar joint (between radius and ulna).

(iv) **Gliding joint** This joint allows articulating bones to slide upon one another, e.g. joints between the carpal bones and between the tarsal bones.

(v) **Saddle joint** This type of joint is like ball and socket joint but not developed fully, e.g. joint between carpal (trapezium) of hand and metacarpal of thumb.

(vi) **Condyloid or Ellipsoid or Angular joint** This allows movement in two planes (i.e. back-forth and side-side), e.g. joint between metacarpals and phalanges (metacarpophalangeal joint) of the fingers.

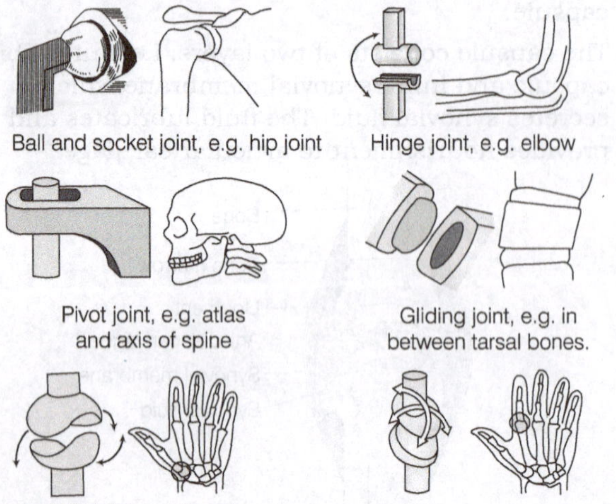

Types of synovial joints

Functions of Joints

Joints serve following functions in human body

(i) These are essential for all types of movement.

(ii) Force generated by muscles is used to carryout movement through joints, where joints act as a fulcrum.

(iii) The joints make body flexible.

(iv) Some joints allow the growth of the structure that they connect to.

Check Your LEARNING...

1 How many bones are present in appendicular skeleton.

2 Name the shoulder and hip bone.

3 Name all the bones of forelimb.

4 Give one example of fibrous joint.

5 Name all the types of synovial joint.

6 Name the type of joint present between atlas and axis.

7 Name the joint which allows movement in two planes.

QUiCK Revision

- **Movement** refers to any change in body position. It is a fundamental characteristic of living beings.
- **Locomotion** is the movement of body parts that leads to change of place.
- Locomotion in human is a function of skeleton system. Other functions of human skeleton include giving shape and support to body, protection to delicate internal organs, formation of different blood cells, etc.
- The skeletal system of humans is divided into two parts, i.e. **axial skeleton** (80 bones) and **appendicular skeleton** (126 bones).
- **Axial skeleton** includes skull, vertebral column, ribs and sternum.
    - **Skull** consists of cranium having 8 bones, ear ossicles with 6 bones (2 malleus, 2 incus and 2 stapes), single hyoid bone and 14 bones that constitute facial bones.
    - **Vertebral column** includes 7 cervical vertebrae, 12 thoracic vertebrae, 5 lumbar vertebrae, 5 sacral and 4 coccygeal vertebrae.
    - **Sternum** is a flat bone lying in the middle of the chest, towards front.
    - **Ribs** are total 24 in number arranged in 12 pairs. First seven pairs are true ribs, 8th to 10th pairs are called false ribs. The last two pairs of ribs, i.e. 11th and 12th, are called floating ribs.
- **Appendicular skeleton** includes forelimbs, hindlimbs, pectoral girdle and pelvic girdle.
    - **Pectoral girdle** is shoulder girdle that consists of right and left halves. Both these halves consist of a triangular bone, scapula and S-shaped, clavicle.
    - **Pelvic girdle** consists two halves, i.e. right and left halves. Each half is made up of three bones, i.e. ilium, ischium and pubis.
    - **Forelimbs** consist of 30 bones of which humerus is present in upper arm. The lower arm has two bones, radius and ulna. Each wrist is composed of 8 small bones called **carpals**. 5 palm bones are called **metacarpals** and 14 bones called **phalanges** form fingers.
    - **Hindlimb** has 30 bones that form thigh, shank, knee and foot. Femur is the longest bone of thigh. Knee cap (patella) is triangular, shank region consists of tibia and fibula. Ankle includes 7 bones called **tarsals**, 5 bones of sole are **metatarsals** and 14 bones called **phalanges** form toe.
- **Joints** are points of contact between bones or between bones and cartilage.
    - **Fibrous joints** do not allow any movement, e.g. sutures of skull which fuse end to end.
    - **Cartilaginous joint** Vertebrae allow slight movement, e.g. joint including the pubic symphysis of pubis and joints between the vertebrae.
    - **Synovial joint** allows considerable movement and characterised by the presence of synovial cavity between the articulating surface of two bones e.g. **ball and socket joint** (between humerus and pectoral girdle), **hinge joint** (knee joint), **pivot joint** (between atlas and axis vertebra), **gliding joint** (between the carpals) and **saddle joint** (between carpals and metacarpals).

Chapter Practice

Section-I

1 Mark Questions

1. Name the following.
   (i) The smallest bone of the body.
   (ii) Large hollow box-like part of the skull that houses brain.
   (iii) The only bone in our body which does not form any joint.
   (iv) The first vertebra of the vertebral column.
   (v) The bone of the pelvic girdle.
   (vi) The name of the cavity in the girdle to which head of femur articulates.
   (vii) The type of joint present in the skull.
   (viii) Freely movable joints.
   (ix) The substance responsible for lubricating the freely movable joint at the shoulder.
   (x) The joint that resembles hinge of a joint.

Ans. (i) Stapes (ii) Cranium
(iii) Hyoid (iv) Atlas
(v) Ilium/Ischium/Pubis (vi) Acetabulum
(vii) Fibrous joint (viii) Synovial joints
(ix) Synovial fluid
(x) Knee joint

2. Correct and rewrite the following statements by changing the underlined words.
   (i) The first seven ribs are called <u>floating</u> ribs.
   (ii) The <u>axial</u> skeleton comprises of 126 bones.
   (iii) Pectoral girdle consists of two bones, i.e. scapula and <u>ilium</u>.
   (iv) The place of articulation between two or more bones is called <u>muscle</u>.
   (v) The joint present between atlas and axis is <u>hinge</u> joint.

Ans. (i) The first seven ribs are called true ribs.
(ii) The appendicular skeleton comprises of 126 bones.
(iii) Pectoral girdle consists of two bones, i.e. scapula and clavicle.
(iv) The place of articulation between two or more bones is called joint.
(v) The joint present between atlas and axis is pivot joint.

3. Give biological reasons for the following.
   (i) The last two pairs of ribs are called floating ribs.
   (ii) Some people in old age complain about stiff joints.

Ans. (i) The last two pairs of ribs are called floating ribs because they do not articulate directly with the sternum but are attached only to the vertebrae.
(ii) In old age, the fluid in the synovial capsule called synovial fluid often dries up and cartilage corrode due to continuous use. As a result, there is no smooth movement possible between joints. Due to this, some people in old age complain about stiff joints. The condition is known as arthritis.

4. (i) Match the following columns.

Column I	Column II
A. Cranium	1. 22
B. Skull (facial and cranial)	2. 8
C. Face	3. 14
D. Hindlimb	4. 12
E. Ribs	5. 30

(ii) Match the following columns.

Column I	Column II
A. Radius	1. 14 bones
B. Carpals	2. 5 bones
C. Metacarpal	3. 8 bones
D. Phalanges	4. 1 bone

(iii) Match the following columns.

Column I	Column II
A. Sternum	1. Synovial fluid
B. Glenoid cavity	2. Vertebrae
C. Freely movable joint	3. Pectoral girdle
D. Cartilaginous joint	4. Flat bone

(iv) Match the following columns.

Column I	Column II
A. Ball and socket joint	1. Between humerus and pectoral girdle
B. Hinge joint	2. Knee joint
C. Pivot joint	3. Between atlas and axis
D. Gliding joint	4. Between the carpals

Ans. (i) A-2, B-1, C-3, D-5, E-4
(ii) A-4, B-3, C-2, D-1
(iii) A-4, B-3, C-1, D-2
(iv) A-1, B-2, C-3, D-4

5. Choose the correct answer from the four options given below.

(i) Our vertebral column is formed by the
(a) 26 serially arranged units called vertebrae
(b) 27 serially arranged units called vertebrae
(c) 33 serially arranged units called vertebrae
(d) 35 serially arranged units called vertebrae

Ans. (c)

(ii) Which one of the following is showing the correct sequential order of vertebrae in the vertebral column of human beings?
(a) Cervical – Lumbar – Thoracic – Sacral – Coccygeal
(b) Cervical – Thoracic – Sacral – Lumbar – Coccygeal
(c) Cervical – Sacral – Thoracic – Lumbar – Coccygeal
(d) Cervical – Thoracic – Lumbar – Sacral – Coccygeal

Ans. (d)

(iii) How many lumbar vertebrae are found in our body?
(a) 5 (b) 4 (c) 7 (d) 12

Ans. (a)

(iv) Ribs are attached to
(a) scapula (b) sternum
(c) clavicle (d) ilium

Ans. (b)

(v) Which pairs of ribs are known as false ribs?
(a) 1st and 2nd (b) 11th and 12th
(c) 8th and 9th (d) 6th and 7th

Ans. (c)

(vi) Which of the following is a part of pectoral girdle?
(a) Ilium (b) Ischium
(c) Acetabulum (d) Glenoid cavity

Ans. (d)

(vii) Number of tarsals, metatarsals and phalanges in human skeleton is
(a) 7, 5, 14 (b) 8, 5, 14
(c) 9, 5, 14 (d) 5, 6, 7

Ans. (a)

(viii) Synovial joints in humans are characterised by
(a) joining of two bones
(b) presence of fluid-filled synovial cavity
(c) rare movement
(d) no movement at all

Ans. (b)

(ix) Knee joint and elbow joint are examples of
(a) saddle joint (b) ball and socket joint
(c) pivot joint (d) hinge joint

Ans.(d)

(x) What is the type of movable joint present between carpal of hand and metacarpal of thumb?
(a) Pivot (b) Saddle
(c) Hinge (d) Gliding

Ans. (b)

6. Fill in the blanks by using suitable words.

(i) .... refers to a change in position of any part of an organism's body.
(ii) Movement of an organism from place to place is called ....
(iii) A structure which provides a rigid framework to the body is called ..... .
(iv) The longest bone in human is ....
(v) The appendicular skeleton in human consists of ...... and ....
(vi) ...... helps in articulation of upper limb with axial skeleton.
(vii) Patella is a ...... bone.
(viii) ...... forms the sole of foot.
(ix) Immovable joint is found in ....

Ans. (i) Movement (ii) locomotion
(iii) skeleton (iv) femur
(v) limbs, girdles (vi) Clavicle
(vii) sesamoid bone (viii) Metatarsals
(ix) skull

7. Choose the odd one out from the following terms given below and name the category to which the other three belong.

(i) Cranium, Facial bones, Backbone, Ear ossicles
(ii) Clavicle, Ilium, Scapula, Sternum
(iii) Humerus, Radius, Patella, Ulna

Ans. (i) **Odd term** Backbone.
Rest three are belong to the bones of skull.
(ii) **Odd term** Sternum.
Rest three are belong to the bones of the appendicular skeleton.
(iii) **Odd term** Patella.
Rest three are belong to the bones of forelimbs.

8. Given below are sets of five terms each. Rewrite the terms in correct order in a logical sequence.

(i) Radius, Phalanges, Humerus, Carpals, Metacarpals
(ii) Clavicle, Sternum, Pelvis, Tibia, Patella

Ans. (i) Humerus, Radius, Carpals, Metacarpals, Phalanges
(iii) Clavicle, Sternum, Pelvis, Patella, Tibia

9. State whether the following statements are true or false. Correct and rewrite the false statements.

(i) Skull in humans consists of 22 bones.
(ii) There are 10 vertebrae in our neck.
(iii) Vertebrae of the chest region are called thoracic vertebrae.
(iv) There are 12 pairs of ribs in human body.
(v) There are three kinds of ribs, known as true, false and floating ribs.
(vi) Last two pairs of ribs are not attached to any other bones is the ribcage.
(vii) Scapula articulates with clavicle through glenoid cavity.

(viii) Pelvic girdle is a part of axial skeleton.
(ix) Sutures are immovable joints between bones of skull.
(x) Hinge joint is a slightly movable joint.
(xi) Joint between radius-ulna is a gliding joint.

Ans. (i) False, skull in humans consists of 29 bones.
(ii) False, there are 7 vertebrae in our neck.
(iii) True
(iv) True
(v) True
(vi) True
(vii) False, scapula articulates with clavicle through acromion process.
(viii) False, pelvic girdle is a part of appendicular skeleton.
(ix) True
(x) False, hinge joint is a freely-movable joint.
(xi) False, joint between radius-ulna is a pivot joint.

10. State the exact location of the following.
(i) Acetabulum
(ii) Patella
(iii) Cartilaginous joint
(iv) Ball and socket joint
(v) Hinge joint

Ans. (i) Acetabulum is a cup-shaped depression in the pelvic girdle.
(ii) Patella is cup-shaped bone in the hindlimb.
(iii) Cartilaginous joint is present between the adjacent vertebrae in the vertebral column.
(iv) Ball and socket joint is present between humerus and pectoral girdle.
(v) Hinge joint is present between humerus and the ulna.

11. Give one example of the following.
(i) Bone of skull
(ii) Bone of pectoral girdle
(iii) Bone of pelvic girdle
(iv) Bone of hindlimb

Ans. (i) Facial bone/Cranial bone/Ear ossicle/ Hyoid
(ii) Clavicle/ Scapula
(iii) Ilium/Pubis/Ischium
(iv) Femur/Tibia/Fibula/Patella/Tarsals/ Metatarsals/ Phalanges.

12. State the main function of the following.
(i) Skeleton (ii) Ribs
(iii) Pectoral girdle (iv) Synovial fluid

Ans. (i) Skeleton provides a support or framework to all the soft parts and gives the definite shape to the body.
(ii) Ribs protect the heart, large blood vessels and lungs.
(iii) Pectoral girdle provides an attachment point for numerous muscles that allow shoulder and elbow joints to move.
(iv) Synovial fluid lubricates and provides nourishment to the articular cartilage.

13. Mention one difference between each of the following pairs on the basis of what is given in the bracket.
(i) Cervical vertebrae and Thoracic vertebrae (number and location)
(ii) True ribs and Floating ribs (number)
(iii) Ball and socket joint and Hinge joint (location)

Ans. (i) Difference between cervical vertebrae and thoracic vertebrae is as follows

Cervical vertebrae	Thoracic vertebrae
Present in neck and are 7 in number.	Present in thoracic region and are 12 in number.

(ii) Difference between true ribs and floating ribs is as follows

True ribs	Floating ribs
The first 7 pairs of ribs make the true ribs.	The last two pairs (11th and 12th) make floating ribs.

(iii) Difference between ball and socket joint and hinge joint is as follows

Ball and socket joint	Hinge joint
Present between upper arm and shoulder and between upper leg and hip.	Present in knee and elbow.

14. Give biological/technical terms for the following.
(i) Skull (ii) Spine
(iii) Shoulder bone (iv) Collar bone
(v) Knee cap (vi) Hip bone

Ans. (i) Cranium
(ii) Vertebral column
(iii) Scapula
(iv) Clavicle
(v) Patella
(vi) Coxal bone

15. Briefly explain the following terms.
(i) Centrum
(ii) Sternum
(iii) Glenoid cavity

Ans. (i) The main body of vertebra is called as centrum.
(ii) Sternum is a flat long bone located on the ventral midline of thorax.
(iii) The outer cup-shaped part of scapula is called glenoid cavity.

16. Answer the following questions briefly.
(i) How is locomotion different from movement?
(ii) What are the different parts of axial skeleton?
(iii) The three tiny bones present in middle ear are called ear ossicles. Write them in correct sequence beginning from eardrum.
(iv) Which bones form the wrist and the ankle?

Ans. (i) Locomotion is movement of body from one place to another. On the other hand, movement is change in position or posture of any body part.
(ii) Skull, vertebral column, ribs and sternum are the different parts of axial skeleton.
(iii) Malleus, incus and stapes.
(iv) Wrist-Carpals
Ankle-Tarsals

2 Marks Questions

17. How many facial bones are present in the skull? Which of them is a movable bone?

Ans. There are 14 facial bones. The lower jawbone, i.e. mandible is the movable bone.

18. The human endoskeleton consists of two parts. Name them with number of bones in each.

Ans. Two parts of human endoskeleton are as follows
(i) **Axial skeleton** It comprises of 80 bones.
(ii) **Appendicular skeleton** It comprises of 126 bones.

19. What are the points for articulation of pelvic and pectoral girdles?

Ans. Pectoral and pelvic girdle bones help in the articulation of the upper and the lower limbs respectively with the axial skeleton.
In pectoral girdle below the acromion, their is a depression called the glenoid cavity which articulates with the head of the humerus to form the shoulder joint.
Pelvic girdle articulates with femur through a cavity called acetabulum forming thigh joint.

3 Marks Questions

20. What is a joint? Name three major classifications of joint with examples.

Ans. The place of articulation between two or more bones or between a bone and a cartilage is called a joint.
There are three major structural types, i.e. fibrous, cartilaginous and synovial.
(i) **Fibrous joint** It is present between the bones of skull.
(ii) **Cartilaginous joint** It is present between sternum and ribs.
(iii) **Synovial joint** It is present between pectoral girdle and the head of humerus.

21. Name the different types of synovial joint with example of each.

Ans. Different types of synovial joints are
(i) **Ball and socket joint** It is present between the femur and the acetabulum.
(ii) **Hinge joint** It is present between phalanges.
(iii) **Pivot joint** It is present between the atlas and axis.
(iv) **Gliding joint** It is present between the carpal and bones.

Section-II [5 Marks]

Structured Questions

1. Axial skeleton comprises of 80 bones which include skull, vertebral column, sternum and ribs.
(i) Which bones of the skull are movable?
(ii) What do you mean by ear ossicles?
(iii) What is the vertebral formula for man?
(iv) How many vertebrae are there in general in neck region of mammals?
(v) Which pairs of ribs are called false ribs?

Ans. (i) Mandible and ear ossicles are the movable bones.
(ii) The bones found in middle ear are called ear ossicles.
(iii) Vertebral formula for man is :
$C_7T_{12}L_5S_{(5)}C_{(4)} = 33$
(iv) Mammals in general have seven cervical vertebrae in neck region.
(v) The 8th, 9th and 10th pairs of ribs are called false ribs.

2. Observe the diagram and answer the questions that follows.

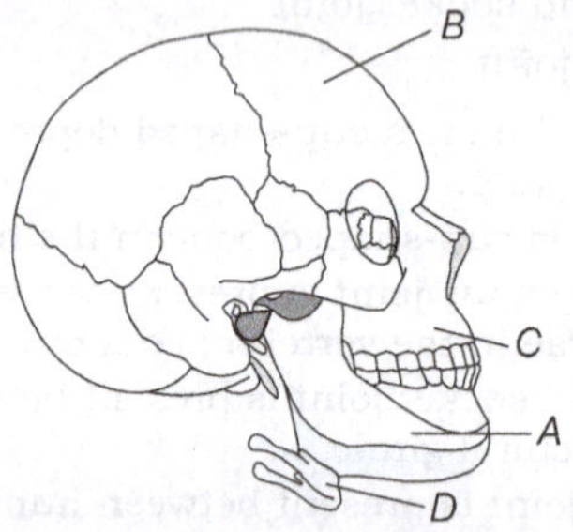

(i) Identify *A*, *B*, *C* and *D* in the given diagram of human skull.
(ii) Name the opening of skull through which spinal cord passes.
(iii) How many bones are present in lumbar vertebrae?
(iv) What is the name given to the hard covering of brain?
(v) Which joint is present in the bones of skull?

Ans. (i) The parts *A*, *B*, *C* and *D* in given digram of human skull are as
A– Mandible
B– Frontal bone
C– Maxilla
D– Hyoid bone
(ii) Foramen magnum is the large opening in the posterior portion of skull through which spinal cord passes.
(iii) 5 bones are present in lumbar vertebrae
(iv) The brain box or cranium
(v) Fibrous joint is present in the bones of skull.

3. Observe the diagram carefully and answer the questions that follows.

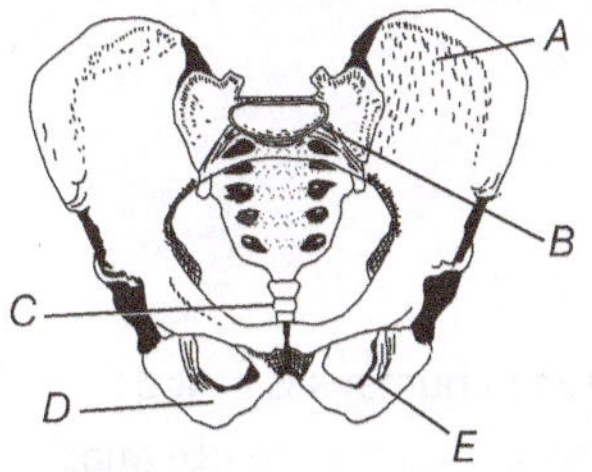

(i) Identify *A* to *E* in the given diagram.
(ii) Name the part where femur articulates.
(iii) Give one function of the part shown in the diagram.
(iv) Which joint is formed by the two halves of pelvic girdle?
(v) The diagram shown above is part of which skeleton, axial skeleton or appendicular skeleton?

Ans. (i) The parts *A* to *E* in the given diagram are as *A*-Ilium, *B*-Sacrum, *C*-Pubic symphysis, *D*-Ischium, *E*-Acetabulum.
(ii) Acetabulum is the part where femur articulates.
(iii) This part is responsible for providing articulation to the bones of the leg.
(iv) Pubic symphysis.
(v) Pelvic girdle is the part of appendicular skeleton.

4. Appendicular skeleton comprises of 126 bones, which include pectoral and pelvic girdles and limb bones.
(i) What is glenoid cavity?
(ii) What is the role of collar bone?
(iii) Give the name of three bones which make up the hip bone?
(iv) Give the name of bones of the hand?
(v) How many bones are present in each limb?

Ans. (i) Glenoid cavity is a depression below the acromion to which head of humerus articulates and form shoulder joint.
(ii) Collar bone (clavicle) helps in articulation of the upper limb with axial skeleton.
(iii) Ischium, ilium and pubis make up the hip bone.
(iv) Humerus, radius, ulna, carpals, metacarpals and phalanges are the bones of the hand.
(v) Each limb is made up of 30 bones.

5. Observe the diagram carefully and answer the questions that follows.

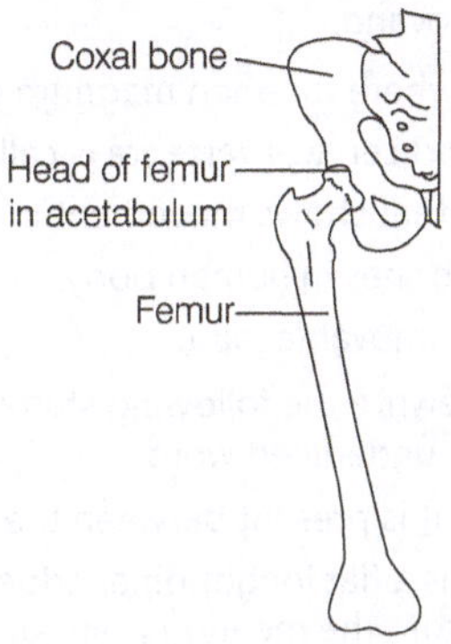

(i) Which joint is shown in the figure?
(ii) Give another example of this joint.
(iii) What is the function of synovial fluid?
(iv) Which joint is present between radius and ulna?
(v) Name the two layers of capsule of synovial joint.

Ans. (i) Ball and socket joint is shown in the figure.
(ii) Another example of this joint is shoulder joint (between pectoral girdle and head of humerus).
(iii) Synovial fluid acts as a lubricant to absorb mechanical shock.
(iv) Pivot joint is present between radius and ulna.
(v) The two layers of capsule of synovial joint are the outer fibrous capsule and inner synovial membrane.

Chapter Assessment

Section-I

1 Mark Questions

1. Name the following.
   (i) The part where foramen magnum is found.
   (ii) The second cervical vertebra is called.
   (iii) The joint that shows movement in one plane only.
   (iv) Irregular bones in human body.
   (v) Slightly immovable joint.
2. Correct and rewrite the following statements by changing the underlined words.
   (i) <u>Hinge joint</u> is present between the tarsals bone.
   (ii) <u>Centrum</u> is a flat longitudinal ridge projecting upward from the meeting point of two neural arches.
   (iii) The humerus and <u>tibia</u> together make up the elbow.
3. Give biological reason for the following.
   The 8th, 9th and 10th pairs of ribs are called false ribs.
4. (i) Match the following columns.

	Column I		Column II
A.	Humerus and shoulder girdle	1.	Partially movable
B.	Two adjacent vertebrae	2.	Gliding
C.	Atlas and axis	3.	Immovable
D.	Bone of brain box	4.	Ball and socket
E.	Between the carpals	5.	Pivot

   (ii) Match the following columns.

	Column I		Column II
A.	Cervical vertebrae	1.	5
B.	Thoracic vertebrae	2.	7
C.	Lumbar vertebrae	3.	12
D.	Coccygeal vertebrae	4.	4

5. Choose the correct answer from the four options given below.
   (i) What is the name of the lower jaw bone?
   (a) Maxilla (b) Mandible
   (c) Clavicle (d) Ossicles
   (ii) First vertebrae in humans is called
   (a) axis (b) atlas
   (b) lumbar (d) cervical
   (iii) Humerus is the bone of
   (a) leg (b) hand
   (c) skull (d) shoulder
   (iv) The joint present in the cranium
   (a) hinge (b) ball and socket
   (c) immovable (d) gliding
   (v) Angular joint is present between
   (a) metacarpels and phalanges
   (b) skull and axis vertebrae
   (c) skull and atlas vertebrae
   (d) axis and first thoracic vertebrae
6. Fill in the blanks by using suitable words.
   (i) The spinal column or vertebral column is commonly called as ....
   (ii) .... ribs are attached to the sternum.
   (iii) ..... and .... comprise the bone of the lower leg.
   (iv) .... and .... comprise the bone of the lower arm.
   (v) The term used for the joint between tibia and fibula is ....
7. Choose the odd one out from the following terms given and name the category to which other three belong.
   (i) Skull, Vertebrae, Sternum, Pelvic girdle
   (ii) Humerus, Ulna, Metatarsal, Phalanges
8. Given below are sets of five terms each. Rewrite the terms in correct order in a logical sequence.
   (i) Patella, Fibula, Femur, Phalanges, Tarsals
   (ii) Cranium, Sternum, Ischium, Ilium, Metatarsals
9. State whether the following statements are true or false. Choose and rewrite the false statements.
   (i) Study of movement is called Arthrology.
   (ii) Axial skeleton includes shoulder and hip girdles.
   (iii) Maxilla of skull is the only movable joint in the head.
   (iv) Vertebrae of the tail region are called cervical vertebrae.
   (v) Humerus of the upper arm is the longest bone.

10. State the exact location of the following.
(i) Centrum (ii) Glenoid cavity

11. Give one example of the following.
(i) Joint present in carpal/metacarpal of thumb
(ii) Joint present in femur/acetabulum
(iii) Joint found between cranial bones
(iv) Joint found between pubic bones in the pelvic girdle

12. State the main function of the following.
(i) Pectoral girdle (ii) Joints

13. Mention one difference between each of the following pairs on the basis of what is given in the bracket.
(i) Axial and Appendicular skeletons (number of bones)
(ii) Pelvic and Pectoral girdles (location)

14. Give biological/technical terms for the following.
(i) Brain box (ii) Breast bone

15. Briefly explain the following terms.
(i) Gristle (ii) Gorilla ribs

16. Answer the following questions briefly.
(i) How is the shank of leg supported?
(ii) What is sesamoid bone? Name it.
(iii) What are constituents of our skeleton?

2 Marks Questions

17. Name the parts of appendicular skeleton along with number of bones in each part.

18. What makes synovial joint freely movable? Give the basic structure of a synovial joint.

3 Marks Question

19. Just as the humerus corresponds to femur, what bones correspond to carpals, metacarpals and ulna, respectively?

Section-II [5 Marks]

Structured Questions

20. Given diagram show the right pectoral girdle and upper arm (frontal view) of human.
Study the diagram and answer the questions that follows.

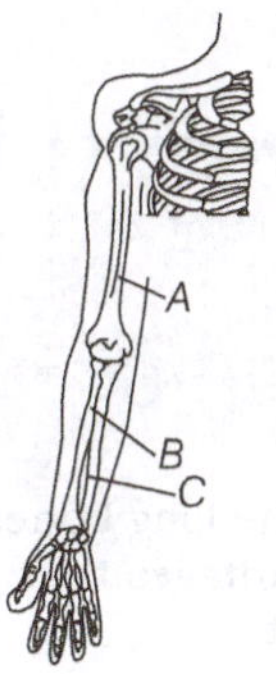

(i) Identify *A* to *C*.
(ii) Name the bones of wrist, palm and fingers.
(iii) Which joint is present between radius and ulna?
(iv) How many wrist bones are present in forelimb?
(v) Which bone contributes to the movement of wrist?

21. The hard, supportive or protective element of the animal body constitutes the skeletal system or skeleton.
(i) How many bones are found in a newborn baby?
(ii) Name the different curves of vertebral column.
(iii) What is the difference between male and female sacrum.
(iv) Which part of scapula articulates with clavicle?
(v) Which bones form the digits of the foot?

22. The following diagram shows the structure of a typical vertebra. Study the diagram and answer the questions that follows.

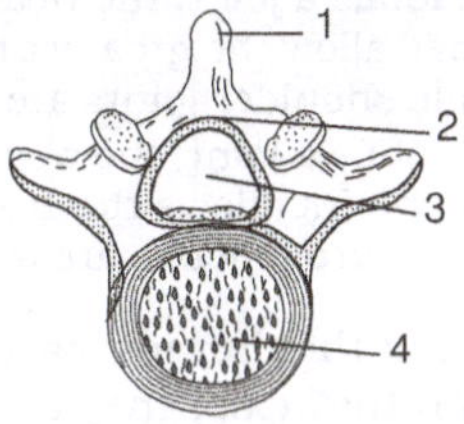

(i) Label the parts 1 to 4.
(ii) How many vertebrae are present in our
(a) Neck (b) Abdomen?
(iii) How many transverse processes project from base of neural arch?
(iv) Which joint is similar to ball and socket ioint?
(v) Which structure provides protection to the spinal cord?

For explanations scan the given QR Code

Olympiad Section*

Brain Teasing Questions asked in Previous Olympiads

1 In vertebrates, the long bones are always hollow. The advantages that this anatomy provides are that [INBO 2010]

I. They harbour and protect marrow.
II. They provide attachment to tendons.
III. They are stronger than solid structures made up of same amount of material.
IV. Only hollow bones can articulate better with one another.

(a) I, II and III
(b) I and III
(c) I, III and IV
(d) I, II, III and IV

2 Why are shoulder dislocations more common than dislocations of the carpal bones in the hand.

(a) The less mobile a joint, the weaker the joint. The shoulder joint allows the greatest range of motion, while carpal bones are more stable
(b) The less mobile a joint, the weaker the joint. Carpal bones allow the greatest range of motion, while shoulder joints are more stable
(c) The more mobile a joint, the weaker the joint. Carpal bones allow the greatest range of motion while shoulder joints are more stable
(d) The more mobile a joint, the weaker the joint. The shoulder joint allows the greatest range of motion while carpal bones are more stable

3 Abnormalities of the thoracic cage are relatively rare, but when they exist they can cause disorders. Which of the following would most be at risk if someone had a defective thoracic cage?

(a) Middle
(b) Brain
(c) Spinal cord
(d) Heart

4 A cricket player is fast chasing a ball in the field. Which one of the following groups of bones are directly contributing in this movement?

(a) Femur, Malleus, Tibia, Metatarsals
(b) Pelvic, Ulna, Patella, Tarsals
(c) Sternum, Femur, Tibia, Fibula
(d) Tarsals, Femur, Metatarsals, Tibia

5 What angular movements occur at the hip joint and knees as you bend down to touch your toes?

(a) Both the hip and knees are flexed
(b) Both the hip joint and knees are extended
(c) The hip joint is extended and the knees are flexed
(d) The hip joint is flexed and the knees are extended

6 Which type of skeletal system of animals is composed of a hard skeletal layer found on the exterior of the organism?

(a) Hydrostatic skeleton (b) Exoskeleton
(c) Axial skeleton (d) Appendicular skeleton

7 Relative rates of red blood cell production in the bone marrow of different bones at different ages are shown in the graph. *A*, *B* and *C* are likely to be, respectively

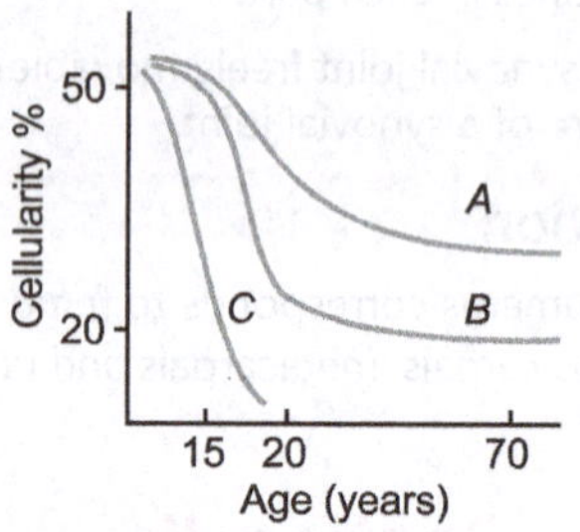

(a) Vertebra, Rib and Tibia
(b) Femur, Carpal and Rib
(c) Tibia, Fibula and Femur
(d) Radius, Sternum and Carpal

Answers

1. (b) **2.** (d) **3.** (d) **4.** (d) **5.** (d) **6.** (b) **7.** (a)

**These questions may or may not be asked in the examination, have been given just for additional practice required for olympiads, scholarship exams etc. For detailed explanations refer Page No. 230.*

CHAPTER 11

The Skin

Chapter Inside

• Skin • Skin Derivatives • Thermoregulation

Skin

It is the outermost protective layer which covers the whole human body. It accounts for 15% of an adult's total body weight.

It is the largest organ of human body in terms of its surface area and forms the first line of defence for the body. This layer is thin and delicate.

The skin (integument) along with its derivatives collectively constitutes integumentary system of the body.

Various parts of integumentary system in mammals are shown in the flowchart below

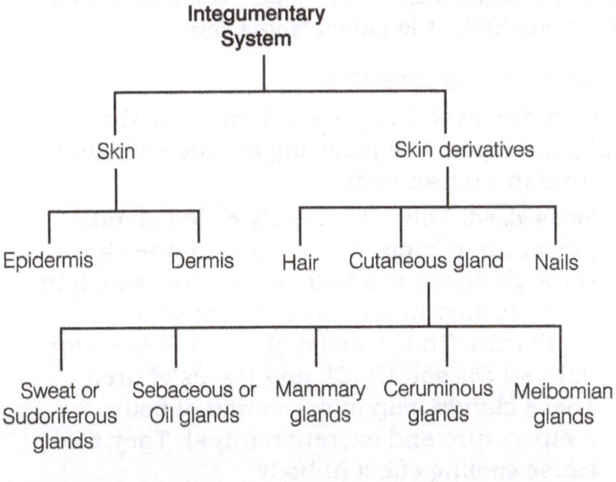

Structure of Skin

Skin is composed of following two layers

1. Epidermis

This is the outermost layer of skin. It originates from **ectoderm** of embryo. It consists of stratified epithelium having three regions namely, **stratum corneum** (outermost cornified layer), **granular layer** (middle part) and **Malpighian layer** (inner germinal layer).

(i) **Cornified layer** (Stratum Corneum) It is the layer containing dead skin cells. These cells are made up of fibrous structural protein called **keratin**.
It forms the tough outer coat which acts as barrier to pathogen, mechanical damage and reduce water loss through evaporation. The cells of this layer are continuously replaced by newly formed cells of germinal layer or Malpighian layer.

(ii) **Granular layer** (Stratum Granulocum) It is made up of two or three sub-layers of flattened living cells.

(iii) **Malpighian layer** (Stratum Malpighi or Germinative layer) This is the innermost layer of epidermis and it is formed by the column shaped living cells. The cells called Malpighian cells divide constantly so as to form new cells that are pushed outwards continuously. The pigment **melanin** is present in these cells which gives characteristic skin colour to the human skin. The pigment melanin present in this layer acts as a protective screen against ultraviolet light as well.

Abnormal Conditions of Skin Pigmentation

Two abnormal conditions related to skin pigmentation are

(i) **Albinism** It refers to the complete loss of pigmentation of the skin all over the body including hair, eyebrows, eyelashes and even the iris. As a result of albinism, affected individuals appear pinkish due to underlying blood capillaries.

(ii) **Leukoderma** It is also called vitiligo. In this condition there is loss of skin pigmentation (melanin) from smaller or larger patches at different areas of the body. However, the exact cause of the condition is not known.

2. Dermis

This layer lies just below epidermis. It originates from the **mesoderm** of embryo. This layer is 2-3 times much thicker than the epidermis. It is made up of thick elastic connective tissue. The dermis consists of blood vessels, nerve fibres, sensory organs, sweat glands, touch receptors, hair follicles, etc. The outer region of dermis which lies next to the epidermis has various small processes called **papillae** which contain blood capillaries and nerve endings. The sense organs and nerve endings are concerned with the sensation of touch and pain.

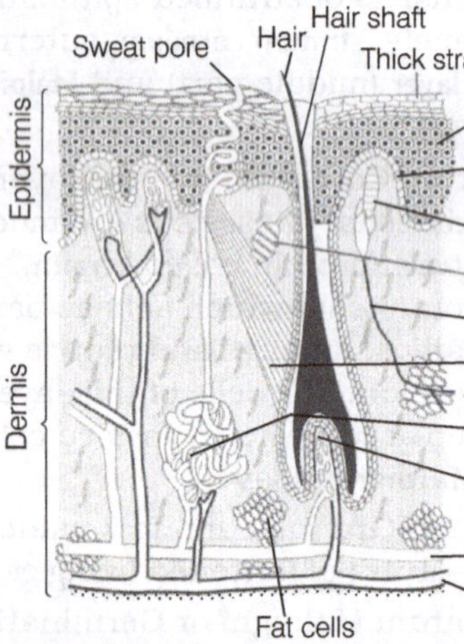

Vertical section of human skin

The fatty or areolar tissue layer lies just beneath the dermis and they are connected with muscles. This layer not only serve as food reserve but also as a heat insulating layer as well as shock absorber.

Functions of Skin

Skin performs many diverse functions which are as follows

(i) Skin acts as protective covering for the body.

(ii) Its dermal layer is impermeable, thus prevents evaporation of water from body.

(iii) The pigment melanin present in skin protects the body from harmful effect of UV radiations.

(iv) It acts as barrier to germs, poisons and foreign particles .

(v) It excretes urea (0.08%), water, NaCl and CO_2.

(vi) It receives stimulus for touch, pain, heat, cold, chemicals, humidity and pressure.

(vii) Subcutaneous layers of skin helps in storage of water and fats.

(viii) Skin acts as a site of vitamin-D synthesis when exposed to sunshine.

Check Your LEARNING...

1 Name the outermost layer of epidermis that forms tough enter coat.

2 Which layer of epidermis divides repeatedly and gives rise to new cells?

3 What is the other name of Malpighian layer?

4 Name the pigment which provides colour to human skin.

Skin Derivatives

The derivatives of human skin include the following structures

1. Hair

These are slender, thread-like outgrowths from a follicle in the skin. A hair consists of three parts, i.e. **hairshaft, hair root** and **hair bulb**. The hair follicle is a structure enclosing the hair root. The roots of hair are supplied with nerve fibres. Therefore, they are sensitive to touch. Hair provides insulation to the body against external temperature of the environment in which the organisms live.
During extreme cold or fright condition, the arrector muscle present in the dermis pull the hair into a verticle position. It is called **'goose flesh'**.

2. Cutaneous Glands

These are the exocrine glands, formed by the Malpighian layer. The following cutaneous glands are found in human body.

(i) **Sweat glands** These are highly coiled glands present in dermis. These open on the skin through ducts as small sweat pores which in turn are surrounded by network of small capillaries. They consist of about 99% water, 0.2 to 0.5% salt (NaCl) and traces of urea. These glands help in regulation of body temperature and excretion (urea). They also cause cooling effect in body.

(ii) **Sebaceous glands** These are lobulated glands consisting of many sacs that open into hair follicle by a common duct. The epithelium layer of these glands secrete an oily secretion called **sebum**. It lubricates the hair, makes skin oily and waterproof and also prevents drying of skin.

Certain problems that relate to sebaceous glands are

(a) **Pimples** They occur due to the accumulation of sebum which promotes the growth of bacteria and leads to pimples.

(b) **Acne** In this, sebaceous glands get inflamed due to hormonal influence occurs usually at puberty.

(c) **Blackheads** When an open pore in the skin gets clogged with dead skin cells and sebum, it turns black upon oxidation by the air and is called black head.

Note
- In humans, oil and sweat glands make the pH of skin acidic (3-5) which discourage the growth of microbes.
- Perception of various stimulus by skin is done by the following cells
  - Pacinian corpuscles Perceive pressure.
  - Meissner's corpuscles Sensory to touch.
  - Ruffini's corpuscles Sensory to high temperature.
  - Krause bulbs Sensory to low temperature.

(iii) **Mammary (milk) glands** These are modified sweat glands which are functional in female and non-functional in males. These glands produce milk in females at the time of birth of young one. Milk secreted by mammary gland is highly nutritious for the baby.

(iv) **Meibomian glands** These are modified sebaceous glands. They open at the margins of the eyelids in the hair follicles of eyelashes. They secrete an oily secretion that keeps them oily, soft, flexible and frictionless. They also prevent over flow of tears.

(v) **Ceruminous glands** These are modified sweat glands found in the auditory canal. The wax-like secretion is called **cerumen** or **earwax**. It lubricates and protects the eardrum.

3. Nails

These are formed by the epidermal layer present at the tips of fingers and toes. Nails are very hard, slightly arched plates formed of **keratin** protein. Nails protect the fingertip and the surrounding soft tissues from injuries.

A nail has three parts

(i) **Plate** It is hard and outer part of the nail which consists of dead, keratinised cells. There are two plates unguis (upper large plate) and subunguis (lower very small).

(ii) **Bed** (root) It is present just below the plate.

(iii) **Matrix** It lies at the base of the nail just below the skin. It is visible as a whitish half moon. It produces new cells which push out the older cells towards the tip of the nails and causes growth of the nail.

Thermoregulation

It is the process of regulation of body temperature, performed by skin through two major mechanisms, i.e. **vasodilation** and **vasoconstriction** of blood vessels.

1. In Hot Weather (Vasodilation)

When the outside temperature increases, the heat regulation centre present in the hypothalamus causes the blood vessels to dilate (widen). This allows more blood to flow through them. Sweat glands produce more sweat. Evaporation by sweating causes more heat loss and thus, brings the body temperature to normal.

2. In Cold Weather (Vasoconstriction)

When the outside temperature is low, the blood vessel will undergo contraction or vasoconstriction (narrowing). As a result, it reduces the blood flow under the skin. This prevents water or heat loss from the skin in colder environment.

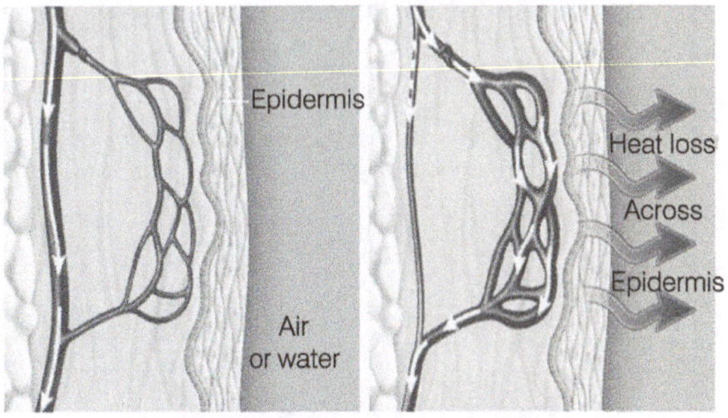

Vasoconstriction Vasodilation

Based on the ability to regulate body temperature, organisms are classified as

(i) **Cold-blooded animals** (Ectotherms) These animals cannot maintain constant body temperature, e.g. bear. These are also called **poikilothermic animals**.

(ii) **Warm-blooded animals** (Endotherms) These animals can maintain a constant body temperature irrespective of change in outer environment, e.g. humans (37°C).

Note **Heat stroke** It is a condition in which sweat production is unable to keep pace with its evaporation in very hot winds. Due to this, the heat loss is reduced, sweating decreases and the body temperature rises, i.e. results in fever. This condition is called heat stroke. That may be sometimes fatal.

Check Your LEARNING...

1 Which layer of skin possess sweat glands?
2 Name the gland responsible for making hair oily.
3 Mammary glands are modified .... glands.
4 State one function of meibomian glands.
5 Name the protein present in nails.
6 What is the main cause of heat stroke?

QUiCK Revision

- **Skin** is the outermost protective covering of the body.
- Skin is composed of **epidermis** which forms the outer layer and **dermis** which is the thick inner layer.
- **Epidermis** consists of three layers, namely **stratum cornified, granular layer** and **stratum Malpighi**.
- **Melanin** is the pigment which provides colour to skin and is present in innermost region of epidermis called **Malpighi layer**.
- The derivatives of skin include hairs, sweat glands, sebaceous glands, nails and mammary glands.
- **Hair** provides insulation to body against external temperature and are formed of external invaginations of dermis.
- **Sweat glands** are present in dermis and their main function is regulation of body temperature.
- **Sebaceous glands** secrete on oily secretion called **sebum**. Accumulation of sebum results in pimples, black head and acne.
- **Mammary glands** and **ceruminous glands** are modified sweat glands.
- **Meibomian glands** are modified sebaceous glands, found at the margins of eyelids.
- **Nails** are hard, keratinised plate-like structures which grow as dead cells from nail roots.
- **Heat regulatory centre** in body is present in hypothalamus.
- **Vasodilation** is dilation of blood vessels in hot weather
- **Vasoconstriction** means constriction of blood vessels in cold weather.

Chapter Practice

Section-I

1 Mark Questions

1. Name the following.
   (i) The complete loss of skin pigmentation from the body.
   (ii) Enlargement of sebaceous glands because of the accumulation of sebum.
   (iii) The modified sebaceous glands which open on the margin of the eyelids.
   (iv) The hard and outer part of nail.
   (v) Rise in body temperature in summer during which heat loss is reduced and sweating decreases.

Ans. (i) Albinism (ii) Pimples
(iii) Meibomian gland (iv) Plate
(v) Heat stroke

2. Correct and rewrite the following statements by changing the underlined words.
   (i) Stratum corneum is the innermost layer of epidermis.
   (ii) The fatty or areolar tissue layer lies just beneath the epidermis.
   (iii) Meibomian glands are the modified sweat glands found in the auditory canal.
   (iv) Nails are formed by dermal layer.
   (v) When the outside temperature increases, the blood vessels contract.

Ans. (i) Malpighian layer is the innermost layer of epidermis.
(ii) The fatty or areolar tissue layer lies just beneath the dermis.
(iii) Ceruminous glands are the modified sweat glands found in the auditory canal.
(iv) Nails are formed by the epidermal layer.
(v) When the outside temperature increases, the blood vessels dilate.

3. Give biological reasons for the following.
   (i) We shiver and our teeth chatter when it is very cold in winter.
   (ii) An otherwise normal healthy young man started perspiring while it was intensely cold outside.

Ans. (i) To maintain constant body temperature in very cold winter, the heat production is increased by speeding up metabolic rate and increasing muscular activity. This activity makes us shiver.
(ii) Fever and sickness or any kind of vigorous activity can lead to perspiration even in cold outside.

4. (i) Match the following columns.

	Column I		Column II
A.	Mammary gland	1.	Earwax
B.	Dermis	2.	Sweat glands
C.	Meibomian gland	3.	Sebaceous glands
D.	Ceruminous gland	4.	Blood vessels

(ii) Match the following columns.

	Column I		Column II
A.	Mammary glands	1.	Hair
B.	Goose flesh	2.	Sweat
C.	Oily secretion	3.	Rudimentary in male
D.	Traces of urea	4.	Sebaceous gland

Ans. (i) A-2, B-4, C-3, D-1
(ii) A-3, B-1, C-4, D-2

5. Choose the correct answer from the four options given below.
   (i) The vascular region of skin is found in
   (a) epidermis (b) dermis
   (c) Malpighian layer (d) cornified layer

Ans. (b)

(ii) Which of the following functions in humans is not performed by skin?
(a) Absorption (b) Circulation
(c) Excretion (d) Protection

Ans. (b)

(iii) The vitamin synthesised by the skin is
(a) vitamin-A (b) vitamin-B
(c) vitamin-D (d) vitamin-C

Ans. (c)

(iv) The structure that covers the hair root is
(a) follicle (b) bulb (c) papilla (d) shaft

Ans. (a)

(v) Sweat glands are situated in
(a) dermis (b) epidermis
(c) Both (a) and (b) (d) None of these

Ans. (a)

(vi) The heat regulating centre is
(a) cerebrum (b) hypothalamus
(c) cerebellum (d) pituitary

Ans. (b)

(vii) The temperature of human body is
(a) 40°C (b) 25°C (c) 37°C (d) 28°C

Ans. (c)

(viii) The main purpose of sweating is
(a) temperature regulation
(b) regulation of water content
(c) removal of excess water
(d) excretion

Ans. (a)

6. Fill in the blanks by using suitable words.
(i) The dead protein present in the stratum corneum is ....
(ii) The melanin pigment is present in .... layer of skin.
(iii) Blood vessels and nerve fibres are absent in the...... of the skin.
(iv) The part of the hair which projects from the skin is ....
(v) Goose flesh is caused due to the contraction of ....
(vi) ...... glands cool the body.
(vii) .... secrete sebum.
(viii) The blood vessels present in the skin .... to allow more blood to flow through skin.
(ix) Contraction of blood vessels due to cold is called ....

Ans. (i) keratin (ii) innermost (Malpighian)
(iii) epidermis (iv) hair shaft
(v) arrector muscles (vi) Sweat
(vii) Sebaceous glands (viii) dilate
(ix) vasoconstriction

7. Choose the odd one out from the following terms given below and name the category to which other three belong.
(i) Sweat glands, Sebaceous glands, Nails, Mammary glands
(ii) Malpighian layer, Cornified layer, Dermal layer, Granular layer

Ans. (i) **Odd term** Nails.
Rest three are types of cutaneous glands.
(ii) **Odd term** Dermal layer.
Rest three are regions of epidermis.

8. State whether the following statements are true or false. Choose and rewrite the false statements.
(i) Skin is the largest organ.
(ii) Stratum corneum is the middle layer of epidermis.
(iii) Cells in the cornified layer are dead.
(iv) Dermis is made up of epithelial tissue.
(v) Temperature regulating centre in the brain is called thyroid.
(vi) Increased body heat causes dilation of blood vessels.

Ans. (i) True
(ii) False, stratum corneum is the outermost layer of epidermis.
(iii) True
(iv) False, dermis is made up of connective tissue.
(v) False, temperature regulating centre in brain is hypothalamus.
(vi) True

9. State the exact location of the following.
(i) Keratin
(ii) Arrector muscles
(iii) Meibomian gland
(iv) Nails

Ans. (i) Keratin is found in nails/horns/skin.
(ii) Arrector muscles run obliquely between the hair follicle and the outer part of dermis.
(iii) Meibomian gland is located on the margin of eyelids.
(iv) Nails are present at the tips of finger and toes.

10. Give one example each of the following.
(i) Skin derivative
(ii) Cold-blooded animal

Ans. (i) Hairs
(ii) Bear

11. State the main function of the following.
(i) Hair
(ii) Sweat glands
(iii) Sebum
(iv) Mammary gland

Ans. (i) Hair provides warmth and protection to the body.
(ii) Sweat glands produce sweat which regulates body temperature and helps in thermoregulation too.
(iii) Sebum lubricates hair, makes it oily and waterproof. It also prevents skin from drying.
(iv) Mammary glands produce milk in females at the time of birth of young ones.

12. Mention one difference between each of the following pairs on the basis of what is given in the bracket.
(i) Cerumen and Sebum (source)
(ii) Vasodilation and Vasoconstriction (blood flow)
(iii) Ectothermal and Endothermal (behaviour)

Ans. (i) Difference between sweat and sebum is as follows

Cerumen	Sebum
It is secreted by ceruminous glands.	It is secreted by sebaceous gland.

(ii) Difference between vasodilation and vasoconstriction is as follow

Vasodilation	Vasoconstriction
Dilated blood vessels have wider lumen which allows more flow of blood.	Constricted blood vessels have narrower lumen so less blood flows.

(iii) Difference between endothermal and ectothermal is as follows

Endothermal	Ectothermal
They maintain the constant body temperature irrespective of change in the environment.	They cannot maintain constant temperature.

13. Give the biological/technical terms for the following.
(i) The innermost layer of epidermis that replaces cells of outermost layer.
(ii) Accumulation of sebum which promotes bacterial growth.
(iii) Animals which cannot maintain constant body temperature.
(iv) Dilation of blood vessels when temperature increases.

Ans. (i) Stratum Malpighi (ii) Pimples
(iii) Cold-blooded animals (iv) Vasodilation

14. Briefly explain the following terms.
(i) Integumentary system
(ii) Goose flesh
(iii) Mammary glands
(iv) Endothermal

Ans. (i) It is the system formed by the skin and its derivatives (nail, hair, etc.)
(ii) Due to extreme cold or fright, the arrector muscle present in the dermis pull the hair into a vertical position. It is called 'goose flesh'.
(iii) Mammary glands are modified sweat glands producing milk to feed young ones in females.
(iv) Endothermal means warm-blooded animals whose body temperature remains same irrespective of the outside temperature.

15. Answer the following questions briefly.
(i) In which form does, fat get stored under the skin?
(ii) How do hair provide touch sensation?
(iii) How is outer surface of skin made waterproof and oily?
(iv) Which inflammed skin glands causes acne?
(v) State in terms of heat. What happens when an individual is engaged in strenous physical work.

Ans. (i) Fat is stored in the form of adipose tissue under the skin.
(ii) It has nerve fibre at its base that makes it sensitive to touch.
(iii) The sebaceous glands of the skin secrete sebum which makes the outer surface of the skin oily and waterproof.
(iv) Sebaceous glands of the face get enlarged due to accumulation of sebum and cause acne.
(v) When a person is engaged in strenous physical work, heat is produced within the body in excess amounts, thus increasing the dilation of blood vessels and blood supply to the skin. This results in greater loss of heat by radiation and by vapourisation.

2 Marks Questions

16. Explain the structure of hair.

Ans. A hair consists of shaft, root and bulb. Hair shaft extends below the epidermal region. The hair bulb contains a projection of the dermis, i.e. hair papilla which receives blood capillaries.
The hair root is made up of hair follicles which contains connective tissue.

17. Give the names of various types of sensory corpuscles present in the skin and give their functions.

Ans. The various types of sensory corpuscles present in the skin and their funcitons are as
(i) **Pacinian corpuscles** Preceive pressure.
(ii) **Meissners corpuscles** Sensory to touch.
(iii) **Ruffinis corpuscles** Sensory to high temperature.
(iv) **Krause bulbs** Sensory to low temperature.

18. What is the importance of secretion of oil and sweat glands in human beings?

Ans. In humans, secretion from oil and sweat glands makes the pH of skin acidic (3-5) which discourage the growth of microbes.

3 Marks Questions

19. What is epidermis? From where does epidermis originate and what are its regions?

Ans. Outermost layer of the skin is known as epidermis. It originates from ectoderm of embryo. It consists of stratified epithelium having three regions that are
(i) Stratum corneum (outermost cornified layer)
(ii) Granular layer (middle part)
(ii) Malpighian layer (inner germinal layer)

20. Describe the structure of nails.

Ans. Nails are formed by the epidermis present at the tips of all fingers and toes. These are hardened keratinous plate-like structures. There are two plates, i.e. upper large, unguis and lower very small, subunguis. Below the unguis, the dermis is richly supplied with blood vessels that impart pink colour to it, called **nail bed**. At the base of the nail, nail root is formed by the invaginations of epidermis. It provides keratin for the growth of the nails.

Section-II [5 Marks]

Structured Questions

1. Observe the diagram carefully and answer the questions that follows.

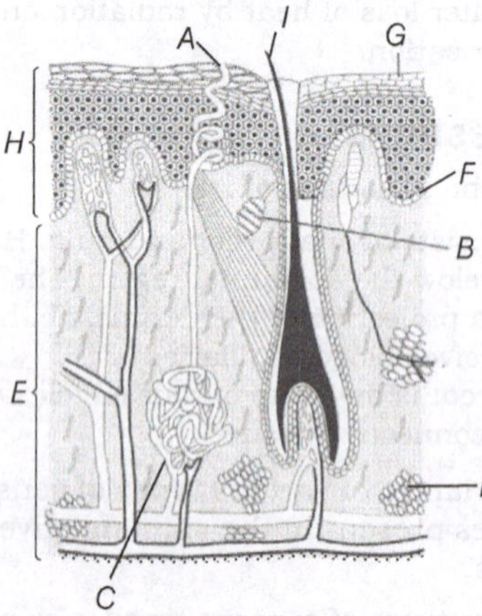

(i) Label the parts *A* to *I*.

(ii) How does skin helps in maintaining body temperature?

(iii) State the functions of parts *C*, *D* and *I*.

(iv) What are the excretory substances present in the sweat?

(v) Name the glands which possess sacs which open into hair follicle by a common duct.

Ans. The parts *A*-*I* are labelled as

(i) *A*-Sweat pore; *B*-Sebaceous gland; *C*-Sweat gland; *D*-Fat cells; *E*-Dermis; *F*-Stratum Malpighi; *G*-Stratum Corneum; *H*-Epidermis; *I*-Hair shaft.

(ii) When temperature rises the skin helps to lose extra heat by sweating and dilation of blood vessels. When temperature falls down, sweating is reduced and the blood vessels constrict.

(iii) The functions of parts *C*, *D* and *I* are as
Part *C* (Sweat gland) produces sweat to control body temperature.
Part *D* (Fat cells) store fat to insulate the body heat.
Part *I* (Hair shaft) keeps the body warm.

(iv) The excretory substances like urea and salt are present in the sweat.

(v) Sebaceous gland.

2. Skin is the outermost protective layer which covers the whole body.

(i) Name the layers of epidermis.

(ii) The cells of which layers are replaced by newly formed cell of Malpighian layer?

(iii) People living in different countries have different skin shades. Justify the statement.

(iv) What is the role of pigment present in the innermost layer?

(v) Name the structures that are present in dermis layer.

Ans. (i) The layers of epidermis are Stratum Corneum, Stratum Granulosum, Stratum Malpighian.

(ii) The cell of cornified layer or stratum corneum are replaced by newly formed cell of malpighian layer.

(iii) People living in different countries have different skin shade due to the presence of different amount of melanin in the body.

(iv) The role of pigment present in the innermost layer is that it acts as a protective screen against ultraviolet light.

(v) Blood vessels, nerve fibres, sweat glands, sense of organs, etc, present in the dermis layer.

3. Study the diagram carefully and answer the questions that follow.

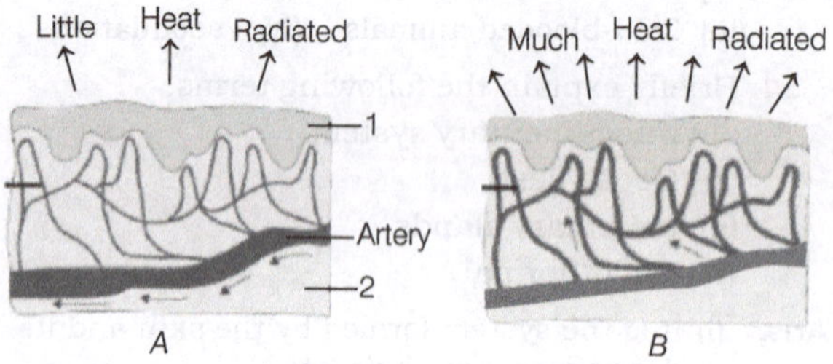

(i) Identify the mechanism in *A* and *B*.

(ii) Identify the labels numbered as 1 and 2.

(iii) What are warm-blooded animals?

(iv) What are your observations in case of vasoconstriction?

(v) How does hypothalamus act as principal body heat regulating centre?

Ans. (i) The mechanism in *A* and *B* is
A-Vasoconstriction
B-Vasodilation

(ii) The labels numbered as 1 and 2 are
1-Epidermis and 2-Dermis

(iii) The animals whose body temperature does not fluctuate according to the atmospheric temperature.

(iv) When the outside temperature is low, the blood vessels get narrowed (vasoconstriction). This results in lowering of blood supply to the skin.

(v) When the outside temperature increases the heat regulation centre present in hypothalamus causes the blood vessels to dilate allowing more blood to flow through them increased rate of water loss leads to lowering back of body temperature to normal, whereas when outside temperature is low the blood vessels undergo contraction which reduces the blood flow under the skin and further prevents heat loss.

Chapter Assessment

Section-I

1 Mark Questions

1. Name the following.
   (i) The receptor present in the skin, which is sensitive to low temperature.
   (ii) The secretion of ceruminous gland.
   (iii) Inflammation of sebaceous glands usually at puberty.
   (iv) Structures collectively responsible for elongation of hair.
   (v) The modified sweat gland which make up earwax.
2. Correct and rewrite the following statements by changing the underlined words.
   (i) <u>Glandular layer</u> consists of pigment melanin which is responsible for skin colour.
   (ii) Mammary glands are modified <u>sebaceous glands</u>.
3. Give biological reason for the following.
   Skin is the best thermoregulatory organ of the body.
4. Match the following columns.

	Column I		Column II
A.	Vasoconstriction	1.	Mammals
B.	Meissner's corpuscles	2.	Less flow of blood in blood vessel
C.	Pacinian corpuscles	3.	Oily secretion
D.	Sebaceous gland	4.	Sense of pressure
E.	Endotherms	5.	Sense of touch

5. Choose the correct answer from the four options given below.
   (i) Which one out of the organs listed below, most actively functions in regulating our body temperature?
   (a) Heart (b) Lungs
   (c) Skin (d) Stomach
   (ii) Integument is usually called the 'jack of all trades' because it
   (a) gives shape to various structures of the body
   (b) protects the body
   (c) performs various functions
   (d) restricts the size of the individual
   (iii) If for some reason, the sebaceous glands fail to function, which of the following will be observed?
   (a) The body will not be able to regulate the body temperature
   (b) The skin will turn darker with more melanin
   (c) The hairs will fail to grow
   (d) The skin will turn dry and rough
   (iv) Secretion of sebaceous glands in humans helps in
   (a) making skin soft and oily
   (b) respiration
   (c) temperature regulation
   (d) All of the above
6. Fill in the blanks by using suitable words.
   (i) Nails develop from .... of the skin.
   (ii) The ...... glands secrete milk.
   (iii) The ...... muscle contracts and thus hair become erect.
   (iv) ...... is the portion of hair that can be visualised easily.
7. State whether the following statements are true or false. Choose and rewrite the false statements.
   (i) The pigment melanin is found in Malpighian layer.
   (ii) Dermis is very thick on palm and soles.
   (iii) Increased body heat causes vasoconstriction.
   (iv) Frog is a cold-blooded animal.
   (v) Humans are ectothermal.
8. State the exact location of the following.
   (i) Sebaceous glands
   (ii) Hair follicle
9. State the main function of the following.
   (i) Stratum corneum (ii) Subcutaneous layer
10. Mention one difference between each of the following pairs on the basis of what is given in the bracket.
    (i) Epidermis and Dermis (location)
    (ii) Leukoderma and Albinism (type of disorder)
11. Give the biological/technical terms for the following.
    (i) The layer of epidermis that provides resistance to mechanical damage.
    (ii) Natural method of conserving body heat.
    (iii) Animals which can maintain their body temperature.

12. Briefly explain the following terms.
(i) Epidermis (ii) Hair papilla

13. Answer the following questions briefly.
(i) What parts come under skin derivatives?
(ii) What is the role of Malpighian layer?
(iii) What is the composition of sweat?
(iv) How does the skin help to conserve body heat in winter season?

2 Marks Question

14. What is goose flesh? How is it brought about?

3 Marks Question

15. How does our skin provide protection to our body from the following?
(i) Entry of germ
(ii) Excessive loss of heat in severe cold
(iii) Entry of harmful ultraviolet rays

Section-II [5 Marks]

Structured Questions

16. The skin along with its derivatives collectively constitutes integumentary system of the body.
(i) What are two main glands present in the skin?
(ii) List two ways in which the skin serves as protective layer in our body.
(iii) What is the role of sense organ and nerve endings in dermis?
(iv) Comment upon the role of ceruminous glands in protecting the eardrum.
(v) Name one condition caused by skin pigmentation

17. Study the diagram and answer the questions that follows

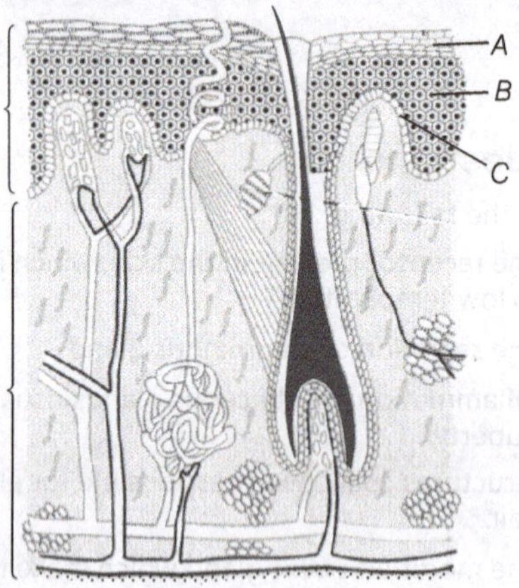

(i) Identify the figure.
(ii) Name the layer of skin that originates from mesoderm of the embryo.
(iii) Label the parts *A* to *C*.
(iv) Name the protein found in nails and hair
(v) State the role of the structure identified in (i) in synthesising vitamin-D.

For explanations scan the given QR Code

Olympiad Section*

Brain Teasing Questions asked in Previous Olympiads

1 Which one of the following is a keratinised tissue?
(a) Stratified compound epithelium
(b) Glandular epithelium
(c) Pseudostratified epithelium
(d) None of the above

2 Accumulations of hardened sebum beneath the skin is called whitehead or
(a) acne
(b) milia
(c) pimple
(d) birthmark

3 Negroes have dark coloured skin, while European have light coloured skin because of the presence of
(a) melanin (b) sweat glands
(c) sebaceous glands (d) nails

4 What is the process that darkens the skin when it is exposed to UV light?
(a) Blackheads
(b) Hyperpigmentation
(c) Tanning
(d) Hypopigmentation

5 Where does mitosis (cell division) or replacement of the skin take place?
(a) Stratum lucidum
(b) Stratum corneum
(c) Stratum granulosum
(d) Stratum germinativum

6 The deterioration of collagen and elastin fibres during the aging process causes
(a) rosacea (b) freckles
(c) macules (d) wrinkles

7 An allergic reaction to cosmetics or chemicals which salon professionals may be susceptible to is called
(a) papules
(b) dermatitis venenata
(c) lentigines
(d) chloasma

8 A solid mass in the skin that could be soft or hard fixed or freely movable and may be elevated or deep is called a
(a) crust (b) callus (c) tumour (d) wheal

9 What may happen to the skin if an area is subjected to pressure or friction over a long period of time?
(a) It may become callused
(b) It may appear thin
(c) It may scale and flake
(d) It may become shiny

10 What is the technical term for a decrease in the activity of melanocytes?
(a) Acne
(b) Verruca
(c) Leucoderma
(d) Melanoderma

Answers

1. (a) **2.** (b) **3.** (a) **4.** (c) **5.** (d) **6.** (d) **7.** (b) **8.** (c) **9.** (a) **10.** (c)

**These questions may or may not be asked in the examination, have been given just for additional practice required for olympiads, scholarship exams etc. For detailed explanations refer Page No. 230.*

CHAPTER

12

Respiratory System

Chapter Inside

- Respiration • Human Respiratory System
- Mechanism of Respiration • Respiratory Volumes and Capacities

Respiration

It is the chemical process by which glucose in the body gets broken down to release energy for metabolic activities. In this catabolic process, there is exchange of gases (*viz.* oxygen and carbon dioxide) between the body and the outside environment. This overall process can be written in the form of equation as

$$\underset{\text{(Glucose)}}{C_6H_{12}O_6} + \underset{\text{(Oxygen)}}{6O_2} \longrightarrow \underset{\text{(Carbon dioxide)}}{6CO_2} + \underset{\text{(Water)}}{6H_2O} + \text{(Energy)}$$

Energy is stored as ATP. Water being an important part of the body is retained inside, whereas CO_2, being toxic beyond certain limit has to be eliminated.

Types of Respiration

Respiration can occur in the presence or absence of oxygen. Depending on it, respiration can be classified as

1. Aerobic Respiration

Respiration taking place in the presence of oxygen with the release of fairly large amount of energy is called **aerobic respiration**.

It can be summarised in the equation given below

$$\underset{\text{(6 carbon molecule)}}{\text{Glucose}} \xrightarrow{\text{In cytoplasm}} \underset{\text{(3 carbon molecule)}}{\text{Pyruvate}} + \text{Energy} \xrightarrow[\text{In mitochondria (Krebs' cycle)}]{\text{Oxygen}} \text{Carbon dioxide} + \text{Water} + 38\ \text{ATP}$$

2. Anaerobic Respiration

Respiration taking place in the absence of oxygen with the release of small amount of energy is called **anaerobic respiration**, e.g. in yeast, bacteria and in the human muscles. It is also known as **fermentation**.

Muscle cells are temporarily anaerobic, when there is lack of enough oxygen (i.e. oxygen debt). Anaerobic respiration produces lactic acid and only two ATP molecules for each glucose molecule. No carbon dioxide is released during this process.

Need for Respiration-Heat production

The breakdown of glucose takes place in a sequential manner with the help of respective enzymes. The overall process of respiration yields energy in the form of heat as well as ATP.

ATP is used in completing the other metabolic activities taking place inside the cell. However, birds and mammals need to produce heat in order to keep themselves warm. This heat is generated through respiration in cells.

Human Respiratory System

All the organs in an organism that carry oxygen and help in the removal of carbon dioxide from body are called respiratory organs. These collectively constitute the respiratory system. In human, pulmonary respiration takes place, i.e. the respiratory organs are a pair of lungs.

The complete respiratory system in human can be categorised into two major components, i.e. respiratory tract and lungs.

1. Respiratory Tract

It is the passage for the air (transport of oxygen to the lungs and return of carbon dioxide from lungs to the exterior). It starts with nostrils up to the terminal bronchioles. In this part, gaseous exchange at cellular level does not take place.

The various parts of the respiratory tract are as follows

(i) **Nostrils** These are the pair of slits at the lower end of the nose, which opens into the nasal chamber. In these chambers, air is filtered (by hairs) and moistened (by mucus). The secreted mucus traps dust particles which can cause harm to respiratory system.

(ii) **Pharynx** It is a wide cavity situated at the back of the mouth. It is a common passage for air and food.

(iii) **Larynx** (Voice box) It is the upper part of trachea. It allows the air to pass into lungs. Pharynx opens through **glottis** of the larynx into trachea. Glottis is a slit-like aperture that remains open except during swallowing. The glottis bears a leaf-like cartilaginous flap (i.e. the **epiglottis**) at its anterior region. It closes the glottis to check the entry of food during swallowing.
Larynx helps in sound production and hence, called the **sound** (voice) **box**.
It is often called the **Adam's apple** and is more prominent in men than in women.

(iv) **Trachea** (Windpipe) It is a thin-walled tube, about 11 cm long and 2.5 cm wide. It extends up to the mid-thoracic cavity. It passes the air to the bronchi.

(v) **Bronchi** These are the immediate branches of the trachea which enter into the two lungs as two tubes, right and left bronchi. They divide and redivide into secondary and tertiary bronchi which further divide to form bronchioles.

(vi) **Bronchioles** The branches of tertiary bronchi are called bronchioles. They are the minute tubules ending in the alveoli of the lungs.

(vii) **Alveoli** (Air sacs) The small terminal bronchioles give off a number of thin, irregular walled, vascular bag-like structure called alveoli. Approximately 600 million alveoli aid in gaseous exchange.

Note
- The wall of **trachea**, **bronchi** and **bronchioles** is composed of fibromuscular tissue and is lined by pseudostratified ciliated columnar epithelium rich in mucus secreting cells.
- Cartilaginous rings support the walls of the trachea and the bronchi prevent them from collapsing.

2. Lungs

Lungs are the site of actual exchange of oxygen and carbon dioxide between blood and the atmospheric air. These are thin-walled, spongy, elastic, pinkish and paired triangular bags that constitute the respiratory organ. They are highly distensible.

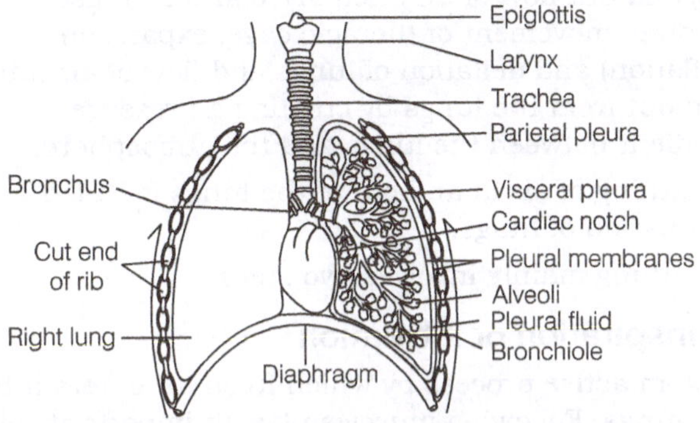

Diagrammatic view of human respiratory system (sectional view)

They lie in the **thoracic cavity** and are enclosed dorsally by thoracic cage (comprised of **ribs, sternum** and a muscular sheet called **diaphragm**).
The **left lung** comprises of two lobes. It also has a cardiac notch, a concavity where the heart lies. On the other hand, **right lung** is slightly bigger and has three lobes.

Each lung is enclosed by two membranes called the **pleura** (i.e. protective covering layer of lung). A very narrow space that exists between the two pleura is termed as **pleural cavity**. It contains the **pleural fluid** secreted by the pleura that reduce friction on the lung surface.

Check Your LEARNING...

1 Define respiration.
2 State the function of epiglottis.
3 Name the protective covering of lungs.
4 Name the minute tubules ending in the alveoli of the lungs.
5 What is ventilation of lungs?

Mechanism of Respiration

The main mechanism of respiration is categorised into following three steps

1. **Breathing** (pulmonary ventilation) It is the inflow of atmospheric air (i.e. O_2) and release or outflow of CO_2 rich alveolar air from the lungs.
2. **Exchange of gases** (O_2 and CO_2) It takes place across alveolar membrane (external respiration) as well as in tissues (tissue respiration or internal respiration).
3. **Transport of gases** It is carried out with the help of blood.

1. Breathing

It is an extracellular, energy consuming and physical process which involves the inflow of atmospheric air (O_2) and out flow of CO_2 rich alveolar air. It also involves movement of thoracic cage, expansion (inflation) and deflation of lungs and flow of air into and out from the lungs by creating a pressure gradient between the lungs and the atmosphere.

Breathing of air in and out of the lungs is called ventilation of lungs.

Breathing mainly involves two steps

(i) Inspiration or Inhalation

It is an active process by which fresh air enters into the lungs. Following muscles play an important role in inspiration

(a) **Diaphragm** It is lowered by the contraction of its muscle fibres and becomes flat. This causes an increase in the volume of thoracic chamber.

(b) **External intercostal muscles** They occur between the ribs. The external intercostal muscles contract and pull the ribs and the sternum upward and outward thus, increasing the volume of thoracic chamber.

Thus, the overall increase in the volume of thoracic cavity causes an increase in the pulmonary volume. As a result, air flows rapidly into the nose, which sequentially leads to alveoli. From the alveoli, O_2 passes into blood and CO_2 diffuses out from the blood to alveoli lumen.

(ii) Expiration or Exhalation

It is a passive process by which CO_2 is expelled out from the lungs. The movement of following muscles are involved in expiration

(a) **Diaphragm** The muscle fibres of the diaphragm relax making it convex and decreasing the volume of thoracic cavity.

(b) **Internal intercostal muscles** These muscles contract thus, pulling the ribs downward and inward, thus, decreasing the thoracic volume.

The overall volume of the thoracic cavity thus, decreases thereby reducing the pulmonary volume. As a result, the expulsion of the air occurs from the lungs. The process of expiration is simpler than inspiration.

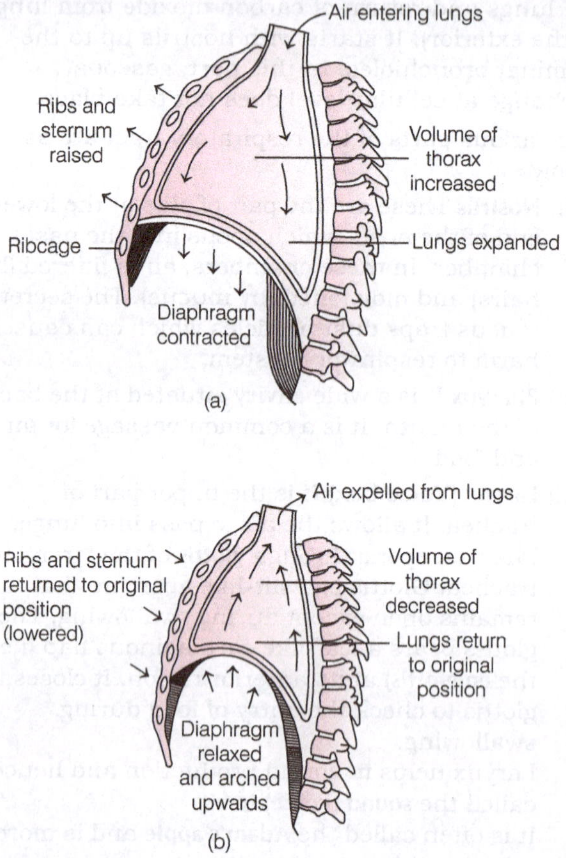

Mechanism of breathing showing: (a) Inspiration, (b) Expiration

■ **Some Important Point Related to Breathing**

At rest, breathing occurs at the rate of about 12-16 times/minute, and is more in children.

The volume of air involved in breathing movements can be estimated by using a **spirometer**. It helps in clinical assessment of pulmonary functions.

Breathing is under **neural control** (respiratory rhythm centre is found in medulla oblongata and pons Varolii) and **chemical control** (chemoreceptors in carotid bodies).

The term breathing and respiration are not same. Breathing is the first step of respiration and a physical process, while respiration is a biochemical process involving exchange of gases and oxidation of food.

2. Exchange of Gases

This occurs across alveolar membrane as well as in tissues.

The exchange of gases (i.e. O_2 and CO_2) between lung alveoli and pulmonary capillaries is called **external respiration.**

The walls of alveoli contain an extensive network of blood vessels. The sequence of exchange of oxygen and carbon dioxide, which occurs between blood vessels and alveoli is as follows

Blood releases carbon dioxide into alveoli that it brings from rest of the body.

↓

Oxygen is taken up by blood from alveolar air to blood vessels.

↓

Haemoglobin takes up oxygen from lungs and carries it to tissues, which are deficient in oxygen.

↓

Oxygen in blood is then transported to all cells in the body by respiratory pigment (haemoglobin) and due to diffusion pressure.

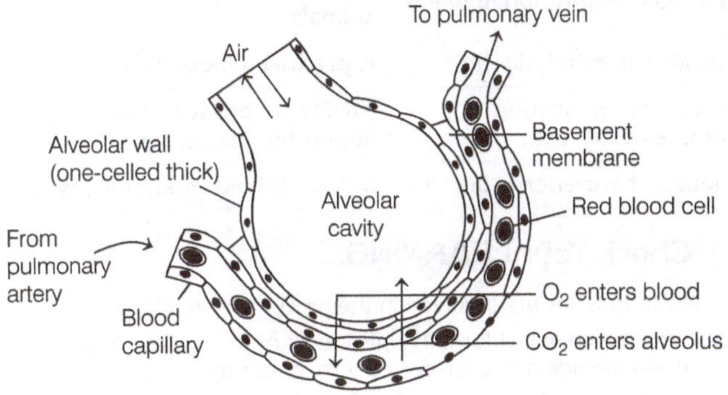

A diagram of a section of an alveolus with a pulmonary capillary

3. Transport of Gases

Blood carries oxygen from the lungs to tissue cells for oxidation and carbon dioxide from the tissue cells to the respiratory surface for elimination.

This exchange of O_2 and CO_2 between the blood and the body tissues is called tissue respiration.

Transport of O_2 and CO_2 is discussed below in detail

(i) Transport of Oxygen

It is done in the following manner

(a) **As dissolved gas** About 3% of oxygen in the blood is carried in dissolved state form through the plasma.

(b) **As oxyhaemoglobin** About 97% of O_2 is carried by RBCs in the blood.

(ii) Transport of Carbon Dioxide

CO_2 in gaseous form diffuses out of the cells into capillaries, where it is transported in following ways

(a) **Transport as dissolved form** About 7% CO_2 is carried in dissolved form through the plasma because of its high solubility.

(b) **Transport as bicarbonate** About 70% CO_2 is carried in plasma as bicarbonate ions (HCO_3^-). At the tissues site, where concentration of CO_2 is high due to catabolism, CO_2 diffuses into the blood (RBCs and plasma) and forms HCO_3^- and H^+.

(c) **Transport as carbaminohaemoglobin** Nearly 20-25% CO_2 is carried by haemoglobin as carbaminohaemoglobin.

Respiratory Volumes and Capacities

The quantity of air, the lungs can receive, hold or expel under different conditions is called **respiratory** (pulmonary) **volumes**. A healthy man can inspire or expire approximately 6000-8000 mL of air per minute.

The different volumes and capacities are as follows

(i) **Tidal Volume** (TV) It is the volume of air inspired or expired during normal breathing in relaxed or resting position. It is about 500 mL.

It consists of **dead air space** (150 mL) which includes tidal air left in respiratory passage and alveolar air (350 mL) which is the tidal air contained in air sacs.

(ii) **Inspiratory Reserve Volume** (IRV) It is the additional amount of air that can be inspired forcibly after a normal inspiration. It is about 2000-3000 mL.

(iii) **Expiratory Reserve Volume** (ERV) It is the additionl volume of air that can be expired forcibly after an normal expiration. It is about 1000-1100 mL.

(iv) **Residual Volume** (RV) It is the volume of air remaining in the lungs even after a forcible expiration. It is about 1100-1200 mL. It cannot be measured by spirometry.

(v) **Inspiratory Capacity** (IC) It is the amount of air that can be inspired with maximum effort after normal expiration. It is about 2500-3000 mL.

(vi) **Vital Capacity** (VC) It is the maximum volume of air a person can breathe in after a forced expiration or the maximum volume of air a person can breathe out after a forced inspiration. This include

TV + IRV + ERV

It varies from 3500-4500 mL depending upon age, sex and height of individual.

(vii) **Total Lung Capacity** (TLC) It is the total volume of air present in the lungs after a forced (maximum) inspiration. It includes (VC + RV) or (RV + ERV + TV + IRV). It is about 5800-6000 mL.

Effect of Altitude on Breathing

Normal comfortable breathing is called **Eupnoea** but as we go higher with increase in altitude, the atmospheric pressure goes on decreasing along with a gradual decrease in oxygen content.

At about 2400 metres and above, the exposure to low oxygen has a pathological effect on humans known as **mountain sickness/altitude sickness**. It leads to a condition of oxygen shortage in the tissues called as **hypoxia**.

Its symptoms include fatigue, dizziness, nausea, loss of appetite, peripheral edema, nosebleed, etc.

Anaemic hypoxia results from reduced oxygen carrying capacity of the blood due to anaemia or carbon monoxide **poisoning.**

Asphyxia (suffocation) is a condition in which the O_2 content of blood falls, while CO_2 content rises. It paralyses the respiratory centre, causes shortage of breathing leading to death.

Respiration in Plants and Animals

Respiration is a characteristic of all living organisms including plants and animals. There are certain similarities found in plants and animals with respect to aerobic respiration.

These similarities are

(i) Free O_2 is required.

(ii) CO_2 and H_2O are produced.

(iii) Energy released is stored as ATP molecules.

(iv) Aerobic repiration takes place in mitochondria.

(v) Respiratory substrate is glucose.

However, there are a few differences as well. These differences are tabulated below

Respiration in plants	Respiration in animals
No breathing takes place.	In aerobic respiration, breathing takes place except in few lower animals.
No transporting system for the transportation of O_2 and CO_2 is present. Gases diffuse from cell to cell.	Blood vascular system is present in most of the animals for the transportation of O_2 and CO_2.
Very small amount of detectable heat is produced.	A considerable amount of detectable heat is produced.
Green plants have additional oxygen source from photosynthesis.	Aerobic animals have either air or water as source of O_2.
Rate of respiration is low.	Rate of respiration is high.
CO_2 produced in respiration is utilised in photosynthesis.	CO_2 produced is released in the atmosphere.

The differences in anaerobic respiration in plants and animals are as follows

Anaerobic respiration in plants	Anaerobic respiration in animals
It produces ethyl alcohol.	It produces lactic acid.
Anaerobic respiration produces CO_2 also.	No CO_2 is produced in anaerobic respiration.
Released heat energy is more.	Released heat energy is less.

Check Your LEARNING...

1 Which muscles are involved in the process of breathing?

2 Name the chemical form in which most of the oxygen and carbon dioxide are transported throughout the body.

3 What is tissue respiration?

4 Tidal volume is .... mL of air.

5 What is anaemic hypoxia?

QUiCK Revision

- **Respiration** is the process of breakdown of glucose to release energy, which is used in various bodily functions. **Aerobic respiration** occurs in the presence of oxygen releasing large number of ATPs per glucose molecule. **Anaerobic respiration** occurs in the absence of oxygen, releases less ATPs per glucose molecule.
- **Human respiratory system** consists of a nose, larynx, trachea, bronchi and bronchioles, alveoli (i.e. parts of respiratory tract) and lungs.
- **Nostrils** initiate the respiratory passage and are used for breathing. Nasal passage has two chambers for respiratory and olfactory (smell) purpose.
- **Larynx** is involved in sound production. **Epiglottis** a leaf-shaped cartilaginous structure which prevents entry of food into larynx.
- **Trachea** is a non-collapsible air conducting tube.
- **Bronchi and bronchioles** The first branching by which trachea enters the lungs are bronchi. Repeated divisions of bronchi form very thin terminal **bronchioles**.
- **Alveoli** are the functional units of lungs, richly supplied with blood cells.
- **Lungs** are the major respiratory organs, present in thoracic cavity, covered by a pleural membrane.
- **Breathing** is the process of exchange of oxygen rich air from the environment with carbon dioxide produced in cells of the body. It includes inspiration and expiration.
- **Inspiration** occurs when diaphragm contracts along with external intercostal muscles while abdominal muscles relax. The volume of thoracic cavity increases and air enters into the lungs.
- **Expiration** involves relaxation of the diaphragm and the external intercostal muscles. This reduces thoracic volume which creates positive pressure leading to exhalation.
- **Exchange of gases** occurs in alveoli of lungs by simple diffusion. It is based mainly on pressure gradients.
- **Transport of gases** like oxygen and CO_2 occurs in blood. These can be transported (a) in physical solution (b) as chemical compound. CO_2 can also be transported as bicarbonates and carbamino compounds.
- **Respiratory volumes** include tidal volume, inspiratory reserve volume, inspiratory capacity, residual volume, expiratory reserve volume, functional residual capacity, vital capacity and total capacity.
- **Asphyxia** (suffocation) is a condition when the O_2 content of blood falls while CO_2 content rises.
- **Hypoxia** is the deficiency of oxygen reaching the tissues.

Chapter Practice

Section-I

1 Mark Questions

1. Name the following.
   (i) The intermediate and the end products of breakdown of glucose in aerobic respiration.
   (ii) A hollow cartilaginous structure located at the start of windpipe.
   (iii) The fluid present between the two membranes of the lungs.
   (iv) Name the respiratory tubes formed by division of windpipe before they enter the lungs.
   (v) A physical process in which atmospheric air is taken in and forced out of the lungs.
   (vi) The complex chemical changes which occur inside the cell to release energy from glucose.
   (vii) The volume of air that can be taken in and expelled out by maximum inspiration and expiration.
   (viii) The volume of air remaining in lungs after normal breathing.
   (ix) The volume of air normally inspired or expired in one breath.
   (x) A condition in which the blood becomes more venous by accumulation of more carbon dioxide and the oxygen supply is diminished.

Ans. (i) Intermediate products are Pyruvic acid + Energy. End products are CO_2+ H_2O + Energy.
(ii) Larynx (iii) Pleural fluid
(iv) Bronchi (v) Breathing
(vi) Cellular respiration (vii) Vital capacity
(viii) Residual volume
(ix) Tidal volume
(x) Asphyxia

2. Correct and rewrite the following statements by changing the underlined words.
   (i) Larynx is more prominent in men and is called <u>amad's apple</u>.
   (ii) Internal intercostal muscles contract pulling ribs <u>upward</u> during expiration.
   (iii) Strenuous physical exercise may cause fatigue due to accumulation of <u>CO_2</u> in blood.
   (iv) Breathing and gaseous transport are <u>same</u> processes.
   (v) Tissue respiration means <u>chemical changes occurring inside the cell</u>.

Ans. (i) Larynx is more prominent in men and is called Adam's apple.
(ii) Internal intercostal muscles contract pulling ribs downward during expiration.
(iii) Strenuous physical exercise may cause fatigue due to accumulation of lactic acid in blood.
(iv) Breathing and gaseous transport are different processes.
(v) Tissue respiration means exchange of gases between the blood and the tissues.

3. Give biological reasons for the following.
   (i) Wall of trachea and bronchi is supported by C-shaped cartilaginous rings.
   (ii) A network of blood capillaries surrounds the wall of each alveolus.
   (iii) At high altitude, it is difficult to breathe.
   (iv) The need for the production of energy is greater in animals than in plants.

Ans. (i) Wall of trachea and bronchi is supported by C-shaped cartilaginous rings in order to keep the trachea and bronchi distended and prevent their collapsing when pressure inside them falls during inspiration.
(ii) The capillary network allow efficient gas exchange in tissues since they have a large surface area and thin walls.
(iii) As we reach the higher altitude, the air we breathe in decrease in pressure accompanied by a gradual decrease in oxygen content. Thus, it becomes difficult to breathe.
(iv) The need for production of energy is greater in animals than in plants because animals consume more energy in doing physical work.
For example, they have to move about for obtaining food or run away to escape their enemies. They have to chew their food and carry out other activites.

4. (i) Match the following columns.

Column I	Column II
A. Nasal chamber	1. Exchange of gases
B. Epiglottis	2. C-shaped rings
C. Air sacs	3. Strengthen within warm air
D. Lungs	4. Drives mucus
E. Alveoli	5. Closes windpipe during swallowing
F. Trachea	6. Network of capillaries
G. Cilia	7. Spongy and elastic

(ii) Match the following columns.

Column I (% of CO_2 transported)		Column II (By)
A. 20-25%	1.	Bicarbonates
B. 70%	2.	RBC
C. About 7%	3.	Plasma

(iii) Match the following columns.

Column I (Respiratory volumes)			Column II (Capacities)
A.	TV	1.	5800 mL
B.	IRV	2.	4600 mL
C.	ERV	3.	1200 mL
D.	RV	4.	1100 mL
E.	VC	5.	3000 mL
F.	TLC	6.	500 mL

Ans. (i) A-3, B-5, C-6, D-7, E-1, F-2, G-4
(ii) A-2, B-1, C-3
(iii) A-6, B-5, C-4, D-3, E-2, F-1

5. Choose the correct answer from the four options given below.

(i) Which portion of the human respiratory system is called sound box?
(a) Larynx (b) Trachea
(c) Nasopharynx (d) Glottis

Ans. (a)

(ii) The ultimate end of trachea
(a) bronchi
(b) bronchioles
(c) alveoli
(d) pharynx

Ans. (c)

(iii) Inspiration is initiated by
(a) extension of the diaphragm
(b) contraction of the diaphragm
(c) extension of the lungs
(d) contraction of the lungs

Ans. (b)

(iv) Which of the following does not occur during breathing?
(a) Brings the air to body temperature
(b) Warms up the air
(c) Diffusion of gases
(d) Clean up the air

Ans. (c)

(v) In humans, exchange of gases occurs
(a) by diffusion
(b) between blood and tissue
(c) between alveoli and pulmonary blood capillary
(d) All of the above

Ans. (d)

(vi) CO_2 is carried by haemoglobin as
(a) carboxyhaemoglobin
(b) carbaminohaemoglobin
(c) carbamidohaemoglobin
(d) deoxyhaemoglobin

Ans. (b)

(vii) Haemoglobin of the human blood forms a stable complex compound with ...... gas, leading to death.
Complete the given statement with an appropriate option.
(a) oxygen (b) carbon dioxide
(c) carbon monoxide (d) hydrogen

Ans. (c)

(viii) Tidal volume is
(a) volume of air inspired or expired
(b) additional volume of air, a person can inspire by a forcible inspiration
(c) additional volume of air, a person can expire by a forcible expiration
(d) remaining volume of air in the lungs even after a forcible expiration

Ans. (a)

(ix) Movement of the air into and out of the lungs is carried out by
(a) imbibition (b) pressure gradient
(c) osmosis (d) diffusion

Ans. (b)

(x) Anaemic hypoxia occurs due to
(a) reduced oxygen carrying capacity of blood due to anaemia
(b) carbon monoxide poisoning
(c) carbon dioxide poisoning
(d) Both (a) and (b)

Ans. (d)

6. Fill in the blanks by using suitable words.
(i) Respiration is a ...... process.
(ii) Anaerobic respiration produces ...... in human.
(iii) The functional unit of lungs is ....
(iv) Nasal passage is lined by ....
(v) The protective covering of lungs is called ....
(vi) The right lung of a man has ...... lobes.
(vii) .... lung is bigger.
(viii) The total lung capacity of human is ...... litres.
(ix) A healthy man can inspire or expire .... of air in one minute.
(x) Asphyxia usually occurs at an altitude of ....

Ans. (i) catabolic (ii) lactic acid
(iii) alveoli (iv) ciliated epithelium
(v) pleura (vi) three
(vii) Right (viii) 5-6
(ix) 6000-8000 mL (above sea level)
(x) 2400 m

7. Choose the odd one out from the following terms given below and name the category to which other three belong.
(i) Bronchioles, Bronchus, Alveolus, Diaphragm
(ii) Ethyl alcohol, Carbon dioxide, Starch, Oxygen absence
(iii) Hairy, Moist, Mucus, Vocal cord

Ans. (i) **Odd term** Diaphragm.
Rest three are parts of lungs.
(ii) **Odd term** Starch.
Rest three are related to anaerobic respiration.
(iii) **Odd term** Vocal cord.
Rest three are present in the nostrils.

8. Given below are sets of five terms each. Rewrite the term in correct order of a logical sequence beginning with the term that is underlined.
(i) Larynx, Pharynx, Bronchioles, <u>Nostrils</u>, Alveoli
(ii) Energy, $C_6H_{12}O_6$, $6H_2O$, $6O_2$, <u>$6CO_2$</u>
(iii) <u>Glucose</u>, 2ATP, Heat, Energy, Lactic acid
(iv) Trachea, Bronchus, Bronchiole, Epiglottis, <u>Pharynx</u>

Ans. (i) Nostrils, Pharynx, Larynx, Bronchioles, Alveoli
(ii) $C_6H_{12}O_2$, $6O_2$, $6CO_2$, $6H_2O$, Energy
(iii) Glucose, Lactic acid, 2ATP, Heat, Energy
(iv) Pharynx, Epiglottis, Trachea, Bronchus, Bronchioles

9. Expand the following biological abbreviations.
(i) TLC (ii) RV
(iii) FRC (iv) ADP (v) TV

Ans. (i) Total Lung Capacity
(ii) Residual Volume
(iii) Functional Residual Capacity
(iv) Adenosine Diphosphate
(v) Tidal Volume

10. State whether the following statements are true or false. Correct and rewrite the false statements.
(i) The most common respiratory substrate is glucose.
(ii) Anaerobic respiration produces lactic acid in animals.
(iii) Respiratory system in man consists of respiratory tract and respiratory organs.
(iv) Anaerobic respiration is a slow process and the reaction can continue for long time.
(v) Strenuous physical exercise may cause fatigue due to accumulation of carbon dioxide in the blood.
(vi) Respiration is controlled by hormones.
(vii) Recording the changes in the volume of air moving into and out of lungs is done by respirometer.
(viii) Krebs' cycle takes place in mitochondria.

Ans. (i) True (ii) True (iii) True
(iv) False, anaerobic respiration is a fast process and the reaction can continue for short time.
(v) False, strenuous physical exercise may cause fatigue due to accumulation of lactic acid in the muscles.
(vi) False, respiration is controlled by medulla oblongata.
(vii) False, recording the changes in the volume of air moving into and out of lungs is done by Spirometer.
(viii) True

11. State the exact location of the following.
(i) Nostrils (ii) Epiglottis
(iii) Alveoli (iv) Lungs

Ans. (i) Nostrils are pair of slits present at the lower end of the nose.
(ii) Epiglottis is a cartilaginous leaf-like structure present in the front of larynx.
(iii) Alveoli are balloon-shaped structures present at the end of bronchioles.
(iv) Lungs lie in the thoracic cavity and are enclosed dorsally by thoracic cage.

12. State the main function of the following.
(i) Mucus (ii) Pharynx
(iii) Vocal cords (iv) Intercostal muscles

Ans. (i) Mucus secreted by the lining of nasal chamber traps dust particle which carry germs.
(ii) Pharynx serves as a common passage for air and food.
(iii) Vibrations of these cords produce sound.
(iv) Intercostal muscles help in expansion and contraction of ribs during inhalation and expiration.

13. Mention one difference between each of the following pairs on the basis of what is given in the bracket.
(i) Right and Left lung (size)
(ii) Oxyhaemoglobin and Carbaminohaemoglobin (formation)

Ans. (i) Difference between right and left lungs is as follows

Right lung	Left lung
It is larger and heavier.	It is smaller and lighter.

(ii) Difference between oxyhaemoglobin and carbaminohaemoglobin is as follows

Oxyhaemoglobin	Carbaminohaemoglobin
It is formed by the combination of oxygen with the Fe^{2+} part of haemoglobin.	It is formed by the combination of CO_2 with the amino group of haemoglobin.

14. Give biological/technical terms for the following.
(i) Oxidation of glucose in the absence of free oxygen.
(ii) Structures which support walls of the trachea.
(iii) The air left in lungs after expiration.
(iv) Animal tissue lining the respiratory organ.

Ans. (i) Anaerobic respiration
(ii) Cartilaginous rings
(iii) Expiratory reserve volume
(iv) Ciliated epithelium

15. Briefly explain the following terms.
(i) Fermentation
(ii) Ventilation of lungs
(iii) Asthma
(iv) Mountain sickness

Ans. (i) It is the incomplete breakdown of sugar into ethanol and carbon dioxide to release energy.
(ii) Breathing of air in and out of lungs is called as ventilation of lungs.
(iii) Asthma is narrowing of bronchi due to spasm in bronchial muscles.
(iv) Mountain sickness is breathlessness, headache, nausea, vomiting, mental fatigue due to deficient availability of O_2 to the body.

16. Answer the following questions briefly.
(i) Name the substance which is oxidised in body during respiration.
(ii) What is Adam's apple? Where is it more prominently found?
(iii) Why lungs are divided into very small sac-like structures?
(iv) Name the two membranes covering the lungs.
(v) What is total lung capacity?

Ans. (i) Glucose is oxidised in the body during respiration.
(ii) Larynx is often called as Adam's apple. It is more prominent in males than in females.
(iii) Lungs are divided into very small sac-like structure to increase the surface area for gaseous exchange.
(iv) The two membranes of lungs are outer parietal layer and inner visceral layer. Both these membranes cover the lungs.
(v) Total lung capacity is the total volume of air present in the lungs after a forced (maximum) inspiration. It includes RV + ERV + TV + IRV. It is about 5800-6000 mL.

2 Marks Questions

17. Compare between alcoholic fermentation and lactic acid fermentation.

Ans. In alcoholic fermentation, pyruvate is broken down into ethanol and carbon dioxide with the release of energy whereas in lactic acid fermentation, pyruvate is broken down into lactic acid with the release of energy.

18. In normal breathing, which is the active process inspiration or expiration? Explain.

Ans. In normal breathing, inspiration is an active process as it is brought about by the contraction of diaphragm and external intercostal muscles, while expiration is a passive process as it simply involves relaxation of inspiratory muscles.

19. Give the condition of the following muscles during expiration.
(i) Diaphragm muscles
(ii) Internal intercostal muscles

Ans. (i) The muscles of the diaphragm are in a relaxed position, making it convex.
(ii) The internal intercostal muscles contract thus, pulling the ribs downward and inward.

20. 'The breathing cycle is rhythmic in nature, whereas exchange of gases is a continuous process'. Comment upon this statement.

Ans. The breathing cycle is rhythmic whereas exchange of gases is always continuous.
This is because the lungs always contain a residual volume of air so that the absorption of oxygen and release of carbon dioxide becomes continuous.

3 Marks Questions

21. How are the lungs designed in human beings to maximise the area for exchange of gases?

Ans. In lungs, balloon-like structures called alveoli are present to provide maximum surface area for the exchange of gases. The alveoli have very thin walls and contain an extensive network of blood vessels to facilitate the exchange of gases.

22. Write the role of diaphragm and intercostal muscles in the inspiratory process.

Ans. The diaphragm and intercostal muscles (external and internal) present between the ribs help in generation of a pressure gradient between the lungs and the atmosphere. During inspiration, diaphragm is lowered by the contraction of its muscle fibres and becomes flat. The external intercostal muscles contract, pulling the ribs and sternum upward and outward. This increases the volume of thoracic cavity and thus, decreases the intrapulmonary pressure. The greater atmospheric pressure outside the body now causes the air to flow rapidly into external nares, which sequentially leads to alveoli. Thus, causing inspiration.

23. For completion of respiration process, write the given steps in sequential manner.
(i) Diffusion of gases (O_2 and CO_2) across alveolar membrane.
(ii) Transport of gases by blood.
(iii) Utilisation of O_2 by the cells for catabolic reactions and resultant release of CO_2.
(iv) Pulmonary ventilation by which atmospheric air is drawn in and CO_2 rich alveolar air is released out.
(v) Diffusion of O_2 and CO_2 between blood and tissues.

Ans. Steps in the process of respiration are as
(i) Pulmonary ventilation by which atmospheric air is drawn in and CO_2 rich alveolar air is released out.
(ii) Diffusion of gases (O_2 and CO_2) across alveolar membrane.
(iii) Transport of gases by blood.
(iv) Diffusion of O_2 and CO_2 between blood and tissues.
(v) Utilisation of O_2 by the cell for catabolic reaction and resultant release of CO_2.

Section-II [5 Marks]

Structured Questions

1. The diagram shows human respiratory system front view.

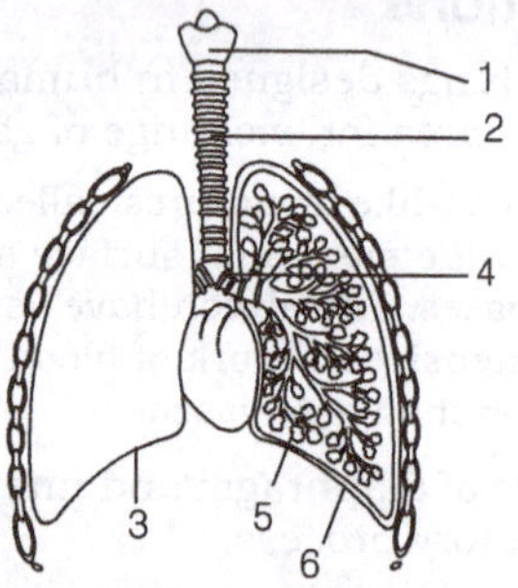

(i) Label the parts numbered 1 to 6.
(ii) Why C-shaped cartilaginous rings are present in part labelled 2?
(iii) How many times a man breathes per minute at rest?
(iv) Why do lungs contract during exhalation?
(v) On entering the lungs, the part 4 divides into fine and then more finer structures. Name these structures.

Ans. (i) The parts numbered 1 to 6 are labelled as

1. Larynx	2. Trachea
3. Right lung	4. Bronchus
5. Alveoli	6. Left lung

(ii) Rings provide flexibility and keep the trachea distended permanently.
(iii) 12 -14 times per minute at rest.
(iv) During exhalation the diaphragm relaxes, and the volume of thoracic cavity decreases and the pressure within it increases. As a result, lungs contract and air is forced out.
(v) Secondary bronchi and tertiary bronchi.

2. The diagram given below shows ribs and diaphragm movements during breathing.

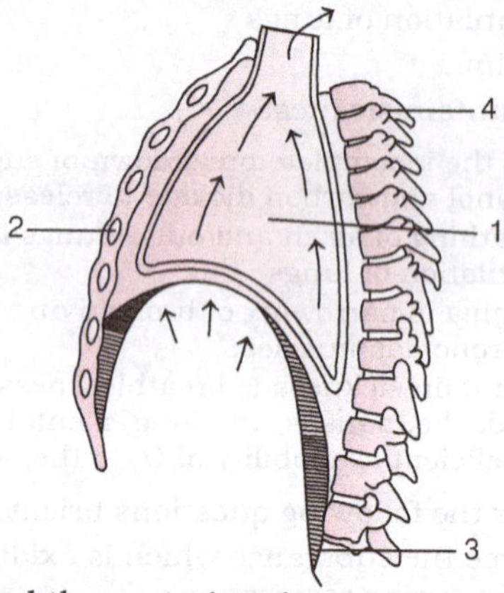

(i) Label the parts 1 to 4.
(ii) Name the phase of breathing shown in the diagram.
(iii) Describe briefly the phase shown in the diagram.
(iv) What do the arrow indicate?
(v) What happens to the volume of thoracic cavity during the above phase?

Ans. (i) The parts 1 to 4 are labelled as
1. Lung
2. Ribs in cross-section
3. Diaphragm
4. Vertebra

(ii) Expiration/exhalation is the phase of breathing shown in the diagram.
(iii) During expiration internal intercostal muscles contract and pull ribs downward and inward. Diaphragm becomes dome- shaped as a result pressure of abdominal content increases and pushes the air out.
(iv) Arrows indicate, movement of air towards outside.
(v) The overall volume of thoracic cavity decreases.

3. The figure shows a diagrammatic sketch of a kind of structure in human lungs.

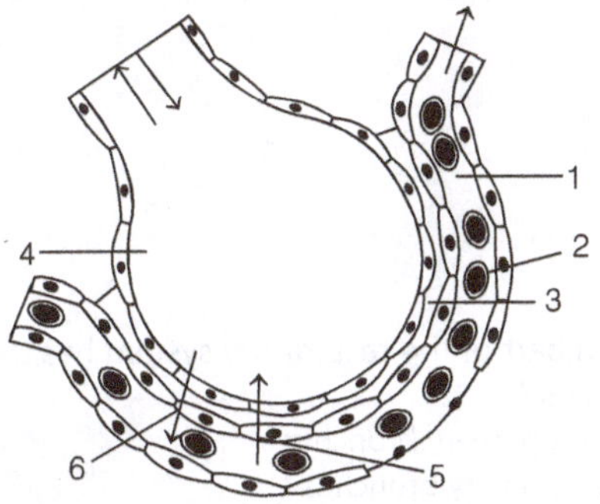

(i) Label the parts 1 to 4.
(ii) What do the arrows 5 and 6 indicate?
(iii) Why is the wall of alveolus extremely thin and moist?
(iv) From which vessel, the blood enters into the alveolus?
(v) What percentage of CO_2 in dissolved form is carried through plasma?

Ans. (i) The parts 1 to 4 are labelled as
1. Blood capillary
2. Red blood cell
3. Basement membrane
4. Alveolar cavity

(ii) The arrows 5 and 6 indicate.
5. CO_2 diffusing out
6. Oxygen diffusing in

(iii) Wall of alveolus is thin and moist since, it has to allow gaseous diffusion through them.
(iv) Pulmonary artery
(v) 7%

4. Respiration is the vital process in all the living organisms. It continues throughout their life.
(i) What is the condition of ribcage and sternum during inspiration?
(ii) What happens to the air pressure inside the thorax and lungs during expiration?
(iii) The walls of trachea and bronchi are lined by which type of tissues?
(iv) Give the dimension of trachea.
(v) Respriatory rhythm centre are found in which part of brain?

Ans. (i) The ribcage and sternum move upwards and outwards during inspiration.
(ii) The air pressure increases inside the thorax and lungs during expiration.
(iii) The walls of trachea and bronchi are lined by pseudostratified ciliated columnar epithelium.
(iv) Trachea is a thin-walled tube, about 11cm long and 2.5 cm wide. It extends up to mid-thoracic cavity.
(v) Respiratory rhythm centre are found in medulla oblongata and pons Varolii.

5. The breathing movements are normally not under the control of the will but to some extent one can consciously increase or decrease the rate of breathing.
(i) How much air per minute a healthy person can inspire or expire?
(ii) Which instrument is used to measure the volume of air involved during breathing?
(iii) How can vital capacity be calculated?
(iv) Name the respiratory volume that cannot be measured by a spirometer.
(v) In which form, CO_2 is transported by haemoglobin?

Ans. (i) Approximately 6000-8000 mL air per min.
(ii) Spirometer instrument is used to measure the volume of air involved during breathing.
(iii) TV+IRV+ERV = VC
(iv) Residual volume
(v) In the form of carbaminohaemoglobin, CO_2 is transported by haemoglobin.

Chapter Assessment

Section-I

1 Mark Questions

1. Name the following.
   (i) The muscular sheet that separates the thoracic cavity from abdominal cavity.
   (ii) Blind end sacs present in lungs.
   (iii) The respiratory pigment contained in human blood.
   (iv) Muscles that help in breathing.
2. Correct and rewrite the following statements by changing the underlined words.
   (i) About 3% of <u>CO_2</u> in the blood is carried in a dissolved state through the plasma.
   (ii) Artificial hypoxia occurs due to insufficient availability of <u>CO</u> to the body.
3. Give biological reasons for the following.
   (i) Inspiration is called as an active process.
   (ii) Cells need constant supply of oxygen.
4. Match the following columns.

	Column I		Column II
A.	Larynx	1.	An inverted Y-shaped tube
B.	Bronchioles	2.	Lined with hair
C.	Nasal chamber	3.	Production of voice
D.	Bronchi	4.	Small air tubes

5. Choose the correct answer from the four options given below.
   (i) Site of aerobic respiration in higher organisms is/are
   (a) Golgi apparatus (b) mitochondria
   (c) Both (a) and (b) (d) lungs
   (ii) During expiration, the diaphragm becomes
   (a) normal (b) flattened
   (c) dome-shaped (d) oblique
   (iii) Larynx is present between
   (a) glottis and epiglottis (b) trachea and bronchiole
   (c) epiglottis and trachea (d) bronchus and epiglottis
   (iv) Which part of the respiratory system has the smallest diameter?
   (a) Right primary bronchus
   (b) Left primary bronchus
   (c) Trachea
   (d) Respiratory alveoli
   (v) Process of exchange of O_2 from the atmosphere with ...*A*... produced by the cells is called ...*B*..., which is commonly known as ...*C*... .
   Choose appropriate options for the blanks *A*, *B* and *C* to complete the given statement.
   (a) *A* – H_2O, *B*–breathing, *C*– respiration
   (b) *A* – O_2, *B*–breathing, *C*– respiration
   (c) *A* – CO_2, *B*–breathing, *C*– respiration
   (d) *A* – NO_2, *B*–breathing, *C*– respiration
6. Fill in the blanks by using suitable words.
   (i) An unstable bright red compound formed between haemoglobin and oxygen to carry oxygen to the body cells is ....
   (ii) During inspiration, diaphragm ....
7. Choose the odd one out from the following terms given below and name the category to which other three belong.
   TV, VC, AV, RV
8. Given below is a set of five terms each. Rewrite the terms in correct order of a logical sequence beginning with the term that is underlined.
   Trachea, Larynx, Glottis, Pharynx, <u>Nasal chamber</u>
9. State whether the following statements are true or false. Correct and rewrite the false statements.
   (i) CO_2 is transported to the lungs by the blood in two forms as carbonates and as carbaminohaemoglobin.
   (ii) Tidal volume is equal to vital capacity of lungs.
   (iii) VC is the maximum capacity of lungs for inhaling air.
   (iv) Tidal volume = Vital capacity + IRV+ ERV
10. State the exact location of the following.
    (i) Bronchi
    (ii) Diaphragm

11. State the main function of the pleural fluid.

12. Mention one difference in each of the following pairs on the basis of what is given in the bracket.
   (i) Anaerobic respiration in plants and Anaerobic respiration in animals (product).
   (ii) Breathing and Respiration (definition)
   (iii) Inspiration and Expiration (definition)
   (iv) Inspiratory Reserve Volume (IRV) and Expiratory Reserve Volume (ERV) (definition)

13. Give biological/technical term for the following.
   (i) Narrowing of bronchi due to spasm in bronchial muscles.
   (ii) Two layered bag-like structure around the lungs.
   (iii) Removal of foul air from lungs.

14. Explain the following terms.
   (i) Inspiratory capacity
   (ii) Inspiratory reserve volume
   (iii) Dead air space

15. Answer the following questions briefly.
   (i) Starting from the nostrils, trace the path in sequence from which the inspired air is taken until it reaches the air sacs.
   (ii) How is the respiratory passage kept free of dust particles?
   (iii) Under what condition would the breathing rate increase?

2 Marks Questions

16. The end product of a process is ethanol and carbon dioxide with the release of energy. Name this process and write the pathway involved in the reaction.

17. How does haemoglobin help in the transport of oxygen from lungs to tissues?

18. How is CO_2 transported in human body?

3 Marks Questions

19. Explain the mechanism of breathing with neat labelled sketches.

20. Diffusion of gases occur in the alveolar region only and not in the other part of respiratory system. Why?

Section-II [5 Marks]

Structured Questions

21. The diagram shows ventral view of human thorax.

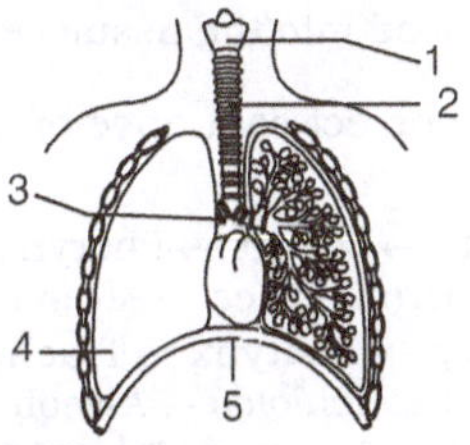

   (i) Label the parts 1 to 5.
   (ii) What is the function of ribcage?
   (iii) What is the difference between voice and speech?
   (iv) Why do the alveoli not collapse even after forceful expiration?
   (v) What is normal comfortable breathing called as?

22. Respiratory system is a biological system consisting of specific organs and structures used for gas exchange in animals and plants.
   (i) Given the name of the two phases of indirect respiration. Also, name the preliminary phase preceding them.
   (ii) Give the name of the site of actual exchange of O_2 and CO_2.
   (iii) What is the role of oxyhaemoglobin after releasing molecular oxygen in the tissues?
   (iv) Why is nose breathing better than mouth breathing?
   (v) Give the names of some respiratory disorders.

For explanations scan the given QR Code

Olympiad Section*

Brain Teasing Questions asked in Previous Olympiads

1 In which direction, does carbon dioxide move during internal respiration? **[INJSO 2019]**

(a) From the tissue cells into the blood
(b) From the blood into the lungs
(c) From the lungs into the blood
(d) From the blood into the tissue cells

2 Which is the correct sequence of air passage in man? **[NSEB 2014]**

(a) Nasal cavity → Larynx → Pharynx → Trachea → Bronchi → Bronchioles → Alveoli
(b) Nasal cavity → Pharynx → Trachea → Larynx → Bronchi → Bronchioles → Alveoli
(c) Nasal cavity → Larynx → Bronchi → Pharynx → Trachea → Bronchioles → Alveoli
(d) Nasal cavity → Pharynx → Larynx → Trachea → Bronchi → Bronchioles → Alveoli

3 The following graph depicts the rate and extent of a person's breathing just before exercise.

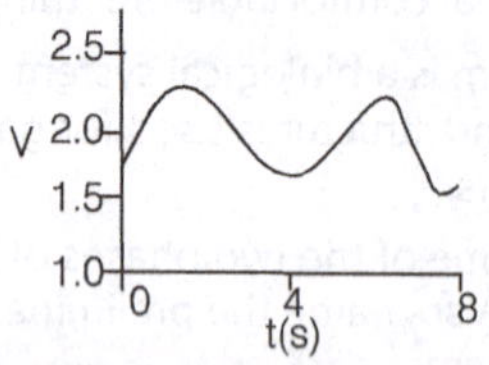

Here V is the volume of air in lungs in dm3 and t is the time in seconds. Which of the following graph best depicts the rate and extent of breathing of the same person immediately after a period of exercise? **[INJSO 2013]**

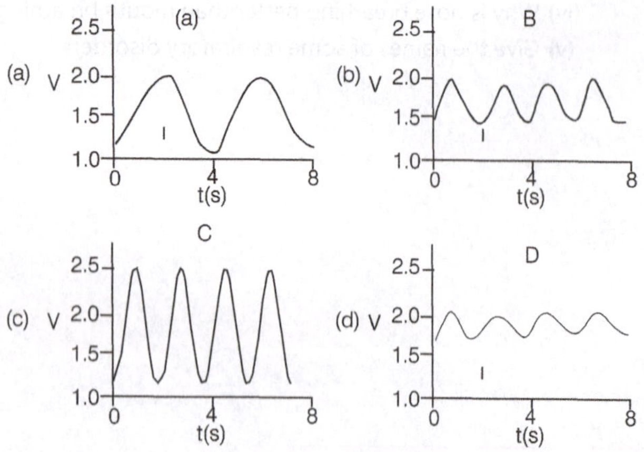

4 From the following relationships between respiratory volume and capacities, mark the correct option.

(i) Inspiratory Capacity (IC) = Tidal Volume (TV) + Residual Volume (RV)
(ii) Vital Capacity (VC) = Tidal Volume (TV) + Inspiratory Reserve Volume (IRV) + Expiratory Reserve Volume (ERV)
(iii) Residual Volume (RV) = Vital Capacity (VC) − Inspiratory Reserve Volume (IRV)
(iv) Tidal Volume (TV) = Inspiratory Capacity (IC) − Inspiratory Reserve Volume (IRV)

Codes

(a) (i) Incorrect, (ii) Incorrect, (iii) Incorrect, (iv) Correct
(b) (i) Incorrect, (ii) Correct, (iii) Incorrect, (iv) Correct
(c) (i) Correct, (ii) Correct, (iii) Incorrect, (iv) Correct
(d) (i) Correct, (ii) Incorrect, (iii) Correct, (iv) Incorrect

5 A person suffers punctures in his chest cavity in an accident, without any damage to the lungs its effect could be

(a) reduced breathing rate
(b) rapid increase in breathing rate
(c) no change in respiration
(d) cessation of breathing

6 In a mammalian lung, the rate at which oxygen could be obtained from the air would increase if

(a) tidal volume decreased
(b) the cells lining the alveoli and capillaries were thinner.
(c) blood haemoglobin content were lower
(d) you ascended to a higher altitude

7 The trachea, bronchi and bronchioles of humans have all of the following functions, except

(a) increasing the surface area available for gas exchange
(b) moistening the incoming air
(c) conducting mucus away from the alveoli
(d) warming the incoming air to body temperature

8 Which of the following produces negative pressure within your thoracic cavity?

(a) Exhalation
(b) Contraction of the diaphragm muscles
(c) Relaxation of the the muscles between the ribs
(d) Contraction of the muscles in the wall of the stomach

Answers

1. (a) **2.** (d) **3.** (c) **4.** (b) **5.** (d) **6.** (b) **7.** (a) **8.** (b)

**These questions may or may not be asked in the examination, have been given just for additional practice required for olympiads, scholarship exams etc. For detailed explanations refer Page No. 230.*

CHAPTER 13

Health and Hygiene

Chapter Inside

• Health • Hygiene • Disease • Common Bacterial Diseases in Humans
• Common Viral Diseases in Humans • Common Protozoan Diseases in Humans
• Common Parasitic Worm Diseases in Humans (Helminthic)

Health

It is a state of complete physical, mental and social well-being. It does not merely mean the absence of disease or infirmity as defined by the WHO (World Health Organisation; 1948). Thus, a healthy person is physically, mentally and socially sound.

Significances of Health

Good health has the following advantages

(i) It increases our working efficiency and helps us to perform various activities at our best.

(ii) It helps us to cope with the social and mental pressures without much difficulty.

(iii) It makes our life joyful.

Good health can be achieved and maintained by

(i) Practicing balanced diet, personal hygiene and regular exercise.

(ii) Practicing yoga to achieve physical and mental health.

(iii) Keeping and spreading awareness about diseases and their effect on different body functions.

(iv) Vaccination (immunisation) against infectious disease.

(v) Proper disposal of waste, control of vectors and maintenance of hygienic food and water resources.

Hygiene

It is the science of practicing and maintaining good health so as to prevent diseases. It can be practiced on both the personal as well as public levels by following personal hygiene and public hygiene, respectively.

(i) **Bathing** Regular bathing removes dirt and grease from the skin, prevents body odour and proliferation of germs.

(ii) **Tooth care** One should brush at least twice a day to maintain clean teeth and avoid dental caries.

(iii) **Care of nails** Overgrown nails can harbour many infectious germs. Nails should be cut a least once a week.

(iv) **Breathe by nose** One must always breathe by the nose and never by mouth. One should blow the nose into a handkerchief.

(v) **Eyecare** Eyes should be washed with clean, plain water two or three times everyday. A soft cloth should be used to remove dust particles from eyes.

(vi) **Ears** Soft cotton buds should be used to clean the wax from ears. A pointed object should never be inserted in the ear as it may harm the eardrum.

(vii) **Hair care** Hair should be cleaned frequently with good quality shampoo and should be properly combed to avoid parasites like lice, etc.

(viii) **Physical exercise** Regular exercise is important for people of all age groups. Regular exercise keeps the body fit and in shape. It helps one to maintain a healthy heart.

(ix) **Rest and sleep** Proper rest is also necessary for a healthy body. For a normal adult, 6-7 hours of undisturbed sleep is necessary.

Public Hygiene and Sanitation

The health of all organisms depends on their personal habits or economic status and physical environment. Personal health refers to the overall well-being of an individual whereas public or community health refers to the maintenance, protection and improvement or overall well-being of the whole community in which an individual lives. Human beings live in communities. Therefore, the health of the community is an important factor for our individual health. Various factors that affect our health are

(i) Social environment
(ii) Public cleanliness
(iii) Personal hygiene
(iv) Social equality and harmony
(v) Good economic conditions

Maintenance of Community Health

The various measures which should be taken in order to maintain community health are

(i) **Public cleanliness** It includes
 (a) Proper sanitation, sewage drainage and garbage disposal.
 (b) Availability of safe drinking water and unadulterated/nutritive food articles which do not contain any contamination.
 (c) Strict rules and norms against pollution.

(ii) **Preventive control** It includes pest control, vaccination against diseases, control of diseases and infections.

(iii) **Health education** It is the best way to make the population aware about the consequences related to health. Health education regarding disease, alcoholism, drug addictions, safe sex should be provided to masses to educate the young as well as adults.

(iv) **Establishment of healthcare services** Services like hospitals, community healthcare centres, maternity and childcare centres, etc., are necessary for medical care of the population.

Disease

It can be defined as any condition which impairs or disturbs the normal functioning of the body.

The diseases can be classified as

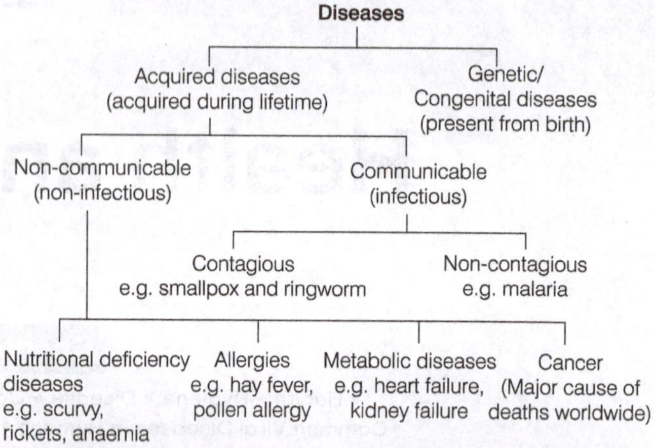

On the basis of mode of transmission, diseases are classified as

(i) **Communicable/Infectious diseases** The diseases that are easily transmitted from one person to another, e.g. influenza, tuberculosis, etc.

(ii) **Non-communicable/Non-infectious diseases** The diseases that cannot be transmitted from one person to another. These occur due to nutritional deficiences or genetic inheritance, e.g. cancer.

On the basis of extent of the occurrence, diseases are categorised into

(i) **Epidemic** When a disease affects large segment of a population in a specific time period at one place, it is said to be epidemic outbreak of a disease, e.g. plague spread in 1994 in India.

(ii) **Endemic** When a disease gets confined to a specific place and reoccurs again and again there only, it is endemic disease, e.g. goitre in hilly areas.

(iii) **Pandemic** When a disease affects the population on a global scale, e.g. AIDS and COVID-19.

(iv) **Sporadic** When there is scattered individual cases of a disease, e.g. malaria and cholera.

Common Terms Related to Disease

- **Pathogenicity** It is the ability of a pathogen to cause a disease.
- **Incubation period** It is defined as the time between the entry of pathogen into the body and the appearance of first disease symptoms.
- **Sign** shows the presence of the pathogen in the affected (diseased) person.
- **Symptoms** are the discomforts felt by the **affected person**.

Modes of Transmission

Infectious diseases can spread from person to person by various means, i.e. food, air, water, vectors, etc.

(i) **Airborne diseases** Diseases which get transmitted through air, i.e. the causative microbes spread *via* air are called airborne diseases. An infected person when sneezes or coughs, release droplets. These droplets can be breathed in by someone standing close and the microbes get a chance to start new infection, e.g. airborne diseases are **common cold, cough, pneumonia** and **tuberculosis**. Air transmitted diseases are easy to catch if we are closer to the infected person. In closed areas, the droplet nuclei recirculate and pose a risk for everyone.
Thus, overcrowded and poorly ventilated housing is a major factor in spreading airborne diseases.

(ii) **Water-borne diseases** Diseases which spread by contaminated water are called water borne diseases, e.g. cholera, typhoid, dysentery, etc.
The contamination of water occurs through the following agents

(a) **Sewage** When improperly disposed off, leaks into sub-soil and may contaminate water supplies and can become the primary source of spread of water-borne diseases.

(b) **Animal wastes** and washings from dairies, poultries, etc., when drained into water bodies, spread infection.

(c) People **defecating** or **urinating** near lakes, rivers or ponds may contribute to contamination of water and become reservoir of infection.

(d) **Tannery wastes** These are wastes from leather industries which contain microbes like *Anthrax bacilli*, responsible for causing anthrax.

(e) **Pesticides** These are the most serious water pollutants, e.g. DDT. Pesticide concentration in humans cause hormonal imbalance, leading to cancer.

(f) **Industrial wastes** They contain mercury which causes abnormalities in the nervous system and is thus a threat to public health.

(g) **Fluorides** These are present in drinking water and cause tooth disorders, bone disorders and if present in higher concentration causes neuro-muscular disorders and may be fatal to all forms of life.

(iii) **Vector-borne diseases** Vector is any agent that acts as an intermediate carrier of a pathogen. There are a number of organisms which spread disease from diseased individuals to healthy ones.
Few of them are as follows

(a) **Houseflies** They spread a large number of diseases like **cholera, dysentery, typhoid**, etc. Flies deposit germs of these diseases on the food materials and contaminate them.

(b) **Rats** These are severe pests and transmit pneumonic plague and anthrax in cattle.

(c) **Cockroaches** These are serious pests as they are omnipresent and are omnivorous. They are suspected to be carriers of many cancer causing viruses, cholera, amoebic dysentery and typhoid germs as they contaminate food materials.

(d) **Mosquitoes** These are also serious vectors of many diseases such as malaria (*Anopheles*), dengue and yellow fever (*Aedes*), etc.

Control of Vectors (Flies, Cockroach, Rats)

(i) Food and drinking material should be covered properly.

(ii) Garbage and refuse should be properly disposed off.

(iii) Insect vectors can be killed and controlled by insecticides and pesticides.

(iv) Rats should be killed by using rat killer chemicals or should be trapped and disposed off.

Check Your LEARNING...

1 Write the full form of WHO.
2 Give one example of an infectious disease.
3 Name one metabolic disorder.
4 What is a pandemic disease?
5 Define incubation period.
6 Name an infectious disease transmitted through
(i) Vector (ii) Water

Common Bacterial Diseases in Humans

Bacteria are the most common cause of diseases in human beings as well as in animals. Most of these diseases are fatal if not treated on time. Bacteria respond to antibiotic treatments so, all bacterial diseases are curable now-a-days.

Few examples of disease caused by bacteria are discussed below

1. Cholera

It is a highly infectious disease caused by *Vibrio cholerae.*

Modes of Transmission

Contaminated food and water spread the disease. Flies also disseminate bacteria in uncovered food sometimes.

Incubation

The incubation period ranges from a few hours to a week.

Symptoms

Watery stools, vomiting and abdominal pain. Cholera results in severe dehydration which can be lethal in case of children.

Prevention and Control

(i) Use of safe drinking water.
(ii) Maintenance of personal hygiene and good sanitation.
(iii) Avoid eating uncooked/raw food.
(iv) Use of antibiotics during infection saves life.
(v) Use of ORS hydrates the body in severe infections.

2. Typhoid

It is caused by *Salmonella typhi.*

Modes of Transmission

The disease gets transmitted by ingestion of food or water contaminated with faecal matter and also by houseflies, etc

Incubation

The incubation period for typhoid fever is 1-3 weeks, depending upon the number of (bacteria) infective dose.

Symptoms

(i) Severe headache.
(ii) Fever that rises in afternoon and keeps increasing for 7-8 days.
(iii) Slow pulse.

Diagnosis The disease is diagnosed by **Widal test.**

Prevention and Control

(i) Proper sanitation and disposal of faecal matter.
(ii) TAB vaccination, typhoid oral vaccine, also chloromycetin drug cures typhoid.
(iii) Ceftriaxone antibiotic is effective. Initially, **ampicillin** and chloramphenicol were the drugs of choice for typhoid.

3. Tuberculosis (TB)

It is caused by *Mycobacterium tuberculosis.*

Modes of Transmission

The bacteria spread from diseased to healthy persons through sneezing, coughing, contaminated utensils, towel and soap used by infected person. It can also spread through milk of infected cattle.

Incubation

Once bacteria enter the body, it takes 2-10 weeks for the symptoms to appear in the infected person.

Symptoms

(i) Loss of weight, appetite and person feels sick and weak.
(ii) Lung infection results into coughing, sputum with blood and pain in chest.
(iii) It shows typical fever patterns and night sweats.
(iv) TB causes swelling and pain in lymph glands specially in legs.

Prevention and Control

(i) Patient should be kept in isolation.
(ii) Disposal of sputum and nasal discharge of infected person should be done safely.
(iii) Healthy person should get immunised by BCG (Bacillus Calmette Guerin) vaccine.
(iv) Treatment with antibiotics like **streptomycin** effectively control the bacteria, but it takes long time to eliminate bacteria from the body.

Check Your LEARNING...

1 Write any two symptoms which relate with cholera in an individual.
2 The disease caused by ***Salmonella*** bacteria is ....
3 Identify the causative agent of tuberculosis.
4 Mention the most common mode of transmission of tuberculosis bacteria.
5 Give names of any two bacterial diseases except tuberculosis.

Common Viral Diseases in Humans

Viruses are the smallest pathogenic entities, which are considered as the connecting link between living and non-livings. They vary in their shape, structure and genetic material. They cannot respire, reproduce and grow independently but use host machinery to perform these functions. All viruses consist of two components

(i) Protein covering called **capsid**. The protein sub-units that form capsid are called **capsomeres**.

(ii) **Genetic material** which may be DNA or RNA. Some viruses may have an additional covering called **envelope**.

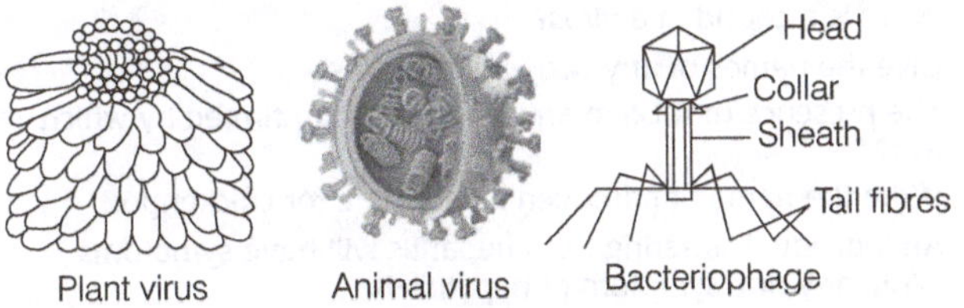

Various kinds of viruses

Few diseases caused by virus are discussed below

1. Acquired Immuno Deficiency Syndrome (AIDS)

AIDS is a disorder caused by **Human Immunodeficiency Virus** (HIV). This virus is pathogenic to human beings as it damages the immune system of human body resulting in loss of natural defence.

The first case of AIDS was reported from California USA in 1981.

Modes of Transmission

HIV gets transmitted generally

(i) by sexual contact with infected person.

(ii) by sharing of infected needles.

(iii) by transfusion of contaminated blood and blood products.

(iv) from infected mother to her child through placenta.

Note
- 1st December is celebrated as AIDS Day.
- HIV/AIDS is not transmitted by mere touch or any physical contact, it only spreads through exchange or contact of body fluids.
- It is hence, imperative for the physical and psychological well-being that HIV/AIDS person should not be isolated from family and society.

Symptoms

(i) The person experiences periods of fever, diarrhoea and weight loss during this period.

(ii) The immunity towards, almost all diseases also decreases.

Diagnosis of AIDS

There are several methods for the diagnosis of HIV infection such as viral culture, Enzyme-Linked Immuno Sorbent Assay (ELISA), PCR test, Western blotting, etc. Out of these, ELISA and Western blotting are widely used.

Prevention

Awareness and precautions are the only options to prevent AIDS. National AIDS Control Organisation (NACO) started in 1991 in India and many other NGOs are doing a lot to spread awareness regarding AIDS. WHO has started a number of programmes to prevent the spread of HIV.

Some common strategies of prevention are

(i) Making blood (in blood bank reserves) safe from HIV.

(ii) Use of only disposable needles and syringes in public and private hospitals and clinics.

(iii) Free distribution of condoms and advocating safe sex.

(iv) Controlling drug abuse.

(v) Promoting regular check-ups for HIV in susceptible people.

(vi) Testing the blood before transfusion and donation.

2. Chickenpox

It is caused by *Varicella zoster* virus, which is passed out in the discharge of respiratory tract of an infected person.

Modes of Transmission

Chickenpox is highly contagious. It is transmitted by direct contact with infected person.

Symptoms

(i) Fever

(ii) Aching muscles

(iii) Loss of appetite

(iv) Appearance of rashes, spots on entire body.

Prevention and Control

(i) The patient should be isolated and direct contact should be avoided by uninfected individuals.

(ii) Calamine lotion can be applied to reduce itching.

(iii) Vaccination for the virus should be given to the children.

3. Hepatitis

It is an infectious inflammation of the liver. Hepatitis can be of following types

(i) **Hepatitis-A** It is caused by Hepatitis-A Virus (HAV). Hepatitis-A is also known as **infectious epidemic hepatitis** or **epidemic jaundice**.

Transmission Virus gains entrance *via* the oral route and can multiply within epithelial lining of the intestinal tract and finally reaches the liver, kidneys and spleen.

Symptoms are nausea, diarrhoea, abnormal discomfort, fever and chills.

These symptoms generally appear in adults. As soon as jaundice disappears, the patient feels better. Symptoms such as yellowing of the skin, whiteness of the eyes and dark urine from last 2-21 days are seen. Mortality is very low. The incubation period ranges from two to six weeks.

Prevention Avoid faecal contamination of food and water.

(ii) **Hepatitis-B or transfusion hepatitis or serum hepatitis** is caused by Hepatitis-B Virus (HBV).

Transmission It takes place through the semen, saliva, vaginal secretion of infected person to other healthy persons. Mother's milk also can be a source of infection to their babies.

The incubation period ranges from 4-26 weeks.

Symptoms of HBV Infection are loss of appetite, low grade fever and joint pain. Jaundice usually appears in the later stage.

Prevention Newly born should be protected from infection by transmission from HBV-positive mothers. There should be the use of barriers during sexual intercourse and donated blood and semen should be used only after testing.

(iii) **Hepatitis-C** It is caused by Hepatitis-C Virus (HCV).

Transmission occurs through cuts, injury, use of contaminated syringes, dental instruments, sexual contact, contaminated blood, etc.

Symptoms involve liver cirrhosis and possibly liver cancer.

(iv) **Hepatitis-D** This is caused by Hepatitis-D Virus (HDV), which is found in nature only as a co-infection with HBV.

Transmission of HDV with the simultaneous infection of HBV is known as **backing.**

Symptoms Liver damage is essentially the same as in other cases of hepatitis but the presence of HDV usually increases the severity.

(v) **Hepatitis-E** It is caused by Hepatitis-E Virus (HEV).

Transmission It spreads through faecal-oral contamination, much like hepatitis-A.

HEV is a major cause of enterically transmitted water-borne hepatitis. The incubation period is 2-8 weeks.

Symptoms of hepatitis-E are similar to that of hepatitis-A. The disease is especially severe in pregnant women.

Check Your LEARNING...

1 What is a capsid in a virus?
2 Give the names of any two viral diseases.
3 The presence of AIDS in an individual is confirmed by which test?
4 Write the name of pathogen responsible for chickenpox.
5 An individual suffering from hepatitis will have symptoms. Write any one symptom of hepatitis-B.

Common Protozoan Diseases in Humans

Some common protozoan diseases are described below

1. Malaria

It is caused by a tiny protozoan called *Plasmodium.* Female *Anopheles* mosquito is the vector of this protozoan and picks it up from the infected person through bite.

Modes of Transmission

Malaria spreads by bite of female *Anopheles* mosquito.

Symptoms

(i) Headache, nausea and muscular pain.
(ii) High fever with specific pattern of cold, hot and sweating stage.

There are 5 parasite species that cause malaria in humans, and 2 of these species *Plasmodium falciparum* and *plasmodium vivax* pose the greatest threat *P. falciparum* causes malignant tertian or subtertian malaria, characterised by fever cycles every 36-48 hrs. While, *Plasmodium vivax* causes benign tertiary malaria. Incubation period ranges from 13-15 days. Fever occurs after 48 hrs.

Prevention and Control

(i) Use mosquito nets and insect repellents to prevent mosquito bites.
(ii) Do not allow stagnation of water anywhere.
(iii) Sprinkle kerosene oil in open drainage or any place where uncovered water gets collected.
(iv) Drugs like quinine is given for controlling malarial infection in patients.

2. Amoebic Dysentery

This is also common cause of intestinal disorder caused by a protozoan. It is caused by the *Entamoeba histolytica.*

Modes of Transmission

(i) Houseflies act as vectors for transmitting the parasite from faeces of the infected person to food and food products. On reaching our body, the parasite establishes in the lining of large intestine, where it feeds by engulfing red blood cells of the patient's intestine.

This *Amoeba* has no contractile vacuole and bears one large blunt pseudopodium.

(ii) When fully mature it forms a cyst which pass out through faeces. The cysts remain active for a long time. On reaching a new host through contaminated water and food, they split off to infect a new individual.

Symptoms

Severe stomach pain with watery stool. Sometimes, blood in stool can also be observed.

Prevention and Control

(i) This can be effectively prevented by maintaining proper hygiene.

(ii) Avoid contamination of food and water.

(iii) Antibiotic treatment is effective in controlling the disease.

(iv) Patients should be given lots of water to avoid dehydration.

3. Sleeping Sickness

It is caused by the protozoan *Trypanosoma gambiense.*

Modes of Transmission

Sleeping sickness is spread by blood sucking tse-tse flies.

Symptoms

(i) Headache, fever, lethargy, anaemia and loss of appetite.

(ii) It affects nervous system, patient feels sleepy and cannot respond to any stimuli.

Prevention and Control

(i) Use of insect repellents to prevent bite of tse-tse flies.

(ii) Treatment includes a course of drugs like melarsoprol, suramin, eflornithine, pentamidine isethionate, etc.

Common Parasitic Worm Diseases in Humans (Helminthic)

Other than bacteria and viruses, many parasites like worms cause certain diseases. Some of the common parasitic worm diseases are discussed below

1. Ascariasis

It is a common helminthic infection caused by *Ascaris lumbricoides.*

Modes of Transmission

(i) worms cysts or eggs are present in soil which grows with rooty vegetables. Usually, uncooked or raw vegetables spread infection.

(ii) Unwashed hands also spread infection.

Symptoms

(i) Abdominal pain in severe infection along with indigestion.

(ii) Vomiting, diarrhoea and restlessness.

Prevention and Control

(i) Sanitation in food habits.

(ii) Proper disposal of faeces.

(iii) Use of antihelminthic drugs.

2. Taeniasis

It is a disease caused by the infection of usually two species of *Taenia*, i.e. *T. solium* and *T. saginata* in human intestine. Their larvae are found in pig and cattle, respectively.

Modes of Transmission

Transmission is through contaminated food and water and unhealthy eating habits.

Symptoms

(i) Indigestion, abdominal pain, anaemia, diarrhoea, etc.

(ii) In severe infection, the cyst flow with blood and reach to the brain and then hatch. It might cause serious problems including paralysis, vision loss, etc.

Prevention and Control

(i) Raw vegetables and uncooked food should not be eaten.

(ii) Proper disposal of faeces.

3. Filariasis

It is also called elephantiasis and is caused by *Wuchereria bancrofti.*

Modes of Transmission

Filariasis is transmitted through the bite of the *Culex* mosquito.

Symptoms

(i) Fever with chills.

(ii) Inflammation of lymph nodes, enlargement of limbs, scrotal sacs and other body parts.

Prevention and Control

(i) The breeding areas of mosquitoes should be destroyed.

(ii) Proper clothing should be worn.

(iii) Antifilarial drugs can be used.

Check Your LEARNING...

1 Malaria is caused by .... and transmitted through ....

2 Severe stomach pain with watery stool are symptoms of which disease?

3 Name any two diseases caused by parasitic worms.

4 Give any one preventive measure for ascariasis.

5 The disease caused by *Wuchereria bancrofti* is ....

QUiCK Revision

- **Health** is a state of complete physical, mental and social well-being. Any deviation from the state of well-being results in a disease.
- **Community health** is an important concept, which aims at the protection, maintenance and health of the community.
- Community health services work in different departments. These are health centres, national programmes, universal immunisation programmes and blood banks.
- Besides personal hygiene and cleanliness, these services aim at generating awareness about health, educating people and helping them in the best possible way.
- **Diseases** are caused by various microorganisms called **pathogens**.
- They enter the body by various routes, multiply and interfere with normal vital activities.
- They are divided into congenital and acquired diseases.
- **Acquired diseases** are further categorised into communicable and non-communicable diseases. These are seen in an organism after birth.
- Congenital diseases are present since birth.
- **Communicable diseases** spread from one person to another. The causative agent or pathogen for the disease could be virus, protozoan, bacteria, fungus, helminthes, etc.

Diseases	Causative agents	Symptoms
Cholera	*Vibrio cholerae*	Watery stool, vomiting and abdominal pain.
Typhoid	*Salmonella typhi*	High fever, weakness, headache and loss of appetite.
Tuberculosis (TB)	*Mycobacterium tuberculosis*	Loss of appetite and weight, persistent cough, etc.
AIDS	Human Immunodeficiency Virus (HIV)	Fever, diarrhoea and weight loss.
Chickenpox	*Varicella zoster*	Malaise, fever, aching muscles, loss of appetite, appearance of rashes and spots.
Hepatitis-A, B, C, D, E	HAV, HBV, HCV, HDV, HEV	Diarrhoea, fever, loss of appetite, joint pain, liver cirrhosis, yellowing of skin, eye and dark urine are combined symptoms of hepatitis group diseases.
Malaria	*Plasmodium* species	High fever, chills, sweating, fatigue, weakness, loss of appetite.
Amoebiasis	*Entamoeba histolytica*	Constipation, abdominal pain and cramps, stools with excess mucus and blood clots.
Sleeping sickness	*Trypanosoma gambiense*	Headache, fever, lethargy, anaemia and loss of appetite.
Ascariasis	*Ascaris lumbricoides*	Include internal bleeding, muscular pain, fever, anaemia and blockage of the intestinal passage.
Taeniasis	*Taenia solium* and *T. saginata*	Indigestion, abdominal pain, anaemia, diarrhoea, etc.
Filariasis	*Wuchereria bancrofti*	Chronic inflammation and deformation of the lower body organ and genitals.

- **Non-communicable diseases** are those diseases which do not spread from an affected person to another healthy person. These can be deficiency diseases, allergies, mental illness, malfunctioning diseases, etc. Among non-communicable diseases, cancer affects large number of individuals worldwide.

Chapter Practice

Section-I

1 Mark Questions

1. Name the following.
   (i) A state of complete physical, mental and social well-being and not merely absence of diseases.
   (ii) The disease group which spreads from place to place affecting many people.
   (iii) The disease which affects the population on a global scale.
   (iv) The period between entry of germs and the appearance of the first symptoms of disease.
   (v) Organisms that transmit microbes that cause disease.
   (vi) A disease that weakens body's defence system against infections.
   (vii) Lotion applied for treatment of chickenpox.

Ans. (i) Health (ii) Epidemic diseases
(iii) Pandemic (iv) Incubation period
(v) Vector (vi) AIDS
(vii) Calamine

2. Correct and rewrite the following statements by changing the underlined words.
   (i) When there are scattered individual cases of a disease, then it is called <u>pandemic</u> disease.
   (ii) Cholera is caused by <u>virus</u>.
   (iii) BCG vaccine provides immunity against <u>AIDS</u>.
   (iv) <u>Chickenpox</u> is transmitted from the infected mother to her child through placenta.

Ans. (i) When there are scattered individual cases of a disease, then it is called sporadic disease.
(ii) Cholera is caused by bacteria *Vibrio cholerae*
(iii) BCG vaccine provides immunity against tuberculosis.
(iv) HIV-AIDS is transmitted from the infected mother to her child through placenta.

3. Give biological reasons for the following.
   (i) One should breathe by nose and never by mouth.
   (ii) Eating places must be kept free of flies.

Ans. (i) One should breathe by nose and never by mouth because nose contains hair and mucus to trap dust and microorganisms, so that the inhaled air becomes clean and the respiratory passage remains free of dust and microorganisms.
(ii) Flies are the carrier of many disease causing germs and bacteria. Therefore, eating places must be kept free of flies to avoid possible contamination of food.

4. (i) Match the following columns.

	Column I		Column II
A.	Sporadic disease	1.	Plague
B.	Pandemic disease	2.	Goitre
C.	Endemic disease	3.	Malaria
D.	Epidemic disease	4.	COVID-19

(ii) Match the following columns.

	Column I		Column II
A.	Cockroaches	1.	Dengue
B.	Rat flea	2.	Cholera
C.	*Culex*	3.	Plague
D.	*Aedes*	4.	Filaria

Ans. (i) A-3, B-4, C-2, D-1
(ii) A-2, B-3, C-4, D-1

5. Choose the correct answer from the four options given below.
   (i) Human health can be maintained by
   (a) balanced diet
   (b) personal hygiene
   (c) regular exercise
   (d) All of these

Ans. (d)

(ii) Which one of these is an unhealthy habit?
(a) Washing hand before eating food
(b) Keeping the mouth closed while breathing
(c) Sleeping for only 6-7 hours
(d) Sharing towels with others

Ans. (d)

(iii) Which one of these is the aim of community health?
(a) Care of infants and the old
(b) Care of women
(c) Healthcare for all
(d) Care of pregnant women

Ans. (c)

(iv) A disease which can easily transmit from one person to another is called
(a) non-infectious disease
(b) infectious disease
(c) viral disease
(d) bacterial disease

Ans. (b)

(v) Among the following, a non-communicable disease is
(a) measles (b) rabies
(c) diphtheria (d) diabetes

Ans. (d)

(vi) Which one of the following non-infectious disease is the major cause of death in humans?
(a) Cancer (b) AIDS
(c) Asthma (d) Typhoid

Ans. (a)

(vii) Which one of these pairs is correctly matched?
(a) Tse-tse – Dengue (b) *Aedes* – Filariasis
(c) *Culex* – Malaria (d) Cockroaches – Typhoid

Ans. (d)

(viii) Amoebic dysentery can be spread by which of these?
(a) Rats (b) Cockroaches
(c) Mosquitoes (d) Houseflies

Ans. (d)

(ix) Which day is celebrated as AIDS Day?
(a) 1st May (b) 1st December
(c) 1st June (d) 1st January

Ans. (b)

6. Fill in the blanks by using suitable words.
(i) Diseases present from the birth are called ....
(ii) The two important contributory factors of diseases are .... and .... make up.
(iii) Cleanliness, rest, sleep and physical exercise are a part of .... hygiene.
(iv) Public and community health can be achieved through .... and ....
(v) The example of infectious disease is ....
(vi) All bacterial diseases can be controlled by ...... treatments.

Ans. (i) congenital, (ii) environment, genetic, (iii) personal, (iv) personal habit, physical environment, (v) AIDS, (vi) antibiotic

7. Choose the odd one out from the following terms given below and name the category to which the other three belong.
(i) Typhoid, AIDS, Cholera, Tuberculosis
(ii) AIDS, Chickenpox, Malaria, Hepatitis
(iii) Malaria, Sleeping sickness, Amoebic dysentery, Ascariasis

Ans. (i) **Odd term** AIDS
Rest three are diseases caused by bacteria.
(ii) **Odd term** Malaria
Rest three are diseases caused by virus.
(iii) **Odd term** Ascariasis
Rest three are diseases caused by protozoans.

8. Expand the following biological abbreviations.
(i) WHO (ii) BCG
(iii) AIDS

Ans. (i) World Health Organisation
(ii) Bacillus Calmette Guerine
(iii) Acquired Immuno Deficiency Syndrome

9. State whether the following statements are true or false. Correct and rewrite the false statements.
(i) Hygiene is the science of health and prevention of diseases.
(ii) All public places should be kept clean to maintain community health.
(iii) Communicable diseases are non-infectious.
(iv) Hepatitis is a non-communicable disease.
(v) Cholera, dysentery and hepatitis are water-borne diseases.
(vi) Sewage is the most common source of contamination of water in cities.
(vii) Cockroaches are not a common household pest.
(viii) AIDS is caused by fungus.
(ix) Ascariasis is a disease which affects the teeth.
(x) Filariasis is transmitted by the housefly.

Ans. (i) True (ii) True
(iii) False, communicable diseases are infectious.
(iv) False, hepatitis is a communicable disease.
(v) True
(vi) True
(vii) False, cockroaches are the common household pest.
(viii) False. AIDS is caused by virus.
(ix) False, ascariasis is a disease which affects small intestine.
(x) False, filriasis is transmitted by *Culex* mosquito.

10. Give one example of each of the following.
(i) Airborne disease
(ii) Pandemic disease
(iii) Sporadic disease
(iv) Disease caused by virus
(v) Disease caused by protozoan

Ans. (i) Common cold
(ii) COVID-19
(iii) Malaria
(iv) AIDS
(v) Amoebiasis

11. Mention one difference in each of the following pairs on the basis of what is given in the bracket.
(i) Personal health and Community health (definition)
(ii) Infectious and Non-infectious diseases (definition)

Ans. (i) Difference between personal health and community health is as follows

Personal health	Community health
Health related to health matters of an individual is called personal health.	Health related to health matters of a community is termed as community health.

(ii) Difference between infectious and non-infectious diseases is as follows

Infectious diseases	Non-infectious diseases
These are the diseases that can transmit from diseased to healthy person.	These are the diseases that cannot transmit from one person to another.

12. Briefly explain the following terms.

(i) Hygiene (ii) Disease
(iii) Disease carrier (iv) Infectious disease

Ans. (i) Hygiene is defined as living conditions or practices performed by an individual or public for maintaining health and thus, prevents the appearance of disease.

(ii) Disease is defined as any condition which impairs or disturb the normal functioning of the body.

(iii) An organism which harbours the germs of the diseases is called disease carrier.

(iv) The infectious diseases are diseases caused by pathogen which spread very fast from one person to another person.

13. Answer the following questions briefly.

(i) What are the dimensions of health according to World Health Organisation (WHO)?

(ii) Write two methods to maintain community health.

(iii) Name two types of acquired diseases.

(iv) Why do we say AIDS is a syndrome and not a disease?

(v) Give the methods of transmission of AIDS.

Ans. (i) According to WHO, a healthy person should be physically, mentally and socially healthy.

(ii) Two methods to maintain community health are as follows

(a) Public cleanliness (b) Health education

(iii) Two types of acquired diseases are

(i) Infectious or communicable diseases

(ii) Non-infectious or non-communicable diseases

(iv) AIDS is caused by HIV. It affects the immune system. So, AIDS patients normally suffer with many diseases. So, it is considered as a syndrome.

(v) AIDS can be transmitted by

- Sexual intercourse with infected person
- Contaminated blood transfusion
- Sharing of infected needles, from infected mother to her child through placenta.

2 Marks Questions

14. What are two ways of maintaining good health?

Ans. Two ways of maintaining good health are

(i) Practicing balanced diet with all required nutrients.

(ii) Maintaining good personal hygiene and regular exercise.

15. What are the significances of good health?

Ans. The significances of good health are

(i) It makes our life joyful.

(ii) It increases our working efficiency and helps us to do various activities at our best.

(iii) It helps us to cope with social and mental pressure without much difficulty.

16. What are the measures to prevent the water- borne diseases?

Ans. To prevent the water-borne diseases, water bodies, ponds, water tanks reservoirs in the city or village should be cleaned periodically. The proper disposal of house wastes, excreta, sewage should be done. At personal level, boiling of water, using aquaguard, washing hands before meals should be practiced.

3 Marks Questions

17. Write three measures for public hygiene.

Ans. Measures for public hygiene are

(i) Proper disposal of wastes and excreta.

(ii) Cleaning and disinfection of pools, water tanks and other water reservoirs.

(iii) Hygienic practices should be adopted at restaurants and hotels.

18. What are the immediate and the contributory causes of diseases?

Ans. (i) Immediate causes of diseases are various microorganisms like viruses, bacteria, fungi, etc.

(ii) Contributory causes of diseases are

(a) poor health due to inadequate diet

(b) genetic disorders

(c) improper functioning of body organ

19. List any three ways of preventing the spread of airborne diseases.

Ans. Measures of preventing airborne diseases are

(i) Avoid direct contact with infected individuals.

(ii) Use mask/gloves/handkerchief in public places.

(iii) Avoid overcrowded areas.

20. Write preventive measures for vector-borne diseases.

Ans. Preventive measures for vector-borne diseases are

(i) Breeding places of vector should be eliminated.

(ii) Stagnation of water should be avoided to control the breeding of mosquitoes.

(iii) Use of mosquito repellents, nets and wire mesh on doors and windows.

(iv) Wearing protective clothes like pants and full sleeves shirt, etc.

Section-II [5 Marks]

Structured Questions

1. Health is a state of complete physical, mental and social-well being and not merely the absence of diseases.
   (i) State any condition essential for good health.
   (ii) What are the different ways by which disease can be spread?
   (iii) How can good health be achieved?
   (iv) What are the various factors that affect our heath?
   (v) What are the various measures which should be taken in order to maintain community health?

Ans. (i) Better sanitation and clean environment are essential for good health.
(ii) Diseases can be spread by different ways such as through air, water and vectors.
(iii) Good health can be achieved by balanced diet, personal hygiene and regular exercise.
(iv) The various factors that affect our health are social environment, public cleanliness, personal hygiene, etc.
(v) The various measures which should be taken in order to maintain community health are as
(a) Proper sanitation, sewage drainage and garbage disposal.
(b) Health education regarding drug addiction and safe sex should be provided to the society.

2. Given below is the figure of a vector. Study this and answer the questions that follows.

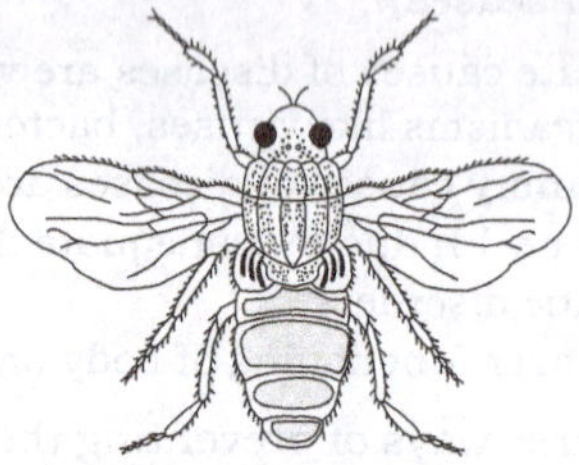

   (i) Name the organism.
   (ii) Name the disease spread by this.
   (iii) How does it spread disease?
   (iv) What are ways by which we can avoid spread of disease by this vector?
   (v) What are the other vectors responsible for spreading diseases?

Ans. (i) The organism is housefly.
(ii) The diseases spread by this are cholera, typhoid.
(iii) Housefly sits on the garbage, faecal wastes, sewage, etc., and the disease causing germs stick to their legs. When it sits on eatables, germs are transmitted to food items which enter into the body of man and cause diseases.
(iv) Spread of diseases by this vector can be controlled by the following actions
(i) Food and drinking material should be kept properly covered.
(ii) They can be controlled by using insecticides and pesticides.
(v) Rats, cockroaches, etc., are the other vectors responsible for spreading diseases.

3. The figure shows the legs of a patient. Study the figure and answer the questions that follows.

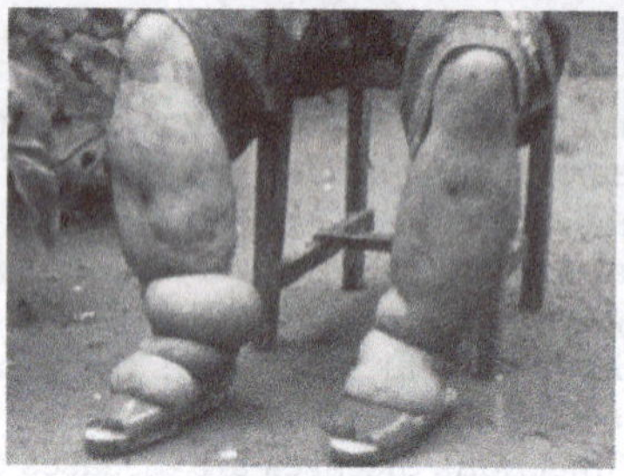

   (i) What is the disease, the patient is suffering from?
   (ii) How does this disease spread?
   (iii) Name the causative agent of this disease.
   (iv) How can this disease be prevented and treated?
   (v) What are the symptoms of this disease?

Ans. (i) Filaria/Elephantiasis
(ii) This disease spread by the bite of male *Culex* mosquito.
(iii) The causative agent of this disease is *Wuchereria bancrofti*.
(iv) Prevention involves protection from mosquito bite. Treatment with antifilarial drugs is found to be effective.
(v) Symptoms of the disease include
- Blocking of lymph nodes in limbs.
- Swelling up of scrotal sacs and other body parts.

Chapter Assessment

Section-I

1 Mark Questions

1. Name the following.
   (i) The smallest structures which are considered as connecting link between living and non-living.
   (ii) The disease which affects large segment of a population in a specific time period at one place.
   (iii) The diseases which cannot be transmitted from one person to another.
   (iv) The discomforts felt by affected person.
   (v) The disease that causes rashes on entire body.
   (vi) The disease that spreads by contaminated water.
2. Correct and rewrite the following statement by changing the underlined words.
   (i) <u>Hygiene</u> is any condition which disturbs the normal functioning of the body.
   (ii) <u>Pandemic</u> disease is confined to a specific place and reoccur again and again there only.
   (iii) <u>Typhoid</u> is caused by parasitic worm called *Ascaris lumbricoides*.
3. Give biological reason for the following.
   Hands must be washed before eating food.
4. Match the following columns.

Column I	Column II
A. BCG	1. Insecticide
B. Suramin	2. Vaccine
C. AIDS	3. Drug
D. DDT	4. HIV

5. Choose the correct answer from the four options given below.
   (i) Which one of these medicines is used in prevention and cure of tuberculosis?
   (a) Chloroquine (b) BCG
   (c) Streptomycin (d) Calamine
   (ii) Which of the following activity will never cause AIDS?
   (a) Sharing infectious needles (b) Sexual contact
   (c) From mother to child (d) Shaking hands
   (iii) Which one is not a symptom of disease caused by *E. histolytica*?
   (a) Stools with excess mucus (b) Constipation
   (c) Abdominal pain (d) Nasal discharge
   (iv) The vector that transmits the malarial pathogen is
   (a) *Culex* mosquito (b) Housefly
   (c) *Anopheles* (d) *Entamoeba*
6. Fill in the blanks by using suitable words.
   (i) The municipal bodies must ensure the supply of clean germ free .... and an efficient .... disposal.
   (ii) One must always breathe by .... not by ....
   (iii) .... is the carrier of pathogen.
   (iv) Bacterial diseases are cured by using ....
   (v) Any organism capable of producing a disease is called ....
   (vi) Chickenpox is caused by ....
   (vii) One example of sexually transmitted disease is ....
7. Choose the odd one out from the following terms given below and name the category to which other three belong.
   (i) Epidemic, Endemic, Pandemic, Infectious disease
   (ii) Ascariasis, Taeniasis, Typhoid, Filariasis
8. Expand the following biological abbreviations.
   (i) HIV (ii) ELISA (iii) TB
9. State whether the following are true or false. Correct and rewrite the false statements.
   (i) AIDS can be transmitted through sexual contacts.
   (ii) Most common worm infection among children is ascariasis.
   (iii) Virus is a non-living pathogen.
   (iv) Dengue causes dehydration which is fatal.
   (v) Sewage is the most common source of contamination of water in the cities.
   (vi) Breeding ground of mosquito is stagnant water present in ditches, water coolers, etc.
   (vii) Cholera is spread by contaminated syringes.
10. Give one example each of the following.
   (i) Endemic disease
   (ii) Disease caused by bacteria
   (iii) Epidemic disease
11. Mention one difference in each of the following pairs on the basis of what is given in the bracket.
   Epidemic and Endemic diseases (definition)
12. Briefly explain the following terms.
   Pathogenicity

13. Answer the following questions briefly.
    (i) Write two healthy habits.
    (ii) Name two means of physical contact by which AIDS does not spread.
    (iii) What are the two types of acquired diseases?
    (iv) Describe the different ways by which the housefly contaminates our food.

2 Marks Questions

14. State the characteristic features of viruses.
15. How are cockroaches and rats harmful to humans?

3 Marks Questions

16. What are the symptoms of cholera and how can it be prevented?
17. What are the symptoms of chickenpox and how it can be prevented?

Section-II [5 Marks]

Structured Questions

18. Given below are few organisms which transmit diseases. Study them and answer the following.

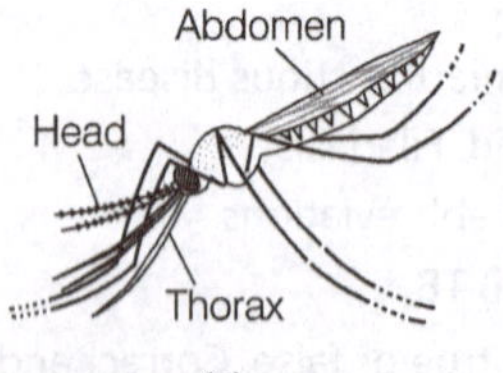

(a)

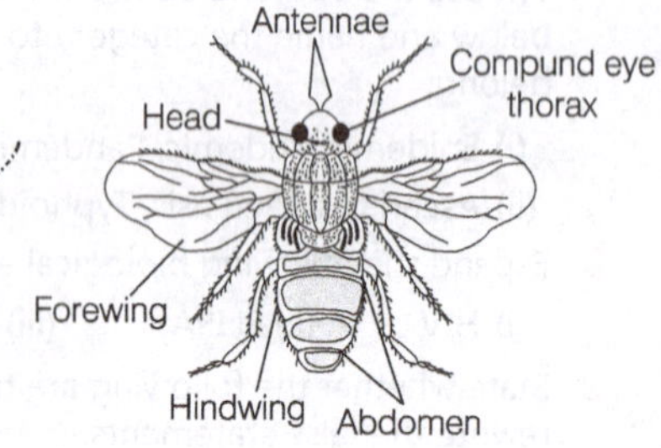

(b)

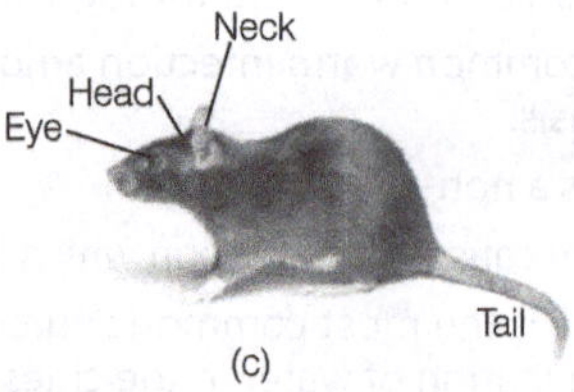

(c)

    (i) Which of the above three organisms can be called a malarial vector?
    (ii) Mention any two diseases transmitted by organism (c).
    (iii) Name the two most common kinds of organism a.
    (iv) How can we control the population of rats?
    (v) Name any one disease transmitted by organism b.

19. Infectious diseases can be spread from person to person by various means, i.e. food, air, water, vectors, etc.
    (i) What are the ways in which contamination of water occurs?
    (ii) Name different vectors which are responsible for spreading diseases.
    (iii) How does the disease causing microbes spread through air?
    (iv) Name the disease caused by contaminated water and food.
    (v) What are the causes of non-infectious diseases?

20. The figure shows the structure of an HIV virus.

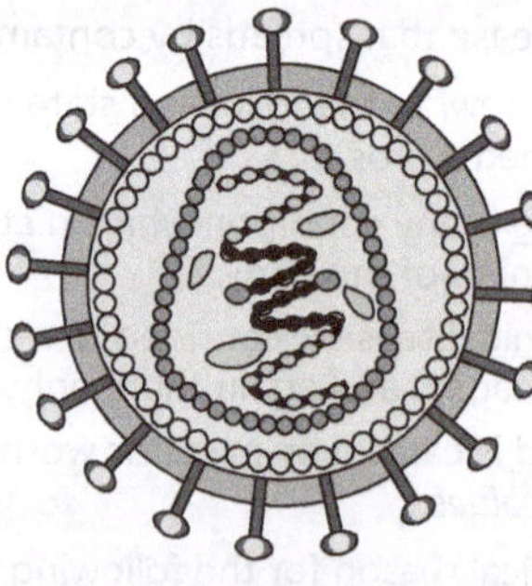

    (i) Which disease does the above virus relate to?
    (ii) How is the disease caused by the above organism transmitted?
    (iii) How can the disease be diagnosed?
    (iv) State any two preventive measures for the disease spread by this virus.
    (v) What are the two symptoms of the disease?

For explanations scan the given QR Code

Olympiad Section*

Brain Teasing Questions asked in Previous Olympiads

1 Which one of the following is the correct matching of a disease with its causative organism and mode of infection?

	Diseases	Causative Organisms	Modes of Infection
(a)	Pneumonia	*Streptococcus pneumoniae*	Droplet infection
(b)	Typhoid	*Salmonella typhi*	With inspired air
(c)	Malaria	*Plasmodium vivax*	Bite of infected male *Anopheles* mosquito
(d)	Elephantiasis	*Wuchereria bancrofti*	With contaminated food and water

2 Making antiviral drugs is more difficult than making antibacterial medicines because

(a) viruses make use of host machinery
(b) viruses are on the border line of living and non-living
(c) viruses have very few biochemical mechanisms of their own
(d) viruses have a protein coat

3 You are moving to Africa and you have heard that the green fever virus disease is common there. Before you leave, you visit your doctor for advice. Which of the following is your doctor most likely to recommend? You should

(a) take a large supply of antibiotics with you
(b) wash your food in an antiseptic before you eat it
(c) get vaccinated against the disease
(d) not worry as viruses only cause diseases in plants

4 In Canada, recent outbreaks of meningitis, caused by a virus, were controlled by immunisation with a vaccine. Unfortunately, AIDS caused by the HIV virus has not yet been controlled by a vaccine because of the

(a) cost of development and production of vaccines
(b) availability of effective antibiotics
(c) high degree of variability in the HIV virus
(d) complex structure of the HIV virus

5 Why do male *Anopheles* do not cause malaria?

(a) They feed on juices of plants
(b) Their population is very less
(c) They are killed by female *Anopheles* after mating
(d) They harbour malarial parasite in their salivary glands

6 The group of diseases carried by insects are

(a) typhoid, jaundice, dysentery
(b) mumps, measles, smallpox
(c) rabies, ringworm, fever
(d) malaria, filaria, yellow fever

7 A person was found to be affected by unilateral swelling of the lower extremity. On getting the history of swelling, it was noticed that it started with number of feed and then spread upwards mainly due to fluid retention. The disease, he is suffering from is caused by

(a) *Taenia solium* (b) *Wuchereria bancrofti*
(c) *Entamoeba histolytica* (d) *Trypanosoma gambiense*

8 The doctor on examining a particular patient found that he has some watery boils on the skin. He is also explaining about fever and muscle pain. From which disease, was the patient suffering?

(a) Hepatitis (b) Malaria
(c) Chickenpox (d) AIDS

9 A doctor was explaining to his students about a particular virus that suppresses the immune system. This disorder leads to decrease in number of T-cells. The doctor was talking about which disorder?

(a) AIDS (b) Hepatitis
(c) Syphilis (d) Chicken pox

10 Refer to the given table, which of the following options correctly identifies *P*, *Q*, *R* and *S* in the table.

	Diseases	Causing agents	Vaccines
1.	*P*	*Salmonella typhi*	TAB vaccination
2.	Tuberculosis	*Q*	*R*
3.	*S*	*Varicella zoster*	CDC

P Q R S
(a) Malaria, *Plasmodium*, BCG, Sleeping sickness
(b) Dengue, *Culex* mosquito, BCG, Hepatitis
(c) Typhoid, *Mycobacterium tuberculosis*, BCG, Chickenpox
(d) Cholera, *Vibrio cholerae*, BCG, Typhoid

Answers

1. (a) 2. (c) 3. (c) 4. (c) 5. (a) 6. (d) 7. (b) 8. (c) 9. (a) 10. (c)

*These questions may or may not be asked in the examination, have been given just for additional practice required for olympiads, scholarship exams etc. For detailed explanations refer Page No. 230.

CHAPTER

14

Aids to Health

Chapter Inside

• Defence System • Other Methods of Defence against Microorganisms • Health Organisations

Health is a state of complete physical, mental and social well-being. It is maintained by the efficient working of the immune or defence system of the body.

We have already discussed health and hygiene concepts in chapter 13. In this chapter, we will study the various aspects involved in aids of maintaining good health, e.g. defence system of body, various health organisations, etc.

Defence System

Human body is constantly under attack by bacteria, fungi, viruses and other microorganisms, but most of the time we remain healthy due to the presence of body's own defence system. Defence system in our body works in two ways as given below

1. Local Defence System

It acts as a type of barrier system to fight with germs/ pathogens at their entry points. This system includes

(i) **Physical barriers** These barriers are first line of defence for our body. These are

(a) **Skin** It prevents the entry of pathogens into the body (which can enter either through cuts or injury on the skin) by its outer tough layer.

(b) **Hair** It interferes with the germ's entry inward or up to the skin, e.g. hair inside the nostrils (nose) trap dust.

(c) **Mucus** It is the slimy secretion of epithelial lining of various organs that prevents the entry of germs inside the body, e.g. mucus secreted in nasal passage, windpipe, etc.

(ii) **Germ-killing secretions** Different body parts secrete several secretions in order to prevent the entry of germs/pathogens, e.g. **saliva** (in mouth), **sweat** (on skin), **tears** (in eyes), **nasal secretions** (in nostrils) and **earwax** (in ears).

Hydrochloric acid (HCl) secreted by stomach kills germs that gain entry along with the food. These secretions contain substances that have ability to kill germs.

(iii) **Coughing, sneezing and vomiting** These are the intense body responses to directly throw out the pathogen or foreign substances entering the body and interfering with the normal respiratory and digestive system.

(iv) **White Blood Cells** (WBCs) Leucocytes or WBCs also take part in body defence system. This is because they have the ability to fight with the germs/foreign substances by engulfing them through the process of **phagocytosis**.

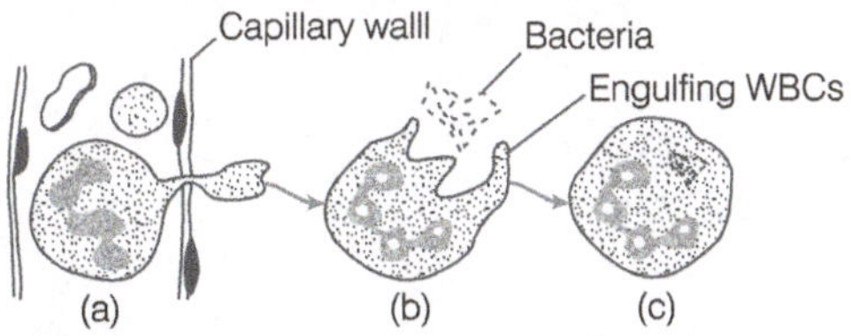

The engulfing of bacteria by white blood cells (phagocytosis).
(a) Cell forcing its way across caplliary wall (diapedesis),
(b) White blood cell attracted towards bacteria,
(c) Bacteria are engulfed by the white blood cell .

Note **Phagocytes** These are named from the Greek word 'phagein' (to eat). Phagocytes are cells that engulf foreign particles, including infectious agents, such as bacteria. Monocytes, neutrophils and macrophages are the main phagocytic cells. They search and embrace foreign particles and destroy them.

Merits of Local Defence System

Local defence system possesses the following merits

(i) It starts working instantaneously.

(ii) It is not dependent on the previous exposure of infections.

(iii) It is effective against almost all types of infectious agents.

2. Immune System

The ability of a person to resist or defend itself from the development of disease due to the entry of foreign organism is called **immunity**. It develops when the local defence system fails or is ineffective due to the poisonous secretions (toxins) of certain microbes entering the deeper tissues and various organ systems. In response, the body fluids such as blood starts fighting against the germs and **antigens**. Blood secretes **antibodies** and **antitoxins** to destroy harmful germs.

Note
- **Antigens** These are foreign substances that have capability to elicit immune responses.
- **Antibodies** These are special chemicals or serum proteins found in blood which are produced in response to specific antigens or their secretions.

Types of Immunity

Immunity is classified into two main types as follows

(i) **Innate immunity** The immunity inherited by organisms from parents since birth, also known as **natural** or **inborn immunity**. It is also called as **non-specific immunity** because it does not differentiate between different type of pathogens. It respond to each foreign substance using same mechanism. It consists of various types of barriers (skin, mucous membrane, etc) that prevent the entry of foreign agents.

(ii) **Acquired immunity** The immunity acquired by an individual after birth, i.e. during its lifetime when he/she gets exposed to certain microorganisms.

Acquired immunity can be of two main types

(a) **Active acquired immunity** The immunity developed within an individual due to encounter with previous infection or antigen, e.g. a person who has suffered from measles, do not normally suffer from it again. It is further divided into two types

(i) **Naturally acquired active immunity** Natural infection by a pathogen generates antibodies and specialised lymphocytes.

(ii) **Artificially acquired active immunity** Vaccines are administered to the body which generates antibodies and specialised lymphocytes.

(b) **Passive acquired immunity** The immunity provided to an individual from an outside source in the form of readymade antibodies, e.g. antibodies provided in case of rabies and snake bite, antibodies received by foetus from mother through placenta and antibodies received by infant through milk.

Passively acquired immunity is also of two types

(i) **Naturally acquired passive immunity** Antibodies will passively pass from mother to foetus *via* placenta and mother to infant *via* milk.

(ii) **Artificially acquired passive immunity** Antibodies formed within other organisms are introduced into the patient's body through injection for defensive purpose against the pathogen.

Differences between Active and Passive Immunity

Active immunity	Passive immunity
Produced by itself.	Received from outside, i.e. cannot be developed by one's own body.
Provides effective and long-lasting protection.	Has immediate effects.
Immunity is effective only after a certain time gap (time is required for antibodies production).	Protection is less effective and does not ensure response against a subsequent infection.
Induced by infection or by contact with immunogens (immunity-producing agents such as vaccines, allergens, etc.).	Provided by readymade antibodies.
No harmful effects.	Has side effects.
e.g. immunity provided for diseases such as polio, hepatitis, etc.	e.g. immunity provided by mother to foetus.

Check Your LEARNING...

1 The first line of defence in our body is formed by?
2 Name the cells performing phagocytosis in human body.
3 Name the immunity developed in our body due to specific antigenic exposure.
4 Give one example of passive acquired immunity.

Other Methods of Defence against Microorganisms

Vaccination or Immunisation

It is the practise of injecting dead or weakened pathogens into the living body in order to develop resistance (immunity) against a particular disease without infection. The substance (antibody provoking agent) which is introduced into the body is called **vaccine**. It induces the formation of certain specific antibodies.
Vaccine can either be given orally (e.g. polio vaccine) or in the form of injections, e.g. TAB vaccine (for typhoid), Salk's vaccine (for poliomyelitis).

National immunisation schedules in India are as follows

Vaccines	Protections	Numbers of doses	Vaccination schedules
BCG (Bacillus Calmette Guerin)-Freeze-dried vaccine	Tuberculosis	1	At birth (up to 1 year if not given earlier).
OPV (Oral Polio Vaccine)- Liquid vaccine	Poliomyelitis	5	Birth dose for institutional deliveries, primary three doses at 6th, 10th and 14th weeks and one booster dose at 16-24th month of age.
Hepatitis– B-Liquid vaccine	Hepatitis-B	4	Birth dose (within 24 hours) for institutional deliveries, primary three doses at 6th, 10th and 14th weeks.
DPT (Diphtheria, Pertussis and Tetanus Toxoid)-Liquid vaccine	Diphtheria, pertussis and tetanus	5	Three doses at 6th, 10th and 14th weeks and two booster doses at 16-24th month and 5-6 years of age.
TT (Tetanus Toxoid) - Liquid vaccine	Tetanus	2	10 years and 16 years of age. For pregnant woman, two doses given (one dose if previously vaccinated within 3 years).
Hi-B (Haemophilus- influenza type B) (given-as pentavalent containing HiB +DPT + Hep-B in selected state)–Liquid vaccine	Hi-B pneumonia and Hi-B meningitis	3	6th, 10th and 14th weeks of age.

Antibiotics

These are chemical substances secreted by microorganisms, used against other pathogens in order to kill or prevent their growth inside the body, e.g. penicillin (first antibiotic that was discovered by **Alexander Fleming** in 1929 from a fungi *Penicillium notatum*), streptomycin, chloromycin, ampicillin, etc. Now-a-days, they can be produced synthetically. These are primarily used as a medicine. They also act as food preservatives, used in treating animal infections and to control plant diseases.

Antiseptics

These are mild chemical substances used to kill germs. These are applied to the living tissue/skin to reduce the possibility of infection or putrefaction, e.g. carbolic acid, iodine, boric acid, benzoic acid, etc.

Disinfectants

These are strong chemical substances applied to non-living objects to destroy microorganisms living on them. As disinfectants are strong in nature, they are harmful for human skin and should be used carefully, e.g. lime, lysol, phenol, formalin (40%), bordeaux mixture, etc.

Differences between Antiseptic and Disinfectant

Antiseptic	Disinfectant
It is applied on the body to kill germs.	It is applied on non-living objects and places where germs can grow and multiply.
It is a mild treatment.	It is a strong treatment.
It does not cause any harm to the body, e.g. iodine	It causes harm to the body, e.g. bordeaux mixture.

Antitoxins

These are chemical substances produced inside the body in response to the entry of foreign poisonous substance or toxins to neutralise its effect, e.g. antivenoms for snake bite is produced inside host.

Note In 1930s, a group of chemicals known as **sulphonamides** were discovered. They proved to be effective in treating many bacterial diseases. These are rarely used now. Examples are sulphadiazine and sulphanilamide.

Serum

It is an antitoxin rich blood preparation (blood plasma) used against a specific disease. This yellow coloured fluid is obtained when blood gets devoid of blood cells and clotting factor or fibrinogen. It contains proteins that are not used in clotting, electrolytes, hormones, antibodies, antigens and external substances (e.g. drugs). Serum can be injected into the body of a patient against a specific disease for which it is prepared. The antibodies present in the serum neutralise the antigens and the patient begins to recover. Serum helps in providing passive immunity.

Check Your LEARNING...

1 How can you immunise an individual against disease?
2 Who discovered the first antibiotic?
3 Name two disinfectants found in our homes.
4 Which substance is released in body against the foreign poisonous substance?
5 What is a serum?

Health Organisations

Organisations that make programmes for the maintenance of public health are known as health organisations. These organisations work at different levels in order to promote proper growth and development of individuals.

Categories of Health Organisations

Each and every country is concerned about the health of its people. Thus, several organisations work at different levels to provide proper facilities. These are divided into three main categories

1. Local Bodies

These organisations look after the sanitation (i.e. removal of garbage, sewage and other wastes), supply of proper drinking water, timely vaccination of children to protect them from diseases, etc. These include town area committees, municipal corporations and other local NGOs, etc.

2. National Organisations or National Programmes

Many national agencies, research centres in India are actively engaged in removing infectious diseases and other health problems of the country, e.g. National Malaria Eradication Programme (NMEP), Tuberculosis Programme (TBP), Pulse Polio Programme (PPP), National Cholera Control Programme (NCCP), etc.

3. International Organisations

Several organisations are working at international level to solve health issues and other related problems of the world. Two such organisations are described in detail below

(i) **World Health Organisation** (WHO) It is a special agency of United Nations Organisation (UNO) which was established in 1948. Its headquarter is situated in **Geneva**. 194 member states are a part of this organisation.

WHO : Emblem

Main activities of WHO are as follows

- To act as the directing and coordinating authority on international health work.
- To promote technical cooperation.
- To assist governments, upon request, in strengthening health services.
- To establish and stimulate the establishment of international standards for biological, pharmaceutical and similar products and to standardise diagnostic procedures.
- To promote and support projects for research on diseases.
- To collect and supply information about diseases of epidemic nature such as plague, ebola, etc.

- To supply information about latest developments related to the use of vaccines.
- To organise campaigns for controlling the spread of various epidemic (widespread) and endemic (local) diseases.
- To suggest quarantine measures (isolation of patient) to prevent spread of disease to others.
- To lay pharmaceutical standards for important drugs to ensure purity and size of the doses.

(ii) **Red Cross** It is an organisation that was formed with the original purpose of providing medical help to the wounded soldiers. It is a national as well as an international agency. This was later extended to include alleviation and prevention of human suffering in both peace and war. Red coloured cross painted on white background is the emblem of Red Cross Organisation. **Red Cross Day** is celebrated on **8th May.**

Red Cross : Emblem

The activities of red cross include

- Care and treatment of soldiers wounded in war.
- Providing relief to victims of natural calamities like earthquake, famine, flood, etc., through procurement and supply of food, medicines, etc., to needy people.
- Providing ambulance services, arranging blood through voluntary donations, etc., for people and supplying the same to the hospitals, etc.
- Looking after maternity and child welfare centres.
- Training of midwives, etc.
- To educate people in road safety.

Check Your LEARNING...

1. Mention any two national level health agencies working in India.
2. Name the special agency which looks after the work of WHO.
3. Name any two epidemic diseases.
4. When is the Red Cross Day celebrated?
5. Write two main activities of WHO.

QUiCK Revision

- **Health** is a state of complete physical, mental and social well-being.
- Human body is exposed to many microorganisms, but does not get diseased every time due to the presence of body's own defence system.
- Defence system in our body works in two ways
  - (i) Local defence system including physical barriers, germ killing secretions, coughing, sneezing, vomiting and White Blood Cells (WBCs)
  - (ii) Immune system
- **Immunity** is the ability of a person to resist or defend itself from the development of disease by the entry of foreign substances. It develops when local defence system becomes ineffective. **Immunity** is of two types
  - (i) **Innate or Inborn immunity** It occurs without any external stimulation or previous infection.
  - (ii) **Adapted or Acquired immunity** Resistance to a disease which an individual acquires during his lifetime. Acquired immunity is of two types, **actively acquired immunity** and **passively acquired immunity.**
- **Antibodies** These are special chemicals produced in response to antigens or their secretions. They are proteins by nature.
- **Vaccination** It is the phenomenon of injecting dead or weakened pathogens into the living body in order to develop resistance (immunity) against a particular disease in individual without infection. The substance (antibody provoking agent) which is introduced is called **vaccine.**
- **Antibiotics** These are strong chemical substances secreted by microorganisms. These are used against other pathogens in order to kill or prevent their growth inside the body, e.g. penicillin.
- **Antiseptics** These are mild chemical substances used to kill germs. These are applied to the living tissue/skin to reduce the possibility of infection or putrefaction, e.g. carbolic acid, lysol, iodine, boric acid, benzoic acid, etc.
- **Disinfectants** These are strong chemical substances applied to non-living objects to destroy microorganisms living on it.
- **Antitoxins** The chemical substance produced inside the body in response to the entry of foreign poisonous substance to neutralise its effect, e.g. antivenoms.
- **Health organisations** make programmes for the maintenance of public health. These organisations work at different levels in order to reduce human sufferings related to their health.
- The **health organisations** are classified into three categories
  - (i) **Local bodies** All municipal corporations and municipalities in cities and town area committees.
  - (ii) **National programmes** NMEP, NCCP, TBP, PPP.
  - (iii) **International organisations** WHO and Red Cross.

Chapter Practice

Section-I

1 Mark Questions

1. Name the following.
   (i) Barrier that prevents entry of pathogens into the body by its outer tough layer.
   (ii) Immunity acquired after first attack of the disease.
   (iii) Immunity received from outside that is short-lived and provides less protection.
   (iv) Immunity effective only after a certain time gap.
   (v) Immunity provided by mother to growing foetus.
   (vi) The vaccine that provides immunity against polio.
   (vii) Organisations that look after removal of garbage, sewage, etc., so as to protect people from diseases.
   (viii) Organisation that directs and coordinates authority on international health work and promote technical cooperation.
   (ix) Organisation that looks after maternal and child welfare centres.

Ans. (i) Skin
(ii) Natural immunity
(iii) Passive immunity
(iv) Active immunity
(v) Naturally acquired passive immunity
(vi) Salk's vaccine
(vii) Local bodies
(viii) WHO (World Health Organisation)
(ix) Red Cross

2. Correct and rewrite the following statements by changing the underlined words.
   (i) <u>Platelets</u> are a part of body's defence system.
   (ii) <u>Acquired</u> immunity is non-specific to antigens.
   (iii) Vaccine induces the formation of certain <u>antigens</u>.
   (iv) Alexander Fleming in 1929, discovered the first antibiotic called <u>streptomycin</u>.
   (v) Disinfectants are <u>mild</u> chemicals applied to non-living objects to destroy the microbes living on them.

Ans. (i) Leucocytes (WBCs) are a part of body's defence system.
(ii) Natural or Inborn or innate immunity is non-specific to antigens.
(iii) Vaccine induces the formation of certain antibodies.
(iv) Alexander Fleming in 1929, discovered the first antibiotic called penicillin.
(v) Disinfectants are strong chemicals applied to non-living objects to destroy the microbes living on them.

3. Give biological reasons for the following.
   (i) We sneeze whenever we inhale any kind of dust particle along with the air that we breathe.
   (ii) WBCs defend the body against various infections and diseases.

Ans. (i) Sneezing is the intense body response to directly throw out the dust particle or any foreign substance inhaled that interferes with normal respiration.
(ii) WBCs have the ability to fight with the germs or foreign substances by engulfing them through the process of phagocytosis. Thus, providing defence against infections and diseases.

4. (i) Match the following columns.

Column I	Column II
A. Penicillin	1. Bordeaux
B. Antiseptic	2. Alexander Fleming
C. Disinfectant	3. BCG
D. Vaccine	4. Boric acid

(ii) Match the following columns.

Column I	Column II
A. Toxin	1. Phagocytosis
B. Slimy secretion	2. Passive immunity
C. WBCs	3. Snake venom
D. Serum	4. Mucus

(iii) Match the following columns.

Column I	Column II
A. BCG	1. Ensure purity of doses
B. Chloromycin	2. Used as food preservative
C. Iodine	3. Antiseptic
D. WHO	4. Tuberculosis
E. Antibiotics	5. Antibiotics
	6. Antigen

(iv) Match the following columns.

Column I	Column II
A. Physical barriers	1. Passive immunity
B. Antigens	2. Induce antibody formation
C. Side effects	3. First line of defence
D. Vaccine	4. Innate immunity
	5. Foreign substances

Ans. (i) A-2, B-4, C-1, D-3
(ii) A-3, B-4, C-1, D-2
(iii) A-4, B-5, C-3, D-1, E-2
(iv) A-3, B-5, C-1, D-2

5. Choose the correct answer from the four options given below.

(i) Which of the following statements is true for health?

(a) A state of complete physical well-being
(b) A state of complete mental well-being
(c) A state of complete social well-being
(d) All of the above

Ans. (d)

(ii) Introduction of dead or weak pathogens into the body is called

(a) antitoxin (b) vaccination
(c) sterilisation (d) immunisation

Ans. (b)

(iii) Which of the following is correct for passive immunity?

(a) It is received from outside
(b) Provides effective protection
(c) It has no side effects
(d) It is induced by immunogens or by infection

Ans. (a)

(iv) The antibiotic penicillin is obtained from

(a) protozoan (b) bacteria
(c) virus (d) fungus

Ans. (d)

(v) Foreign invaders which affect our health badly, include

(a) bacteria (b) fungi
(c) viruses (d) All of these

Ans. (d)

(vi) Which of the following cells show phagocytosis?

(a) Erythrocytes
(b) Thromboplasts
(c) Leucoplasts
(d) None of these

Ans. (c)

6. Fill in the blanks by using suitable words.

(i) ...... is a state of complete physical, mental and social well-being.

(ii) Our skin acts as a ...... barrier.

(iii) ...... also act as a part of our body's defence system.

(iv) ...... are the foreign molecules that enter the body and induce the formation of an antibody.

(v) Immunity developed by an individual after birth is called ...... immunity.

(vi) ...... are mild chemical substances used to kill germs.

(vii) The headquarter of WHO is in ....

Ans. (i) Health (ii) physical
(iii) WBCs (leucocytes) (iv) Antigens
(v) acquired (vi) Antiseptics
(vii) Geneva

7. Choose the odd one out from the following terms given below and name the category to which other three belong.

(i) Skin, Saliva, Hair, Mucus
(ii) Iodine, Boric acid, Phenol, Benzoic acid
(iii) Lysol, Mercurochrome, Lime, Bordeaux mixture

Ans. (i) **Odd term** Saliva.
Rest three act as physical barriers to defend body against diseases and infections.

(ii) **Odd term** Phenol.
Rest three are antiseptics used to kill germs.

(iii) **Odd term** Mercurochrome.
Rest three are are disinfectants.

8. Given below is a set of five terms each. Rewrite the terms in correct order in a logical sequence beginning with the term that is underlined.

<u>Active immunity</u>, Antigen, Antibody, Bacteria, Lymphocytes

Ans. Active immunity, Bacteria, Antigen, Lymphocytes, Antibody

9. Expand the following biological abbreviations.

(i) OPV (ii) TT (iii) NMEP
(iv) TBP (v) WHO

Ans. (i) Oral Polio Vaccine
(ii) Tetanus Toxoid
(iii) National Malaria Eradication Programme
(iv) Tuberculosis Programme
(v) World Health Organisation

10. State whether the given statements are true or false. Correct and rewrite the false statement.

(i) Innate immunity is also called natural or inborn immunity.

(ii) Active immunity is produced by itself.

(iii) The vaccine used to immunise the person against typhoid is BCG vaccine.

(iv) Penicillin obtained from *Penicillium notatum* is an antibody.

(v) Antibiotics are obtained from fungi and bacteria.

(vi) Chemicals applied to spots and places to kill harmful microorganisms are called disinfectants.

(vii) DDT is an example of disinfectant.

(viii) Serum includes proteins that are not used in clotting and all electrolytes.

(ix) Antibodies and hormones are both present in serum.

(x) Red cross day is celebrated on 8th May.

Ans. (i) True (ii) True

(iii) False, the vaccine used to immunise the person against typhoid is TAB vaccine.

(iv) False, penicillin obtained from *Penicillium notatum* is an antibiotic.

(v) True (vi) True
(vii) False, DDT is a pesticide
(viii) True (ix) True
(x) True

11. Give one example of the following.
(i) Passive acquired immunity
(ii) Oral vaccine
(iii) A disinfectant

Ans. (i) Antibodies provided in case of snake bite.
(ii) Oral polio vaccine (for polio)
(iii) Formalin (40%)

12. State the main function of the following.
(i) Mucus (ii) Antigens
(iii) Antibiotics (iv) Serum

Ans. (i) Mucus is the slimy secretion of epithelial lining of various organs that prevents the entry of germs inside the body.
(ii) Antigens are foreign substances which are capable of eliciting immune response.
(iii) Antibiotics are used against other pathogens in order to kill or prevent their growth inside the body.
(iv) Serum provides passive immunity.

13. Mention one difference in each of the following pairs on the basis of what is given in the bracket.
(i) Active and Passive immunity (effect)
(ii) Vaccine and Vaccination (definition)
(iii) DPT and BCG (used against)
(iv) Antibiotic and Antibody (source)

Ans. (i) Difference between active and passive immunity is as follows

Active immunity	Passive immunity
It is effective and long lasting.	It is less effective and short- lived.

(ii) Difference between vaccine and vaccination is as follows

Vaccine	Vaccination
A preparation that consists of weakened or dead germs to develop immunity against the germs of a specific diseases.	It is the introduction of any kind of disease causing microbes into the body of living beings to develop immunity.

(iii) Difference between DPT and BCG is as follows

DPT	BCG
It is used against diphtheria pertussis and tetanus.	It is used against tuberculosis.

(iv) Difference between antibiotic and antibody is as follows

Antibiotic	Antibody
It is secreted by microorganisms.	It is found in blood of organisms.

14. Give biological/technical terms for the following.
(i) Ability of a person to resist or defend itself from the development of diseases due to entry of foreign particles.
(ii) An antitoxin rich blood preparation containing proteins.
(iii) Organisation that look after sanitation supply of proper drinking water timely vaccination of children, etc.

Ans. (i) Immunity (ii) Serum (iii) Local bodies

15. Briefly explain the following terms.
(i) Immunity (ii) Active acquired immunity
(iii) Antitoxins

Ans. (i) Immunity is the ability of a person to resist or defend itself from the development of diseases due to the entry of foreign particles.
(ii) Active acquired immunity developed within an individual due to previous encounter with the antigen.
(iii) Antitoxins are chemical substances produced inside the body in response to the entry of toxins to neutralise its effect.

16. Answer the following questions briefly.
(i) When does the immunity of a person starts functioning?
(ii) How are vaccines supplied to an individual's body?
(iii) How is serum inserted into the body of the patient?
(iv) When was World Health Organisation (WHO) established?

Ans. (i) Immunity of a person starts functioning when the local defence system fails or is ineffective due to the poisonous secretions of certain microbes entering deeper tissues and various organ systems.
(ii) Vaccines can either be given orally (e.g. polio vaccine) or in the form of injections, e.g. TAB vaccine.
(iii) Serum is injected (and not given orally) into the body of a patient against a specific disease.
(iv) WHO is special agency of United Nations Organisation (UNO) which was established in 1948.

2 Marks Questions

17. Write any two merits of local defence system.

Ans. Two merits of local defence system are
- It starts working instantaneously.
- It is not dependent on the previous exposure to infections.

18. How is immunity classified?

Ans. Immunity is classified into two main types
- **Innate immunity** It is present since birth.
- **Acquired immunity** It is acquired by an individual during lifetime.

19. What are sulphonamides? What are their uses?

Ans. Sulphonamides are group of chemicals which proved effective in many types of bacterial diseases. They interfere with the metabolism of bacteria which kills them.

20. Write the names of any four defence methods against microorganisms.

Ans. The four methods of defence are
(i) Vaccination (ii) Antibiotics (iii) Antitoxins
(iv) Antiseptics

3 Marks Questions

21. What are the various parts and secretions of the body that constitute the first line of defence?

Ans. The following parts and secretions of the body constitute the first line of defence
(i) **Skin** It secretes sweat in order to prevent entry of germs/pathogens.
(ii) **Nasal secretions** These do not allow the entry of foreign substances in the nasal passage.
(iii) **Earwax** in the ear has the ability to kill germs.

22. Write three major functions of WHO.

Ans. Three major functions of WHO are
(i) It assists countries to improve health and sanitation services.
(ii) It promotes medical education and training.
(iii) It regulates quarantine measures to prevent the spread of disease to unaffected areas.

Section-II [5 Marks]

Structured Questions

1. Study the diagram given below and answer the questions that follows.

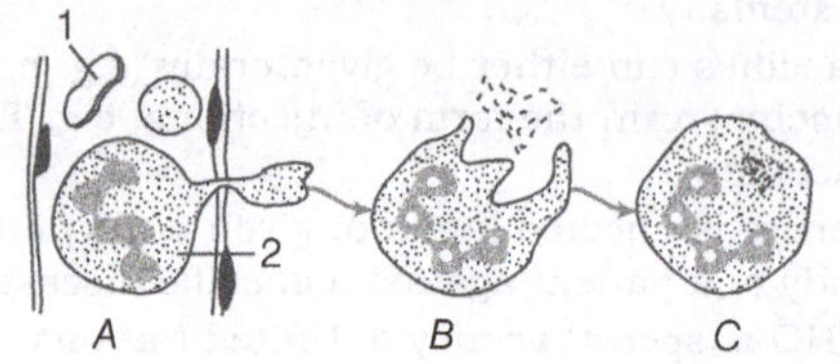

(i) Name the cell labelled 1.
(ii) Identify the phenomenon occurring in *A*.
(iii) Mention two structural differences between 1 and 2.
(iv) Name the process occurring in *B* and *C*.
(v) State the importance of the above process (iv) in the human body.

Ans. (i) The cell labelled 1 is white blood cells.
(ii) The phenomenon occurring in *A* is diapedesis.
(iii) Two structural differences between WBCs (2) and RBCs (1) are as follows

RBCs	WBCs
Biconcave in shape.	Amoeboid in shape.
They lack nucleus	They have nucleus.

(iv) The process phagocytosis is occurring in *B* and *C*.
(v) During phagocytosis, WBCs engulf bacteria and destroy them. Thus, protecting the body from infections and diseases.

2. Our body is invaded by various harmful pathogen, but most of the time we remain healthy due to the presence of body own's defence system.
(i) Name any two secretions which prevent entry of germs into the body.
(ii) How is local defence system beneficial?
(iii) Name the two secretions from blood that destroy harmful germs.
(iv) Which type of immunity does not show any side effects?
(v) How can immunity be boosted?

Ans. (i) Tears (in eyes) and nasal secretion (nostrils) prevent entry of germs into the body.
(ii) Local defence system is effective against almost all types of infectious agents and starts working instantly.
(iii) Antibody and antitoxin secretions from blood can destroy harmful germs.
(iv) Active immunity does not show any side effects.
(v) Immunity can be boosted by eating a healthy diet and avoiding junk food. This keeps the immune system strong.

Chapter Assessment

Section-I

1 Mark Questions

1. Name the following.
   (i) Name the disease for which TT vaccine is given.
   (ii) The germ killing substances found in saliva and tears.
   (iii) A strong germ killing substance applied on non-living object.
   (iv) One combined vaccine given to babies in order to build immunity against three diseases.
   (v) Organisation that educates people in accident prevention.
2. Correct and rewrite the following statements by changing the underlined words.
   (i) Vaccination is the artificial development of immunity.
   (ii) Sulphuric acid is present in stomach to kill germs.
   (iii) Local defence system is effective against non-infectious diseases.
   (iv) WHO and Red Cross are national organisations.
3. Give biological reasons for the following.
   The stomach cavity is filled with a strong acid like HCl that act as local defence system of body.
4. (i) Match the following columns.

Column I	Column II
A. Lymphocytes	1. Smallpox
B. Skin	2. Passive immunity
C. Immediately effective	3. Tetanus
D. Living fully poisonous germs	4. Physical barrier
	5. Produce killer cells

   (ii) Match the following columns.

Column I	Column II
A. TAB	1. Diphtheria
B. Salk's vaccine	2. Polio
C. Toxoids	3. Tuberculosis
D. BCG	4. Typhoid

5. Choose the correct answer from the four options given below.
   (i) The immunity induced in one's own body with the help of vaccination is
   (a) active
   (b) passive
   (c) natural
   (d) None of the above
   (ii) TAB vaccine is used to build immunity against
   (a) tuberculosis
   (b) typhoid
   (c) malaria
   (d) All of the above
   (iii) Antitoxins are available for
   (a) tetanus
   (b) snake venom
   (c) diphtheria
   (d) All of the above
6. Fill in the blanks by using suitable words.
   (i) Penicillin is a/an ....
   (ii) Number of doses for DPT vaccine is ....
   (iii) WHO was established in the year ....
7. Choose the odd one out from the following terms given below and name the category to which other three belong.
   (i) Lime, Phenol, Ampicillin, DDT
   (ii) BCG, Cholera, Rabies, Tuberculosis.
8. Expand the following biological abbreviations.
   (i) DPT (ii) PPP (iii) NCCP
9. State the following statements are true or false. Correct and rewrite the false statements.
   (i) OPV is a vaccine against tetanus.
   (ii) Lysol is an antibiotic.
   (iii) Antibodies eat up germs.
   (iv) Antigens induce the formation of antibodies.
10. Give one example of the following.
   (i) Antiseptic
   (ii) Local bodies
   (iii) Antibiotics

11. Mention one difference in each of the following pairs on the basis of what is given in the bracket.
   (i) DPT and BCG (expanded form)
   (ii) Antiseptic and Disinfectant (functions)
   (iii) WHO and Red Cross (activity)

12. Give suitable biological/technical terms for the following.
   (i) Resistance developed to disease causing germs or their toxins by introducing killed germs.
   (ii) Chemical substances which are also used in controlling plant diseases.

13. Answer the following questions briefly.
   (i) Which part of the body is responsible for maintaining an individual's health?
   (ii) What role is played by WBCs in providing prevention against germs?
   (iii) What is the emblem of Red Cross Organisation?

2 Marks Questions

14. Write the names of two vaccines and mention the diseases against which they are effective.

15. Write down any two roles of the Red Cross Organisation.

3 Marks Questions

16. Mention three uses of antibiotics?

17. What are health organisations? What is their role? Name the different categories of health organisations.

Section-II [5 Marks]

Structured Questions

18. Study the given figure and answer the questions that follows.

   (i) Which organisation does the above figure emblem, represent?
   (ii) Under which agency, does the above organisation fall?
   (iii) Where is its headquarter located?
   (iv) In which year, was WHO established?
   (v) How many members are a part of this organisation?

19. The ability of a person to resist or defend itself from the development of disease due to the entry of foreign particles is called immunity.
   (i) Name the two types of acquired immunity.
   (ii) What is the name given to the proteins produced in the blood to fight and destroy harmful bacteria?
   (iii) Which type of immunity has no harmful effect?
   (iv) Why innate immunity is known as non-specific immunity?
   (v) Give example of active acquired immunity.

For explanations scan the given QR Code

Olympiad Section*

Brain Teasing Questions asked in Previous Olympiads

1 Immunity is the state of protection against foreign agents. It can be conferred either actively by activating a person's immune system or passively without activating his own immune system. Following are different examples of how immunity can be attained.

I. Antibodies passed from mother to the child through breastfeeding.
II. Treatment of humans bitten by venomous snakes with antivenin, a serum from sheep or horses that have been immunised against the venom.
III. Infection with hepatitis-A virus and subsequent recovery from it.
IV. Administration of hepatitis-A vaccines.

Which of the above are examples of passive immunity? **[INJSO 2018]**

(a) I and II (b) II and III
(c) Only I (d) I and IV

2 Which of the following defences of the body against foreign particles constitute innate immunity? **[NSEB 2016]**

I. Antimicrobial proteins
II. Mucous membrane
III. Antibodies
IV. Phagocytic cells
V. Inflammatory response
VI. Cytotoxic lymphocytes

(a) I, III, IV and V (b) II, IV, V and VI
(c) III, IV, V and VI (d) I, II, IV and V

3 Which of the following is an example of active acquired immunity? **[INJSO 2014]**

(a) Nursing mother transfers some antibodies to infant through colostrum (breast milk)
(b) Person recovered from measles does not get measles again
(c) Injection of antitetanus is given after injury
(d) We do not suffer from Distemper, a fatal canine disease

4 If you suspect major deficiency of antibodies in a person, to which of the following would you look for confirmatory evidence?

(a) Serum globulins
(b) Fibrinogen in the plasma
(c) Number of RBCs
(d) Number of WBCs

5 Which of the following is not a natural way of destroying bacterial infection?

(a) Antibodies produced in the body
(b) Production of HCl in the stomach
(c) Antibiotics taken orally or by injection
(d) Phagocytosis by WBCs

6 Antivenom against snake poison contains

(a) antigens (b) antigen-antibody
(c) antibodies (d) enzymes

7 Why does the human body need more than its skin to function as a barrier to infecting pathogens?

(a) Skin works only against some types of bacteria. To prevent the entry of other pathogens, other physical or chemical barriers are needed
(b) Skin does not provide a broad coverage against invasion of the body by any foreign particle, so it is not a very effective barrier
(c) Pathogens could enter the body through several places that are not covered by skin that need to have a barrier to prevent infection
(d) Skin acts only as a chemical barrier against pathogens. The body also needs physical barriers to prevent various types of infection

8 What is the mechanism that skin uses to protect against diseases caused by organism?

(a) High pH
(b) Mucus
(c) Tears
(d) Desiccations

Answers

1. (a) **2.** (d) **3.** (b) **4.** (a) **5.** (c) **6.** (c) **7.** (a) **8.** (b)

**These questions may or may not be asked in the examination, have been given just for additional practice required for olympiads, scholarship exams etc.* *For detailed explanations refer Page No. 230.*

CHAPTER 15

Waste Generation and Management

Chapter Inside

• Wastes and their Sources • Waste Management

Ever since the human society has been evolving with huge population growth, an ever increasing demand for primary needs of food, shelter and clothing, etc., was observed along with rapidly growing industrialisation and urbanisation, the amount of waste being generated is also increasing. In this chapter, we will focus on the different types of waste and their management.

Wastes and their Sources

One of the disturbing issues leading to environmental imbalance is the improper management of generated waste.

The useless, left-over or discarded substances are called as **waste substances**. These are of three types, such as **solid** in the form of household wastes, farm wastes, industrial wastes, etc., **liquid** in the form of chemical wastes and **gaseous** in the form of smoke from chimney and automobiles, etc.

Sources of Wastes

Wastes are generated from a number of activities and sources such as

(i) Domestic Wastes

The wastes generated due to daily household work in our surroundings are classified as domestic wastes. An average home produces the following types of wastes

(a) **Kitchen waste** includes waste generated from the kitchen, e.g peelings of vegetables and fruits, any stale or rotten food items, etc.

(b) **Plastic** used in packing and wrapping of objects, discarded or broken plastic, objects including bottle, toys, etc.

(c) **Glass** in the form of broken glass utensils, mirrors, containers, window panes, etc.

(d) **Rags** include a huge variety of waste pieces of cloth, torn towel, handkerchief, old bed sheets, blankets, etc.

(e) **Paper** includes daily newspapers and magazines.

(ii) Industrial Wastes

The waste materials in this category are most threatening to the environment as compared to the other wastes. Industrial waste materials are typically constituted by toxic chemicals, metals, plastic, paints, oils, inorganic chlorinated solvents, ashes, etc. Some of the industries that release maximum toxic waste products are

(a) **Mining operations** India alone consists of hundreds of mines, which extract copper, silver, gold, zinc, iron, coal, etc. During their processing, huge amount of wastes are produced. These wastes are generally called **mine tailing**. The mine tailing mixed with other materials can be used for making tiles, masonry, cement, etc.

(b) **Cement factories** Cement manufacturing produces solid, liquid and gaseous wastes. Solid wastes are used in construction activities or dumped in landfills.

The liquid wastes including wash off are treated to remove harmful substances and then released into the rivers, ponds, etc. Gaseous wastes like fly ash, which contain solid particles are released into the environment.

(c) **Oil refineries and petrochemical units** Release mixture of hydrocarbon containing organic acids, styrofoam, motor oil, SO_2, soot, etc.

(d) **Construction units** Construction sites produce wastes like broken bricks, waste stones, pebbles, wood wastes, concrete, plaster, metal, etc.

(e) **Paper and pulp industries** Release toxic effluents like wood chips, cellulose fibres, chemicals, etc.

(iii) Agricultural Wastes

Agricultural waste is a waste produced as a consequence of agricultural operations. Modern technologies of agricultural practices incorporate extensive use of chemicals like pesticides, insecticides, fertilisers, etc. Agricultural wastes mainly include

(a) **Animal wastes** from fields, dairy farming, excreta, etc.

(b) **Plant wastes** from harvesting, threshing, winnowing, etc. It includes organic matter like carbohydrates, fats, crop residues, etc.

(c) **Bagasse** is the plant residue (as of sugarcane after extracting the sugarcane juice). These are used as fire wood or in paper industry.

(d) **Pesticides** and **fertilisers** collect into the soil and are washed off with the irrigation and rainwater, leading to water pollution.

Note Threshing is the beating action of separating the seeds from husk and stem of the plant using thresher machine. This process generates maximum wastes among all agricultural practices.

The crop residues should not be burned as it destroys the biological components of soil and pollutes air. Instead, it should be used to generate energy.

(iv) Municipal Wastes

These include the solid and liquid wastes produced due to activities in home or offices, restaurants and other public places.

They also include papers, foils and kitchen washings and faecal matter from toilets. Sewage is the waste water that runs into the drains. It is categorised as degradable and non-biodegradable. It carries human excreta along with other materials.

Contaminants/Constituents of the sewage can be studied as

Organic impurities	Human excreta, animal wastes, oil, fruits, vegetables, etc.
Inorganic impurities	Nitrates, phosphates, metals, pesticides and fertilisers.
Microbes	Bacteria, fungi and viruses.

Septic tanks are used to degrade the degradable part. The non-degradable part is dumped or buried at safe places.

(v) E-Waste

It is a common, informal name for the electronic wastes.

Generation of E-waste

These wastes are considered dangerous as certain components of these products contain materials that are hazardous, depending upon their condition and density, e.g. old computers, television, mobile phones, DVD players, printers, refrigerators, electronic toys, lead-acid batteries, fluorescent tubes, etc.

Effects on the Environment and Human Health

E-wastes are the most rapidly increasing solid waste problem in today's world. The potential crisis is not just the amount but also the toxicity of their constituents. Adverse effects that are produced, if these wastes are not properly handled are

- Contamination of water resources
- Air pollution
- Leaching of toxicants in soil
- Disturbance in ecological system

Chemical toxins released from e-waste include lead, mercury, cadmium, nitrates, etc. Most of these wastes are non-biodegradable and non-recyclable.

Disposal of E-waste

- Large scale e-wastes repair and refurbishment programmes are required worldwide.
- Many of these products can be reused or recycled in an environmentally sound manner.
- Special 'e-bins' should be placed at various points for dumping of discardable e-waste units.

Note Certain wastes that emit radioactive radiations are called **radioactive wastes**. Their disposal needs a lot of care as any carelessness can prove to be a threat to human life, e.g. uranium is a radioactive material that can be threatening to human life if disposed carelessly.

Biodegradable and Non-biodegradable Wastes

Waste materials can be in the form of solid, liquid or gas. On the basis of their decomposition by environmental factors, they can be classified as

(i) Biodegradable Wastes

These are the waste materials that can be broken down in the soil by the action of soil microbes and other decomposers like fungi, e.g. fruit and vegetable peels, leaves, grasses, woods, clothes, papers, etc.

(ii) Non-biodegradable Wastes

These are the waste materials that cannot be decomposed in the soil. There is no natural process available for decomposition of these wastes, e.g. plastic bags, synthetic clothes, metal containers, radioactive and electronic wastes, etc. Some non-biodegradable wastes however can be recycled like plastic goods, metals, glasses, etc. Recycling is the only non-polluting and feasible solution for controlling non-biodegradable wastes.

Check Your LEARNING...

1 List an example of waste released from industrial activities.
2 Name the waste generated in oil refineries.
3 Mention one problem associated with e-waste.
4 What is biodegradable waste?
5 Enlist few examples of non-biodegradable wastes.

Waste Management

Accumulation of wastes poses serious problems to the environment. Use of technology contributes very little to solve this problem. But, without the involvement of people and their efforts, this cannot be achieved. It involves collection, processing and disposal of accumulated waste materials. It is a necessary step to control the increasing amount of waste materials.

Methods of Safe Disposal of Wastes

As we already know that wastes are produced in three forms, i.e. solid, liquid and gas. Their disposal also requires different suitable methods.

Forms of wastes	Methods of disposal
Solid wastes	Segregation, dumping, composting and incineration
Liquid wastes	Drainage and effluent treatment before discharge
Gaseous wastes	Use of scrubbers and electrostatic precipitators

1. Solid Wastes Disposal

The important methods of solid wastes disposal are as follows

(i) **Segregation** It refers to the separation of waste materials into different categories of wastes. The first step is to separate materials into reusable, biodegradable and non-biodegradable wastes.
The waste materials can also be segregated according to their features like
(a) Sharp-edged wastes like blades and knives.
(b) Inflammable wastes like batteries and spray cans.
(c) Recyclable wastes like plastic and glass.
(d) Infectious wastes like hospital wastes.

(ii) **Dumping** The process of depositing the collected wastes in an area is called dumping. Several sites are landmarked as waste disposal sites, known as **landfills**.
Proper method of disposal involves spreading of uniform thin layer which gets solidified. Before adding another layer of waste, a 3m layer of clean Earth is also added.

(iii) **Composting** It is a method of solid wastes disposal where the organic waste matter is allowed to decompose by microbes and soil organisms. In this method, the waste not only gets disposed but converts into fertiliser by natural process.

Following are the steps of composting
- A pit of about 5 m long, approximately 1.5 m wide and 1.5 m deep is dugged in the soil.
- The organic or biodegradable waste is piled up and layered in a loose manner for air passage.
- The layer is fully wetted with a watery mixture of cowdung and some mud.
- A second layer of mixed refuse is spread after few days so that decomposition of matter becomes faster.
- About 50-60 days later, the compost or manure is ready. It can be applied in the agricultural fields, garden, etc., for good growth.
- Composting with the help of earthworms is called **vermicomposting**.

Uses of Compost
- In nurseries, landscape sites, greenhouse, etc.
- Used by farmers and gardeners.

(iv) **Incineration** It is the disposal of waste materials by burning. The waste is subjected to controlled combustion releasing incombustible residues along with gaseous release. The end products are ashes and clinkers. Ashes are dumped in low land areas while clinkers are used as aggregate in low grade concrete.
Incineration is carried out to
- reduce the volume of waste materials.
- convert toxic wastes into less toxic residues.
- reduce the requirement of landfill sites.
- allow hygienic disposal of wastes.

2. Liquid Wastes Disposal

(i) **Drainage** The removal of surface or sub-surface water from any given area is called drainage. A functional drainage system
- prevents land/soil erosion.
- prevents accumulation of soluble salts.

Drainage system provides an open, adequate and readily accessible channel for uninterrupted flow of surface water.

(ii) **Effluent treatment before discharge** The waste in liquid form originates mainly from domestic and industrial sources. The sewage is treated in wastewater treatment plants before dumping it in the water bodies. The process involves physical, chemical and biological processes in order to remove the impurities.

The treatment of sewage is carried out in the following stages

(a) **Primary treatment** It is a process that involves physical removal of large as well as small particles from the sewage through filtration and sedimentation in primary settling tanks. Initially, the floating debris is removed by sequential filtration and then, soil and small pebbles are removed by sedimentation.
All solids undergo sedimentation and settle down to constitute the **primary sludge**. The supernatant left after removing primary sludge, constitutes the **effluent**. This effluent is taken out for **secondary treatment**.

(b) **Secondary treatment** It involves microbial degradation of organic matter. The primary effluent is passed into large aeration tanks, where it is constantly agitated mechanically. Air containing heterotrophic microorganisms is constantly pumped into the effluent to allow growth of aerobic microbes.
While growing, these microbes consume a major part of the organic matter, present in the effluent which significantly reduces the BOD (Biochemical Oxygen Demand).
The sewage water is further treated till the BOD reduces significantly. Then, the effluent of aeration tank is passed into a settling tank, where the bacterial 'flocs' are allowed to sediment. This sediment is called **activated sludge**.
A small part of the activated sludge is pumped back into the aeration tank to serve as bacterial inoculum. The remaining major part of the sludge is pumped into large tanks called **anaerobic sludge digesters** in which methanogenic bacteria digest the bacteria, fungi present in the sludge and a mixture of gases such as methane, hydrogen sulphide and carbon dioxide is produced. These gases form biogas which can be used as the source of energy as it is inflammable.
The effluent from the secondary treatment plant is generally released into natural water bodies like rivers and streams.

(c) **Tertiary treatment** It is a physio-chemical process. It involves disinfecting the water if it is to be used for domestic purposes. It is done by various methods such as reverse osmosis, treating with chlorine (chlorination), ozone gas or perchlorate salts.

3. Gaseous Wastes Disposal

Gaseous wastes occur in the form of smoke from factories, vehicles, etc. Increased production of CO_2, SO_2, NO_2, CO, etc., have led to problems like acid rain, global warming and greenhouse effect. Efforts have been made to minimise the gaseous release in environment in order to control air pollution. Some of these regulations are discussed below

(i) **Scrubbers** These are a simple and effective devices that are used to remove particulates and effluents from polluted air. They are also used to remove gases from the industrial exhausts, e.g. sulphur dioxide (SO_2). The exhaust is passed through a spray of lime or water. Water dissolves the gases and lime reacts with SO_2 to form a precipitate of calcium sulphate and sulphide. It washes out undesirable gases from the exhaust.

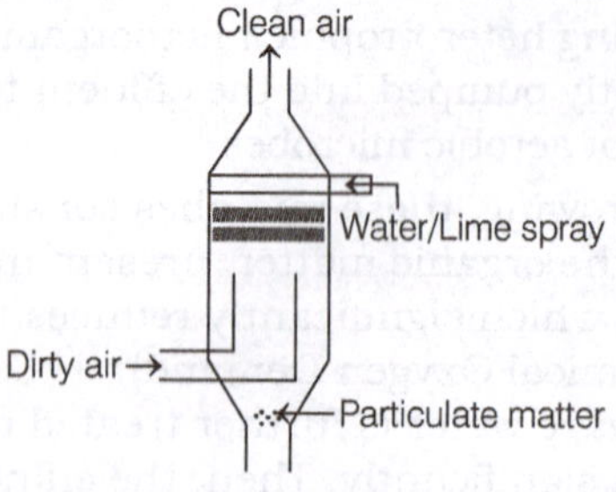

Scrubber

Scrubber can be of two types
- Wet scrubber
- Dry scrubber

(ii) **Electrostatic precipitator** It is the most widely used method and can approximately remove 99% of particulate matter from exhaust of thermal power plant. It has electrode wires of high voltage maintained at several thousands volts, which produces a corona that releases electrons.

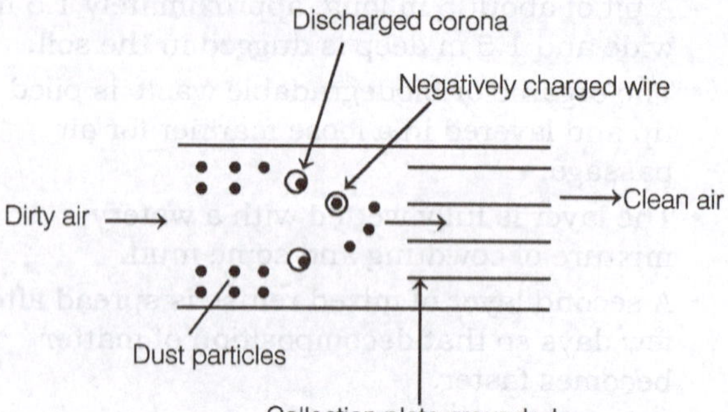

Electrostatic precipitator

These electrons get attached to the dust particles and give them negative charge. A collecting plate is there, which is grounded and positively charged and attracts the negatively charged dust particles.
When the air passes through the collecting plate, it gets cleaned. Velocity of air between the plates is maintained low to allow the dust particles to fall in.

Check Your LEARNING...

1. Explain the significance of a functional drainage system.
2. Define incineration.
3. Name the method of disposal of liquid wastes.
4. Name the two methods employed for quick sedimentation during secondary treatment of wastes.
5. Give one difference between scrubbers and electrostatic precipitators.

QUiCK Revision

- **Wastes** are discarded or left over materials. The terms 'rubbish' and 'trash' are often used interchangeably for waste materials. The waste materials can be either solid, liquid or gas. The various sources of wastes are municipal wastes, industrial wastes, mining wastes, hazardous wastes, defunct ships and electronic wastes.
- **Domestic wastes** mainly include newspapers, kitchen wastes, rags, plastic, glass, etc.
- **Industrial wastes** include scrap, effluents, sludge and fly ash. It consists of oxides of silica, aluminium and iron along with small quantities of heavy metals. **Mining wastes** include mine dust, rock tailings, slack and slag. Toxic metals and chemicals present in the mining waste destroy vegetation and produce many deformities in animal and human beings.
- **Agricultural wastes** are plant parts that are left after obtaining usable portions, animal wastes, fertilisers, etc.
- **Municipal wastes** are wastes from homes, shops, offices, school, street and road sweepings which are collected and disposed off by municipalities. The major components are waste paper, textiles, leather, metals, glass, plastic and polythene, food wastes, etc.
- **Electronic wastes** (e-waste) include irreparable computers, mobiles and other electronic goods.
- Control of **solid wastes** involves collection and categorisation of wastes, transport to disposal site and disposal of wastes. Disposal of wastes consists of recovery and recycling, source reduction, burning and dumping.
- The articles which can be recovered and recycled are tins, cans and other metal wastes, glass, plastic, rags, paper and cardboard.
- In source reduction, garbage and other organic wastes are taken out of urban areas and used for formation of compost to produce biogas and manure.
- **Burning** is combustion of solid wastes containing organic compounds in open places. It, however, produces offensive odours and air pollutants. Better methods for this are incineration and pyrolysis. Incineration is controlled aerobic combustion of wastes inside chambers at temperature of 900-1300°C.
- **Dumping** is piling of wastes on selected low lying land. It is of two types, open and sanitary.
- **Liquid wastes disposal** is done by sewage treatment plant before they are released into water bodies. It occurs *via*, physical removal of debris, i.e. **primary treatment**, biological degradation of organic matter, i.e. **secondary treatment** and disinfection of water, i.e. **tertiary treatment**.
- **Gaseous wastes disposal** is needed to reduce the level of toxic gases from the environment. Some most widely used devices of gaseous wastes disposal are electrostatic precipitators, gas scrubbers, catalytic converters, etc.

Chapter Practice

Section-I

1 Mark Questions

1. Name the following.
   (i) Any substance that is discarded after primary use or is useless.
   (ii) Waste that is generated as pieces of torn towel, old bed sheets, etc.
   (iii) Wastes that are typically constituted by toxic chemicals and are the most threatening.
   (iv) Waste generated after extraction of minerals from ores.
   (v) Industries which release toxic effluents like wood chips, cellulose fibres, etc.
   (vi) Waste generated from agricultural activities.
   (vii) Waste material excreted from the body of living organism.
   (viii) Solid and liquid wastes produced due to activities in home, offices or any other public places.
   (ix) Wastes which can be decomposed *via.* microbial activity.
   (x) The wastewater from different sources which runs-off into the drains.

Ans. (i) Waste
(ii) Rags
(iii) Industrial waste
(iv) Mine tailing
(v) Paper and pulp industries
(vi) Crop residue/Plant remains/Agricultural waste
(vii) Excreta
(viii) Municipal waste
(ix) Biodegradable waste
(x) Sewage

2. Correct and rewrite the following statements by changing the underlined words.
   (i) Stale or rotten food items are a part of municipal waste.
   (ii) Plastic comes in the form of mirrors, window panes, etc.
   (iii) Liquid wastes constitute farm waste.
   (iv) Excessive use of pesticides, insecticides, etc., contribute towards industrial waste.
   (v) E-wastes like old mobile phones are considered beneficial.

Ans. (i) Stale or rotten food items are a part of domestic waste categorised as kitchen waste.
(ii) Glass comes in the form of mirrors, window panes, etc.
(iii) Liquid wastes constitute chemical waste.
(iv) Excessive use of pesticides, insecticides, etc., contribute towards agricultural waste.
(v) E-wastes like old mobile phones are considered harmful.

3. Give biological reasons for the following.
   (i) Plant residues left after obtaining usable parts should not be burnt.
   (ii) E-wastes are generally considered hazardous.
   (iii) Nuclear power plants are harmful.
   (iv) Broken glass materials are considered as non-biodegradable.
   (v) Vehicles used for transportation of waste should not be rendered open.

Ans. (i) Plant residues left after obtaining usable parts should not be burnt as it destroys the biological components of soil and pollutes air.
(ii) E-wastes are generally considered hazardous because certain components of these products contain materials which are harmful in nature.
(iii) Nuclear power plants are harmful because the radioactive materials used in the generation of power (e.g. uranium) also generates a large amount of energy and remains active for thousands of years.
(iv) Broken glass materials are considered as non-biodegradable because they cannot be further decomposed to simpler forms due to which they persist in the environment for a very long period of time.
(v) Vehicles used for transportation of waste should not be rendered open rather should be covered so as to prevent waste from being scattered which will further prevent infections caused due to waste materials.

4. (i) Match the following columns.

	Column I		Column II
A.	Magazines and newspaper	1.	Paper and pulp industry
B.	Wood chips	2.	Inorganic chlorinated solvents
C.	Industrial waste	3.	Toxin released from e-waste
D.	Cadmium	4.	Vegetable peels
		5.	Paper waste

(ii) Match the following columns.

	Column I		Column II
A.	Catalytic converter	1.	Particulate matter
B.	Electrostatic precipitator	2.	SO_2 from industrial exhausts
C.	Ear cuffs	3.	High noise level
D.	Landfills	4.	Solid wastes

(iii) Match the following columns.

	Column I		Column II
A.	Plastic	1.	Non-biodegradable waste
B.	Infectious waste	2.	Reduce the requirement of landfill sites
C.	Landfills	3.	Physical removal of large and small particles
D.	Primary treatment	4.	Disposal sites
		5.	Hospital waste

(iv) Match the following columns.

	Column I		Column II
A.	Gaseous waste	1.	Acid rain
B.	Activated sludge	2.	Incineration
C.	Prevents land/soil erosion	3.	Drainage
D.	Reduce the volume of waste materials	4.	Removes majority of particulate matter
		5.	CO_2, SO_2, NO
		6.	Liquid waste disposal

Ans. (i) A-5, B-1, C-2, D-3
(ii) A-2, B-1, C-3, D-4
(iii) A-1, B-5, C-4, D-3
(iv) A-5, B-6, C-3, D-2

5. Choose the correct answer from the four options given below.

(i) The waste generated by human activities can be
(a) solid (b) liquid
(c) gas (d) All of these

Ans. (d)

(ii) The discarded solid materials which are produced due to various human activities are called
(a) solid wastes (b) industrial wastes
(c) electronic wastes (d) hospital wastes

Ans. (a)

(iii) Wastes commonly released from mining industry are
(a) coal (b) zinc
(c) copper (d) All of these

Ans. (d)

(iv) Which of the following is a degradable waste among those given below?
(a) Newspapers (b) Vegetable peels
(c) Plastic bags (d) Both (a) and (b)

Ans. (d)

(v) Which one of the following is the most harmful waste in today's time?
(a) Pesticides (b) E-waste
(c) Plastics (d) Sewage

Ans. (b)

(vi) Which among the following is an e-waste?
(a) Electronic motherboards
(b) Computer
(c) CDs
(d) All of the above

Ans. (d)

(vii) Separating the waste materials into different categories is called
(a) recycling (b) segregation
(c) composting (d) dumping

Ans. (b)

(viii) Among the options given below, which method is a long term process?
(a) Composting (b) Scrubbing
(c) Dumping (d) Incineration

Ans. (a)

(ix) In the effluent treatment of water, which step facilitates the killing of germs in water?
(a) Flocculation (b) Coagulation
(c) Chlorination (d) Filtration

Ans. (c)

(x) Air scrubbers are used to remove
(a) liquid (b) particulate matter
(c) solid wastes (d) Both (b) and (c)

Ans. (b)

(xi) Electrostatic precipitator works on which principle?
(a) Magnetism
(b) Current
(c) Thermal effect of electricity
(d) Static electricity

Ans. (b)

6. Fill in the blanks by using suitable words.

(i) Domestic wastes include ...... and ....
(ii) Glass objects are .... wastes.
(iii) .... is a type of industrial waste.
(iv) .... is a waste generated in oil refineries.
(v) Computer parts and mobile phones constitute .... wastes.
(vi) For vermicomposting, the use of .... is required.
(vii) The waste disposal method which employs burning is ....

Ans. (i) paper, rags
(ii) non-biodegradable
(iii) Fly ash
(iv) Stryofoam
(v) electronic
(vi) earthworms
(vii) incineration

7. Choose the odd one out from the following terms given below and name the category to which other three belong.
(i) Stale bread, Rotten apple, Tissue paper, Vegetable peel
(ii) Soot, Bricks, Waste stones, Concrete
(iii) Organic acids, Styrofoam, Coal, Soot
(iv) Old refrigerators, DVD, Lead-acid batteries, Gold
(v) Segregation, Primary treatment, Dumping, Composting

Ans. (i) **Odd term** is tissue paper.
Rest three are categorised under kitchen waste.
(ii) **Odd term** is soot.
Rest three are wastes obtained from construction units.
(iii) **Odd term** is coal.
Rest three are wastes generated from oil refineries and photochemical units.
(iv) **Odd term** is gold.
Rest three are categorised under e-waste.
(v) **Odd term** is primary treatment.
Rest three are methods of solid waste disposal.

8. Expand the BOD.

Ans. Biochemical Oxygen Demand

9. State whether the following statements are true or false. Correct and rewrite the false statements.
(i) The wastewater discharged from the industries is called effluents.
(ii) Segregation refers to drainage of wastewater or sewage from a given area.
(iii) Dumping of waste is better suited for non-biodegradable wastes.
(iv) Composting is a practice that is beneficial for farmers and gardeners as it yields organic manure.
(v) Electrostatic precipitators are used to overcome the emissions of poisonous gases like CO_2 and NO_2 from automobiles.

Ans. (i) True
(ii) False, segregation is the separation of waste based on some categories.
(iii) True
(iv) True
(v) True

10. Give one example of the following.
(i) Waste from mining operations.
(ii) Waste from pulp and paper industry.
(iii) Recyclable material
(iv) Liquid waste

Ans. (i) Coal/Copper (ii) Cellulose fibres
(iii) Metals (iv) Chemicals (from industries)

11. State the main function of the following.
(i) Scrubbers
(ii) Electrostatic precipitators

Ans. (i) Scrubbers are used to remove gases from the industrial exhausts.
(ii) Electrostatic precipitators are widely used devices to remove majority of particulate matter from exhaust of thermal power plant.

12. Mention one difference between each of the following pairs on the basis of what is given in the bracket.
(i) Domestic waste and Industrial waste (examples)
(ii) Biodegradable and Non-biodegradable waste (definition)
(iii) Composting and Dumping (definition)
(iv) Segregation and Incineration (definition)

Ans. (i) Difference between domestic waste and industrial waste is as follows

Domestic waste	Industrial waste
Paper, vegetable peels, etc.	Wood waste, cellulose fibres, etc.

(ii) Difference between biodegradable and non-biodegradable is as follows

Biodegradable	Non-biodegradable
These are wastes that can be broken down into simple substances *via* microbial decomposition.	These are wastes that cannot be broken down into simpler substances *via* microbial decomposition.

(iii) Difference between composting and dumping is as follows

Composting	Dumping
It is a method of waste disposal where organic matter is allowed to decay.	It is the process of depositing the collected wastes in an area.

(iv) Difference between segregation and incineration is as follows

Segregation	Incineration
It is the separation of waste materials into biodegradable and non-biodegradable wastes.	It is the disposal of waste materials by burning.

13. Give scientific/biological terms for the following.
(i) Substances which lack a natural process of decomposition.
(ii) Act of throwing away waste materials.
(iii) Fertilisers produced from animal dung.
(iv) Large tanks into which remaining major part of sludge is pumped.

Ans. (i) Non-biodegradable substances
(ii) Discard
(iii) Manure
(iv) Anaerobic sludge digesters

14. Briefly explain the following terms.
(i) Waste substances (ii) Plant wastes
(iii) E-Waste (iv) Composting (v) Effluent

Ans. (i) The useless, left-over or discarded substances are called waste substances.
(ii) Plant wastes are agricultural wastes which include organic matters like fats, carbohydrates, etc., and are obtained *via* processes like threshing, winnowing, etc.
(iii) E-wastes are a common, informal name for electronic wastes that consist of discarded electrical appliances like old television, mobile phones, etc.
(iv) Composting is a method of solid wastes disposal in which the organic waste matter is allowed to decompose by microbes and soil organisms.
(v) The supernatant left after removing primary sludge during primary treatment of sewage is called effluent.

15. Answer the following questions briefly.
(i) What is meant by the term segregation of waste?
(ii) Open landfill sites are potential centres to harm the environment. How?
(iii) Incineration, the disposal method of solid wastes leads to pollution. Comment.
(iv) State the purpose behind the study of waste management.

Ans. (i) It refers to the segregation of waste materials into different categories of wastes, e.g. reusable, biodegradable and non-biodegradable wastes.
(ii) Open landfill sites are potential centres to harm environment as leaching of chemicals and toxins may contaminate the environment.
(iii) Incineration involves burning of wastes which release fumes and harmful substances.
(iv) To reduce the generation of waste by living beings.

2 Marks Questions

16. What are toxic wastes? Where are they released?

Ans. Toxic wastes are materials which can cause death or injury to living creatures since they contain poison. They are released on land, in air and water.

17. What are the two major categories of waste seen in everyday life?

Ans. Two major categories of waste seen in everyday life are
(i) Domestic waste (ii) Industrial waste

18. What are the sources of radioactive waste?

Ans. Sources of radioactive wastes are
(i) Accidental leakage of nuclear material or radiation from nuclear power plants.
(ii) Improper disposal of radioactive material.

19. Name any two methods of solid waste disposal.

Ans. Two methods of solid waste disposal are
(i) Segregation (ii) Composting

20. How do farmers make use of animal waste?

Ans. Animal waste has many useful constituents like organic wastes which can be used as fertiliser and manure for growing crops. The manure can also be processed to produce fuels for heating and transportation purposes.

21. State the constituents of sewage.

Ans. Constituents of sewage include organic impurities like human excreta, animal waste, inorganic impurities like phosphates, nitrates and microbes like bacteria, fungi and viruses.

3 Marks Questions

22. It is considered necessary to separate the constituents of municipal sewage before any treatment for disposal. Give reason.

Ans. The municipal sewage waste is first segregated into two categories of biodegradable and non-biodegradable wastes. This segregation is important for selecting a proper disposal method.

The biodegradable wastes are isolated and converted into compost which can be used by farmers and gardeners as manure. Since, non-biodegradable wastes cannot be decomposed they are treated further to decrease their toxicity. After this, they are dumped in landfill sites in proper manner.

23. Briefly explain the treatment of liquid wastes.

Ans. Treatment of liquid wastes is carried out in three stages
(i) **Primary treatment** Large objects like cans, sticks, etc., are removed by passing the liquid through coarse screen. After this, the liquid is passed through a grit chamber to remove grit and sand and then sent to a flocculation tank where processes like sedimentation and precipitation are carried out.
(ii) **Secondary treatment** In this, the wastewater is treated with anaerobic bacteria to change sludge into harmless substances. Then, liquid is aerated so that aerobic bacteria can remove other wastes. After that, liquid is subjected to chlorination to kill harmful germs in water.

(iii) **Tertiary treatment** This is an advanced stage of water treatment. It removes nitrogenous wastes from water.

24. How does an electrostatic precipitator work to remove particulate pollutants released from the thermal power plants?

Ans. Electrostatic precipitator removes the particulate matter with 99% efficiency. It has electrode wires maintained at high voltage, which produces a corona that releases electrons.

These electrons get attached to the dust particles and give them negative charge. A positively charged collecting plate is also there, which attracts the negatively charged dust particles. Thus, separating them from the air and collecting them on itself. Afterwards, the air passes through the collecting plate and gets cleaned.

Section-II [5 Marks]

Structured Questions

1. Composting recycles organic matter like leaves and food scraps and is a natural process.
   (i) What do you mean by a compost?
   (ii) What is the ideal location of a compost?
   (iii) How many layers should be there in a compost pit?
   (iv) Define vermicomposting.
   (v) State two advantages of compost.

Ans. (i) The decomposed matter obtained after recycling organic matter is called a compost.
(ii) The ideal location of compost is a dry and shady spots.
(iii) There should be three layers in a compost pit.
(iv) Vermicomposting is a type of composting in which certain species of earthworms are used to enhance the process of organic waste conversion.
(v) Two advantages of compost are
(i) It prevents soil erosion.
(ii) It promotes healthier plant growth.

2. Study the diagram given below and answer the questions that follows.

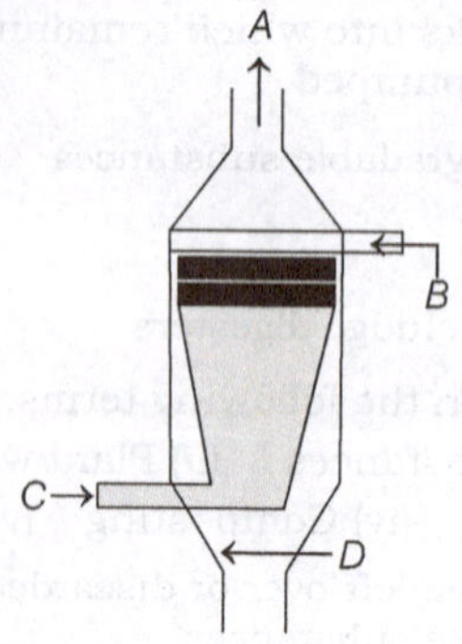

(i) Identify the above device.
(ii) Identify the parts labelled as *A*, *B*, *C* and *D*.
(iii) How many types of such devices are available in the market?
(iv) Give one example of a gaseous waste that can be removed using the above device.
(v) What is the role of lime in the above method?

Ans. (i) The above device is scrubber.
(ii) The part labelled as *A*, *B*, *C* and *D* are
A-Clean air
B-Water/Lime spray
C-Dirty air
D-Particulate matter
(iii) Scrubbers are of two types
(i) Wet scrubber
(ii) dry scrubber
(iv) Sulphur dioxide (SO_2) is example of a gaseous waste that can be removed using the above device (scrubber).
(v) Lime reacts with SO_2 and forms a precipitate of calcium sulphate and sulphide.

Chapter Assessment

Section-I

1 Mark Questions

1. Name the following.
   (i) Plant residue of sugarcane after extracting sugarcane juice.
   (ii) Solid precipitate material produced during secondary treatment of wastewater.
   (iii) Harmful electronic waste material.
   (iv) Useful electronic waste material.

2. Correct and rewrite the following statements by changing the underlined words.
   (i) Composting constitutes conversion of solid organic waste by <u>chemical</u> process.
   (ii) All solids undergo sedimentation and settle down to constitute the <u>activated sludge</u>.

3. Give biological reasons for the following.
   (i) Waste segregation is a key to waste management.
   (ii) We should avoid using plastic bags.

4. Match the following columns.

	Column I		Column II
A.	Paper, leather, textile, rubber	1.	Municipal solid wastes
B.	Scraps, fly ash	2.	Industrial solid wastes
C.	Pesticides and fertilisers	3.	Agricultural waste
D.	Electronic toys, printers	4.	E-waste

5. Choose the correct answer from each of the four options given below.
   (i) The waste materials come from various sources. Identify the correct sources of waste material from those given below.
   (a) Domestic (b) Industrial
   (c) Hospitals (d) All of these
   (ii) Which of the following does not come under domestic waste?
   (a) Broken glass (b) Paper packet
   (c) Faecal matter (d) Newspaper
   (iii) The most convenient reusable waste is
   (a) old newspaper (b) broken glass
   (c) fly ash (d) medical instruments
   (iv) Which of the following is not a domestic waste?
   (a) Kitchen waste
   (b) Plastic waste
   (c) Paper
   (d) Mobile phones

6. Fill in the blanks by using suitable words.
   (i) Two important constituents of domestic wastes are .... and ....
   (ii) .... are used to degrade the degradable part of municipal waste.
   (iii) The municipal sewage wastes can contain both the .... and .... wastes.
   (iv) The biological treatment in treatment of effluents occurs in .... tank with the help of ....
   (v) Emissions from the power plants can be treated efficiently by the use of ....

7. Choose the odd one out from the following term given below and name the category to which other three belong.
   Gravel, Concrete, Pesticides, Wood scrap

8. State whether the following statements are true or false. Correct and rewrite the false statements.
   (i) Solid wastes can be biodegradable or non-biodegradable.
   (ii) Irreparable computers and electronic goods are known as radioactive wastes.
   (iii) E-wastes contain harmful toxicants.

9. Give one example of the following.
   (i) Non-biodegradable material
   (ii) Material that can be used in composting
   (iii) Gaseous effluents removed by scrubbers

10. Mention one difference between each of the following pairs on the basis of what is given in the brackets.
   (i) Composting and Incineration (end products)
   (ii) Secondary treatment and Tertiary treatment (definition)

11. Give scientific/biological terms for the following.
    (i) A physio-chemical process that involves chlorination of water.
    (ii) Sediment obtained after treating effluent of aeration tank with bacteria.
12. Briefly explain the following terms
    (i) Primary treatment of sewage
    (ii) Sludge
13. Answer the following questions briefly.
    (i) List one waste which you generate at home and school that can be easily reduced.
    (ii) Mention any one way in which e-wastes can be disposed in the environment.
    (iii) What is the characteristic of a functional drainage system?

2 Marks Questions

14. Cloth bags are considered better than plastics. Comment.
15. What are the two advantages of incineration?

3 Marks Question

16. Discuss the following.
    (i) Radioactive waste
    (ii) Agricultural waste

Section-II [5 Marks]

Structured Questions

17.

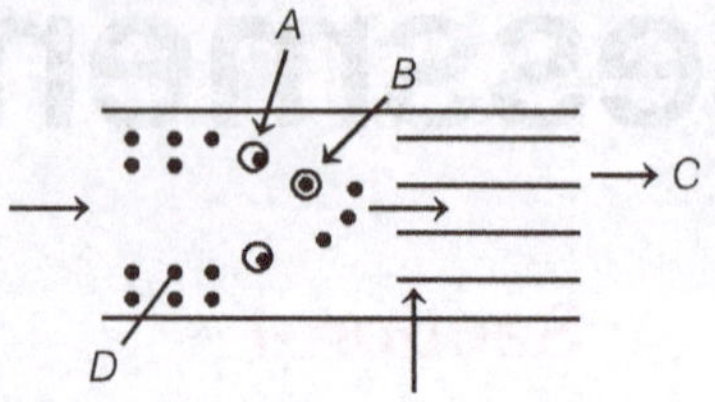

(i) Identify the above device.
(ii) Identify the parts labelled as *A*, *B*, *C* and *D*.
(iii) In the above device, electrode wires of high voltage are maintained at several thousand volts. Why?
(iv) Where is the above device used and for what purpose?
(v) Why is the velocity of air between the plates is maintained low?

18. Waste management is devoted to services like waste minimisation, collection and proper disposal.
    (i) What is an effective way to minimise waste/kitchen waste?
    (ii) How can one make use of industrial waste?
    (iii) Does an improper waste disposal system affect an individual's health?
    (iv) State any two ways to manage waste?
    (v) What is the best method to reduce waste?

For explanations scan the given QR Code

Olympiad Section*

Brain Teasing Questions asked in Previous Olympiads

1 Raja's mother collects all the kitchen waste every day and puts it in a pot. She then adds a few cut pieces of old papers, a spoonful of sour buttermilk and some soil. She covers the pots and keeps it aside with intermittent mixing. After several days, it turns into a nutrient-rich compost to grow plants. In the context of decomposition in this composting process, the most appropriate statement among the following is **[INJSO 2021]**

(a) Paper acts as a good source of carbon while buttermilk gives the correct acidity to the mixture
(b) Soil acts as a good source of inorganic nitrogen while buttermilk is a good source of proteins
(c) Paper is a good source of carbon while buttermilk is a good source of starter bacteria
(d) Paper is a good source of fibre while buttermilk is a good source of fat

2 Anita buried the following in a corner of her garden to dispose them off

I. A broken egg shell
II. Pencil shavings
III. Dry leaves
IV. Plastic carry bags
V. Fruit and vegetable peels

If the corner is dug up 5 years later, which of these is most likely to have remained the same?

(a) Dry leaves
(b) Broken egg shell
(c) Plastic carry bags
(d) Fruit and vegetable peels

3 Indiscriminate disposal of plastic wastes can cause environmental pollution. Which of the following statements is/are true?

(a) Plastics are made by chemicals
(b) Plastics are non-biodegradable
(c) Plastic produces toxic gases when burnt
(d) All of the above

4 Ravi separated items mentioned below in the garbage into red, green and blue containers for their transfer to landfill, composting pit and recycling unit, respectively. These items include.

I. Plastic bags
II. Newspapers
III. Screw and nuts
IV. Vegetable peels
V. Metal chips
VI. Egg shells

Which items were transferred to which bin?

	Red	Green	Blue
(a)	I and IV	II and III	V and VI
(b)	I and III	II and V	IV and VI
(c)	I, III and V	IV and VI	II only
(d)	I and V	II and IV	III only

5 In some cities, we find dustbins of two different colours for collection of garbage. These dustbins are usually of which of the following two colours?

(a) Green and yellow
(b) Green and red
(c) Blue and red
(d) Blue and green

6 Ravi collected three different types of wastes *P*, *Q* and *R* from a human dwelling and left wastes *P* and *Q* in an open field while disposed off *R* by a manual method of waste disposal as it was toxic. The given graph shows the changes in amount of *P*, *Q* and *R* with time.

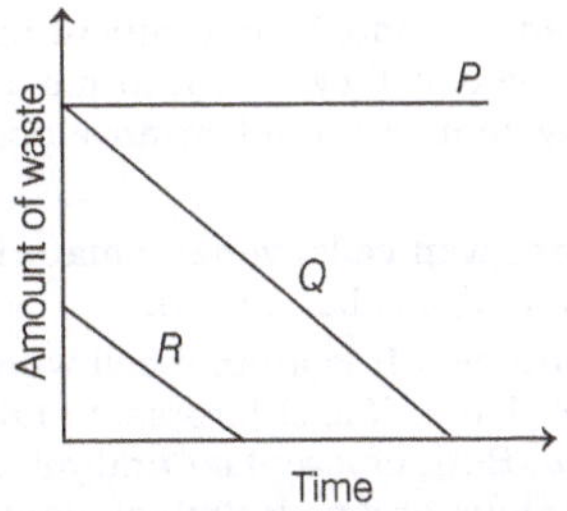

Refer to the above given graph and select the incorrect option regarding *P*, *Q*, *R*.

(a) *P* could be a man-made object whereas *Q* is derived from living organism
(b) The method used for disposing off *R* is often employed in disposal of hospital wastes
(c) Management of waste *P* and *R* by manual method will always increase air and water pollution
(d) *Q* is disposed off by decomposition process which is slow but completely disposed off the waste

7 From the below-mentioned options, pick the substances that should not be added to a vermicompost pit as it will hinder the process of vermicomposting.

(a) Egg shells
(b) Dried leaves
(c) Synthetic fertilisers
(d) Fruit peels

Answers

1. (c) **2.** (c) **3.** (d) **4.** (c) **5.** (d) **6.** (c) **7.** (c)

*These questions may or may not be asked in the examination, have been given just for additional practice required for olympiads, scholarship exams etc. For detailed explanations refer Page No. 230.

Explanations to Olympiad Section

Chapter 1. Cell : The Unit of Life

1. (b) Statements I and II are true whereas statement III is false. It can be corrected as

   Large surface area to volume ensures that the cell is efficient in circulating and moving the nutrients, waste material, etc., around through the process of diffusion. This process is intercellular and not intracellular. Thus, surface area to volume ratio has no relation with diffusion inside the cells.

2. (c) Statements II, IV and VI are correct whereas I, III and V are incorrect. These can be corrected as
   - Animal and plant cells are eukaryotic cells which contain true nucleus whereas nucleoid is present in prokaryotic cells.
   - Bacterial cell has a cell wall which is made up of peptidoglycan.
   - The plant cell wall is mainly composed of cellulose.

3. (d) Statement in option (d) is incorrect about prokaryotes and can be corrected as

   Centrosomes are microtubule organising centres in eukaryotic cells. These are not found in prokaryotes.

4. (c) The nuclear membrane around the newly formed cells is formed by endoplasmic reticulum during the telophase stage of cell cycle. ER forms a continous membrane system with nuclear envelope in eukaryotic cells.

5. (d) Among the given cells, genetic material could be found in *X* and *Y* of cells I and II.

   Here, I is plant cell, II is animal cell whereas III is bacterial cell. Thus, *X* is chloroplast and *Y* is mitochondria. Both chloroplast and mitochondria are semi-autonomous organelles which contain their own genetic material.

6. (b) Plasma membrane is permeable to some molecules which can pass through it freely. Among given options, cholesterol will diffuse faster as it is the structural component of plasma membrane. Water moves across membrane through osmosis. Glycerol diffuses very slowly because it contains three polar OH-groups which make it insoluble in lipids.

7. (a) The vesicles in the ER fuse with the plasma membrane and release their content outside the cell in extracellular fluid. Thus, the PO_4 groups which were labelled toward the lumen, would be translocated outside when ER buds-off vesicles.

8. (c) Cytomembrane system is a system of organelles consisting of endoplasmic reticulum, Golgi apparatus and vesicles. In this system, the membranes are physically connected.

Chapter 2. Tissues

1. (a) Collenchyma and chlorenchyma are primary simple permanent tissues therefore they will turn pink. Xylem and phloem are secondary complex tissues which will turn blue.

2. (b) Assimilatory roots are modified root which are capable of carrying out photosynthesis. They synthesise carbon dioxide, water and carbohydrates in the presence of sunlight. Thus, these act as source. The meristematic region of plant is the site of active cell division which require energy for division all the time. Thus, this region would act as sink.

3. (c) Statement in option (c) is most likely to be correct. The transport of water occurs through xylem, whereas food transport is facilitated by phloem. Xylem is located in the centre of the vascular bundle, deep in the plant. Phloem is located on the outer side of the vascular bundle. Thus, in given situation, water transport from root to leaves will not be obstructed but food transport down the leaves stops at the ring.

4. (a) The matrix of cartilage is predominantly composed of proteins and sugars. These include glycosaminoglycans, proteoglycans, collagen fibres and sometimes elastin.

5. (b) Transitional epithelium is a type of tissue that changes shape in response to stretching (stretchable epithelium). Thus, it can accommodate fluctuation of volume of the liquid in urinary bladder. It lines the organs of the urinary system and here, it is known as urothelium.

6. (d) Statement in option (d) is correct about the function of cells described.

   Tracheids are elongated cells that transport water and mineral salts through the xylem of vascular plants. They are elongated tube-like cells with tapering ends. At maturity, the cells are no longer alive and the mature cells are devoid of protoplast. The secondary cell wall is heavily lignified and the cells are angular and polygonal in cross-section.

7. (d) Option (d) is odd pair out.

   Periderm is a protective tissue that replaces the epidermis during secondary growth. It is produced by phellogen or cork cambium

Chapter 3. The Flower

1. (c) If the AP3 and PI genes lose their activity, only A gene will be expressed and thus, only sepals would be formed at position 1 and 2. Similarly in whorl 3 and 4, only gene C will be expresesed and thus only carpels would be formed.

Note According to ABC model of flowering, A gene alone produce sepals, A+B produce petals, B+C produce stamens and C alone produce carpel.

2. (b) If the activity of genes AP1 and AP2, i.e. gene A is lost, sepals and petals will not form. Thus, first whorl would be formed by carpels (C alone), then stamens (B + C) and then carpels again.
Thus, correct answer is carpel, stamens, stamens and carpels.
3. (c) The given case signifies that *Atriplex lampa* is a dioecious plant as the flowers are present on separate plants. Being unisexual, the plant would either contain staminate (male) or carpellate or pistillate (female) flower. These flowers would not be found together.
4. (a)
5. (b)

Chapter 4. Pollination and Fertilisation

1. (b) Anemophily is a form of pollination in which pollens are distributed by wind.
2. (a) The zygote develops into an embryo during the post-fertilisation events. The process of development of embryo from diploid zygote is called embryogenesis and it involves cell division and cell differentiation.
3. (a) I–Endosperm, II–Ovule and III– Embryo
4. (a) Statement in option (a) is correct regarding pollen grain. Tapetum is the innermost layer which nourishes the developing pollen.
Other statements are incorrect and corrected as follows
   - Sporogenous tissue is diploid.
   - Endothecium is the wall of microsporangium which help in protection and dehiscence of anther to release pollen grains.
   - Intine is the inner layer of pollen. Hard outer layer is exine.
5. (d) II and IV
6. (c) AEF, BCD

Chapter 5. Structure and Germination of Seed

1. (d) Clay and humus have more water and nutrient content than sand. Whereas humus and sand have more oxygen availability than clay.
2. (b) Etiolation is defined as the process of bleaching and altering the natural development of a green plant by excluding them from sunlight.
3. (a)
4. (d) All the given statements are correct except given in option (d) because the diagram represents epigeal seed germination which occurs in bean seeds. In this type of seed germination cotyledons are pushed out of the soil by greater growth of hypocotyl. Hypocotyl grows actively and becomes curved to protect the plumule and cotyledons from friction of soil. After coming out of the soil surface, the hypocotyl straightens. The loosened seed coats fall down, cotyledons turn green and become photosynthetic to function as first leaves of the seedling.

Chapter 6. Respiration in Plants

1. (c) Aerobic respiration proceeds in a series of steps, which also increases efficiency. Since, glucose is borken down gradually and ATP is produced as needed, less energy is wasted as heat. If this energy is released at a single step, maximum amount of energy will be wasted in form of heat.
2. (a)
3. (b)
4. (c) The immediate product of photosynthesis is glucose and later it is stored as starch.
5. (a) Photosynthesis utilises energy to build carbohydrates, while cellular respiration metabolises carbohydrates.
6. (c) In the test tube full of mercury (figure A), there is no air and therefore the introduced soaked seeds do not get air for their respiration. But they are capable of respiration in the absence of oxygen as indicated by the evolution of carbon dioxide (figure B). Therefore, anaerobic respiration takes place in the seeds in the absence of free oxygen. The experiment also shows that CO_2 is evolved in anaerobic respiration of seeds.
7. (d)
8. (a) The seeds are boiled with an antiseptic to avoid bacterial decay.
9. (b) CO_2 produced by germinating seeds was absorbed by KOH, so vaccum was created in system. This results in the rise of water level in delivery tube of flask B.
10. (b)

Chapter 7. Diversity in Living Organisms

1. (d) A–pseudroelomate, B–*Ascaris*
2. (a) P-1, Q-IV, R-V, S-II
Bryophytes and pteridophytes are cryptograms. Vascular bundles are absent and seeds are not produced in this group, e.g. *Marchantia*, *Marsilea*. Gymnosperms possess naked seeds, e.g. *Pinus*. In angiosperms, seeds are either monocotyledon (e.g. maize) or dicotyledon (e.g. rice, legume).
3. (c) Tapeworm exhibit pseudo-segmentation whereas *Nereis* and centipede show metameric segmentation.
4. (b) A–2, B–4, C–3, D–1
5. (b) Among given sets, II and I correctly represent Pteridophyta and Algae, respectively.

Chapter 8. Economic Importance of Bacteria and Fungi

1. (c) Nitrogen-fixing bacteria are responsible for conversion of atmospheric nitrogen into inorganic nitrogenous compounds (nitrate, nitrite and ammonia). This process is called biological nitrogen fixation.
2. (a) The enzyme nitrogenase is a Mo-Fe protein and catalyses the conversion of atmospheric N_2 to NH_3. If

this enzyme is inactivated then there will be no nitrogen-fixation in legumes.

3. (a) Plants that are in a mutalistic relationship with nitrogen-fixing bacteria would receive nitrogen in the form of ammonium ions.

4. (b) Nitrogen cycle is mainly composed of four important processes that occur in the following sequence.

(i) **Nitrogen fixation** (Atmospheric N_2 converted to inorganic compounds like nitrate, nitrite and ammonia)

(ii) **Ammonification** (Conversion of amino acids into ammonia)

(iii) **Nitrification** (Conversion of ammonia and other ammonium compounds)

(iv) **Denitrification** (Nitrate in soil is reduced back to free N_2).

Chapter 9. Nutrition and Digestion in Humans

1. (c) HCl is involved in the activation of pepsinogen that is responsible for protein digestion. Thus, in the absence of HCl, protein metabolism will be affected. Digestion of carbohydrates will continue and fats digestion will not be influenced as it begins in small intestine.

2. (d) Substances that are absorbed in small intestine travel first to the liver for processing before reaching to the heart. From heart, they get distributed to different target organs through a network of arteries.

3. (b) Salivary amylase works at an optimum pH of 6-8 in order to convert starch into sugar. This pH is provided by the sodium phosphate buffer.

4. (c) Bile does not contain any enzyme as gastric juice and helps in emulsification of fats.

5. (a) Gall bladder is the site for the storage of bile which is needed for fat emulsification. Removal of gall bladder singifies that there is no concentration of bile which will cause problems in digestion of fats. High amount of fats in food cannot be digested and will result in accumulation of gas and bloating.

Chapter 10. Movement and Locomotion

1. (b) In vertebrates, the long bones are always hollow because they harbour and protect marrow and they are stronger than solid structures made up of same amount of material.

2. (d) The joints with more mobility are the weakest joints. These joints do not offer joint stability and have greater range of motion. Carpal bones are not highly movable joints while the shoulder joint allows the greatest range of motion.

3. (d) The thoracic cage protects the heart and lungs. Any disorder related to abnormalities of thoracic cage will risk the heart and lungs .

4. (d) Tarsals, femur, metatarsals, tibia are part of hindimb bones that mainly take part during chasing a ball in the field by a cricket player.

5. (d) When we bend down to touch our toes then the hip joint is flexed and the knees are extended.

6. (b) An exoskeleton is a hard external skeleton that protects the outer surface of an organism.

7. (a) All the large bones contain bone marrow. With the increase in age, RBC production decreases. In vertebra, the decrease rate is not that significant. So, *A* represents vertebra. Ribs will show higher decrease rate as compared to vertebra. So, *B* represents rib. Tibia will show a higher decrease rate as compared to rib. So, *C* represents tibia.

Chapter 11. The Skin

1. (a) Cells present on the surface of stratified squamous epithelium are flattened and dead. These are filled with a protein called keratin that makes our skin waterproof.

2. (b) Sebaceous glands secrete an oily substance called sebum. Due to the overgrowth of oil producing cells, sebum becomes trapped inside the gland causing it to swell and form a bump under the skin thus, the condition of milia arises.

3. (a) Colouration of the skin (complexion of the face) is due to the pigment melanin contained in the cells of the germinative layer (Malpighian layer). The different quantities of this pigment in different human races lead to a variety of skin colourations ranging from dark coloured skin (e.g. African Negroes) to whitish (e.g. Europeans) and to wheatish (e.g Indians).

4. (c) Tanning is a protective response wherein melanin (the pigment responsible for skin colouration) is produced in excess amounts when the skin is exposed to ultraviolet radiations. As a result the colour of the skin darkens.

5. (d) The basal layer (Stratum Germinativum) is the innermost layer of epidermis which divides continuously and push older worn out cells towards the surface of the skin for shedding.

6. (d) Elastin and collagen both act as elastic tissues. The loss of the elastic tissues in skin with age causes the skin to lose its elasticity. Thus, causing wrinkles.

7. (b) The allergic reaction which results from exposure to allergens or irritants like chemicals or cosmetic products is called dermitites venenata. It is also called contact dermititis and results in large burning and itchy rashes.

8. (c) A mass of tissue often results in tumours. This mass is formed due to uncontrolled growth of cells taking place at a place. These may be soft or procure as hard outgrowths which may be fixed as a place or spread from one region to another.

9. (a) Corns and calluses develop from repeated friction, rubbing, irritation or pressure on the skin.

10. (c) Leucoderma (or vitiligo) is a skin disorder in which patches appear on a persons skin. In other words, the disorder causes the skin to lose its colour.

Chapter 12. Respiratory System

1. (a) Since the concentration of carbon dioxide is more in body tissues and cells as compared to blood, it will move from tissue cells into the blood.

2. (d) Air enters the human body *via* nostrils and moves through the nasal cavity. From the nasal cavity, air enters the pharynx and then larynx. From the voice box (larynx), air enters the windpipe (trachea). The trachea bifurcates into bronchi and then to bronchioles, i.e. air moves towards bronchioles and then to air sacs-alveoli.

3. (c) After heavy exercise oxygen availability get decreased. In order to balance this decrease in volume of oxygen there is an increase in respiration rate accompanied with deep breathe.

4. (b) Inspiratory Capacity (IC) is the amount of air that can be inspired with maximum effort after normal expiration.

$$IC = IRV + TV$$

Vital capacity (VC) is the maximum amount of air that can be taken in after a forced expiration or the maximum volume of air that can be given out after a forced inspiration.

$$VC = TV + IRV + ERV$$

Residual volume (RV) is the volume of air remaining in lungs after a forcible expiration.

$$RV = TLC - VC$$

Tidal volume (TV) is the volume of air inspired or expired during normal breathing in relaxed position.

$$TV = \text{Alveolar space} + \text{Dead air space}$$

5. (d) Breathing involves inhalation and exhalation of air. In order to breath there must be a pressure gradient maintained in the lungs with respect to the atmosphere.

In case of an accident wherein the chest cavity of a person gets punctured the pressure gradient in the lungs would become zero. As a result, the breathing would cease.

6. (b)Cells lining the alveoli and capillaries are thin so as to allow diffusion of gases. If the cell lining had been thinner diffusion of oxygen would increase and thus the rate at which oxygen could be obtained from air would increase.

7. (a) Alveoli in the lungs allow large surface area for the gaseous exchange. So, the trachea, bronchi and bronchioles of humans have all of the following functions except option (a).

8. (b) The contraction of the diaphragm muscles produces negative pressure within the thoracic cavity as a result the air from the atmosphere enters inside the lungs.

Chapter 13. Health and Hygiene

1. (a) Denotes the correct match of a disease with its causative organism and the related mode of infection.

- Pneumonia is a bacterial disease caused by *Streptococcus pneumoniae*. It is transmitted by air or by direct contact resulting in inflammation of the lungs, high fever, breathing problems and fatigue.
- Typhoid is yet another bacterial disease caused by *Salmonella typhi*. It spreads through contaminated water, milk and through flies. Person suffering from typhoid fever, experiences acute headache, fever, diarrhoea, etc.
- Malaria is caused by a protozoan *Plasmodium vivax* and is spread to humans through the bite of an infected female *Anopheles* mosquito.
- Elephantiasis or filariasis is caused by the filarial worm *Wuchereria bancrofti*. The infection is transmitted through the bite of *Culex* mosquito.

2. (c) Making antiviral drugs is more difficult than making antibacterial medicines because viruses have very few biochemical mechanisms of their own. These make use of the host machinery to replicate. Thus, it becomes difficult to find targets where these drugs will interfere by not harming the host organism. Thus, antiviral drugs with high safety and effectiveness cannot be designed.

3. (c) Vaccines help in developing immunity by initating an infection. The infection induced by the vaccine does not cause illness but it does cause the immune system to produce T-lymphocytes and antibodies vaccines reduce the risk of infection by stimulating body's natural immune response against the virus. Thus, the doctor would suggest to get vaccinated against the disease.

4. (c) Virus responsible for causing AIDS, i.e. HIV or Human Immunodeficiency Virus mutates rapidly and thus, a single vaccine cannot eradicate all strains of the virus.

5. (a) Male *Anopheles* mosquito have been found to feed on nectar and fruit juices and not bite humans in order to suck blood, whereas in female *Anopheles* mosquito feed on the blood of humans. It nourishes the future mosquitoes.

6. (d) Malaria is caused by a protozoan *Plasmodium* and is spread by the bite of female *Anopheles* mosquito.

Filaria or filariasis is caused by *Wuchereria bancrofti* and is transmitted by the bite of *Culex* mosquito.

Yellow fever is a rare viral disease caused by the *Flavivirus* and transmitted by *Aedes aegypti* mosquito.

7. (b) *Wuchereria bancrofti* a worm causes a tropical disease called filariasis or elephantiasis. It is transmitted through the bite of *Culex* mosquito. The disease causes swelling of legs as there is inflammation of lymph glands and lymph vessels. Person suffering from elephantiasis also experiences fever with chills.

8. (c) Chickenpox is a contagious disease caused by the *Varicella zoster* virus. It is more common in children but also affects adults. Its symptoms include rashes which first appear as pink spots and rapidly change to watery blisters.

The blisters get dry soon and form scabs. The person suffering from chickenpox also experience muscle pain.

9. (a) The HIV (Human Immunodeficiency Virus) responsible for causing AIDS affects specific type of immune system cells in the body known as CD4 cells or T cells. These cells help us in fighting infections. HIV virus on entering the T-cells makes copies of itself and kill the T-cells.

This in turn affects the immune system negatively. As a result, the individuals immune system loses its ability to fight infections which later turn lethal.

10. (c) (P) Typhoid is caused by the bacterium *Salmonella typhi* which attacks the individuals intestines and the person infected with this fever passes out germs in his excreta.

TAB vaccine has proved to be an effective treatment for typhoid fever.

Tuberculosis is a bacterial disease caused by (Q) *Mycobacterium tuberculosis*. It is usually a disease of the lungs, but affects other parts like brain, kidney and

(R) BCG vaccine has been found useful in developing immunity against TB.

(S) Chickenpox is caused by a herpes virus *Varicella zoster*. This disease spreads quickly by close contact with an infected person. Symptoms include rashes which later turn into watery blisters.

Chapter 14. Aids to Health

1. (a) Antibodies through mother milk and antivenom are examples of passive immunity.
2. (d) Antimicrobial proteins, mucous membrane, phagocytic cells and inflammatory responses are various defence that constitute innate immunity.
3. (b) In active acquired immunity, person exposed to a live pathogen develops disease and then become immune to it. Therefore, person recovered from measles does not get measles again.
4. (a) An antibody is defined as a protein molecule generated in the living body which particularly inactivates an antigen molecule. Antibodies belong to a class of serum protein which are called gamma globulins. Therefore, the antibodies are also known as immunoglobulins and are produced by lymphocytes. Therefore to prove the deficiency of antibodies in person, serum globulins will be tested.
5. (c) The natural way of destroying bacterial infection is the production of the antibodies by the plasma B-cells in the body. The production of HCl also kills the harmful becteria. The WBCs or leucocytes are cells which can perform phagocytosis and destroy bacterial cells.

   Thus, the intake of antibiotics is not the natural way.
6. (c) Snake antivenom is a biological product that typically consists of venom neutralising antibodies derived from host animals such as a horse or sheep, it is not considered as antigen or antigen antibody complex or enzyme.
7. (a) Skin can provide defence against some types of bacteria to stop the entry of other pathogens, other physical or chemical barrier is required.
8. (b) Mucus secreted by mucous membrane trap the microbes and immobilises them.

Chapter 15. Waste Generation and Management

1. (c) Paper is a valuable material for composting because it is a great source of carbon while buttermilk consists of many bacteria which are good source of starter bacteria that make compost.
2. (c) Plastic bags are non-biodegradable waste so they are most likely to have remained the same after 5 years.
3. (d) Accumulation of plastics in the environment results in pollution, which causes an imbalance in ecological cycle. Plastics are composed of chemicals. Plastic products produce toxic gases when burnt and take around 450 years for decomposing and after that approximately 50 years to decay. Hence, we can state that a plastic product takes arround 500 years to decompose.

   Thus, option (d) is correct.
4. (c) Egg shells and vegetable peels are organic waste so they will be separated in green container. Plastic bags, screw and nuts and metal chips will be separated in landfills (red containers). Newspapers can be recycled so these will be separated in blue container.
5. (d) The green dustbin is used for wet wastes, while the blue dustbin is used for dry wastes.
6. (c) Option (c) is incorrect because *R* is disposed off by manual method and is decreasing in amount with time thus, not causing or increasing air and water pollution. Whereas *P* is not decomposing with time and may cause air and water pollution even if it is decomposed by manual method.
7. (c) Vermicomposting is a proces by which worms are used to convert organic materials (usually wastes) into humus-like material. Egg shells, dried leaves and fruit peels are organic whereas synthetic fertiliser is inorganic). Also, synthetic fertiliser due to its toxic nature can affect worms and cause their death thus, stopping the process.

Internal Assessment of Practical Work

Plant Life

Experiment 1

Aim

To examine an onion peel under the microscope and study various parts of the cell.

Materials Required

Onion bulb, glass slide, coverslip, methylene blue or glycerine, safranin solution, dropper, mounting needle, blotting paper, compound microscope, blade, watch glass, brush, a pair of forceps, water.

Theory

All living organisms are composed of cells. New cells arise by the division of pre-existing cells. Cell is the structural and functional unit of life. In plants, cells have an outermost rigid cell wall present beneath, which is cell membrane.
The cell membrane encloses cytoplasm, cell organelles and a nucleus.

Procedure

(i) Take a fleshy scaly leaf of an onion. Using a pair of forceps, pull out a thin membranous peel adhering to the inner surface of the leaf. This is the epidermal peel.

(ii) Place the peel in a watch glass containing water and cut it into small rectangular pieces.

(iii) Mix 1 or 2 drops of methylene blue or safranin in a small quantity of water taken in another watch glass and transfer the peel into it. Leave the peel for about 3 minutes. Dip the peel in water to remove excess stain.

(iv) Take a clean slide with a drop of glycerine in the middle and using a brush, transfer the washed and stained peel on to it.

(v) Place a coverslip over it by slowly lowering it with the help of a needle. Avoid entry of air bubbles.

(vi) Remove excess glycerine from the edges of coverslip with the help of a piece of blotting paper.

(vii) Observe the slide under the microscope, first in low power (10×) and then in high power (45×).

(viii) Draw a labelled diagram of the cells as seen under microsope.

(ix) Observe and record its features.

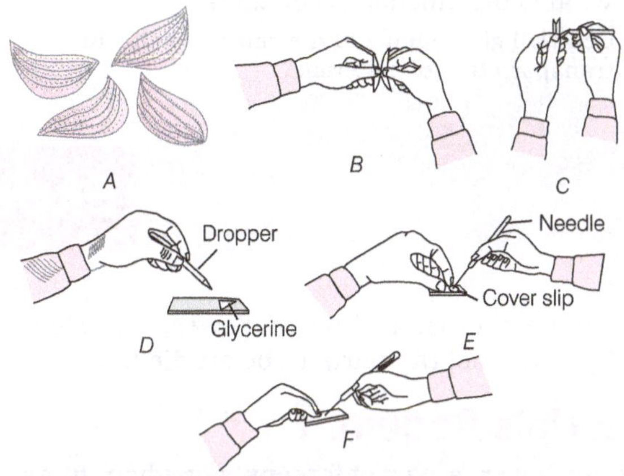

A, B, C- Method of removing peel from onion. D, E, F-Steps showing mounting procedure

Observations

(i) There are a large number of brick-shaped (rectangular) epidermal cells lying side by side (compactly arranged).

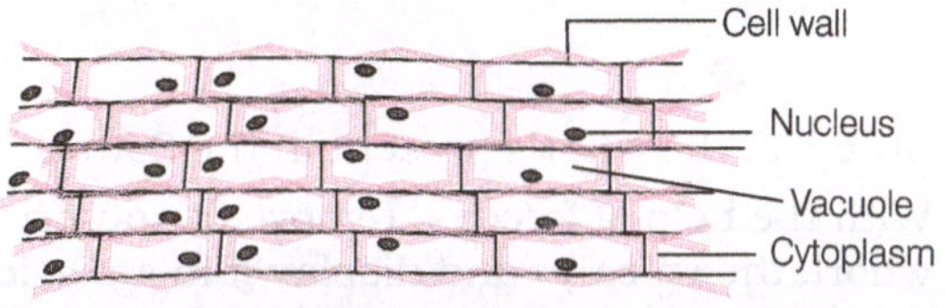

Cell structure of an onion peel

(ii) Each cell has a distinct cell wall and there are no intercellular spaces.

(iii) A darkly stained distinct nucleus is present in each cell.

(iv) A prominent vacuole is seen in the centre and cytoplasm is present in the periphery of every cell.

Conclusion

The cells observed under microscope are plant cells. Each cell has a distinct cell wall and a large vacuole in the centre.

Precautions

(i) Always hold the slide from its edges.

(ii) The slide and coverslip should be cleaned before use.

(iii) Staining of peel should be appropriate. Avoid understaining or excessive staining of the peel.

(iv) Keep the coverslip gently so as to avoid the formation of air bubbles.

(v) Extra glycerine from the edges of the coverslip should be soaked with blotting paper.

(vi) Use a brush to transfer the peel on the slide.

Viva-Voce

1. What is the shape of cells in onion peel?

Ans. The cells of onion peel are elongated and rectangular.

2. How will you remove excess stain from the peel?

Ans. Excess stain can be removed by putting the peel in water for 2-3 minutes.

3. What is the function of cell wall?

Ans. Cell wall gives shape to the cell and helps in transportation of materials.

4. State the role of vacuole in plant cell.

Ans. Vacuole helps in the storage of food materials.

5. Where are all the organelles present in cell?

Ans. All the organelles are present in cytoplasm, which fills up the space in a cell.

6. Explain the function of nucleus.

Ans. Nucleus controls all the activities that take place inside a cell.

Experiment 2

Aim

To examine a cross-pollinated flower, e.g. *Hibiscus*, identify and label the parts to be studied.

Materials Required

Hibiscus flower, a pair of forceps, petridish, filter paper, sharp blade and hand lens.

Theory

Flower forms the most important, attractive and brightly coloured part of the plant. It helps in reproduction and development of fruit. *Hibiscus* is said to be a complete flower.

Procedure

(i) Study all the whorls present in the flower.

(ii) With the help of forceps, remove the outermost whorl, the epicalyx and display it in a petridish lined with filter paper.

(iii) Then, display the calyx by removing it carefully with the help of forceps.

(iv) After removing the calyx, remove the petals one by one and display them in a separate pertidish.

(v) Carefully represent androecium and gynoecium.

(vi) Remove the stamens carefully in order to get the ovary intact.

(vii) Carefully cut a transverse section of the ovary with the help of blade and put it on slide, add glycerine solution and observe with the help of dissecting microscope.

(viii) Draw the labelled sketches of flower and all its parts.

Observations

The *Hibiscus* flower is bright red in colour. It is a bisexual flower, complete, large and showy. The various whorls are

(i) **Epicalyx** 5-8 epicalyx are present as the outermost whorl.

(ii) **Calyx** There are 5-sepals, green in colour and they are united at their ends.

(iii) **Corolla** There are five large petals, red in colour. They are free.

(iv) **Androecium** Numerous stamens are there which are united in a bundle and form a staminal tube which is united with the corolla.

(v) **Gynoecium** There are 5 carpels which are fused. Style passes through the staminal tube.

(vi) **Ovary** It has five locules with many ovules in each locule. It shows axile placentation.

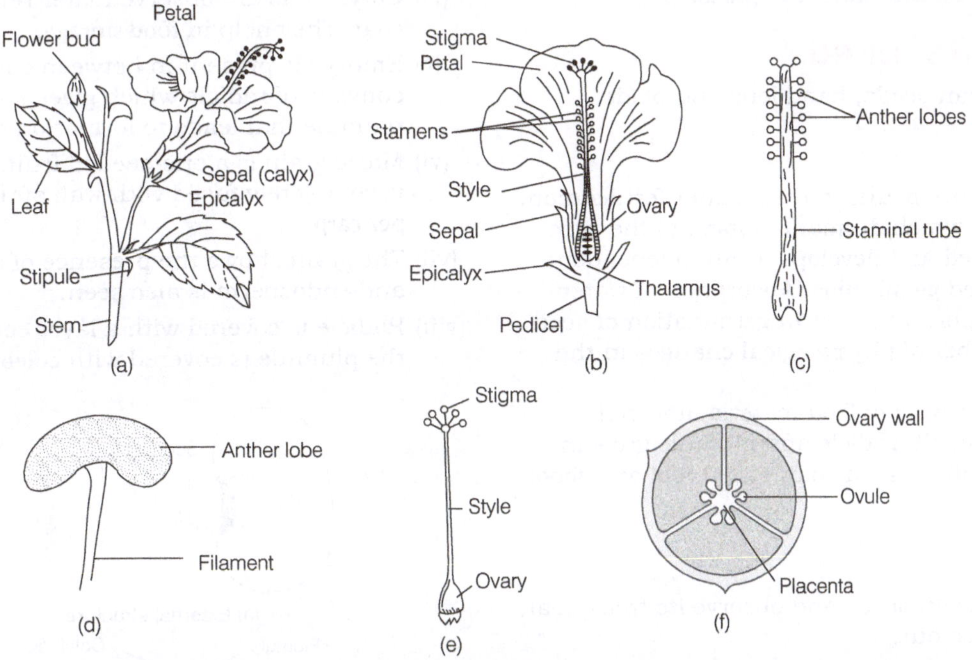

Hibiscus rosa-sinensis : (a) A flower twig, (b) Vertical section of flower, (c) Staminal tube, (d) A stamen, (e) Gynoecium, (f) TS of ovary

Conclusion

Hibiscus is a complete flower as all the four whorls, i.e. calyx, corolla, androecium and gynoecium are present in it.

Viva-Voce

1. What type of flower is *Hibiscus*?

Ans. *Hibiscus* is a bisexual flower, i.e. it contains both male and female reproductive parts on a single flower.

2. How many sepals and petals does a *Hibiscus* flower have?

Ans. It has 5 sepals and 5 petals.

3. What type of placentation is shown by the ovary of a *Hibiscus* flower?

Ans. The ovary shows axile placentation.

4. A flower is bright in colour. What type of pollination will it show?

Ans. It will show cross-pollination by insects.

5. What is a staminal tube?

Ans. Staminal tube is formed by the filaments of stamen, which are fused.

Experiment 3

Aim

To examine the specimens of germinating seeds with plumule and radicle (the bean seed and maize grain) and identify, draw and label the parts.

Materials Required

Maize grain, bean seeds, hand lens and blade.

Theory

A seed is a mature ovule produced after fertilisation. The process by which dormant embryo of the seeds grows out of seed and develops as an independent seedling is called **germination.** Absorption of water, which is an important factor in germination of seed induces a number of physiological changes in the seed.

It includes hydrolysis of food material and cell division. As a result, radicle and plumule grow in size and come out of seed coat, called **root** and **shoot**, respectively.

Procedure

(i) Take dry bean seeds and observe its thick coat, brown in colour.

(ii) Observe the white scar present on one side, called **hilum.**

(iii) Now take germinated seeds and observe them.

(iv) Press the seeds. Observe that water in a germinated seed comes out of a pore called **micropyle.**

(v) Observe the two fleshy structures, which are seen after removing the seed coat. These are cotyledons.

(vi) With the help of hand lens, observe the embryo present between the two cotyledons.

(vii) Take the dry maize grain, pale yellow in colour.

(viii) Soak the grains in water and then cut them lengthwise.

(ix) Observe the cotyledon, endosperm and embryo with the help of hand lens.

Observations

(i) The bean is kidney-shaped covered with a coat. It is made up of two layers, i.e. outer called **testa** and inner one is **tegmen.**

(ii) The seeds show presence of hilum.

(iii) The presence of micropyle through which seed absorbs water and oxygen is required for germination.

(iv) Cotyledons are observed after removal of seed coat. They help in **food storage.**

(v) Embryo is present in between cotyledons. It consists of radicle which gives rise to root and plumule that leads to formation of shoot.

(vi) Maize grain is a one-seeded fruit. Its seed coat is completely fused with wall of the fruit called **pericarp.**

(vii) The grain shows the presence of one cotyledon and endosperm is also seen.

(viii) Radicle is covered with a layer **coleorhiza** and the plumule is covered with **coleoptile.**

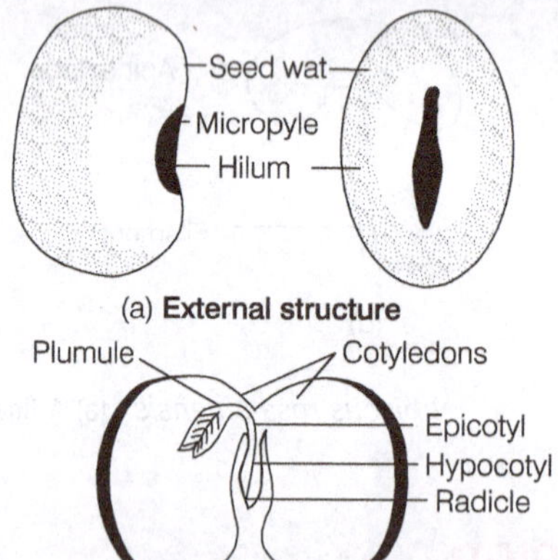

(a) **External structure**

(b) **Internal structure**

Structure of bean seed

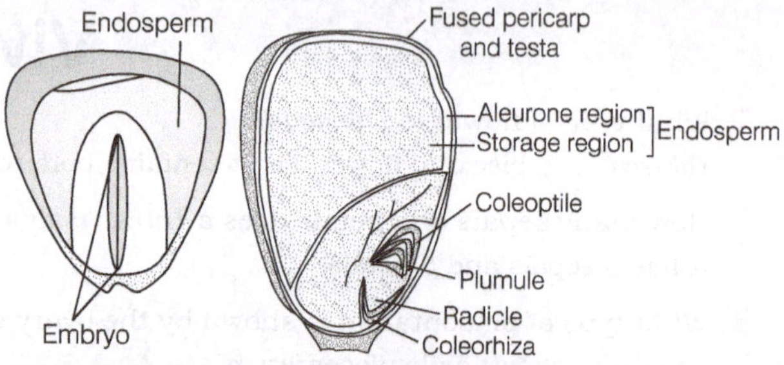

(a) **External structure** (b) **Internal structure**

Structure of a maize seed

Conclusion

The bean seed observed in experiment has two cotyledons and endosperm is not present. Maize grain has one cotyledon and has endosperm. Coleoptile and coleorhiza are also present.

Viva-Voce

1. What is the function of micropyle?

Ans. Micropyle is a minute opening present on seeds, which helps in absorption of water and exchange of gases.

2. How can we easily locate micropyle in a seed?

Ans. Micropyle can be easily located in a soaked seed. Water and air bubble oozes out of the pore when we press it.

3. Where is food stored in a seed?

Ans. Cotyledons or endosperm.

4. Give an example of dicot and monocot seeds.

Ans. Bean is an example of dicot seed. Maize is an example of monocot seed.

5. What is germination?

Ans. The process by which a seed gives rise to plant in favourable conditions.

6. What gives rise to the root?

Ans. Radicle gives rise to root.

7. Name the part that gives rise to the shoot.

Ans. Plumule gives rise to shoot.

Animal Life

Experiment 1

Aim

To prepare a temporary mount of human cheek cells under the microscope and to study the characteristics of various parts of the cell.

Materials Required

Methylene blue stain, glycerine, a compound microscope, slide, cover slip, a clean spatula or a toothpick, a brush, a needle and a piece of blotting paper, dropper, watch glass.

Theory

The body of all animals including humans is composed of cells. Unlike plant cells, animal cells do not have cell wall. The outermost covering of an animal cell is a cell membrane. The cytoplasm, nucleus and other cell organelles are enclosed in it. Epithelial tissue is the outermost covering of most organs and cavities of an animal body.

Procedure

(i) Rinse your mouth with freshwater.

(ii) With the help of a clean spatula or a toothpick, gently scrape the inner side of your cheek.

(iii) Transfer the scrapped material into a drop of water taken on a clean slide.

(iv) With the help of a needle, spread the material uniformly.

(v) Add a drop of methylene blue stain. After about 3 minutes put a drop of glycerine over it.

(vi) Place a clean coverslip over the glycerine. Remove the excess glycerine from the edges of coverslip with the help of a piece of blotting paper.

(vii) Examine the slide under the microscope, first under low power (10×) and then under high power (45×).

(viii) Draw diagrams of cells as seen under the microscope. Observe and record the features.

Observations

(i) A large number of flat polygonal cells arranged compactly are observed under the microscopic field.

(ii) Each cell is bounded by a thin cell membrane.

(iii) Cell contains jelly-like substance called **cytoplasm**.

(iv) Cytoplasm is granular.

(v) A dark stained distinct nucleus is observed in each cell.

(vi) Cells lack cell wall and large vacuoles.

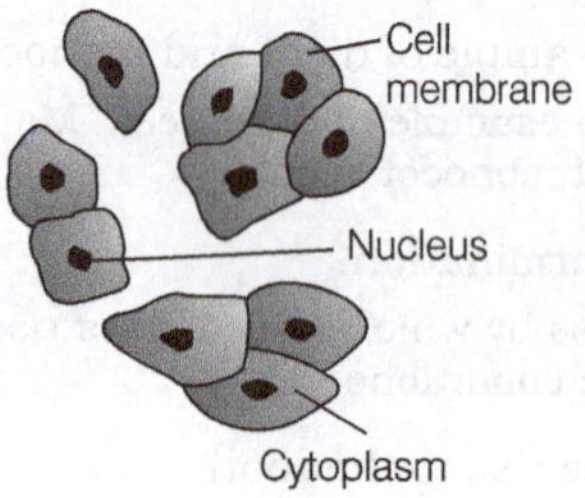

Cheek epithelial cells

Conclusion

The cells observed under the microscope are animal cells as each cell has a cell membrane as outer boundary enclosing a distinct nucleus and a dense cytoplasm. Cell wall and central prominent vacuoles are absent.

Precautions

(i) Clean your mouth cavity with warm water before scraping the cheek.

(ii) Scrape the cheek gently to avoid bleeding.

(iii) Scraping should be properly done so that the cells are widely separated.

(iv) The coverslip should be kept gently to avoid entry of air bubbles.

(v) Always hold the slide by its edges to avoid fingerprints.

(vi) Avoid overstaining or understaining of the material.

Viva-Voce

1. Name the organelles which are not present in human cheek cells?

Ans. Cell wall and chloroplast.

2. What is cell membrane?

Ans. The outer membrane in animal cell which allows transport of substances is called cell membrane or plasma membrane.

3. What should be done to spread the cells?

Ans. Scraping should be done properly to spread the cells.

4. What kind of cells were observed under the microscope?

Ans. Compactly arranged polygonal cells were observed under the microscope.

5. What is used as stain to observe the cell?

Ans. Methylene blue stain is used to observe the cell.

Experiment 2

Aim

To identify the presence of sugar, starch, protein and fats in given food samples.

Materials Required

Test tubes, funnel, beakers, water bath, test tube holder, test tube stand, droppers, spirit lamp, distilled water,
reagents-Benedict's solution, saturated solution of NaOH, dilute iodine solution, copper sulphate, ammonium hydroxide, fruit juices of apple, grape or banana, extracts of potato, sugarcane or rice, egg albumin, etc., as sources of carbohydrates, proteins and fats.

Theory

Carbohydrates or **sugars** are the organic compounds made up of carbon, hydrogen and oxygen. They are the main source of energy in our body.

When excess of carbohydrates are present, they are converted into fats and stored in the body.

The word 'protein' was first coined by **Berzelius** (1837) and **Mulder** (1838). Proteins are the complex biomolecules containing carbon, hydrogen, oxygen, nitrogen and small amount of sulphur and phosphorus.

These are the linear polymers of amino acids that are held together by peptide bonds. Proteins are responsible for maintenance of body cells and tissues. Eggs are a rich source of protein.

Fats are a rich source of energy. There is 9 kcal of energy yield per gram of fat. They get stored in body in the adipose tissues. These tissues provide warmth and necessary padding in areas like thighs. In plants, fat molecules have a role in providing buoyancy in some or all parts of a plant.

Some of the sources of fats are butter, ghee, meat, milk, fish, groundnut oil, coconut oil, etc.

Procedure

The tests and procedure for identifying the components are given below in tabular form.

Experiment	Observation	Inference
• **Test for Starch**		
Take an extract of potato in a test tube and put 2-3 drops of iodine solution in it		
Shake the test tube.	Extract will turn blue-black in colour.	Blue-black colour confirms presence of starch.
• **Test for Sugar**		
(Benedict's test)		
Take 2 mL of freshly prepared apple or banana juice in a test tube.		
Add equal amount of Benedict's solution and boil it.	Formation of brick red precipitate.	Presence of sugar confirmed.
• **Test for Protein**		
(a) (Xanthoproteic test)		
Take egg white in a clean and dried test tube and add 4-5 drops of concentrated nitric acid to it using dropper.		
Heat the test tube.		
Now add ammonium hydroxide to solution. Shake the test tube and keep it undisturbed for 5 minutes.	Formation of yellow precipitate and then colour changes to orange precipitate.	Confirms presence of proteins.
(b) (Biuret test)		
Take egg white in a test tube and addd few drops of NaOH solution to make it dilute.		
Add 1-2 drops of dilute copper sulphate.		
Heat the test tube.	Formation of red or violet colour.	It shows the presence of proteins.
• **Test for Fats**		
(Translucence test)		
Take butter and rub it on a piece of white paper.	Paper becomes translucent.	It shows the presence of fats.

Precautions

(i) Always use small quantities of sample extracts and chemicals to avoid wastage.

(ii) All the test tubes should be washed thoroughly before and after use.

(iii) Use separate droppers for adding different reagents.

(iv) Care must be taken that excess of copper sulphate is not added in Biuret test otherwise there will be blue colour instead of violet colour.

(v) Proper care should be taken while heating the samples in test tube. Keep the mouth of the test tube away from yourself and your friends.

(vi) Proper care should be taken while using acids like HCl and HNO_3 as they may harm your skin.

Viva-Voce

1. In which forms does the carbohydrates get stored in plants and animals?

Ans. Carbohydrates are stored in the form of starch in plants and in the form of glycogen in animals.

2. What are the major sources of protein?

Ans. The major sources of protein are milk, cheese, egg albumin, pulses and nuts.

3. What are the two major tests for the detection of protein in plant and animal samples?

Ans. Biuret test and xanthoproteic test are the two major tests for the detection of protein in plant and animal samples.

4. Why are only few drops of $CuSO_4$ solution added during Biuret test?

Ans. Only few drops of $CuSO_4$ solution should be added during Biuret test because, excess $CuSO_4$ will produce blue colour instead of violet colour.

5. What are the building blocks of proteins?

Ans. Amino acids are the building blocks of proteins, which are held together by peptide bonds.

6. Which test for fats can be done without the use of chemicals?

Ans. When fat or oil is rubbed on white paper, it makes the paper translucent. This translucence test for fats is done without using any chemical.

Experiment 3

Aim

To examine and identify the species belonging to different groups of animals.

Materials Required

Specimens of animals.

Theory

Animals are eukaryotic, multicellular and heterotrophic organisms. Their cells do not have cell walls and most of them are mobile. Kingdom–Animalia is thus classified on the basis of the extent and type of body design as discussed below

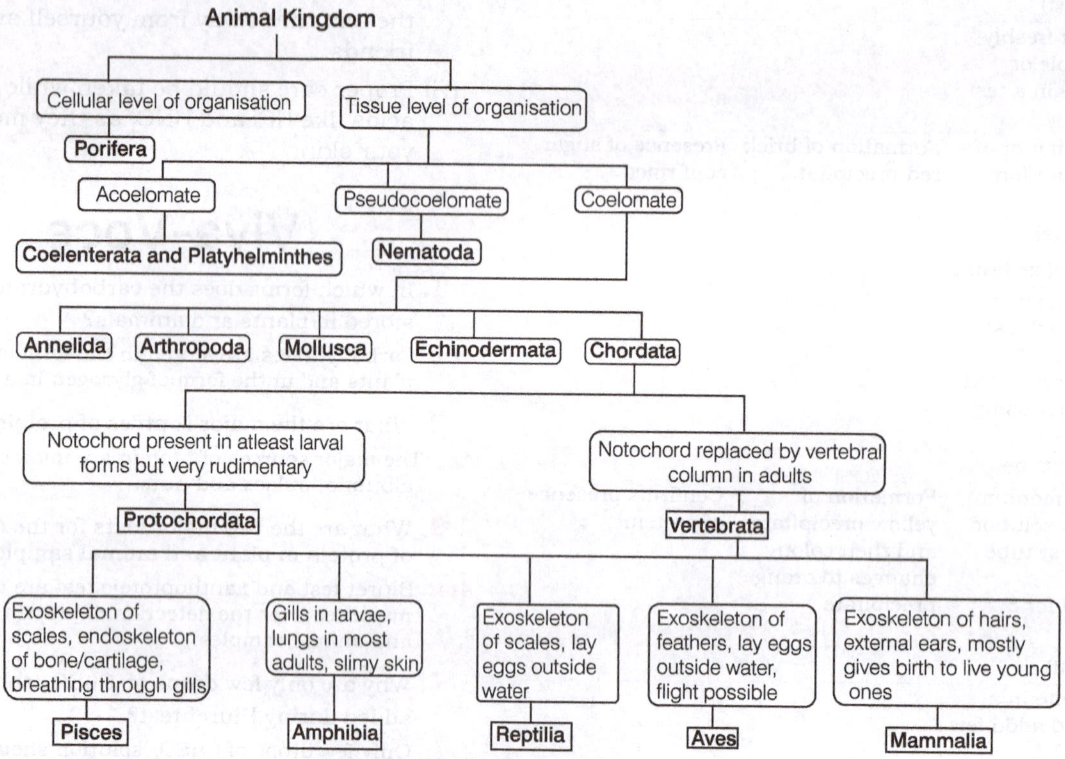

All phyla are grouped under the category invertebrates (animals without backbone) except, the phylum–Chordata. The phylum–Chordata has a **category vertebrates** or animals with a backbone.

Procedure

(i) Observe the preserved specimen carefully. (ii) Note down the characteristics of organism.
(iii) Draw well-labelled diagrams.

Observations

Phylum–Porifera

The characteristics possessed by poriferans are as follows

These are the simplest multicellular organisms.

- Animals that belong to this phylum are commonly called **sponges**.

- The animals show a cavity called **spongocoel**.
- They are mostly found in sea, but few species are found in freshwater like *Spongilla*.
- They may be vase-like, rounded, sac-like or branched.
- Their body is covered with a hard layer or skeleton from outside made up of spicules of calcium carbonate.
- They consist of porous body with innumerable pores called **ostia** which lead to a canal system that helps in circulation of water throughout the body.
- Their single exhalent pore is called **osculum**.
- Young forms or larvae are motile. In adult stage, they attach themselves to submerged (solid) objects and become stationary (sessile).
- Respiration and excretion take place by diffusion through the general surface of the body, e.g. *Spongilla* (freshwater sponge), *Leucosolenia* (simplest sponge), *Euspongia* (bath sponge), *Sycon*, *Euplectella* (venus flower basket), etc.

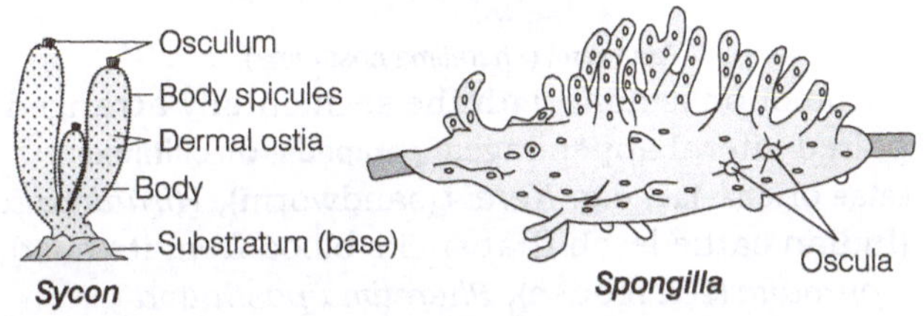

Poriferans

Phylum–Coelenterata

The characteristics possessed by coelenterates are as follows

- These animals show more body design differentiation.
- These organisms are multicellular, diploblastic and acoelomate animals having tissue level of organisation.
- These animals mostly live in marine water and have tentacles (appendages) for locomotion.
- Coelenterates have a central cavity called **coelentron** or **gastrovascular cavity**.
- These exist in two forms, i.e. the **polyps** and **medusae**.
- A gelatinous layer called **mesoglea** or **mesophyll** persists between the ectoderm (epidermis) and endoderm (gastrodermis).
- Body of these animals show radial symmetry.
- The phenomenon of **polymorphism** occurs, which is the specialisation of individuals of colonial species for the division of labour.
- Most of the forms are soft and may have transparent appearance.

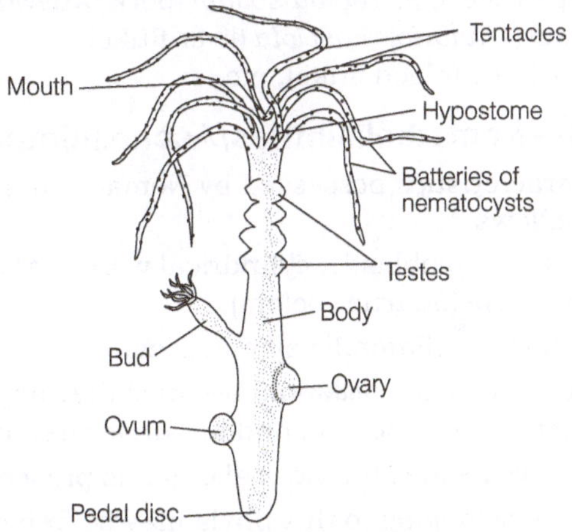

Hydra (Coelenterata)

- Asexual reproduction by budding and sexual reproduction by gametes formed by medusae, e.g. *Hydra*, *Metridium* (sea anemone) and *Aurelia* (jellyfish).

Phylum–Platyhelminthes

The characteristics possessed by Platyhelminthes are as follows

- These are triploblastic, dorsoventrally flattened, leaf-like animals with organ level of organisation. So, these are also called **flatworms**.
- These have bilateral symmetry.
- Body cavity (coelom) is totally absent in these animals.
- Their excretory system consists of blind tubules called **protonephridia**.
- Blind end of a tubule bears a tuft or cilia or a flagellum and is called **flame bulb or flame cell**.
- They can be free-living (*Planaria*) or parasitic (*Fasciola*).

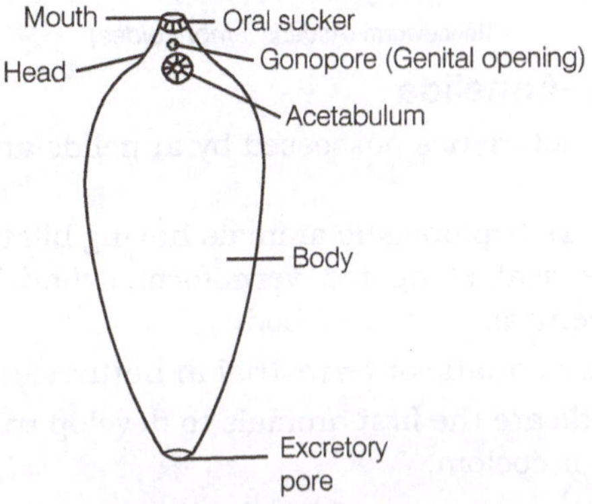

Liver fluke (*Fasciola hepatica*)

- Both male and female reproductive organs are present in the same individual, i.e. they are **hermaphrodite**, e.g. *Taenia solium* (pork tapeworm), *Dugesia* (*Planaria*), *Fasciola* (liver fluke), *Schistosoma* (blood fluke), etc.

Phylum–Nemathelminthes/Aschelminthes

The characteristics possessed by Nemathelminthes are as follows

- These are triploblastic, cylindrical worms having **pseudocoelom** (no true coelom).
- Their body is bilaterally symmetrical.
- These are called **roundworms** because they appear circular in cross-section and are unsegmented.
- They have tissues but no real organ is present.
- Animals belonging to this phyla may be free living or parasitic.
- Their digestive system consists of mouth and anus.
- In these animals, sexes are separate (unisexual), e.g. *Ascaris* (roundworm), *Ancylostoma* (hookworm), *Wuchereria bancrofti* (filarial worm causing elephantiasis), *Enterobius* (pinworm of human), etc.

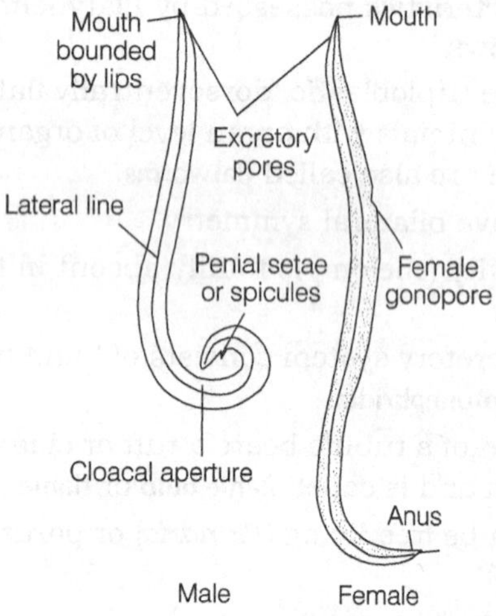

Roundworm (*Ascaris lumbricoides*)

Phylum–Annelida

The characteristics possessed by annelids are as follows

- These are triploblastic animals having bilaterally symmetrical, elongated, vermiform, cylindrical or dorsoventrally flattened body.
- They are aquatic or terrestrial in nature.
- Annelids are the first animals to develop true body cavity or coelom.
- Their alimentary canal is tube-like, complete and extends straight from mouth to anus.
- This differentiation occurs in a segmental fashion, with the segments lined up one after the other from head to tail (metameric segmentation).
- They respire through skin.
- Excretion in these animals occurs by paired segmental nephridia. Their sexes may be **hermaphroditic** (separate).

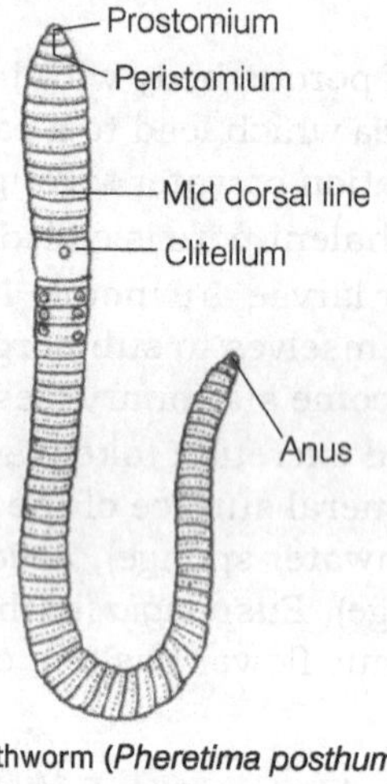

Earthworm (*Pheretima posthuma*)

- Locomotion is done with the segmentally arranged paired lateral appendages, **parapodia** or **chitinous setae** or **chaetae**, e.g. *Nereis* (sandworm), *Hirudinaria* (Indian cattle leech that sucks blood from its host), *Aphrodite* (sea mouse), *Pheretima posthuma* (earthworm), etc.

Phylum–Arthropoda

The characteristics possessed by arthropods are as follows

- These are triploblastic, bilaterally symmetrical and segmented animals.
- Body segments are grouped into two regions, i.e. **cephalothorax** (head and thorax together) and **abdomen** or three regions, i.e. head, thorax and abdomen.
- It consists of an impermeable exoskeleton, composed of structural polysaccharide called **chitin**.
- Muscular system with exoskeleton for attachment is present and cilia are absent.
- Body segment of these animals (somite) usually bears paired lateral and jointed legs or appendages.
- Body cavity is filled with blood, they have open circulatory system.
- **Compound eyes** are present with mosaic vision.
- A pair of antenna is attached to the head which have sensory function.

- Sexes are separate, e.g. cockroach, prawn, mosquitoes, etc.

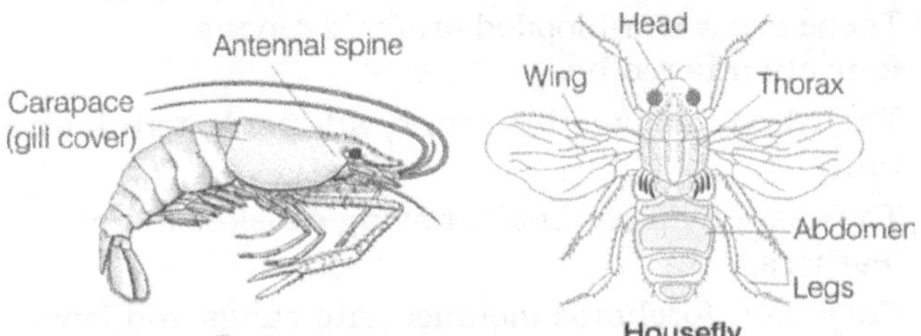

Prawn Housefly

Phylum–Mollusca

The characteristics possessed by molluscs are as follows

- Body is soft and has bilateral symmetry.
- Little segmentation is present without appendages.
- The coelomic cavity is reduced and restricted to the pericardial cavity and lumen of the gonads and nephridia.
- Open circulatory system is present. Kidney-like structures or a pair of **metanephridia** are present for excretion.
- They respire through **gills** (called **ctenidia**) or **mantle**.
- Their sexes are usually separate.
- A muscular foot is present for locomotion, e.g. *Dentalium* (tusk shell), *Pila* (apple snail), *Unio* (freshwater mussel), *Pinctada* (Indian pearl oyster), *Chiton*, *Octopus*, etc.

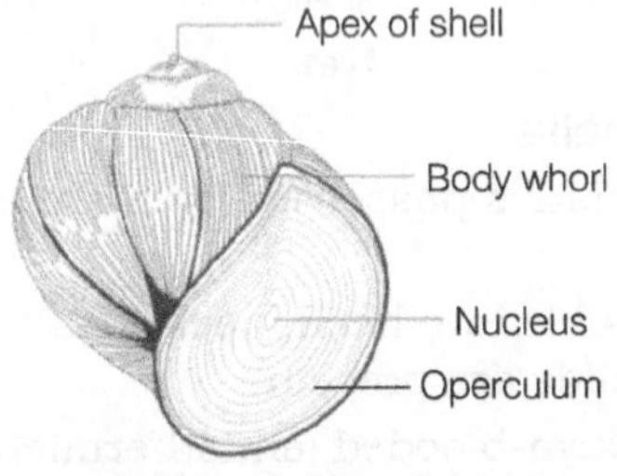

Apple snail (*Pila globosa*)

Phylum–Echinodermata

The characteristics possessed by echinoderms are as follows

- These are simple spiny skinned animals which may be star-like, spherical or elongated.
- These are triploblastic, coelomate, unsegmented and show radial symmetry (bilateral in larval); pentamerous symmetry in case of adults.
- These are marine animals.
- Tube feet are present which help in locomotion and exchange of gases.
- Body wall is covered with spiny plates (ossicles) that form a rigid or flexible endoskeleton.
- Their sexes are separate, e.g. *Antedon* (feather star), *Holothuria*, *Echinus* (sea urchin), *Asterias* (starfish or sea star), *Ophiura* (brittle star), etc.

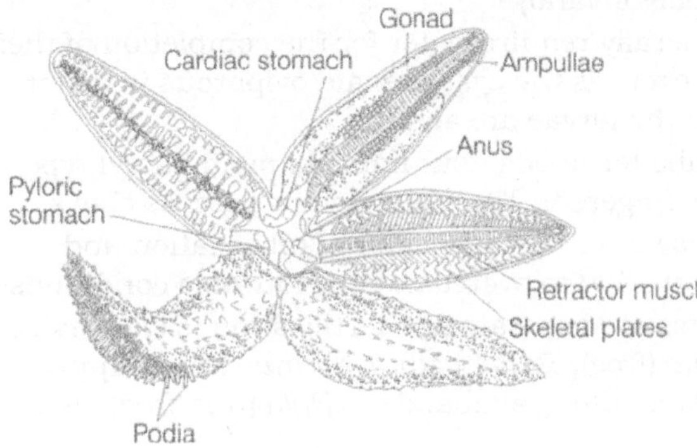

Starfish

Class–Pisces (Fishes)

The characteristics possessed by Pisces are as follows

- These are exclusively aquatic animals.
- They have stream lined body covered with scales that ends in a muscular tail (which helps in movement).
- Fins are present, but limbs are absent.
- Respiration occurs by gills by taking oxygen dissolved in water.

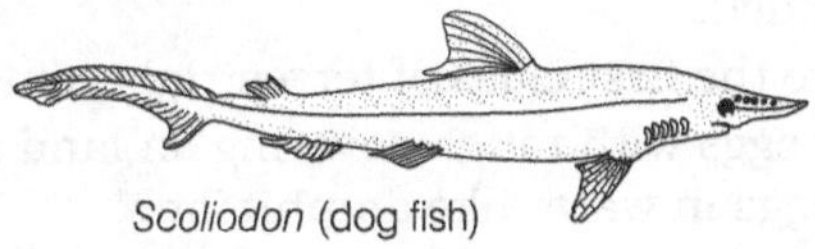

Scoliodon (dog fish)

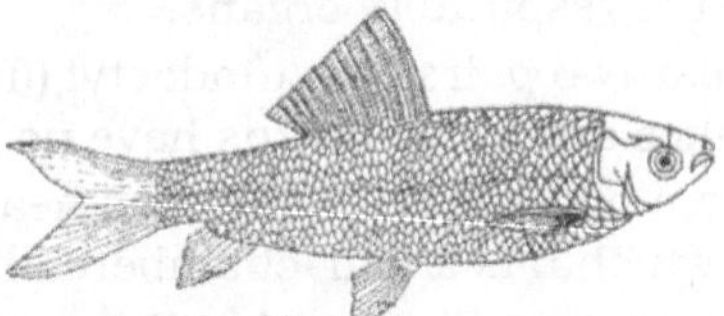

Labeo rohita

- They are cold-blooded (ectothermic) and have two-chambered heart.
- Most of them lay eggs, e.g. *Chimaera* (rat fish), angler fish, lion fish, rohu, *Catla catla*, *Scoliodon*.

Class–Amphibia

The characteristics possessed by amphibians are as follows

- They are amphibious in nature, *viz*, can live on land as well as in water and were the first chordates to live on land.
- They lack scales and have mucous glands in their skin which secrete mucus that keeps the skin moist.
- Amphibians are cold-blooded and have three-chambered heart.

- They have distinct head and trunk. Neck and tail may or may not be present.
- Respiration can be either by gills (in water) or by lungs (on land).
- Generally require water for the completion of their life cycle as the eggs are laid oviparous in water and the larvae are aquatic.
- Limbs tetrapods (four limbed), pentadactyl type (five fingered). The digits do not possess claws.
- These have peculiar habit of hibernation and aestivation to overcome unfavourable conditions.
- Sexes are separate and fertilisation is external, e.g. *Rana* (frog), *Bufo* (toad), *Necturus* (mud puppy), *Salamandra* (salamander), *Hyla* (tree-frog), etc.

(a) Salamander (b) Toad

Amphibians

Class–Reptilia

The characteristics possessed by reptiles are as follows

- These animals possess dry skin, with scales and mostly live in warmer regions. They are cold-blooded.
- These are the first class of terrestrial animals.
- They lay eggs with tough covering on land and do not lay eggs in water like amphibians.
- Lungs are the respiratory organs.
- Reptiles bear two pairs of pentadactyl (five digits) limbs (snakes and some lizards have no limbs).
- Most of them have three-chambered heart except crocodile, which has a four-chambered heart.
- Sexes are separate. Fertilisation is internal.

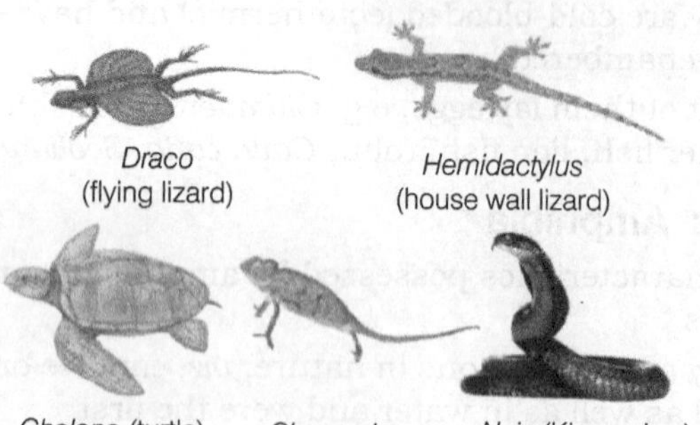

Draco (flying lizard) *Hemidactylus* (house wall lizard)

Chelone (turtle) *Chamaeleon* *Naja* (King cobra)

Reptiles

- Embryo of these animals is protected inside the egg by extraembryonic membrane, e.g. *Chelone* (turtle), *Chamaeleon, Naja* (cobra), *Hemidactylus* (house wall lizard), *Testudo* (tortoise), *Draco* (flying lizard), etc.

Class–Aves

The characteristics possessed by Aves are as follows

- These are warm-blooded animals having four-chambered heart.
- Their body is divisible into head, neck, trunk and tail.
- These are flying animals, having exoskeleton of feathers.
- They have forelimbs modified into wings and jaws modified into horny toothless beak.
- Bones are light in weight because of air spaces (pneumatic bones) and body is streamlined to reduce air resistance during flight.
- Lungs with air sacs are present for double respiration.
- The syrinx is responsible for production of sound.
- Birds are egg-laying where egg possesses large amount of yolk and the shell covering the yolk is hard and calcareous.
- Sexes are separate and fertilisation is internal, e.g. *Ciconia ciconia* (white stork), *Aythya fuligula* (male tufted duck), *Struthio camelus* (ostrich), pigeon, crow, sparrow, etc.

Pigeon Sparrow Crow

Aves

Class–Mammalia

The characteristics possessed by mammals are as follows

- Body is divisible into head, neck, trunk and tail. Movable eyelids are present.
- These are warm-blooded (endothermic) animals which have four-chambered heart. Females have mammary glands for the production of milk to nourish the young ones.
- These are known to be the advanced group of animals with a very well-developed brain.
- Skin is covered with hair and has sweat glands and oil glands.
- Mammalia is the first class to mark the presence of ear pinna (external fleshy ear). Middle ear is with three ossicles, i.e. malleus, incus and stapes.
- Different types of teeth are in jaw socket present in these animals, i.e. heterodont and thecodont.
- Each digit ends up with claws, hoofs or nails.

- Limbs are adapted for walking, running, swimming, burrowing and even flying (bats).
- Most mammals produce live young ones (i.e. they are viviparous) but some like platypus and echidna produce eggs (i.e. are oviparous) and some like kangaroos give birth to poorly developed young ones.
- Respiration is through lungs only.
- They excrete urea (ureotelic animals) and fertilisation is internal, e.g. *Rattus* (rat), *Homo sapiens* (human), *Felis* (cat), bat, *Canis* (dog), chimpanzee, *Macropus* (kangaroo), whale, dolphins, walrus (aquatic mammals).

Mammals

Viva-Voce

1. What is the common name for animals that belong to phylum–Porifera?

Ans. Sponges.

2. State reason for the following. Platyhelminthes are called flatworms.

Ans. They are called so because their body is dorsiventrally flattened.

3. Write the type of body cavity and symmetry possessed by nematodes.

Ans. Body cavity–Pseudocoelom.
Symmetry–Bilateral

4. State the phylum to which liver fluke and *Planaria* belong.

Ans. Liver fluke and *Planaria* belong to the phylum–Platyhelminthes.

5. Name a herbivorous mollusc that leads an amphibious life

Ans. *Pila globosa* (Apple snail).

6. Echinoderms are marine animals. What is their skeleton made up of?

Ans. Their skeleton is made up of calcium carbonate.

7. Name the substance with which coelomic cavity of arthropods is filled. What types of symmetry do they have?

Ans. In Arthropoda, the coelomic cavity is filled with blood (haemolymph). Arthropods have bilateral symmetry.

8. State any two features which belong to class-Aves.

Ans. Two features which belong to class-Aves are as follows
(i) They are warm-blooded animals with a four-chambered heart.
(ii) Their body is divisible into head, neck, trunk and tail.

9. State the phylum which do not have true coelom.

Ans. Phylum-Nematoda.

10. How does excretion take place in Annelida?

Ans. Excretion takes place through nephridia.

Experiment 4

Aim

To identify the structures of lungs and skin of humans.

Materials Required

The chart, specimen or model of lungs and skin.

Theory

1. **Lungs** These are the respiratory organs present in human body.
2. **Skin** It is the largest organ of human body. It forms the outermost covering of the body and is stretched to form a layer. It performs many important functions such as protection, temperature regulation, excretion and synthesis of vitamin-D. It serves as sensory organ for various stimuli such as touch, pressure, pain, etc.

Observation

Characteristic features of lungs of humans are as follows

(i) The lungs are thin-walled, elastic, spongy, pinkish, triangular and highly distensible structures.

(ii) A pair of lungs is present in the thoracic cavity of humans.

(iii) Right and left lungs are well-protected by bony structures called **rib cage.**

(iv) The intercostal muscles of rib cage help in breathing movements.

(v) Each lung is covered by internal and external pleural membranes.

(vi) These membranes are filled with pleural fluid which acts as shock absorber and also as lubricant to facilitate free expansion and relaxation.

(vii) Trachea (windpipe) branches into two bronchi in the chest cavity.

(viii) Each bronchus divides into smaller bronchioles on each side of the left and right lungs.

(ix) Each small bronchiole leads to the alveolar ducts which form alveolar sacs.

(x) A large number of alveolar sacs are present in human lungs.

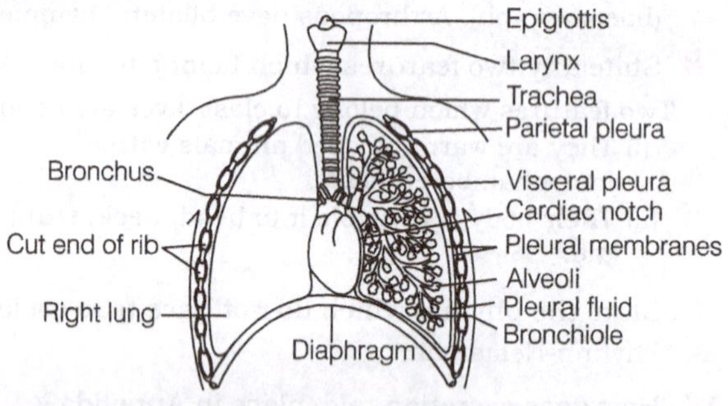

Human respiratory system (sectional view)

Characteristic features of human skin

(i) Skin is composed of epidermis and dermis, both layers are separated by thin basement membranes.

(ii) The epidermis consists of flattened cells having keratin. This layer is called **stratum corneum.**

(iii) The cells above the basement membrane are called **Malpighian**, forming a layer of cuboidal epithelial cells.

(iv) Colouration of the skin is due to melanin contained in the cells of Malpighian layer.

(v) The dermal layer is rich in fibres, blood capillaries, lymph vessels, sensory cells, sebaceous glands, sweat glands and hair follicles.

(vi) Sebaceous glands secrete oily sebum whereas sweat glands open on the surface of epidermis by a sweat pore.

(vii) The thickness of the skin is not same on the different parts of the body.

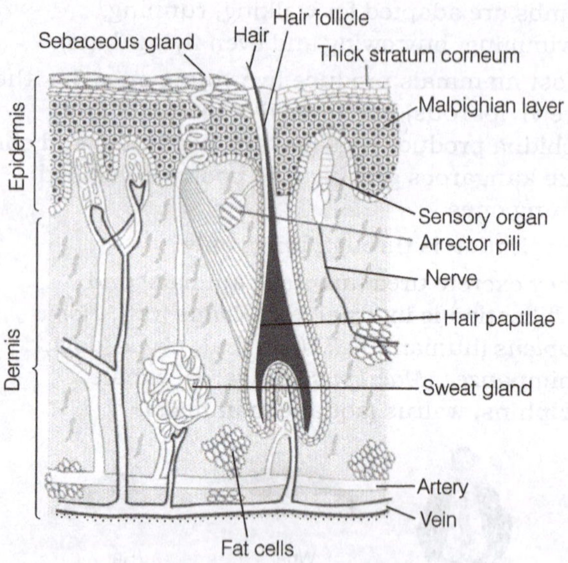

Vertical section of human skin

Viva-Voce

1. State the structure which protects the lungs.

Ans. Bony rib cage is present around the lungs in the human body which protects them.

2. Explain the mechanism of expansion and contraction of lungs.

Ans. The intercostal muscles present in the rib cage move the thoracic cavity up and down. This helps in expansion and contraction of lungs.

3. Which structures of lungs are responsible for gaseous exchange?

Ans. Alveoli are blind end sacs in lungs where gaseous exchange occurs.

4. State the function of pleural fluid.

Ans. It reduces the friction on the lung surface.

5. Which type of cells are found in the lining of air sacs?

Ans. Alveolar sac is lined by squamous epithelial cells.

6. What is the basement membrane found in skin?

Ans. It is a cellular membrane found between epidermis and dermis layer of skin.

7. State two functions of skin.

Ans. Two function of skin are as follows

- Skin covers all body organs and protects them against various shocks and harmful UV rays.
- It acts as a sense organ for touch, pain and other sensations.

8. What is keratin?

Ans. It is a kind of protein found in skin which is produced by the cells of stratum corneum.

9. Name the outermost layer of the skin.

Ans. Epidermis is the outermost layer of skin.

Experiment 5

Aim

To show the mechanism of breathing by using bell jar setup.

Materials Required

A bell jar, balloons, Y-shaped glass tube, rubber stopper and thread.

Procedure

(i) Tie the rubber sheet at the bottom of bell jar.

(ii) At the opposite end of bell jar, put up a rubber stopper.

(iii) Insert the Y-shaped glass tube in the jar with balloons attached to its two arms with thread.

(iv) Tube represents windpipe and bronchi.

(v) Two balloons represent lungs and the tied rubber sheet represents diaphragm.

(vi) Now, pull the rubber sheeting down with the help of thread and observe any change in it.

(vii) Slowly allow the rubber sheet to get to its original position.

Observations

(i) At first, when we pull rubber sheet downwards with the help of thread, the balloons expand and air gets inside, *via*. Y-tube.

(ii) When rubber sheet is pushed upwards the balloons collapse as air rushes out.

Conclusion

(i) When the rubber sheet is pulled down, the balloons (lungs) inflate because the volume of bell jar (thoracic cavity) and its pressure decreases.
Thus, the air rushes in through the tube and fills the balloons (inspiration).

(ii) When the rubber sheet is pulled up the balloons deflate because the volume of bell jar and pressure in it increases, thus the air rushes out from the balloons (expiration).

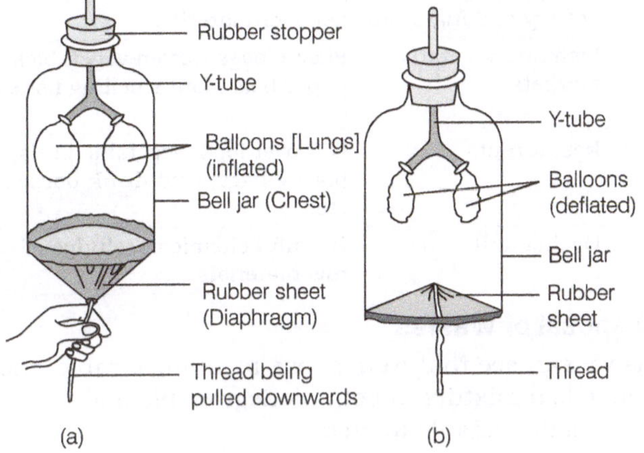

Bell jar experiment for mechanism of breathing

Viva-Voce

1. Define breathing.

Ans. The mechanical process of taking in of oxygen and releasing out carbon dioxide is called breathing.

2. What do balloons represent in above experiment?

Ans. Balloons represent a pair of lungs.

3. How is windpipe represented in experiment?

Ans. Windpipe is represented with the help of glass tube.

4. How are lungs protected?

Ans. Lungs are protected with the help of ribs.

5. What is the significance of Y-shaped tube?

Ans. Y-shaped tube signifies bronchi, when we compare it with human respiratory system.

Experiment 6

Aim

To visit a few establishments in the locality and study the type of waste produced and methods for their disposal.

Theory

Any thing or material which is of no use to us and is discarded is called **waste**. Different sources generate different kinds of waste.

A visit to some of the establishments gave us the insight on the kind of waste generated is there. These are listed in a table below

Source/Establishment	Waste generated
Motor repair workshop	Discarded batteries, machine parts, chemicals, paints.
Kilns	Produces solid, liquid and gaseous waste.
Pottery making units	Leftover material.
Fish and vegetable markets	Plastic bags, rotten vegetables, paper bags, foul smelling fishes.
Restaurants	Left over food, vegetable peels, plastic bags, cold-drink bottles, etc.
Dyeing units	Harmful chemicals, sludge of raw materials.

Disposal of Wastes

As we can see that from above mentioned table, the waste is a mixture of both biodegradable and non-biodegradable wastes.

Biodegradable waste includes rotten vegetables, left over food, vegetable peels, etc, while non-biodegradable is discarded batteries, harmful chemicals, plastic bags, etc. Safe disposal of wastes includes segregation of wastes into different categories and then disposing it off. Some common methods of disposal are composting (for biodegradable wastes like vegetable peels, left over food, etc), landfills, incineration and sewage treatment (for non-biodegradable wastes like plastic bags, glass bottles, machine parts, etc).

Viva-Voce

1. Can office waste be reduced at individual level? If yes how?

Ans. Office waste can be reduced at individual level by

(i) Using both sides of the paper to write or print in, order to reduce paper waste.

(ii) Adopting paperless ways to communicate, e.g. *via* mails.

2. Which type of waste is produced by motor repair workshop?

Ans. The waste produced is more of non-biodegradable type such as batteries, chemicals or motor parts.

3. Is domestic waste biodegradable?

Ans. No, most of domestic waste is biodegradable, which includes stuff from kitchen. But some non-biodegradable substances are also present like plastic bags, bottles, etc.

4. Give two examples of agricultural waste.

Ans. Crop residues, pesticides.

5. Which industry produces most toxic waste?

Ans. Nuclear reactors release more toxic waste.

Experiment 7

Aim

To visit a water treatment plant, sewage treatment plant, garbage dumping or vermicomposting sites in the locality and study their working.

Theory

Any undesirable thing present on land, soil or air which is useless or unwanted is called **waste.**

Waste is categorised into domestic, industrial, agricultural depending upon the source from where it is generated. The waste so generated is either disposed off or treated in water treatment plant for reuse.

Observation

Sewage Treatment

The waste in liquid form originates mainly from domestic and industrial sources. The sewage is treated in waste water treatment plants before dumping it into the water bodies. The treatment involves various physical, chemical and biological processes in order to remove the physical, chemical and biological impurities.

The treatment of sewage is carried out in the following stages

(i) **Primary treatment** It is a physical process that involves physical removal of large as well as small particles from the sewage through filtration and sedimentation in primary settling tanks. Initially, the floating debris is removed by sequential filtration and then, soil and small pebbles are removed by sedimentation. All solids undergo sedimentation and settle down to constitute the primary sludge. The supernatant left after removing primary sludge, constitutes the effluent. This effluent is taken out for secondary treatment.

(ii) **Secondary treatment** It involves microbial degradation of organic matter. The primary effluent is passed into large aeration tanks, where it is constantly agitated mechanically. Air containing heterotrophic microorganisms is constantly pumped into the effluent. This allows a vigorous growth of aerobic microbes into flocs, i.e. masses of bacteria associated with fungal filaments to form mesh-like structures.

While growing, these microbes consume the major part of the organic matter, present in the effluent which significantly reduces the BOD (Biochemical Oxygen Demand). The sewage water is further treated till the BOD reduces significantly. Then, the effluent of aeration tank is passed into a settling tank, where the bacterial 'flocs' are allowed to sediment. This sediment is called **activated sludge.**
A small part of the activated sludge is pumped back into the aeration tank to serve as bacterial inoculum. The remaining major part of the sludge is pumped into large tanks called **anaerobic sludge digesters.** Here, methanogenic bacteria, which grow anaerobically, digest the bacteria and fungi present in the sludge.

During this digestion, bacteria produce a mixture of gases such as methane, hydrogen sulphide and carbon dioxide. These gases form biogas which can be used as the source of energy as it is inflammable.
The effluent from the secondary treatment plant is generally released into natural water bodies like rivers and streams.

(iii) **Tertiary treatment** It is a physio-chemical process. It involves disinfecting the water if it is to be used for domestic purposes. It is done by various methods such as reverse osmosis, treating with chlorine, ozone gas or perchlorate salts.

Dumping

The process of depositing the collected wastes in an area is called dumping. Several sites are landmarked as waste disposal sites, also known as **landfills.** Proper method of disposal involves spreading of uniform thin layer which gets solidified. Before adding another layer of waste, a 3m layer of clean soil is also added.

Composting

It is a method of solid waste disposal where the organic waste matter is allowed to decompose by microbes and soil organism. In this method, the waste not only gets disposed but fertiliser is also made by natural process. Following are the steps of composting

- A pit of about 5 m long, approximately 1.5 m wide and 1.5 m deep is dugged in the soil.
- The organic or biodegradable waste is piled up and layered in a loose manner for air passage.
- The layer is fully wetted with a watery mixture of cowdung and some mud.
- A second layer of mixed refuse is spread after few days so that decomposition of matter is faster.
- About 50-60 days later, the compost or manure is ready. It can be applied in the agricultural fields, garden, etc., for good growth.
- Composting with the help of earthworms is called **vermicomposting.**

Uses of Compost

- In nurseries, landscape sites, greenhouse, etc.
- Used by farmers and gardeners as it provides nutrition to growing crops.

Viva-Voce

1. What do you mean by domestic waste?

Ans. The waste which comes out from homes is called domestic waste.

2. What is non-biodegradable waste?

Ans. The waste which cannot be decomposed in nature is called a non-biodegradable waste, e.g. plastic.

3. Give example of biodegradable wastes.

Ans. Vegetable peels, left over food, etc.

4. How can we decompose biodegradable waste?

Ans. Biodegradable waste can be converted into compost.

5. What kind of worms are used for vermicomposting?

Ans. Redworms.

LATEST
ICSE Specimen PAPER
Biology (Fully Solved)

General Instructions

1. You will not be allowed to write during the first 15 minutes. This time is to be spent in reading the question paper.
2. The time given at the head of this paper is the time allowed for writing the answers.
3. Attempt all questions from Section I and any 4 questions from Section II.
4. The intended marks for questions or parts of questions are given in brackets [ ].

Time : 2 Hrs **Max. Marks : 80**

Section-I [40 *Marks*]

1. (a) Name the following [5]

(i) The region of the axis between the point of attachment of cotyledons and the plumule.

(ii) The undigested cellulose which is fibrous in nature.

(iii) A vaccine for poliomyelitis.

(iv) A large hole at the back of the cranium through which the spinal cord passes.

(v) A serious food poisoning disease caused due to bacterium in tinned foods.

(b) Given below are sets of five terms each. Rewrite the terms in correct order in a logical sequence beginning with the term that is underlined. [5]

(i) Sacrum, Thoracic, Coccyx, <u>Cervical</u>, Lumbar

(ii) Larynx, Pharynx, Bronchioles, <u>Nostrils</u>, Alveoli

(iii) Pollen tube, Stigma, Ovary, <u>Pollen grain</u>, Embryo sac

(iv) Rectum, <u>Pharynx</u>, Oesophagus, Duodenum, Stomach

(v) Nuclear membrane, <u>Cell wall</u>, Cytoplasm, Nucleolus, Cell membrane

(c) Differentiate between the following pairs on the basis of what is given in the brackets [5]

(i) Tendon and Ligament (Function).

(ii) Parotid gland and Sublingual gland (Location).

(iii) Tidal volume and Residual volume (Volume of air).

(iv) Leucoderma and Albinism (Type of disorder).

(v) Epidemic disease and Endemic disease (Example).

(d) Mention the exact location of the following [5]

(i) Pancreas (ii) Ovules

(iii) Centrosome (iv) Sternum

(v) Ceruminous glands

(e) Choose the correct answer from each of the four options given below [5]

(i) The barrier between the protoplasm and the outer environment in a plant cell is

A. nuclear membrane

B. plasma membrane

C. tonoplast

D. cell wall

(ii) The term neuter is given to a flower in which both

A. calyx and corolla are present.

B. calyx and corolla are absent.

C. androecium and gynoecium are present.

D. androecium and gynoecium are absent.

(iii) In *Vallisneria*, pollination takes place by the agency of

A. water B. wind C. birds D. insects

(iv) The group of plants having naked seeds

A. Angiosperms B. Bryophyta

C. Pteridophyta D. Gymnosperms

(v) Mammary glands are modified
A. sweat glands B. gastric glands
C. tear glands D. sebaceous glands

(f) Match the items given in **Column A** with the most appropriate ones in **Column B** and rewrite the correct matching pairs. [5]

	Column A		Column B
A.	Patella	1.	Maize flowers
B.	Adult man	2.	*Plasmodium*
C.	*E*-waste	3.	Knee joint
D.	Anemophilous	4.	Plastic
E.	Malaria	5.	16 teeth in each jaw
		6.	Mobile batteries
		7.	Elbow joint
		8.	14 teeth in each jaw

(g) Choose the **odd** one out from the following terms given and name the catgory to which the others belong [5]
(i) Carbolic acid, Boric acid, DDT, Benzoic acid
(ii) Hepatitis, Cholera, Chicken pox, AIDS
(iii) Vegetable peel, Syringes, CDs, Styrofoam
(iv) Shark, Dogfish, Starfish, Trout
(v) Gram seed, Pea seed, Rice, Bean seed

(h) Given below is a diagram depicting a physiological process in man.
Study the same and answer the following questions [5]

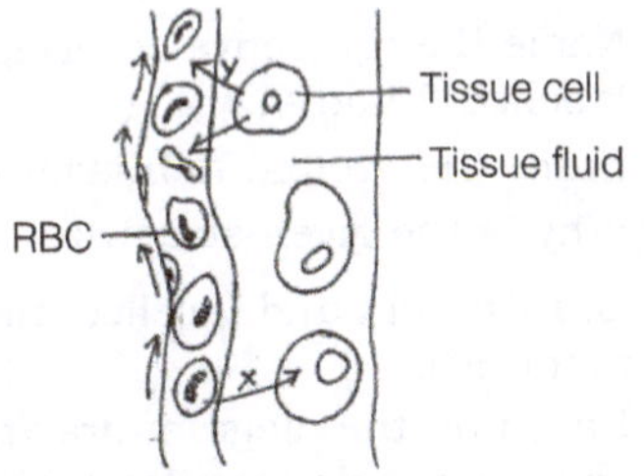

(i) Name the process occurring in the diagram.
(ii) Explain the process mentioned in part (i).
(iii) Label the gases '*X*' and '*Y*'.
(iv) Write a balanced chemical equation for the process shown.
(v) Name the organelle where cellular respiration takes place.

Section-II [40 Marks]

2. (a) Study the diagram and answer the questions that follows [5]
(i) Label the parts 1 – 4.
(ii) Give the function of parts labelled 3, 4 and 6.
(iii) Name the protein present in the part labelled '1'.
(iv) Name the pigment that gives colour to the skin.
(v) Name the fluid secreted by the part labelled '5'.

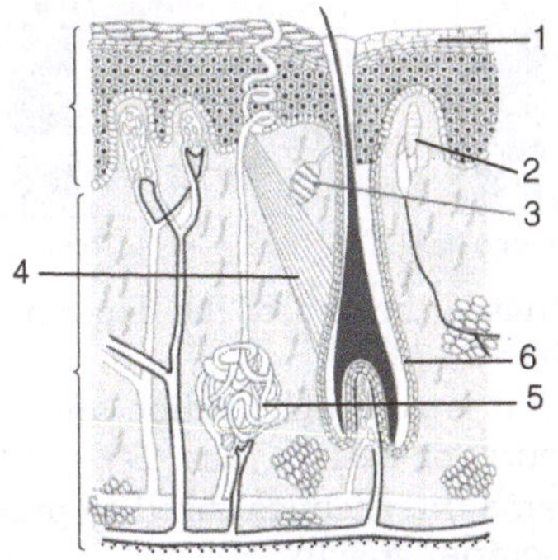

(b) Complete the following paragraph by filling in the blanks (i) to (x) with appropriate words: [5]
The hindlimb consists of a long bone __(i)__ in the thigh, two long bones, the inner __(ii)__ and the outer __(iii)__ in the shank, seven __(iv)__ bones in the ankle, five long __(v)__ bones in the middle of the foot and fourteen __(vi)__ in the toes. The forelimb consists of a long bone __(vii)__ in the upper arm and two long bones __(viii)__ and __(ix)__ in the lower arm. The wrist has eight bones called __(x)__ .

3. (a) Study the diagram given below and answer the questions that follows [5]

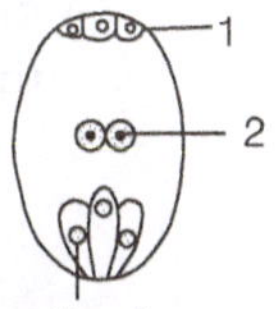

(i) Identify the above structure and mention its location in a flower.
(ii) Label the parts numbered 1 and 2.
(iii) Explain the term 'double fertilisation'.
(iv) What is the fate of the calyx and corolla after fertilisation?
(v) Draw a neat, labelled diagram of a pollen grain.

(b) Give an example for each of the following [5]
(i) A poriferan
(ii) An antibiotic
(iii) A coelenterate
(iv) A deficiency disease
(v) A mammal
(vi) An annelid worm
(vii) A reptilian
(viii) A fat soluble vitamin
(ix) An amphibian
(x) A protein deficiency disease.

4. (a) Study the experimental set up given below and answer the following questions [5]

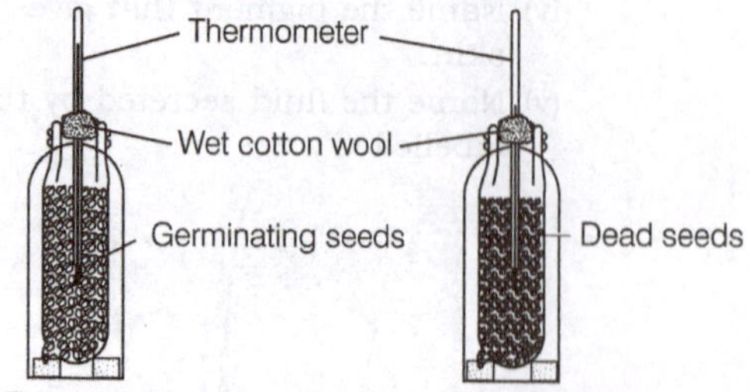

(i) What is the aim of the experiment shown above?

(ii) What is your observation after a few hours for flask 'A' and 'B'?

(iii) Name the chemical used to prevent bacterial growth.
Explain how the bacteria would interfere with the experiment.

(iv) Why do we use thermos flasks specifically for the experiment?

(v) Which is the control setup and why?

(b) Fill in the blanks with suitable words [5]

(i) (1) .... $\xrightarrow{\text{Renin}}$ (2) ....

(ii) (3) .... $\xrightarrow{\text{Maltase}}$ (4) ....

(iii) Emulsified fat $\xrightarrow{\text{Lipase}}$ (5) .... + (6) ....

(iv) (7) .... $\xrightarrow{\text{Erepsin}}$ (8) ....

(v) (9) .... $\xrightarrow{\text{Pepsin}}$ (10) ....

5. (a) Study the diagram given below and answer the questions that follows [5]

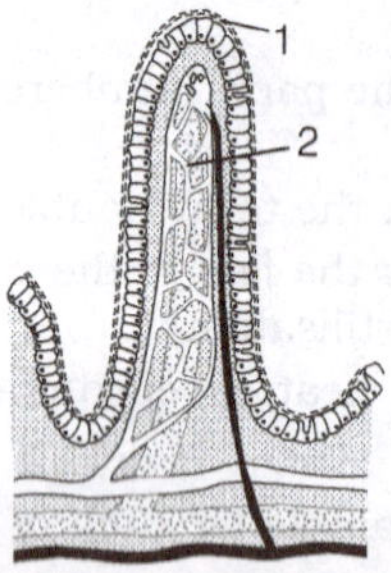

(i) Name the structure shown in the diagram.
State in which part of small intestine, it is present?

(ii) How is this structure well-adapted for absorption of digested food?

(iii) Label the parts numbered 1 and 2.

(iv) Name the lymph vessel present inside the structure.

(v) Name the digestive juice secreted by the liver.
What are the two pigments present in it?

(b) Give appropriate biological/technical terms for the following [5]

(i) The mode of arrangement of flowers on the axis of the plant.

(ii) The type of waste generated in hospitals and pathological laboratories.

(iii) Different timings of maturation of androecium and gynoecium.

(iv) The process of formation of a seedling from the embryo.

(v) The energy currency of the cell.

(vi) The category of immunity required in the treatment of a snake bite.

(vii) The outermost covering of a vacuole.

(viii) The membrane that encloses the lungs.

(ix) The tissue which stores fat.

(x) The device used to remove gaseous and particulate air pollutants.

6. (a) Study the diagram given below and answer the questions that follows [5]

(i) Name the structure shown and label its parts 1 and 2.

(ii) Is the given structure albuminous or non-albuminous?
Give reason for your answer.

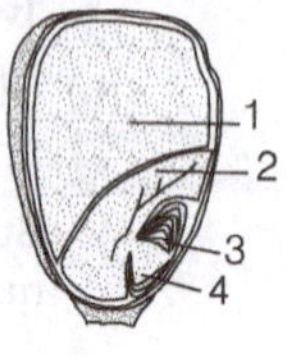

(iii) Name the protective coverings of part labelled 3 and 4.

(iv) Name the protein rich layer of endosperm.

(v) Why is the given structure called a grain?

(b) (i) Draw a neat and labelled diagram of a plant cell.

(ii) Based on the diagram drawn above in (i), give a suitable term for each of the following descriptions

1. The site of protein synthesis.
2. A cell organelle that is absent in a plant cell.
3. The supporting framework of the cell.
4. The plastids that contain DNA and have the capacity to divide.
5. The structures that carry the hereditary units.
6. The cell organelle that regulates all the metabolic functions.
7. The structure that is semipermeable in nature. [5]

7. (a) Given below are four living structures. Study the same and answer the questions given below [5]

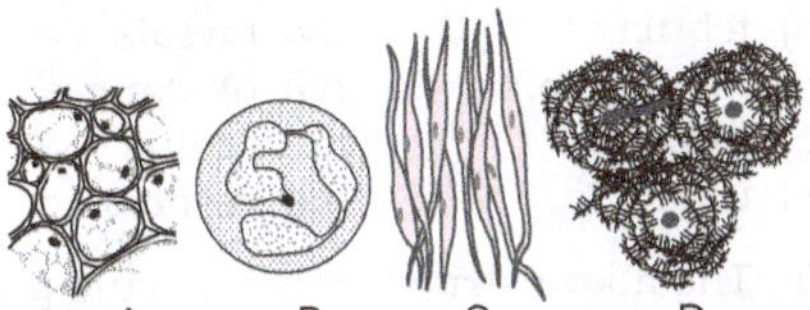

(i) Name the structure A, B, C and D.
(ii) State the living cells in the structure 'D'.
(iii) Name the fluid in which the structure 'B' is found.
(iv) What is the function of the structure 'C'?
(v) Draw a neat, labelled diagram of a neuron.

(b) Answer the following questions briefly [5]
(i) State two activities of the red cross.
(ii) State any two ways by which food can be preserved.
(iii) One should breathe through the nose and not through the mouth. Explain.
(iv) The wall of the trachea is supported by 'C'-shaped cartilaginous rings.
Give a suitable reason.
(v) State two activities of WHO.

Answers

Section-I

1. (a) (i) Epicotyl
(ii) Roughage
(iii) Salk's vaccine and sabin vaccine
(iv) Foramen Magnum
(v) Botulism

(b) (i) Cervical, Thoracic, Lumbar, Sacrum, Coccyx
(ii) Nostrils, Pharynx, Larynx, Bronchioles, Alveoli
(iii) Pollen grain, Stigma, Pollen tube, Ovary, Embryo sac
(iv) Pharynx, Oesophagus, Stomach, Duodenum, Rectum
(v) Cell wall, Cell membrane, Cytoplasm, Nuclear membrane, Nucleolus

(c) (i) Tendon and Ligament (function)

Tendon	Ligament
Tendons attaches bone to muscles and help in movement of bones.	Ligaments attaches bone to bone and keep them stable.

(ii) Parotid gland and Sublingual gland (Location)

Parotid gland	Sublingual gland
These glands are located an either side of mouth and in front of both ears.	These glands are located inferior to the tongue (in floor of our mouth).

(iii) Tidal volume and Residual volume (Volume of air)

Tidal volume	Residual volume
Tidal volume is the volume of air inspired and expired during normal breathing. Its volume is about 500 mL.	Residual volume is the amount of air that remains in an individual's lung after a forceful exhalation. It is about 1100-1200 mL.

(iv) Leucoderma and Albinism (Type of disorder)

Leucoderma	Albinism
In this disorder skin pigmentation is lost from smaller or larger patches at different regions of the body.	In this disorder, the pigment is completely lost from all over the body.

(v) Epidemic disease and Endemic disease (Example)

Epidemic disease	Endemic disease
When a disease affects large segment of a population, e.g. plague spread in 1994 in India.	When a disease is confined to a specific place and reoccurs frequently, e.g. goitre in hilly areas.

(d) (i) **Pancreas** is located across the back of the abdomen, behind the stomach.
(ii) **Ovules** are present in the ovary.
(iii) **Centrosome** is present near the nucleus of the animal cell.

(iv) **Sternum** is located on the ventral midline of thorax (centre of the chest).

(v) **Ceruminous glands** are present in the external auditory canal.

(e) (i) (D) cell wall

(ii) (D) androecium and gynoecium are absent.

(iii) (A) Water is used for pollination in *Vallisneria* (Hydrophily).

(iv) (D) Gymnosperms have naked seeds.

(v) (A) Mammary glands are modified sweat glands.

(f) The correct matches are as follows

A.	Patella	3.	Knee joint
B.	Adult man	5.	16 teeth in each jaw
C.	E-waste	6.	Mobile batteries
D.	Anemophilous	1.	Maize flowers
E.	Malaria	2.	*Plasmodium*

(g) (i) **DDT** is insecticide and all others are antiseptics.

(ii) **Cholera** is bacterial disease and hepatitis, chicken pox and AIDS are viral diseases.

(iii) **Vegetable peel** is biodegradable waste and others are non-biodegradable wastes.

(iv) **Starfish** belong to phylum-Echinodermata and dogfish, shark and trout belong to class–Pisces.

(v) **Rice** is monocotyledons and gram, pea and bean seeds are dicotyledons.

(h) (i) The process occurring is tissue respiration.

(ii) It involves gaseous exchange between blood in a capillary and tissue cells. The terminal blood vessels (capillaries) deliver oxygen to body tissues, similarly capillaries take up carbon dioxide released by them.

(iii) *X*-Oxygen, *Y*-Carbon dioxide.

(iv) Cellular respiration

$C_6H_{12}O_6 + 6O_2 \rightarrow 6CO_2 + 6H_2O + 38$ ATP

(v) Cellular respiration occurs in the mitochondria.

Section-II

2. (a) (i) 1. Stratum corneum 2. Sensory corpuscle 3. Sebaceous gland 4. Erector muscle of hair

(ii) **Functions of Parts 3, 4 and 6**

Part 3 (Sebaceous gland) releases an oily secretion called sebum. It lubricates the hair, makes skin oily and waterproof.

Part 4 (Erector muscle of hair) It causes piloerection, i.e. lifting of hair during winters.

Part 6 (Hair follicle) It is responsible for growth and elongation of the hair.

(iii) Keratin is the protein present in part labelled 1 (Stratum corneum).

(iv) Melanin is the pigment responsible for skin colouration.

(v) Part labelled 5 is sweat gland, it secretes sweat (mixture of water, salts and traces of urea).

(b) (i) femur (ii) tibia

(iii) febula (iv) tarsals

(v) metatarsals (vi) phalanges

(vii) humerus (viii) radius

(ix) ulna (x) carpals

3. (a) (i) The above structure is an ovule present in the ovary of a flower.

(ii) 1. Antipodal cells

2. Polar nuclei

(iii) **Double fertilisation** The process in which male gamete fuses with the egg cell forming zygote and other male gamete fuses with secondary (2n). As a result, a diploid zygote and triploid primary endosperm nucleus are formed.

(iv) Calyx and corolla wither away after post-fertilisation.

(v) **Pollen grain**

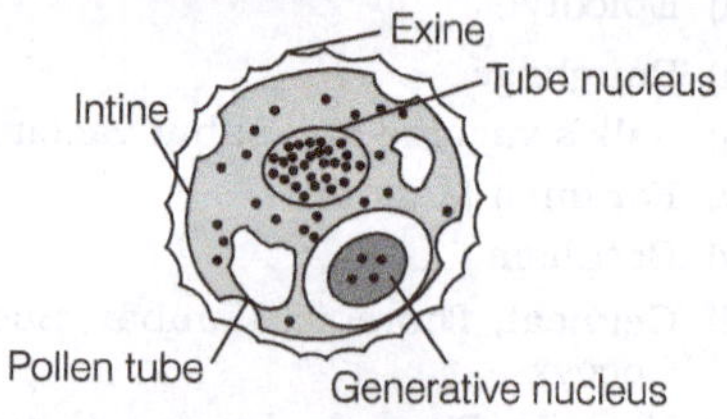

Muture pollen grain

(b) (i) A poriferan – *Spongilla*

(ii) An antibiotic – Penicillin

(iii) A coelenterate – *Hydra*

(iv) A deficiency disease – Goitre due to iodine deficiency.

(v) A mammal – *Homo sapiens* (Human beings)

(vi) An annelid worm – *Nereis* (Sand worm)

(vii) A reptilian – Turtle

(viii) A fat soluble vitamin – Retinol (Vitamin-A)

(ix) An amphibian – Toad (*Bufo*)

(x) A protein deficiency disease – Kwashiorkor.

4. (a) (i) **Aim** is to prove that heat is produced during respiration.

(ii) **Observation**

In flask A – Temperature is raised

In flask B – No change in temperature

(iii) The chemical used to prevent bacterial growth is diluted formalin or carbolic acid. The bacterial growth will cause the decay of boiled seeds.

(iv) Thermos flasks are specifically used for this experiment in order to insulate the seeds and prevent heat loss.

(v) Setup B is control for this experiment. This is because dead seeds (boiled seeds) are placed in B, will not respire (as enzymes have been denatured) thus, no heat will be produced.

(b) 1. Milk protein (casein) 2. Paracasein
3. Maltose 4. Glucose
5. Fatty acids 6. Glycerol
7. Peptides 8. Amino acids
9. Protein 10. Peptides

5. (a) (i) The structure shown is villi of small intestine. Villi are numerous, finger-like projections present in inner lining of small intestine.
(ii) The villi increase the surface area for absorption of food.
(iii) 1-Epithelial, 2-Blood capillaries
(iv) Lacteals are the lymphatic vessels of the small intestine (villi).
(v) Liver secretes bile juice. The pigments present in bile juice are bilirubin and biliverdin.

(b) (i) Inflorescence (ii) Biomedical waste
(iii) Dichogamy (iv) Germination
(v) ATP (vi) Passive immunity
(vii) Tonoplast (viii) Pleural membrane
(ix) Adipose tissue
(x) Electrostatic precipitator

6. (a) (i) Internal structure of maize seed.
Part-1 Endosperm, Part-2. Scutellum
(ii) The given structure is an albuminous seed because endosperm is present surrounded by thick aleurone layer.
(iii) Part 3-Plumule, it is covered with protective sheath called coleoptile.
Part 4-Radicle, it is covered by protective covering called coleorhiza.
(iv) Aleurone layer is rich in protein and enzymes.
(v) Maize grain is a one-seeded fruit, formed by fusion of the seed coat and the fruit wall as a protective layer. Such fruit is called a grain.

(b) (i)

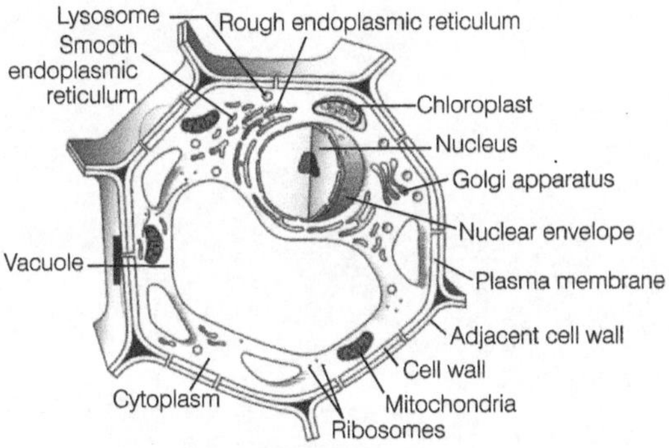

Plant cell

(ii) 1. Site for protein synthesis – Ribosome
2. A cell organelle absent in plant cell-Centrosome
3. Endoplasmic reticulum
4. Chloroplast
5. Nucleus
6. Nucleus
7. Plasma membrane

7. (a) (i) A – Parenchyma cells
B – Neutrophil (WBC)
C – Smooth muscle cell
D – Bone
(ii) The living cells in structure D (i.e. bone) is osteoblasts.
(iii) Blood is the body fluid in which neutrophils (WBCs) are found.
(iv) The unstriated (smooth) muscle cells are found in the walls of intestine helping in passage of food, movement of the iris of the eye, etc.
(v)

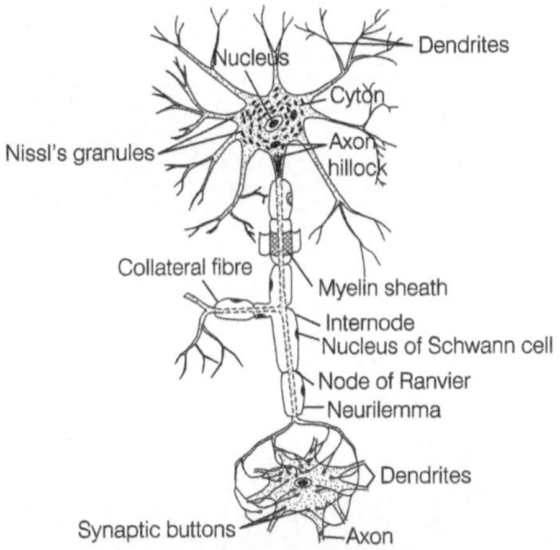

(b) (i) The activities of red cross include
1. Care and treatment of war wounded soldiers.
2. Providing relief to victims of natural disasters like earthquake, famine, etc., by procurement and supply of essentials like cloths, medicine, etc.
(ii) Preservation of food can be achieved by
1. **Pasteurisation** (usually applied to milk). It is a technique of partial sterilisation.
2. Salting is a common method of preserving food like fishes, pickles, etc. It prevents biodegradation of food.
(iii) We should breathe through the nose not mouth, because, the inner lining of the nasal chambers of nose
• warms the air as it passes through
• adds moisture to the air
• entraps harmful particles by mucus secretion.
(iv) The C-shaped cartilaginous rings provide flexibility and keep the trachea permanently distended.
(v) Main activities of WHO are as follows
1. To act as the directing and coordinating authority on international health works.
2. To assist governments, upon request, in strengthening the health services.

SAMPLE
QUESTION PAPERS (1-3)

SAMPLE QUESTION PAPER 1

A HIGHLY SIMULATED Sample Question Paper for ICSE Class IX

Biology (Unsolved)

General Instructions

1. You will not be allowed to write during the first **15** minutes. This time is to be spent in reading the question paper.
2. The time given at the head of this paper is the time allowed for writing the answers.
3. Attempt **all** questions from **Section-A** and **any 4** questions from **Section-B**.
4. The intended marks for questions or parts of questions are given in brackets [ ].

Time : 2 Hrs **Max. Marks : 80**

Section-A [40 Marks]

1. Choose the correct answer from the four options given below. [15]

(i) It is believed that sleeping under a tree at night can be harmful. Which of the following provides the most scientific explanation for this belief? • *Recall*

(a) Trees release carbon dioxide at night, reducing oxygen levels

(b) Trees attract insects at night, increasing the risk of bites

(c) Trees absorb all the moisture during the night

(d) Sleeping under a tree causes bad dreams due to spiritual reasons

(ii) **Assertion** (A) Passive immunity provides immediate protection through pre-formed antibodies.

Reason (R) The mother provides passive immunity to the foetus by transferring ready-made antibodies through the placenta. • *Understanding & Application*

(a) A is true, but R is false

(b) A is false, but R is true

(c) Both A and R are true

(d) Both A and R are false

(iii) **Assertion** (A) The colour of bile is due to certain pigment called bilirubin.

Reason (R) The biliverdin is produced by the breakdown of worn-out white blood cells. • *Understanding*

(a) A is true, but R is false

(b) A is false, but R is true

(c) Both A and R are true

(d) Both A and R are false

(iv) The introduction of dead or weak pathogens into the body is called ......P...... which helps in ......Q...... . • *Understanding*

(a) P- immunisation, Q- disease spread

(b) P- pathogenesis, Q- immune suppression

(c) P- vaccination, Q- immunity development

(d) P- antigen processing, Q- infection control

(v) A student falls, while playing and injures the joint between the humerus and ulna, experiencing pain and swelling in the elbow region. What type of joint is affected in this injury? • *Recall*

(a) Ball and socket joint (b) Hinge joint

(c) Pivot joint (d) Saddle joint

(vi) During an exam, a student is asked to look at a cell under the microscope. The student sees the cell in the image below and is asked to identify its main function. • *Analysis*

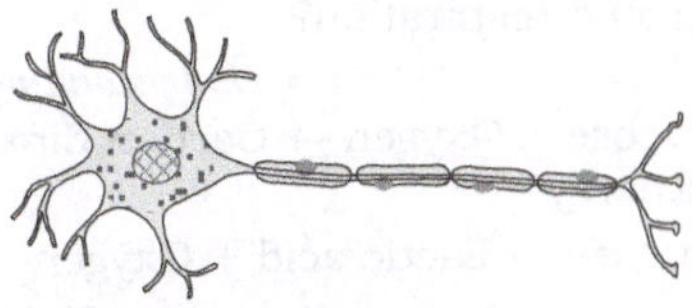

(a) Transport of oxygen

(b) Removing waste from cell

(c) Conduction of impulse from brain to muscles

(d) Storage of genetic information

(vii) The cellular organelle that are present in plant cells, but absent in animal cells are • *Understanding*

(a) centrosome and cell wall

(b) vacuoles and plastids

(c) plastids and cell wall

(d) Ventrosome and vacuole

(viii) The tissue which helps aquatic plants to float in water • *Recall*

(a) chlorenchyma (b) aerenchyma
(c) sieve tubes (d) sieve elements

(ix) **Assertion** (A) Inspiration occur due to the combined action of the ribs and the diaphragm.

Reason (R) The anaerobic respiration in muscles result in the production of lactic acid. • *Analysis*

(a) A is true, but R is false
(b) A is false, but R is true
(c) Both A and R are true
(d) Both A and R are false

(x) Mrs. Verma asked her students to provide examples of muscular tissue. • *Understanding*

Ravi said: Connective tissue and skeletal muscles.

Meera said: Smooth muscles and cardiac muscles.

Karan said: Skeletal muscle and voluntary muscles.

Which statement is correct? Choose the correct option.

(a) Ravi (b) Meera
(c) Karan (d) Both (a) and (b)

(xi) **Assertion** (A) Nectaries are situated usually at the base of leaves.

Reason (R) Sepaloid perianth is green in colour like sepals. • *Application*

(a) A is true, but R is false
(b) A is false, but R is true
(c) Both A and R are true
(d) Both A and R are false

(xii) The expanded tip of pedicel from where floral parts arise is called • *Recall*

(a) thalamus (b) receptacle
(c) Both (a) and (b) (d) None of these

(xiii) Which of the following is the correct equation for aerobic respiration? • *Understanding & Application*

(a) Glucose + Oxygen → Carbon dioxide + Water + Energy
(b) Glucose → Lactic acid + Oxygen
(c) Oxygen + Carbon dioxide → Glucose + Water
(d) Glucose → Alcohol + Carbon dioxide

(xiv) Radhika tried to match the joints with their respective locations in the body. She tabulated the pairs as follows.

Joints	Location in the body
P	Present between bones of wrist.
Q	Present between humerus and ulna.

Identify the correct pair of joints. • *Recall & Application*

(a) *P*- Gliding joint, *Q*- Hinge joint
(b) *P*- Hinge joint, *Q*- Pivot joint
(c) *P*- Pivot joint, *Q*- Hinge joint
(d) *P*- Pivot joint, *Q*- Gliding joint

(xv) Which of these are known for producing seeds? • *Recall*

(a) Pteridophyta and gymnosperms
(b) Bryophyta and gymnosperms
(c) Gymnosperms and angiosperms
(d) Angiosperms and pteridophytes

2. (a) Name the following. [5]

(i) Plant containing filaments that are united in two bundles. • *Understanding*
(ii) Fishes with gill slits concealed under a gill cover. • *Analysis*
(iii) Alternative term used for vitamin-B_{12}. • *Recall*
(iv) A blood cell without nucleus. • *Understanding*
(v) Site of occurrence of glycolysis in plants. • *Recall*

(b) Given below are sets of five terms each. Rewrite the terms in correct order of a logical sequence beginning with the term that is underlined. • *Analysis* [5]

(i) Genus, <u>Kingdom</u>, Order, Phylum, Family
(ii) Cement, Dentine, Root, <u>Enamel</u>, Pulp
(iii) Corolla, <u>Epicalyx</u>, Androecium, Calyx, Gynoecium
(iv) Radicle, Plumule, <u>Seed coat</u>, Coleoptile, Scutellum
(v) Egg cells, <u>Micropyle</u>, Nucellus, Polar nuclei, Antipodal cells

(c) Given below is a cross section of pistil, showing germination and fertilisation. Match the structures marked (*A*) to (*E*) with their correct functions. • *Analysis* [5]

Cross section of pistil, showing germination and fertilisation	Functions
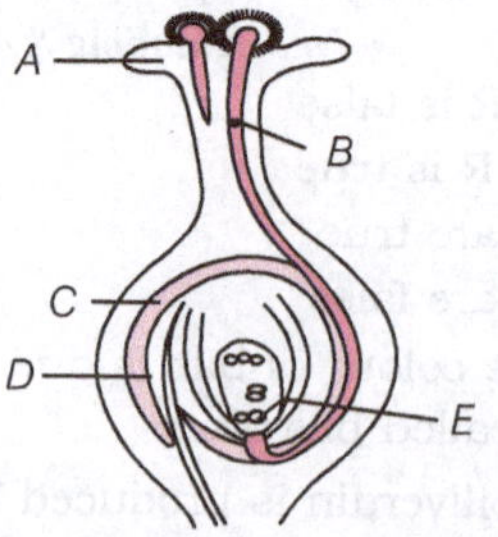	1. It stores ovules and facilitates fertilisation.
	2. It nourishment to the developing ovule.
	3. It captures pollen and facilitates fertilisation.
	4. It guide the pollen tube to the egg cell for fertilisation.
	5. It carries male gametes to the ovule for fertilisation.

(d) Given below is an image of human immunodeficiency virus. Read the information below diagram and fill in the blanks. • *Recall & Application* [5]

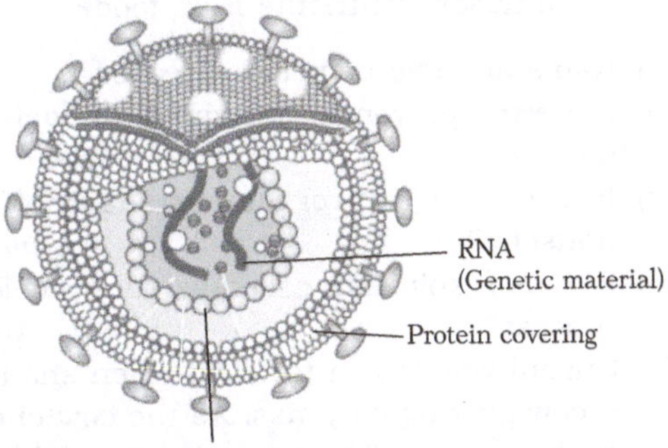

Viruses are tiny, non-living particles that consist of genetic material (DNA or RNA) enclosed in a protein coat called a capsid. They cannot reproduce on their own and must infect a host cell to replicate. Viruses cause a variety of diseases in humans, animals and plants.

The causative germ of .....(i)..... is a virus named HIV (Human Immunodeficiency Virus). It has been detected in .....(ii)..... like blood, semen, saliva and urine. It attacks the .....(iii)..... and the patient suffer from even .....(iv)..... or other diseases. Even .....(v)..... appear when the immune system fails.

(e) Read the explanation given below and name the structure. • *Understanding* [5]
  - (i) The highly branched and small projections of neuron.
  - (ii) Glands located on the margin of eyelids.
  - (iii) Tissue composed of long, narrow and dead cells.
  - (iv) The region of axis between the point of attachment of cotyledons and the plumule.
  - (v) The glands lying close to the inner side of the lower jaw on each side.

Section-B
[40 Marks]

3. (a) Define *e*-wastes. • *Recall* [1]
   (b) Name the diseases for which the following vaccines are given. • *Recall* [2]
   - (i) Salk's vaccine
   - (ii) BCG

   (c) Differentiate between personal health and community health. • *Understanding* [2]
   (d) What is Adam's apple? Is it more prominent in male or female? • *Analysis* [2]
   (e) Given below is the diagram of a open seed cut which show various parts. Study the diagram and answer the questions that follows. • *Analysis & Application* [3]

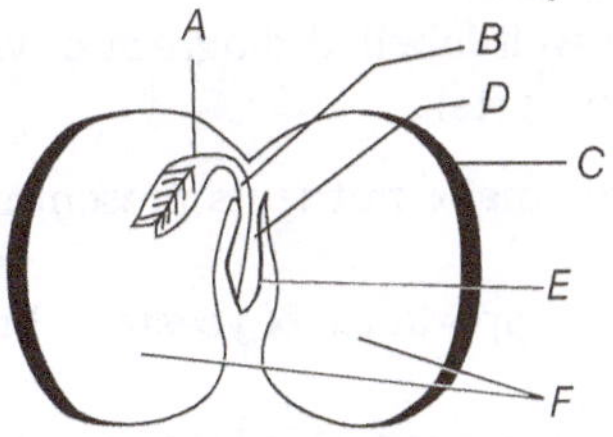

   - (i) Label the parts *A* to *F*.
   - (ii) Name the seed.
   - (iii) What is the function of part labelled as *C*?

4. (a) Expand the abbreviation PEC. • *Recall* [1]
   (b) Define cleistogamy. Give examples of the plants which showing this adaptation. • *Recall* [2]
   (c) Name the structure of seed that develops into shoot and root, respectively. • *Understanding* [2]
   (d) Why anaerobic respiration is less efficient? • *Analysis* [2]
   (e) Draw a labelled diagram of bean seed. • *Recall* [3]

5. (a) What happens to the energy released in respiration? • *Understanding* [1]
   (b) Give reason, why blue-green algae are classified along with bacteria and placed in kingdom–Monera. • *Analysis* [2]
   (c) Observe the diagram carefully and answer the following questions. • *Application* [2]

   - (i) Name the essential whorl of the flower.
   - (ii) Which part is responsible for the formation of pollens?

   (d) State the functions of small and large intestine. • *Recall* [2]
   (e) Draw a labelled diagram of nitrogen cycle. • *Understanding & Creative skills* [3]

6. (a) Name the proenzymes found in pancreatic juice. • *Recall* [1]
   (b) How many facial bones are present in the skull? Which of them is a movable bone? • *Recall* [2]

(c) What happens with blood vessels in cold weather? • *Understanding* [2]

(d) Compare alcoholic fermentation and lactic acid fermentation. • *Application* [2]

(e) Draw a well-labelled diagram of villus (label ateast 6 parts). • *Recall* [3]

7. (a) Name the major nutrients present in the food. • *Understanding* [1]

(b) State the importance of yeasts in breweries and bakeries. • *Application* [2]

(c) Given below are two groups of organisms. Identify the kingdom to which they belong. • *Recall* [2]

Group 1 *Amoeba, Paramicium, Euglena.*

Group 2 Escherichia coli, streptococcus spirilum

(d) Explain why, a land plant dies if roots remain waterlogged for a long time? • *Analysis* [2]

(e) Observe the diagram given below and answer the following questions. • *Analysis & Application* [3]

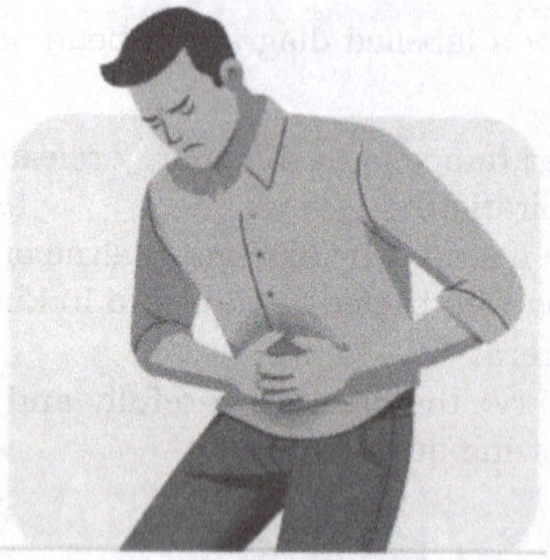

(i) Rahul is suffering from indigestion of food for quite some time. Name the organ system responsible for his condition.

(ii) If Rahul has trouble in digesting fatty foods, which digestive juice might not be produced properly?

(iii) Which part of the digestive system helps to absorb nutrients from food?

8. (a) Name any two bacterial diseases. • *Recall* [1]

(b) State the preventive measures of bacterial diseases. • *Understanding* [2]

(c) How can we control the population of housefly? • *Application* [2]

(d) Why is respiration called as energy releasing process? • *Analysis* [2]

(e) Surbhi was out in the field when she noticed a cow grazing on grass. As the cow chewed on the grass, she saw that it was nibbling on the top parts of the plants, including the tender, growing tips. • *Applicaiton & Analysis* [3]

(i) Name the meristem that is responsible for growing of the grass after being eaten by the cow.

(ii) Why is the apical meristem important for a plant's growth?

(iii) Give two characteristic features of meristematic tissue.

Answers

1. (i) (a) (ii) (c) (iii) (a) (iv) (c) (v) (b) (vi) (c) (vii) (c) (viii) (b)
(ix) (c) (x) (b) (xi) (c) (xii) (b) (xiii) (a) (xiv) (a) (xv) (c)

SAMPLE QUESTION PAPER 2

A HIGHLY SIMULATED Sample Question Paper for ICSE Class IX

Biology (Unsolved)

General Instructions

1. You will not be allowed to write during the first **15** minutes. This time is to be spent in reading the question paper.
2. The time given at the head of this paper is the time allowed for writing the answers.
3. Attempt **all** questions from **Section-A** and **any 4** questions from **Section-B**.
4. The intended marks for questions or parts of questions are given in brackets [ ].

Time : 2 Hrs **Max. Marks : 80**

Section-A [40 Marks]

1. Choose the correct answer from the four options given below. [15]

(i) The ultimate end of trachea is • *Recall*

(a) bronchi (b) bronchioles
(c) alveoli (d) pharynx

(ii) Maize is pollinated by .....*P*...... which helps in ......*Q*....... • *Understanding*

(a) *P*- insects, *Q*- cross-pollination
(b) *P*- water, *Q*- self-pollination
(c) *P*- wind, *Q*- cross-pollination
(d) *P*- animals, *Q*- vegetative propagation

(iii) *Aedes* spreads • *Recall*

(a) malaria (b) yellow fever
(c) elephantiasis (d) typhoid

(iv) **Assertion** (A) Biodegradable materials can be broken down by natural processes, while non-biodegradable materials cannot.

Reason (R) Biodegradable materials are decomposed by microorganisms, whereas non-biodegradable materials remain in the environment for a long time because they resist natural decomposition. • *Understanding*

(a) A is true, but R is false
(b) A is false, but R is true
(c) Both A and R are true
(d) Both A and R are false

(v) **Assertion** (A) The Krebs' cycle helps produce energy in the form of ATP for the cell.

Reason (R) The Krebs' cycle occurs in the thylakoid membranes of the chloroplasts.

(a) A is true, but R is false • *Application*
(b) A is false, but R is true
(c) Both A and R are true
(d) Both A and R are false

(vi) The discarded solid materials which are produced due to various human activities are called • *Recall*

(a) solid wastes (b) industrial wastes
(c) electronic wastes (d) hospital wastes

(vii) Mr. Sharma asked his students to identify examples of biodegradable waste.

Riya said: Fruit peels and plastic bottles.
Vikas said: Vegetable scraps and paper.
Neha said: Polythene bags and metal cans.

Which statement is correct? Choose the correct option. • *Understanding*

(a) Riya (b) Vikas
(c) Neha (d) Both (a) and (c)

(viii) Which of the following statement is true for health? • *Understanding*

(a) A state of complete physical well-being
(b) A state of complete mental well-being
(c) A state of complete social well-being
(d) All of the above

(ix) Mohit tried to match the diseases with their causative agents and tabulated pais as

Diseases	Agents
P	*Aedes aegypti*
Q	*Escherichia coli*

Identify the correct pair of diseases. • *Recall*

(a) *P*- Dengue, *Q*- Diarrhoea
(b) *P*- Malaria, *Q*- Dengue
(c) *P*- Ringworm, *Q*- Filariasis
(d) *P*- Diarrhoea, *Q*- Malaria

(x) Riya and her friends recently returned from a trip to a hill station. A week later, Riya started feeling unwell with high fever, chills and surating.
She also complained body aches and fatigue. Concerned her family took her to the doctor, who recommended a blood test.
Which of the following disease is most likely based on Riya's symptoms? • *Application*

(a) Malaria
(b) Tuberculosis
(c) Common cold
(d) Food poisoning.

(xi) A disease which can easily transmit from one person to another is called • *Recall*

(a) non-infectious disease
(b) infectious disease
(c) viral disease
(d) bacterial disease

(xii) **Assertion** (A) Breathing involves the intake of oxygen and the release of carbon dioxide, while respiration is the process of energy production in cells. • *Analysis*
Reason (R) Breathing is a physical process, while respiration is a biochemical process that takes place within the cells of the body.

(a) A is true, but R is false
(b) A is false, but R is true
(c) Both A and R are true
(d) Both A and R are false

(xiii) Inspiration is initiated by • *Application*

(a) extension of the diaphragm
(b) contraction of the diaphragm
(c) extension of the lungs
(d) contraction of the lungs

(xiv) **Assertion** (A) Anaerobic respiration occurs in the absence of oxygen and produces less energy compared to aerobic respiration.
Reason (R) In anaerobic respiration, glucose is partially broken down into lactic acid or ethanol. • *Analysis*

(a) A is true, but R is false
(b) A is false, but R is true
(c) Both A and R are true
(d) Both A and R are false

(xv) The diagram given below shows the structure of an antibody. Based on the diagram, answer the following questions. • *Understanding & Application*

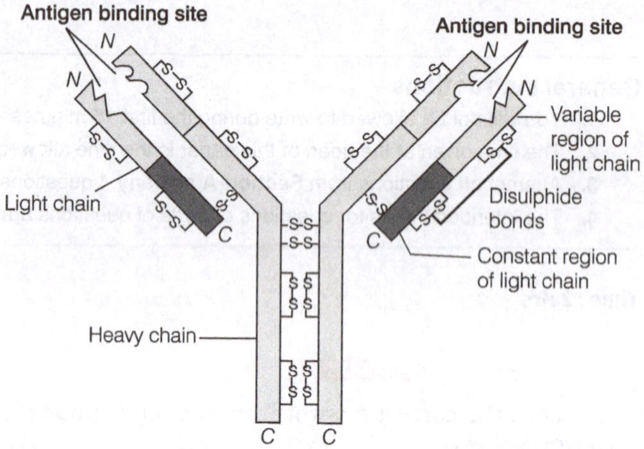

What is the main function of antibodies?

(a) To help in digestion
(b) To carry oxygen in the blood
(c) To fight infections by recognising and neutralising harmful substances
(d) To produce energy for the body

2. (a) Name the following. [5]

(i) The class to which rohu belongs. • *Recall*
(ii) A flying mammal. • *Understanding*
(iii) A condition in which petals are fused. • *Understanding*
(iv) The fluid present in synovial joint. • *Analysis*
(v) An enzyme present in saliva. • *Recall*

(b) Given below are sets of five terms each. Rewrite the terms in correct order of a logical sequence beginning with the term that is underlined. • *Analysis* [5]

(i) Preservation, Harvesting, Spawning, Composting, Casting.
(ii) Cell wall, Nucleus, Cell membrane, Cytoplasm, Nucleolus.
(iii) Mollusca, Chordata, Arthropoda, Echinodermata, Porifera.
(iv) Oesophagus, Mouth, Small intestine, Stomach, Anus.

(v) Skull, Pectoral girdle, Pelvic girdle, Vertebral column, Hindlimb

(c) Match the following columns. • *Analysis* [5]

Structure of neuron	Functions
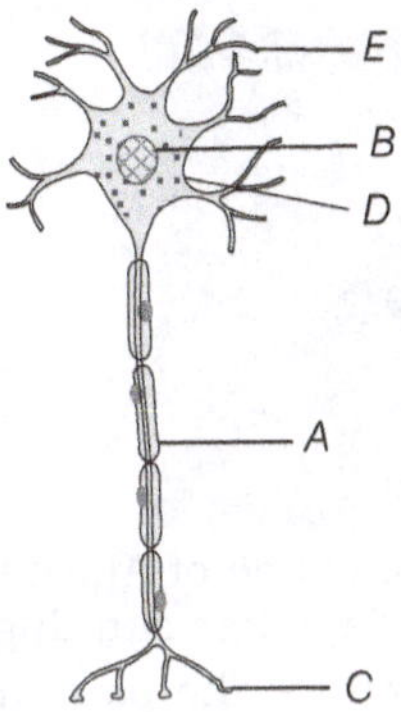	1. Processes incoming signals and maintains the neuron's health.
	2. Receive signals from other neurons and transmit them to the cell body.
	3. Gaps in the myelin sheath that speed up nerve imuplse transmission through saltatory conduction.
	4. Transmits electrical impulses away from the cell body to other neurons or effectors.
	5. Controls the neuron's activities and contains genetic material.

(d) Fill in the blanks. • *Recall & Application* [5]

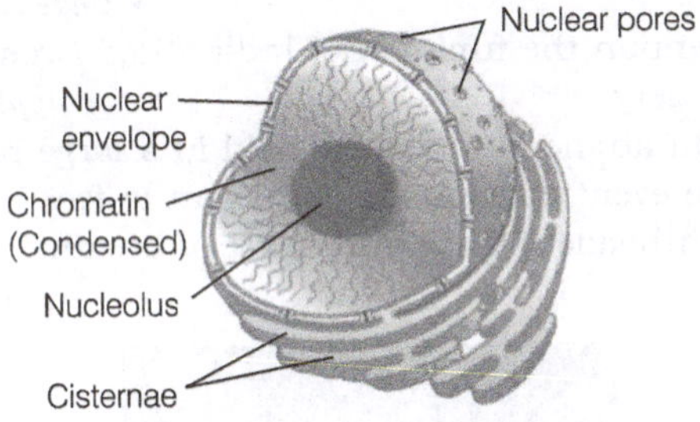

A eukaryotic cell is a complex cell with a true nucleus and membrane-bound organelles, found in plants, animals, fungi and protists. Its nucleus houses genetic material (DNA) and controls cell activities through gene expression and regulation of cellular processes.

Nucleus is a spherical structure located in the .....(i)..... . It has delicate nuclear membrane which is filled with a relatively dense .....(ii).... . In nucleoplasm there are certain thread-like structures called ......(iii)...... . During cell division these fibres become thick and .....(iv)..... and known as .....(v)..... .

(e) Read the following statement and identify the correct term. • *Recall & Application* [5]

(i) Teeth present on either side of the incisors in each jaw.

(ii) The substance which forms the exoskeleton of arthropods.

(iii) It protects the brain and forms the structure of face.

(iv) It contains the ovules and after fertilisation, develops into the fruit with the ovules becoming seeds.

(v) Substances can be broken down naturally by microorganisms, reducing environmental pollution.

Section-B

[40 Marks]

3. (a) Why most of the organisms cannot survive without oxygen? • *Understanding* [1]

(b) What is common in aerobic and anaerobic respiration? • *Recall* [2]

(c) The human endoskeleton consists of two parts. Name them with number of bones in each. • *Recall* [2]

(d) Why do you shiver and your teeth chatter when it is very cold in winter? • *Understanding* [2]

(e) Draw the diagram of a typical stamen. • *Recall* [3]

4. (a) What is a group of flowers on a twig called? • *Recall* [1]

(b) Some pollen grain are rough and spiny. Justify. • *Analysis* [2]

(c) Name the parts of pistil which develop into fruit and seeds. • *Recall* [2]

(d) State two differences between kwashiorkor and marasmus. • *Recall* [2]

(e) Observe the figure and answer the questions that follows. • *Application* [3]

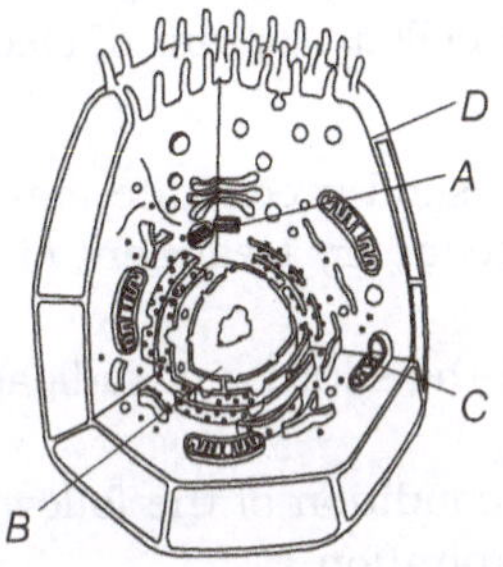

(i) Label the parts *A-D*.

(ii) State the function of part *B*.

(iii) Name the part concerned with production of energy.

5. (a) Locomotion requires perfect coordinated activities of different system. Name these systems. • *Understanding* [1]

(b) State the role of fats in humans. • *Application* [2]

(c) Humerus is the bone of the upper arm. Similarily, name the bones that form the forearm, wrist, palm and fingers. • *Recall* [2]

(d) Name any two antibiotics derived from each
(i) Bacteria
(ii) Fungus • *Recall* [2]

(e) Meena noticed her grandmother planting seeds in the garden. After a few days, she saw small green shoots emerging from the soil. She was curious about how the seeds transformed into tiny plants. [3]

(i) What process is taking place when seeds turn into young plants? • *Recall*
(ii) Which part of the seed grows into the shoot that appears above the soil? • *Understanding*
(iii) Which part of the seed forms the root system of the plant? • *Understanding*

6. (a) Which are the first land plants to have vascular tissues? • *Recall* [1]
(b) How are bacteria helpful in curing of tea and tobacco? • *Analysis* [2]
(c) Cellulose is not digested in our body. Yet it is an important component of a balanced diet. Why? • *Understanding* [2]
(d) Why do we say AIDS is a syndrome and not a disease? • *Understanding* [2]
(e) Draw a labelled diagram of electrostatic precipitator. • *Recall* [3]

7. (a) Name the solid precipitate material produced during secondary treatment of wastewater. • *Application* [1]
(b) What are the sources of radioactive wastes? • *Understanding* [2]
(c) Give the condition of the following muscles during expiration. • *Analysis*
(i) Diaphragm muscles
(ii) Internal intercostal muscles [2]
(d) Give the location of ball and socket joint in a human body. • *Recall* [2]
(e) Amrita started running after a long break from physical activity. Initially, she felt fine during the run, but the next day, she experienced pain and soreness in her legs. She also noticed that her legs felt stiff and heavy. • *Analysis & Application* [3]

(i) What might be the cause of Amrita's leg pain and soreness the day after running?
(ii) How can Amrita reduce the pain in her legs after running?
(iii) During this exercise tidal volume is increase or decreased?

8. (a) What are air scrubbers? • *Recall* [1]
(b) Glycolysis is considered as an important stage of respiration. Why? • *Analysis* [2]
(c) What is fate of integuments after fertilisation? • *Understanding* [2]
(d) Mention the function of Indian Red Cross Society. • *Application* [2]
(e) Rita attended a concert held in a large hall. As the event continued, she began to feel lightheaded, dizzy and short of breath. • *Analysis* [3]

(i) What condition might Rita be suffering from based on her symptoms?
(ii) What might be the cause of Rita feeling lightheaded and dizzy during the concert?
(iii) How might Rita's condition improve?

Answers

1. (i) (c) (ii) (c) (iii) (b) (iv) (c) (v) (a) (vi) (a) (vii) (b) (viii) (d) (ix) (a) (x) (a) (xi) (b) (xii) (c) (xiii) (b) (xiv) (c) (xv) (c)

SAMPLE QUESTION PAPER 3

A HIGHLY SIMULATED Sample Question Paper for ICSE Class IX

Biology (Unsolved)

General Instructions

1. You will not be allowed to write during the first **15** minutes. This time is to be spent in reading the question paper.
2. The time given at the head of this paper is the time allowed for writing the answers.
3. Attempt **all** questions from **Section-A** and **any 4** questions from **Section-B**.
4. The intended marks for questions or parts of questions are given in brackets [ ].

Time : 2 Hrs **Max. Marks : 80**

Section-A [40 Marks]

1. Choose the correct answer from the four options given below. [15]

(i) An endospermic seed is • *Recall*

(a) bean (b) maize
(c) pea (d) gram

(ii) **Assertion** (A) *Azotobacter* and *Clostridium* are free-living nitrogen fixing bacteria.

Reason (R) Wine is produced by fermentation of sugar with a bacteria. • *Understanding*

(a) A is true, but R is false
(b) A is false, but R is true
(c) Both A and R are true
(d) Both A and R are false

(iii) Bone of hand is • *Recall*

(a) tibia (b) tarsal (c) humerus (d) femur

(iv) Riya tried to match the vitamins with their respective functions. She tabulated the pairs as follows. • *Understanding & Application*

Vitamins	Functions
P	Needed for normal clotting of the blood
Q	Promotes health of skin

Identify the correct pair of vitamins.

(a) *P*-Vitamin-C, *Q*-Vitamin-B_1
(b) *P*-Vitamin-E, *Q*-Vitamin-E
(c) *P*-Vitamin-K, *Q*- Vitamin-E
(d) *P*-Vitamin-D, *Q*-Vitamin-E

(v) Fungi are saprophytes because they • *Understanding*

(a) do not contain chlorophyll
(b) feed on fresh matter
(c) feed on decayed matter
(d) possess cell walls

(vi) Our vertebral column is formed by the • *Recall*

(a) 26 serially arranged units called vertebrae
(b) 27 serially arranged units called vertebrae
(c) 33 serially arranged units called vertebrae
(d) 35 serially arranged units called vertebrae

(vii) Identify *A*, *B* and *C* in the given diagram. • *Analysis*

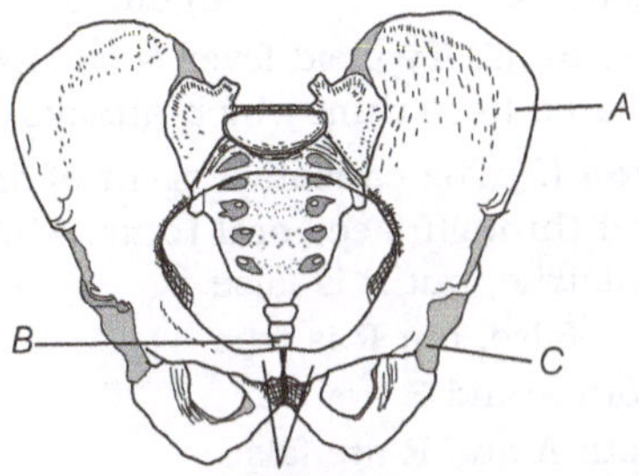

(a) *A*-Ilium, *B*- Coccyx, *C*- Acetabulum
(b) *A*- Ilium, *B*- Ischium, *C*- Pubis
(c) *A*- Coccyx, *B*- Pubis, *C*- Sacrum
(d) *A*- Coccyx, *B*- Ischium, *C*- Ilium

(viii) **Assertion** (A) Skin account for 15% of an adult human's total body weight.

Reason (R) Sweat consists of 0.5 per cent salt and 0.08 per cent urea. • *Recall & Understanding*

(a) A is true, but R is false
(b) A is false, but R is true
(c) Both A and R are true
(d) Both A and R are false

(ix) Priyanka tried to match the following layers of skin with their respective functions. She tabulated the following pair. • *Application*

Layers	Their Functions
P	It forms ridges that make fingerprints.
Q	This provides strength to the skin and serves as a home for hair follicles and sebaceous glands.

Identify the correct pair of functions.
(a) *P*- Granulosa layer, *Q*- Reticular layer
(b) *P*- Malpighi layer, *Q*- Substratum layer
(c) *P*- Cornified layer, *Q*- Germinative layer
(d) *P*- Papillary layer, *Q*- Reticular layer

(x) Amar is walking on a treadmil as part of his exercise routine. After a few minutes, he starts breathing faster to keep up with his increasing need for oxygen. When Amar breathes faster during exercise, which lung volume is most likely to increase? • *Understanding*
(a) Tidal volume
(b) Residual volume
(c) Expiratory reserve volume
(d) Inspiratory reserve volume

(xi) Movement of the air into and out of the lungs is carried out by
(a) imbibition (b) pressure gradient
(c) osmosis (d) diffusion

(xii) **Assertion** (A) Typhoid fever is caused by a flagellated bacterium which attacks intestine.
Reason (R) The causative agent of cholera spread through faeco-oral route. • *Understanding*
(a) A is true, but R is false
(b) A is false, but R is true
(c) Both A and R are true
(d) Both A and R are false

(xiii) **Assertion** (A) The plant cells have larger vacuoles in comparison to animal cell.
Reason (R) The function of vacuole is to capture solar energy for the production of starch and sugar. • *Analysis*
(a) A is true, but R is false
(b) A is false, but R is true
(c) Both A and R are true
(d) Both A and R are false

(xiv) Mr. Verma asked his students about the harmful components and recycling methods of *e*-waste. • *Application*
Riya said: E-waste contains lead and it can be recycled through incineration.
Amit said: E-waste contains cadmium and it can be recycled through bioleaching.
Sneha said: E-waste contains mercury and it can be safely disposed of in landfills.
Kunal said: E-waste contains chromium and it can be recycled through hydrometallurgical processes.
Who gave the correct answer? Choose the correct option given below.
(a) Riya and Kunal (b) Amit
(c) Sneha (d) Kunal

(xv) Separating the waste materials into different categories is called • *Application*
(a) recycling
(b) segregation
(c) composting
(d) dumping

2. (a) Name the following. [5]
(i) A cell organelle which helps in cellular respiration. • *Understanding*
(ii) Name the group of organisms to which Protozoa belongs. • *Understanding*
(iii) The kingdom to which protozoans belong. • *Recall*
(iv) A heterotrophic plant. • *Recall*
(v) The end product of glycolysis. • *Analysis*

(b) Given below are sets of five term each. Rewrite the terms in correct order of a logical sequence beginning with the term that is underlined. • *Analysis* [5]
(i) Pollen tube, Stigma, Ovary, <u>Pollen grain</u>, Embryo sac.
(ii) Rectum, <u>Pharynx</u>, Oesophagus, Duodenum, Stomach.
(iii) Larynx, Pharynx, Bronchioles, <u>Nostrils</u>, Alveoli.
(iv) Sacrum, Thoracic, Coccyx, <u>Cervical</u>, Lumbar
(v) <u>Episepalous</u>, Stamens, Pistil, Sepals, Petals.

(c) Given below is a cross-section of bisexual flower. Match the structures marked (*A*) to (*E*) with their respective functions. • *Analysis* [5]

Cross section of bisexual flower	Functions
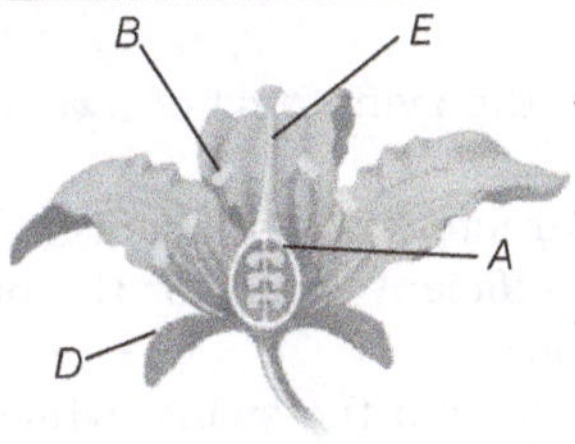	1. Produce male gametes.
	2. Protect the young flower bud.
	3. It encloses the egg cell.
	4. Serves as landing platform for pollen grains.
	5. Attract insects for pollination.

(d) Given below is an image of child suffering from nutrient deficiency. Read the information below the diagram and fill in the blanks. • *Recall & Application* [5]

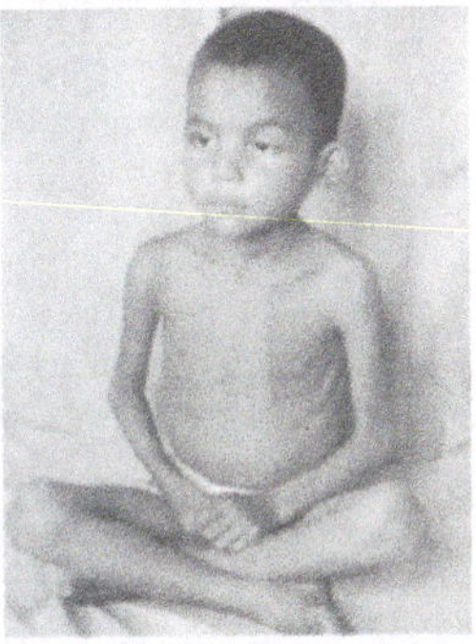

Nutrient deficiency occurs when the body or plants do not get enough essential nutrients, such as vitamins, minerals or macronutrients. It can lead to health issues in humans, such as weakness, poor immunity and growth problems, and in plants, it may cause stunted growth, yellowing leaves and reduced yield. ......(i)...... usually effects infants below the age of ......(ii)...... and is due to the deficiency of ......(iii)......, ...(iv)...... and proteins in the diet. This disease is due to the sudden stoppage of ......(v)......, followed by a diet poor in energy-giving foods.

(e) Read the explanation given below and name the structure. • *Understanding* [5]

(i) Small opening present in the outer layer of an ovule.

(ii) The site in human body where tapeworm reach a length of a metre.

(iii) Green colour plastids found in plant cell.

(iv) Living parenchyma cell closely associated with sieve tube cell.

(v) Salivary gland situated below the tongue.

Section-B

[40 Marks]

3. (a) List atleast two wastes which you generate at home and school that could be easily reduced. • *Recall* [1]

(b) Two materials are given to you, a plastic and a cotton bag. How will you determine these materials as biodegradable and non-biodegradable? • *Understanding* [2]

(c) Distinguish between the following on the basis of what is given in bracket. • *Application*[2]

(i) DPT and BCG (expanded form of the vaccine).

(ii) Antiseptic and disinfectant (functions).

(d) Explain the role of blood in respiration. • *Recall* [2]

(e) Draw a labelled diagram of nervous tissue. • *Recall* [3]

4. (a) Name the bacteria used for retting of fibres. • *Recall* [1]

(b) What is a vaccine? Can it be obtained from bacteria? • *Understanding* [2]

(c) The role of bacteria in industries is widespread. Justify. • *Analysis* [2]

(d) List few advantages of five kingdom classification over two kingdom classification. • *Recall* [2]

(e) Study the figure and answer the questions. • *Application* [3]

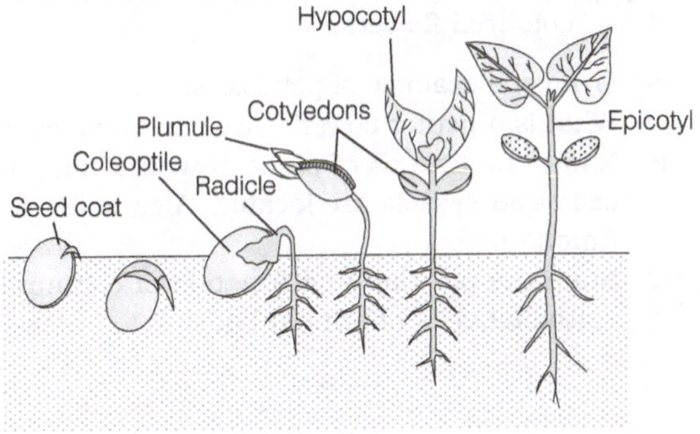

(i) What type of germination is shown in the figure? Define it.

(ii) State the role of coleorhiza.

(iii) What conditions are required for germination? Explain any one.

5. (a) Name the group of organisms to which Protozoa belongs. • *Recall* [1]

(b) Mention the advantages of seed producing plants over those which do not produce seeds. • *Understanding* [2]

(c) Why is there heat and light produced when some materials burns? • *Analysis* [2]

(d) Write about any two steps of aerobic respiration. • *Understanding* [2]

(e) Draw a labelled diagram of an animal cell. • *Understanding & Creative skill* [3]

6. (a) What is seed coat? • *Recall* [1]

(b) Differentiate between monocot and dicot seed. • *Understanding* [2]

(c) Write a note on the need and significance of pollination in plants. • *Application* [2]

(d) Why are pollen grains produced in enormous quantities in maize? • *Analysis* [2]

(e) Jyoti observed a variety of plants her mother had carefully planted in the garden. She noticed different shapes, sizes and colours, each adding beauty and life to the space. • *Analysis & Application* [3]

(i) Why do flowers possess different colours?

(ii) Why do not all plants have colourful flowers?

(iii) Write two common characteristics of brightly coloured flowers.

7. (a) Write one example of petaloid sepals. • *Recall* [1]

(b) What is a neuter flower? Give one example. • *Recall* [2]

(c) Name the tissues of plant in which companion cells and vessels are located. Also write its function. • *Application* [2]

(d) State the position and function of columnar epithelial cells of animal body. • *Application* [2]

(e) Draw a well-labelled structure of pollen grain. • *Recall* [3]

8. (a) Why is nose breathing better than mouth breathing? • *Understanding* [1]

(b) What is the role of fungi in industry? • *Recall* [2]

(c) What are the symptoms of kwashiorkor diseases? • *Recall* [2]

(d) What characteristics of small intestine makes it efficient organ for the process of absorption? • *Understanding* [2]

(e) Raghav fell from the swing, while playing and hurt his right forearm. The doctor put a plaster on it to help it heal and advised him to rest. • *Analysis & Application* [3]

(i) Which bone in Raghav's hand might have been affected when he fell from the swing?

(ii) Name the joints associated with this bone.

(iii) How many bones are there in the wrist?

Answers

1. (i) (b) (ii) (a) (iii) (b) (iv) (c) (v) (c) (vi) (a) (vii) (b) (viii) (c) (ix) (d) (x) (a) (xi) (b) (xii) (c) (xiii) (a) (xiv) (b) (xv) (a)